Cyberfeminism and Gender Violence in Social Media

Deepanjali Mishra
KIIT University, India

IGI Global
PUBLISHER of TIMELY KNOWLEDGE

A volume in the Advances in Human and Social Aspects of Technology (AHSAT) Book Series

Published in the United States of America by
IGI Global
Information Science Reference (an imprint of IGI Global)
701 E. Chocolate Avenue
Hershey PA, USA 17033
Tel: 717-533-8845
Fax: 717-533-8661
E-mail: cust@igi-global.com
Web site: http://www.igi-global.com

Library of Congress Cataloging-in-Publication Data

Names: Mishra, Deepanjali, 1981- editor.
Title: Cyberfeminism and gender violence in social media / edited by: Deepanjali Mishra.
Description: Hershey PA : Information Science Reference, [2023] | Includes bibliographical references. | Summary: "The book provides an interdisciplinary approach, making it relevant to a wide range of fields such as social science, humanities, technology, and management. It creates awareness among people, especially women, about the prospects of cybersecurity and its impact on their wellness. It is expected to enrich the audience about the impact of social media on the general public and how cyber security education can make people aware of their security and well-being. This book is ideal for researchers, academicians, and students who are interested in new and innovative techniques for the safety of people irrespective of their gender. Overall, the book is a significant contribution to the ongoing conversation on women's rights and violence against them in the digital age"-- Provided by publisher.
Identifiers: LCCN 2023022585 (print) | LCCN 2023022586 (ebook) | ISBN 9781668488935 (hardcover) | ISBN 9781668488942 (paperback) | ISBN 9781668488959 (ebook)
Subjects: LCSH: Internet and women. | Cyberfeminism. | Online hate speech. | Gender-based violence. | Women--Violence against. | Misogyny.
Classification: LCC HQ1178 .C927 2023 (print) | LCC HQ1178 (ebook) | DDC 004.67/8082--dc23/eng/20230629
LC record available at https://lccn.loc.gov/2023022585
LC ebook record available at https://lccn.loc.gov/2023022586

This book is published in the IGI Global book series Advances in Human and Social Aspects of Technology (AHSAT) (ISSN: 2328-1316; eISSN: 2328-1324)

British Cataloguing in Publication Data
A Cataloguing in Publication record for this book is available from the British Library.

Advances in Human and Social Aspects of Technology (AHSAT) Book Series

Mehdi Khosrow-Pour, D.B.A.
Information Resources Management Association, USA

ISSN:2328-1316
EISSN:2328-1324

Mission

In recent years, the societal impact of technology has been noted as we become increasingly more connected and are presented with more digital tools and devices. With the popularity of digital devices such as cell phones and tablets, it is crucial to consider the implications of our digital dependence and the presence of technology in our everyday lives.

The **Advances in Human and Social Aspects of Technology (AHSAT) Book Series** seeks to explore the ways in which society and human beings have been affected by technology and how the technological revolution has changed the way we conduct our lives as well as our behavior. The AHSAT book series aims to publish the most cutting-edge research on human behavior and interaction with technology and the ways in which the digital age is changing society.

Coverage

- ICTs and human empowerment
- End-User Computing
- Activism and ICTs
- Cultural Influence of ICTs
- Gender and Technology
- Computer-Mediated Communication
- Information ethics
- Technoself
- Public Access to ICTs
- Philosophy of technology

The Advances in Human and Social Aspects of Technology (AHSAT) Book Series (ISSN 2328-1316) is published by IGI Global, 701 E. Chocolate Avenue, Hershey, PA 17033-1240, USA, www.igi-global.com. This series is composed of titles available for purchase individually; each title is edited to be contextually exclusive from any other title within the series. For pricing and ordering information please visit http://www.igi-global.com/book-series/advances-human-social-aspects-technology/37145. Postmaster: Send all address changes to above address.

Titles in this Series

For a list of additional titles in this series, please visit: www.igi-global.com/book-series

Analyzing New Forms of Social Disorders in Modern Virtual Environments
Milica Boskovic (Faculty of Diplomacy and Security, University Union Nikola Tesla, Serbia) Gordana Misev (Ministry of Mining and Energy Republic of Serbia, Serbia) and Nenad Putnik (Faculty of Security Studies, University of Belgrade, Serbia)
Information Science Reference • copyright 2023 • 284pp • H/C (ISBN: 9781668457603) • US $225.00 (our price)

Adoption and Use of Technology Tools and Services by Economically Disadvantaged Communities Implications for Growth and Sustainability
Alice S. Etim (Winston-Salem State University, USA)
Information Science Reference • copyright 2023 • 300pp • H/C (ISBN: 9781668453476) • US $225.00 (our price)

Investigating the Impact of AI on Ethics and Spirituality
Swati Chakraborty (GLA University, India & Concordia University, Canada)
Information Science Reference • copyright 2023 • 300pp • H/C (ISBN: 9781668491966) • US $225.00 (our price)

Philosophy of Artificial Intelligence and Its Place in Society
Luiz Moutinho (University of Suffolk, UK) Luís Cavique (Universidade Aberta, Portugal) and Enrique Bigné (Universitat de València, Spain)
Engineering Science Reference • copyright 2023 • 320pp • H/C (ISBN: 9781668495919) • US $215.00 (our price)

Advances in Cyberology and the Advent of the Next-Gen Information Revolution
Mohd Shahid Husain (College of Applied Sciences, University of Technology and Applied Sciences, Oman) Mohammad Faisal (Integral University, Lucknow, India) Halima Sadia (Integral University, Lucknow, India) Tasneem Ahmad (Advanced Computing Research Lab, Integral University, Lucknow, India) and Saurabh Shukla (Data Science Institute, National University of Ireland, Galway, Ireland)
Information Science Reference • copyright 2023 • 271pp • H/C (ISBN: 9781668481332) • US $215.00 (our price)

Handbook of Research on Perspectives on Society and Technology Addiction
Rengim Sine Nazlı (Bolu Abant İzzet Baysal University, Turkey) and Gülşah Sari (Aksaray University, Turkey)
Information Science Reference • copyright 2023 • 603pp • H/C (ISBN: 9781668483978) • US $270.00 (our price)

Impact of Disruptive Technologies on the Socio-Economic Development of Emerging Countries
Fredrick Japhet Mtenzi (Institute for Educational Development, The Aga Khan University, Tanzania) George S. Oreku (The Open University of Tanzania, Tanzania) and Dennis M. Lupiana (Institute of Finance Management, Tanzania)

IGI Global
PUBLISHER of TIMELY KNOWLEDGE

701 East Chocolate Avenue, Hershey, PA 17033, USA
Tel: 717-533-8845 x100 • Fax: 717-533-8661
E-Mail: cust@igi-global.com • www.igi-global.com

Editorial Advisory Board

Table of Contents

Detailed Table of Contents

Indian society has never freed itself from the shackles of patriarchy and its age-old norms. In a diverse nation like India, with age-old gender stereotypes, beliefs, and tradition, the concept of marital rape stands as vague and hence isn't illegal. As all the three pillars of democracy—judiciary, legislature, and executive—stand blindfolded, the only ray of hope lies with the media as they play a major role in shaming the attackers and holding them accountable. The current study is central to understanding the role of social media in shaming the attackers of marital rape by analyzing the possible impact of physical force used by the perpetrator and sexual assault severity on post-trauma stress disorder and coping self-efficacy in particular in marital rape victims. Thus, in this ground, social media can be an effective medium to bring forth the conversations about marital rape into the public sphere by conducting debates, seminars, and interviews in order to effectively engage the public to understand their mindset.

Research on digital articulations of patriarchal violence—sexual gender-based violence, harassment, intimidation, and bullying—as experienced by women and femmes globally is still exploratory. Despite the continued research development, feminist academics and activists still have challenges designing online platforms that are safe spaces for all genders and expressions of sexuality. Thus, this chapter extends current research and focuses on the root causes of digital violence. This chapter also focuses on the uses of social media, mainly Twitter, and the developments of feminist discourses by activist organizations in Southern Africa: @womenforchange5 and @SisterNambia. This chapter discusses the use of feminist organizations as tools in building community, developing social change strategies, and the ability to combat cis-heterosexist patriarchal conditioning and violence. Consequently, this chapter aims to contextualize social media as an echo chamber of societal violence. Moreover, social media affordances result in digital realms becoming field sites of misogyny and misogynoir.

The latter half of the 20th century witnessed rapid growth in the domain of science and technology especially information and communication technology (ICT). The impact of ICT can easily be seen in the different domains of humans like science, education, professional career, culture, and politics, explicitly and implicitly or negatively. There are different types of digital violence exercised against women. Some of the forms range from hacking, controlling, or manipulating information, doxing, dissemination of intimate photos or private information, use of spyware, surveillance, faking identity, cyberbullying like posting or sharing embarrassing or threatening pictures, defamation, harassment, stalking in the form of sending online unsolicited or unwanted sex-based materials, and rape threats. The chapter attempts to explore role of the digital technology and online platforms as intermediaries in rendering gender-based violence, digitalization of gender-based violence, verbal or nonverbal sexual assaults, and online sexual politics to prolong women's subjection in India.

Online trolling is the practise of engaging in dishonest, harmful, or disruptive behaviour in a social setting over the internet without any apparent gain. If a target falls for their trick, the trolling gets worse for even more heinous enjoyment. Trolling may be distinguished from other forms of online antisociality by its dishonest and "pointless" disruptive features, in contrast to which the perpetrators' names and objectives are usually more transparent. Trolling has adverse negative effects on mental health. Therefore, there is an urgent need to address this issue. This chapter attempted to look into the causes of trolling which is damaging the mental health of people and why people become victims of trolling. Secondly, it assessed whether the damage in mental health vary with age or not. Thematic analysis was conducted on the transcribed data and the findings were discussed.

Intimate partner violence (IPV) against women is a pervasive global issue. The media plays a significant role in shaping society's perceptions and understanding of IPV. This study focuses on the representation of femicide in Turkish newspapers, with a specific focus on the context of Turkey as an honor culture characterized by a distinct emphasis on female sexual purity and male dominance. Honor cultures often justify violence against women in the name of preserving honor. This research aims to investigate how newspapers depict honor-based IPV through quantitative analysis, content analysis, discourse analysis, and frame analysis of femicide cases. The findings reveal that newspapers frame IPV within an honor culture by victim-blaming and justifying men's violent behavior. Additionally, news coverage often

interventions, evaluating existing policies, and understanding evolving dynamics to achieve a violence-free digital future.

Cyber victimization is a phenomenon where people are subjected to cyber bullying through online harassment, exposure to unsolicited sexual content, and hurtful comments. This phenomenon is said to induce embarrassment, traumatic experiences, and in severe cases, psychopathological cascades. Social withdrawal, shame, and social anxiety are commonly witnessed in victims of cyber bullying. According to previous research and substantiated theories, women are more commonly the victims of online abuse. In such a scenario, a discussion regarding clear definition of cyber victimization, social media addiction processes, prevalence of gender differences, and effects of cyber victimization is important. This chapter aims to review all these relevant topics and discuss neuropsychological mechanisms underlying these processes.

The study aims to determine how board diversity affects cybersecurity information disclosure for financial companies listed on S&P BSE 150. To create a CSD scorecard, the authors rely on past studies as well as SEC guidelines. The empirical research is based on data from 30 financial companies that were listed in India between 2013 and 2022. Panel data estimation technique was used to examine the connection between board diversity and CSD. The results demonstrate that CSD in Indian financial companies is in its infancy. CSD and independence diversity are significantly and favourably related. Gender diversity has no effect on CSD. Additionally, having an IT specialist on board considerably raises CSD levels and moderates the association between independence diversity and CSD, but does not successfully moderate the association between gender diversity and CSD. This study contributes to the literature through empirical evidence on the extent of CSD practises, relationship between board diversity and CSD, and the importance of an IT specialist on the board in defining CSD practises.

Various definitions of violence exist, ranging from those that only consider physical assaults to those that also take into account sexual assault, psychological abuse, and economic exploitation. Both genders are discursively represented in their heterogeneity. (The feminine is frequently portrayed as a commodity, while the masculine is frequently portrayed as weak and pathological.) What is more important, though, is the understanding that there are specific types of gender violence that target women and utilize sexist language and images to harm and oppress them. This incident is categorized in the study as semiotic violence. Women are not the only ones who may experience this type of assault; anybody can. Even though it is the most pervasive, covert, and despised kind of violence committed against a person, it is generally ignored. The main goal of this study on semiotic violence is to improve understanding of this kind of violence.

The internet is directly proportional to the influence it has on society. Although contacting others has become quite simple with the internet, it has its own disadvantages. Privacy invasion, internet abuse, cyberbullying, and many more negative effects are just a few of its downsides. The purpose of this chapter is to provide a succinct analysis of the notion of cyberbullying. Not every internet user in the digital world identifies what they encounter as cyberbullying since it seems to be becoming more commonplace. Finding solutions to problems becomes challenging if the cause of the issue cannot be located. To have an in-depth understanding of the issue, it is essential to first define cyberbullying and examine its characteristics. This chapter attempts to understand cyberbullying in its many forms and causes in addition to examining people's, especially youths', idea on this deadly phenomenon that is rapidly growing.

Cyber-feminism is a concept that has emerged in response to the increasing use of technology and the internet in our daily lives. At its core, cyber-feminism is about challenging the gender biases that exist in the technology industry and ensuring that women have equal access to technology and digital spaces. The chapter covers the history of cyber-feminism, including key thinkers and activists who have contributed to its development. The chapter discusses strategies for staying safe online, including the importance of digital literacy and education. This chapter explores the role of cyber-feminism in the digital space through a case study approach. Specifically, it examines the impact of the #MeToo Movement, the Women's March, and the story of Malala Yousafzai. By highlighting the successes and challenges of cyber-feminist movements, this chapter offers insights into how we can work towards a more inclusive and feminist digital future. The chapter provides a unique and original perspective on the topic of Cyber-feminism. While existing literature on the subject tends to focus on theoretical discussions, this chapter employs a case study methodology to examine the impact of Cyber-feminism on real-world events such as the #MeToo Movement, Women's March, and the story of Malala Yousafzai. This approach provides a deeper understanding of the practical applications of Cyber-feminism and how it can affect change in society. Furthermore, the chapter highlights the potential impact that Cyber-feminism can have in promoting gender equality in the digital space and beyond. By analyzing the key issues of Cyber-feminism and offering potential solutions, the chapter adds significant value by providing actionable insights for those interested in promoting gender equality.

in the chapter, connecting the dots and linking every other issue in cyber security to master the art of living in the digital space, deriving optimum output from the same without being masqueraded by the pretentious elements with ulterior motives.

The increasing use of digital technologies and the internet has provided immense opportunities for communication, information sharing, and social interaction. However, alongside these benefits, the cyber world has also become a platform for the perpetration of offences against women. This chapter investigates the problem of violations and crimes targeting women in the cyber world, with particular emphasis on India. It explores the various forms of cyber offence women face, the underlying factors contributing to such crime, and the legal and policy framework in India. The chapter also highlights the challenges in addressing cyber offences against women and proposes strategies for prevention and support.

Th chapter presents an empirical study on a Brazilian cyber-activism movement on Instagram associated with the hashtag #CorpoLivre (#FreeBody in Portuguese). This movement, which was established in 2018, has published more than 3,000 posts and has over 400,000 followers, disseminates anti-fatphobia and real body discourses, and promotes a positive relationship between women and their bodies beyond traditional beauty standards. The study analyses the posts made by the feminist movement on Instagram in December 2022, with a sample size of 101 posts. The study adopted the framework developed by Khurana and Knight for the analysis, which enables the classification of the sample posts in terms of message appeal, orientation, engagement, popularity, and image characteristics. This framework was used to examine the relationship between content characteristics and engagement. Additionally, the study includes a content analysis of the posts' comments, specifically evaluating the valence (positive, negative, or neutral) to assess the effectiveness of the characteristics of the posts.

Cyber security has always been critical for safeguarding sensitive information, but in recent years, its impact on physical health has become increasingly apparent. The need for cyber security has become more critical in the digital age, as cyber threats have become more sophisticated and pervasive. As healthcare becomes increasingly digitized, the need for robust cyber security measures has become more important than ever. Cyber-attacks on healthcare systems can have devastating consequences on patient care, as the loss of crucial patient information can lead to delays or errors in medical treatment.

Moreover, the pandemic has accelerated the shift to remote healthcare and telemedicine, leading to an increase in cyber-attacks on personal devices used for medical purposes, such as laptops and smartphones. These attacks can compromise personal health data, leading to delayed or ineffective medical treatment.

The use of social media has become increasingly prevalent over the past decade, with platforms such as Facebook, Twitter, and Instagram boasting billions of active users. Social media platforms provide users with a variety of ways to connect with others, including the ability to share photos, videos, and messages in real-time. However, this increased connectivity has also led to a rise in cyber-bullying. Cyber-bullying refers to the use of electronic devices and technology, such as social media platforms, to harass, intimidate, or embarrass others. Cyber-bullying can take many forms, including spreading rumors, making threats, and posting hurtful or humiliating comments or images. Unlike traditional forms of bullying, cyber-bullying can occur 24/7, and the anonymity afforded by social media platforms can make it difficult to identify perpetrators.

Digital revolution experienced by the human race has made great impact on presentation of bodies and self. Observing the (re)presentation of self in the social constructed phenomenon of 'selfie' through sociological lens opens up gate for variety of conceptual and theoretical perspectives. The study aims to make inquiry in complex interplay among body, technology, and social control reflected in selfie. For this purpose, the study employs Netnography techniques along with thematic analysis under frameworks like dramaturgy, sociosemiotic, and dialectic to explore and describe sociologically relevant theories to grasp novel avenues of social control and (re)presentation of women's bodies through selfie. The chapter intend to develop space for further sociological research that enables the perception of selfies not only as socially constructed phenomenon but also a tool for social control over (re)presentation of self and objectification women bodies in cyberspace.

Cyber-feminism is a concept that has emerged in response to the increasing use of technology and the internet in our daily lives. At its core, cyber-feminism is about challenging the gender biases that exist in the technology industry and ensuring that women have equal access to technology and digital spaces. The chapter covers the history of cyber-feminism, including key thinkers and activists who have contributed to its development. The chapter discusses strategies for staying safe online, including the importance of digital literacy and education. This chapter explores the role of cyber-feminism in the digital space through a case study approach. Specifically, it examines the impact of the #MeToo Movement, the Women's March, and the story of Malala Yousafzai. By highlighting the successes and challenges of cyber-feminist movements, this chapter offers insights into how we can work towards a more inclusive and feminist digital future.

Foreword

Gender violence and social media is one trending topic which specifies victimization of women on social media. This mostly happens due to lack of understanding technology and its advancements thereby leading to victimisation resulting in abuses, suicide, personal injury and even impact on mental health. The book, *Cyberfeminism and Gender Violence on Social Media* is a very much promising book which is enriched with basket of research work that are qualitative in nature and are from various countries across the globe. It not only has chapters on the concept of social media, but also on the roles of the peers in preventing such violence. The book will surely be hugely popular for which one of the reasons being that it is being published by one of the most leading publishers of the world, IGI Global. I wish this book and the author, Deepanjali Mishra, all success in this publication.

Le Anh Ngoc
Swinburne University, Australia and Vietnam

Preface

Cyber feminism is a new term which advocates for fighting for those women who are victims of social media. It has emerged from the movement of "Feminism" which was formed to provide equal rights to women in legal, social, and academic aspects. Social Media has proved to be a platform where users can interact with people and share their feelings, expressions, using multimedia irrespective of location, time, status and recognition. Even though it is considered to be beneficial in various aspects, like academics, research, developing contacts, at the same time it has various negative impacts (Cammaerts, 2015). There have been various cases where women fall victims of extortion, forgery, manipulation, etc. by people using pseudo names which make the victims difficult to recognize. Women are victims of criminal activities like cyber trolling, Online pornography, body morphing, texting objectionable contents etc. just to name a few (Creswell, 2007). There are various situations where women lose mental stability and do not hesitate to do anything or take drastic steps which may bring harm to their reputation and also to their family. These led to suicides, harming oneself in order to escape from the culprits. The major advantage of the victim is when he commits a crime online, it is easy to escape unharmed. The government has formulated certain laws and guidelines for such type of cases, but they are not enough. The Information technology laws also are not stringent to nab the culprits (Amnesty International, 2018). Awareness and creating platform for awareness is the only way to make the victims realize the negative and positive impact of social media and they should also be trained to use social media which would protect them from falling into the prey of the digital mafia. Therefore, the basic objective of this paper is to make an explicit analysis of various types of victimization of women on social media through case analyses and real life experiences.

The book, *Cyberfeminism and Gender Violence on Social Media* is an exploration of various aspects on asserting women's rights, victimization of women and subsequently means and measures to overcome the subjugation and violence using social media. The chapters are a plethora of vast intellectual research from various nations across the globe.

Deepanjali Mishra
KIIT University, India

REFERENCES

Amnesty International. (2018). *Toxic Twitter - A Toxic Place for Women.* Amnesty International. https://www.amnesty.org/en/latest/research/2018/03/online-violence-against-women-chapter-1/

Cammaerts, B. (2015). Social Media and Activism. In The International Encyclopedia of Digital Communication and Society. doi:10.1002/9781118767771.wbiedcs083

Creswell, J. W. (2007). *Qualitative Inquiry & Research Design*. In Sage Publications, Inc. doi:10.1111/1467-9299.00177

Acknowledgement

At the outset, I would like to express my heartfelt gratitude to my parents for their constant support. I would also like to express my unconditional gratitude to my most revered Vice Chancellor, Professor Sasmita Samanta for her motivation for all my academic endeavours.

Chapter 1
Antecedents of Marital Rape Cases:
Disgracing Assailants via Social Media Forums

Sugyanta Priyadarshini
Kalinga Institute of Industrial Technology, India

ABSTRACT

Indian society has never freed itself from the shackles of patriarchy and its age-old norms. In a diverse nation like India, with age-old gender stereotypes, beliefs, and tradition, the concept of marital rape stands as vague and hence isn't illegal. As all the three pillars of democracy—judiciary, legislature, and executive—stand blindfolded, the only ray of hope lies with the media as they play a major role in shaming the attackers and holding them accountable. The current study is central to understanding the role of social media in shaming the attackers of marital rape by analyzing the possible impact of physical force used by the perpetrator and sexual assault severity on post-trauma stress disorder and coping self-efficacy in particular in marital rape victims. Thus, in this ground, social media can be an effective medium to bring forth the conversations about marital rape into the public sphere by conducting debates, seminars, and interviews in order to effectively engage the public to understand their mindset.

INTRODUCTION

From a woman's salad days, she is being edified to bide in a hunky-dory mythus world. Unfortunately, this bubble of fallacy bursts when she gains muleibrity and steps into the pandemonium and bedlam Janus-faced society where in one hand, she is prayed in culture as goddess and on the other hand, she is preyed by men for pleasure. This bacillus of men of preying on women for pleasure for aeons has metamorphosed into the culture of rape. The society has always been grappled with the scourge of rape turning it into one of the challenging crime as it is the most underreported practice of assault in the criminal justice system (Randall & Haskall, 1995; Yamasaki & Tschanz, 2005; Ullman & Siegel, 1993;

DOI: 10.4018/978-1-6684-8893-5.ch001

Mahoney & Williams, 1998; Adinkrah, 2011). Rape can be defined as a kind of sexual penetration, irrespective of how slight or deep, into the vagina or anus, using any body part or object by the perpetrator without the prior consent of the victim (Koss & Oros 1982; Koss & Gidycz, 1985; Koss et al., 2007). Dolefully, the prejudiced pyramid of rape does not reckon the heinous strata of marital rape. The act of marital rape has been a culturally acceptable and fostered means of suppressing women sexually. Marital rape refers to the rape committed by the victim's spouse. The definition of marital rape remains same as rape, but the only contrast is the nuptial bond between the victim and the perpetrator. The visibly invisible atrocious phenomenon of marital rape is even tougher to study and has remained to be the least studied form of sexual assault (Martin et.al., 2007). The reasons behind the arduous challenge to study this very phenomenon could be low reporting rates (Basile, 2002) and diminutive conviction rates (Ferro et.al., 2008).

Marriage in India is pristine and this is a license for permissible sex. Traditionally, it is considered that one of the duties of a married woman is to bear children. So, a lot of non-consensual sex goes on in Indian households and our society seems to be fine with it. World Health Organization declared that women are mostly unsafe at their respective homes following the estimates according to which, one in every three women have experienced physical or sexual abuse in the hands of their spouse in 2017. India is counted among the countries with highest incidence of intimate partner sexual violence. Further, Thomson Reuters Foundation survey has confirmed India to be the most dangerous nation for married woman as they are subjected to a wide range of physical and sexual assaults in the hands of their husband (Shah, 2018). However, the situation is more perturbing in India where spousal sexual violence inform of marital rape is either mostly normalized or ignored widely by the persisting patriarchal society. Unfortunately, the government and the supporting law enforcement agencies are a product of the patriarchal ethos resulting in confining the continuation of sexual assault of wives in the hands of their husbands. With all doors shut, the only ray of hope lies with the media as they play a major role in shaming the attackers and holding them accountable. Moreover, the social media provides an interactive climate with no gatekeepers that gives freedom to the victims of marital rape to express their agony and shame the purveyors (Armstrong & Mahone, 2016).

Marriage isn't equal to consent. Being married is not a valid justification for sexual abuse. But, unfortunately cases of marital rapes are growing in number irrespective of voluminous research works and policy framework. However, after several studies by eminent scholars on consequences of marital rape on the victim; it was observed that marital rape has a significant impact on physical, psychological and social well-being of the wives (Gelles & Straus, 1988; Kilpatrick et al., 1988). In the immediate hours of sexual abuse, victims were exposed to severe shock and disbelief and its aftermath is experienced in the later period (Burgess & Holmstrom, 1974). During the initial weeks following a marital rape, victims are witnessed with acute somatic manifestations including Physical trauma (general soreness and bruising in throat, neck, breasts, thighs, legs, and arms), skeletal muscle tension (Tension headaches and fatigue, as well as sleep pattern disturbances), gastrointestinal irritability (stomach ache, lowered appetite, loosing taste) and genitourinary disturbance (vaginal discharge, itching, a burning sensation on urination). The long-term effects of marital rape resulted in increase in motor activity (including changing residence and phone number as a precautionary measure from threatening or obscene phone calls), fear of indoors, fright of resuming sexual relations with others and prolonged nightmares which could be quite upsetting (Burgess & Holmstrom, 1974).

Purpose of the Study

The literature on marital rape is voluminous, but it has overlooked the psychological and physical impact on victim. The current study deals with the sexual assault severity, force applied by perpetrator, psychological distress, physical injury and copying efficiency of the victims of marital rape. The present pragmatic study aims to explore the relationship among the above-mentioned assault characteristics by addressing few questions such as

What is the possible impact of the force used by the perpetrator and sexual assault severity on the coping self-efficacy of the victim?
Whether any stern reaction of victim restrain the frequency of marital rapes by perpetrator?
What is the possible situation instigating the perpetrator to conduct marital rape and which situation highly triggered the physical force used in the misconduct?
What is the role of social media in shaming the attackers of marital rape?

Research Methodology

In order to find out the possible determinants and consequences of marital rape on victims, 125 women were interviewed who have once reported a complaint against their spouse for sexual assault and domestic violence. The data is collected from the respondents aging 20-40 years through convenient sampling and then through snowball sampling. The data is collected from nine north eastern states of India (Odisha, West Bengal, Mizoram, Manipur, Meghalaya, Nagaland, Arunachal Pradesh, Assam, Meghalaya and Sikkim). The data was collected from these least developing states keeping in mind the high rate of women victimization to domestic violence and sexual assaults in hands of husband. They were communicated through telephonic survey and personal visits by the investigator. The questions were phrased in different forms, such that subjects themselves could define marital rape in their words. In context of domestic violence, questions related to marital rape were asked. Such as respondents were asked if ever their spouse made attempts to conduct sexual intercourse unpleasantly by force. Further, it was also asked if her husband ever pressurized her to have sex and how had he pressurized her. Additionally, after asking questions related to forced sex, the respondents were asked if they were ever raped by their husband. If they answered it as yes, then they were further asked to describe the situation that resulted in rape, her reactions after being raped and her feelings about this misconduct. Out of 125 respondents, 50 women agreed to the fact that they were at least once raped by their husband in their marital relationship. A standard set of 4 questionnaires is prepared for a structured interview in a prearranged order. First set of question was regarding the demographic characteristic of the victim that included her age, years to her marriage, current marital status and financial status of the victim and her husband. Secondly, the next questionnaire was forwarded which focused on the reaction of the victim after the very first time victimized to marital rape, situation triggering the perpetrator to forcefully attempt sexual intercourse, frequency of the misconduct, and reasons for not restraining the misconduct of marital rape. Third questionnaire was regarding the construct of assault severity and physical force used during the act and lastly, they were investigated on post assault trauma, physical injury and copying self-efficiency. The interviewer was a woman who reciprocated with the subjects regarding their reactions and bitter experiences of marital rape. Few respondents emotionally broke down but were then encouraged to talk about their deep-down feelings by providing emotional support by the interviewer. In order to learn about the post trauma symptoms in victim and relative efforts of victim for copying self-efficacy, a 17-item PTSD scale (Post Trauma Stress disorder) and 26-item CSES (Coping Self-Efficacy Scale) was used respectively. Further, the criterion validity and significance of the relationship among the assault characteristics (assault severity, physical force used by perpetrator), physical injury, coping self-efficacy and post assault distress was assessed through regression analysis. Bivariate correlations were conducted in order to examine the relationship between stern reaction of victim after the very first-time forced sex with the frequency of marital rapes by perpetrator. Both regression and correlation analysis were conducted through SPSS (Statistical Package for Social Sciences). The process of data collection took a period of approximately eleven months to meet the sample size and to conduct in-depth analysis of the matter.

DISCUSSION

Even though, the country is vocal about the issues of domestic violence, rape, trafficking, forced prostitution, but it turns blind eye in the name of culture and tradition when it comes to marital rape. However, a victim of marital rape who is unable to leave her husband due to certain obligations was asked about her experience to which she responded:

Now these days, I fear to go to bed at night. I am scared of what my husband will do with me. It's a never-ending pain. My fear is inside the house, not outside. I feel safer outside and trapped inside. It remains visibly invisible to my family. Am dependent on my husband financially, so I can't leave him. Now, this is my destiny.

Similarly, another victim of marital rape who divorced her husband due to repeated forced sex by him mentioned that:

I have developed a fear of men and an instinctive dislike towards sex. Sex just means pain is the only presumption set in my mind because of what happened in my marital life. I am in a relationship where I fear to share my bed with my boyfriend. I am still getting those nightmares. It haunts me every day. I can't forget that pain and scream. I am trying to forget it but can't help it.

A Detail Analysis of Demographic Characteristics of the Victim to Marital Rape

Figure 1 shows the detail demographic division in terms of age (I), marital status (II), years to marriage (III), employment status (IV), if employed their respective income (V) and income of their spouse (VI) with its respective frequency. After complete analysis it was found that none of the wives are earning more than their husband except in case of two couples where the income of wives falls under the range of Rs 50,000 and above and Rs 40,000-50,000 but their spouse earns within a range of Rs 30,000-40,000 in both the cases. Out of these two cases, in one case the wife is divorced and is living independently but in the other case the wife is still stuck in the marital bond where she is still facing forced sex but is unable to leave her husband because of the fear of losing the dignity in the society. Out of 28 employed wives, 35.71% are still married after coming across repeated marital rapes because they either don't want to spoil their child's future or due to the fear of losing dignity in the society whereas 64.29% have divorced their husband for such misconduct. Similarly, out of 22 unemployed wives, 86.36% are still

Figure 1. Demographic characteristics of victim of marital rape

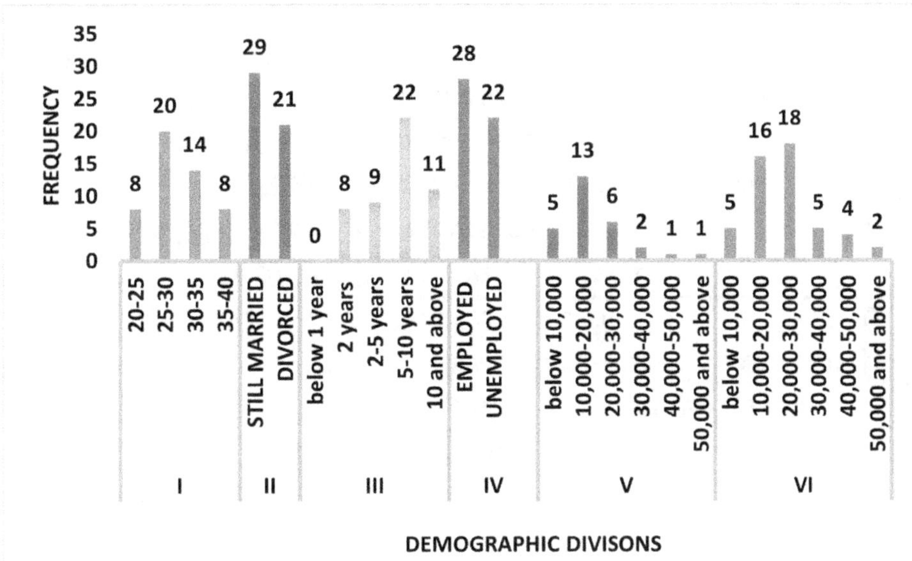

married whereas 13.64% have divorced their husband as they either could not take it anymore or have found a better person for remarriage. Consequently, it was found that majorly, financially independent women have preferred to divorce their husband due the misconduct but financially dependent housewives could not manage to leave their husband after being forcefully raped by several times.

Additionally, data was also collected regarding situation behind marital rapes, frequency of forced sex, reaction of victim after first forced sex, and finally reasons for not restraining the misconduct by husband in Figure 2. It was found that there are four major actions that instigate husbands to go for marital rape. 80% husbands endorsed consuming alcohol (25% of perpetrators had 2-4 drinks, 60% had 5-6 drinks, and 15% had 7 or more drinks)which is considered as a significant reason behind provoking the perpetrator for forced sex; followed by 60% husbands bringing the frustration of job back to their home and taking out the anger on their wives by forcefully raping her; 40% husbands rape their wives as they can't stand any offensive words by their wives which badly hurt their male ego and then ultimately use muscle power to physically injure her and rape her to let them know their limits; and then ultimately 20% husbands believe in BDSM (Bondage and discipline, dominance and submission, sadochism and masochism) where they receive pleasure by constantly conducting sex with their wife by giving immense pain without pre-sex negotiations, disclosure, consent and safe words.

Impact of Physical Force Used and Sexual Assault Severity on CSE of Victims of Marital Rape

A complete rape where the perpetrator uses extreme physical force is considered as the most severe type of sexual assault. The current study examines level force and sexual assault severity used in the rape scenario and its impact on coping efficacy of the victims perceived marital rape. The independent variable, level of physical force is segregated into three levels: subtle force (ignored the victims' response and embraced her, lifted her skirt and completed the act of intercourse), moderate force (ignored the

Figure 2. Data on pre- and post-marital rape scenario

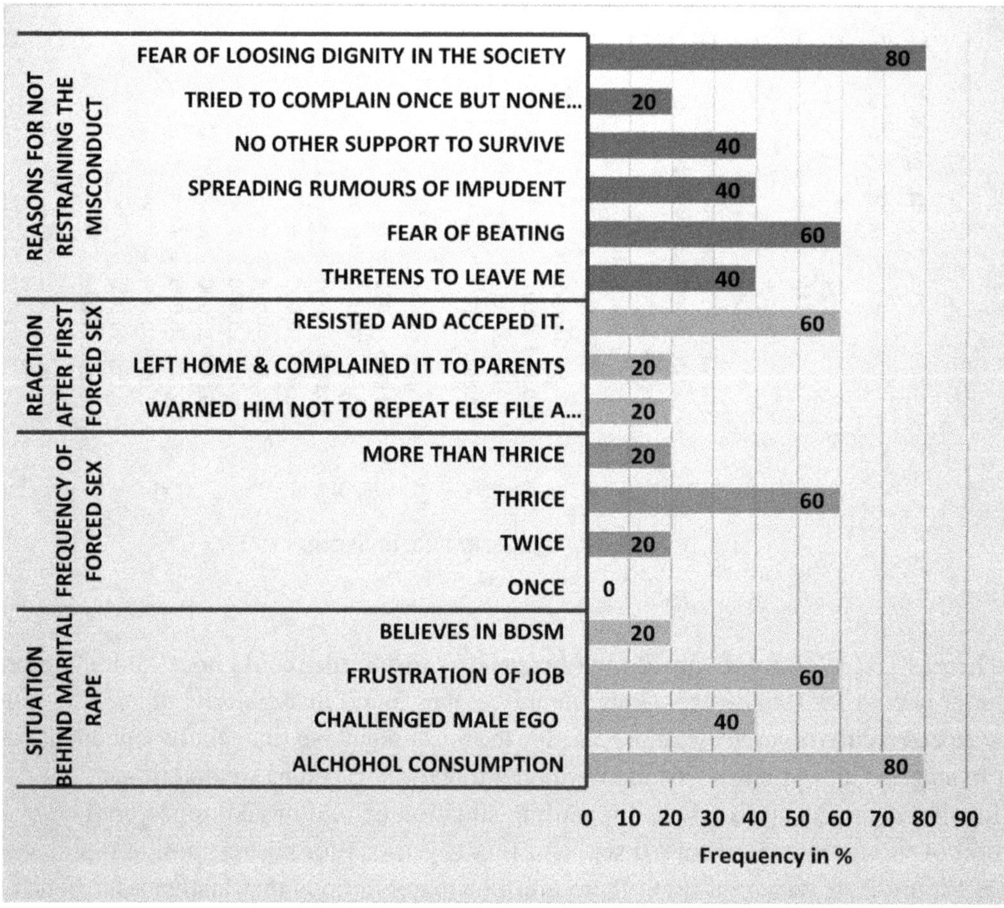

victim's response and grabbed the shoulders, pinned her down and completed the act of intercourse.) and extreme force (ignored the victim's response and grabbed her by the hair, threw her to the couch, forced himself on top of her and completed the act of intercourse). After taking into account, the actions involved during unwanted sex, these three levels of force were constructed to explore the physical force engaged during the marital rape. The respondents scored the intensity of force by using a Likert type scale ranging from 1(subtle force) to 3 (maximum force) when asked about 'What was the possible extent of physical injury on the victim just after the misconduct?'. The dependent variable is the participant rating on the coping self-efficacy by the use of 26 item Coping Self-Efficacy Scale (Chesney et al.,2006). Respondents were requested to rate on 11-point Likert Scale ranging from 0 to 10 (0- "fail to do at all", 5- "can do till certain extent", 10- "can do it certainly"). The score ranges from 26 to 260. The higher the score gained from the statements, higher will be the level of victim's coping self-efficacy. The internal consistency of the scale in the current study is excellent (α = .91). Further, victimization severity or sexual assault severity is measured by using a mutually exclusive ordinal ranking order ranging from 1 to 9 by asking to range the statement: "How far the unwanted sexual act was enforced on you?" (Sexual touching = 1, attempted oral sex = 2, attempted vaginal sex = 3, attempted anal sex = 4, offender attempted to make victim perform oral sex = 5, completed oral sex = 6, victim made to

Table 1. Significant association between physical force, assault severity and coping self-efficacy

Model		Unstandardized Coefficients		Standardized Coefficients	Sig.
		B	Std. Error	Beta	
1	(Constant)	411.800	7.890		.000
	PHYSICAL FORCE	-86.100	8.126	-.636	.000
	ASSAULT SEVERITY	-14.500	2.379	-.366	.000

perform oral sex = 7, completed vaginal sex = 8, and completed anal sex = 9). This scale ranges from not so severe (sexual touching) to extreme harm (completed anal sex). Higher the score gained, higher is perceived assault severity (Swinson, 2013).

Regression analysis is conducted to assess whether perceived physical force and sexual assault severity serve as a predictor to the coping self-efficacy of the victims of marital rape. It was evident that physical force (α= 0.00) and assault severity conditions (α=0.00) were significantly more likely to limit the victim to cope self-efficacy after the misconduct. Both perceived physical force (β= -0.636) and sexual assault (β= -0.366) severity were negatively related to coping self-efficacy in victims. Approximately, 76% of the respondents scored within a range of 80-100 which signifies low coping self-efficacy among the victims. The analysis magnified the fact that 67% of victims have come across completed vaginal sex by imposing extreme force by the perpetrator and 26% have faced unwanted complete anal sex with a massive force by the perpetrator. These two types of severity combined with extreme force was evident in maximum number of cases. It was observed that mostly wives have low coping self-efficacy if she was subjected to extreme force during forced anal intercourse as she is likely to perceive the situation as impossible and experience intense fear. Consequently, the victim may develop maladaptive coping strategies which may result in PTSD. Therefore, it can also be considered that low CSE can be a significant component of assault severity and physical force perceived by the perpetrator on victim which is examined through regression analysis in Table 1.

Negative Reaction of Victim After First Forced Sex Limiting the Frequency of Forced Sex

It was evident from the study that 60% of victims have been raped thrice in a month by their husband, followed by 20% have been raped twice and 20% have been raped more than thrice a month. No subject was raped just for once in a month. After facing marital rape for the very first time, 60% victims resisted and accepted it where as 20% victims left their homes and complained it to their parents and 20% warned their husband for divorce after being raped by them. Out of the 30 victims who preferred resisting and accepting the non-consensual sex, 20 women faced it thrice a month and 10 women faced it more than thrice a month. Out of 10 victims who left their homes and complained regarding the same to their parents, 7 of them were victimized to marital rape twice a month and 3 of them faced it thrice. On the other hand, out of 10 victims who warned their husband for divorce after being raped by them, 3 of them were victimized to marital rape twice a month and 7 of them faced it thrice a month reason being hurting their partner's male ego of not subjugating themselves to bestow the desire of their husband. However, it was observed that the negative reaction after first forced sex and frequency of forced sex is significantly

Table 2. Association between negative reaction after first forced sex and frequency of forced sex

Correlation between negative reaction after first forced sex and frequency of forced sex		REACTION	FREQUENCY
NEGATIVE REACTION	Pearson Correlation	1	-.791**
	Sig. (2-tailed)		.000
	N	50	50
FREQUENCY	Pearson Correlation	-.791**	1
	Sig. (2-tailed)	.000	
	N	50	50

**. Correlation is significant at the 0.01 level (2-tailed).

negatively correlated. Negative reaction includes leaving respective homes, complaining parents and in-laws, warning husband for divorce which condenses the frequency of repeated non-consensual sex. The correlation between negative reaction after first forced sex and frequency of forced sex is -0.791 which exhibits high degree of negative correlation between the variables. Further, the correlation coefficient is more than seven times the probable error, establishing a significant relationship between the variables.

Possible Situation Instigating the Perpetrator to Conduct Marital Rape on Victim and the Probable Extent of Injury

While examining the substance use by the perpetrator, it was observed that 80% husbands endorsed consuming alcohol (25% of perpetrators had 2-4 drinks, 60% had 5-6 drinks, and 15% had 7 or more drinks) which is considered as a significant reason behind provoking the perpetrator for forced sex; followed by 60% husbands bringing the frustration of job back to their home and taking out the anger on their wives by forcefully raping her; 40% husbands rape their wives as they can't stand any offensive words by their wives which badly hurt their male ego and then ultimately use muscle power to physically injure her and rape her to let them know their limits; and then ultimately 20% husbands believe in BDSM where they receive pleasure by constantly conducting sex with their wise by giving immense pain without pre-sex negotiations, disclosure, consent and safe words which is shown in Figure 3. However, the victims confessed that their drunk husband (irrespective of n number of drinks) applied massive force on them while the conduct of nonconsensual sex which resulted in swallow cut (50% victims faced it) and deep cut (other 50% victims faced it) in their vaginal area. Further, out of the 60% husbands who brought the frustration of job back to their home and took out the anger on their wives by forcefully raping her, 70% applied moderate force, 20% applied subtle force and 10% applied massive force which caused bruising (25% victims faced it), swelling (40% victims faced it), swallow cut (30% victims faced it) and deep cut (5% victims faced it) in vaginal areas. Additionally, out of 40% husbands who raped their wives as they hurt their male ego, 56.66% applied moderate force, 26.67% applied subtle force and 16.67% applied massive force which caused bruising (33.33% victims faced it), swelling (30% victims faced it), swallow

Figure 3. Possible situation instigating the perpetrator to conduct marital rape on victim

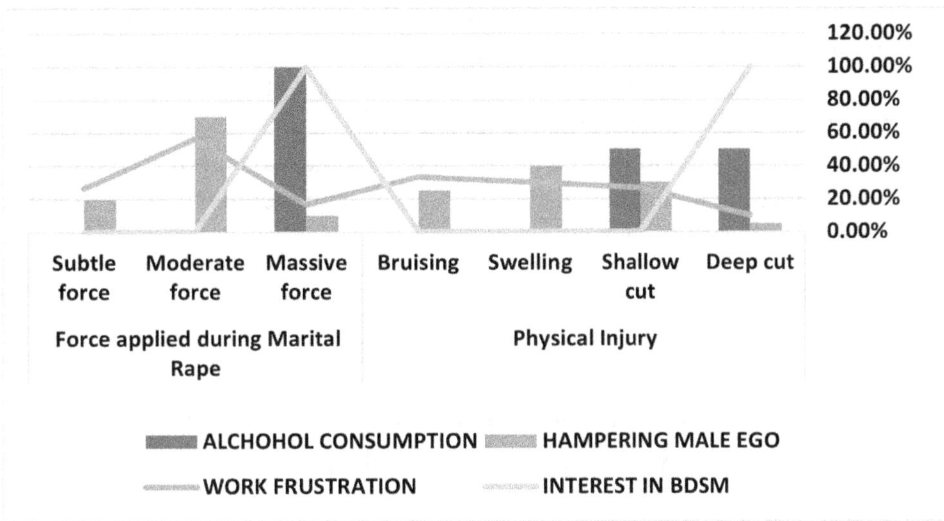

cut (26.67% victims faced it) and deep cut (10% victims faced it) in vaginal areas. However, it was sad to note that, 98% of victims did not seek medical treatment following the assault.

Role of Social Media in Shaming the Attackers of Marital Rape

Marital rape isn't illegal in India. It is not included in the list of sexual offences as mentioned in IPC. According to Exception 2 of Section 375 of the Indian Penal Code (IPC), it is not considered as rape when a man engages in sexual activity with his own wife. Interestingly, Indian courts have never been on the same page when it comes to marital rape. The views and verdicts of the courts stand polar opposite of each other. A court in Maharashtra (Punekar, 2021) granted anticipatory bail to a man while coming to the conclusion that having forcible intercourse with his wife was not an "illegal thing," despite the fact that she claimed it left her paralysed; whereas the Kerala High Court (Srmtech, 2022) endorsed marital rape as a legitimate basis for divorce. A plethora of cases support marital rape whereas many disregard the concept (Rajagopal, 2021). Although, the supreme court in a historic judgement recognised marital rape but still it doesn't stand illegal (Outlook Web Desk, 2022). Moreover, the Government also doesn't support the decision to frame laws to punish the marital rape perpetuators. Centre believes that India shouldn't blindly follow the west and make marital rape illegal as India has its own unique problems and criminalising marital rape will disrupt families and the dignity of women (Garg, 2022).

As the centre and judiciary fails to understand the pain and agony of women, the media can play a vital role in creating awareness and shaming the purveyors of marital rape. Studies on internet activism, social media, and rape culture are becoming more and more common (Zaleski et al., 2016). Within a very short span of time, social media has established itself as a very effective instrument for raising awareness, disseminating information, and organising campaigns on a range of subjects over time (Agbasiere, 2021). With the help of this tool, anyone can instantly share content and thoughts with a global audience. This medium has proved to be a potential podium for traumatised women who want to share their painful experiences, sufferings and start a clarion call on the prevailing injustice towards them. Further, the media can contribute towards digital feminism and activism (Rentschler, 2014) in amending the laws and making marital rape illegal in India. It has the potential to play a potent role in shaping the opinions and perspective of people, organisations, government and judiciary about the legality of marital rape culture. Moreover, social media can be an effective medium to bring forth the conversations about marital rape into the public sphere by conducting debates, seminars and interviews in order to effectively engage the public to understand their mindset (Stubbs-Richardson et al., 2018). The journalists can collect the data and statistics of marital rape victims in order to create awareness and change the old aged mindset of people.

RESULTS

It was evident from the study that the Perceived physical force and Sexual assault severity serve as a predictor to the coping self-efficacy of the victims of marital rape. These two factors significantly limit the victim to cope self-efficacy after the misconduct. Additionally, it can be said that higher the Perceived physical force and Sexual assault severity imposed on victim, lower is the probability of coping self-efficacy. Further, it was analyzed that the negative reaction after first forced sex and frequency of forced sex is significantly negatively correlated. If the victim tried to restrain the spouse from committing such immoral conduct by negative reactions such as leaving home, complaining parents and in-laws, warning for divorce, then the frequency of forced sex reduced significantly. On the other hand, remaining silent or bearing the forced sex increases the frequency of the misconduct. Additionally, the possible situation instigating the perpetrator to conduct marital rape on victim are found to be alcoholic consumption (80%) followed by job frustration (60%); then clashing male ego (40%) and ultimately fond of BDSM (20%). However, massive force was imposed mostly after alcoholic consumption by perpetrator and often by the perpetrators who are fond of BDSM. The marital rape has so tightly grappled the society and created bigots in existing patriarchy that men have considered marital rape as their birth right. This virulent and malignant thought must be eradicated from the society and for this awareness creation is the most effective vaccine. Strategies by use of social media like Instagram, YouTube, poster campaign, advertised slogan, sharing of real-life stories and delivering statics and information in several podiums can be fruitful in changing the mindset of the society. Educating students and youth is the best approach to bust sex related violence in the community. Further, medical curriculum should accommodate education on gender violence with courses on how to manage sexually harassed victims and providing them love, care and support.

CONCLUSION

The voyage of a woman in the soaring tides of social atrocities has never been a hunky-dory ride. Marital rape, being one of the major social atrocities has always bullwhipped the dignity, self-respect, psychological and physical wellbeing of women. Marital rape is rape; irrespective of the victim being the wife of the perpetrator. Unfortunately, since what could have been done has not been done so far therefore, it is high time for government to bring in comprehensive legislation without further dawdle to penalize marital rape and proclaim it as an act of paramount violence rather than the issue of conjugal rights. However, every coin has two sides. On one hand, the legislation to penalize marital rape will empower women and protect them from violence whereas, on the other hand, the above said legislation can be misused by women for her personal interests which may place an innocent behind the bars. Even though, the upper hand lies in criminalizing marital rape as no women would slap, hit and injure herself to cite it as a marital rape and earn disgrace in the society. However, it is sad to note that Government has turned a blind eye towards the issue and is loathful to legalize marital rape. What flabbergasting is, government has used the excuse of prevailing societal, cultural and traditional ethos to deny in framing stringent laws against marital rape. The quietude around marital rape as maintained by social system and lawlessness has empowered the perpetrator to conduct this heinous act without any culpability. The social media serves as a 'technology of non-violence' (Hart & Mitchell, 2015) to address the issue of marital rape and shame the perpetuators. In this techno savvy world, with the rampant use of social media, it can definitely play a pivotal role in making vocal the years of pain and screams of marital rape victims. It will encourage other women to come forward and punish their attackers, although they are their better half. It has the power to change the mindset of people, who believe rape as conjugal right of husband and to stay silent as good wife's duty. With Government and Judiciary taking little to no action, the onus to create awareness about marital rape and shame the purveyors lies on the hands of social media. And the social media activism on marital rape will continue till the perception of people haven't been changed and definite laws to punish the purveyors haven't been framed.

REFERENCES

Adinkrah, M. (2011). Criminalizing rape within marriage; perspectives of Ghanaian University Students. *International Journal of Offender Therapy and Comparative Criminology*, *55*(6), 982–1010. doi:10.1177/0306624X10371800 PMID:20516292

Agbasiere, C. (2021). Assessing the Role of social media in the Fight Against Sexual Assault. *Path of Science, 7*, 5001–5006.

Armstrong, C. L., & Mahone, J. (2016). *"It's On Us." The Role of Social Media and Rape Culture in Individual Willingness to Mobilize Against Sexual Assault: Mass Communication and Society*. https://www.tandfonline.com/doi/abs/10.1080/15205436.2016.1185127

Basile, K. C. (2002). Prevalence of wife rape and other intimate partner sexual coercion in a nationally representative sample of women. *Violence and Victims*, *17*(5), 511–524. doi:10.1891/vivi.17.5.511.33717 PMID:12477095

Burgess, A. W., & Holmstrom, L. L. (1974). Rape Trauma Syndrome. *The American Journal of Psychiatry*, *131*(9), 981–986. doi:10.1176/ajp.131.9.981 PMID:4415470

Chesney, M. A., Neilands, T. B., Chambers, D. B., Taylor, J. M., & Folkman, S. (2006). A validity and reliability study of the coping self-efficacy scale. *British Journal of Health Psychology*, *11*(3), 421–437. doi:10.1348/135910705X53155 PMID:16870053

Ferro, C., Cermele, J., & Saltzman, A. (2008). Current perceptions of marital rape: Some good and not-so-good news. *Journal of Interpersonal Violence*, *23*(6), 764–779. doi:10.1177/0886260507313947 PMID:18272725

Garg, A. (2022, January 29). Don't blindly follow West in criminalising marital rape: Govt. *The Times of India*. https://timesofindia.indiatimes.com/india/dont-blindly-follow-west-in-criminalising-marital-rape-govt/articleshow/89188920.cms

Gelles, R. J., & Straus, M. A. (1988). *Intimate Violence*. Simon & Schuster.

Kilpatrick, D. G., Best, C. L., Saunders, B. E., & Veronen, L. J. (1988). Rape in marriage and in dating relationships: How bad is it for mental health? *Annals of the New York Academy of Sciences*, *528*(1 Human Sexual), 335–344. doi:10.1111/j.1749-6632.1988.tb50875.x PMID:3421605

Koss, M. P., Abbey, A., Campbell, R., Cook, S., Norris, J., Testa, M., Ullman, S., West, C., & White, J. (2007). Revising the SES: A collaboration process to improve assessment of sexual aggression and victimization. *Psychology of Women Quarterly*, *31*(4), 357–370. doi:10.1111/j.1471-6402.2007.00385.x

Koss, M. P., & Gidycz, C. A. (1985). Sexual experiences survey: Reliability and validity. *Journal of Consulting and Clinical Psychology*, *53*(3), 422–423. doi:10.1037/0022-006X.53.3.422 PMID:3874219

Koss, M. P., & Oros, C. J. (1982). Sexual experiences survey: A research instrument investigating sexual aggression and victimization. *Journal of Consulting and Clinical Psychology*, *50*(3), 455–457. doi:10.1037/0022-006X.50.3.455 PMID:7096751

Mahoney, P., & Williams, L. M. (1998). Sexual assault in marriage: Prevalence, consequences, and treatment of wife rape. Academic Press.

Martin, E. K., Taft, C. T., & Resick, P. A. (2007). A review of marital rape. *Aggression and Violent Behavior*, *12*(3), 329–347. doi:10.1016/j.avb.2006.10.003

Outlook Web Desk. (2022, September 30). *SC's Observations "Welcome" But Marital Rape Still Not Illegal In India, Here Are Countries Where It Is*. Https://Www.Outlookindia.Com/. https://www.outlookindia.com/national/sc-observations-welcome-but-omarital-rape-still-not-illegal-in-india-here-are-countries-where-it-is-news-226913

Punekar. (2021, August 14). Mumbai: Woman Claims Marital Rape Led To Her Paralysis, Court Says "It Is Not Illegal To Have Relationship With Wife Without Her Consent." *Punekar News*. https://www.punekarnews.in/mumbai-woman-claims-marital-rape-led-to-her-paralysis-court-says-it-is-not-illegal-to-have-relationship-with-wife-without-her-consent/

Rajagopal, K. (2021, August 14). Courts continue to differ in views on marital rape. *The Hindu*. https://www.thehindu.com/news/national/courts-continue-to-differ-in-views-on-marital-rape/article61430217.ece

Randall, M., & Haskell, L. (1995). Sexual violence in women's lives: Findings from the Women's Safety Project, a community-based survey. *Violence Against Women*, *1*(1), 6–31. doi:10.1177/1077801295001001002 PMID:12346573

Rentschler, C. (2014). Rape Culture and the Feminist Politics of Social Media. *Girlhood Studies, 7*.

Shah, B. (2018, June 27). *India snags the first rank—It's the world's most dangerous country for women*. YourStory.Com. https://yourstory.com/2018/06/india-snags-first-rank-list-worlds-worst-places-live-women

Srmtech. (2022, March 24). *2021 Kerala HC remarks on marital rape that set a precedent.* The Federal. https://thefederal.com/analysis/2021-kerala-hc-remarks-on-marital-rape-that-set-a-precedent/

Stubbs-Richardson, M., Rader, N. E., & Cosby, A. G. (2018). Tweeting rape culture: Examining portrayals of victim blaming in discussions of sexual assault cases on Twitter. *Feminism & Psychology*, *28*(1), 90–108. doi:10.1177/0959353517715874

Swinson, K. C. (2013). *The Sexual Assault Severity Scale: A Comprehensive Measure of Assault Severity*. Dissertations. 199.

Ullman, S. E., & Siegel, J. M. (1993). Victim-offender relationship and sexual assault. *Violence and Victims*, *8*(2), 121–134. doi:10.1891/0886-6708.8.2.121 PMID:8193054

Yamasaki, N., & Tschanz, B. T. (2005). Rape perception differences between Japanese and American college students: On the mediating influence of gender role traditionality. *Sex Roles*, *52*(5/6), 379–392. Advance online publication. doi:10.100711199-005-2680-7

Zaleski, K. L., Gundersen, K. K., Baes, J., Estupinian, E., & Vergara, A. (2016). Exploring rape culture in social media forums. *Computers in Human Behavior*, *63*, 922–927. doi:10.1016/j.chb.2016.06.036

Chapter 2
Tweeted Articulations of Resistance Against Patriarchal Violence:
Imagining Digital Black Fem/ Womanism in Southern Africa

Kutlwano Mokgwathi
https://orcid.org/0000-0002-3819-4280
University of Botswana, Botswana

ABSTRACT

Research on digital articulations of patriarchal violence—sexual gender-based violence, harassment, intimidation, and bullying—as experienced by women and femmes globally is still exploratory. Despite the continued research development, feminist academics and activists still have challenges designing online platforms that are safe spaces for all genders and expressions of sexuality. Thus, this chapter extends current research and focuses on the root causes of digital violence. This chapter also focuses on the uses of social media, mainly Twitter, and the developments of feminist discourses by activist organizations in Southern Africa: @womenforchange5 and @SisterNambia. This chapter discusses the use of feminist organizations as tools in building community, developing social change strategies, and the ability to combat cis-heterosexist patriarchal conditioning and violence. Consequently, this chapter aims to contextualize social media as an echo chamber of societal violence. Moreover, social media affordances result in digital realms becoming field sites of misogyny and misogynoir.

INTRODUCTION

#Justicefor, #ShutItAllDown, #AmINext, #IBelieveHer, #SayHerName, #EnoughisEnough — all are hashtags that have trended on *Twitter* periodically, cross-culturally (Southern African Development Community – SADC) and transnationally throughout the African diaspora. Other hashtags, such as

DOI: 10.4018/978-1-6684-8893-5.ch002

#OurBodiesNotWarZones (Mutsvairo, 2020) locally (SADC) and #WhyIStayed, (Linabary et al., 2020) globally, were created to discuss critical issues affecting women in violent patriarchal societies. Therefore, social media is an extension of activist work and feminist/womanist praxis. For example, in the tradition of women like Ida B. Wells and Fanie Lou Hamer in North America (McArthur & Muhammad, 2022) and Wangari Maathai (Kenya), Winnie Mandela (South Africa) who used their voices through print, imagery, and political activism to combat state violence, so too do contemporary feminists/womanist use social media platforms such as YouTube, Blogs, Instagram, Tik Tok, and Twitter to denounce and resist violent patriarchy — misogyny, sexism, racism, capitalism, and cultured violence. Through videos, digital sources (e-books and blogs), and hashtags, women have the capability and accessibility to reach audiences cross-culturally which amplifies their activist work.

Moreover, the abovementioned hashtags were a means to 'talk back' (hooks, 2014) and raise awareness about i. The crisis of violent masculinity/patriarchy, and ii. The abduction, rape, and murder of cis-hetero-women, children, or members of the LGBTQ+ community. This way, using hashtags and media is crucial for women, Black women in particular, to voice their rage and mourning and implement strategies of resistance. Social media offers marginalized and silenced voices the necessary cross-cultural channels to challenge violence, amplify advocacy, and reclaim agency. Feminist practitioners and theoreticians are driven by pursuing solutions to real problems faced by 'real people' (Code, 2006), such as hunger, poverty, and reproductive justice; the focus is on justice and liberation.

This chapter engages with the crimes perpetrated against Southern African women, mainly in South Africa and Namibia and the activist work, digital resistance, and digital disobedience in two organizations — @womenforchange5 and @SisterNambia. Digital disobedience in this chapter is defined as the intentional disruption of violent patriarchy, creating visibility and amplifying marginalized voices, creating alternative, more so, authentic African women's identities and speaking against oppressive cultural regimes. Oppressive cultural regimes include homophobia, transphobia, misogyny, sexism, and rape culture, which leads to femicide. As such, the countries and organizations mentioned above were selected due to their geographic proximity, culture(s), histories, and the exchange of encounters on social media by women from these varying locations who use their platforms to build community and increase digital visibility.

Furthermore, this chapter will focus on the developing and continued development of Black Cyberfeminism (McMillan Cottom, 2016; Matos, 2017; Brown, 2018; Steele, 2021) and digital womanism. Scholarship on Womanism is vast; however, digital womanist praxis must be conceptualized more theoretically. Knowledge production and intellectualizing are not under the sole possession of a singular demographic; feminist epistemologies are multivocal exchanges of lived experiences applicable to the broader society (Code, 2006). Much like feminism(s) discussed in academic text and the physical realm, there are nuances to the varied frameworks in cyberspace. Hence the pluralization and emphasis on Black Cyberfeminism(s) and digital Womanism(s). Which is the intentional focus on Black women across digital and physical geographies; this chapter extends the idea of geography within the virtual realm (Ash et al., 2018). Black women's oppression is nuanced and intersectional (Gqola, 2001); therefore, solutions must adhere to the specificity of Black trauma. Nevertheless, what is more significant is that digital activism, whether womanist or feminist, was needed due to the violence perpetrated against marginalized and minoritized groups, mainly women, primarily Black and indigenous, on various social media and digital platforms (Brown, 2018; Sobande, 2021).

Digital feminists or cyberfeminists fight against and raise awareness of the fact that social media is a breeding ground for rape culture, which is the normalization of violent rhetoric, harassment, intimidation, and, as theorized by Henry and Powell (2015), technology-facilitated sexual assault under violent patriarchy and toxic masculinity. The treatment of girls, women, and femmes evidences violent behaviours. As stated by Toyana (2020), "Oppression has been of a highly gendered nature, disproportionately affecting the lives of women" (p. 2). As such, oppression occurs through capitalism, racism, sexism, misogyny, and violence (i.e., physical, psychological, emotional, and financial) — "mechanism(s) for maintaining heteropatriarchy" (Boyer, 2022, p. 399). Therefore, social media is an integral field site of study in analyzing and ascertaining knowledge in all matters listed above. Social media platforms are not divorced from realities; they act as echo chambers and amplify misogynistic perceptions. However, on the other hand, it also allows activists to resist and combat violent digitized regimes.

This chapter outlines digital violence, digital activism, and cyberfeminist practices. It is critical, to begin with a contextualized framework of digital masculinities and digital violence to situate the crisis of cyberharassment and other forms of digitized violence or, more aptly, technologically facilitated assault/violence (Henry & Powell, 2015; Morris & Ratajczak, 2019).

Digital Masculinities

Research indicates that constructions of masculinities are dictated by power, domination, and the ability to exert control—political, environmental, social, and financial (Katz et al., 1999). Regarding African masculinities, research indicates that Apartheid, colonialism, and slavery are embedded generationally through psychological wounds. These wounds are found in constructions of contemporary masculinities (Ratele, 2016; Hooks, 2014). In the Southern African context in particular, colonial and religious disruption were socially and consciously engrained and thus resulted in the composite formulation of masculinity (Jaji, 2020) coupled with historicized paternalism (Toyana, 2020), what conspiratorially African men adhere to for their maintenance of power, which translates to state power which translates to state violence.

Additionally, there is a parallel between white privilege and male privilege; power, control, domination, the inherent bias and perception of leadership, intellect, and righteousness. Hence, arguments are made for dismantling violent patriarchy, encompassing sexism, misogynoir, racism, and capitalism. However, masculinities in this study refer specifically to the performativity of cis-gendered heterosexual males and the reinforcement of various performances of masculinity by digitized versions; developing theories of masculinity include digital or virtual constructions (Morris & Ratajczak, 2019). In other words, gender is performative; various factors further police these performances. Factors include culture, religion, environment, socio-economic class, education and societal capital.

Furthermore, Steiner (2014) writes, "Various forms of masculinities come into existence in specific historical circumstances; what is currently hegemonic masculinity has displaced older forms but eventually will itself be displaced" (p. 367). Hence, the development of digital masculinities, including but not limited to incel culture and alpha and beta males' reliance upon coerced performances (Ging, 2017). Coerced performances include collective social practices interpreted as purposeful and intentional harm against women aided by peer support and male solidarity (Morgan, 2006). It is more befitting, however, to interpret male peer support as coercion. As such, the foundation of coercion is fear. However, fear is double-edged; it is crippling and debilitating and is a corrective measure for cis-gendered heterosexual males. The fear of being emasculated, unmasked and revealed as fraudulent based on hypothetical or socially constructed manhood scales determined by patriarchal instruction is what polices men and boys, which encourages the adoption of hypermasculine performances "like violence, sexual aggression…

threats, and verbal manipulation to coerce women into sexual compliance" (Avery et al., 2016, p. 164). It is, therefore, crucial for future research to delve into performances of digital masculinities whereby a cult of personality is achieved through overtly and subconsciously targeting males threatened by developing perceptions of gender and sexuality.

As cited by Ging (2017), Connell and Messerschmidt (2005, p. 840) write, "masculinity' represents not a certain type of man but, rather, a way that men position themselves through discursive practices" (p. 643). It is, therefore, safe to assert, based on Morgan's (2006) definition, it is evident that masculinity is, in fact, in crisis; he writes, "the notion of crisis conveys a sense of widespread serious concern, located within an identifiable time period and representing some kind of convergence of different forces, events, changes, and anxieties" (p. 110). Additionally, media representations coupled with cultural instructions of masculinity/manhood are limited to power through wealth and physique, giving men social capital. Those without, compensate with demonstrations of violence or targeted humiliation against those perceived as a threat against the claims mentioned above. As such, it is womanist/feminist organizations that, similar to Black Consciousness Movements, offer strategies of resistance and correction (Gqola, 2001).

However, parallel to Linabary et al. (2020), African/Black feminists have been cautious of disclosing violence and abuse for fear of perpetuating state violence on Black/African men. Research highlights and emphasizes that crime is due to spatial and cultural proximity due to the remnants of apartheid and segregationist practices (Lemanski, 2004). As such, African/Black feminism(s) emphasizes racial discrimination as a countermeasure to not align with white supremacist beliefs. On the one hand, minoritized women and digital activists are cognizant of the effects of social media. On the other hand, challenges of interrogating contemporary Black/African masculinities include white heteronormative positions inaccessible to marginalized communities; the ideal baseline criterion of whiteness, heterosexuality, class status, and wealth is beyond the scope of what is achievable by most (Code, 2006).

Thus, either disassociation or assimilation occurs—disassociation through countercultures, assimilation through mimicry, and subjugating group members who are in close proximity. Lastly, just as cyberfeminists and digital activists created hashtags, so too have detractors, for example, #NotAllMen; however, as Code (2006) argues, "it is a hard-won product of consciousness-raising and socio-political engagement that exposes the false presuppositions of the 'myth of the neutral man' on which domination and subordination rely" (p. 156). In other words, neutrality and the emphasis on 'the good' is moot when statistically, women experience violence.

Digital Violence

Digital violence is defined as intimidation, the threat of bodily harm, sexual assault, and murder; it also includes the malicious intent of exposure known as doxing (disclosure of location, private information), which is a legitimate concern used as a social media sport to coerce obedience (Henry & Powell, 2015). These crimes are likely committed by men (Matos, 2017). Therefore, gender studies do not benefit from separationism. It is critical to study digital Black feminism and activist work and simultaneously include masculinity studies, not as adversarial but as a means of creating solution-based research. Additionally, according to the World Health Organization (WHO), one-third of the female population has been physically, sexually, and psychologically assaulted (Venditto et al., 2022). The statistical indicators also represent online behaviours where 85% of women have been subjected to online violence and abuse, particularly during the Covid pandemic. Violence increased physically and digitally (Venditto et al., 2022). Research (Henry & Powell, 2015; Barker & Jurasz, 2020; Boyer, 2022) indicates that violence against women is prevalent and is expressed in various ways, such as hatred, humiliation, and fear derived from the threat of bodily harm or sexual assault. These factors are driving forces behind misogyny, whether online or off.

Online violence against women (OVAW) is a digitally replicated form of gender-based violence that includes but is not limited to "image-based sexual abuse" – rape pornography, revenge pornography (Barker & Jurasz, 2020, p. 3), "technology-facilitated sexual assault" (Morris & Ratajczak, 2019, p. 1988) and "technology-facilitated sexual violence" (Henry & Powell, 2015, p. 759). The three subcategories mentioned constitute sexualized aggression and domination. However, other forms of violence are exhibited online; digital violence consists of displays of power and control. However, the focus is on i. Coercion and threats, and ii) intimidation due to the nature of digital realms; the other six argued by Morris and Ratajczak (2019), for example, "minimizing, denying and blaming are also pertinent regarding developing and understanding of violence" (p. 1984). It is critical to note the detrimental effects of digital violence and targeted digital sexual harassment on the victim's psyche, self-conceptualization, and mental health (Venditto et al., 2022).

Henry and Powell (2015) write, "TFSV might be understood as gendered harms explicitly or implicitly fixated on the objectification of the "feminine body" — maimed, brutalized and defaced (p.768). It is important to note that the feminine body is not restricted by the sex assigned at birth or gender; for example, effeminate males and transmen are also susceptible and vulnerable to abuse. Relevant case studies which demonstrate the aforementioned are the #WhyIStayed (Linabary et al., 2020) and #ZimbabweLivesMatter (Toyana, 2020), where the amplification of activist voices through social media and intentional disruption of patriarchal narratives was the objective; the hashtags were intended to combat systemic oppression and forced silence. Interestingly, Morris and Ratajczak (2019) posit that "violence against women can be interpreted as a compensatory manhood act" (p. 1992); they further state, "incels marshall the flexibility of digital platforms to compose a homosocial space in which they can seek patriarchal "peer support" to reinforce their misogyny" (p. 1997). Male peer support is expounded in Henry and Powell (2015), and this concept speaks specifically to men in the SADC region. In that, so-called incel behaviour does not apply, instead the cultural expectation of women's inferiority and submission (Biwa, 2021). Which leads to other expressions of African femininity being ostracized and labelled as whore or prostitutes (Toyana, 2020).

However, the self-described disenfranchised male uses social media as an echo chamber for anti-feminist rhetoric and misogynistic vitriol (Barker & Jurasz, 2019). Much like popular feminism exists, so too does popular misogyny, which, as stated by Trusolino (2022), is "a response to popular feminism where men see their 'rightful place in the social hierarchy being undermined" (p. 140). Popular misogyny is formulated by harassment, co-opting hashtags, digital noise, and denouncing feminist narratives (Linabary et al., 2020).

It is, therefore, necessary to continue to study, research, theorize, and critique social media use; social media is a fieldsite of misogyny due to capitalist masculinist benefits where all voices are given platforms. However, feminists must reconcile with the consequences that online harm may translate to offline violence (Barker & Jurasz, 2019). Hence, the various feminist organizations on spaces such as *Instagram, Twitter, online podcasts* and *YouTube* use their platform to educate, raise awareness, network, and support social movements to dismantle systemic oppression. This chapter discusses two examples of Black cyberfeminist work: Sister Namibia and WomenForChange, South Africa. Again, Black cyberfeminism is necessary to speak specifically to, as "research indicates that Black women are 84% more likely than White women to be mentioned in abusive Twitter comments" (Sobande, 2021, p. 134).

On cyberharassment, self-constraint is a requisite for women; however, Boyer (2022) writes about physical space (transport, walking); the digital realm has also become a site of violence and harassment women endure. Furthermore, "gender discrimination and racism can intertwine suggested in the portmanteau misogynoir, coined by Moya Bailey" (Boyer, 2022, p. 400). Social media reinforces rape culture, which consists of perpetuating rape myths, victim blaming, slut-shaming, and re-victimization through targeted non-belief (Boyer, 2022).

In the case of Lemanski's (2004) research, although an indication of violence between 1994 – 2002, demonstrates the violence embedded in South African societies. Arguably, violence (Apartheid, colonialism) is socially ingrained. Therefore, the physical violence perpetuated translates digitally through harassment, intimidation, threats of sexual assault, and doxing (Trusolini, 2022). Fear of sexual violence is weaponized by patriarchy to silence and paralyze women (Boyer, 2022) and minoritized communities. As such, some women apply "self-censorship" for self-preservation and protection (Mutsvairo, 2020). In the European context, no concrete or standardized measures are set in place to comprehensively address the nuances within the range of online violence against women, primarily due to a lack of definition and global comprehension or uniformity in belief (Barker & Jurasz, 2020).

Similarly to Europe, within the SADC region, policy reforms have not included the breadth of violence women experience. One may posit that the lack of legislation is based, in part, due to i. Lack of research and the continued development of technology of which the legal system has yet to acquire knowledge and ii ignorance of the psycho-social implications of online harassment and OVAW.

As cited in Linabary et al. (2020), Megarry (2017) argues that "the encoding of male bias in platforms and practices should be of greater concern to feminist scholarship" (p. 5). Hence, recommendations for regulations have been made to curtail abusive behaviour online (Mutsvairo, 2020). Recommendations should, however, include confronting patriarchal masculinities to dismantle "white supremacist capitalist patriarchy" (hooks, 2014), which is culturally engrained in the global south, evidenced by internalized racism, colonial patriarchy and violent masculinists beliefs.

Situating Digital Activism

As previously mentioned, social media affordances enable activists, most significantly, Black women from varying geographic locations, to build community as part of digital citizenship across digital geographies (Ash et al., 2018). Moreover, within digital activism exists cyberfeminism and Digital Black feminism, which constitute disseminating information, mobilizing, fundraising, knowledge production, and feminist theorizing — "producing feminist content online" (Truslino, 2022, p. 131). Another area of focus for digital feminists/activists is combatting digital violence. Digital violence exists because violent patriarchy exists. The normalization of hierarchical stratification of society where women are pronounced less than manifests as violence off/online (Barker & Jurasz, 2020).

Within hierarchization is the inherent inferior/superior dichotomy where in [some] African cultures, women are infantilized and stripped of agency (Venditto et al., 2022), in other words, subjected to state, cultural, and patriarchal violence. Thus the critical use of social media for liberation. Toyana (2020) writes, "Information technology, mainly the internet, could be to the 21st-century African activists what the Ak-47 was to African nationalists fighting colonial rule in the 20th century" (p. 4). To some, the previous statement might read as hyperbolic; however, it is evidenced through such hashtags as #MenAreTrash, #OurBodiesNotWarZones (Southern Africa), #12DaysofRage, #MeToo (North America). These hashtags demonstrate the pertinence of community participation and collective consciousness-raising through social media platforms.

Thus the premise of the fourth wave of feminism— the continued theoretical and practical developments are made possible through technological advancements, mainly social media. The fourth wave, or technologically enhanced social media, consists of cross-border, cross-cultural, transnational liberationist efforts (Jackson, 2018). Women's active participation in web technology is evidenced by opportunities social media affords, such as amplification of voice, visibility, sharing and acquiring information (Steiner, 2014), open yet secret networks, i.e., Black Twitter and the formulation of relationships, most significantly for this chapter, Black sisterhood relationships (McMillan Cottom, 2015; Steele, 2021).

Although there is a multitude of benefits, the most significant obstacle, however, is the digital divide. Access, connectivity, affordability, and technophobia are hindrances to full participation by women of various socio-economic statuses (McMillan Cottom, 2015; Mutsvairo, 2020). On the African continent, in particular, other issues include load-shedding and censorship; therefore, the attempted legislation against social media must be recognized, as it further hinders access and free speech (Mutsvairo, 2020). Research (Trusolino, 2022) indicates that digital feminism has circumvented and positively impacted communities of women where media is censored.

Cyberfeminism ↔ Black Digital Feminism

As previously mentioned, feminism(s) include media technology — film, photography, digitized music, and radio. The fourth wave is increasingly digital. Digital media is imperative to the feminist movement, and social media is crucial to global organizing efforts and the broader distribution of knowledge (Trusolino, 2022). Hence, terms associated with newer forms of feminism— digital feminism, cyberfeminism, xenofeminism. Though there is scepticism about the comprehensiveness of digital feminism, it is, therefore, critical to implement safety networks and create digital spaces free of violence (Barker & Jurasz, 2019).

Black cyberfeminism is more specific to Black women globally and centres on feminist theoretical frameworks (McMillan Cottom, 2015). Black cyberfeminism, therefore, consists of Black/African feminism that focuses on not only race, gender, culture, and religion but how intersectional identities interact with technology (McMillan Cottom, 2015). Moreover, it is pertinent to highlight the specificities of focus in African/Black thought where African women's activism embodies the "historical, cultural, and localized" (Biwa, 2021, p. 51), meaning focused on the community, the collective whole. Although it is beyond the scope of this chapter are intergenerational and intercultural issues of contention. Nnaemeka proposes African feminism rooted in negotiation, accommodation, and compromise (Biwa, 2021). However, fourth-wave feminists, according to popular discourse, stand opposed. Although the negotiation is written as "finesse" or strategic manipulation, it speaks to again the doubly efforted need to humanize African women and femmes to African men as feminized subjects are deemed vessels of culture which contradictorily are perceived as less than others.

African women cross-generationally, nevertheless, fight for economic freedom, education, and fundamental human rights (Biwa, 2021). Furthermore, African feminism works to mitigate the deficiencies of Western activists' thinking; they are located in specific cultural and decolonial movements (Venditto et al., 2022). These movements are amplified on social media by way of sharing, liking, and uploading audiovisual data (speeches, lectures, panel discussions, interviews), documentary films, book excerpts, blogs, and other forms of feminist/womanist messaging noted as alternative media which counteracts patriarchal domination (Steiner, 2014). Feminist uses of media challenge normative standards that align with cis-hetero-sexist patriarchy. One method of community 'speak' and mobilization is using hashtags. Feminist/womanist hashtags are political, social, environmental, and cultural artefacts (Trusolini, 2022).

Hashtags have possible transformative implications, such as the development of language, interruptions of governments, reformation of policies, and community building (Trusolini, 2022).

There is no separation between Black feminist theorization and Black feminist digital activism; Black theoretical frameworks are the cornerstones of Black digital feminism (McMillan Cottom, 2015). The theoretical framework derives from previous research, focusing significantly on cyberfeminism (Matos, 2017) and Black digital feminism (McMillan Cottom, 2015; Steele, 2021). Additionally, constructions of Black feminist technology (Brown, 2018) are utilized to develop an analytical framework to discuss issues of violence, gendered uses of social media, African feminist organizations on Twitter, and the creation of digital resistance measures. It is critical to place Black women and femmes at the centre of this study; Black women's experiences differ from other communities (Brown, 2018; Sobande, 2021). Black women are often left unprotected and erased while facing hypervisibility and scrutiny.

Therefore, a comprehensive framework is relevant to contemporary research; social media platforms are constantly developing essentially due to capitalist determinants. However, users bring themselves (ideologies, belief systems) to social media, hence, the perpetuation of racism, sexism, capitalism, and misogynoir. The danger, however, is the creation of violent echo chambers and the glamorization of violence perpetuated and wholly consumed by those easily susceptible to media communication without critical discernment. The lack of critical discernment creates a volatile environment for social justice activists, feminists, women, femmes, and other "othered" bodies. Hence, Black women must use digitized spaces to develop a body of knowledge intrinsic to Black liberation. Black digital spaces, created in predominantly owned white spaces though contradictory, is, on the other hand, a strategic development in community consciousness-raising. Other critical areas of focus for feminists online and offline are, as discussed in Code (2006), projected subordinate positions in women, which in turn become internalized patriarchal conditioning.

One legacy of Apartheid and other oppressive regimes is the exclusiveness of information, where community gatherings and information sharing were in sole control of the elites (Kivikuru, 2005). Thus, the advantage of social media is the inclusion of various voices. However, it must be noted that due to connectivity and the digital divide, social media also excludes various community members. Other exclusionary factors include digital literacy.

Although Kivikuru (2005) discusses the uses of radio, the parallel is in the gendered uses of media where women speak primarily of "concrete, practical issues, while men often widely discuss political matters and religion" (p. 332); similarly, on social media platforms such as Twitter, men speak of hypothetical happenstances and womxn speak to their current realities.

Consequently, despite critical advancements in feminists' uses of social media, patriarchal violence—misogyny, harassment, intimidation, doxxing, sexual aggression, rape, and death threats are used against prominent women and activists (Morris & Ratajczak, 2019; Venditto et al., 2022; Linabary et al., 2020). Sexual assault and harassment online are global issues that affect women in Zimbabwe, Namibia, South Africa, the United Kingdom, and the United States. The socialization of boys through violent patriarchal structures manifests through violent acts perpetrated by men.

Feminist uses of social media, such as those demonstrated below, are necessary in the epistemological frameworks of Black cyberfeminism. Each entity differs in its communication and messaging. They speak to African/Black feminist issues within the borders of SADC — Trans rights, Gay identities, immigration, land, access to education, sexual gender-based violence, gender-based violence, and femicide. African feminism(s) as a theoretical framework or Black digital feminism in southern Africa is complimentary in that the framing of argumentations of human rights and, thusly, women's rights rely on the inherent belief that African women are humanized, are women, and no longer dehumanized subjects—each organization— Sister Namibia and Women For Change, centres on marginalized's voices. African women are marginalized within cis-heterosexist patriarchal African societies formerly colonized (Tamale, 2020). Thus social media affordances offer the ability to utilize counternarratives for African socialization.

There are parallels between Code's (2006) arguments and the practical significance of feminist knowledge production, feminist consciousness, and empowering, informing, and building community online. The purpose is to disrupt male-dominated spaces and heterosexist supremacy and create a knowledgebase that centres women, femmes, and gender-nonconforming— the formerly stripped of agency and silenced. Silence is no longer normalized.

METHODOLOGY

As previously stated, two social media accounts have been identified through digital ethnographic methods, such as social listening, the 'following' of digitized trails, and searches on the Internet, especially Twitter. There are nuances in ethnographic research that are determined by the nature of the research focus and the researcher. Ethnographers are tasked with paying great attention to participants' beliefs and values, distinguishing them from their own. Similarly, cyberethnographers are tasked with examining digital cultures and studying online behaviours (Grasseni et al., 2022). Ethnographic research examines, explores, or investigates phenomena by studying people in their natural environment as they interact with those around them (Underberg & Zorn, 2013), which provides an in-depth understanding of culture.

The data included in this study are digital texts, audiovisual data created and published on *Twitter*, *Instagram* and *Tik Tok*. With technological advancements in media, research must reflect on and be open to utilizing tools to redefine and expand research methods. Search parameters on *Google* included "African women organizations," however, due to the specificity of the Southern African regions, search parameters included "South African feminist organizations," "feminist organizations in South Africa," and the like. Moreover, much like Venditto et al. (2022), the methodological approach first combined literature on online violence against women and cyberfeminism to contextualize digital violence and virtual realities of African/Black women. However, the significance of this study is not to offer a discursive analysis; instead, the intent is to develop and extend an understanding of cyberfeminism, Black digital cyberfeminism, and digital womanist praxis in Southern Africa mainly, Namibia and South Africa.

Second, data collected included i. Tweets from both accounts @SisterNamibia and @WomenForChange5, between January 1st 2021 – May 1st 2023. ii. Tik Tok videos from @WomenForChange.SA and iii. Instagram posts from @SisterNambia and @WomenForChange.SA. Note that @WomenForChange5 and @WomenForChange.SA are under the same Women For Change organization. The messages across platforms are uniformly created and cohesive. Information was discounted if it was repetitive, gave little contextual information, and was retweeted from various accounts without additional relevant information. Below are descriptive summaries of each organization's message and content. Words written in italics are quotes from each organization that demonstrate the intent and purposeful communication.

@WomenForChange5

#JusticeforReeva. #EndGBV. #EndViolenceAgainstWomen. #SayHerName. #AmINext?. #WomenForChange. Women For Change was created on *Twitter* in September 2019. The dates of creation on other platforms are not available. The focus of the organization is branched into two major areas 1. Awareness/Death notices—Femicide and 2. Critique of the justice system. From the thousands of posts, it is evident that their philosophy is confrontation. They act as a mirror of society, communicating the realities of women in South Africa. Their strategy intentionally disrupts the status quo, demonstrating cyberfeminism's relevance and power. As written above, cyberfeminism is centred on combatting silence and shifting power balances away from cis-heterosexist patriarchy. Thus, WomenForChange stands as a mouthpiece to speak for victims' families and provide unanimous support to victims against perpetrators of violence, where typically, in [some] African societies, patriarchs are protected (Tamale, 2020). For example, #JusticeforReeva was illustrated when the page spoke out against the possibility of Oscar Pistorius being paroled.

We are standing with June and Berry Steenkamp, and we oppose the parole application of Oscar Pistorius.

The words above accompanied a photograph of the parents of Reeva, worn down by grief, public scrutiny, and perceived empathy for Pistorius rather than their daughter Reeva Steenkamp. It is, therefore, critical that pages such as WomenForChange act as intermediaries between the public and media and display unabated support to victims' families. It is also crucial for feminist organizations to communicate reality rather than sexist narratives, as is the modus operandi of several journalists.

From a Tik Tok video consisting of photographs and typed messages, shared on March 7th 2023, Women For Change wrote;

In March 2016, our Women For Change movement was founded because two beautiful souls, Sinoxolo Mafevuka and Franziska Blöchliger, were brutally murdered in Cape Town – only a few days apart... It is our duty and a privilege to engage in social matters, especially concerning our women and youth. The continuous attacks in homes, on the streets, in places of education, and outdoors in nature are a potential threat. As women, we want to unite to end violence against women and children.

In South Africa, it is safe to assert that children as young as one year old are victims of sexual abuse and murder. Victimhood is not a distinction of morality. In other words, accusations of sexual promiscuity and questions of clothing and piety can no longer exist, although these are patriarchal strategies employed to vindicate perpetrators of violence.

If I am next, leave me in front of parliament. – February 4th, 2023

Images and information that speak to a woman or child who has been murdered either by a partner, boyfriend or someone close to the victim of femicide are posted regularly. The tweet above, thus, speaks to the inaction of the government and critique of the justice system. As stated, the second category of Tweets expresses discontent with how government officials fail to prioritize the safety of women and girls. "*If I am next*", in other words, murdered, "*leave me in front of parliament*" so that those in positions of power take accountability for how they trivialize the femicide crisis. The sentiments are further stated by *"Our women and children are terrorized by male violence in South Africa."* Through these actions and confrontational communicative acts, Women For Change resists patriarchal violence or the cultural expectation of using coded language that protects perpetrators of violence. "*Terrorized by male violence*" is a powerful statement and needs further interrogation. It is also a demonstration of the significance of understanding violent patriarchal masculinities, hegemonic masculinities, and other categorizations in the Southern African context. Terrorism connotes various imagery; however, it is often linked to patriarchal men in South Africa.

Furthermore, it is evident from analysis of the exchanges between varied audiences that women are blamed for their rape and or murder. It is also apparent that much of the centre of the discussion is on an attempt to assert blame. Victims are often re-victimized, and the people behind the posts are often subjected to violent rhetoric. The violent rhetoric and digital violence offer supporting evidence of the need to disrupt current education and gendered socialization.

Every 29 seconds, a woman is raped, and 12 women are killed each day by a man!

Statistic occurrences are essential and integral in confronting societal oppressions that constrict the movements and liberation of women and children. The statistics are alarming. The statistics are a reminder that the protest image shared on Instagram (Figure 2), "*It is easier to get raped than to get a job,*" is relevant. Thus, societally, more attention and intentional responses from the government and citizens are needed to make significant changes.

The image in Figure One is the pinned Tweet on the WomenForChange Twitter page, meaning it is the first engagement and introduction to WomenForChange that audiences see. Figure Two is a screenshot of six Instagram posts that typify the messages shared by the organization. There is cohesiveness in the messages across pages, where the faces of young girls and women are shared. Also shared are the brutal ways in which they were murdered or raped. There is unrecognizable brutality in their murders. Physically and spiritually, these women are doubly dehumanized. It is thus essential to note that vicarious victimization and digitally embedded trauma are possible. It is challenging to view death daily. However, it has become normalized due to social media. The images of the women shared seemingly daily on the various Women For Change platforms are mirror images of the women across South Africa. In other words, in the faces and bodies of the countless women shared, South African, African, Black, Indian, and White women see themselves. Vicarious victimization and trauma are not the focus of this study. However, future studies may further research social media's effects on audiences' psychological deterioration.

The organization also has a website with a link to a Blog. The blog stories are categorized as Activism, Information, and Ambassador. Interestingly, a petition, Fire Bheki Cele, Minister of Police, is active with 12,316 signatures. Also, on the website, "*We are tired of creating 'Missing Child' and 'Memorial posts.' We are tired of trending hashtags. We are tired of thinking, 'Am I Next?'*. The other noted petition, End GBV has 8, 856 signatures. Bheki Cele, the current Minister of Police, is under scrutiny for his perceived apathy and lack of urgency in confronting rape and femicide. WomenForChange has, in various communications, called for his dismissal/removal from the ministry. They have also called out the current President, Ramaphosa, for his apparent lack of action against sexual-gender and gender-based violence.

As evidenced by Figure Three, social media offers many organizations platforms and abilities to participate in activists' work and make the plights of various communities visible. Without social media, Black and Indigenous women would continually be relegated to obscurity by persistent erasure or

Figure 1. Tweet by @WomenForChange5 (Women For Change) February 27th, 2023. "3843 women were murdered in 2022 in South Africa."

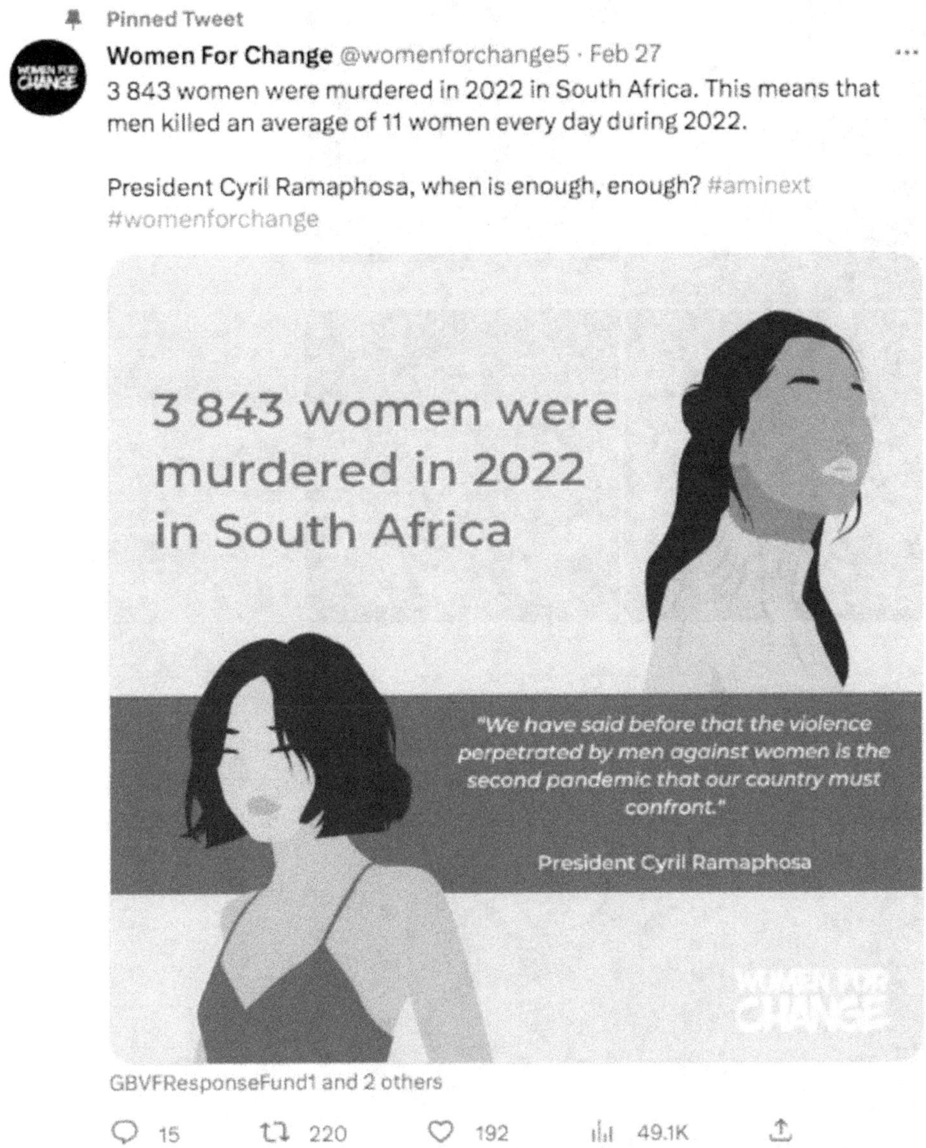

dismissal. Inversely, social media platforms may participate in silencing marginalized communities with acts of shadowbanning or censorship. Shadowbanning consists of acts by the digital platform to restrict viewership from broader audiences without the knowledge of the account owners. Shadowbanning is as it sounds, accounts are relegated to obscurity, and visibility is reduced. In the post above WomenFor-Change write, "*While Instagram continues to censor and shadow-ban our account and the accounts of many other activists and people who use their platform to speak up, it doesn't remove or ban men who are harassing and verbally abusing women.*" As the literature above demonstrates, social media is still

Figure 2. (Screenshot) Instagram posts by Women For Change (@WomenForChangesa) May 11-17th, 2023. Societal Commentary.

Figure 3. Instagram post by Women For Change (@WomenForChangesa) May 11th, 2023. "Many times this past year, Instagram has deleted posts and stories and censored and/or shadow-banned our account."

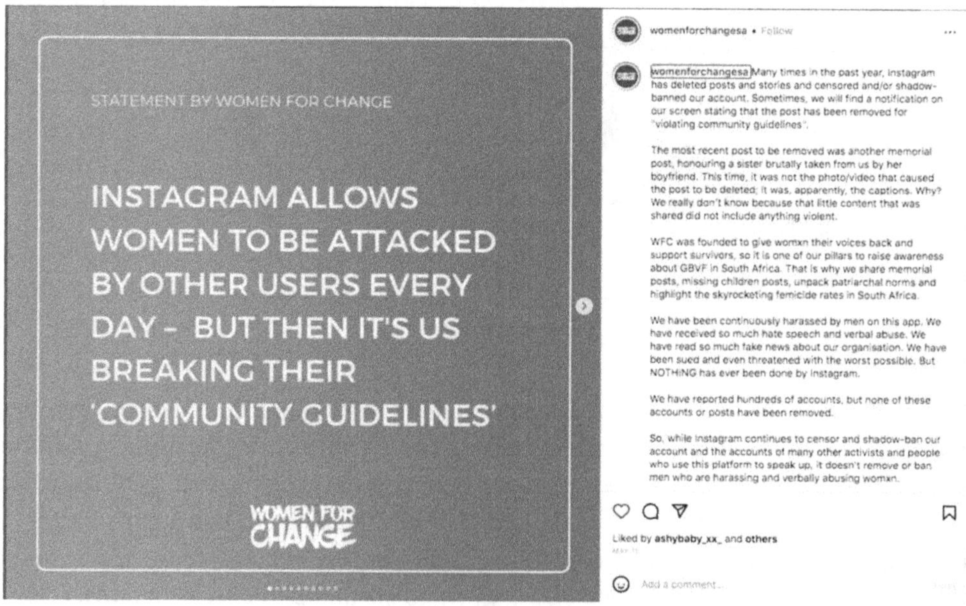

a tool for cis-heterosexist capitalist gain. Therefore, the work of Black, Indigenous, and first nations activists transformed the intent and significance.

However, one critique of the organization is that although it is critical to make murder, trauma, and women's realities visible in South Africa, it is also crucial to humanize victims. The women on this page existed prior to their death. They led lives beyond what is communicated on social media pages. With rightful concern, this page is cautioned against perpetrating what they resist. The organization would benefit from increasing its educational components and creating strategies to combat violence, such as providing community resources and adding informational material explaining why violence occurs. The violence and social ills have been diagnosed strategically; what will be implemented for social change moving forward?

@SisterNamibia

#ShutItAllDown. #TeenagePregnancyCrisis. #NamibiaLGBTQ. #SodomyLaw. #Abortion. #FreeMenstrualProducts. Hashtags are key indicators of a position held or supported by an individual or an organization. Hashtags are also indicators of current issues of debate, ideological, cultural disharmony, or contestation. Shut It All Down, for instance, as tweeted by several organizations and people in Nambia in 2020, demonstrates the above position. Where women in various communities protested and marched against sexual-gender-based violence. As a collaborative advocacy group, Sister Nambia works to amplify the voices of women, children, and marginalized groups in Namibia.

Culture should not be made to be a stagnant chassel that it never was to begin, simply to conform to the views of Christianity and colonial patriarchy. – Frieda Mukufa

The quote above was Tweeted on September 16th, 2021; it is wholly relevant to African feminists fighting against patriarchal socialization due to colonization. Molara Ogunidpe Leslie theorized that it is one of the mountains on African women's backs (Gqola, 2001). The colonial gendered project through missionary schools dictated womanhood, wifehood, and motherhood. The binary of man and woman, masculine and feminine, created rules of acceptability disguised as Christian morality. The friction arises when women no longer accept confinement or isolationist enforcement and men cannot perform their prescribed roles. Moreover, it is vital to speak about culture as a manufactured creation and recognize that it continually evolves, regardless of the preferred stagnancy.

Compared to WomenForChange, Sister Namibia needs to be more narrowly focused and defined. They are educational and informative, focusing on gender identity and expression, homosexuality, reproductive justice, SGBV and domestic violence, gender justice, and equity. The organization expands across various social media, with Twitter and Instagram leading frequency of use. Their website is just as detailed in structure, with the focus separated into six main branches. More so, unlike Women For Change, they have incorporated a podcast as part of their reachability. They began their platform on Twitter in 2011, which gives them the maturity and advantage that comes with time in creating a voice and a message. However, this does not translate to broader audiences as they still need to develop a large online following. Their digital community remains small.

Cross-cultural and transnational communication acts occur where similar messages speak to similar issues. For example, *In my country, it is easier to get raped than to get a job*, is shared on Twitter by Sister Namibia and on Instagram by Women For Change. This message speaks to the emergent state of both countries where women have communicated their fear. Biwa (2021) writes, "Namibia is ranked 108 out of 159 countries on the UN's 2015 Gender Index" (p. 44). Protests illustrate this reality and call for action with the #ShutItAllDown movements that occurred across Namibia to fight against sexual gender-based violence and to confront authorities with the violence marginalized communities experience.

What stands out and is noted as womanist within Sister Namibia is the equitable concentration on LGBTQ+ communities and male participation. These tweets demonstrate the collective consciousness-raising that is relied on within womanist praxis. These tweets also illustrate the importance of including all community members in creating relevant and significant changes. The most current posts and informational material focuses on LGBTQ+ rights as they follow the justice system and the recent historic trial of Same-Sex marriage rights; #RecognizeUs is utilized. On May 16th, 2023, they tweeted:

We're in court today, waiting for the Supreme Court to deliver its judgment in the recognition of same-sex marriages concluded abroad! The court is in session from 10 am - it's a huge day for the fundamental rights of queer Namibians.

Figure 4. (Screenshot) Instagram posts by Sister Namibia (@SisterNamibia) February 14th - March 6th, 2023. Social Commentary.

Figure 5. Tweet by Sister Namibia (@SisterNamibia) April 8th, 2022. Informational on Slut Shame Walk 2022.

As demonstrated below, Sister Namibia focuses on human rights, queer rights, and women's rights to life, choice, and bodily autonomy. They are knowledgeable about legal matters, legitimizing their position as advocates. Legal jargon must often be more understandable and accessible for laypersons to understand. However, Sister Namibia provides detailed information about various state and cultural issues in a language that broad audiences may realize.

Faithful to the activist commentary on Sister Namibia, Figure five demonstrates other foundational concerns in Namibia. The Slut Shame Walk (SSW) began in Namibia in 2019 by intersectional activist Nsozi Mwazi. The Slut Shame Walk as a global continuation started in 2011 in Toronto, Canada, when a police officer said, quoting Michell Martin of NPR, "that to avoid being sexually assaulted, women should quote, "avoid dressing like sluts." The comment caused an uproar in the global North, which resulted in protests. Protests, influenced by social media activism and cross-cultural dissemination of information, took place in various countries worldwide. The word slut was taken and co-opted to reduce denigration and humiliation. The SSW was created to combat the heterosexist perception of blame, where victims/survivors of sexual assault are condemned for the perpetrators' actions. Victim-blaming, slut-shaming, and guilt are often targeted at victims because we live in violent patriarchal societies where sexual assault is normalized.

However, Sister Namibia must incorporate the emotive connection illustrated by Women For Change, perhaps indicated by a need for more engagement across their various platform uses. Interestingly, Sister Namibia and Women For Change must incorporate what the other does well. Women For Change is evocative more than informative, and Sister Namibia is informative more than evocative.

CONCLUSIVE THOUGHTS

The use of social media as an act of creating space and language for liberation, education, knowledge production, and activism is similar to as written by McArthur and Muhammad (2022) to the practices of Ida B. Wells-Barnett's use of "journalistic talents to educate and engage readers" (p. 755). Using journalism, Wells-Barnett educated readers on matters that plagued the Black community, such as lynching and the critical inclusion of rape and violence against Black women, which was erased from the public. As such, contemporary Black feminists, through social media, employ similar strategies of storytelling and investigation to educate Black/African communities. Moreover, through advanced technologies and social media, education is done cross-culturally across digital geographies and perceptions of borders.

Furthermore, feminist epistemologies are critical and centred on various theoretical positions that force broader societies to interrogate limited ways of knowledge production and thinking (Code, 2006). The relevance of social media, as parallel to acts of writing, is that "society does not choose to centre Black girls' ways of knowing and being but instead seek to keep Black girls trapped in monolithic or false profiles that are negative in opposition to the ways they see themselves" (McArthur & Muhammad, 2022, p. 771). Social media is a corrective measure for false narratives of Blackness and colonial scripts of African/Black womanhood. Through social media discourses, Black women have amplified themselves and each other. Through social media affordances, Black women have created visible spaces to resist violence and counter negligible patriarchal instructions that render Black girls and women less than — the dehumanized other.

As feminist theory expands with the inclusion of technology, it is crucial to be conscious of the fundamental tenet — liberation. At the centre of digital cyberfeminism as constructed by Black women, in particular, the core of digital social movements is the pursuit of freedom, including social justice, reproductive justice, safety, bodily autonomy, development of the community, and most significantly, living a life free from harm. The two organizations discussed in myriad ways have demonstrated various uses of social media and cyberfeminist praxis.

@WomenForChange focuses on confronting femicide and abduction in South Africa. Their objectives include refusing to placate patriarchal denialism of violence and the negligible manner in which broader society, mainly the justice system, dismisses violence against women. Hence, research must include gender, masculinity, and violent patriarchy. It is crucial to study and further develop masculinity and gender studies at the intersection of culture and media. Research (Ratele, 2016; Hooks, 2014) indicates that Apartheid, colonialism, and slavery are foundational to understanding the causes of SGBV and GBV. Therefore, studying both articulations of resistance and violence is significant. Future research may explore masculinity, not as a male trait but inherently a colonial, capitalist, patriarchal condition amplified by media images and cultural contexts.

@SisterNamibia focuses on equity. They create targeted messages centred on educating and raising awareness against harassment and violence, LGBTQ+ rights, and freedom. Twitter, Instagram and Facebook have revealed that there are several African feminist organizations, and that number is steadily growing. There are organizations such as @BlackWomenRadicals, @WCOZimbabwe and @ShutItAll-Down, much like Sister Namibia, focus on myriad injustices and construct messages that speak toward equity for women in Africa and the diaspora. The focus is also primarily on financial freedom, which offers choice. As stated at the beginning of this chapter is the possibility of harassment and violence that women experience online, mainly due to social media as a corporate space that benefits from so-called freedom of speech, which allows for all voices to build platforms; Linabary et al., (2020) therefore dispels the idea of social media as a feminist utopia, however, with the development of Black cyberfeminism social change is made possible.

REFERENCES

Ash, J., Kitchin, R., & Leszczynski, A. (2016). Digital Turn, Digital Geographies? *Progress in Human Geography*, *42*(1), 25–43. doi:10.1177/0309132516664800

Avery, L. R., Ward, L. M., Moss, L., & Üsküp, D. (2016). Tuning gender. *The Journal of Black Psychology*, *43*(2), 159–191. doi:10.1177/0095798415627917

Bailey, M. (2022). *Misogynoir transformed: Black Women's Digital Resistance*. New York University Press.

Barker, K., & Jurasz, O. (2019). Online Misogyny: A Challenge for Digital Feminism? *Journal of International Affairs*, *72*(2), 95–114. https://www.jstor.org/stable/26760834

Biwa, V. (2021). African Feminisms and co-constructing a collaborative future with men: Namibian women in Mining's discourses. *Management Communication Quarterly*, *35*(1), 43–68. doi:10.1177/0893318920973988

Boyer, K. (2021). Sexual Harassment and the Right to everyday life. *Progress in Human Geography*, *46*(2), 398–415. doi:10.1177/03091325211024340

Brown, N. M. (2018). Methodological Cyborg as Black Feminist Technology: Constructing the Social Self-Using Computational Digital Autoethnography and Social Media. *Cultural Studies ↔ Critical Methodologies, 19*(1), 55–67. doi:10.1177/1532708617750178

Code, L. (2006). Women Knowing/Knowing Women: Crititical-Creative Interventions in the Politics of Knowledge. In K. Davis, M. Evans, & J. Lorber (Eds.), Handbook of gender and women's studies (pp. 146–166). Sage.

Ging, D. (2017). Alphas, Betas, and Incels: Theorizing the masculinities of the Manosphere. *Men and Masculinities*, *22*(4), 638–657. doi:10.1177/1097184X17706401

Gqola, P. D. (2001). Ufanele Uqavile: Black women, Feminisms and Postcoloniality in Africa. *Agenda (Durban, South Africa)*, *16*(50), 11–22. doi:10.1080/10130950.2001.9675990

Grasseni, C., Barendregt, B. A., de Maaker, E., Musso, D. F., Littlejohn, A., Maeckelbergh, M., Postma, M., & Westmoreland, M. R. (2022). *Audiovisual and Digital Ethnography: A Practical and Theoretical Guide*. Routledge.

Henry, N., & Powell, A. (2015). Embodied harms. *Violence Against Women*, *21*(6), 758–779. doi:10.1177/1077801215576581 PMID:25827609

hooks, b. (2015). *Talking Back: Thinking feminist, thinking black*. Routledge, Taylor & Francis Group.

Jackson, S. (2018). Young Feminists, Feminism and Digital Media. *Feminism & Psychology*, *28*(1), 32–49. doi:10.1177/0959353517716952

Jaji, R. (2021). Youth Masculinities in Zimbabwe's Congested Gerontocratic political space. *Africa Development. Afrique et Developpement*, *45*(3), 77–96. doi:10.57054/ad.v45i3.635

Lemanski, C. (2004). A new Apartheid? The Spatial Implications of Fear of Crime in Cape Town, South Africa. *Environment and Urbanization*, *16*(2), 101–111. doi:10.1177/095624780401600201

Linabary, J. R., Corple, D. J., & Cooky, C. (2019). Feminist activism in Digital Space: Postfeminist contradictions in #WhyIStayed. *New Media & Society*, *22*(10), 1827–1848. doi:10.1177/1461444819884635

Martin, M., Jarvis, H., & Fry, A. (2011, June 9). *"Slutwalk" Goes Global To Protest Sexual Assault*. National Public Radio. NPR.

Matos, C. (2017). New Brazilian feminisms and online networks: Cyberfeminism, protest and the female 'Arab Spring.'. *International Sociology*, *32*(3), 417–434. doi:10.1177/0268580917694971

McArthur, S. A., & Muhammad, G. E. (2020). Pens Down, Don't Shoot An Analysis of How Black Young Women Use Language to fight back. *Urban Education*, *57*(5), 751–778. doi:10.1177/0042085919893734

McMillan Cottom, T. (2016). Black CyberFeminism: Ways Forward for Intersectionality and Digital Sociology. In J. Daniels, K. Gregory, & T. McMillan Cottom (Eds.), Digital Sociologies (pp. 211–232). Policy Press.

Media Education Foundation. (1999). *Tough Guise: Violence, Media & the Crisis in Masculinity*. Retrieved from https://www.toughguise2.org/

Morgan, D. (2006). The Crisis in Masculinity. In K. Davis, M. Evans, & J. Lorber (Eds.), Handbook of gender and women's studies (pp. 109–123). Sage. doi:10.4135/9781848608023.n7

Morris, E. W., & Ratajczak, K. (2019). Critical masculinity studies and research on Violence Against Women: An Assessment of past scholarship and Future Directions. *Violence Against Women*, *25*(16), 1980–2006. doi:10.1177/1077801219875827 PMID:31718529

Mutsvairo, B. (2020). *Disenchanting or Demoralizing: Zimbabwean Women Share their Social Media Experience*. Women Empowerment for Leadership (WE4L). https://hivos.org/resource/disenchanting-or-demoralizing-zimbabwean-women-share-their-social-media-experience/

Ratele, K. (2016). *Liberating masculinities*. HSRC Press.

Sobande, F. (2021). Spectacularized and Branded Digital (Re)presentations of Black people and Blackness. *Television & New Media*, *22*(2), 131–146. doi:10.1177/1527476420983745

Steele, C. K. (2021). *Digital Black Feminism*. New York University Press. doi:10.18574/nyu/9781479808373.001.0001

Steiner, L. (2014). Feminist Media Theory. In M. Fackler & R. S. Fortner (Eds.), The Handbook of Media and Mass Communication theory (pp. 359–379). John Wiley & Sons, Inc. doi:10.1002/9781118591178.ch20

Stevens, G. (2007). Tactical Reversal or Re-Centring Whiteness? A Response to Green, Sonn, and Matsebula. *South African Journal of Psychology. Suid-Afrikaanse Tydskrif vir Sielkunde*, *37*(3), 425–430. doi:10.1177/008124630703700303

Tamale, S. (2022). *Decolonization and Afro-Feminism*. Daraja Press.

Toyana, M. (2020). Essay Series: African Journalism And Media In The Time Of Covid-19. Hashtags and Spectacles: Zimbabwe's Feminist Activists Find Online Avenues to Tackle Government's COVID-19 Clampdown, 1–13.

Trusolino, M. (2022). 'I wanna kill my rapist': Margaret Cho's #12daysofrage campaign as Promotional Digital Activism. *Communication and the Public*, *7*(3), 130–145. doi:10.1177/20570473221111200

Underberg, N. M., & Zorn, E. (2014). *Digital Ethnography: Anthropology, Narrative, and New Media*. University of Texas Press.

Venditto, B., Set, B., & Amaambo, R. N. (2022). Sexualization and Dehumanization of Women By Social Media Users in Namibia. *Sexes*, *3*(3), 445–462. doi:10.3390exes3030033

ADDITIONAL READING

Jordan-Zachery, J. S., & Harris, D. (2019). *Black Girl Magic Beyond the Hashtag: Twenty-First Century Acts of Self-Definition*. University of Arizona Press. doi:10.2307/j.ctvqc6hbp

Knight Steele, C. (2021). When The Black Lives That Matter Are Not Our Own: Digital Black Feminism and a Dialectic of Self and Community. *Feminist Media Studies*, *21*(5), 860–863. doi:10.1080/14680777.2021.1949370

Mendes, K., Ringrose, J., & Keller, J. (2019). *Digital Feminist Activism: Girls and Women Fight Back Against Rape Culture*. Oxford University Press. doi:10.1093/oso/9780190697846.001.0001

Monier, M. (2023). "Rest As Resistance:" Black Cyberfeminism, Collective Healing And Liberation On @TheNapMinistry. *Communication, Culture &amp. Communication, Culture & Critique*, *16*(3), 1–7. doi:10.1093/ccc/tcad022

Reneses, P. A., & Bosch, T. (2023). The limitations of Hashtag Feminist Activism on South African Twitter: A case study of #MenareTrash and #WomenareTrash. *Men and Masculinities*, 1–19. doi:10.1177/1097184X231188681

Williams, S. (2021). Revisiting Digital Defense and Black Feminism on Social Media. *Feminist Media Studies*, *21*(8), 1373–1377. doi:10.1080/14680777.2021.1996429

KEY TERMS AND DEFINITIONS

Black Cyberfeminism: Like African, Black, and Women of Color Feminism, Black Cyberfeminism is specific to the digital experiences of Black and African diaspora women.

Cultured Violence: Beliefs that are normalized in a society that manifest in physical and other forms of harm against marginalized and minoritized communities.

Digital Literacy: Navigating, comprehending, and evaluating digital media across platforms.

Digital Womanism: The digital praxis of womanism is much like Black cyberfeminism; however, womanism is founded in African cultures and beliefs that uphold liberation and justice for all community members.

Misogynoir: The specific targeted hatred and prejudice toward Black women due to the intersections of race and gender enacted both digitally and physically.

Popular Feminism: May be understood as the use of social media and popular culture for empowerment.

Xenofeminism: A posthumanist interpretation of feminism where technology is at the core rather than limited understanding and uses of gender.

Chapter 3
Role of Information and Communication Technology in the Digitalization of Violence and Sexual Politics in the Indian Scenario

Rabindra Kumar Verma
Manipal University Jaipur, India

Ashish Kumar Gupta
https://orcid.org/0000-0002-0436-3744
Government Post-Graduate College, Rudrapur, India

ABSTRACT

The latter half of the 20th century witnessed rapid growth in the domain of science and technology especially information and communication technology (ICT). The impact of ICT can easily be seen in the different domains of humans like science, education, professional career, culture, and politics, explicitly and implicitly or negatively. There are different types of digital violence exercised against women. Some of the forms range from hacking, controlling, or manipulating information, doxing, dissemination of intimate photos or private information, use of spyware, surveillance, faking identity, cyberbullying like posting or sharing embarrassing or threatening pictures, defamation, harassment, stalking in the form of sending online unsolicited or unwanted sex-based materials, and rape threats. The chapter attempts to explore role of the digital technology and online platforms as intermediaries in rendering gender-based violence, digitalization of gender-based violence, verbal or nonverbal sexual assaults, and online sexual politics to prolong women's subjection in India.

DOI: 10.4018/978-1-6684-8893-5.ch003

INTRODUCTION

In academia, the terms 'digitalization' and 'digitization' are often used interchangeably, but it is crucial to understand the distinction between these terms as they represent different processes. Mistaking one for the other leads to a confusion between a social process and a technological process. Digitization primarily involves the representation of sensory aspects of the social world through binary codification and decoding. On the other hand, digitalization encompasses the description of the social changes that accompany digitization. While digitization is predominantly controlled by the actors and knowledge involved in technological development, digitalization extends its reach to every member of society and encompasses a broader spectrum of forces, interests, values, and visions. It is important to note that digitalization carries significant implications for the concept of emancipation, as it introduces normative questions that are often overlooked in the process of digitization. (Duff, 2012).

Digitization serves as the technical aspect, involving the conversion of analog information into digital formats, enabling storage, manipulation, and transmission of data. It focuses on the transformation of physical or analog artifacts into digital representations, utilizing binary code as the medium. Conversely, digitalization transcends the mere technical conversion and delves into the social, cultural, and economic impacts of digitization. It encompasses the broader implications of the widespread adoption and integration of digital technologies in various spheres of life. Digitalization entails understanding the transformative effects, both positive and negative, that arise from the utilization of digitized information and technologies in society.

To comprehend digitalization fully, one must acknowledge its multidimensional nature. It involves not only the implementation of digital tools but also the reconfiguration of societal structures, norms, and practices. The scope of digitalization extends beyond the realm of technology developers and experts. It necessitates the active participation of individuals, communities, organizations, and policymakers to navigate the challenges and opportunities presented by the digital era. Furthermore, digitalization raises important normative questions related to ethics, privacy, power dynamics, access to information, and social equality. These questions require thoughtful consideration and collective engagement to ensure that digitalization serves the interests of all members of society. By addressing these normative aspects, digitalization can contribute to the advancement of societal well-being, empowerment, and inclusivity.

DISCUSSION

A widely acknowledged definition of cyberbullying characterizes it as a purposeful and aggressive act or behavior, executed by an individual or a group, utilizing electronic means of communication consistently and over an extended duration. The target of cyberbullying often faces significant challenges in defending themselves against these acts of aggression (Smith, 2013). It is crucial to recognize the various mediums and tactics employed in cyberbullying to fully comprehend its impact and develop effective strategies to combat this form of harassment.

According to Shivika Agrawal (2020), cyberbullying refers to deliberate and aggressive behavior targeted at another individual through electronic means. Agrawal highlights various manifestations of cyberbullying, such as ignoring, disrespecting, teasing, or harassing someone. Additionally, she notes more severe forms, including spreading rumors, stalking, or using technology-based devices and electronic communications to physically threaten others. Agrawal emphasizes that a key aspect of cyberbullying is the anonymity of the perpetrator, which leads the victim to constantly fear being monitored. She further asserts that women and members of the LGBTQ community are particularly vulnerable to the detrimental effects of cyberbullying. Agrawal states, "Rape threats or threats to reveal the sexual orientation of a person cause unique stress. Teens choose not to involve or seek the assistance of elders due to the fear of being called a coward and in turn facing the chance of being bullied even more". In recent times, there has been a distressing surge in the prevalence of sexist remarks, misogyny, and gender-based comments within various digital platforms. This alarming trend has gradually infiltrated online spaces, affecting individuals across different demographics. The impact of these offensive behaviors is far-reaching, perpetuating harmful stereotypes and contributing to a hostile environment for marginalized genders in the virtual realm. "At present, women and girls cannot escape sexism, misogyny or gender-based violence in digital spaces" (United Nations Office of the High Commissioner for Human Rights [UN OHCHR] 2017). "Unlike physical violence, which requires people to be in the same place, technology-facilitated violence can happen across geographical locations, with abusers being able to access their victims even when they are not in close physical proximity" (Bailey and Mathen, 2019).

The different forms of cyberbullying are prevalent on social media websites, and other web sources. Some of them are equally as offensive and pernicious as physical forms of violence against women. For instance, Nancy Willard (2006) describes "various forms of cyberbullying, including flaming, harassment, denigration, impersonation, outing, trickery, exclusion, and cyberstalking." Manpreet Kaur and Munish Saini (2022) claim Cyber victimization can be attributed to various factors, including social media usage, online activity duration, parental supervision, individual awareness, and social involvement. Despite the implementation of stringent measures by both local and national authorities to combat cyberbullying, the frequency of such incidents continues to escalate steadily.

Grace Xess et al. claim as thus:

Turning to official data, we find that there were 8,379 cases of r-crime which related to sexual harassment or exploitation reported across India in 2019 as per data released by the National Crime Records Bureau. These crimes included cyber-stalking, harassment, pornography, defamation, morphing, etc. A total of 289 cases of fake profiles under the IT Act were filed in the same year.

In the last two decades, the use of ICT to access web sources, and use social networking platforms has confronted the world with the different types of cyberbullying and multiplied cases of bullying, cyberstalking, doxing, morphing, harassment, intimidation, humiliation, impersonation, and denigration. Helen Moestue and Robert Muggah (2014) rightly comment:

Indeed, bullying, sexual violence and human trafficking are activities that can be alternately enabled and prevented through the use of ICTs. Child trafficking is a particularly good example. On the one hand, new technologies ranging from social media outlets to cloud-based computing can be used for communications and transactions between traffickers, to recruit victims, and transmit pornographic images of trafficked persons.

It is crucial to highlight that the primary motivation behind these acts is rooted in the victim's gender, specifically targeting women due to their gender or disproportionately impacting them. Acts of violence against women in the digital landscape can manifest in diverse forms, including but not limited to:

For cyberstalking and harassment, the perpetrators exploit ICTs to engage in persistent and unwanted online behaviors, such as sending threatening messages, making derogatory comments, or spreading explicit content, with the intention of intimidating, demeaning, or controlling women. On the other hand, the online sexual exploitation through the internet and social media platforms, women are increasingly vulnerable to various forms of sexual exploitation, including non-consensual distribution of intimate images (often referred to as "revenge porn"), sextortion, and grooming for sexual purposes.

ICTs provide a platform for the dissemination of misogynistic and sexist ideologies, resulting in the proliferation of hate speech targeting women. Such harmful narratives contribute to the normalization of violence against women and perpetuate gender inequality. While it has been found that the abusive partners may employ ICTs as tools for exerting control and power over their intimate partners. This can include monitoring their online activities, invading their privacy by accessing personal accounts or devices without consent, and using digital means to manipulate or coerce them. The digital sphere has become a breeding ground for the propagation of harmful stereotypes and false information about women, which further perpetuate discrimination, bias, and gender-based violence. However, the emergence of artificial intelligence introduces new dimensions to violence against women in the digital realm. Automated systems can be programmed to discriminate against women, perpetuating biased decisions in areas such as employment, lending, and criminal justice, thereby reinforcing gender inequalities and exacerbating violence. Therefore, it is essential to recognize and address the digital dimension of violence against women, as it has severe and far-reaching consequences on the lives of women. Efforts to combat this issue require a comprehensive approach that combines legal measures, policy frameworks, education, awareness-raising, and technological advancements that prioritize the safety and empowerment of women in the digital space.

The paper titled "The digital dimension of violence against women as addressed by the seven mechanisms of the EDVAW Platform" discusses the different dimensions of violence against women. It states:

The digital dimension of violence against women can include any act of gender-based violence against women that is committed, assisted or aggravated in part or fully by the use of information and communication technologies (ICTs), such as mobile phones and smartphones, the internet, social media platforms or email, geolocation tracking devices, drones and non-internet connected recording devices, and artificial intelligence (AI), against a woman because she is a woman, or affects women disproportionately.

India has also witnessed a tremendous upsurge in the cases of morphing reported by the newspapers. In a tragic incident, a young girl took her own life on 26 June 2014 due to the distressing actions of her friends, Satish and Deepak. These individuals manipulated her photographs and proceeded to publish them on Facebook, along with her personal contact details (Tnn, 2014). Similarly, on 9 January 2018, another distressing case emerged, involving a 20-year-old Hindu woman who faced harassment on WhatsApp. The harassment was directed towards her friendship with a Muslim man in Karnataka, eventually leading to her untimely demise (BBC News, 2018). A separate incident took place on 4 May 2020, when the Delhi police initiated legal proceedings against a 15-year-old boy involved in the 'Bois Locker Room' Instagram group. This group facilitated the sharing of inappropriate photographs of underage girls, accompanied by vulgar remarks. The Delhi police successfully apprehended the culprits involved in this disturbing affair (Staff, 2020). However, Adrija Dey (2020) expressed that India experienced a significant utilization of digital technologies during the widespread protests that ensued after the horrific Delhi Nirbhaya rape case on December 16, 2012. This movement stands out as one of the largest gender-related movements ever witnessed in the country. The case itself ignited a profound contemplation on various aspects of Indian society, including its deep-rooted patriarchy, and shed light on the shortcomings of the existing government structures in delivering justice to the women of the nation. The protests not only served as a powerful expression of public outrage but also opened up a broader dialogue on the societal structures and values that perpetuate gender-based violence.

Cyberstalking is a serious problem in India and around the world, especially when it affects women. It describes the act of harassing, threatening, intimidating, or monitoring someone without consent via electronic communication tools like social media, email, or messaging applications. The victims of this kind of online abuse may experience serious repercussions, such as mental discomfort, psychological trauma, and even bodily harm. The prevalence of cyber-stalking in India has grown as a result of the internet's and technology's increased accessibility. Women are frequently the targets of different types of online abuse, including online bullying, blackmail, defamation, and the non-consensual posting of intimate photographs (revenge porn). Cyberstalking frequently serves as a continuation of the harassment and violence that women encounter in the real world.

Cyberstalkers frequently hide behind anonymity, making it challenging to find them and prosecute them. They may act with impunity thanks to their anonymity, which gives them more leeway. Social standards that blame the victim or discourage reporting also make the problem worse. Legal, technological, and sociological comprehensive measures are required to combat cyber-stalking on all fronts. Governments should implement and strictly enforce laws that prohibit internet harassment, ensuring that offenders get just punishment. Law enforcement organizations should receive training on how to effectively and sensitively handle reports of online stalking.

Parallel to this, digital firms and platforms need to put in place strong security controls and simple methods for reporting harassers. To reduce the risk of online stalking, measures like two-factor authentication, privacy settings, and content moderation may be used. To successfully fight cyber-stalking, awareness-raising is essential. Online safety education, consent promotion, and victim empowerment should be the main goals of educational campaigns, workshops, and community participation initiatives. The issue might also be lessened by promoting an atmosphere of respect and empathy online. Thus, combating cyber-stalking necessitates a team effort from people, communities, governmental organizations, and technological corporations. Together, we can make online environments for women safer and assure their safety from harassment and abuse.

Radhika Gajjala (2018) rightly remarks:

While most people recognize that in physical space—the bodies doing the calling out are very clearly vulnerable and can be exposed, they forget that even in digital spaces, whether Facebook, Twitter or Google Docs, there is still a serious risk of exposure through hacking and doxing.

According to the National Crime Records Bureau (NCRB), a total of 50,035 cases were registered under the category of Cyber Crimes, indicating an 11.8% increase in registration compared to 2019's figure of 44,735 cases. The data provided by the NCRB reveals that in 2020, 60.2% of the registered cyber crime rate saw a rise from 3.3 in 2019 to 3.7. Upon analyzing the motive behind these registered cyber crime cases, it becomes evident that fraud was the primary objective in a significant number of instances, accounting for 30,142 out of the total 50,035 cases. Sexual exploitation constituted 6.6% of the cases (3,293 cases), while extortion accounted for 4.9% (2,440 cases). These statistics shed light on the prevalent motivations driving cyber-criminal activities.

Moreover, the advent of online communication channels has emerged as a crucial platform for the propagation of social movements, especially for those that encounter challenges in finding an offline voice. Scholars such as Fenton (2008) and Travers (2003) have emphasized the growing significance of online platforms in enabling social movements that struggle to gain offline visibility. Briefly, the NCRB's records indicate a notable increase in the number of cyber-crime cases registered, particularly in the context of fraud, sexual exploitation, and extortion. Furthermore, online communication channels have played a pivotal role in empowering marginalized social movements that face obstacles in expressing their concerns offline (Fenton 2008; Travers 2003).

In their study on Indian government initiatives on cyberbullying, Manpreet Kaur and Munish Saini (2022) argue that certain social, cultural, and ethical behaviours can help reduce cyberbullying or its different forms. For example, social acceptance, parental support and monitoring, and social engagement can eradicate cyberbullying. Similarly, it is a great matter of concern for the experts in the domain who have also suggested that the use of technology should aptly be interlinked with the society. Urvashi Aneja and Vidisha Mishra (2017) emphasize upon the appropriate use of technology, technological platforms, and devices so that gender gaps can be eliminated, and marginalization of women can be prevented. They state that It is imperative to recognize that technology alone is not inherently empowering; rather, its effectiveness relies on its integration with comprehensive policy interventions spanning various social sectors. Failure to do so will result in the digital age further marginalizing already marginalized communities and intensifying gender-based hierarchies.

Describing the role of technology in cyber-crime, and cyberbullying in the context of India, Samundeeswari, and Vijaya (2022) assert that on the one hand the 'digital India' has witnessed internet plans at lower costs to facilitate people with internet access through computers, tablets or mostly mobile devices, on the other hand, the cases of cyberbullying have surprisingly been higher year by year. However, the threat of cyberbullying is dangerous and its evaluation and prevention seek urgent and remedial action to curb technology-enabled harassment of girls and women in the different states of India. In their opinion, the most vulnerable population includes children and teenagers, and India ranks third in cyberbullying. In his scholarly work, Hadeel Al-Alosi (2017) utilizes the terms 'cyber-violence' and 'technology-facilitated domestic abuse' interchangeably. He provides a clear definition, stating that cyber-violence encompasses repeated acts of abuse committed by an individual, "referred to as the abuser, against their current or former intimate partner using digital technology" (p. 1573). This concept encompasses a broad range of controlling and coercive behaviors, including but not limited to threatening phone calls, cyber-stalking, tracking the location of individuals through "smartphones, harassment on social media platforms, and the non-consensual dissemination of intimate images of partners, commonly known as 'revenge porn'" (Shimizu, 2013).

Furthermore, Garner (2004) offers a comprehensive definition of 'stalking,' which involves two key aspects. First, it refers to the act or instance of surreptitiously following another person. Second, stalking can also encompass offenses such as loitering near someone with the intention of annoying, harassing, or committing further crimes like assault or battery (p. 1440).

By combining these scholarly perspectives, it becomes evident that cyber-violence and technology-facilitated domestic abuse are terms used to describe the repetitive mistreatment carried out through digital means by one person against their current or former intimate partner. This includes a wide array of controlling behaviors such as threatening phone calls, cyber-stalking, tracking locations via smartphones, social media harassment, and the unauthorized sharing of intimate images, commonly referred to as 'revenge porn.' Stalking, as defined by Garner, involves covertly following someone and engaging in activities that are meant to harass or annoy the targeted individual, potentially leading to further criminal acts like assault or battery. In India, the second decade of the 21st century has recorded a high volume of cases about cybercrimes that gained attention of the intellectual, policy makers, government regulatory bodies, and feminist activists. For example, the year 2012 witnessed the case of digital threatening of an eminent Dalit writer, poet, and activist Meena Kandasamy at the different social networking platforms accessible to the worldwide visitors. The multiple Twitter account holders passed derogatory remakes by using abusive language due to the writer's opinions expressed on her personal Twitter account, on a beef-eating festival in the southern city of Hyderabad. The author faced severe threats of acid attacks and televised gang rape. Kandasmay, belonging to the Dalit community, which is considered lower in the Hindu caste system, participated in a festival organized by a marginalized caste group. Another incident occurred in 2013 when Indian journalist Sagarika Ghose received rape threats on Twitter after her daughter's name and school were discovered and published by users. Ghose stated that these tweets were directed by right-wing nationalists targeting "liberal and secular women." Concerned for her safety, Ghose decided to refrain from sharing her personal views on Twitter. Similarly, in the same year, Kavita Krishnan, a prominent women's rights activist based in Delhi, experienced harassment during an online discussion on violence against women on the news website Rediff. The individual using the handle @ RAPIST continuously harassed her until she had to leave the conversation. Additionally, in 2015, both Krishnan and Indian actress Shruti Seth received abusive language and violent threats on Twitter for criticizing the prime minister's social media campaign called 'Selfie With Daughter,' which encouraged fathers to share photos with their daughters to promote girls' education. On February 19, 2015, Richa Kaul Padte reported that Rega Jha, Buzzfeed's India editor, received rape threats for praising Pakistani players on Twitter during an India-Pakistan cricket match. Many Indian men, including renowned writers Chetan Bhagat and Suhel Seth, made abusive comments. The relationship between India and Pakistan has been tense since the partition of India in 1947 (Pasricha, 2021).

It is argued that digital oppression of women occurs because of the gender-based digital divide due to patriarchy in Indian society. Elizabeth Isaac (2023) is one of the critics who states as follows:

India's culture is quite patriarchal in nature and the degree of discrimination and oppression intensifies as we move from urban areas into rural spaces. This overrule of agency often prevents them from having personal access to the internet in the domestic sphere, and when they do it is often governed by the male figures in the family. . . Women in public often refrain from having conversations on their phones in the public domain fearing judgement. Thus, resulting in widening the gender-based digital divide.

However, the different dating web sites, and social networking sites have been one of the major and serious concerns for scholars advocating women's equality in the digital era. For example, In their scholarly work, Vishal Sharma et al. (2019) put forth a compelling argument advocating for the implementation of stringent measures by government authorities in matrimonial websites. Their proposal revolves around the necessity for these platforms to enforce user verification through phone number and email address authentication. This response aims to build upon their ideas, further expanding on the recommended practices without resorting to plagiarism or errors. To begin with, the authors assert that verification should be made obligatory through the utilization of One-Time Passwords (OTPs), ensuring a secure login process. Such OTPs should be generated uniquely for each user and remain valid for a single login attempt. By adopting this approach, matrimonial websites can establish a robust authentication system, enhancing the overall security and trustworthiness of their platforms.

Sharma et al. (2019) emphasize the importance of comprehensive profile screening before making them publicly accessible. This initial screening process acts as a crucial filter, enabling website staff to assess the authenticity and appropriateness of the profiles. However, the authors propose taking this screening a step further by suggesting that subsequent profile updates trigger a repeated screening procedure. By continuously monitoring and scrutinizing profile modifications, the website staff can ensure that the information displayed remains accurate and relevant, providing users with a reliable platform for their matrimonial pursuits.

The authors recommend a transparent approach by advocating for matrimonial websites to explicitly state on their homepages that their services are exclusively intended for marriage seekers. This clarification serves to set clear expectations for users, helping to minimize any potential misunderstandings and ensuring that individuals utilizing these platforms are genuinely interested in pursuing marriage-related connections. By openly communicating their primary objective, matrimonial websites can create a focused and dedicated community of like-minded individuals, facilitating meaningful interactions and promoting successful matches. For instance, Jeevansathi.com says: "Jeevansathi is only meant for users with a bonafide [sic] intent to enter into a matrimonial alliance and is not meant for users interested in dating only." Once documents are uploaded and verified, the websites provide trust badges. Moreover, like Jeevansathi.com, there are a few other popular websites as well that facilitate sharing of such information. They may include—shaadi.com, and bharatmatrimony.com but these networking sites need adhere to the guidelines stipulated by the government for the safety of women, and prevention of the misuse of identity.

It is noticeable that the traditional ways of women's sexual harassment have been replaced by digital devices and platforms. But, patriarchal notions of women's oppression, antifeminist thinkers have been defending women's traditional roles in every walk of life on digital platforms too. Consequently, the cases of women's physical, mental, and sexual harassment in different forms, explicit or implicit, have found manifestation irrespective of caste, class, race, and ethnicity. According to Jordan Fairbairn (2015), "Similar to how sexual harassment and domestic violence were once considered an unavoidable reality for women in the past, there has been a shift in the perspective of advocates and activists towards online abuse and harassment. They are now rejecting the idea that such digital mistreatment is an unfortunate but inevitable part of girls' and women's lives. Instead, there is a growing recognition that the rampant abuse and harassment experienced online stems from deeper societal problems, including misogyny, racism, and homophobia. Consequently, there is a strong belief that these issues should be addressed seriously and urgently (229).

In the past, society often trivialized or dismissed online abuse targeting women, treating it as harmless or inconsequential. However, the perspective has changed as the devastating impact of such harassment has become increasingly evident. Victims of online abuse often suffer tremendous psychological distress, including anxiety, depression, and even suicidal ideation. This recognition of the profound negative effects has amplified the demand for action against online abuse and harassment.

Moreover, advocates and activists now view online mistreatment as an extension of the broader societal inequalities that persist in our world. They understand that online platforms simply provide a new avenue for existing prejudices and discrimination to manifest. Misogyny, racism, and homophobia, which infiltrate our societies offline, effortlessly permeate the digital realm. Therefore, addressing online abuse requires tackling the structural and cultural issues that perpetuate these forms of oppression.

By taking online abuse seriously and recognizing it as a reflection of systemic social problems, advocates and activists hope to create meaningful change. This involves pressuring tech companies to prioritize user safety and implement robust measures to combat harassment. It also calls for enhancing legal systems to hold perpetrators accountable for their actions online. Moreover, educators, parents, and community leaders play a vital role in promoting digital literacy and creating safe online spaces for girls and women. It has been shown great resentment and dissatisfaction against the presentation of women on online social networking websites, and web sources because these websites have not been safeguarding women from violence, abuse, molestation, impersonation, threats against their male counterparts. Philips and Morrissey (2004) wryly observe: "[T]he online world is not [entirely] a safe place and the internet is not necessarily a superhighway to love". Jordan Fairbairn (2015) deliberates upon the notion of violence especially online violence against women. He aptly remarks, "Violence is an abuse of power that hinders a person's ability to be physically and emotionally safe in the world. This world includes the Internet" (245).

Moral and ethical dishonesty while using digital platforms has accelerated online fraud, especially against women. Such users of the internet hide or fake their identities and disseminate unwanted text messages, captions, snaps, and images. Clare Sullivan (2011) states:

I argue that dishonest misuse of an individual's registered transaction identity by another person should be considered theft of identity. This approach accurately describes the nature of the wrong, and the consequences for the individual whose identity is misused by another person. Unlike the general fraud offences, theft designates that individual as the victim of the crime.

Sherry Turkle (1999)opines that the digital realm offers individuals the opportunity to engage in a transformative exploration of identity, particularly evident within virtual communities centered around "role playing," such as Multi-User Domains (MUDs). These immersive environments allow users to craft and embody multiple personas, marking the inception of their participation. However, this phenomenon is not exclusive to these distinctive settings.

Fear of the patriarchy, social norms, and cybercriminals in women and girls has become one of the major reasons behind the low reporting of the cases of victimization of women to the different regulatory bodies of the government. The different studies have shown that women and girls as victims of cybercrimes are reluctant to report the police or other regulatory bodies, and even they do not want to inform, discuss, and disclose about their victimization to their family members, and friends due to social issues or fear of social pressure that can affect their lives in future. A survey conducted by Halder and Jaishankar (2015) discovered that a significant portion of the 131 respondents (67.9%) expressed their openness to discussing potential victimization with their family members. Conversely, 29.0% of the participants showed disinterest in engaging in such discussions, while a smaller proportion (3.1%) chose not to provide a response. Among the respondents, 55.0% confirmed their willingness to report any form of victimization via WhatsApp, but surprisingly, they had not yet reported these incidents to the police. Interestingly, only one person out of the entire group of 131 respondents mentioned having actually reported an incident to the police. In contrast, 41.2% stated their intention not to report such incidents, and 3.8% opted not to answer.

Black's Law Dictionary (2004) defines harassment as "words, conduct, or action (usually repeated or persistent) that, being directed at a specific person, annoys, alarms, or causes substantial emotional distress in that person" The definition emphasizes the repetitive or persistent nature of such behavior. Furthermore, it highlights that while certain forms of harassment may warrant legal action, not all instances necessarily qualify for a lawsuit.

It is crucial to note that the definition provided by *Black's Law Dictionary* offers a comprehensive understanding of harassment, encompassing a broad range of behaviors that can cause harm to individuals. By emphasizing the repetitive or persistent nature of harassment, the definition acknowledges that isolated incidents may not meet the threshold for legal action. However, when harassment is ongoing and has a detrimental impact on an individual's well-being, it may be deemed legally actionable, and individuals have the option to seek legal recourse by filing a lawsuit.

This definition underscores the significance of recognizing the various forms that harassment can take, including verbal, non-verbal, physical, or digital means. It acknowledges that the intent behind harassment is to cause distress and harm to the targeted individual. By emphasizing the requirement of substantial emotional distress caused by the harasser's words, conduct, or actions, the definition establishes a benchmark for evaluating the severity of the harm inflicted.

It is essential to consult legal authorities and specific jurisdictional regulations to fully comprehend the nuances and variations of harassment within a particular legal framework. The definition provided by Black's Law Dictionary serves as a starting point to grasp the general concept of harassment, but it should be supplemented with further legal research to gain a more comprehensive understanding of its applicability and implications in specific contexts.

Jordan Fairbairn (2015) asserts, "Online harassment is understood as a form of sexual violence in part because of the emotional distress and breach of an individual's sense of safety" (234). However, these online violent behaviours range from harassment and public intimidation to the intention to inflict physical and sexual assaults, murders, and induced suicides. The proliferation of the Internet due to technology-facilitated digital platforms has not only multiplied online violence against women but it has also resulted in the different global dimensions. It has also been found that Cyber-VAWG is emerging as a global problem with serious implications for societies and economies around the world (1). Online crimes are not a limited to specific demography or the 'first world' but such crimes depend on the spread of the Internet and access to the web sources. Further, the different sets and dimensions of anti-social, aggressive, and intimidating contents expressing cybercrimes in multifaceted behaviours have become common to any individual who logs on to the Internet or social networking websites, regardless of age, gender, culture or values because Multiple studies have unequivocally demonstrated that violence against women and girls (VAWG) transcends all boundaries, transcending borders, race, culture, and income disparities, causing profound harm to the victims, those in their immediate vicinity, and society as a whole (Broadband Commission). The comprehensive reports from the Broadband Commission have shed light on the escalating influence of the Internet, the rapid proliferation of mobile information and communication technologies (ICTs), and the widespread prevalence of social media, thereby presenting novel opportunities and facilitating diverse initiatives to combat VAWG. In the era of the interconnected online world, networks empowered by "distributed intelligence" and easily accessible mobile platforms are extending their reach to even the most remote corners of the globe. With the advent of mobile Internet access, instances of VAWG can transpire at any time, in any location, relentlessly haunting their victims.

Poonam Muttreja and Andrea Wojnar (2023) advocate for educated, economically productive, empowered and socially aware women and girls in the digital era. They suggest that digital literacy for women is a necessity of the time if India needs to achieve the ultimate goal of gender equality and eliminate gender disparity either it is offline or online. However, the argument of these scholars may help overcome the problem of women's subordination and maltreatment especially by anti-women thinkers yet women's literacy will not merely be sufficient to prevent online physical, and sexual assault on them. In the study conducted by Kowalski et al. (2008), the concept of denigration is explored as an additional form of cyberbullying. Denigration involves spreading derogatory and false information about another individual, either through the creation of web pages or by sharing it via email or instant messaging platforms. Furthermore, this particular type of cyberbullying encompasses the act of distributing digitally manipulated photographs of someone, often with the intention of portraying them in a sexualized or harmful manner.

The researchers emphasize that denigration is a significant component of the broader cyberbullying phenomenon. It entails the dissemination of harmful content that not only damages the victim's reputation but also perpetuates a hostile online environment. Instances of denigration can cause severe emotional distress and have lasting psychological effects on the targeted individual. Therefore, the significant opinions can be taken into consideration to overcome such effects. For instance, the study of Kowalski et al. (2008) sheds light on the multifaceted nature of cyberbullying by highlighting the specific tactics employed in denigration. This form of online harassment goes beyond mere name-calling or teasing and involves the deliberate fabrication and circulation of defamatory material. The researchers' findings underscore the urgent need for effective prevention strategies and interventions to address this insidious form of digital aggression.

The study of the role of ICT in the digitalization of violence and sexual politics against women reveals that ICT plays a double-edge role, especially with women because digital technologies have presented activists with a valuable tool to closely monitor the actions of elites and government bodies, fostering increased awareness and encouraging self-regulation. However, this same advancement has also granted authorities the ability to surveil dissent activities, resulting in the restriction of social action. (Garrett 2006). In other words, it is also explicit that on the one hand, ICT is one of the key factors in the digitalization of data, on the other hand, it becomes a tool for presenting women and girls as diminished personalities destined to be treated as subject of men's desires, and dreams. This subversive nature of men's behaviour towards women has also been perpetuated in the digital era, especially everyday incidents of cyber bullying, hacking, and doxing have been responsible for women's harassment from private to the public spheres or home to the world.

CONCLUSION

To sum up, the discussion on the role of ICT in the digitalization of violence and sexual politics in India reveals that there has been an unexpected upsurge in the cases of projected violence against women and girls in India for the last two decades. The nature of violence has changed its forms due to ICT, and online platforms but the forms of violence have become rigid, implicit, intricate, and pernicious. Similarly, sexual politics in the digital age has also transformed its roles from traditional to digital due to the advancement of technology, and access to the website from anywhere, anytime with the help of ICT, and technological devices. Consequently, vulnerability against women has increased rapidly. While the initiatives taken by the government against such malpractices have not been sufficient to curb online frauds against women and girls, insults, derogatory remarks, misuse of digital identity or faking identity, cyberbullying in different forms and behaviours, online sexual assault, rape, and pornography directed against women. One of the instances of the initiatives of the Home Ministry, Government of India include the online portal for its citizens to register their complaints against cybercrime. It is known as CCPWC (Cyber Crime Prevention against Women and Children). But, an extensive awareness amongst the public about this portal needs to be calculated so that women and girls or victims of cybercrime especially Dalit women and girls can record their complaint on CCWPC. Therefore, the government needs to encourage women report online threats, and harassment cases, and issue safety majors and guidelines for monitoring online or digital vulnerability against women. It is also recommended that similar studies may help and identify such social ills, and malpractices to curb them for quality and harmony between sexes, and betterment of humanity.

REFERENCES

Agrawal, S. (2020, September 22). Cyber bullying. *ProBono India.* http://probono-india.in/blog-detail.php?id=168

Al-Alosi, H. (2017). Cyber-violence: Digital abuse in the context of domestic violence *Thematic: Cyber-Violence, 40*(4), 1573-1603. https://www.unswlawjournal.unsw.edu.au/wp-content/uploads/2017/11/404_13.pdf

Aneja. (2017, May 25). Digital India is no country for women. Here's why. *The Wire.* https://thewire.in/economy/digital-india-women-technology

BBC News. (2018, January 9). India woman kills self "over WhatsApp bullying." *BBC News.* https://www.bbc.com/news/world-asia-india-42617237

Broadband Commission for Sustainable Development. (n.d.). http://www.broadbandcommission.org/resources/Pages/default.aspx

Cyber Violence against Women and Girls: A World-Wide Wake-Up Call. (n.d.). https://en.unesco.org/sites/default/files/genderreport2015final.pdf

Dey, A. (2020). Sites of exception: Gender violence, digital activism, and Nirbhaya's zone of anomie in India. *Violence Against Women, 26*(11), 1423–1444. doi:10.1177/1077801219862633 PMID:31379258

Directorate of Communications, Council of Europe. (2022). *The digital dimension of violence against women as addressed by the seven mechanisms of the EDVAW platform.* https://www.ohchr.org/sites/default/files/documents/hrbodies/cedaw/statements/2022-12-02/EDVAW-Platform-thematic-paper-on-the-digital-dimension-of-VAW_English.pdf

Duff, A. S. (2012). *A Normative Theory of the Information Society.* Routledge. doi:10.4324/9780203137758

Fairbairn, J. (2015). Rape threats and revenge porn: Defining sexual violence in the digital age. In J. Bailey & V. Steeves (Eds.), *eGirls, eCitizens: Putting Technology, Theory and Policy into Dialogue with Girls' and Young Women's Voices* (pp. 229–252). University of Ottawa Press. https://www.jstor.org/stable/j.ctt15nmj7f.13

Fenton, N. (2008). Mediating solidarity. *Global Media and Communication, 4*(1), 37-57.

Gajjala, R. (2018). When an Indian whisper network went digital. *Communication, Culture & Critique, 11*(3), 1–5. doi:10.1093/ccc/tcy025

Garner, B. A. (2004). *Black's Law Dictionary.* West Group.

Halder, D., & Jaishankar, K. (2015). *Harassment via WHATsAPP in Urban & Rural India. A Baseline Survey Report (2015)*. https://www.cybervictims.org/CCVCresearchreport2015.pdf

Isaac, E. (2023). IAMAI Report: Digital gender divide lingers in India. *Feminism in India*. https://feminisminindia.com/2023/03/08/digital-gender-divide-lingers-in-india-as-per-new-report/

Kaur, M., & Saini, M. (2022). Indian government initiatives on cyberbullying: A case study on cyberbullying in Indian higher education institutions. *Education and Information Technologies*, *28*(1), 581–615. doi:10.100710639-022-11168-4 PMID:35814802

Kowalski, R. M. (2008). *Cyber Bullying: Bullying in the Digital Age*. Blackwell Publishing. doi:10.1002/9780470694176

Moestue & Muggah. (2014). *Digitally enhanced child protection: How new technology can prevent violence against children in the Global South*. Igarape Institute. https://www.jstor.org/stable/resrep20658

Muttreja & Wojnar. (2023, March 5). India needs to double down on bridging its digital gender gap. *Mint*. https://www.livemint.com/opinion/columns/india-needs-to-double-down-on-bridging-its-digital-gender-gap-11678040421197.html

NCRB. (n.d.). *Crimes in India 2020: Statistics Volume I*. National Crime Records Bureau (Ministry of Home Affairs). https://ncrb.gov.in/sites/default/files/CII%202020%20Volume%201.pdf

Padte, R. K. (2015, February 19). *Sexist remarks, stalking and rape threats: how women are punished for speaking online*. Scroll.in. https://scroll.in/article/707639/sexist-remarks-stalking-and-rape-threats-how-women-are-punished-for-speaking-online

Pasricha, J. (2021). *"Violence" Online in India: Cybercrimes against women and minorities on social media*. https://feminisminindia.com/wp-content/uploads/2021/08/Cyberviolence-Against-Women-in-India_Research-Report_FII.pdf

Philips, F., & Morrissey, G. (2004). Cyberstalking and cyberpredators: A threat to safe sexuality on the internet. *Convergence (London)*, *10*(1), 66–79. doi:10.1177/135485650401000105

Samundeeswari, S., & Vijaya, K. (2022). Cyberbullying: Harmful impact of technology. *International Journal of Creative Research Thoughts*, *10*(2), 850–855. https://ijcrt.org/papers/IJCRT2202339.pdf

Sharma, Nardi, Norton, & Tsaasan. (2019, Sep). Towards safe spaces online: A study of Indian matrimonial websites. *17th IFIP Conference on Human-Computer Interaction (INTERACT)*, 43-66. . hal-0255387910.1007/978-3-030-29387-1_4

Shimizu, A. (2013). Recent developments: domestic violence in the digital age: Towards the creation of a comprehensive cyberstalking statute. *Berkeley Journal of Gender, Law & Justice*, 116–117.

Smith, P. K., del Barrio, C., & Tokunaga, R. S. (2013). Definitions of bullying and cyberbullying: how useful are the terms? In S. Bauman, D. Cross, & J. Walker (Eds.), *Principles of Cyberbullying Research: Definitions, Measures, and Methodology* (pp. 26–40). Routledge/Taylor & Francis Group.

Staff, F. P. (2020, May 6). Delhi Police arrests Instagram group admin in bois locker room case; 27 other members identified. *Firstpost*. https://www.firstpost.com/india/delhi-police-arrests-instagram-group-admin-in-bois-locker-room-case-27-other-members-identified-8337451.html

Sullivan, C. (2011). Digital identity — protection. *Digital Identity: An Emergent Legal Concept,* 107–136. https://www.jstor.org/stable/10.20851/j.ctt1sq5wqb.12

TNN. (2014, June 25). Girl kills self over Facebook harassment. *The Times of India*. https://timesofindia.indiatimes.com/city/kolkata/girl-kills-self-over-facebook%20harassment/articleshow/37211521.cms?utm_source=contentofinterest&utm_medium=text&utm_campaign=cppst

Travers, A. (2003). Parallel subaltern feminist counter publics in cyberspace. *Sociological Perspectives*, *46*(2), 223-237.

Turkle, S. (1999, November). Cyberspace and identity. *Contemporary Sociology*, *28*(6), 643–648. doi:10.2307/2655534

Willard, N. (2006). *Cyber bullying and cyberthreats: Responding to the challenge of online social cruelty, threats, and distress*. Center for Safe and Responsible Internet Use.

Xess, G. (n.d.). *Cyber-bullying, cyber-stalking and sexism: A case study of women students of Delhi University*. https://www.jmc.ac.in/uploads/staticfiles/societies/Final%20WSC%20Project%20Report%20(Cyber%20Stalking%20Cyber%20Bullying%20&%20Sexism%20-%20Case%20Study%20of%20Women%20Students%20of%20DU).pdf

Chapter 4
Trolling and Victims' Perception of Trolling:
A Thematic Analysis

Shravani Minesh Kapse
Banasthali Vidyapith, India

Sandhya Gupta
Banasthali Vidyapith, India

ABSTRACT

Online trolling is the practise of engaging in dishonest, harmful, or disruptive behaviour in a social setting over the internet without any apparent gain. If a target falls for their trick, the trolling gets worse for even more heinous enjoyment. Trolling may be distinguished from other forms of online antisociality by its dishonest and "pointless" disruptive features, in contrast to which the perpetrators' names and objectives are usually more transparent. Trolling has adverse negative effects on mental health. Therefore, there is an urgent need to address this issue. This chapter attempted to look into the causes of trolling which is damaging the mental health of people and why people become victims of trolling. Secondly, it assessed whether the damage in mental health vary with age or not. Thematic analysis was conducted on the transcribed data and the findings were discussed.

1. INTRODUCTION

Trolls act in ways intended to "annoy, degrade, disrupt, mock, incite, or encourage individuals to respond passionately to the individuals they target" in order to have fun. Assaultive, stimulating discriminatory, racist, or offensive language can be used in trolling on social media, electronic newspapers, news comments, or other media outlets on the internet Trolls are not conscious that they are injuring actual individuals; instead, they view online interaction platforms as accessible venues for their peculiar sense of humour. They view other internet consumers as a kind of technological abstraction rather than as true people. As a result, they are unmoved by the suffering they have brought about on the opposite side. In reality,

DOI: 10.4018/978-1-6684-8893-5.ch004

they are more effective the more agony they inflict. Trolls are utterly immune to any kind of productive or bothersome comments or criticisms. One cannot bargain with them, implore them to show generosity or contrition, or appeal to their sense of guilt. However, trolls do not feel constrained by the laws of compassion or social obligation, for whatever cause. Such acts of trolls leave a deep scar on the lives of human beings. Therefore, there is an urgent need to address the issue of trolling. This chapter attempted to look into the causes of trolling, why people become victim of trolling and the impact of trolling on mental health of two age groups, viz, 18-35 years and 36-55 years, with the help of thematic analysis.

2. BACKGROUND

2.1 What Is Trolling?

It's ambiguous where the terms "troll" and "trolling" emerged from or when they started to be used. A common view among scientific articles is that the application of the term trolling, regarding its use on the internet, springs from a form of fishing where a baited line is set in the water and dragged slowly by a boat to encourage the fish to bite (Cambria, Chandra, Sharma & Hussain, 2010; Binns, 2012; Bishop, 2014a; Golf-Papez & Veer, 2017; Jussinoja & Terho, 2018). According to Hardaker (2013) said that Usenet, one of the first worldwide discussion systems on computers has been recognised as the place where trolling started, even though there is no direct convincing proof for it.

Despite decades of research that aims to create typologies, shed light on trolls' motives and motivations, and theorise the wider ramifications of the phenomena, scholars cannot agree on how to define or operationalize trolling. Comparing studies on trolling is extremely challenging due to the wide variety of theoretical frameworks, contexts, and sampling frames. Indeed, researchers contend that trolling is contextually dependent and irrational; what users see as trolling in one area, like Wikipedia, may not be considered such in another, like Instagram (Hardaker, 2010; Ortiz, 2022). However, researchers cited that "Trolls" are those who take pleasure in stirring up conflict online, seeking to initiate conversations, and upsetting other people (Aydn et al., 2021). Presenting purposefully offensive content in a specific context with the intention of misleading other people into responding angrily is one common form of trolling, according to Hardaker (2010). According to many researchers (Buckels et al., 2014; Hardaker, 2010; Phillips, 2015; Sanfilippo et al., 2018), trolling is effectively an umbrella word encompassing a spectrum of multifaceted, hostile, antisocial, or deviant behaviours and motivations online. Trolling is an identity-deception game that is performed without the consent of other players. He also noted that trolls try to pose as real users, interrupt conversations, and undermine confidence (Jussinoja & Terho, 2018).

There is no agreed-upon definition for trolling, but it is a phrase that is used in the literature to refer to a wide range of offensive online behaviours. The practise of trolling is a recent phenomenon that is changing from a rather anarchic kind of individual internet harassment to one that is more systematic. It defines trolling as an online behaviour that takes place in settings where debate is encouraged (e.g., social media platforms, online forums, comment and discussion threads, online gaming, chat groups, etc.). Investigators defined trolling as a situation-specific, intentional, controversial and repetitive (Fichman & Sanfilippo, 2016) behaviour by a person towards other people or groups (Sanfilippo, Yang & Fichman, 2017). The cross-national variability of online trolling was noted by Phillips (2015), who also discussed the diverse causes of trolling behaviour in Australia, Britain, and the US, respectively (Sun & Fichman, 2018). The idea of trolling has undergone a significant transformation from a distinctive type of online behaviour to an archetypically anti-social person in online communities—the troll—as the obnoxious and deceitful features of trolling behaviour become more common (Cruz, Seo, & Rex, 2018).

2.2 What Is Internet Trolling?

Over the past decades, the phenomenon of internet trolling has gained increased notoriety (Fichman & Sanfilippo, 2016; Maltby et al., 2016; Molenda, et al., 2022). Since the 1980s, people who use email, chat relays, and forums on the Internet for communication have encountered several specific behaviours that are seen as abnormal, dishonest, hostile, or confrontational (Ortiz, 2020). As a result, considering previous theories and studies on antisocial internet phenomena (Moor & Anderson, 2019), they defined internet trolling as a potentially dangerous online behaviour (Molenda, et al., 2022). In order to differentiate between sincere/insincere or genuine/deceptive interactions, this "trolling" behaviour had to be identified, which required insider knowledge of the standards of these specific websites (Ortiz, 2020). The posting of messages that are excessively offensive rather than just offensive should be addressed to as online trolling in legal contexts (Starmer, 2013; Bishop, 2014). According to a vast body of investigation (Buckels et al., 2014; Cheng et al., 2017; March & Marrington, 2019; March & Steele, 2020), Internet trolling behaviours are associated with hostile personality traits, low self-esteem, and an elevated level of negative mood (Molenda, et al., 2022). Due to the large audience and potential anonymity, there is still an additional explanation why trolls might post unpleasant or derogatory content (Cambria et al., 2010). Internet trolls (Gemiharto & Sukaesih, 2020), post inflammatory or off-topic statements using fictitious online personas in an effort to stifle conversations and elicit strong feelings from other users. Online harassment is described as "a recurring, disruptive online deviant behaviour by an individual targeting other individuals or groups" (Fichman & Sanfilippo, 2016; Case & King, 2017).

Online trolling, according to a researcher (Xavier, 2022), is the act of acting dishonestly, destructively, or disruptively in a social setting over the Internet for no discernible reason. Scholars have also noted that online trolling has grown to be of major importance in influencing the movements for politics and society on social media (Tuna et al., 2016). While it is impossible to disregard social media firms' attempts to stop online harassment, the impact of trolling on society has gotten a lot of attention in both mainstream and alternative media (Bharati, Lee & Syed, 2019).

2.3 Who Are Trolls?

The Old Norse word "troll" means giant or monster and is the source of the English noun "troll" in its common sense of unattractive dwarf or giant, which dates to 1610. The phrase conjures up the trolls from children's stories and Scandinavian folklore, which are sociopathic, argumentative, and slow-witted beings that make life unpleasant for travellers (Xavier, 2022). A troll tries to disrupt a newsgroup by posing a controversial question, which they frequently succeed in doing. The troll may be overtly or covertly offensive to stir up conflict or attempt to drag people into pointless debate (Binns, 2012, p. 548).

Internet trolls first cause havoc by, for instance, publishing divisive remarks or disseminating dubious material online. They frequently discuss the so-called "hot spots" that elicit strong emotional responses (Papapicco & Quatera, 2019; Molenda et al., 2022). An active member of a social media platform who consciously seeks to disrupt, assault, offend, or otherwise create difficulty within the group by publishing particular remarks, images, videos, or other types of online content is known as an Internet troll (Moreau, 2017).

According to studies to date, trolls are predisposed by their temperament and genetic makeup to trolling (Cheng et al., 2017; Case & King, 2017). The "dark tetrad" of narcissism, psychopathy, Machiavellianism, and commonplace sadism stands out among the many psychological characteristics that studies consistently mentioned (Buckels, 2014; Paulhus, 2014; Craker & March, 2016; Maltby, 2016; Molenda, et al., 2022). Because trolls conceal information that may be used to identify them and because they can pretend to be a different gender or age (Phillips, 2013), it is impossible to confirm their accurate demographics (Jussinoja & Terho, 2018; Zezulka & Seigfried-Spellar, 2016). According to Sest and March (2017), who also utilised a poll to try to identify the demographics of trolls, the typical troll is a male with psychological characteristics comparable to those of the "dark tetrad" but low affective empathy, allowing them to grasp other people's emotional anguish without empathising. In specific research (Buckels et al., 2014; Craker & March, 2016), it has been shown that men used trolling more frequently than women. Phillips (2011) had observed female trolls and others who were pretending to be women using language that was comparable to the male trolls' usage.

Shachaf and Hara (2010) examined Wikipedia trolling and hypothesised that the three most frequent motivations for trolling were boredom, retaliation, and attention seeking (Jussinoja & Terho, 2018). As stated by Cheng et al. (2017), trolling undermines productive discourse in online communities. Although previous research implies that trolls are a vociferous and antisocial minority, it has been shown that regular people are capable of participating in such behaviours as well. The mood of the individual and the setting of a debate (such as prior exposure to trolling behaviours) were suggested as the two main trigger factors in the study (Xavier, 2022).

2.4 Categorization of Trolling and Trolls

Trolling may variate in complexity from relatively insignificant events, such as "accidental trolls" (someone simply expressing their opinion), to more serious variants, in which people intentionally inflict anguish to bereaved families (Hardaker, 2010, 2013).

Trolls come in a variety of forms and even subtypes, and while studies have highlighted this (Bishop, 2012c), they are all frequently regarded in a negative manner. Research investigations have discussed various types of internet trolls, including gender trolls (Mantilla, 2013), RIP trolls (Phillips, 2011), Wikipedia trolls (Shachaf & Hara, 2010), McCann trolls (Synnott et al., 2017), political and social trolls (Sanfilippo et al., 2017a), and more. In addition, Bishop also sorted the trolls into four distinct categories—haters, lolcows, bzzzters, and eyeballs—and looked at them in detail using a total of 12 subcategories (Aydn et al., 2022).

Aggressive trolling is when a user is insulted, words are used incorrectly on purpose, and personal remarks are sent to the target user. Provocative trolls, on the contrary, use comments meant to frustrate people to try to draw attention to themselves or to stop the topic from moving forward (Case et al., 2017). In a similar vein, Fichman and Sanfilippo (2016) labelled trolls into six categories: grieving, remembrance, ideological, LOL, nonideological, religious, and political. However, they did it by using the themes and reasons as the dividing lines. In his most updated classification, Sanfilippo et al. (2018) identified four distinct behavioural types: serious trolling, serious non-trolling, humorous trolling, and humorous non-trolling (Jussinoja & Terho, 2018).

2.5 Impact of Trolling on Mental Health

Based on the work of Binns (2012) "trolling can have severe impact on both the offenders and the target of such behaviours, not only in their online domains but also in their everyday lives" (Jussinoja & Terho, 2018). Multiple research studies (Myers & Cowie, 2017; Maltby, 2017; Jenaro et al., 2017; Seigfried-Spellar & Chowdhury, 2017; Pearson, 2016) addressed the same behavioural effects, such as abuse of substances, disgrace, humiliation, diminished self-worth, anxiety, abandonment of social life, and negative effects on interpersonal relationships (for example, with other family members, intimate partners). Online trolling has also been connected, in some more extreme cases, to an increased risk of attempted suicide and self-harm (Maltby, 2017; Pearson, 2016). Coles and West (2016a) communicated an equivalent view that trolling could even cause victims to consider hurting themselves. In Griffiths' (2014) work, he also discovered that recipients of trolling had a poor linkage between their self-esteem and the trolling attacks.

The victims who feel more personally under attack and experience offline threats as a result of online trolling are more likely to suffer grave repercussions (Maltby et al., 2016; Barlow & Awan, 2016); they are more likely to have their private data revealed online or to receive threats against their friends and family. Retribution porn in which footage of sexual acts are released online to discredit ex- intimate partners, is a prime instance of this type of direct threat. This kind of internet abuse is very intimate and frequently accompanied by physical threats like stalking and physical assault. According to Henry and Powell (2016), the effects of this kind of activity can be very severe and include accusing victims, disengagement from social situations, diminished self-worth, paranoia, and disrupted relationships with others. Ofcom (2017) discovered that 44% of the 1,000+ social media users who responded to the study concurred that the possibility of receiving offensive comments or reactions discourages them from sharing content.

Online trolling is more tolerable for victims who believe it is driven by attracting attention habits; therefore, they do not suffer the same detrimental effects on their physical and mental health (Maltby et al., 2016). But even when individuals exhibit relatively high levels of psychological adaptability, they might nevertheless alter their online activities in reaction to trolling. Trolling victims may experience humiliation in front of other internet users after being targeted and may even come under ridicule from other users for ending up becoming a prey to the troll (Hardaker, 2015).

The negative effects of trolling extend beyond just harming people or communities; they also have an impact on monetary corporations. Publications with internet followings have a stake in keeping their name and community engaging to their readers, but even a small number of devoted trolls can change the vibe and turn off frequent visitors (Binns, 2012). The phrase "Don't feed the troll" has been used frequently recently in an effort to prevent trolls from being the centre of everybody's focus as a result of all the foregoing negative effects (Aydın et al., 2022). Additionally, trolling can have negative effects on the trolls themselves. There have been numerous instances where trolls have been prosecuted and imprisoned for their actions, and trolling occasionally errs on the side of unlawful behaviour. The opposite is also true, according to some Investigators (Phillips, 2015), who think that trolling behaviour has also beneficially impacted popular internet culture (such as through memes). Coles and West's (2016b) argument that trolls who are effective in igniting controversies in an online newspaper's comment area may actually boost readership and generate more income for a news site. Certain research studies contend that trolling, even when done unintentionally (e.g., on online forums), can produce valuable discourse and appropriate societal critique (Phillips, 2015; Jussinoja & Terho, 2018).

The review of literature suggests that trolling has adverse negative effects on mental health. Therefore, there is an urgent need to address this issue. This chapter attempted to look into the causes of trolling, why people become victim of trolling and the impact of trolling on mental health of two age groups, viz, 18-35 years and 36-55 years.

3. METHODOLOGY

3.1 Participants

The study included two groups of people, viz, 18-35 years and 36-55 years. For this purpose, 40 people were interviewed. The participants were selected to ensure a diverse sample in terms of gender, race, and socioeconomic status. A qualitative analysis (thematic analysis) was done.

3.2 Procedure

The purpose of this study was to investigate the causes of trolling, causes of victimisation of trolling, and impact of trolling on the mental health of individuals in the age groups of (18–35years) and (36–55 years) using a qualitative research methodology. The consent of the respondents was obtained before the interview, and they were promised that the information they provided would be kept confidential. To investigate the causes, victimisation, and effects of trolling on mental health, unstructured interviews were done with a sample of individuals from the age groups (18-35 years) and (36-55 years). The participants' homes or another suitable venue was the setting for the in-person interviews. For analysis, the interviewees' audio was taped and analysed. Thematic analysis was used to examine the data in order to find recurring themes and patterns among the participants' responses.

4. RESULTS

Thematic analysis was used to analyse the data. Themes and sub-themes were extracted from the audio recordings through extensive study and analysis.

5. CAUSES OF TROLLING:

5.1 Leisure Time/Entertainment

Trolls cause discomfort and intentionally provoke people online for their own amusement. They participate in trolling as a form of leisure and entertainment. They get pleasure from stirring up strong feelings and upsetting internet exchanges. Excerpt of Respondent 7 emphasizing on it – *"I think trolls tend to troll for fun and their own entertainment.... it's like a leisure activity for them"*

Table 1. Themes and sub-themes for causes, victimization, and impact of trolling on mental health (age group: 18-35 years)

S.No.	Themes	Sub-Themes	Findings
		Causes of Trolling	
1.	Leisure Time/ Entertainment	For fun, Enjoyment, Mockery	People enjoy making fun of others
2.	Popularity	Gaining fame, Publicity, Attention-seeking	People who urge for popularity, name and fame
3.	Emotional Immaturity	Anger, Irritability, Frustration, Jealousy	When people are not able to control their frustrations arising out of life challenges exhibitlack of emotional control
4.	Premature thinking	Immaturity, Narrow-minded thoughts, Lack of reasoning	People who can't think logically and have backwardness in thoughts
5.	Cognitive Incongruence	Incongruent beliefs, Clash of belief systems	People cannot tolerate beliefs different than theirs'
6.	Anonymity	Lack of accountability for the actions	When people feel they are undercover or "behind the curtains" their inhibitions lower
7.	Sadism	Aggression, Enjoy hurting others	People seek pleasure by hurting others
8.	Meddling	Unnecessary intrusion in people's lives, Jealousy, Attention-seeking	People like to interfere in others' lives reason being their own unsatisfied lives
		Why People Become Victims of Trolling	
1.	Cyber bullying	Irresponsibility in posting content, Lack ofAccountability, Derogatory comments, Misuse of information	When people post content tactlessly, unintelligently and be negligent towards their postings
2.	Lack of self-awareness	Inadequate self, Discrepancy between ideal and real self, Self-doubt, Lack of self-confidence	When people have very scarce knowledge of themselves and easily believe whatever others' say about them even negative things
3.	Need of Approval	Compulsive need of validation, Craving for attachment, Unable to handle rejection	People become vulnerable because of their need for approval and validation which results in their exploitation by trolls
4.	Publicity	Popularity, Fame, Approval of others, Attention-seeking	When people post irresponsibly just for name, fame and attention
5.	Personal Insecurities	Insecurities of oneself are targeted, Inadequacy, Vacillation, Anxious	When people' personal insecurities are attacked and their made to feel inadequate
6.	Negativity Bias	Over-emphasis on negativity, More focus on negative information, Strong response to negative information, Proclivity to attend negative information	When people focus on the negative feedback far more than positive feedback
7.	Weird/Unusual Content	Extraordinary, bizarre, odd, curious content	People posting explicit content which is non-conforming to society's norms
		Impact of Trolling on Mental Health	
1.	Mental Disorders/ MentalHealth Issues	Eating disorders, Depression, Anxiety, Suicidal thoughts or even committing Suicide.	People become depressed, anxious and have suicidal tendencies. they are also prone to eating disorders
2.	Worthlessness	Feelings of uselessness, unworthiness	People start feeling useless and unworthy when they are trolled
3.	Negative MoodState	Negativity enters mind, Irritability, Aggression	People become aggressive, pessimistic and irritable in day-to-day lives
4.	EmotionalInsecurity	Increased insecurities, Lack of confidence, Self-doubt, Hesitancy, Indecisiveness	People start undervaluing themselves, lose confidence and there comes feeling of incompetence
5.	Identity Crisis	Change in identity, Confusion, Uncertainty	People fail to recognize themselves, they become unclear about their identity and who they are
6.	Personality	Change in personality of a person, Introversion	People change themselvescompletely and also become introverts and remain in a shell
7.	Seclusion/Solitude	Social isolation, Absence of social relationships, lack of approval	People tend to isolate themselves from society and prefer being left out
8.	Rumination	Overthinking, Repeatedly dwell on same situations, Thinking too much about situation	People start overthinking unimportant things and make it difficult to move on by dwelling on same situations

5.2 Popularity

Seeking popularity, name and fame is a motivation for some individuals who engage in trolling, Trolls often resort to offensive or inflammatory remarks to elicit strong reactions and garner attention. By provoking others and generating controversy, they may attract a following or gain a temporary sense of notoriety within certain online communities. Excerpt of Respondent 5 emphasizing on it – *"According to me, their (trolls) motive is to gain name, fame and mainly attention.... this is the main reason they troll"*.

5.3 Emotional Immaturity

Trolls engage in trolling due to emotional immaturity. Their behaviour often stems from anger, irritability or a desire to alleviate their own personal frustrations, which they express through provocative and hurtful actions towards others which shows their lack of emotional control. Excerpt of Respondent 15 emphasizing on it – *"In my opinion, trolls are very immature and so they project their anger and frustrations on others"*.

5.4 Premature Thinking

Trolling behaviour often stems from a lack of maturity in thinking, narrow minded thoughts and lack of reasoning. Trolls may display backwardness and illogicality while trolling in order to hurt others. Excerpt of Respondent 17 emphasizing on it – *"I think the main reason of trolling is narrow-mindedness...they lack reasoning as they are not very mature"*.

5.5 Cognitive Incongruence

Trolls engage in trolling behaviour because they have a low tolerance for beliefs or opinions that differ from their own. They seek to provoke and harass individuals who hold contrasting views as a way to assert their own superiority or to disrupt online discussions. Their actions reflect intolerance for diverse perspectives and a desire to impose their own beliefs on others. Excerpt of Respondent 3 emphasizing on it – *"I think that trolls have a belief system and people who go against this belief system are trolled"*.

5.6 Anonymity

Trolls engage in trolling behaviour primarily due to the anonymity it provides, allowing them to avoid accountability for their actions. When people feel they are undercover or hidden behind the curtains of the internet, their inhibitions lower, leading them to engage in provocative and disruptive behaviour for the sake of amusement or to incite reactions from others. Excerpt of Respondent 11 emphasizing on it – *"According to me, trolling occurs because there is no accountability.... trolls are behind veils and so they troll"*.

5.7 Sadism

Trolls engage in trolling because they derive pleasure from causing harm and distress to others. They exhibit sadistic and aggressive tendencies, finding enjoyment in the suffering and emotional reactions of their targets. Their actions reflect a deep-seated desire to inflict pain and disrupt online interactions for their own gratification. Excerpt of Respondent 18 emphasizing on it – *"In my opinion, trolls are sadistic people and they get pleasure by trolling..."*

5.8 Meddling

Trolls engage in trolling because they have a propensity for meddling in people's lives, often driven by jealousy and a desire for unnecessary intrusion. They derive satisfaction from disrupting the personal lives and online experiences of others, seeking to create chaos and dissatisfaction in an attempt to alleviate their own negative feelings or insecurities. Excerpt of Respondent 9 emphasizing on it – *"I think that people who like meddling in other's lives, pointing out the wrongs of others.... I think they are jealous of people's success. I guess this can be the reason they troll"*.

6. WHY PEOPLE BECOME VICTIMS OF TROLLING

6.1 Cyber Bulling

People become victims of trolling due to a combination of factors that come under the label of cyberbullying that is irresponsible posting of content, lack of accountability, derogatory comments, and the misuse of information. Trolls exploit these vulnerabilities to harass and harm people online, causing emotional distress and potentially damaging reputations. Excerpt of Respondent 16 emphasizing on it – *"In my perspective people who are irresponsible about what they are posting on social media are prime victims of trolling"*.

6.2 Lack of Self-Awareness

People become victims of trolling due to factors such as inadequate self-perception, a discrepancy between their ideal and real self, self-doubt, and a lack of self-confidence. Trolls target these vulnerabilities, deliberately attacking and provoking individuals to further undermine their self-esteem and amplify their insecurities. Excerpt of Respondent 7 emphasizing on it – *"I think when people are unclear about themselves, they don't know who they are and what are their goals then they are prone to become victim of trolling"*.

6.3 Need of Approval

People become victims of trolling due to their compulsive need for validation and approval, often driven by a craving for attachment and an inability to handle rejection. Trolls exploit these needs and vulnerabilities, intentionally targeting individuals who seek external validation, and deriving satisfaction from the emotional reactions and disruption they cause. Excerpt of Respondent 1 emphasizing on it – *"According to me people who have extreme urge of validation from others and who crave attachment are the ones who become victims of trolling"*.

6.4 Publicity

People become victims of trolling when they engage in irresponsible posting solely for the sake of gaining name, fame, attention, and approval of others on internet. Trolls seize this opportunity to exploit their vulnerable desire for validation, intentionally targeting and harassing individuals who seek recognition and validation through their online presence. Excerpt of Respondent 19 emphasizing on it – *"In my opinion, people who don't take responsibility of what they are posting on social media, they are negligent and post just for name, fame and attention…."*

6.5 Personal Insecurities

People become victims of trolls due to their personal insecurities, which can include feelings of inadequacy, vacillation, and anxiety. Trolls specifically target these vulnerabilities to provoke and harass individuals, exacerbating their insecurities and causing emotional distress. The trolls' intention is to exploit these weaknesses for their own amusement or to derive a sense of power and control. Excerpt of Respondent 20 emphasizing on it – *"I think people who are insecure about themselves and feel that they are not enough they are always anxious about themselves…"*

6.6 Negativity Bias

People become victims of trolling due to several factors, including an over-emphasis on negativity, a tendency to focus more on negative information, a strong response to negative stimuli, and a proclivity to pay attention to negative information. Trolls exploit these tendencies, deliberately provoking negative reactions and targeting individuals who are more likely to be affected by their hurtful behaviour. Excerpt of Respondent 4 emphasizing on it – *"I believe that victims of trolling are only those who tend to give emphasis on negativity more…they ignore 20 likes and focus unnecessarily on those 5 dislikes."*

6.7 Weird/Unusual Content

People can become victims of trolling when they share or post weird, unusual, or extraordinary content that draws attention. Trolls may specifically target such individuals, exploiting their unique content as a way to provoke and harass them, capitalizing on the curiosity or shock value to elicit negative reactions and disrupt online interactions. Excerpt of Respondent 12 emphasizing on it – *"According to me people who post explicit and extraordinary content nonconforming to our norms become victims of trolling."*

7. IMPACT OF TROLLING ON MENTAL HEALTH

7.1 Mental Disorders/Mental Health Issues

Trolling can have a significant impact on mental health, leading to various negative outcomes such as eating disorders, depression, anxiety, and even suicidal thoughts or actions. The relentless harassment, derogatory comments, and emotional distress caused by trolls can contribute to a deterioration of one's mental well-being, exacerbating existing vulnerabilities and potentially pushing individuals towards severe psychological struggles. Excerpt of Respondent 5 emphasizing on it – *"I think the main aftereffects of trolling on mental health are depression, anxiety and sometimes the harassment forces the person to even commit suicide"*.

7.2 Worthlessness

Trolling can have a profound impact on mental health, often resulting in feelings of uselessness and unworthiness. The constant barrage of derogatory comments and targeted harassment from trolls can undermine an individual's self-esteem, exacerbating feelings of inadequacy and worthlessness, which can contribute to negative mental health outcomes such as depression and low self-worth. Excerpt of Respondent 13 emphasizing on it – *"In my perspective people who are trolled being to feel unworthy and useless they start doubting themselves...."*

7.3 Negative Mood State

Trolling has a major impact on mental health, leading to negative mood states characterized by increased negativity, irritability, and aggression. The constant exposure to provocative and hurtful comments from trolls can infiltrate one's thoughts, triggering negative emotions and potentially contributing to heightened levels of irritability and aggression. Excerpt of Respondent 8 emphasizing on it – *"I think people when trolled very harshly become negative they start filling themselves with negative emotions .... they become angry and irritable too."*

7.4 Emotional Insecurity

Trolling impact mental health by exacerbating emotional insecurity, resulting in elevated insecurities, reduced confidence, heightened self-doubt, hesitancy, and indecisiveness. The relentless harassment and targeted attacks from trolls contribute to a negative self-perception, amplifying individuals' emotional vulnerabilities and undermining their overall mental well-being. Excerpt of Respondent 9 emphasizing on it – *"In my opinion, when individuals experience trolling, they often undergo emotional instability, experience a decline in confidence, and develop self-doubt."*

7.5 Identity Crisis

Trolling can profoundly affect mental health, leading to an identity crisis marked by changes in self-perception, confusion, and uncertainty. The persistent harassment and targeted attacks from trolls can cause individuals to question their sense of identity and struggle with recognizing themselves, resulting in a lack of clarity and self-understanding. Excerpt of Respondent 10 emphasizing on it – *"As per my knowledge trolling causes a person to forget their original identity, they become someone else they are confused and live with low self-esteem."*

7.6 Personality

Trolling can have a serious impact on mental health, leading to personality changes and a shift towards introversion. Individuals who experience trolling may undergo significant transformations in their personality, becoming more withdrawn, hesitant to engage with others, and preferring to remain in their shells as a protective measure against further harassment. Excerpt of Respondent 15 emphasizing on it – *"In my opinion, individuals who experience trolling often undergo significant changes, transforming their entire personality and adopting introverted tendencies, choosing to withdraw and shield themselves within a shell of protection."*

7.7 Seclusion/Solitude

Trolling can have a detrimental impact on mental health, leading individuals to seclude themselves and experience social isolation due to a lack of approval. The negative experiences and harassment from trolls can cause individuals to withdraw from social interactions, preferring solitude and avoiding social relationships to protect themselves from further harm. This seclusion can contribute to feelings of loneliness and further exacerbate the negative effects of trolling on mental well-being. Excerpt of Respondent 7 emphasizing on it – *"According to me after being trolled harshly people stop talking and mingling with people.... They isolate themselves from everyone"*.

7.8 Rumination

Trolling also impact mental health by rumination and overthinking. The persistent harassment and negative experiences from trolls can cause individuals to continuously dwell on the same situations, overthinking and excessively analysing unimportant matters, making it challenging to move on and impacting their overall well-being. Excerpt of Respondent 6 emphasizing on it – *"I think that people who are trolled start thinking too much on everything, they become overthinkers and it becomes extremely challenging for them to take decisions"*.

8. CAUSES OF TROLLING

8.1 Cognitive Incongruence

Trolls engage in trolling behaviour due to cognitive incongruence, which arises from the clash between their own opinions and views and those of others. Their inability to tolerate beliefs that differ from their own leads them to provoke and harass individuals who hold contrasting perspectives, as they struggle to accept or accommodate differing beliefs. This cognitive incongruence fuels their trolling behaviour as a means to assert their own views and impose their beliefs on others. Excerpt of Respondent 11 emphasizing on it – *"According to me trolls tend to troll when their beliefs don't match the views of another person. In this case of contrasting perspectives trolls troll."*

8.2 Emotional Immaturity

Trolls engage in trolling behaviour due to emotional immaturity, which manifests as jealousy, insecurity, and a desire to vent their anger or seek revenge. Their actions reflect a lack of emotional control, as they struggle to cope with these negative emotions arising from personal challenges. Trolling becomes a means for them to project their own unresolved issues onto others, deriving a distorted sense of power

Table 2. Themes and sub-themes for causes, victimization, and impact of trolling on mental health (age group: 36-55 years)

S.No	Themes	Sub-Themes	Findings
Causes of Trolling			
1.	Cognitive Incongruence	Incongruency in opinions and views, Clash among different perspectives	People cannot tolerate beliefs different than theirs'
2.	Emotional Immaturity	Jealousy, Insecurity, Venting out anger, Revenge	When people are not able to control their emotions like jealousy, insecurity, anger arising out of life challenges showcase lack of emotional control
3.	Past Experience	Trolled in past start trolling others	People troll because they were trolled in the past by others
4.	Free Time	Leisure activity, recreation time	When people have too much free time, they troll others as a part of their leisure activity
5.	Social Media Addiction	Dependence, overuse of social media, difficult to refrain	When people become addict of social media, they cannot refrain themselves from indulging in every aspect of it including trolling
6.	Paid Trollers in Politics	Interference in political decision-making, lack of belief in postingcontent, biases political opinion	People are backed by political parties to troll their opposition party in order to defame them
7.	Lack of Empathy and Sympathy	Lack of concern for others, Low affect, Inability to internalize others' emotions	People who are emotionally detached and immature tend to lack concern for others feelings
8.	Feeling of Superiority	Feeling of better than others, Control over environment, Exaggerated claims pertaining to one's abilities	When people think of themselves greater than others and exaggerate their capabilities, they tend to look down on other people
9.	Popularity	Attention seeking, Fame, Approval, Publicity	People having a strong desire of name, fame and attention
Why People Become Victim of Trolling			
1.	Popularity	Fame, Approval, Publicity	When people are popular and famous, they are prone and open to everyone' criticism
2.	Naïve Sense of Self	New to social media, Lack of awareness	People who are new and unaware about the functioning of social media
3.	Emotional Insecurity	Increased insecurities, Lack of confidence, Self-doubt, Hesitancy, Indecisiveness	People start undervaluing themselves, lose confidence and there come feeling of incompetence
4.	Attention to trolls	Attention-seeking, receive attention from others	When people feed trolls by responding to them in order to get attention and validation
5.	Cyber bullying	Irresponsibility in posting, Posting controversial things, Lack ofAccountability, Derogatory comments, Misuse of information	When people post content tactlessly, unintelligently and be negligent towards their postings
6.	Attitude of "trolling anyoneand everyone"	No reason for trolling but just troll	When there is no reason for people to get trolled but still the trolls troll them
Impact of Trolling on Mental Health			
1.	Mental Disorders/ Mental Health Issues	Constantly living in fear, depression, suicidal tendencies, stress	People become depressed, have suicidal tendencies and live in fear
2.	Emotional Insecurity	Increased Aggression, irritability, Sensitivity, Self-doubt, Loss of confidence	People become very sensitive, they lose their confidence and doubt themselves, they also become aggressive in day to day lives
3.	Personality	Major shift and changes in personality	People change themselves completely and lose their original self
4.	Seclusion/ Solitude	Social isolation, Absence of social relationships, Lack of approval	People tend to isolate themselves from society and prefer being left out
5.	Unhappiness	Makes a person unhappy	People become unsatisfied and unhappy with themselves which makes them depressed
6.	Rumination	Overthinking, Repeatedly dwell on same situations,Thinking too much about situation	People start overthinking on unimportant things and make it difficult to move on by dwelling on same situations
7.	Masking Emotions	Hiding one's emotions from others. Uneasiness to share feelings	People hide their original feelings and never reveal what they actually feel to others

or satisfaction from their harmful behaviour. Excerpt of Respondent 8 emphasizing on it – *"According to me, when a person is trolled they become emotionally unstable, loose their confidence and start doubting themselves."*

8.3 Past Experience

Trolls engage in trolling behaviour because they have been trolled in the past by others. Negative experiences of being targeted and harassed online can lead some individuals to adopt trolling as a means of retaliation or defence, perpetuating a cycle of online harassment and aggression. The past trauma of being trolled can influence their decision to troll others as a misguided coping mechanism or as an attempt to regain a sense of control in the online environment. Excerpt of Respondent 7 emphasizing on it – *"In my perspective sometimes people tend to troll because they have faced trolling in past and thus, they troll....".*

8.4 Free Time

Trolls engage in trolling behaviour because they have excessive free time and see it as a recreational activity. With an abundance of leisure time, some individuals turn to trolling as a way to entertain themselves, finding satisfaction in provoking and harassing others online. Trolling becomes a part of their leisure or recreational activities, allowing them to pass time and derive a sense of amusement from their harmful behaviour. Excerpt of Respondent 5 emphasizing on it – *"I think that some people are so free that they troll in their free time just for entertainment it's their recreational activity".*

8.5 Social Media Addiction

Trolls engage in trolling because of their social media addiction and the difficulty they face in refraining from overusing social media platforms. When individuals become dependent on social media, they struggle to control their impulses and engage in various aspects of online behaviour, including trolling others, as it becomes an integral part of their addictive behaviour patterns. Excerpt of Respondent 1 emphasizing on it – *"In my opinion people who are social media addicts are ones who troll because they just can't keep themselves away from social media and have an urge to take part in each activity there".*

8.6 Paid Trollers in Politics

Trolls engage in trolling as paid operatives in politics, seeking to interfere with political decision-making processes. They are hired by political parties to attack and harass the opposition, using derogatory and manipulative tactics to defend their own party's stance. These paid trolls operate with the intention of manipulating public opinion by spreading misinformation and sowing discord among opposing political groups. Excerpt of Respondent 15 emphasizing on it – *"As per my knowledge I don't think there's single troll but there are armies of trolls who have political backing and they troll get paid for trolling opposition..."*

8.7 Lack of Empathy and Sympathy

Trolls engage in trolling due to a lack of empathy and sympathy, as well as an inability to internalize and understand the emotions of others. People who are emotionally detached and lack maturity often exhibit low concern for the feelings and well-being of others, leading them to engage in trolling behaviour without considering the negative impact it may have on their victims' emotions. Excerpt of Respondent 2 emphasizing on it – *"I think that trolls are very insensitive people and they lack empathy or sympathy .... they just don't care about anyone".*

8.8 Feeling of Superiority

Trolls engage in trolling behaviour due to their feelings of superiority, which lead them to believe they are better than others. They seek control over their online environment and often make exaggerated claims about their abilities or knowledge, using these inflated self-perceptions to demean and look down upon others, perpetuating a cycle of online harassment and trolling. Excerpt of Respondent 19 emphasizing on it – *"In my opinion people who have superiority complex troll they think they are better than everyone......this inflated sense of self makes them troll."*

8.9 Popularity

Trolls engage in trolling because they have a strong desire for popularity, attention, and fame. By seeking notoriety through provocative and disruptive behaviour online, they aim to garner attention and gain approval from others, even if it means resorting to negative and harmful actions. Excerpt of Respondent 14 emphasizing on it – *"I feel that trolls troll because they want name, fame, and attention.... they want to be seen by hook or by crook".*

9. WHY PEOPLE BECOME VICTIMS OF TROLLING

9.1 Popularity

People become victims of trolling due to their popularity, fame, and the public scrutiny that comes with it. When individuals achieve a certain level of recognition or success, they become more visible and exposed to a wider audience, making them susceptible to criticism, judgment, and trolling from those who may seek to undermine or attack their achievements. The desire for approval and publicity that often accompanies fame can also attract attention, both positive and negative, making them more vulnerable to trolling behaviour. Excerpt of Respondent 3 emphasizing on it – *"I think that people who are famous, popular and who have a public account are more prone to become a victim of trolling because they have a large audience and have kept themselves open for criticism, trolling etc."*

9.2 Naïve Sense of Self

People become victims of trolling due to their lack of awareness and understanding about the functioning of social media platforms. When individuals are new to social media or lack knowledge about its potential risks and dynamics, they may unknowingly engage in behaviours or share content that attracts trolling. Their limited familiarity with online etiquette and the consequences of their actions makes them more susceptible to becoming targets of trolling behaviour. Excerpt of Respondent 10 emphasizing on it – *"In my perspective people who are very naïve, who don't know much about social media and trolling become victims of trolling."*

9.3 Emotional Insecurity

People become victims of trolling due to emotional insecurity, which leads to increased insecurities, lack of confidence, self-doubt, and hesitancy in decision-making. When individuals are targeted and harassed by trolls it undermines their self-esteem and reinforces feelings of incompetence and inadequacy. Excerpt of Respondent 3 emphasizing on it – *"As per my knowledge I think that people who are emotionally weak, insecure ... they doubt themselves much and have no confidence become victims of trolling."*

9.4 Attention to Trolls

People become victims of trolling because they inadvertently give attention to trolls, seeking validation and attention from others. When individuals engage with or respond to trolling behaviour, they inadvertently reinforce and encourage the trolls' actions, as trolls thrive on the attention and reaction they receive. This attention-seeking behaviour from victims inadvertently perpetuates the cycle of trolling, as trolls continue to target those who respond and provide them with the attention they seek. Excerpt of Respondent 7 emphasizing on it – *"In my opinion only people who feed trolls, give them attention and respond to them are victims of trolling"*.

9.5 Cyber Bullying

People become victims of trolling due to cyberbullying, which often stems from the irresponsibility in posting, posting controversial content without considering the consequences. Trolls take advantage of the lack of accountability, making derogatory comments and misusing personal information shared online. When individuals are negligent and careless in their posting behaviour, they become more vulnerable to trolling. Excerpt of Respondent 2 emphasizing on it – *"I think that irresponsibility while posting on social media is the prime reason why people become victim of trolling"*.

9.6 Attitude of "Trolling Anyone and Everyone"

People become victims of trolling because some trolls adopt an attitude of "trolling anyone and everyone" without any specific reason or justification. These trolls target individuals indiscriminately, seeking to provoke, harass, and demean them for their own amusement or satisfaction. The lack of a specific reason for targeting someone makes it difficult for victims to understand why they are being trolled, leaving them susceptible to the arbitrary and senseless actions of the trolls. Excerpt of Respondent 9 emphasizing on it – *"I don't think that there is something that people do which makes them victim of trolls.... trolls can troll anyone and everyone there is no particular reason."*

10. IMPACT OF TROLLING ON MENTAL HEALTH

10.1 Mental Disorders/Mental Health Issues

The impact of trolling on mental health can be severe, leading to mental disorders, such as depression and increased suicidal tendencies. Constant exposure to trolling can create a stressful environment, causing individuals to experience fear, anxiety, and a decline in overall mental well-being. Excerpt of Respondent 2 emphasizing on it – *"In my view, the primary consequences of trolling on mental well-being include depression, anxiety, and, in extreme cases, the relentless harassment may even push individuals to commit suicide".*

10.2 Emotional Insecurity

The impact of trolling on mental health can lead to emotional insecurity, heightened aggression, increased irritability, sensitivity, and self-doubt. Individuals who are subjected to trolling may develop a sense of emotional vulnerability, becoming more reactive and defensive. They may experience heightened irritability and sensitivity towards others, as well as self-doubt and a loss of confidence in themselves and their abilities. Excerpt of Respondent 12 emphasizing on it – *"According to me, when a person is trolled, they become emotionally unstable, loose their confidence and start doubting themselves."*

10.3 Personality

The impact of trolling on mental health can result in significant changes in a person's personality. Trolling can cause individuals to undergo a transformation where they lose touch with their original personality and sense of self, adopting defensive or guarded behaviours as a response to harsh trolling behaviours. Excerpt of Respondent 10 emphasizing on it – *"In my opinion people who are trolled extremely change completely, they change their complete personality and become introverts and live in a shell."*

10.4 Seclusion/Solitude

The impact of trolling on mental health can result in significant changes in a person's personality. Trolling can cause individuals to undergo a transformation where they lose touch with their original personality and sense of self, adopting defensive or guarded behaviours as a response to harsh trolling behaviours. *"In my opinion, when people experience severe trolling, they tend to withdraw from social interactions and avoid engaging with others, ultimately isolating themselves from everyone."*

10.5 Unhappiness

The impact of trolling on mental health can be profound, often resulting in unhappiness and dissatisfaction. Trolling can lead individuals to feel unsatisfied and unhappy with themselves, as they may internalize the negative comments and criticism directed towards them, affecting their self-esteem and overall well-being. Excerpt of Respondent 15 emphasizing on it – *"According to me when a person is trolled, they feel unhappy, sad and hurt.... they feel they are wrong and what they do is not enough."*

10.6 Rumination

Trolling can significantly affect mental well-being as it often leads individuals to engage in rumination and overthinking. This excessive focus on negative situations and the tendency to dwell on them can make it difficult for people to move forward and let go, trapping them in a cycle of repetitive thoughts that hinder their overall mental health. Excerpt of Respondent 6 emphasizing on it – *"In my perspective, individuals who face trolling tend to engage in excessive overthinking, transforming into individuals who find it immensely challenging to make decisions."*

10.7 Masking Emotions

Trolling can have a profound impact on mental health by causing individuals to mask their emotions and feel uneasy about sharing their true feelings with others. As a result, people may hide their genuine emotions and never fully reveal how they truly feel, leading to a sense of emotional isolation and potential long-term psychological distress. Excerpt of Respondent 18 emphasizing on it – *"I think that trolling causes a person to mask their emotions and hide their true feelings from everyone.... they become emotionally distant."*

11. DISCUSSION

Due to their vast audience and potential anonymity, online social networks are increasingly being used by trolls to post offensive or defamatory content (Bharti et al., 2018; Cambria et al. 2010). People in the age group of 18-35 years were of the view that the trolling is done for a number of causes, such as, entertainment, popularity, emotional immaturity, premature thinking, cognitive incongruence, sadism, anonymity and meddling. Similarly, people in the age group of 36-55 years thought that factors like, past experience, free time, social media addiction, paid trollers in politics, lack of empathy and sympathy, feeling of superiority is responsible for trolling.

Findings of the study further revealed that there are certain factors which led to the victimization of trolling. As per respondents of 18-35 years, these factors include lack of awareness, cyber bullying, need for approval, publicity, personal insecurities, negativity bias. Whereas, respondents of 36-55 years viewed emotional insecurity, attention to trolls, attitude of "troll anyone and everyone" are factors for becoming the victim of trolling.

The impact of trolling on mental health can be severe, leading to mental disorders, such as depression and increased suicidal tendencies. Constant exposure to trolling can create a stressful environment, causing individuals to experience fear, anxiety, and a decline in overall mental well-being. Both the groups were of the opinion that emotional insecurity, changes in personality, seclusion, rumination, masking of emotions, identity crisis, negative mood state contributes to the deterioration in mental health. It was also found that the impact of trolling does not vary with age.

12. FUTURE DIRECTIONS

Trolling plays a crucial role in common man's life. There is a need for further research in this area based on demographic information of trollers or being trolled among others. Furthermore, various disruptive online behaviour that try to interfere with how online social networks and media typically operate.

13. CONCLUSION AND LIMITATIONS OF THE STUDY

Digital trolling has grown to be a significant influence affecting people's lives. The impact of trolling on community has drawn a lot of interest in both the mainstream media and the public debate. The results of this study offered insight on the causes of trolling, causes of being victimized of trolling and will help to inform future research and policy decisions.

REFERENCES

Aydın, A., Arda, B., Güneş, B., & Erbaş, O. (2021). Psychopathology of Cyberbullying and Internet Trolling. *Journal of Experimental and Basic Medical Sciences*, *2*(3), 380–391.

Barlow, C., & Awan, I. (2016). "You need to be sorted out with a knife": The attempted online silencing of women and people of Muslim faith within academia. *Social Media + Society*, *2*(4), 2056305116678896. doi:10.1177/2056305116678896

Bharati, P., Lee, C., & Syed, R. (2018). Trolls and social movement participation: An empirical investigation. *Trolls and Social Movement Participation*, 1-5.

Bharati, P., Lee, C., & Syed, R. (2019, July). Influence of trolling on social media participation: An empirical investigation. In Academy of Management Proceedings (Vol. 2019, No. 1, p. 18645). Academy of Management.

Binns, A. (2012). Don't Feed the Trolls! Managing troublemakers in magazines' online communities. *Journalism Practice*, *6*(4), 547–562. doi:10.1080/17512786.2011.648988

Bishop, J. (2012c). Tackling internet abuse in Great Britain: Towards a framework for classifying severities of 'flame trolling'. In *Proceedings of the 11th International Conference on Security and Management*. SAM.

Bishop, J. (2014a). 'U r bias love:' Using 'bleasure' and 'motif' as forensic linguistic means to annotate twitter and news blog comments for the purpose of multimedia forensics. *Proceedings of the 11th International Conference on Web Based Communities and Social Media.*

Bishop, J. (2014b). 'YouTube if you want to, the lady's not for blogging': Using 'bleasures' and 'motifs' to support multimedia forensic analyses of harassment by social media. *Oxford Cyber Harassment Research Symposium.*

Cambria, E., Chandra, P., Sharma, A., & Hussain, A. (2010). *Do not feel the trolls.* ISWC.

Case, C. J., & King, D. L. (2017). Internet Trolling in Social Networking Sites: A Preliminary Investigation of Undergraduate Student Victimization. *ASBBS Proceedings, 24*(1), 143.

Cheng, J., Danescu-Niculescu-Mizil, C., Leskovec, J., & Bernstein, M. (2017). Anyone can become a troll. *American Scientist, 105*(3), 152. doi:10.1511/2017.126.152 PMID:29399664

Coles, B. A., & West, M. (2016b). Weaving the internet together: Imagined communities in newspaper comment threads. *Computers in Human Behavior, 60*, 44–53. doi:10.1016/j.chb.2016.02.049

Craker, N., & March, E. (2016). The dark side of Facebook®: The Dark Tetrad, negative social potency, and trolling behaviours. *Personality and Individual Differences, 102*, 79–84. doi:10.1016/j.paid.2016.06.043

Cruz, A. G. B., Seo, Y., & Rex, M. (2018). Trolling in online communities: A practice-based theoretical perspective. *The Information Society, 34*(1), 15–26. doi:10.1080/01972243.2017.1391909

Donath, J. S. (2002). Identity and deception in the virtual community. In *Communities in cyberspace* (pp. 37–68). Routledge.

Fichman, P., & Sanfilippo, M. R. (2016). *Online trolling and its perpetrators: Under the cyberbridge*. Rowman & Littlefield.

Golf-Papez, M., & Veer, E. (2017). Don't feed the trolling: Rethinking how online trolling is being defined and combated. *Journal of Marketing Management, 33*(15-16), 1336–1354. doi:10.1080/0267257X.2017.1383298

Hardaker, C. (2010). Trolling in asynchronous computer-mediated communication: From user discussions to academic definitions. *Journal of Politeness Research, 6*(2), 215–242. doi:10.1515/jplr.2010.011

Hardaker, C. (2013). "Uh.... not to be nitpicky, but… the past tense of drag is dragged, not drug": An overview of trolling strategies. *Journal of Language Aggression and Conflict, 1*(1), 58-86.

Hardaker, C. (2015). 'I refuse to respond to this obvious troll': An overview of responses to (perceived) trolling. *Corpora, 10*(2), 201–229. doi:10.3366/cor.2015.0074

Henry, N., & Powell, A. (2015). Embodied harms: Gender, shame, and technology-facilitated sexual violence. *Violence Against Women, 21*(6), 758–779. doi:10.1177/1077801215576581 PMID:25827609

Jussinoja, T. (2018). Life-cycle of Internet trolls [Unpublished doctoral work]. University of Jyväskylä.

Maltby, J., Day, L., Hatcher, R. M., Tazzyman, S., Flowe, H. D., Palmer, E. J., Frosch, C. A., O'Reilly, M., Jones, C., Buckley, C., Knieps, M., & Cutts, K. (2016). Implicit theories of online trolling: Evidence that attention-seeking conceptions are associated with increased psychological resilience. *British Journal of Psychology, 107*(3), 448–466. doi:10.1111/bjop.12154 PMID:26403842

Maltby, J., Day, L., Hatcher, R. M., Tazzyman, S., Flowe, H. D., Palmer, E. J., Frosch, C. A., O'Reilly, M., Jones, C., Buckley, C., Knieps, M., & Cutts, K. (2016). Implicit theories of online trolling: Evidence that attention-seeking conceptions are associated with increased psychological resilience. *British Journal of Psychology, 107*(3), 448–466. doi:10.1111/bjop.12154 PMID:26403842

Maltby, W. (2017). *The reign of Charles V*. Bloomsbury Publishing.

Mantilla, K. (2013). Gendertrolling: Misogyny adapts to new media. *Feminist Studies*, *39*(2), 563–570. doi:10.1353/fem.2013.0039

March, E., & Marrington, J. (2019). A qualitative analysis of internet trolling. *Cyberpsychology, Behavior, and Social Networking*, *22*(3), 192–197. doi:10.1089/cyber.2018.0210 PMID:30720370

March, E., & Steele, G. (2020). High esteem and hurting others online: Trait sadism moderates the relationship between self-esteem and internet trolling. *Cyberpsychology, Behavior, and Social Networking*, *23*(7), 441–446. doi:10.1089/cyber.2019.0652 PMID:32364769

Molenda, Z. A., Marchlewska, M., Rogoza, M., Michalski, P., Górska, P., Szczepańska, D., & Cislak, A. (2022). What makes an Internet troll? On the relationships between temperament (BIS/BAS), Dark Triad, and Internet trolling. *Cyberpsychology (Brno)*, *16*(5). Advance online publication. doi:10.5817/CP2022-5-11

Moor, L., & Anderson, J. R. (2019). A systematic literature review of the relationship between dark personality traits and antisocial online behaviours. *Personality and Individual Differences*, *144*, 40–55. doi:10.1016/j.paid.2019.02.027

Moreau, E. (2017, June 2). *10 Popular Social Media Posting Trends*. Retrieved from Life wire: https://www.lifewire.com/popular-social-media-posting-trends-3486028

Myers, C. A., & Cowie, H. (2017). Bullying at university: The social and legal contexts of cyberbullying among university students. *Journal of Cross-Cultural Psychology*, *48*(8), 1172–1182. doi:10.1177/0022022116684208

Ofcom. (2017). *Rise of the Social Seniors revealed*. Ofcom. Available at: *https://www.ofcom.org.uk/about-ofcom/latest/media/media-releases/2017/rise-social-seniors*

Ortiz, S. M. (2020). Trolling as a collective form of harassment: An inductive study of how online users understand trolling. *Social Media + Society*, *6*(2). doi:10.1177/2056305120928512

Papapicco, C., & Quatera, I. (2019). "Do not Make to eat to Troll!": The Dark Side of Web. *Online Journal of Communication and Media Technologies*, *9*(2), e201910. doi:10.29333/ojcmt/5764

Paulhus, D. L. (2014). Toward a taxonomy of dark personalities. *Current Directions in Psychological Science*, *23*(6), 421–426. doi:10.1177/0963721414547737

Pearson, J. (2016). *Scientists invented a tool to expose 4chan's racist trolling campaigns*. Motherboard. Available at: https://motherboard.vice.com/en_us/article/block-4chan-to-stopthe-alt-right-from-spreading-racist-memes-scientists-say

Phillips, W. (2011). Meet the trolls. *Index on Censorship*, *40*(2), 68–76. doi:10.1177/0306422011409641

Phillips, W. (2013). The house that fox built: Anonymous, spectacle, and cycles of amplification. *Television & New Media*, *14*(6), 494–509. doi:10.1177/1527476412452799

Phillips, W. (2015). *This is why we can't have nice things: Mapping the relationship between online trolling and mainstream culture*. MIT Press. doi:10.7551/mitpress/10288.001.0001

Sanfilippo, M., Yang, S., & Fichman, P. (2017). Managing online trolling: From deviant to social and political trolls. *Proceedings of the 50th Hawaii International Conference on System Sciences*. 10.24251/HICSS.2017.219

Sanfilippo, M. R., Fichman, P., & Yang, S. (2018). Multidimensionality of online trolling behaviors. *The Information Society*, *34*(1), 27–39. doi:10.1080/01972243.2017.1391911

Sanfilippo, M. R., Yang, S., & Fichman, P. (2017a). Trolling here, there, and everywhere: Perceptions of trolling behaviors in context. *Journal of the Association for Information Science and Technology*, *68*(10), 2313–2337. doi:10.1002/asi.23902

Seigfried-Spellar, K. C., & Chowdhury, S. S. (2017). Death and Lulz: Understanding the personality characteristics of RIP trolls. *First Monday*. Advance online publication. doi:10.5210/fm.v22i11.7861

Sest, N., & March, E. (2017). Constructing the cyber-troll: Psychopathy, sadism, and empathy. *Personality and Individual Differences*, *119*, 69–72. doi:10.1016/j.paid.2017.06.038

Shachaf, P., & Hara, N. (2010). Beyond vandalism: Wikipedia trolls. *Journal of Information Science*, *36*(3), 357–370. doi:10.1177/0165551510365390

Starmer, K. (2013). *Guidelines on prosecuting cases involving communications sent via social media*. Crown Prosecution Service.

Sun, H., & Fichman, P. (2018). Chinese collective trolling. *Proceedings of the Association for Information Science and Technology*, *55*(1), 478–485. doi:10.1002/pra2.2018.14505501052

Synnott, J., Coulias, A., & Ioannou, M. (2017). Online trolling: The case of Madeleine McCann. *Computers in Human Behavior*, *71*, 70–78. doi:10.1016/j.chb.2017.01.053

Tuna, T., Akbas, E., Aksoy, A., Canbaz, M. A., Karabiyik, U., Gonen, B., & Aygun, R. (2016). User characterization for online social networks. *Social Network Analysis and Mining*, *6*(1), 1–28. doi:10.100713278-016-0412-3

Xavier, S. (2022). Impact of Trolling and Its Effects on the Popularity of social media. *International Journal of Scientific Development and Research*, 760-768.

Zezulka, L. A., & Seigfried-Spellar, K. (2016). Differentiating cyberbullies and internet trolls by personality characteristics and self-esteem. *Journal of Digital Forensics, Security and Law*, *11*(3), 7–26.

Chapter 5
Unveiling the Portrayal of Intimate Partner Violence Against Women in the Media:
Insights From an Honor Culture

Gülçin Akbaş
Atilim University, Turkey

Suzan Ceylan-Batur
TOBB University of Economics and Technology, Turkey

ABSTRACT

Intimate partner violence (IPV) against women is a pervasive global issue. The media plays a significant role in shaping society's perceptions and understanding of IPV. This study focuses on the representation of femicide in Turkish newspapers, with a specific focus on the context of Turkey as an honor culture characterized by a distinct emphasis on female sexual purity and male dominance. Honor cultures often justify violence against women in the name of preserving honor. This research aims to investigate how newspapers depict honor-based IPV through quantitative analysis, content analysis, discourse analysis, and frame analysis of femicide cases. The findings reveal that newspapers frame IPV within an honor culture by victim-blaming and justifying men's violent behavior. Additionally, news coverage often portrays honor-based IPV as isolated incidents, failing to recognize its reflection of the broader honor culture. These portrayals inadvertently perpetuate and legitimize IPV, discouraging women from seeking assistance and support.

INTRODUCTION

The analysis of violence against women in the media holds significant importance due to its broader societal implications beyond individual relationships. Through mass media, individuals are exposed to acts of violence and influenced by their portrayal (Bullock & Cubert, 2002). The media's reporting style

DOI: 10.4018/978-1-6684-8893-5.ch005

and presentation of violence play a crucial role in shaping people's perceptions of such acts. While the media is not the primary cause of violent behavior, it has the potential to impact people's attitudes and responses to violence against women, potentially exacerbating its effects and providing justifications for such behavior (Fairbairn & Dawson, 2013). Therefore, alongside addressing the underlying causes of violence, it is crucial to examine its portrayal in the media to effectively combat this issue. Hence, this paper aims to investigate how violence against women is depicted in the media, with a specific focus on intimate partner violence (IPV) in Turkey. Turkey is characterized as an honor culture with a strong emphasis on patriarchy (Sakallı-Uğurlu & Akbaş, 2013) and has experienced a rise in the number of incidents of violence against women (the Digital Monument Counter, anitsayac.com). Given this context, this study will explore media representations of violence against women from an honor-based perspective.

Intimate Partner Violence

Intimate Partner Violence (IPV) is formally defined by the World Health Organization (WHO, 2012; 2021) as behavior occurring within an intimate relationship that inflicts physical, sexual, or psychological harm, encompassing acts of physical aggression, sexual coercion, psychological abuse, and controlling behaviors. This definition applies to violence perpetrated by both current and former spouses and partners (apps.who.int).

According to the WHO, IPV against women is a pervasive global issue affecting individuals worldwide (2012, 2018). Their estimates indicate that 27% of women, aged 15 to 49 (referred to as the reproductive age group), who have ever been in a partnership, have experienced physical and/or sexual IPV at least once in their lives (2018). However, IPV against women is not confined solely to this particular age group; rather, it is prevalent across all age groups (Roberto et al., 2013). Turkey, specifically, exhibits alarmingly high rates of IPV against women. WHO records (2018) show that 32% of women in Turkey, aged 15 to 49, reported experiencing lifetime IPV (see also Boyacıoğlu, 2016; Hacettepe Üniversitesi Nüfus Etütleri Enstitüsü, 2015). Furthermore, these records indicate that Turkey has the highest rates of IPV in Europe.

This paper will specifically focus on physical violence instances committed by an intimate partner that results in death in Turkey. Research on Domestic Violence Against Women (VAW) conducted in Turkey reveals that 36% of women have been subjected to physical violence at least once in their lifetime (Hacettepe Üniversitesi Nüfus Etütleri Enstitüsü, 2015). Between the years 2010 and 2022, a total of 4,205 women in Turkey lost their lives due to various reasons, including jealousy, divorce requests, suspicion of infidelity, and disputes (the Digital Monument Counter, see anitsayac.com).

Numerous studies conducted globally and specifically in Turkey have aimed to identify the underlying causes of violence against women (e.g., Flood & Pease, 2009; Sakallı, 2001). Various factors have been associated with domestic violence. According to the World Health Organization (WHO, 2012), individual factors (such as substance abuse and acceptance of violence), relationship factors (including relationship conflict and male dominance), and community and societal factors (such as weak legal sanctions against IPV and gender-inequitable social norms) are considered causes and risk factors for IPV on a global scale (p. 4). Similarly, Boyacıoğlu (2016) summarized the factors associated with violence against women in Turkey, including demographic variables, personality traits, alcohol and substance use, childhood abuse, victim-blaming, attitudes toward divorce, lack of social support, low status of women in society, migration, media influences, sexism, and the presence of an honor culture. In this paper, we will specifically focus on honor driven IPV.

Honor values hold significant endorsement in Turkey (Sakallı-Uğurlu & Akbaş, 2013). The emphasis on honor may normalize and condone abusive behavior by men for honor-related reasons, while submissive women may accept this violence (Vandello & Cohen, 2003). Therefore, comprehending and preventing IPV necessitates a thorough understanding of honor dynamics. Additionally, the portrayal of violence by the media can contribute to justifying violence, absolving the perpetrator of responsibility, and blaming the victim. Hence, it is crucial to gain insights into how the news media presents honor-based intimate partner violence.

Media Representations of Domestic Violence

Individuals rely on various media platforms, including visual, audio, written, and social media, as essential tools for accessing news and information (Jewkes, 2015). As the primary source of information for many people, the media plays a pivotal role in shaping public knowledge and understanding of social issues. It has the power to shape people's worldview, and previous research (Bullock, 2007; Bullock & Cubert, 2002; Carlyle et al., 2008; Fairbairn & Dawson, 2013; Taylor, 2009) has demonstrated that media platforms can provide extensive information about violence against women and influence people's opinions and knowledge on the subject. Consequently, individuals' interpretations of violence incidents as social problems can be heavily influenced by the media's portrayal of such violence.

However, media tools often frame news in various ways to capture the attention of readers and audiences, rather than providing an accurate reflection of real-life information (Bullock & Cubert, 2002; Lee & Wong, 2020). The framing of news in the media significantly shapes society's perception of the problem and the potential solutions (Bullock & Cubert, 2002). Media framing possesses the capacity to exert influence over the ways in which individuals perceive and interpret presented issues (Easteal et al., 2015). However, the manner in which the media presents news can be misleading, leading to inaccurate evaluations and perceptions about violence against women (Lee & Wong, 2020). Moreover, how the media portrays violence against women can contribute to the perpetuation of existing gender inequalities between men and women (Easteal et al., 2015). These distorted views can have a profound impact on society's perception of risk, reactions to violence, as well as the development of public policies and legal regulations concerning violence against women.

Given the widespread prevalence and far-reaching consequences of violence against women, including domestic violence and honor-based violence, along with the significant influence of the media in shaping people's perceptions of reality, it is imperative to examine the representation of violence in the media. Previous research highlights that serious incidents of domestic violence are often inaccurately portrayed in newspapers (Bullock & Cubert, 2002; Lee & Wong, 2020). Scholars (Meyers, 1994; Taylor, 2009) argue that news coverage of domestic violence tends to reinforce the existing patriarchal system, perpetuating notions of male superiority and female subordination. Such portrayals may contribute to the normalization of violence within intimate relationships (Carlyle et al., 2008). Furthermore, Bullock and Cubert (2002) discovered that newspapers frequently report domestic homicides as "isolated instances" of murder rather than recognizing them as domestic violence (p. 475). Similarly, Lee and Wong (2020) conducted a content analysis of news articles on domestic homicides in selected Canadian newspapers from 2004 to 2015. They found that the failure to label domestic violence as such in newspapers leads the public to believe that it is a rare occurrence confined to specific groups, rather than recognizing it as a societal problem rooted in traditional gender roles. In a similar vein, Carlyle et al. (2008) examined 395 articles reporting intimate partner violence in daily newspapers and observed that these articles predominantly focused on the victim, attributing responsibility for their victimization while overlooking contextual factors. Identifying intimate partner violence as a public issue at the societal level, necessitating collective efforts, rather than treating it as isolated incidents, would encourage victims to seek assistance and facilitate the implementation of legal regulations and preventive policies by the criminal justice system and the government (Hammond et al., 2006). Shifting the focus from individual incidents of male violence against women to a singular act of homicide diverts society's attention away from the broader issue of domestic violence and perpetuates victim-blaming rather than acknowledging the need for comprehensive societal action against domestic violence (Bullock & Cubert, 2002; Lee & Wong, 2020; Meyers, 1994).

Moreover, the presence of patterns that excuse the perpetrators and employ a victim-blaming approach in shaping news reports further exacerbates the situation. Extensive research on domestic violence consistently demonstrates the prevalence of victim blaming and the tendency to excuse the perpetrators in media coverage. Bullock and Cubert (2002) conducted groundbreaking research in which they qualitatively analyzed news articles covering domestic violence incidents in 1998. Their analysis revealed that 47.8% of the articles mentioned "at least one motivation or excuse for the perpetrator" (p. 484), thereby reducing the responsibility of men for their violent actions. These motivations or excuses included factors such as "mental and physical health problems, substance abuse, and a history of growing up in an abusive home environment" (p. 485). Additionally, they reported that 17% of the articles blamed the victim for the violent act, citing "unacceptable behaviors (such as drug use and infidelity)" (p. 485) and suggesting that the victim somehow played an active role in bringing about the violence in her own life (p. 486). The inclusion of the "why he did it" aspect in news coverage exonerates the perpetrator, justifies violence, and attributes the responsibility for the violence to the abused women (Bullock & Cubert, 2002). Meyers (1994) argues that this victim-blaming portrayal by the media diverts attention from the true source of the problem, which is abusive men and the underlying structural causes of their behavior, and instead focuses on female victims. According to Meyers (1994), this creates a significant barrier to achieving social change and preventing violence against women.

The extensive body of research confirms that media content and messaging have a powerful influence on shaping individuals' perspectives and responses to violent incidents, the perpetrators, and the victims. A notable example is the exposure to rape myths in newspaper articles, which experimental studies have shown to lead individuals to adopt more defensive attitudes toward the rapist and offer less support for the victim (Franiuk et al., 2008a). This effect is particularly pronounced among men, as exposure to rape myth-endorsing headlines makes them less likely to hold the attacker accountable and more likely to believe that the victim somehow provoked the assault (Franiuk et al., 2008b). These findings highlight the significant role of media language in shaping attitudes toward violence against women, often excusing the perpetrators and blaming the victims. Considering that people rely heavily on the media as a major source of information, newspapers, in particular, can be seen as a significant medium that reinforces victim-blaming narratives (Franiuk et al., 2008b).

In Turkey, several studies have been conducted that align with these findings. İnam and Şahin (2020) conducted a review of eleven research articles focusing on media discourses related to violence against women in Turkey. Their analysis revealed that instances of violence against women were often portrayed as isolated incidents rather than being acknowledged as a broader societal issue in written media news. Moreover, the news coverage frequently justified violence by adopting a patriarchal perspective that perpetuated sexism and intruded upon the victims' privacy. For instance, Serdar Tekeli (2016) highlighted that certain cases of violence against women were presented in a manner that legitimized the perpetrator's actions, often by linking the incidents to allegations of infidelity.

As demonstrated by the extensive literature reviewed earlier, media representations of violence against women play a significant role in perpetuating and promoting patriarchal gender norms related to femininity and masculinity. Unfortunately, these representations often fail to challenge widespread misconceptions about violence and address the issue of male violence against women. Given the influence of honor in contributing to gender-based inequalities, it is crucial to examine media portrayals of honor-based femicide. Such an examination helps shed light on socially accepted norms surrounding honor-based violence. The subsequent section will delve into honor cultures and their manifestations in Turkey, drawing upon studies that explore honor-based violence against women.

Honor Cultures and Turkey

Turkey is widely recognized as an honor culture, as indicated by research (see Glick et al., 2016; Sakallı-Uğurlu & Akbaş, 2013). Honor can be defined as the value attributed to an individual, both in their own eyes and in the eyes of others (Pitt-Rivers, 1977). In honor cultures, maintaining a positive reputation within society holds significant importance. Individuals belonging to honor cultures are highly conscious of how they are perceived by others, and their honor is largely determined by the respect and social approval they receive from others (Peristiany, 1965). Gender roles play a crucial role in shaping the social norms within these cultures, as honor cultures establish a consensus on how both men and women should behave in an honorable manner (Baker et al., 1999).

Research conducted by Rodriguez Mosquera and colleagues (2002a, 2002b) indicates that honor codes, which encompass values and norms related to honorable and dishonorable actions, emphasize the significance of family honor, moral integrity, masculine honor, and feminine honor. Family honor is associated with the values and norms pertaining to the reputation of one's family, which is determined by the collective reputation of each family member within society. Individuals are expected to be concerned about public evaluations of their family, the impact of their own behavior on family honor, and the defense of their family's reputation. The honor code related to moral integrity entails fostering strong social relationships and maintaining harmony through qualities such as hospitality, humility, and generosity. Moral integrity also involves living in accordance with societal expectations.

In honor cultures, gender-specific honor codes dictate distinct expectations and responsibilities for men and women in order to gain societal respect. The feminine honor code places considerable emphasis on female sexual purity and modesty. Women are expected to preserve their sexual purity throughout their lives (Sever & Yurdakul, 2001; Vandello & Cohen, 2003, 2008). Adhering to feminine honor entails experiencing sexual shame, which necessitates women to restrict their sexuality by maintaining virginity before marriage and refraining from adultery. Women's sexual shame not only affects their individual honor but also impacts the reputation of their families; if they fail to safeguard their honor, it tarnishes the honor of their entire family. Moreover, women are expected to conform to male authority within the family (Baker et al., 1999). On the other hand, men are regarded as protectors of the family's reputation. They bear the responsibility of ensuring that all family members, particularly females, uphold sexual shame. The masculine code of honor emphasizes qualities such as toughness, hypersensitivity to threats against honor, the ability to retaliate against offenses, sexual activity, and procreation (Sever & Yurdakul, 2001; Vandello & Cohen, 2003).

Honor codes, primarily rooted in traditional gender roles, exert pressure on both men and women in honor cultures to conform to these codes and behave accordingly. Members of these cultures are driven to protect their honor throughout their lives (Leung & Cohen, 2011; Rodriguez-Mosquera et al., 2008), as violating these codes can undermine individuals' self-worth (Bosson et al., 2009), their personal reputation (Vandello & Cohen, 2003), and their family's reputation (Nisbett & Cohen, 1996). Social norms in Turkey reflect these honor codes, placing strong emphasis on female modesty and male strength (see Sakallı-Uğurlu & Akbaş, 2013). Women are expected to maintain sexual purity and refrain from engaging in any sexual activity with men, while men are expected to exert control over their family members and safeguard their honor, even through the use of violence.

The attributed significance of honor makes it fragile, compelling men in honor cultures to protect their reputation at any cost. Honor can be besmirched by various actions, including infidelity, rape, extramarital affairs, and a desire for divorce, and honor culture norms justify and perpetuate violence against women. Men may employ violence against women within their families or against other men in order to assert their honor (Vandello & Cohen, 2008). In this context, honor-related threats can trigger violence, which may be tolerated by members of society (Ceylan-Batur et al., 2021).

Similarly, honor-based violence against women remains prevalent in honor cultures (Amnesty International, 2004). Traditions deeply rooted in honor can serve as justifications for violence against women and contribute to its acceptance (Amnesty International, 2004). Violence against women is legitimized, perpetuated, and reinforced within these cultures through legal practices and traditional norms (Vandello & Cohen, 2003, 2008). Furthermore, honor codes demand that men possess the courage to restore their honor by any means necessary (Vandello & Cohen, 2008). All male members of the family bear the responsibility of reclaiming honor. Women may be subjected to violence in order to prevent them from engaging in behaviors considered dishonorable, and if they are deemed to have dishonored, they can face various forms of violent punishment, including physical harm and femicide, as a means of restoring honor (Sev'er & Yurdakul, 2001). In honor cultures, violence against women in response to acts that taint honor is regarded as a prerogative of men (Vandello & Cohen, 2003).

Research indicates that individuals from honor cultures, when compared to those from non-honor cultures, perceive men whose wives have been unfaithful as less trustworthy and less masculine (Vandello & Cohen, 2003). Conversely, individuals from non-honor cultures tend to view women's infidelity as a reflection on women themselves, rather than something connected to men. Vandello and Cohen (2003) also demonstrated that both men and women from honor cultures perceive husbands who engage in domestic violence for honor-related reasons as more masculine.

Furthermore, additional studies have shown that individuals from honor cultures exhibit tolerance toward intimate partner violence against women when it is justified by honor-related motives (Ceylan-Batur et al., 2021; Vandello et al., 2009). A recent study conducted in Turkey by Ceylan-Batur and her colleagues (2021) revealed that participants displayed greater acceptance of intimate partner violence when it was motivated by concerns related to honor, such as infidelity, as opposed to violence stemming from non-honor-related reasons like overspending on a credit card. Similarly, a study involving women of low socioeconomic status in Turkey (Efe & Ayaz, 2010) found that half of the women considered intimate partner violence acceptable in cases of adultery. These findings suggest that honor-based violence is perceived as permissible and justified by both men and women living in Turkey.

There is currently a lack of published studies specifically investigating the representation of honor-based violence in the media. However, based on existing research on media portrayals of violence against women in Turkey and worldwide, it is likely that the media adopts a traditional patriarchal perspective when depicting honor-related violence. In line with prevailing notions of honor, media representations of honor-based violence may tend to blame the victim and offer justifications for the perpetrator.

If media representations of honor-based violence follow a victim-blaming and patriarchal approach, these portrayals can contribute to the perpetuation of honor and hinder efforts to prevent violence against women. They can significantly influence how violence is perceived, justified, and internalized. Therefore, it is crucial to investigate honor violence and identify how the media represents it in order to reduce or prevent its prevalence. It is worth noting that in Turkey, research suggests that people are more likely to tolerate violence against women when it is based on honor-related reasons compared to financial reasons (Ceylan-Batur et al., 2021). Although laws allowing reduced penalties for honor-based violence have been abolished in Turkey, any form of media support for honor-based violence may still increase support for such violence.

Overview

Considering the widespread occurrence of honor-based violence against women and the influential role of the media in shaping societal attitudes, examining the media's representation of violence against women with a specific focus on honor-based violence seems essential. With the intention of achieving this objective, our aim was to ascertain the portrayal of honor-based intimate partner violence (IPV) against women by examining the news coverage in newspapers pertaining to IPV.

This study can help identify how patriarchy and honor codes contribute to the justification of violence. It can serve as a valuable step towards reducing victim blaming and finding excuses for men's violence against women in Turkey and other honor cultures that share similar characteristics. Understanding these representations will raise public awareness and may guide the development of solutions to address honor-based violence.

Analytical Approach

The present study employed three analytical frameworks: content analysis, discourse analysis, and frame analysis to investigate newspapers. Content analysis encompasses a diverse set of techniques employed to effectively organize and comprehend text collections, enabling quantitative analysis and comparison of textual data (Stemler, 2001). On the other hand, discourse analysis employs qualitative methodologies to explore various aspects of text, examining not only their presence or absence, but also the underlying meanings that shape their inclusion or exclusion (Mogashoa, 2014). Lastly, frame analysis involves a comprehensive examination of the entire story structure, including the selection of words, phrases, and imagery, to reveal the intended meaning (Pan & Kosicki, 1993). By employing these three complementary frameworks, the study aimed to provide a comprehensive analysis of the social context surrounding honor-based femicide as portrayed in newspaper articles.

The following research questions guide the current study:

1. How is blame and responsibility attributed in cases of honor-based intimate partner femicide?
2. How is the social context portrayed in newspaper articles reporting honor-based femicide?

METHOD

Sample

A purposive sampling procedure was employed to develop the sample for this study. The data for this study were collected from an online digital platform called "anitsayac.com," which serves as an archive for cases involving women who have been victims of femicide in Turkey. A total of 1559 murder cases, spanning from 2008 to 2023, were included in the analysis. The age of the women who were killed ranged from 15 to 81 years, with a mean age of 34.52 years.

Materials

The primary material used in this study was the database of murder cases available on the anitsayac.com website, focusing specifically on cases within Turkey. This database provided detailed information about each case, including the date of the murder, the age of the victim, the location where the event occurred (within Turkey), the relationship of the murderer to the victim (e.g., spouse, father, acquaintance), the age of the murderer, the reason for the murder, the legal outcome or punishment imposed on the murderer, and a link to the news report describing the case. By accessing the provided news report links, researchers were able to gather additional information regarding the method used by the killer to commit the murder (e.g., firearm, physical assault, poisoning).

Procedure

To examine the representation of violence against women in media, the researchers accessed the anitsayac.com website and retrieved information on the murder cases. The database was searched for cases that occurred between 2008 and 2023. The researchers collected data on the total number of murders (1559).

Ethical Considerations

As the data for this study were collected from a publicly available online database, no direct contact or interaction with participants was involved. However, ethical considerations were taken into account by ensuring the confidentiality and anonymity of the victims. The researchers treated the data with utmost sensitivity and used aggregate statistics to present the findings, thereby avoiding any potential harm or identification of individuals.

RESULTS

Quantitative Analysis

Table 1 presents the detailed data on the location of the murder, the relationship of the murderer to the victim, the method used by the murderer, and the outcome of the murderer. The table shows the distribution of these variables among the murder cases. The analysis revealed that the majority of murders occurred in İstanbul (17.1%), followed by İzmir (6.5%) and Ankara (5.6%). These three cities accounted for the

Table 1. Profile of cases

Variables	Frequency	Percentage
Location of murder		
İstanbul	267	17.1
İzmir	101	6.5
Ankara	88	5.6
Adana	72	4.6
Antalya	72	4.6
Bursa	63	4.0
Gaziantep	50	3.2
Other cities in Turkey	845	54.4
The relationship of the murderer to the victim		
Husband	1004	64.4
Boyfriend	279	17.9
Ex-husband	165	10.6
Ex-boyfriend	80	5.1
Fiancé	14	0.9
Ex-fiancé	11	0.7
Others (e.g., family of the husband)	5	0.4
The method used by the murderer		
Firearm	814	52.2
Sharp object (e.g., knife)	472	30.3
Choking	107	6.9
Battery	47	3.0
Others (e.g., poisoning)	118	7.6
Outcome of the murderer		
Arrested	884	56.7
Died by suicide	292	18.7
Could not be determined	122	7.8
Fugitive	119	7.6
Defendant	97	6.2
Not taken into custody / Released	16	1.0
Others (e.g., being killed)	9	0.6

highest proportions of murder cases in the dataset. Regarding the relationship between the murderer and the victim, the findings indicated that the most prevalent categories were husbands (64.4%), boyfriends (17.9%), and ex-husbands (10.6%). These intimate relationships represented the primary associations between the perpetrators and the victims in the examined murder cases. Regarding the methods employed by the murderers, the analysis revealed that the most commonly utilized means were firearms (52.2%), sharp objects (30.3%), and choking (6.9%). These methods represented the predominant approaches employed by the perpetrators to carry out the murders. With regard to the outcomes of the murder cases, the majority of perpetrators were arrested (56.7%) and taken into custody by law enforcement. A notable proportion of perpetrators died by suicide (18.7%), while a smaller percentage remained fugitives (7.6%) and were still sought by the authorities at the time of data collection.

Qualitative Analysis

Reported Rationales for Intimate Partner Femicide

Figure 1 presents the reported reasons for intimate partner femicide based on an analysis of newspaper articles in the scope of the current study. The findings highlight distinct categories of motivations and circumstances surrounding the incidents.

Honor-Based Femicide: To establish this category, newspaper articles were systematically coded utilizing a coding scheme rooted in the existing research on honor cultures. Among the reported cases, the most frequently cited reason for intimate partner femicide was honor-based femicide. Within this category, the leading reported reasons included man's jealousy (182 cases) and man's inability to accept abandonment (120 cases). Additionally, woman's infidelity (60 cases) and woman's rejection of man's reconciliation request (48 cases) were also significant factors. Other reasons within this category, such as woman's assertion of autonomy, insulting remarks, post-breakup romantic engagement, and other unspecified factors, were also reported.

Figure 1. Reported rationales for intimate partner femicide

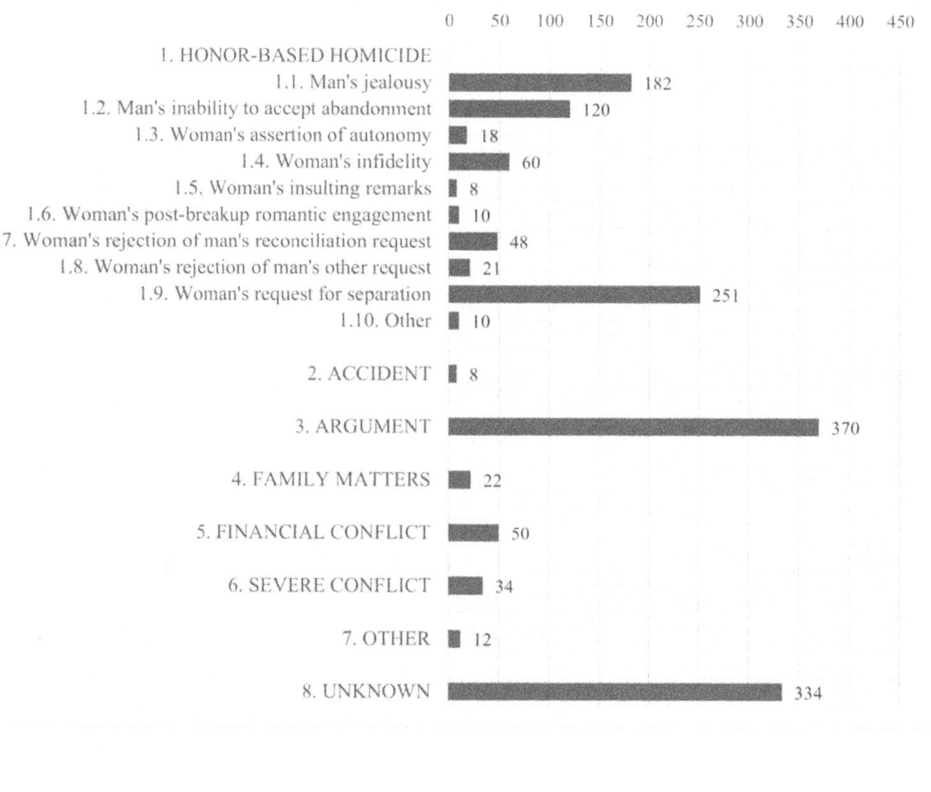

Other Categories: Apart from honor-based femicide, the analysis revealed other reasons reported for intimate partner femicide. Argument-related incidents accounted for a substantial proportion, with 370 cases documented in the newspaper articles. Family matters (22 cases), financial conflict (50 cases), and severe conflict (34 cases) were also identified as contributing factors. Additionally, a smaller number of cases were categorized as accidents (8 cases), while some incidents fell under the broad category of "other" (12 cases). A significant number of cases (334) remained classified as unknown due to the absence of sufficient information in the analyzed newspaper articles. In these instances, the articles did not provide explicit details or clear reasons regarding the motivations behind the intimate partner femicide.

Moving forward, the analysis will now concentrate solely on honor-based homicide, as this category aligns with the primary focus of our study on honor-based femicide. The decision to exclude the "Other Categories" ensures a more targeted investigation into the specific motivations and dynamics surrounding honor-based femicide incidents. By narrowing our scope to this specific context, we aim to provide a comprehensive understanding of the factors contributing to honor-based femicide and its implications for individuals involved in honor-based violence.

Outcomes in Relation to Research Questions

1. Blame and Responsibility

The influence of news and information media in shaping perceptions of violence against women has been widely recognized in many previous studies. One notable aspect explored in the literature is the phenomenon referred to as "victim blaming." This term pertains to the portrayal of crime victims in a manner that suggests their own responsibility for the transgressions perpetrated against them. Based on previous research, this section will encompass 3 distinct parts, each examining key aspects within the broader context of the topic. These parts aim to provide a comprehensive understanding and analysis of the subject matter, drawing upon the existing body of research and literature.

1.A. Behavior of Woman

In accordance with previous research, it is noteworthy to highlight the influence of media in shaping perceptions of violence against women. While direct "victim blaming" may not always be explicitly employed, subtle cues and details are often present in media narratives that subtly suggest the potential involvement or responsibility of women in the violence perpetrated against them (Morgan & Politiff, 2012).

Analyzing the reasons behind honor-based femicide, we observed recurring themes related to women's behavior, which align with victim-blaming narratives often found in the literature. These themes include woman's assertion of autonomy, infidelity, insulting remarks, post-breakup romantic engagement, rejection of man's reconciliation request, rejection of man's other request, and request for separation. The presence of these themes in the media's portrayal of femicide cases underscores the prevalence of victim-blaming attitudes. By focusing on women's behavior, the media subtly suggests that they may have played a role or contributed to the violence directed towards them.

1.B. Excuses for Men

The media often presents justifications or explanations for why men resort to violence against women or commit intimate partner femicide, providing a range of excuses that aim to rationalize their actions. In our analysis, we observed two common themes related to such excuses: man's jealousy and man's inability to accept abandonment. These reasons were consistently portrayed in the newspaper articles as underlying factors that allegedly motivated men to engage in femicide. This finding aligns with the existing literature on the subject.

However, our analysis revealed an intriguing observation that deviates from the conventional narrative. In the literature, researchers have frequently reported additional situational factors such as drug use, alcohol use, mental health issues, and financial problems, which have been presented as potential justifications or excuses for men's violent behavior, serving to diminish their responsibility. Nonetheless, in our study focusing on honor-based femicide, these situational factors were notably absent within the identified categories (as depicted in Figure 1). It appears that when honor is at stake, these additional justifications or excuses become unnecessary, as the concept of honor itself is deemed sufficient to mitigate the perpetrators' responsibility. Consequently, victim-blaming narratives take precedence over the presentation of excuses or justifications for male perpetrators, as they seem to be deemed unnecessary in honor-based cases.

This finding underscores the predominance of victim-blaming attitudes within the context of honor-based femicide. It highlights how the focus shifts towards scrutinizing and attributing responsibility to the female victims, while simultaneously disregarding the need for additional excuses or justifications for the male perpetrators. This pattern indicates the deeply entrenched influence of honor-related beliefs and norms, which supersede other situational factors often considered in the broader literature on intimate partner violence.

1.C. Mutuality

In the context of domestic violence and intimate partner homicide, previous studies have noted that media often attribute a mutual responsibility for violence against women by highlighting the presence of arguments or disputes preceding the violent acts (e.g., Roberto et al., 2013). However, in the case of honor-based femicide, the inclusion of disputes or arguments as indicators of mutuality becomes irrelevant. This is because, within the framework of honor-based violence, any conflicts or arguments that arise are categorized as part of the honor dynamics, rather than being viewed as separate and mutually exclusive factors. Therefore, the concept of mutuality, as traditionally understood, does not apply in the context of honor-based femicide.

Additionally, it is worth noting that some newspaper articles in our study reported instances of murder-suicides, which were sometimes portrayed as a form of justification or even romanticized in certain cases. As shown in Table 1, approximately 18.7% of the reported cases involved the perpetrators dying by suicide. However, it is crucial to approach such portrayals with caution, as they can contribute to the normalization or romanticization of violent acts and should be critically analyzed within the broader context of intimate partner femicide.

2. Social Context

Previous research (e.g., Lee & Wong, 2019) has identified a common occurrence of "episodic framing" in media coverage of violence against women. Episodic framing refers to a reporting approach that emphasizes specific incidents or events while neglecting the broader social context in which such acts of violence take place. In contrast, "thematic framing" incorporates an understanding of the social factors that contribute to the occurrence of violence against women, providing a different and more comprehensive perspective. In the current study, a random selection of 20 newspaper articles was made to analyze the framing employed in news coverage.

To select the 20 cases, we initially identified news articles that prominently featured the most common reason for violence against women: the woman's request for separation. From this subset, we chose every 12th news article to ensure random sampling. Using critical discourse analysis, we examined these 20 news reports for specific criteria. We investigated whether they (1) addressed concepts such as gender inequality and violence against women, (2) provided information for women on where to seek help, (3) delved into the history of violence by perpetrators, (4) positioned violence against women as an individual or private issue, and (5) included relationship labels.

Our findings indicate that only one out of the 20 news articles incorporated concepts related to gender-based violence and violence against women. None of the articles provided information on support resources for women. However, in 15 of the 20 articles, there was documentation of a history of violence by the perpetrators. Furthermore, 19 out of the 20 articles framed violence against women as an individual or private problem rather than a societal issue. Notably, all of the articles included relationship labels to describe the victims and perpetrators.

These findings underscore the limited use of thematic framing and the predominance of episodic framing in news coverage of violence against women. The lack of attention to gender inequality, the absence of information for women seeking help, and the individualistic framing of the issue contribute to a narrow understanding of the complex social dynamics underlying violence against women.

DISCUSSION

The aim of this study was to examine how news coverage in the Turkish media portrays honor-based intimate partner violence (IPV) against women resulting in death. Through conducting quantitative analysis, content analysis, discourse analysis, and frame analysis, we sought to investigate how news articles attribute blame and responsibility for violence and portray the social context of IPV.

Research indicates that biased media coverage of IPV can significantly impact societal perceptions of violence and the importance attributed to it (Fairbairn & Dawson, 2013). Presenting IPV against women as a personal matter rather than a social problem can hinder progress and perpetuate gender inequality, which, in turn, encourages violence. Therefore, it is crucial to address the minimization of honor-based IPV in media coverage by recognizing the role of honor beliefs. Fairbairn and Dawson (2013) assert that identifying IPV against women as a social problem, rather than a mere conflict between partners, is key to developing strategies to overcome socially sanctioned values.

Previous research consistently demonstrates a strong association between people's evaluation of instances of violence against women and their willingness to take action, both of which are strongly influenced by newspaper coverage of such incidents (Bullock, 2007). Considering the significant role that the media plays in shaping individuals' perceptions and understanding of reality, particularly their interpretations of violence against women (Franiuk et al., 2008a, 2008b), it can be argued that the print media in Turkey may reinforce the endorsement of honor and patriarchal gender roles rather than challenging existing notions of masculinity and femininity.

The results of the quantitative analysis reveal a distressingly high incidence of femicide, thereby underscoring the severity of the issue in Turkey. Such figures demand the attention of both society and the government, urging immediate action to combat violence against women. Furthermore, the rationales reported for femicide in newspapers predominantly revolve around honor-based motives. While non-honor-related femicide cases are also prevalent, honor appears to be the primary underlying cause of violence against women in Turkey. These alarming statistics and the pervasive presence of honor concerns place a responsibility on the media to exercise particular sensitivity in their reporting of intimate partner violence, refraining from employing language that may serve to justify such acts.

In the qualitative analysis, we examined media reports regarding the attribution of blame and responsibility for violence, focusing on three key aspects: women's behavior, excuses for men, and mutuality. Consistent with prior research (Lee & Wong, 2020), we identified themes of victim-blaming, wherein news reports subtly attribute blame to women by discussing their behavior. Moreover, nearly all news articles engaged in justifications for violence, aiming to exonerate the perpetrators by citing reasons such as jealousy and intolerance of abandonment. For instance, a femicide case from Turkey was portrayed in newspapers as follows: The husband, who murdered his wife despite her seeking refuge in a shelter due to ongoing spousal abuse, justified his act by claiming that he was driven to it because of the woman's alleged infidelity and the perceived challenge to his masculinity (sosyalistfeministkolektif.org, 2012). Such victim-blaming and excusing of perpetrators in media coverage of violence serve as powerful obstacles to gender equality, social change, and violence prevention (Meyers, 1994). Furthermore, within honor cultures, where patriarchal roles are expected in intimate relationships, men are anticipated to control and dominate women (Sakallı & Akbaş, 2013; Sev'er & Yurdakul, 2001; Vandello & Cohen, 2003). Acts of violence by men, justified under the pretext of threats to honor, infidelity, or abandonment, are deemed acceptable. As previously mentioned, consistent research findings (Ceylan-Batur et al., 2021; Vandello et al., 2009) indicate that individuals from honor cultures are more likely to justify intimate partner violence when it is rooted in honor-related concerns. Yirmibeşoğlu (2007) investigated 300 honor killing legal cases and concluded that men tend to claim committing the murder in the name of honor, regardless of the actual reason behind the violence. This strategy is known to lead to reduced prison sentences. Consequently, media coverage that emphasizes honor ideologies as explanations for IPV may foster support for the perpetrator, acceptance of violence, and victim-blaming due to violations of honor codes. To break this cycle, it is crucial for the media to exercise caution in framing intimate partner violence from an honor perspective.

Previous studies (Bullock & Cubert, 2002) have documented that news reports often place emphasis on the aspect of 'why he did it' and provide excuses for the perpetrator's behavior, such as the influence of drugs or mental health issues. Surprisingly, in cases of honor-based femicide, we found no situational explanations justifying men's violence, such as attributing it to the influence of alcohol or psychopathology. It is likely that when honor concerns are at stake, individuals become deeply entrenched in justifying violence, without seeking additional reasons. Honor concerns appear to automatically and completely drive individuals to justify acts of violence.

In addition to justifying violence through victim-blaming and excusing the perpetrator, the media also minimizes the severity of the situation by regarding intimate partner violence (IPV) as isolated incidents. In our analysis of 20 cases of honor-based IPV reported in the news, we observed that the media fails to recognize honor-based IPV as deeply rooted in cultural values. None of the articles address gender inequality or acknowledge the cultural and social factors that contribute to IPV, such as patriarchal values perpetuating gender inequality and prevailing honor ideologies. By focusing solely on individual instances, there is a missed opportunity to identify and address the underlying cultural and social factors that drive IPV (Fairbairn & Dawson, 2013). Furthermore, this narrow focus may hinder efforts to combat gender inequality and discourage abused women from seeking help. IPV should be viewed as a social problem rather than an isolated issue limited to specific groups or regions, necessitating the implementation of public policies and legal regulations (Bullock & Cubert, 2002; Hammond et al., 2006; Lee & Wong, 2020; Meyers, 1994). Particularly in honor cultures, it is crucial to highlight the role of honor ideologies in perpetuating violence at a societal level. By raising awareness about these societal factors, there is a potential to reduce tolerance for honor-based IPV.

CONCLUSION

Our findings have revealed that the media's understanding of violence against women is largely influenced by cultural codes and regulations. Given the influential role of media in shaping public attitudes, it is concerning that a tendency to victim-blame and exonerate perpetrators in media coverage can obscure the root causes of the problem and undermine efforts to address it. These representations may inadvertently contribute to gender inequality by normalizing violent acts and instilling the belief that such behavior is justifiable. Additionally, framing intimate partner violence as isolated incidents between partners rather than a deep-rooted social problem can dissuade victims from seeking help and perpetuate a cycle of justification based on honor ideologies.

To address this issue, it is crucial for all media outlets to be mindful of the adverse consequences of their news framing on achieving gender equality. Steps should be taken to avoid reinforcing existing stereotypes related to masculinity and femininity, refrain from victim-blaming, and avoid excusing the perpetrators' actions. By challenging and reframing news coverage of intimate partner violence, particularly within the context of honor-based IPV, the media can play a vital role in breaking the cycle of violence perpetuated by honor ideologies.

However, we recognize that media efforts alone cannot fully prevent the perpetuation of honor-based crimes. Therefore, our findings serve as a call to action for governments, policymakers, individuals in society, and non-governmental organizations to collaborate and address the underlying cultural and social factors that fuel violence rooted in honor ideologies.

Limitations and Future Research

Our research focused solely on print media. Considering the significant impact of social media platforms on individuals and the influential power of visual media, it would be valuable to include different types of media in future studies. Visual media and social media, with their ability to provide videos and audio content, may have distinct effects compared to simply reading news articles. In addition, the study focused specifically on the Turkish context, and the findings may not be directly applicable to other countries or cultures with different social, cultural, and media landscapes. Further research is needed to explore the dynamics of media coverage of honor-based IPV in different honor culture contexts.

REFERENCES

Amnesty International. (2004). *Turkey: Women confronting family violence*. https://www.amnesty.org/en/documents/eur44/013/2004/en/

Baker, N., Gregware, P., & Cassidy, M. (1999). Family killing fields: Honor rationales in the murder of women. *Violence Against Women, 5*(2), 164–184. doi:10.1177/107780129952005

Bosson, J. K., Vandello, J. A., Burnaford, R. M., Weaver, J. R., & Wasti, S. A. (2009). Precarious manhood and displays of physical aggression. *Personality and Social Psychology Bulletin, 35*(5), 623–634. doi:10.1177/0146167208331161 PMID:19202132

Boyacıoğlu, İ. (2016). Violence against women and the past and present of women's studies in Turkey: A call for psychological research. *Turkish Psychological Articles, 19*(Special Issue), 146-149. https://search.trdizin.gov.tr/tr/yayin/detay/236984/dunden-bugune-turkiyede-kadina-yonelik-siddet-ve-ulusal-kadin-calismalari-psikolojik-arastirmalara-davet

Bullock, C. F. (2007). Framing domestic violence fatalities: Coverage by Utah newspapers. *Women's Studies in Communication, 30*(1), 34–63. doi:10.1080/07491409.2007.10162504

Bullock, C. F., & Cubert, J. (2002). Coverage of domestic violence fatalities by newspapers in Washington State. *Journal of Interpersonal Violence, 17*(5), 475–499. doi:10.1177/0886260502017005001

Carlyle, K. E., Slater, M. D., & Chakroff, J. L. (2008). Newspaper coverage of intimate partner violence: Skewing representations of risk. *Journal of Communication, 58*(1), 168–186. doi:10.1111/j.1460-2466.2007.00379.x PMID:21297889

Ceylan-Batur, S., Sakallı, N., & Gunaratne, S. (2021). Predictors of tolerating violence against women: Honor concerns and fundamentalist religious orientation. *Current Psychology (New Brunswick, N.J.), 42*(12), 9720–9733. doi:10.100712144-021-02276-4

Easteal, P., Holland, K., & Judd, K. (2015). Enduring themes and silences in media portrayals of violence against women. *Women's Studies International Forum, 48*, 103–113. doi:10.1016/j.wsif.2014.10.015

Efe, S. Y., & Ayaz, S. (2010). Domestic violence against women and women's opinions related to domestic violence. *Anatolian Journal of Psychiatry, 11*(1), 23–29. https://www.proquest.com/openview/9adf1e5f0804b9acd8cb7bef255723d5/1?cbl=136214&pq-origsite=gscholar&parentSessionId=hhyqfcP%2FxaqGYN3TR9w4USQToGyvMvOjiDq1ir32N%2FQ%3D

Fairbairn, J., & Dawson, M. (2013). Canadian news coverage of intimate partner homicide: Analyzing changes over time. *Feminist Criminology, 8*(3), 147–176. doi:10.1177/1557085113480824

Flood, M., & Pease, B. (2009). Factors influencing attitudes to violence against women. *Trauma, Violence & Abuse, 10*(2), 125–142. doi:10.1177/1524838009334131 PMID:19383630

Franiuk, R., Seefelt, J. L., Cepress, S. L., & Vandello, J. A. (2008a). Prevalence and effects of rape myths in print journalism: The Kobe Bryant case. *Violence Against Women, 14*(3), 287–309. doi:10.1177/1077801207313971 PMID:18292371

Franiuk, R., Seefelt, J. L., & Vandello, J. A. (2008b). Prevalence of rape myths in headlines and their effects on attitudes toward rape. *Sex Roles*, *58*(11-12), 790–801. doi:10.100711199-007-9372-4

Glick, P., Sakallı-Uğurlu, N., Akbaş, G., & Metin Orta, İ. (2016). Why do women endorse honor beliefs? Ambivalent sexism and religiosity as predictors. *Sex Roles*, *75*(11), 543–554. doi:10.100711199-015-0550-5

Hacettepe Üniversitesi Nüfus Etütleri Enstitüsü. (2015). *Türkiye'de kadına yönelik aile içi şiddet araştırması*. Elma Teknik Basım Matbaacılık.

Hammond, W. R., Whitaker, D. J., Lutzker, J. R., Mercy, J., & Chin, P. M. (2006). Setting a violence prevention agenda at the Centers for Disease Control and Prevention. *Aggression and Violent Behavior*, *11*(2), 112–119. doi:10.1016/j.avb.2005.07.003

İnam, Ö., & Şahin, N. (2020). Kadına yönelik şiddetin Türk medyasindaki temsil şekli: Sistematik derleme araştirmasi. *Marmara Üniversitesi Kadın ve Toplumsal Cinsiyet Araştırmaları Dergisi*, *4*(1), 1–15. doi:10.35333/mukatcad.2020.212

Jewkes, Y. (2015). *Media & Crime*. Sage.

Lee, C., & Wong, J. S. (2020). 99 reasons and he ain't one: A content analysis of domestic homicide news coverage. *Violence Against Women*, *26*(2), 213–232. doi:10.1177/1077801219832325 PMID:30835161

Leung, A. K. Y., & Cohen, D. (2011). Within-and between-culture variation: Individual differences and the cultural logics of honor, face, and dignity cultures. *Journal of Personality and Social Psychology*, *100*(3), 507–526. doi:10.1037/a0022151 PMID:21244179

Meyers, M. (1994). News of battering. *Journal of Communication*, *44*(2), 47–63. doi:10.1111/j.1460-2466.1994.tb00676.x

Mogashoa, T. (2014). Understanding critical discourse analysis in qualitative research. *International Journal of Humanities Social Sciences and Education*, *1*(7), 104–113. doi:10.5901/mjss.2014.v5n9p452

Morgan, J., & Politoff, V. (2012). *Victorian print media coverage of violence against women: A longitudinal study*. VicHealth.

Nisbett, R. E., & Cohen, D. (1996). *Culture of honor: The psychology of violence in the South*. Westview Press.

Pan, Z., & Kosicki, G. M. (1993). Framing analysis: An approach to news discourse. *Political Communication*, *10*(1), 55–75. doi:10.1080/10584609.1993.9962963

Peristiany, J. G. (1965). *Honor and shame: The values of Mediterranean society*. Weidenfeld and Nicolson.

Pitt-Rivers, J. A. (1977). *The fate of shechem: Or, the politics of sex: Essays in the anthropology of the Mediterranean*. Cambridge University Press.

Roberto, K. A., McCann, B. R., & Brossoie, N. (2013). Intimate partner violence in late life: An analysis of national news reports. *Journal of Elder Abuse & Neglect*, *25*(3), 230–241. doi:10.1080/08946566.2012.751825 PMID:23627429

Rodriguez Mosquera, P. M., Fischer, A. H., Manstead, A. S. R., & Zaalberg, R. (2008). Attack, disapproval, or withdrawal? The role of honour in anger and shame responses to being insulted. *Cognition and Emotion*, *22*(8), 1471–1498. doi:10.1080/02699930701822272

Rodriguez Mosquera, P. M., Manstead, A. S. R., & Fischer, A. H. (2002a). Honor in the Mediterranean and Northern Europe. *Journal of Cross-Cultural Psychology*, *33*(1), 16–36. doi:10.1177/0022022102033001002

Rodriguez Mosquera, P. M., Manstead, A. S. R., & Fischer, A. H. (2002b). The role of honor concerns in emotional reactions to offenses. *Cognition and Emotion*, *16*(1), 143–163. doi:10.1080/02699930143000167

Sakallı, N. (2001). Beliefs about wife beating among Turkish college students: The effects of patriarchy, sexism and sex difference. *Sex Roles*, *44*(9/10), 599–611. doi:10.1023/A:1012295109711

Sakallı Uğurlu, N., & Akbaş, G. (2013). "Honor" and "honor violence" against women in honor cultures: Social psychological explanations. *Turkish Psychological Articles*, *16*(32), 76–91. https://www.psikolog.org.tr/tr/yayinlar/dergiler/1031828/tpy1301996120130000m000089.pdf

Serdar Tekeli, E. (2016). Kadın cinayetlerinin haberleştirilmesi bağlamında medya etiğini yeniden tartışmak: Habertürk gazetesi örneği. *Abant Kültürel Araştırmalar Dergisi*, *1*(1), 129-142. https://dergipark.org.tr/en/pub/akader/issue/28202/299477

Sev'er, A., & Yurdakul, G. (2001). Culture of honor, culture of change: A feminist analysis of honor killings in Turkey. *Violence Against Women*, *7*(9), 964–998. doi:10.1177/10778010122182866

Sosyalistfeministkolektif.org. (2012). *Şefika Etik davası: Kadın bedeninden ölüme gerekçe yaratmak.* Retrieved from http://www.sosyalistfeministkolektif.org/kampanyalar/istanbul-feminist-kolektif/kadn-cinayetlerine-isyandayz/efika-etik-davas-kadn-bedeninden-oelueme-gerekce-yaratmak/

Stemler, S. (2001). An overview of content analysis. *Practical Assessment, Research & Evaluation*, *7*(17), 1–6. doi:10.7275/z6fm-2e34

Taylor, R. (2009). Slain and slandered: A content analysis of the portrayal of femicide in crime news. *Homicide Studies*, *13*(1), 21–49. doi:10.1177/1088767908326679

Vandello, J. A., & Cohen, D. (2003). Male honor and female fidelity: Implicit cultural scripts that perpetuate domestic violence. *Journal of Personality and Social Psychology*, *84*(5), 997–1010. doi:10.1037/0022-3514.84.5.997 PMID:12757144

Vandello, J. A., & Cohen, D. (2008). Culture, gender, and men's intimate partner violence. *Social and Personality Psychology Compass*, *2*(2), 652–667. doi:10.1111/j.1751-9004.2008.00080.x

Vandello, J. A., Cohen, D., Grandon, R., & Franiuk, R. (2009). Stand by your man: Indirect prescriptions for honorable violence and feminine loyalty in Canada, Chile, and the United States. *Journal of Cross-Cultural Psychology*, *40*(1), 81–104. doi:10.1177/0022022108326194

World Health Organization. (2018). *Violence against women prevalence estimates.* https://www.who.int/publications/i/item/WHO-SRH-21.9

World Health Organization. (2021). *Global and regional estimates of violence against women: Prevalence and health effects of intimate partner violence and non-partner sexual violence*. https://www.who.int/publications/i/item/9789241564625

World Health Organization & Pan American Health Organization. (2012). *Understanding and addressing violence against women: Intimate partner violence*. https://apps.who.int/iris/handle/10665/77432

Yirmibeşoğlu, V. (2007). *Toprağa düşen sevdalar*. Hürriyet Yayınları.

ADDITIONAL READING

Gillespie, L. K., Richards, T. N., Givens, E. M., & Smith, M. D. (2013). Framing deadly domestic violence. *Violence Against Women, 19*(2), 222–245. doi:10.1177/1077801213476457 PMID:23420837

United Nations Population Fund (UNFPA) & International Center for Research on Women (ICRW). (2009). *Intimate partner violence high costs to households and communities*. New York: UNFPA. Retrieved from https://www.icrw.org/wp-content/uploads/2016/10/Intimate-Partner-Violence-High-Cost-to-Households-and-Communities.pdf

Uskul, A. K., Cross, S. E., Günsoy, C., & Gul, P. (2019). Cultures of honor. In S. Kitayama & D. Cohen (Eds.), *Handbook of Cultural Psychology* (pp. 793–821). The Guilford Press.

Warshaw, C., Brashler, P., & Gil, J. (2009). Mental health consequences of intimate partner violence. In C. Mitchell & D. Anglin (Eds.), *Intimate partner violence: A health-based perspective* (pp. 147–171). Oxford University Press.

KEY TERMS AND DEFINITIONS

Femicide: The deliberate murder of women, generally based on gender ideologies.

Honor Culture: Cultures which put significant emphasis on reputation, a good standing on the society which is based on male authority and female chastity. These cultures justify male violence against women for honor related reasons.

Intimate Partner Violence (IPV): Acts of physical, emotional, or psychological harm perpetrated by current or former partner on the other.

Isolated Incidents: The attempt to present negative events (e.g., violence against women) as a singular occurrence specific to the involved parties, detached from similar events and broader cultural influences.

Justifications for Violence: Attempts to find excuses for violence, seeking to justify the perpetrator's actions and imply that the victim's behavior warranted the violence.

Media Depictions: Media's representation, explanation, and presentation of the news and events.

Victim Blaming: The notion that the victim is at fault for what happened to them. The occurrence of negative incident attributed to victim's failure to behave in a well manner.

Chapter 6
The Role of Social Media in the Fight Against Gender Violence

Katharina Miller
Founding Partner of 3C Compliance, Spain

Muhammet Demirbilek
Faculty of Education, Suleyman Demirel University, Turkey

ABSTRACT

Gender violence is a pervasive global issue that demands urgent attention and action. Social media platforms have emerged as powerful tools in the fight against this form of violence, providing opportunities for awareness raising, advocacy, and support. It enables individuals and organizations to share information, personal stories, and resources related to gender violence. It serves as a platform for survivors to break their silence, share their experiences, and find solidarity. Social media campaigns raise public awareness, challenge societal norms, and encourage discussions surrounding gender-based violence, fostering a sense of collective responsibility. Social media plays a crucial role in the fight against gender violence, providing a space for survivors, activists, and advocates connecting and educating. This chapter explores the role of social media in the fight against gender violence, focusing on its impact on awareness raising, survivor support, and community mobilization.

INTRODUCTION

Social media is a tool for communicating, sharing information and connecting people with each other. Today, the widespread use of the Internet, especially social media, has emerged as an alternative medium that women can use to seek their rights and express themselves. Social media can play an important role in empowering women and protecting their rights. From the "MeToo" movement to the Women's March, social media has been sed in many areas for women to express themselves and seek their rights. Thus, social media has provided women, women's rights violations and women's movements with the opportunity to capitalize on the unique awareness-raising potential of social media.

DOI: 10.4018/978-1-6684-8893-5.ch006

One of the most important ways in which social media has influenced women's rights is by giving women a platform to talk about issues once considered taboo. With the rise of social media, women can share their stories of harassment, abuse and discrimination. For example, the #MeToo movement has brought to light the extent of sexual harassment and assault that women face in their daily lives. Women from all communities of society can share their stories through social media and create a collective voice for change.

Social media plays a vital role in promoting gender equality and challenging traditional gender roles. Women can raise awareness and use social media by creating hashtags to exhibit their skills and talents, challenge gender stereotypes, end violence and discrimination, and demand equal opportunities. For example, by launching social media campaigns such as #LikeAGirl, #WomenInSTEM and #WomenInLeadership, they can highlight their achievements, raise awareness and claim their rights (Gianniri, 2021). Another important way in which social media empowers women is through its use as a platform for activism and rights advocacy. Women can use social media to raise awareness on issues that affect them, such as reproductive rights, equal pay and access to health care. Through social media, women may be able to connect with activists in their own countries, around the world, organize events, and create a space for collective action. Social media can be used to make women' voices heard and seek their rights such as equality, freedom, rights, bias, and stereotype.

However, in addition to the advantages of social media channels in terms of women's rights, there are also negative aspects in terms of digital violence against women. The anonymity of social media channels can sometimes lead to cyberbullying and online harassment (Cybersafe, 2021). Especially women who are outspoken about their views or have a large following are often the target of online harassment.

Violence Against Women on Social Media

The internet especially social media is a double-edged sword for women. On the one hand, it provides vital spaces for women seeking self-expression and opportunities, and on the other hand, it creates a space for abusers who target women. Violence on Social Media - Digital / Cyber Violence refers to all forms of harassment, abuse, humiliation, insult, abuse, threats, blackmail, bullying, hate speech, non-consensual sharing of pictures and images and sharing of unwanted sexually explicit messages against women through information technologies such as the internet, smartphones or video games.

Digital violence against women is widespread and alarming, affecting millions of women worldwide. While social media has the potential to play a critical role in preventing violence against women, it can also be a digital medium through which violence against women is perpetuated and normalized. Digital violence against women, cyberbullying, online harassment and revenge sexual posts are a growing concern.

One of the most important forms of violence against women on social media is cyberbullying. Cyberbullying refers to all forms of bullying that occur online, including harassment, humiliation and threats. Women are disproportionately affected by cyberbullying. Research shows that women are more likely to experience online harassment than men. Cyberbullying has a negative impact on women's mental health and well-being and can lead to anxiety, depression and even suicide (Cybersafe, 2021).

Online harassment is another form of violence against women on social media. Women who express their opinions or challenge traditional gender roles are often the target of online harassment, which can take many forms, including threats of violence, hate speech and malicious intent, including searching for and posting information about women. Online harassment negatively impacts women's lives and can lead to feelings of isolation, fear and reluctance to express themselves online.

Revengeful sexting is another form of violence against women on social media. Revengeful sexting refers to the non-consensual sharing of intimate images or videos, often as a form of revenge or control. Women are disproportionately affected by revenge sexting. Research shows that 90% of victims of revenge sexting are women (Mckinlay & Lavis, 2020). The impact of revenge sexting on women's lives can be devastating, leading to shame, humiliation and, in some cases, loss of employment or relationships.

One of the challenges of preventing violence against women on social media is the lack of accountability. Social media platforms have been criticized for their inadequate response to online violence against women, with many women reporting that their complaints are not taken seriously or ignored altogether.

Violence against women on social media is a growing concern that needs to be addressed. Cyberbullying, online harassment and revenge sexting are forms of digital violence against women that can have a profound impact on women's lives (Council of Europe, 2023). Social media platforms have a responsibility to take action to prevent and respond to violence against women, including by developing policies and tools to combat digital violence, providing resources and support for victims, and addressing gender bias and discrimination. Working together, we can create a world where all women can live free from violence and abuse, both online and offline.

Types of Violence Against Women on Social Media

Digital violence harms women and girls by restricting their right to freedom of expression and reducing their self-esteem and confidence. According to a report by Plan International, 50 percent of women reported experiencing more online harassment than street harassment (Cybersafe, 2021). Online violence has been identified as a leading cause of the global gender digital divide, which prevents women and girls from advancing in science, technology, engineering and math (STEM) fields. Women and girls are more likely to experience digital violence than men. Globally, 38 percent of women report having experienced direct online abuse (Cybersafe, 2021). Women aged 18-24 in particular are at greater risk of experiencing all forms of cyber violence (Council of Europe, 2023).

Some of the most common forms of violence against women on social media:

1. Cyberbullying: Cyberbullying refers to all forms of bullying that take place online, including harassment, threats and humiliation. Women are disproportionately affected by cyberbullying; research shows that women are more likely to experience online harassment than men. Cyberbullying has a significant impact on women's mental health and well-being and can lead to anxiety, depression and even suicide.
2. Online harassment: Online harassment refers to any unwanted or offensive behavior directed at women online, including hate speech, threats and maliciously searching for and posting someone's information. Women in particular are targets of online harassment. Online harassment can harm women in many ways. Because the harassment is visible to anyone connected to the internet and the victim may be constantly bombarded with abusive messages or comments
3. Retaliatory sexting: Revengeful sexting refers to the non-consensual sharing of intimate images or videos, often as a form of revenge or control. Women are the segment of society most negatively affected by revenge sexting. Research shows that 90% of victims of revenge sexting are women (Henry, Flynn & Powell, 2020). The impact of revenge sexting on women's lives can be devastating, leading to shame, humiliation and even loss of employment or relationships.

4. Sexual objectification: Sexual objectification refers to treating an individual as a sexual object rather than as a whole person. Women are often subjected to sexual objectification on social media, where their bodies or appearance are commented on or used to sell products. Sexual objectification is dangerous in that it can contribute to a culture of misogyny in which women are judged primarily on their physical attributes.
5. Impersonation: This is a type of violence perpetrated through fake accounts with names similar to the person's screen name and using their profile picture. Real pictures of the victim can also be used in this type of violence. The bully impersonating the victim tries to damage the victim's social identity, usually by having sexually explicit conversations with people, or by defending opposing views, or by committing crimes, or by making statements as if they were confessions from the victim's own mouth. This bullying is sometimes also practiced by taking over the victim's account.

Social media has given rise to a range of forms of violence against women, including cyberbullying, online harassment, revenge sexting, sexual objectification and impersonation. These forms of violence can have a profound impact on women's lives, leading to anxiety, depression and even job or relationship loss. It is crucial to recognize the harm that these forms of violence can cause and to take action to prevent and respond to violence against women on social media.

Causes of Violence Against Women on Social Media

Social media has provided a platform for individuals to communicate and interact with each other, but it has also facilitated the spread of violence and abuse against women. Violence against women on social media has become a serious problem in today's society. There are many reasons for the emergence of violence against women on social media (Jankowicz, 2022). These reasons are:

1. Gender-based discrimination: Gender-based discrimination is one of the main reasons for the emergence of violence against women on social media. Women are often subjected to online harassment and abuse because of their gender, with men using social media as a way to exert power and control over women. This discrimination can take the form of sexist jokes, threats or comments about women's bodies or appearance.
2. Anonymity: Anonymity is another reason for the emergence of violence against women on social media. Many social media platforms allow users to create anonymous accounts, which can be used to harass or abuse women without any consequences. Anonymity can also make it easier for perpetrators to spread misinformation or rumors about women without having to be held accountable.
3. Normalization of violence: Normalization of violence against women in the media. Social media plays an important role in this normalization. There are those who believe that online harassment, abuse is part of internet culture, and that women should ignore it. This normalization of violence makes it difficult for women to talk about their experiences and seek help.
4. Lack of accountability/responsibility: Social media platforms have been criticized for their lack of accountability when it comes to violence against women. Many social media platforms do not have adequate policies to address online harassment and abuse and perpetrators often go unpunished. This lack of accountability can embolden perpetrators of digital violence and make women feel that there is no point in reporting abuse.

5. Misogyny: Misogyny is the hatred or dislike of women and is a major factor in violence against women on social media. Many men see women as inferior and use social media as a way to express their misogynistic views. Misogyny can take many forms, including sexist jokes, threats and comments about women's bodies or appearance.

In addition, jealousy, revenge, individual desires, ideological reasons, family unrest, political reasons, anger, greed to make money, economic reasons and psychological disorders can be counted among the causes of violence against women on social media. In conclusion, knowing the causes of violence against women on social media is crucial for taking action to prevent and respond to violence against women on social media.

Using Social Media in the Prevention of Violence Against Women

Violence against women is a widespread and alarming issue affecting millions of women around the world and in our country. Social media, with its widespread reach and accessibility, has the potential to play a critical role in preventing violence against women. By providing a platform for education, awareness raising and advocacy, social media can help change attitudes, behaviors and social norms that perpetuate violence against women.

One of the most important ways social media can prevent violence against women is through education and awareness raising. Social media can be a powerful tool to spread information about violence against women, including its causes, effects and ways to prevent it. Through social media campaigns, organizations can share facts and statistics, raise awareness about the signs of violence, and provide resources for survivors.

Social media can also be used to change attitudes and behaviors that contribute to violence against women. For example, campaigns such as #NotAllMen and #MeToo have highlighted the prevalence of sexual harassment and assault and encouraged men to take responsibility for their actions. Social media can also challenge harmful stereotypes and gender norms that contribute to violence against women by promoting positive images of women and girls and raising awareness about the effects of gender-based violence.

Social media has an important place in the prevention of violence against women as it provides a platform for women to assert their rights and use as an activist. Social media can also be used to build support for policies and programs aimed at preventing violence against women. Women's rights advocacy campaigns such as #TimesUp and #EndVAW have been successful in drawing attention to the issue of violence against women and pushing for legal and policy changes.

Social media can provide a space for women who have experienced violence and injustice to share their stories and seek support. In this way, women can connect with other survivors, stand in solidarity and find support in claiming their rights. Social media can also be used as a tool to help women access resources and support services, such as hotlines, counseling and legal services, in cases of violence and injustice. However, social media also has limitations when it comes to preventing violence against women. For example, disadvantaged communities, including rural women, low-income women and women with disabilities, have very limited access to social media.

Social media can be used as a powerful tool in preventing violence against women. Social media can contribute to changing attitudes, behaviors and social norms that perpetuate violence against women through trainings, raising awareness, encouraging women to defend their rights and creating spaces where women can share their stories of violence. By using the reach and influence of social media and working together, progress can be made in preventing violence against women and a world where all women can live free from violence and abuse can be established.

How to Report Violence on Social Media

Social media platforms have become a powerful tool for communication and social networking. But it has also become a platform for digital violence and abuse. Violence on social media can take many forms, including cyberbullying, harassment and hate speech. If you experience violence on social media, it is important to know how to report it.

Some steps to follow when reporting violence on social media (Jankowicz, 2022):

1. Take screenshots: The first step to reporting violence on social media is to take screenshots of the offending content. This evidence will be crucial when reporting violence to the platform or law enforcement.
2. Report to the platform: Most social media platforms have a reporting feature that allows users to report violence or abuse. The reporting process can vary depending on the platform, but usually involves filling out a form or selecting the offending content to report. When reporting, it is important to provide as much detail as possible, including the nature of the violence, date and time, and other relevant information
3. Contact law enforcement: If the violence on social media is serious or involves threats of physical harm, it is crucial to contact law enforcement. In many cases, social media platforms will also work with law enforcement to address the issue. Give the authorities the evidence you collect, including screenshots.
4. Seek support: Violence on social media can be traumatic and have a significant impact on mental health. If you or someone you know has experienced violence on social media, it is important to seek support from friends, family or a mental health professional.
5. Follow up: After reporting violence on social media, it is crucial to follow up with the platform or law enforcement to ensure that action is taken. If the violence continues, you may need to continue reporting and seeking support until the issue is resolved.

Reporting violence on social media is of great importance for preventing and addressing the problem. Reporting the digital violence, you are exposed to by taking screenshots, reporting it to the platform, contacting law enforcement, seeking support and following up is of great importance in preventing violence. We should not forget that violence on social media is unacceptable and that we all have a responsibility to speak out and take action against it.

What to Consider When Using Social Media

Social media has become an integral part of our daily lives, providing a platform for communication, social networking and entertainment. However, with the increasing use of social media, it is important to be aware of the potential risks and negative effects of social media use. Here are some things to be aware of when using social media (Jankowicz, 2022):

1. Privacy: Privacy is an important issue when using social media. It is necessary to understand how social media platforms use and store your personal information and take steps to protect your privacy. This requires setting privacy settings, avoiding sharing sensitive information and being careful when interacting with strangers online.
2. Cyberbullying: Cyberbullying is a serious issue that can have a significant impact on mental health. It is crucial to be aware of the signs of cyberbullying and take steps to prevent it. This includes reporting any incidents of bullying or harassment, blocking the perpetrator and seeking support from friends, family or mental health professionals.
3. Addiction: Social media addiction is a growing problem. Many internet users spend hours every day scrolling through social media news and feeds. It is important to be aware of the signs of addiction, such as feeling anxious or restless when unable to access social media, and to take steps to limit social media use.
4. Misinformation: Social media has become a breeding ground for misinformation, with misinformation and conspiracy theories spreading rapidly across platforms. It is important to verify information before sharing it and avoid spreading misinformation.
5. Online predators: Online predators are a real threat, especially for children and young people. It is important to be aware of the risks of interacting with strangers online and take steps to protect yourself and your children. This includes setting privacy settings, monitoring online activities and educating children about the dangers of online predators.

Social media can be a valuable tool for communication and networking, but it is important to be aware of the potential risks and negative impacts. By paying attention to privacy, cyberbullying, addiction, misinformation and online predators, we can use social media safely and responsibly. It is important to never forget that your safety and peace of mind are paramount and that it is okay to take a break from social media when needed.

Awareness-Raising Through Social Media

Social media can be a powerful tool in the fight against gender violence. It can provide an avenue for both victims and advocates to speak up and share their stories, creating greater awareness about the reality of gender-based violence. Social media also allows people from all walks of life to come together and take collective action against gender violence. Organizations such as UN Women use social media platforms to educate people on gender-based violence and advocate for change. They want to spread awareness and fight for change in how society treats victims of this type of violence. Through research, UN Women has seen that many survivors are not receiving the support they need because of the stigma surrounding their experiences (UN Women, 2019). Therefore, UN Women is determined to do their part to end this injustice by raising awareness and encouraging public discussion on the issue, as well as advocating for more effective laws and policies that protect those affected by such violence. UN Women's goal is to empower survivors of gender-based violence so they can get the justice they deserve and help create a world where everyone feels safe. These digital efforts have proved to be successful in amplifying voices of victims, raising global awareness about the issue, and engaging more people in the movement. Another international activist who uses social media in its fight against Gender based Violence is Zonta International, a global organization dedicated to empowering women through service and advocacy. The 16 Days of Activism against Gender-Based Violence is an international campaign calling for the elimination of all forms of violence against women and girls around the world, which starts on November 25 (International Day for the Elimination of Violence against Women) and ends on December 10 (Human Rights Day). During these 16 days, people from all walks of life participate in activities to raise awareness and take action to prevent further gender-based violence. During the pandemic, Zonta has been using social media as a platform to signify their support online. By using hashtags such as "16Days" or "OrangeTheWorld", people can spread messages of solidarity and reach a wider audience (Zonta, 2023).

However, virtual actions alone are not enough to combat gender-based violence. It is important for everyone—individuals, organizations—to continue engaging in persistent activism and advocacy to make lasting change within our societies. This includes supporting those affected by gender-based violence, advocating for better legislation and frameworks that protect victims' rights, and making sure there is adequate access to services such as healthcare or legal aid. Through social media, it is possible to connect with a wider audience and create an inclusive environment for everyone who wants to fight against gender-based violence. From online petitions to hashtag campaigns, social media can help bring attention to issues that otherwise may go unnoticed or unacknowledged. By utilizing this powerful tool, more people will be able to stand in solidarity and work together towards creating a safer world free of gender violence.

Social media channels offer survivors of gender violence an important platform to find support and solidarity from friends, family members, and other individuals in the same situation. This form of survivor support is especially crucial for those who may feel distant or alienated from their physical social environments due to the stigma surrounding gender-based violence. Additionally, social media allows survivors to connect with broader online communities that can provide advice on how to navigate through legal systems or access mental health services. There are a number of organizations across the world that specialize in providing specialized counseling and guidance tailored specifically towards survivors of gender violence. These organizations often use platforms such as Facebook, Twitter, Instagram, and YouTube as a means to spread awareness and provide links to helpful resources for victims and advocates alike. By utilizing the power of social media, these organizations are able to reach millions of people in a short amount of time and contribute to the larger fight against gender violence.

In the end, social media has become an invaluable tool for survivors in their quest for support and justice. Not only does it provide a platform to share stories and seek advice from others in similar situations, but also allows them to access vital information about various services and resources available that can better assist them in their journey towards recovery. Social media is helping lead the charge against gender-based violence, by connecting victims with supporters across the world and giving a voice to those who have experienced such injustice. Through its use as a powerful medium for communication and education, social media continues to be an essential resource in the fight against gender violence.

Community Mobilization Through Social Media

Social media has become a key tool for community mobilization in the fight against gender-based violence. By creating networks of activists and survivors' intent on putting an end to this type of violence, it enables people around the world to raise awareness about gender-based issues and pressure their leaders into taking action. Additionally, social media provides access to support systems, resources and correct information for those affected by this form of violence, helping them find safety and wellbeing. Moreover, campaigns like #MeToo or Time's Up have utilized social media to bring together individuals from all over the world and create a powerful movement that is turning the tide against gender-based violence.

It is evident that social media has an important role to play in this fight, and its potential should not be disregarded.

CONCLUSION AND DISCUSSION

In conclusion, social media has the potential to be an effective tool in raising awareness and combating gender violence. It is important to recognize that it can both positively and negatively affect the fight against gender violence. While on one hand, it can help spread awareness and generate support for victims, it can also be used as a platform to propagate hate speech or perpetuate stereotypes about women. As such, it is important for users of social media to exercise caution when engaging with content related to this issue. Social media should not be seen as a replacement for traditional methods of fighting gender violence, but rather as a complement or supplement. Organizations looking to leverage social media should ensure that they have a clear strategy in place that outlines how they will use these platforms to maximize their effectiveness. This may include training for staff on how to use social media responsibly and ethically, as well as putting in place mechanisms that monitor activity and quickly remove hateful content or comments. By working together, both online and offline, we can make a greater impact in the fight against gender violence, which will ultimately benefit everyone. We must all recognize our role in stopping gender violence – whether through education or policy changes – and take a stand: by using social media responsibly, supporting victims, and positively influencing public opinion. In this way we can ensure that future generations of women are provided with the support they need to live free from fear.

REFERENCES

Baker, C., & Carreño, P. (2016). Understanding the Role of Technology in Adolescent Dating and Dating Violence. *Journal of Child and Family Studies*, *25*(1), 308–320. doi:10.100710826-015-0196-5

Council of Europe. (2023). *Activities to address gender and gender-based violence with young people.* Available in https://www.coe.int/en/web/gender-matters/activities

Cybersafe. (2021). *Cyber Violence against Women & Girls – Report on Cyber VAWG and CYBERSAFE Framework.* Final report on WP2 UL FDV. Funded by the European Union's REC Programme (2014–2020).

Gianniri, L. (2021). "Here too": Some media representations of the intersectoral #Metoo in Greece, in ENA Institute for Alternative Policies (2021). The Greek #Metoo and Public Discourse.

Henry, N., Flynn, A., & Powell, A. (2020). Technology-Facilitated Domestic and Sexual Violence: A Review. *Violence Against Women*, *26*(15-16), 1828–1854. doi:10.1177/1077801219875821 PMID:32998673

Jankowicz, N. (2022). *How to Be a Woman Online: Surviving Abuse and Harassment, and How to Fight Back.* Bloomsbury Academic. doi:10.5040/9781350267602

Mckinlay, T., & Lavis, T. (2020). Why did she send it in the first place? Victim blame in the context of 'revenge porn'. *Psychiatry, Psychology and Law*, *27*(3), 386–396. doi:10.1080/13218719.2020.17349 77 PMID:33071547

UN Women. (2019). *Listen, believe, support: the power of mental health care for survivors of violence*. Available in: https://www.unwomen.org/en/news/stories/2019/3/feature-story-mental-health-care

Whiting, J. B., Davies, B. N., Eisert, B. C., Witting, A. B., & Anderson, S. R. (2022). Online Conversations About Abuse: Responses to IPV Survivors from Support Communities. *Journal of Family Violence*, 1–11.

Zonta (2023). Zonta Says No. Available in: https://zontasaysno.com/zontasvision/campaign/ (last access on 07/06/2023)

KEY TERMS AND DEFINITIONS

Cyberbullying: Cyberbullying refers to electronic bullying, Internet bullying, cyber aggression, online bullying.

Digital Violence: Digital violence refers to actions or words that inflict harm through the misuse of digital technologies.

Misogyny: Misogyny refers to the hatred or dislike of women.

Online Harassment: Online harassment the use of information and communication technologies by an individual or group to cause harm to another person.

Social Media: Social media refers to a tool for communicating, sharing information and connecting people with each other.

Chapter 7
Marginalization at Cyberspace: A New Dimension of Violence Against Women and Girls

Geeta Ajit
V.E.S. Institute of Technology, India

ABSTRACT

Cyberspace has been acknowledged as a free space, opening opportunities regardless of caste or gender. But this notion that this technology liberates users into a more democratic genderless world with equality still remains a fallacy. Neither has gender been erased nor has everyone been welcomed into this cyberspace. Not only are girls and women targeted more in this space; they also suffer serious consequences resulting in permanent psychological suffering. Male perpetrators not only dominate the mixed-sex electronic conversation; they have also been identified as frequent instigators of on-line sexual harassment-observations difficult to reconcile with the notion of a gender-neutral utopia. While women enter into this space in hope of a common genderless language, they soon end up unsubscribing from this digital space and also withdraw themselves into silence and isolation thereon.

INTRODUCTION

The virtual world, 'Internet', often described as 'Cyberspace', has entered our homes, schools and workplace and is said to have opened opportunities to people, regardless of caste, creed or gender. It has a self-governing capacity and has changed our lives in all dimensions and also kept us updated on world news and events. This internet access has been established as a new fundamental human right and is celebrated as equal opportunities for public expression regardless of a person's identity or status. It is celebrated as an utopian world that is '(n)either male (physically) nor female (genetically) nor their simple reversal, but something else: a virtual sex. floating in an elliptical orbit around the planet that it has left behind, finally free of the powerful gravitational pull of the binary signs of the male/female antinomies in the crowded earth scene of gender. (Kroker & Kroker 1993). Moreover, the recent COVID-19 pandemic has added to the impetus on the increased reliance on digital technologies in everyday activities.

DOI: 10.4018/978-1-6684-8893-5.ch007

Gender Diversity in Cyberspace

The Cambridge Dictionary defines Cyberspace as 'the internet considered as an imaginary area without limits where you can meet people and discover information about any subject.' IGI Global Dictionary describes it as a 'Digital space navigable in virtual mode by people from different realities communicating with each other within a computerised world of digital networks.' For institutions it is a terrain that design hardware and software to meet the needs for entrance into a high-end techno world. But this terrain is not in the neutral zone as largely perceived rather, an immersion into the internet, virtuality and cyberspace have a price.

In this chapter, I would like to highlight how the notion that this futuristic technology will liberate the users from the physical world with limitations into a more democratic genderless world with equality still remains a fallacy. Investigative unfolding in this service provides insight to the embodied differences that are ingrained and a systematic pattern of activities and representation. Though many social groups have embraced the internet as an iconic representation, perceiving it as a utopian medium which neutralizes physical distinctions of gender, race, and sexual orientation, what is suppressed or rather, less addressed are the ways how these utopian theories correspond to the reality of gender in cyberspace. Despite it being a field that is rapidly changing and expanding, it has rendered people other than the dominant forces invisible or submissive, in other words, a world that is still primarily male dominated. Neither has gender been erased nor has everyone been openly welcomed into this cyberspace. It has been found that any education or socialization in this technological world are male gendered domains. 'When females manipulate complex technology in a productive or creative manner, it is often viewed and treated as a deviant act that deserves punishment.' (Daniels, 2009) While women do use this complex technology, it is generally in a passive manner. Women are invited to help out mostly with the mundane work that men do not want to be bothered with. Daniels compares it to a situation where husbands bought their wives a car to facilitate their domestic chores. In the same way, access to technology assists women to become better bureaucrats because it is a 'structural economic necessity' (Daniels, 2009).

History seems to repeat itself in cyberspace, twining its way again into the phallogocentric hegemony that prevailed over the years. It has been referred to as the 'Virtual Wild West' by Jeffery Look, where the area of law has been dramatically affected. He compares it to the old wild west 125 years ago, when the western states in the US were seen by men to have free use over to run their cattle or space for their crop. They did not seek permission and trampled down those who got into their way. They wanted control on those who came on their property and violently terrorised those who came to share their space. (Look, 1999) Statistics have shown how women are considered as intruders and face violent virtual assault when they refuse to comply. 'The digital arena has become a breeding ground for a range of exclusionary and violent discourses and beliefs, expressed and disseminated in a context of anonymity and impunity. Both women and men can be victims of cyber violence. However, evidence shows that women and girls are highly exposed to it.' (EIGE, 2022). According to Lenhart, 95% of 12–17-year-olds are online and 80% use social media… and more girls report being the victim of cyberbullying more often than boys.

Transgression of Boundaries

New technologies enable fluid spaces where there is a transgression of the boundaries. '...users leave their bodies behind when entering virtual spaces and become free to explore new forms of identity and textual interaction.' (Paasonen, 2011). 'Real' or 'designed' identities forge new relationships and networks, often taking on multiple identities. These identities spread their control in cyberspace, and frequently, the dominant identity becomes abusive and violent. The attributes of anonymity and facelessness not only empower the dominant identities to force submissiveness of the female gender but also allow these perpetrators of women to get away without any fear. And since law controls in this space are few and lax, they continue to ride without fear. Kendall argues that digital technologies reproduce rather than subvert white hetrosexual, masculine cultures and hierarchies of power' (Lori Kendall, 1996, 1998, 2000, 2002).

'Usage of images in the harassment of women has been one of the prominent ways in silencing them in digital spaces. The sophistication of new technologies enables morphing and the constructions of fake images or videos which are often perceived to be 'real' and 'authentic' (Gurumurthy, 2009). In June 2014, a seventeen-year-old schoolgirl committed suicide when a 23-year-old youth, Faisal, uploaded morphed pictures of her on a social networking site. This was a revenge scheme by Faisal, when the young girl refused to reciprocate his advances. Angered by the refusal, he uploaded morphed photographs of the young girl and posted them with her mobile number and message that she was 'seeking friends' and was 'open to relationships' (TNN, 2014). Lecherous predators lurking around, soon swooped in with obscene calls. Feeling trapped and seeing no way out of this predicament, the young girl hung herself. The easy widespread internet access on the internet has made images of women into an immensely sought -after object. It has unprecedented reach and a huge audience who are constantly roving the internet searching for images of willing and unwilling women, to seek and hunt their prey. No sooner than they find one on the internet than they jump in for their kill. 'In the Indian context, images on the internet or through mobile telephones have often been used by stalkers to denigrate, intimidate and harass women on - and off-line (Gurumurthy, 2009). It is interesting to know that Faisal first posted morphed photographs of himself, before uploading pictures of the young girl. The assured confidence that men would not have to face such traumatic phone calls, dared him to carry out this act.

Not only are girls and women targeted more in this space; they also suffer serious consequences; resulting in permanent psychological suffering. The implications of participation of women in cyberspace and the biased rules of the society for women in masculine space are very clearly defined in this case. Faisal was confident that, being a man, his pictures cannot impair his image or his position in society. He also understood that it took just one event of a morphed photograph to intimidate, wreck or destroy the life of a young girl. Unlike men, women are judged and subjected to humiliation by society, often reduced to a 'sex' object. Society does not take kindly to girls who 'dare' in society. Women victims of cybercrime are characterized as emotionally 'weak or unstable'. The girls have to follow the dictum of patriarchy even in cyberspace! 'Despite the indisputable ground-breaking contributions by women to the invention and development of computing technology, today's internet is a contested zone that historically originated as a system to serve war technologies and is currently part of masculinist institutions' (Wilding, 1998).

On November 15, 2017, 23 year old Ooshmal Ullas, an MBBS student of KMCT Medical College in Mukkam, Kerala committed suicide by jumping off the fourth floor of her college building. She was trolled anonymously on her Facebook account which finally led to her death. (TNN, 2017). Most women hesitate to admit and report cases of cyber violence. Studies have highlighted the lack of awareness of the accessible legal support and assistance when encountered such attacks. 'While it is estimated that the number of internet users globally will grow to 5.3 billion by 2023, data regarding cybercrimes on women are not easily available' (O'Dea, 2022). Men are unhesitant go to the authorities to complain on their email or social media used in an unauthorized way. But women can be blacklisted which can submerge them into an abyss of shame and embarrassment. "We are told women who report harassment are "drama queens" and the men who harass them are simply "frat boys" or sad men sitting in their underwear in their mothers' basements. We are blamed for wanting to equitably engage in the public sphere" (Jankowicz, 2022). Moreover, an attack against the image or private life of a person is still not viewed as a cybercrime in many countries including India. Since most violations involving harassment or sexual content online are aimed against women, the gaps in policy and law inevitably compromises on women's rights.

Gendered Power Relations in Digital Spaces

When 20 year old Gurmehar Kaur, in February 2017, launched a campaign on twitter, condemning the Akhil Bharatiya Vidyarthi Parishad, a student's organization with political affiliation, over a campus literary fest, she was trolled mercilessly. Even celebrities, ministers and people from respectable positions joined in, without waiting or looking for the real picture (Shantanu, 2017). This gave a free licence to trolls to get more abusive and issue rape threats. Fake video of a young woman, claiming to be Gurmehar Kaur, seen drinking, singing and dancing in a car began circulating in the social media. The young girl deactivated from social media, unable to withstand the abuse (India Today, 2017). In contrast, during the same time a year before, JNU's Kanhaiya kumar was also trolled allegedly for being an anti-national, but he could not be silenced like Gurmeher Kaur (Jenefa, 2017). EIGE reports how young people's aggressive behaviour online has been largely normalised and that 12 % of 15-year-old girls have been cyber bullied at least once (EIGE, 2018).

When fake images and videos are posted, the women immediately bear the brunt of violence and this force is not just contained within the digital spaces, but extends to a loss of freedom that the internet offers to women. The anonymous constructions of identities in cyberspace have been a multifold increase in the penetration by perpetrators of violence against women. While women enter into this space in hope of a common genderless language, they soon end up unsubscribing from this digital space and also withdraw themselves into silence and isolation thereon. This eventually results in losing opportunities to build a bright career, greater educational opportunities and support networks. 'This type of abuse is the norm for many women engaged in public discourse, particularly those with marginalized identities. We accept that harassment of women is simply the cost of their social media engagement, or worse, that women are expected to endure harassment and silencing in the name of "free speech." It is long past time for that to change (Jankowicz, 2022). When a bully posts something online, without the knowledge of the victim, it can be viewed by hundreds and thousands, before the victim even hears about it. Scores of people would have had the opportunity to view the post or web site and draw their own conclusions. With the internet working ceaselessly, day and night, the victims cannot have time off from bullying. 'At that point, the damage has been done' (Heirman & Walrave, 2008). With people's opinions and judgements still consciously and unconsciously valued in our society, the victim is caught in a terrifying situation when encountered with this news, even if it is fake.

Cyber violence against women continues to be on a rise all over the world, sparing not even the celebrities, social activists or news correspondents. In Jan 2017, Zaira Wasim, the 16 year old 'Dangal' actress from Kashmir, was abused online for acting in the movie. Her actions were called Un-Islamic and her parents were criticised for allowing her to deviate from Islamic teachings (Jenefa, 2017). Matters subdued only after Zaira posted an apology and requested that she not be followed as a role model. Surprisingly male actors like Aamir Bashir from Kashmir are not given the same treatment. "Watching them objectify me is not easy. Watching them deny me and other women our basic democratic and human rights is not easy. And watching these attacks be ignored as "the cost of doing business" in an age where an online presence is all-but-required is enraging (Jankowicz, 2022).

In Mumbai, two 21 year old girls were arrested and humiliated for questioning the complete shutdown of the city of Mumbai after a senior political leader passed away. While it was a harmless question to society, where no names were taken, these young girls were arrested and remanded to 15 days judicial custody. Though the charges were dropped at a later stage, the incident left a deep impression on the girls who have since withdrawn from the social networking sites (Nair, TNN 2012). Senior police have since admitted that it was done in haste and all charges were withdrawn. But it was not until the girls were made to apologise and retreat their comments. These kinds of highhandedness by law enforcers have the potential to restrict women's agency online, potentially undermining their equal participation in digital society. Hall remarks how male interactants have not only been shown to dominate mixed-sex electronic conversation, they have also been identified as frequent instigators of on-line sexual harassment-observations difficult to reconcile with the notion of a gender-neutral utopia. What might be viewed as ''disruptive of the academic social order'' by male participants, is being perceived by an increasing number of female participants as gender-based verbal abuse (Hall, 1996).

TNN reports of how one-third of all cybercrime cases filed in Maharashtra are by women who are victims of stalking, blacking, pornography, fake profiling or morphing and fraud such as cheating and forgery. A report by the National Crime Records Bureau (NCRB) shows that of the total 19536 cyber offences registered from 2018-2021, over 6000 were committed against women (Narayan, TNN, 2022). Cyber psychologists allude to this act by most criminals to be driven by vengeance or sadistic pleasure. Revenge on their minds and the anonymity that the internet provides are the main reasons for cyber offences against women and children. The feel of having powerful control over another makes the whole act pleasurable for these criminals. The internet has given these criminals easy access to spot and approach their targets.

In the name of safety and security, the dominant forces impose restrictions on women's freedoms online. Policies and institutional establishment controlled by reigning forces add narratives and fear around new technologies that can effectively constrain women's freedom to use digital spaces. Many laws are reticent on cyber right and individual protection under the law. For e.g. the International Technology Act of 2000 does not address consent and free will. Therefore, if women engage online in sexual acts of their own violations, they can still be booked under ITA2000, because consent of the parties involved is not considered (Gurumurthy, 2009). Moreover, newer technologies are employed by cyber stalkers and sex industry not only to create more violent forms of pornography material, but they are also used actively to circumvent laws. Many companies simply locate servers in countries where they will not be prosecuted. And with the absence of a global governance framework and lack of territorial jurisdiction over the internet, it becomes difficult to identify the abusers and prosecute the guilty.

Furthermore, women's opinions and sentiments are given little voice in digital spaces. For example, Facebook Inc., which controls Facebook social networking space disallowed advertisement for abortion clinics in several nations, including those which do not prohibit abortions. Thus this network creates new exclusive disadvantages to those voices and participation where many rights depend on their digital citizenship. 'This "brave new world" foreseen by early cyberfeminists has become an anti-utopia fraught with gendered risk, which can then be used to justify current trends in legal responses that include responsibilization, criminalization, and surveillance of women online' (Trevor, 2015). These spaces have the potential to restrict women's agency online, subverting their equal participation in digital society.

Redefining the Gendered Cyberspace

It's time for a broader reflection about women's space in cyberspace and wake up to the response to issues of violence against women in cyberspace. The challenge lies in addressing the realities and restructuring the framework. 'If cyberfeminists wish to avoid making the mistakes of past feminists, they must understand the history of feminist struggle (Wilding, 1998). Questions on how feminists can provide empowerment to women, especially those who have been victimized or targeted should be addressed. The demand for policies to protect and safeguards the privacy of women, have transparency and accountability in all server domains should be stepped up. 'By far the most urgent feminist response that is required is to stop seeing digital and online spaces as a different realm confined to technological users, by an important site of power that requires a feminist intervention' (Gurumurthy, 2009).

It should also emphasise on the freedom of self-expressions with concerns of protection from exploitation. Those engaged in violence against women, and those infringing on women's privacy should be prosecuted by law enforcers while sending a message of warning to those who trespass the boundaries. Such prosecution will 'begin to challenge arbitrary normative standards of online gender performance and ultimately critique online spaces and current policy initiatives for how they entrench these sexist narratives (Trevor, 2015).

Opportunity and flexibility should be offered to girls and women on online platforms in ways that enable them to manifest their embodied selves. The possibility of an utopian platform may be a far-fetched vision, but ideal alternative societies built on positive and creative positions is a fair vision to explore. To work towards this, forces have to work stronger to ensure that women and girls have a voice in discourses on gender and virtual space. This would be crucial to move beyond patriarchal binary thought, thereby increasing women's and girls' online agency, and constructing virtual spaces that reflect better gender equality. In order to be both effective and impressive, narratives would need to move beyond the negativity and shift towards more productive engagements with possible solutions for current social and economic inequalities.

REFERENCES

Braidotti, R. (1994). *Nomadic Subjects: Embodiment and Sexual Difference in Contemporary Feminist Theory*. Columbia University Press.

Cross-cultural Perspectives. (1996). John Benjamins Publishing Company.

Daniels, J. (2009, Spring - Summer). Rethinking Cyberfeminism(s): Race, Gender, and Embodiment. *Women's Studies Quarterly*, *37*(1-2), 101–124.

EIGE. (2022). *Combating Cyber Violence against Women and Girls*. European Institute for Gender Equality. https://eige.europa.eu/publications/cyber-violence-against-women-and-girls-key-terms-and-concepts

EIGE. (2017). *Cyber violence against women and girls*. https://eige.europa.eu/publications/cyber-violence-against-women-and-girls

Enzer, M. (2023). *Glossary of Internet Terms*. https://www.matisse.net/files/glossary.html

Gill, R. (2005). Review: Techno feminism! *Science as Culture*, *14*(1), 97–101. doi:10.1080/09505430500042130

Girl Kills self over Facebook Harassment. (2014). https://timesofindia.indiatimes.com/city/kolkata/girl-kills-self-over-facebook-harassment/articleshow/37211521.cms

Gurumurthy, A., & Menon, N. (2009). Violence against Women via Cyberspace. *Economic and Political Weekly*, *44*(40), 19-21.

Haraway, D. J. (1990). *Simians, Cyborgs and Women: The Reinvention of Nature*. Routledge.

Heirman, W., & Walrave, M. (2008). Assessing concerns and issues about the mediation of technology in cyberbullying. *Cyberpsychology (Brno)*, *2*(2), 1.

Jankowicz, N. (2022). *How to be a woman online: Surviving Abuse and Harassment and How to Fight Back*. Bloomsbury Publishing.

Jenefa, S. (2017). Social Media as a Tool of Violence against Women. *World Journal of Science and Research*, *2*(2), 77–82.

Kendall, L. (1998). Meaning and identity in 'Cyberspace': The Performance of Gender, Class and Race Online. *Symbolic Interaction*, *21*(2), 129–153. doi:10.1525i.1998.21.2.129

Kroker, Arthur, & Marilousie. (1993). *The Last Sex: Feminism and Outlaw Bodies*. New World Perspectives Culture Texts Series.

Lenhart, A., Madden, M., Smith, A., Purcell, K., Zickuhr, K., & Rainie, L. (2011). *Teens, kindness and cruelty on social network sites*. Retrieved on 17 March 2015 from https://www.pewinternet.org/2011/11/09/teens-kindness-and-cruelty-on-social-network-sites/

Look, J. J. (1999). The Virtual Wild, Wild West (www): Intellectual Property Issues in Cyberspace—Trademarks, Service Marks, Copyrights, and Domain Names. *U. Ark. Little Rock. Rev., 22*(49).

Milford, T. S. (2015). Chapter. In J. Bailey & V. Steeves (Eds.), Revisiting Cyberfeminism: Theory as a Tool for Understanding Young Women's Experiences, eGirls, eCitizens (pp. 55–81). University of Ottawa Press.

Nair, S. (2012). *Shame: 2 girls arrested for harmless online comment*. https://timesofindia.indiatimes.com/city/mumbai/shame-2-girls-arrested-for-harmless-online-comment/articleshow/17286105.cms

O'Dea, S. (2022). *Global internet user growth 2018-2023*. https://www.statista.com/statistics/1190263/internet-users-worldwide/

Pokin, S. (2007, Nov. 13). Megan Meier story. *St. Charles Journal*.

Police suspect cyber bullying behind MBBS student's death TNN. (2017). https://timesofindia.indiatimes.com/city/kozhikode/police-suspect-cyber-bullying-behind-mbbs-students-death/articleshow/61684722.cms

Stanley, A. (1995). *Mothers and Daughters of Invention: Notes for a Revised History of Technology*. Rutgers University Press.

Susanna, P. (2011). Revisiting cyberfeminism. *Communications*, *36*, 335–352.

Today, I. (2017). *Gurmehar Kaur's mother to India Today*. https://www.indiatoday.in/india/story/gurmehar-kaur-mother-rajvinder-kaur-ramjas-college-delhi-university-963358-2017-03-01

Wilding, F. (1998). *Where is the Feminism in Cyberfeminism?* Paradoxa, 2.

Wilding, F., & Ensemble, C. A. (1998, Summer). Notes on the Political Condition of Cyberfeminism. *Art Journal*, *57*(2), 46–59. doi:10.1080/00043249.1998.10791878

Women targets in 30% Maharashtra cybercrime cases: NCRB by Narayan Namboodiri. (2022). https://timesofindia.indiatimes.com/city/mumbai/women-targets-in-30-maharashtra-cybercrime-cases-ncrb/articleshow/94124534.cms

Chapter 8
Towards a Cyberfeminist Framework for Addressing Gender-Based Violence in Social Media:
An Introduction

Subhajit Panda
https://orcid.org/0000-0002-1578-1159
Chandigarh University, India

ABSTRACT

This chapter provides a comprehensive overview of gender-based violence in social media and explores strategies to combat this issue. Objectives include examining various types of violence, exploring offline impact, investigating COVID-19 effects on gender-based violence in India, and discussing intersectionality, embodiment, resistance, and community-based interventions. Intersectionality's crucial role in understanding violence is highlighted, emphasizing the need to validate survivors' experiences. It evaluates social media companies' involvement and stresses grassroots activism's significance in challenging oppression. The conclusion emphasizes the urgency for action, sustained research, and advocacy to establish safe and inclusive online environments. It recommends exploring innovative interventions, evaluating existing policies, and understanding evolving dynamics to achieve a violence-free digital future.

INTRODUCTION

Social media has become an integral part of modern society, revolutionizing communication, interaction, and information sharing (Dwivedi et al., 2021). Its widespread usage has opened up unprecedented avenues for individuals to connect, express their thoughts, and engage in public discussions. However, this digital realm has also facilitated the emergence of disturbing forms of gender-based violence, which have a disproportionate impact on women and marginalized communities.

DOI: 10.4018/978-1-6684-8893-5.ch008

Gender-based violence (GBV) stands as a highly pervasive infringement upon human rights, prevailing extensively across the globe. GBV is commonly defined as "any form of violence that results in, or is likely to result in, physical, sexual or psychological harm or suffering to women, including threats of such acts, coercion or arbitrary deprivations of liberty, whether occurring in public or in private life" (United Nations 1993). In social media, GBV encompasses a range of harmful behaviors and actions directed at individuals based on their gender, perpetuated through digital platforms. Online gender-based violence (OGBV), such as, online harassment, doxxing, revenge porn, and cyberstalking are just a few examples of the pervasive and damaging violence that can occur in these digital spaces (Dunn, 2020) (European Institute for Gender Equality, 2022). What makes this form of violence particularly troubling is its potential to extend beyond the online realm, infiltrating the offline lives of its victims and causing long-lasting harm.

In response to the intricate challenges posed by gender-based violence in social media, cyberfeminism has emerged as a critical framework. Cyberfeminism combines feminist principles (Plant, 2020) with a critical examination of technology, aiming to illuminate power dynamics, societal inequalities, and the intersections of gender, race, sexuality, and other identities within digital spaces (Allen, 2022). By employing a cyberfeminist lens, a deeper understanding of the nature and implications of gender-based violence in social media can be gained, while also exploring strategies to effectively challenge and combat it.

This chapter explores the intersection of cyberfeminism and gender-based violence on social media, offering insights and solutions. It examines various types of violence and their impact, highlighting principles such as intersectionality, embodiment, and resistance. By integrating these principles, the chapter aims to promote accountability, empowerment, and equitable online communities. It addresses challenges, including social media company accountability, and proposes technological, educational, and community-based strategies. Overall, it contributes to the literature on cyberfeminism and gender-based violence, advocating for a comprehensive approach centered on accountability, empowerment, and resistance.

BACKGROUND STUDY

Cyberfeminism has emerged as a critical field of study that examines the relationship between women and the Internet, with a focus on investigating power dynamics, access to technology, and the potential perpetuation of gender inequities in digital spaces. While research on cyberfeminism originated in the late 1990s, there is ongoing exploration and investigation due to the evolving nature of digital threats. The following research studies contribute to the foundational understanding of cyberfeminism and provide insights into current trends and challenges in the field:

Cunningham and Crandall (2014) argued that nonprofit organizations, heavily reliant on social media, offered opportunities to apply cyberfeminist goals and explore the interplay of gender and technology. Schlesselman-Tarango (2014) incorporated feminist pedagogy and critical information literacy, emphasizing the empowerment of students through digital technologies to challenge dominant narratives and foster inclusion and diversity in information resources.

Mohanty and Samantaray (2017) explored the potential of cyberspace for female emancipation, highlighting women's utilization of digital platforms for personal empowerment and advocating for countering the predominant male influence in information and communication technology. They emphasized the importance of incorporating a female perspective in the perception of technology. Verma et al. (2018) analyzed successful online campaigns on social media platforms like Facebook, Twitter, and Instagram, illustrating their contribution to women's empowerment and global feminist discourse.

Koo (2019) investigated the South Korean cyberfeminist community, Womad, within the context of trolling. The study explored the interaction between Womad's identity politics and trolling tactics, influenced by the specific characteristics of its platform and the broader South Korean cultural context, shedding light on the formation of a distinct counterpublic. Lestari et al. (2020) conducted qualitative research on cyberfeminism through the Female Daily Network's #YourBeautyRules campaign in Indonesia, highlighting its potential to educate and develop women by prioritizing character and self-development.

Tazi and Oumlil (2020) examined the role of information and communication technologies in fourth-wave feminism during the Arab Spring in the MENA region. Through case studies from Egypt, Tunisia, and Lebanon, the authors explored how feminist activists utilized online platforms to advocate for gender equality and broader social justice issues, emphasizing their significant contributions during the Arab Spring.

Gurunathan (2022) focused on the treatment of women in video games and analyzed cyberfeminist perspectives within The Witcher 3: Wild Hunt, shedding light on gender stereotypes and normative policing in online gaming. The study explored how cyberfeminism viewed technology as a liberating force, empowering women to express themselves and succeed in various domains. Toto and Scarinci (2022) delved into cyberfeminism as the "third wave" of feminism, examining its social and cultural aspects, including the impact of digital products such as online magazines, YouTube channels, and webinars in challenging gender inequalities and shaping societal perceptions.

Kiani et al. (2023) adopted a cyberfeminist perspective to investigate the role of cyberworlds and virtual tourism in providing liberating travel experiences for women, focusing on Iranian women in the vTime virtual world. The study explored the extent to which virtual tourism allowed women to overcome travel-related constraints and achieve self-determination. The findings revealed that while virtual tourism offered some freedom, women's self-expression and activities were still restricted by patriarchal concerns, surveillance, legal consequences, harassment, stigma, and Western dominance.

Collectively, these studies contributed to the literature on cyberfeminism by exploring various aspects of its application and impact, including nonprofit organizations, feminist pedagogy, online campaigns, cultural contexts, video games, media representation, and virtual experiences. They shed light on the potential of cyberfeminism to empower women, challenge gender inequalities, and advocate for social justice in both online and offline spheres.

STATUS OF WOMEN IN G20 COUNTRIES

The Group of Twenty (G20) consists of 19 nations, including Argentina, Australia, Brazil, Canada, China, France, Germany, India, Indonesia, Italy, Japan, Republic of Korea, Mexico, Russia, Saudi Arabia, South Africa, Turkey, United Kingdom, and United States, along with the European Union. Together, the G20 member countries represent about 85% of the world's GDP, over 75% of global trade, and approximately two-thirds of the global population (National Portal of India, n.d.). Given the impracticality of studying each country and continent individually, the G20 can serve as a means to obtain a comprehensive overview of the social status of women worldwide.

Table 1. Gender-based violence (OGBV or TF GBV), preventive measures, gender inequality, and gap index in G20 countries

Country	Violence*		Measures*		Gender Inequality Index Rank**	Global Gender Gap Index Rank***
	Forms	Numbers	Types	Numbers		
Argentina	6	104	10	131	69	33
Australia	9	247	10	208	19	43
Brazil	4	12	3	11	94	94
Canada	9	208	9	220	17	25
China	5	35	9	34	48	102
France	9	195	10	132	22	15
Germany	9	108	9	102	19	10
India	8	148	9	124	122	135
Indonesia	6	31	6	33	110	92
Italy	7	40	8	28	13	63
Japan	6	77	8	59	22	116
Republic of Korea	5	56	9	53	15	99
Mexico	6	112	10	82	75	31
Russia	5	25	6	23	50	Data not available
Saudi Arabia	4	19	6	24	59	127
South Africa	8	30	6	24	97	20
Turkiye	9	54	7	44	65	124
United Kingdom	9	156	9	105	27	22
United States	7	58	7	45	44	27

*Source: UN Women (2023)
**Source: United Nations (2022)
***Source: World Economic Forum (2022)

Table 1 presents data on violence against women, available preventive measures, the gender inequality index rank, and the global gender gap index rank for all G20 countries. The data reveals that Canada and Germany exhibit the highest level of gender equality, while India and Indonesia rank the lowest. Taking a broader perspective, it becomes evident that the South Asian region lags significantly behind in achieving gender equality.

NEED OF THE STUDY

The aforementioned results clearly indicate that our world is significantly lagging behind in bridging the gender gap. According to the Global Gender Gap Report 2022 (World Economic Forum, 2022), the North American regions are projected to be the closest to achieving gender parity, with an estimated time frame of 59 years (Figure 1). On the other hand, the South Asian regions face a daunting timeline

Figure 1. At current space when the regions are likely to close the gender gap
Source: World Economic Forum (2022)

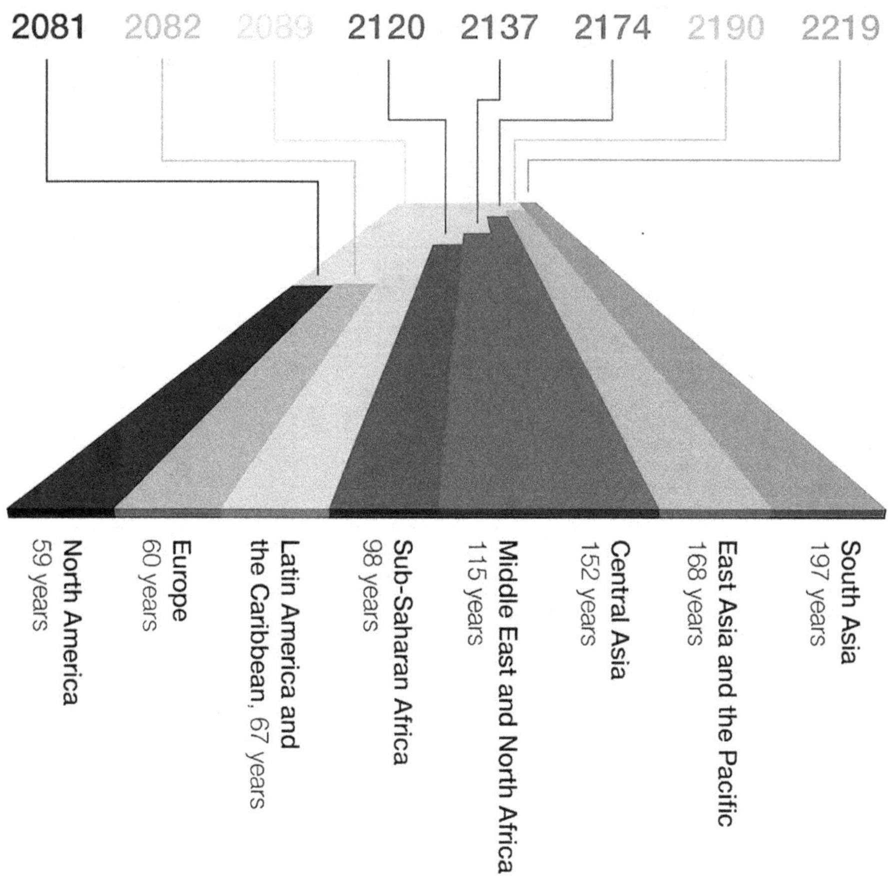

of 197 years to close the gender gap (Figure 1). These findings emphasize the urgent need for increased awareness regarding the status of women in our society and the pervasive violence they endure in their daily lives. Furthermore, in the age of social media, it is crucial to examine their representation and experiences in digital spaces. This study is essential to meet the social needs of our era, as it aims to shed light on the realities faced by women and address the pressing issues surrounding gender-based violence in digital spaces.

STUDY OBJECTIVES

The primary objectives of the book chapter are to:

1. Provide an overview of gender-based violence in social media, examining its various types and manifestations.
2. Explore the offline impact of online gender-based violence (OGBV) or tech-facilitated gender-based violence (TF GBV), emphasizing the interconnectedness between online and offline experiences.

3. Investigate the specific effects of COVID-19 on OGBV or TF GBV, with a focus on the Indian context.
4. Examine the concept of intersectionality and its relevance in understanding the multiple dimensions of gender-based violence, considering the intersecting identities and experiences of individuals.
5. Explore the principle of embodiment, emphasizing the emotional impact of gender-based violence and the importance of recognizing and validating survivors' experiences.
6. Discuss the role of resistance in shifting power dynamics and working towards change, highlighting strategies and approaches that challenge oppressive structures.
7. Identify and analyze the challenges faced in addressing OGBV or TF GBV in social media, including barriers, limitations, and complexities associated with combating this issue.
8. Evaluate the role of social media companies in combating OGBV or TF GBV, examining their response, policies, and enforcement mechanisms.
9. Explore grassroots activism and community-based interventions as effective strategies for addressing gender-based violence, emphasizing the importance of community engagement and empowerment.
10. Propose a multi-faceted approach to address the challenges associated with OGBV or TF GBV in social media, emphasizing collaboration, regulation, and advocacy for accountability, empowerment, and resistance.

RESEARCH METHODOLOGY

The current study primarily adopts a qualitative approach to analyze and structure evidence-based report data, aiming to identify the underlying causes behind OGBV or TF GBV. The data used in this study was collected from various survey reports conducted by government bodies, NGOs, and other organizations. Additionally, the principles studied here are drawn from several previous research studies. The challenges and future scope identified in this research stem from gaps and limitations observed in both previous and current research. Furthermore, this study highlights areas where further investigation is required to gain a comprehensive understanding of OGBV or TF GBV and to develop effective strategies for combating it.

GENDER-BASED VIOLENCE IN SOCIAL MEDIA: OVERVIEW AND CASE STUDIES

In recent years, gender-based violence has infiltrated the realm of social media, presenting substantial challenges for individuals and communities alike. While online platforms were once celebrated for fostering connectivity and self-expression, they have now become breeding grounds for diverse forms of gender-based violence, particularly targeting women and marginalized groups. A study by the Economist Intelligence Unit revealed that an average of 85% of 4,500 women surveyed across 45 countries reported experiencing or witnessing online abuse, with even higher percentages in regions such as the Middle East, Latin America, and Africa (Meco & MacKay, 2022). Tactics such as misinformation and defamation are commonly employed to silence women, limiting their ability to voice their opinions online and, in some cases, effectively excluding them from the digital political landscape.

This section aims to provide an overview of gender-based violence in social media, examining its manifestations and impact, and presenting case studies that highlight its alarming prevalence and consequences.

What Is Online Gender Based Violence (OGBV) or Technology-Facilitated Gender-Based Violence (TF GBV)?

According to UN Women (2022), "Online Gender Based Violence (OGBV) or Technology-facilitated gender-based violence (TF GBV) is any act that is committed, assisted, aggravated or amplified by the use of information communication technologies or other digital tools which results in or is likely to result in physical, sexual, psychological, social, political or economic harm or other infringements of rights and freedoms."

Types of OGBV or TF GBV in Social Media

There is an alarming array of gender-based violence (OGBV or TF GBV) that manifests in social media platforms. These types of violence target individuals based on their gender and can have severe consequences for their well-being.

Recognizing the diverse manifestations of OGBV or TF GBV is essential for effectively addressing and combating these issues. Some of the prominent types (Figure 2) of OGBV or TF GBV observed in social media include (Dwivedi, 2022) (WMC, n.d.):

Figure 2. Types of online or technology facilitated gender-based violence
Source: The Dart Center (2018)

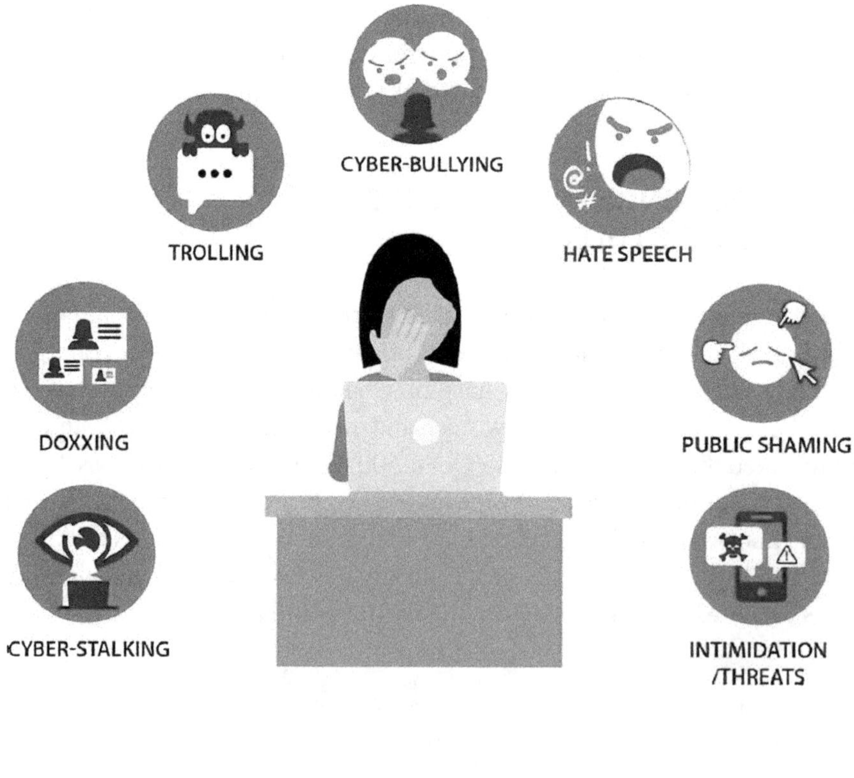

Online Harassment

Online harassment is the deliberate and persistent targeting of individuals with abusive, threatening, or offensive behavior on social media platforms. It involves the use of derogatory language, hate speech, or threats to intimidate, humiliate, or instill fear in the victim.

Doxxing

Doxxing is the act of publicly revealing and sharing someone's private and personal information without their consent. This includes details such as their real name, home address, phone number, workplace, or other sensitive data. Perpetrators engage in doxxing with the intention to expose, shame, threaten, or incite harm against the targeted individual, leading to severe consequences such as offline harassment, stalking, or physical violence.

Revenge Porn

Revenge porn, or non-consensual pornography, refers to the distribution or sharing of intimate or sexually explicit images or videos of a person without their consent. Perpetrators use these materials to seek revenge, exert control, or humiliate the victims, causing severe emotional distress and damaging personal relationships. The act is a serious violation of consent and privacy, leading to social, professional, and psychological consequences for the victims.

Cyberstalking

Cyberstalking is the persistent and unwanted surveillance, tracking, and monitoring of an individual's online activities. It involves using digital tools to harass, intimidate, and frighten the victim, causing distress and impacting their sense of security and well-being.

Image Manipulation and Deepfake

Image manipulation is the unauthorized alteration of someone's images to demean, degrade, or misrepresent them. It involves digitally modifying photographs or creating fake images, including deepfakes, to depict the targeted individual in explicit or compromising situations. These techniques are used to perpetuate harm, humiliation, and harassment.

Online Bullying and Trolling

Online bullying involves repetitive and intentional hurtful or threatening behavior targeting individuals, often carried out by a group to provoke emotional distress. Trolling, on the other hand, entails deliberately inciting others through offensive statements and actions. Both practices create toxic online environments and harm the mental health of victims.

Non-Inclusive Online Spaces

Non-inclusive online spaces exclude and marginalize individuals based on their identity factors, perpetuating systemic inequalities and silencing marginalized voices. This occurs through restrictive rules, biased algorithms, and discriminatory attitudes and behaviors, limiting the participation and expression of marginalized groups.

The Offline Impact of OGBV or TF GBV

The OGBV or TF GBV also involves attempts to silence and discredit women online, including threats of offline violence (UN Women, 2022). The offline consequences of digital gender-based violence are significant, with studies showing psychological distress, physical safety concerns, social isolation, professional and educational repercussions, and negative impacts on health and well-being (General Assembly, United Nations, 2022; World Wide Web Foundation, 2020).

Psychological Distress

The OGBV or TF GBV can have significant psychological effects on its victims. Studies have found that individuals subjected to online harassment, cyberstalking, or revenge porn often experience increased levels of anxiety, depression, and stress (Sánchez et al., 2018; Felt et al., 2016). The emotional toll of these experiences can spill over into various aspects of their lives, affecting their mental well-being and overall quality of life.

Physical Safety Concerns

In some cases, OGBV or TF GBV can escalate to physical threats or acts of violence in offline spaces. Research has highlighted instances where online harassers transition from online abuse to real-life stalking, assault, or harassment (Douglas et al., 2019). This crossover poses significant risks to the physical safety and security of victims, necessitating the need for proactive measures to prevent offline harm.

Social Isolation and Withdrawal

Victims of OGBV or TF GBV may also face social repercussions, including social isolation and withdrawal. The fear of continued abuse or public humiliation can lead individuals to limit their social interactions, both online and offline, and withdraw from activities they once enjoyed (Douglas et al., 2019). This isolation can have detrimental effects on their social relationships, support networks, and overall sense of belonging.

Professional and Educational Consequences

The offline impact of OGBV or TF GBV extends to professional and educational domains. Victims may face reputational damage, job loss, or reduced employment opportunities due to the dissemination of harmful content or the targeting of their online presence (EPRS, 2021). Similarly, students who experience digital gender-based violence may encounter difficulties in their academic performance, concentration, and overall educational experience.

Health and Well-Being

The OGBV or TF GBV can have a direct impact on the physical health and well-being of individuals. Research has demonstrated links between online harassment, cyberstalking, and negative health outcomes, including sleep disturbances, somatic symptoms, and self-reported health issues (Douglas et al., 2019; Nixon, 2016). The stress and trauma associated with these experiences can undermine one's overall health and contribute to long-term health complications.

COVID-19 AND ITS IMPACT ON OGBV OR TF GBV

Violence against women (VAW) is a violation of human rights that affects individuals, families, and communities worldwide. The COVID-19 pandemic has exacerbated this issue as economic and social stress, coupled with movement restrictions and social isolation measures, have led to a significant increase in gender-based violence (United Nations, 2020). During the pandemic, violence against women has taken various forms, including domestic violence and online and technology-facilitated violence (UN Women, 2020). These forms of violence occur within a broader context of pervasive gender-based discrimination.

Women disproportionately face online and technology-facilitated violence, with certain groups experiencing higher risks. Research shows that women and girls are targeted more frequently than men, and the forms of violence they encounter are interconnected. Specific groups at heightened risk include human rights defenders, women in politics, journalists, bloggers, ethnic minorities, indigenous women, lesbian, bisexual, transgender women, and women with disabilities. In Europe, young women aged 18 to 29 are particularly vulnerable European Union, 2018). For example, in the United States, two out of every ten young women in this age group have experienced online sexual harassment, and half have received unsolicited explicit images (UN Women, 2020).

Amid the COVID-19 pandemic, women and girls have been increasingly utilizing the internet, although a gender digital divide persists (Foleon.com, 2019). This global health crisis has been characterized as the first major pandemic in the era of social media, with over half of the world's population subjected to lockdown measures by early April, 2020 (Molla, 2020). As quarantine and self-isolation policies have been implemented, internet usage has surged by 50% to 70% (Beech, 2020), as individuals, including women and men, rely on the internet for work, education, and social interactions. However, individuals with limited digital skills are particularly vulnerable to cyberviolence during this period. It is alarming to note that the digital gender divide exacerbates the risk for women and girls, heightening their susceptibility to various forms of online violence (OECD, 2018).

In this context, online violence against women and girls has emerged as a shadow pandemic alongside violence against women. Physical threats, sexual harassment, stalking, zoombombing, and sex trolling are prevalent forms of online violence experienced by women and girls. Media reports and women's rights organizations have documented cases of unsolicited pornographic videos displayed during online social events, threats of violence, sexist content, and racially charged and sexually explicit material "zoombombing" video calls, catching participants off guard (Glaser et al., 2020; Loots et al., 2020; Mudgway & Jones, 2020).

Data from the eSafety Commissioner in Australia shows a 50% increase in online abuse and bullying in the starting months of pandemic (Australia News, 2020). Europol reports a rise in online activity related to child abuse material in Europe, while the Commission on Human Rights in the Philippines has observed a surge in peer-to-peer online violence against women and girls during the quarantine period (Europol, 2020). Additionally, pornographic traffic has dramatically increased, heightening the risk of sextortion globally (UNODC, 2020).

Furthermore, the reduced number of specialized justice officers in cyberviolence during 2020 poses a greater risk of OGBV or TF GBV. As a result, cases of OGBV or TF GBV against women and girls are likely to continue rising even after the emergency phase, as enforcement weakens and internet usage remains high.

Indian Context

Online violence in India has witnessed a steady surge, with women reporting a higher incidence of such violence compared to men. Extensive research conducted by the International Center for Research on Women (ICRW) and Quilt.AI delved into the prevalence of online violence and associated behaviors in India, both prior to and during the pandemic (ICRW & Quilt.AI, 2021).

The research study focused on four urban areas, namely Bengaluru, Delhi, Mumbai, and Kolkata, along with four rural areas, including Assagao, Kangra, Palakkad, and Gaya. By analyzing discourse across various social media platforms and search engines, key trends were identified. These findings served as the basis for formulating recommendations targeting technology companies, policymakers, and non-governmental organizations (NGOs), aimed at enhancing preparedness for future crises.

Upon analyzing the search results in four urban areas, namely Bengaluru, Delhi, Kolkata, and Mumbai (Table 2), several significant findings emerge. Firstly, keywords related to exploitation garnered the highest search volumes across all four cities, closely followed by the domain of hacking. The emerging trend of doxxing, the act of publicly revealing personal information, exhibited notable increases in search interest, with Delhi experiencing a growth of 214% and Mumbai following closely at 211%. Bengaluru and Kolkata also demonstrated substantial interest with growth rates of 191% and 169% respectively. Additionally, there was increased curiosity surrounding image-based abuse and gender trolling. Hacking emerged as a persisting issue, with high search volume and growth across all four cities, suggesting its long-standing presence as a problem in these geographical areas. Notably, Delhi showcased the highest growth in searches for doxxing and image-based abuse (214% and 120% respectively) compared to the other cities, both before and during the COVID-19 pandemic.

In the study of rural areas, data from Assagao, Kangra, Palakkad, and Gaya were examined (Table 3). The search volumes of keywords in the Hacking and Exploitation category were generally well-established, while Doxxing was observed to be growing in many cities. During the COVID-19 period, there was a significant increase in help-seeking searches in Kangra, with a growth rate of 174%. Palakkad followed with a growth rate of 129%, and Gaya with 71%. These findings highlight the evolving search behaviors and concerns of individuals in rural areas, shedding light on the specific challenges they face in terms of online security and seeking assistance during times of crisis.

Table 2. A snapshot of search volume and growth: Sample urban cities in India

Category	Bengaluru, Karnataka		Kolkata, West Bengal		Mumbai, Maharashtra		New Delhi, Delhi	
	Search Volume during COVID	Growth in Interest*	Search Volume during COVID	Growth in Interest*	Search Volume during COVID	Growth in Interest*	Search Volume during COVID	Growth in Interest*
Doxxing	10%	191%	6%	169%	9%	211%	8%	214%
Exploitation	34%	37%	37%	49%	34%	33%	36%	48%
Gendertrolling	4%	62%	3%	65%	3%	67%	3%	54%
Hacking	38%	70%	34%	65%	38%	61%	34%	66%
Image based abuse	0%	55%	1%	58%	0%	96%	0%	120%
Sexual harassment	1%	9%	1%	28%	1%	-8%	1%	13%
Stalking	6%	20%	9%	53%	9%	43%	7%	23%
Threatening	1%	39%	1%	57%	1%	3%	1%	57%
Using fake accounts	6%	15%	8%	-2%	6%	41%	9%	33%

Source: ICRW and Quilt.AI (2021)
*pre vs during COVID

Table 3. A snapshot of search volume and growth: Sample rural cities in India

Category	Assagao, Goa		Gaya, Bihar		Kangra, Himachal Pradesh		Palakkad, Kerala	
	Search Volume During COVID	Growth in Interest*	Search Volume During COVID	Growth in Interest*	Search Volume during COVID	Growth in Interest*	Search Volume During COVID	Growth in Interest*
Doxxing	22%	600%	11%	267%	8%	132%	6%	150%
Exploitation	34%	-21%	28%	78%	22%	51%	23%	117%
Gendertrolling	6%	20%	6%	256%	6%	83%	8%	58%
Hacking	19%	-14%	29%	89%	42%	107%	47%	147%
Image based abuse	0%	0%	0%	0%	0%	0%	1%	67%
Sexual harassment	3%	0%	3%	30%	2%	50%	1%	22%
Stalking	9%	-25%	15%	95%	14%	95%	10%	58%
Threatening	3%	10%	3%	0%	1%	-27%	1%	13%
Using fake accounts	3%	10%	5%	115%	5%	93%	4%	147%

Source: ICRW and Quilt.AI (2021)
*pre vs during COVID

INTERSECTIONALITY: UNDERSTANDING THE MULTIPLE DIMENSIONS OF GENDER-BASED VIOLENCE

The Principle of Intersectionality in Cyberfeminism

Intersectionality, introduced by Kimberlé Williams Crenshaw in 1989, recognizes the simultaneous discrimination faced by Black women due to racism and sexism. Crenshaw criticized prevailing approaches for their narrow focus on privileged members within marginalized groups. Intersectionality refers to how multiple forms of inequality compound and create unique obstacles beyond conventional thinking (Crenshaw, 1989).

Intersectionality in cyberfeminism acknowledges that individuals possess interconnected identities that influence their experiences in digital spaces. It recognizes that gender-based violence cannot be examined in isolation and must be understood in relation to other social categories such as race, class, sexuality, and disability (Figure 3). This principle highlights the need to consider how power structures and systems of oppression operate online, taking into account the intersections of gender with other identities. By recognizing the unique challenges faced by marginalized women and amplifying their voices, cyberfeminism aims to dismantle inequalities and discrimination in digital spaces. An inclusive and intersectional approach is essential for understanding and addressing gender-based violence, promoting change, and creating safer online environments for everyone.

Figure 3. Visual representation of intersectionality

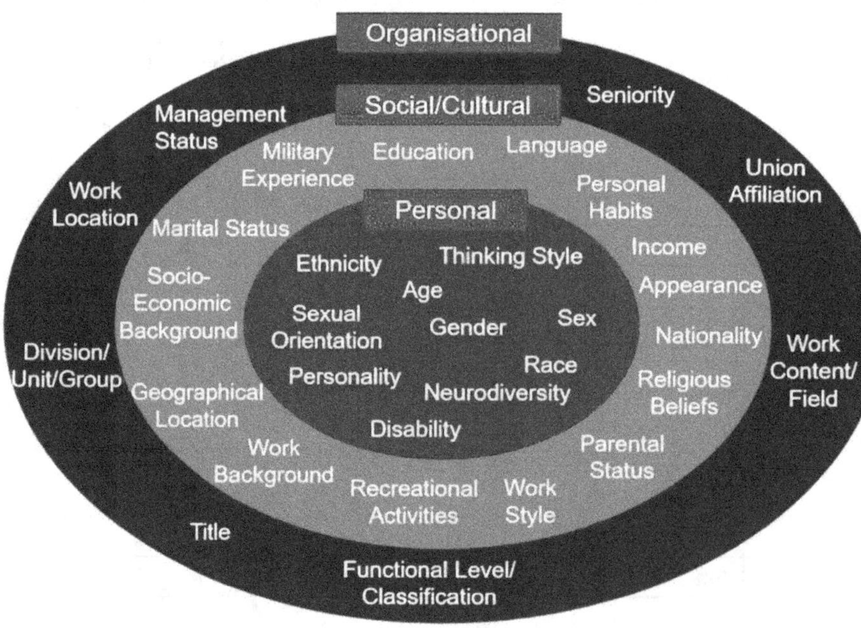

Identity Intersections and Gender-Based Violence in Digital Spaces

Intersectionality acknowledges that gender-based violence in digital spaces is influenced by the intersection of different social identities. Understanding the complex dynamics requires considering how various identities intersect with experiences of gender-based violence. Here are key points on identity intersections and online gender-based violence:

Race and Gender

Women from racial and ethnic minority backgrounds often face unique forms of gender-based violence online, such as racialized sexism or misogynoir. Their experiences are influenced by both their gender and racial identities, leading to specific types of harassment and discrimination.

Class and Gender

Socioeconomic factors intersect with gender to shape experiences of online violence. Women from lower socioeconomic backgrounds may face economic exploitation, cyberbullying related to their social status, or limited access to resources and support.

Sexuality and Gender

LGBTQ+ individuals, particularly transgender and non-binary people, are disproportionately targeted with online violence. They face specific forms of harassment, including transphobic and homophobic abuse, which intersect with their gender and sexual identities.

Disability and Gender

Women with disabilities encounter unique challenges in digital spaces, including ableist discrimination and online harassment that targets their disability. Their experiences of gender-based violence are influenced by both their gender and disability status.

Age and Gender

Different age groups may experience distinct forms of gender-based violence online. Young women and girls are particularly vulnerable to online harassment, cyberbullying, and revenge porn, while older women may face ageist discrimination and exclusion.

Addressing Multiple Forms of Oppression

In addressing gender-based violence in digital spaces, it is crucial to acknowledge and respond to the interconnected nature of multiple forms of oppression. Gender-based violence intersects with racism, ableism, homophobia, transphobia, and classism, requiring a comprehensive approach. Understanding these intersections provides insights into the complex dynamics contributing to online gender-based violence. Neglecting the interconnected forms of oppression overlooks the unique challenges faced by individuals with multiple marginalized identities. Taking a holistic approach involves challenging systemic inequalities and power structures that perpetuate discrimination and violence. Inclusive and intersectional policies and interventions are necessary to address multiple forms of oppression and prioritize marginalized individuals' experiences. Amplifying the voices of those most impacted by intersecting systems of oppression and involving them in decision-making processes is crucial. By adopting this approach, safer and more equitable online environments can be created for all.

EMBODIMENT: RECOGNIZING THE EMOTIONAL IMPACT OF GENDER-BASED VIOLENCE

The Principle of Embodiment in Cyberfeminism

Female embodiment refers to how a woman's self-perception is shaped by her body's experiences in the world, impacting her body image and identity. Embracing positive female embodiment empowers women to reclaim their bodies, strengthen their sense of self, express themselves freely, and live without societal pressures (Chrisler & Johnston-Robledo, 2018). This concept draws from Merleau-Ponty's philosophical ideas (Moya, 2014) that emphasize the role of bodily experiences in shaping our understanding of the world. In psychology, embodiment recognizes the inseparable connection between our physical experiences and our thoughts, emotions, and behaviors.

The principle of embodiment in cyberfeminism recognizes the importance of the body's relationship to technology and digital spaces. It challenges the separation between the physical and virtual realms, acknowledging that individuals are embodied beings with physical experiences and vulnerabilities online. This principle examines how gendered power structures shape our interactions with technology, perpetuating stereotypes, biases, and inequalities. It addresses the objectification and violation of the body in digital spaces, leading to gender-based violence. Cyberfeminism seeks to redefine the body in digital contexts, promoting agency, empowerment, and inclusivity. It advocates for diverse bodies, challenges normative ideals, and calls for safe and inclusive online spaces that respect bodily autonomy and privacy. Overall, the principle of embodiment in cyberfeminism aims to challenge gendered power dynamics, creating a more inclusive and equitable online environment.

Emotional Impact of Online Harassment and Violence

Online harassment and violence cause emotional harm, impacting individuals' well-being and psychological state. Understanding the depth of this harm is crucial for effective intervention. Being targeted with online harassment evokes negative emotions such as fear, anxiety, humiliation, anger, and distress. These emotions disrupt individuals' sense of safety, personal identity, and self-esteem. Key domains affected include:

Emotional Toll

Online harassment and violence can cause significant emotional harm to individuals, leading to negative emotional experiences such as fear, anxiety, humiliation, anger, and distress.

Sense of Threat and Insecurity

Repeated and sustained attacks in online harassment create a constant sense of threat and insecurity, disrupting an individual's sense of safety and well-being.

Loss of Control and Invasion of Personal Space

Online harassment can make victims feel a loss of control over their online presence, resulting in a violation and invasion of their personal space.

Psychological Consequences

The psychological toll of online harassment can be profound, leading to increased stress levels, social withdrawal, and a loss of trust in online platforms and communities.

Impact on Relationships

Online harassment can have ripple effects on relationships, both personal and professional, as victims may struggle to trust others and engage in online interactions.

Loneliness, Depression, and Anxiety

The emotional harm caused by online harassment can contribute to feelings of loneliness, depression, and anxiety among victims.

Healing and Recovery

Understanding the emotional harm is crucial for providing appropriate resources and support to help individuals heal and recover from the effects of online harassment.

Prevention and Education

Proactive measures such as education, awareness campaigns, and policies promoting online safety are important for preventing emotional harm and fostering a culture of respect and inclusivity in digital spaces.

Strategies to Validate and Address Emotional Experiences in Digital Spaces

Creating Safe and Supportive Environments

Establishing online spaces that prioritize safety, empathy, and respect can help validate and address the emotional experiences of individuals. This includes implementing clear guidelines and policies against harassment and violence, and fostering a culture of inclusivity and support.

Active Listening and Validation

Encouraging active listening and providing validation to individuals who have experienced emotional harm online is essential. This involves acknowledging their feelings, experiences, and concerns without judgment or dismissal. Validating their emotions helps individuals feel heard and understood.

Empowering Individuals to Share

Promoting platforms and channels where individuals can openly express their emotional experiences can be beneficial. This can include online support groups, forums, or helplines dedicated to addressing the emotional impacts of online harassment and violence. Creating a space for sharing can facilitate healing and reduce feelings of isolation.

Offering Mental Health Support

Recognizing the potential psychological consequences of online harassment and violence, it is important to provide accessible mental health support. This can include offering resources such as counseling services, helplines, or online therapy platforms. Connecting individuals with trained professionals who specialize in addressing the emotional effects of online harm can aid in their recovery.

Educating and Raising Awareness

Promoting education and raising awareness about the emotional impact of online harassment and violence is crucial. This can be done through campaigns, workshops, or educational programs that emphasize the importance of empathy, respect, and digital well-being. By increasing understanding and empathy, we can collectively work towards creating a more compassionate and supportive digital environment.

Empowering and Advocating for Change

Encouraging individuals to speak out against online harassment and violence and empowering them to be agents of change can help address emotional experiences in digital spaces. This includes promoting bystander intervention, supporting victims/survivors, and advocating for stronger policies and regulations to prevent and address online harm.

Collaborative Efforts

Recognizing that addressing emotional experiences in digital spaces requires collective action, fostering collaboration among various stakeholders is essential. This includes collaboration between social media platforms, policymakers, organizations, and communities to develop comprehensive strategies and initiatives that validate and address the emotional impacts of online harassment and violence.

By implementing these strategies, the goal is to work towards validating and addressing the emotional experiences of individuals in digital spaces, promoting healing, and creating a safer and more supportive online environment for all.

RESISTANCE: SHIFTING POWER DYNAMICS AND WORKING TOWARDS CHANGE

The Principle of Resistance in Cyberfeminism

Gender resistant feminisms center their attention on particular actions and group dynamics that perpetuate women's subordinate status, even within subcultures that ostensibly espouse gender equality. Various forms of resistance draw upon the potential for repetition to weaken the impact of standardization. By reiterating, rearticulating, and repeatedly introducing fresh ideas, established discourses are confronted and subverted. Subversive repetitions can be understood as a form of resistance that spreads and creates a network of adaptable resistance points (Verma, 2021). This type of resistance generates novel truths and standards.

The principle of resistance in cyberfeminism acknowledges the need to challenge and subvert oppressive power structures in digital spaces. It recognizes the occurrence of gender-based violence and discrimination online and calls for active resistance to create a more inclusive and equitable online environment. This resistance takes the form of speaking out against online harassment, advocating for marginalized groups, and dismantling systems that perpetuate inequality. It emphasizes collective action, reclaiming narratives, and using technology for activism. By embracing the principle of resistance, cyberfeminism aims to create a safer and more empowering online space.

Challenging Dominant Power Structures in Social Media

In social media, challenging power structures is vital for inclusivity and equality. This involves questioning and disrupting hierarchical dynamics that shape online spaces. To counter these power structures, the following strategies can be employed:

1. Counter-narratives:
    - Sharing alternative perspectives, stories, and experiences to challenge prevailing norms and narratives.
    - Amplifying marginalized voices to disrupt dominant discourse and promote diversity and inclusivity.
2. Critiquing social media platforms and institutions:
    - Calling out instances of bias, discrimination, and censorship.
    - Advocating for transparent and inclusive policies.
3. Promoting digital and media literacy:
    - Empowering individuals with critical analysis skills to navigate social media platforms.
    - Recognizing and questioning algorithms and mechanisms that perpetuate inequality and power imbalances.
4. Collaboration and collective action:
    - Forming alliances and partnerships with like-minded groups.
    - Participating in advocacy campaigns and supporting initiatives to challenge and transform social media spaces.

Strategies for Fostering Accountability, Activism, and Community-Based Interventions

Promoting accountability, activism, and community-based interventions is vital for positive change and addressing societal issues. In social media and digital spaces, effective strategies can create a responsible, engaged, and supportive online community. Here are some strategies to employ:

Promoting Digital Citizenship

i. Encouraging individuals to be responsible and ethical online.
ii. Promoting respectful and constructive dialogue while discouraging hate speech and cyberbullying.
iii. Educating users about their rights and responsibilities in digital spaces.

Holding Platforms Accountable

i. Advocating for transparency and accountability from social media platforms and technology companies.
ii. Pressuring platforms to address issues related to privacy, misinformation, and algorithmic biases.
iii. Supporting initiatives that promote user safety and well-being.

Empowering Individuals Through Digital Activism

i. Encouraging users to raise awareness and advocate for social causes through online platforms.
ii. Sharing information about online campaigns, petitions, and initiatives for collective action.
iii. Providing resources and tools for individuals to engage in digital activism effectively.

Community-Based Interventions

i. Establishing and participating in online communities that promote positive engagement and support.
ii. Creating spaces for dialogue, education, and awareness-building on social issues.
iii. Collaborating with local organizations, activists, and influencers to address specific challenges within communities.

Education and Awareness Programs

i. Developing educational initiatives to promote digital literacy and responsible online behavior.
ii. Organizing workshops, webinars, and training sessions on topics such as online safety, digital rights, and media literacy.
iii. Encouraging critical thinking and media analysis skills to navigate the digital landscape effectively.

Challenges in Addressing OGBV or TF GBV in Social Media

When striving to build an inclusive social platform for all, several challenges are commonly faced. The following are a few of the most prevalent challenges in this regard:

Lack of Awareness and Understanding

i. Many individuals may not be fully aware of the extent and impact of OGBV or TF GBV in social media.
ii. Lack of understanding about the different forms of online violence, such as harassment, doxxing, stalking, and revenge porn.

Online Anonymity and Impunity

i. Perpetrators of OGBV or TF GBV in social media often hide behind anonymous accounts, making it difficult to hold them accountable.
ii. Limited mechanisms and legal frameworks to address online violence effectively, leading to a sense of impunity.

Inadequate Reporting and Response Mechanisms

i. Underreporting of incidents due to fear of retaliation, victim-blaming, and lack of trust in the platforms' response.
ii. Inconsistent or ineffective response from social media platforms in addressing reports of OGBV or TF GBV.

Intersectional Challenges

i. The OGBV or TF GBV in social media intersects with other forms of oppression, such as racism, ableism, and homophobia.
ii. Understanding and addressing the unique experiences of individuals with multiple marginalized identities can be complex.

Cybersecurity Concerns

i. Concerns about privacy and the security of personal information when reporting incidents of OGBV or TF GBV.
ii. Fear of online attacks and potential exposure to further harm while seeking help or support.

Digital Literacy and Skills Gap

i. Limited digital literacy skills among some individuals, particularly marginalized communities, making it challenging to navigate and protect themselves online.
ii. Lack of awareness about safety measures and strategies to prevent and respond to OGBV or TF GBV in social media.

Online Misogyny and Cultural Norms

i. Prevalence of online misogyny and harmful cultural norms that perpetuate OGBV or TF GBV in social media.
ii. Overcoming deeply entrenched societal attitudes and biases is a significant challenge.

ROLE OF SOCIAL MEDIA COMPANIES IN COMBATING OGBV OR TF GBV

The role of social media companies in combating OGBV or TF GBV can be explained by discussing the following three areas:

Critiques of Social Media Companies' Response to OGBV or TF GBV

Inadequate Measures

Social media companies have faced criticism for not implementing sufficient measures to address OGBV or TF GBV on their platforms, with concerns that their response has been reactive rather than proactive.

Slow Response Time

Critiques highlight the slow response time of social media companies in addressing reports of OGBV or TF GBV. Delays in taking action can perpetuate harm and allow abusive content to remain visible for extended periods.

Inconsistent Enforcement

There are concerns about the inconsistent enforcement of policies related to OGBV or TF GBV across different social media platforms. This inconsistency leads to a lack of trust and confidence in the platforms' commitment to combating such violence effectively.

Insufficient Content Moderation

Criticism has been directed towards social media companies regarding their content moderation practices, with claims that they are not adequately equipped to detect and remove abusive and harmful content in a timely manner.

Lack of Transparency

Critics argue that social media companies need to be more transparent about their policies, actions, and outcomes related to OGBV or TF GBV. Improved transparency can help hold these companies accountable and build trust with users.

Social media companies must address critiques and take concrete steps to improve their response to gender-based violence. By implementing stronger policies, enhancing moderation practices, improving response times, ensuring consistent enforcement, and increasing transparency, they can create safer online environments.

The Importance of Stronger Policies and Enforcement Mechanisms

Clear Guidelines and Policies

Stronger policies are essential to clearly define what constitutes OGBV or TF GBV on social media platforms. Clear guidelines help users understand what is unacceptable behavior and enable platforms to take appropriate action against violators.

Proactive Approach

Stronger policies should focus on a proactive approach rather than reactive measures. Platforms should actively identify and address potential instances of OGBV or TF GBV, rather than relying solely on user reports.

Swift and Consistent Enforcement

It is crucial to have robust enforcement mechanisms in place to promptly address instances of OGBV or TF GBV. Timely action helps prevent further harm and sends a strong message that such behavior will not be tolerated.

Training and Resources

Social media companies should invest in training their staff to effectively identify and respond to OGBV or TF GBV. This includes providing resources and support to content moderators who play a crucial role in enforcing policies.

Collaboration With External Organizations

Platforms should collaborate with external organizations, such as NGOs and experts in OGBV or TF GBV, to develop and improve their policies and enforcement mechanisms. These partnerships can bring diverse perspectives and expertise to the table, leading to more effective solutions.

By prioritizing stronger policies and enforcement mechanisms, social media companies can create a safer and more inclusive online environment. These measures not only protect users from OGBV or TF GBV but also contribute to fostering a culture of respect, equality, and accountability on their platforms.

Advocating for Accountability and User Safety

Transparent Reporting Mechanisms

Social media platforms should provide clear and accessible channels for users to report instances of OGBV or TF GBV. These reporting mechanisms should be easy to use, well-publicized, and ensure the privacy and safety of individuals reporting the incidents.

Improved Response to Reports

Platforms need to demonstrate a commitment to addressing reports of OGBV or TF GBV promptly and effectively. This includes conducting thorough investigations, taking appropriate action against perpetrators, and providing timely updates to the individuals who reported the incidents.

User Support and Resources

Advocating for user safety involves providing adequate support and resources for individuals who have experienced OGBV or TF GBV. This can include offering guidance on how to report incidents, providing access to helplines or support services, and promoting educational resources on online safety and digital literacy.

User Empowerment and Education

Social media companies should invest in initiatives that empower users to protect themselves and others from OGBV or TF GBV. This can be achieved through educational campaigns, awareness programs, and providing resources that promote digital literacy, consent, and healthy online behaviors.

Collaboration with External Organizations

Platforms should actively collaborate with external organizations, such as advocacy groups and nonprofits working in the field of OGBV or TF GBV, to develop and implement effective strategies for promoting accountability and user safety. This collaboration can help leverage expertise and resources to create more impactful initiatives.

By advocating for accountability and user safety, social media companies can play a vital role in combatting OGBV or TF GBV on their platforms. Prioritizing these measures helps to create a safer and more inclusive online environment, where individuals are protected from harm, and their voices are heard and respected.

Overall, addressing these challenges requires a collective effort involving social media companies, users, policymakers, and civil society organizations to create a safer and more inclusive online environment that actively combats OGBV or TF GBV.

GRASSROOTS ACTIVISM AND COMMUNITY-BASED INTERVENTIONS

Grassroots activism and community-based interventions play a vital role in addressing and combating OGBV or TF GBV in digital spaces. These approaches involve individuals and communities coming together to drive change from the ground up, emphasizing empowerment, support, and collective action.

Empowerment and Resistance as Guiding Principles

Grassroots activism and community-based interventions are grounded in the principles of empowerment and resistance. They recognize the importance of empowering individuals affected by OGBV or TF GBV to reclaim their agency and resist oppressive systems. By fostering a sense of empowerment, these approaches enable individuals to challenge societal norms and actively participate in creating safer digital environments.

Community-led Initiatives and Online Activism

Grassroots activism often involves community-led initiatives that aim to address OGBV or TF GBV. These initiatives can take various forms, such as support groups, workshops, awareness campaigns, and online activism. Community-led initiatives provide spaces for survivors to share their experiences, seek support, and access resources. Online activism, through social media platforms and digital networks, helps amplify voices, raise awareness, and mobilize communities to advocate for change.

Examining Successful Models for Combating OGBV or TF GBV in Digital Spaces

Studying successful models and strategies that have effectively addressed OGBV or TF GBV in digital spaces provides valuable insights into effective approaches. Collaborations between grassroots organizations, community networks, NGOs, and technology companies play a crucial role. These collaborations focus on prevention, education, robust reporting mechanisms, and survivor support. By learning from these models, we can develop effective strategies to combat OGBV or TF GBV and create safer online environments for all.

Building Inclusive and Supportive Communities

Grassroots activism and community-based interventions prioritize building inclusive and supportive communities. These initiatives aim to create safe spaces where survivors can find validation, support, and resources. By fostering a sense of community, individuals affected by OGBV or TF GBV can share their stories, access relevant services, and work collectively to address the issue.

Collaboration and Partnerships

Grassroots activism and community-based interventions thrive on collaboration and partnerships. By forging alliances with various stakeholders, including NGOs, tech companies, policymakers, and academic institutions, these approaches can leverage diverse expertise, resources, and networks to create lasting change. Collaboration enables the pooling of knowledge, sharing of best practices, and collective efforts towards combating OGBV or TF GBV.

Grassroots activism and community-based interventions are powerful tools in the fight against OGBV or TF GBV in digital spaces. These approaches recognize the importance of community mobilization, empowerment, and collective action, ultimately working towards creating inclusive and supportive environments for all individuals online.

ADDRESSING THE CHALLENGES: A MULTI-FACETED APPROACH

To effectively address the challenges associated with OGBV or TF GBV in digital spaces, a comprehensive and multi-faceted approach is necessary. This approach involves considering various factors and implementing strategies that work in tandem to create a safer and more inclusive online environment. The following points outline key elements of this approach:

Collaboration Between Stakeholders

Addressing OGBV or TF GBV in digital spaces necessitates collaboration between different stakeholders, including social media companies, policymakers, activists, and communities. By working together, these groups can pool their resources, knowledge, and expertise to develop comprehensive solutions. Collaborative efforts can involve sharing data and research, designing and implementing policies, and creating effective reporting and response mechanisms.

Regulating Online Spaces and Countering Backlash

Regulating online spaces is crucial for countering OGBV or TF GBV. It involves implementing policies and guidelines that explicitly address harassment, hate speech, and other forms of online abuse. Social media companies play a vital role in this process by enforcing their policies consistently and providing transparent mechanisms for reporting and removing harmful content. Additionally, countering backlash requires actively challenging and debunking harmful narratives that perpetuate OGBV or TF GBV, promoting inclusive and respectful online discourse.

Advocating for Greater Accountability, Empowerment, and Resistance

Advocacy efforts are essential in combating OGBV or TF GBV in digital spaces. This includes advocating for greater accountability from social media companies, urging them to strengthen their policies and enforcement mechanisms. It also involves promoting empowerment by supporting initiatives that empower survivors and marginalized communities, providing resources, and fostering resilience. Additionally, advocating for resistance involves challenging oppressive systems and promoting alternative narratives that counter OGBV or TF GBV.

By addressing these key aspects through a multi-faceted approach, significant strides can be made in combating OGBV or TF GBV in digital spaces. Collaboration between stakeholders, effective regulation, and advocacy for accountability, empowerment, and resistance are crucial elements in creating a safer and more inclusive online environment for all individuals.

CONCLUSION AND FUTURE DIRECTIONS

This book chapter has delved into the critical topic of online gender-based violence (OGBV) or tech-facilitated gender-based violence (TF GBV) in digital spaces. Through a comprehensive exploration of various dimensions, challenges, and strategies, several key insights and findings have emerged, underscoring the pressing need for action and further research.

First and foremost, this book chapter has emphasized the significance of intersectionality as a crucial lens for understanding the multifaceted nature of gender-based violence. Recognizing the interconnected forms of oppression individuals may face based on their race, class, sexuality, or gender identity is vital for developing comprehensive interventions. The chapter has also highlighted the urgent need to validate and address survivors' experiences, acknowledging the emotional toll of online harassment and violence. Creating supportive spaces that prioritize well-being is essential to mitigate psychological consequences and foster a sense of safety. The critical examination of social media companies' role in combating gender-based violence has revealed the progress made and the areas requiring further improvement. Strengthening policies and enforcement mechanisms is imperative to ensure accountability and establish safer online environments. Additionally, grassroots activism and community-based interventions have emerged as powerful strategies for challenging oppressive dynamics and promoting positive change. Through empowerment, resistance, and community-led initiatives, societal norms can be reshaped, creating inclusive spaces where gender-based violence is actively challenged. By addressing these aspects, we can work towards a future free from gender-based violence in digital spaces.

In conclusion, addressing gender-based violence in digital spaces is an urgent and imperative task. The emotional well-being and psychological safety of individuals are at stake, necessitating continued research, advocacy, and the implementation of effective strategies. By fostering collaboration, regulation, and advocacy for accountability, empowerment, and resistance, we can work towards creating a safer and more equitable online environment for all. It is our collective responsibility to ensure that gender-based violence becomes a thing of the past, and that online spaces become platforms for empowerment, dialogue, and positive social change.

Looking ahead, future research should focus on exploring innovative interventions, evaluating the impact of existing policies and initiatives, and understanding the evolving dynamics of gender-based violence in an ever-changing digital landscape. Continually pushing boundaries and advancing understanding can pave the way for a future where gender-based violence becomes a thing of the past in digital spaces. Together, let us strive for a world where all individuals can participate in online communities free from fear, harassment, and violence.

REFERENCES

Allen, K. R. (2022). Feminist theory, method, and praxis: Toward a critical consciousness for family and close relationship scholars. *Journal of Social and Personal Relationships*, *40*(3), 026540752110657. https://doi.org/10.1177/02654075211065779

Australia News. (2020, April 11). *Cyber abuse up by 50 percent amid COVID-19 restrictions.* https://www.skynews.com.au/australia-news/cyber-abuse-up-by-50-percent-amid-covid19-restrictions/video/0e8534dc15a01707ab2e065cb6a14178

Beech, M. (2020, March 25). *COVID-19 Pushes Up Internet Use 70% And Streaming More Than 12%, First Figures Reveal*. Forbes. https://www.forbes.com/sites/markbeech/2020/03/25/covid-19-pushes-up-internet-use-70-streaming-more-than-12-first-figures-reveal/#73bc35303104

Chrisler, J. C., & Johnston-Robledo, I. (2018). Woman's embodied self: An introduction. In J. C. Chrisler & I. Johnston-Robledo (Eds.), Woman's embodied self: Feminist perspectives on identity and image (pp. 3–14). American Psychological Association. https://doi.org/10.1037/0000047-001.

Crenshaw, K. W. (1989). Demarginalizing the Intersection of Race and Sex: A Black Feminist Critique of Antidiscrimination Doctrine, Feminist Theory and Antiracist Politics. *University of Chicago Legal Forum*, 149.

Cunningham, C. M., & Crandall, H. M. (2014). Social Media for Social Justice: Cyberfeminism in the Digital Village. In *Feminist Community Engagement* (pp. 75–91). doi:10.1057/9781137441102_5

de Meco, L., & MacKay, A. (2022, January 19). *Social media, violence and gender norms: The need for a new digital social contract*. https://www.alignplatform.org/resources/blog/social-media-violence-and-gender-norms-need-new-digital-social-contract

Douglas, H., Harris, B. A., & Dragiewicz, M. (2019). Technology-facilitated Domestic and Family Violence: Women's Experiences. *British Journal of Criminology*, *59*(3), 551–570. https://doi.org/10.1093/bjc/azy068

Dunn, S. (2020). *Technology-Facilitated Gender-Based Violence: An Overview*. https://www.cigionline.org/static/documents/documents/SaferInternet_Paper%20no%201_0.pdf

Dwivedi, A. (2022, December 18). Crime against women through social media. *The Times of India*. https://timesofindia.indiatimes.com/readersblog/aashank-dwivedi/crime-against-women-through-social-media-48132/

Dwivedi, Y. K., Ismagilova, E., Hughes, D. L., Carlson, J., Filieri, R., Jacobson, J., Jain, V., Karjaluoto, H., Kefi, H., Krishen, A. S., Kumar, V., Rahman, M. M., Raman, R., Rauschnabel, P. A., Rowley, J., Salo, J., Tran, G. A., & Wang, Y. (2021). Setting the Future of Digital and Social Media Marketing research: Perspectives and Research Propositions. *International Journal of Information Management*, *59*(1), 1–37.

European Institute for Gender Equality. (2022). *Combating Cyber Violence against Women and Girls*. https://eige.europa.eu/sites/default/files/documents/combating_cyber_violence_against_women_and_girls.pdf

European Parliamentary Research Service (EPRS). (2021). *Combating gender-based violence: Cyber violence European added value assessment*. https://www.europarl.europa.eu/RegData/etudes/STUD/2021/662621/EPRS_STU(2021)662621_EN.pdf

European Union. (2018). *Cyber violence and hate speech online against women*. https://www.europarl.europa.eu/RegData/etudes/STUD/2018/604979/IPOL_STU(2018)604979_EN.pdf

Europol. (2020, April 3). *Catching the virus cybercrime, disinformation and the COVID-19 pandemic*. https://www.europol.europa.eu/publications-events/publications/catching-virus-cybercrime-disinformation-and-covid-19-pandemic

Foleon.com. (2019). *Measuring Digital Development - Gender gap*. https://itu.foleon.com/itu/measuring-digital-development/gender-gap/

General Assembly, United Nations. (2022). *Advancement of women Intensification of efforts to eliminate all forms of violence against women and girls | Report of the Secretary-General*. https://www.unwomen.org/sites/default/files/2022-10/A-77-302-SG-report-EVAWG-en.pdf

Glaser, A., Kesslen, B., & Solon, O. (2020, March 26). *In video chats, familiar forms of online harassment make a comeback*. NBC News. https://www.nbcnews.com/tech/security/video-chats-familiar-forms-online-harassment-make-comeback-n1168806

Gurunathan, S. (2022). Cyberfeminism in Online Video Games. *International Journal of Interdisciplinary Research in Arts and Humanities*, *7*(2), 4–8. https://www.researchgate.net/publication/361983718

International Center for Research on Women (ICRW) & Quilt.AI. (2021). *COVID-19 and Online Violence in India: Digital Intelligence Report*. https://www.icrw.org/wp-content/uploads/2021/10/Online-Violence_Full-Report-Quilt.AI-and-ICRW.pdf

Kiani, M., Tavakoli, R., & Mura, P. (2023). Iranian Women Traveling in vTime—A Cyberfeminist Approach. *Journal of Travel Research*. doi:10.1177/00472875221149202

Koo, J. (2019). South Korean cyberfeminism and trolling: The limitation of online feminist community Womad as counterpublic. *Feminist Media Studies*, *20*(6), 1–16. https://doi.org/10.1080/14680777.2019.1622585

Lestari, N., Fadilah, A. N., & Wuryanta, E. W. (2020). Empowered Women & Social Media: Analyzing #YourBeautyRules in Cyberfeminism Perspective. *Jurnal ASPIKOM, 5*(2), 280–293. doi:10.24329/aspikom.v5i2.664

Loots, L., Dartnall, E., & Kelly, J. (2020, April 16). Online safety in a changing world – COVID-19 and cyber violence. *Sexual Violence Research Initiative (SVRI)*. http://www.svri.org/blog/online-safety-changing-world-%E2%80%93-covid-19-and-cyber-violence

Mohanty, J. R., & Samantaray, S. (2017). Cyber Feminism: Unleashing Women Power through Technology. *Rupkatha Journal on Interdisciplinary Studies in Humanities, 9*(2), 328–336. doi:10.21659/rupkatha.v9n2.33

Molla, R. (2020, March 12). *How coronavirus took over social media*. https://www.vox.com/recode/2020/3/12/21175570/coronavirus-covid-19-social-media-twitter-facebook-google

Moya, P. (2014). Habit and embodiment in Merleau-Ponty. *Frontiers in Human Neuroscience*, *8*, 542. https://doi.org/10.3389/fnhum.2014.00542

Mudgway, C., & Jones, K. (2020, April 8). *As use of digital platforms surges, we'll need stronger global efforts to protect human rights online*. The Conversation. https://theconversation.com/as-use-of-digital-platforms-surges-well-need-stronger-global-efforts-to-protect-human-rights-online-135678

National Portal of India. (n.d.). *The Group of Twenty (G20)*. Retrieved June 5, 2023, from https://www.india.gov.in/spotlight/group-twenty-g20

Nixon, C. (2016). Current perspectives: The impact of cyberbullying on adolescent health. *Adolescent Health, Medicine and Therapeutics*, *5*(5), 143–158. https://doi.org/10.2147/ahmt.s36456

OECD. (2018). *Bridging the digital gender divide*. https://www.oecd.org/internet/bridging-the-digital-gender-divide.pdf

Plant, S. (2020). On the Matrix: Cyberfeminist simulations. In T. Thomas & U. Wischermann (Eds.), Feminist Theory and Critical Analysis of Media Culture (pp. 337–346). Transcript Verlag. https://doi.org/10.14361/9783839440841-030.

Schlesselman-Tarango, G. (2014). Cyborgs in the Academic Library: A Cyberfeminist Approach to Information Literacy Instruction. *Behavioral & Social Sciences Librarian*, *33*(1), 29–46. https://doi.org/10.1080/01639269.2014.872529

Tazi, M., & Oumlil, K. (2020). The Rise of Fourth-Wave Feminism in the Arab region? Cyberfeminism and Women's Activism at the Crossroads of the Arab Spring. *CyberOrient, 14*(1), 44–71. doi:10.1002/j.cyo2.20201401.0002

The Dart Center. (2018, May 16). You Can Help! Online Harassment Survey. *Dart Blog*. https://dartcenter.org/blog/2018/05/you-can-help-online-harassment-survey

Toto, G. A., & Scarinci, A. (2022). Cyberfeminism: A Relationship between Cyberspace, Technology, and the Internet. *Elementa. Intersections Between Philosophy, Epistemology and Empirical Perspectives, 1*(1-2), 135–151. doi:10.7358/elem-2021-0102-tosc

United Nations. (1993). *Declaration on the Elimination of Violence against Women*. https://www.un.org/documents/ga/res/48/a48r104.htm

United Nations. (2020). *UN Secretary-General's policy brief: The impact of COVID-19 on women*. https://www.unwomen.org/-/media/headquarters/attachments/sections/library/publications/2020/policy-brief-the-impact-of-covid-19-on-women-en.pdf?la=en&vs=1406

United Nations. (2022). Uncertain times, unsettled lives: Shaping our future in a transforming world. *Human Development Report 2021-22*. https://hdr.undp.org/system/files/documents/global-report-document/hdr2021-22pdf_1.pdf

UNODC. (2020). *UNODC Cybercrime and Anti-Money Laundering Section*. https://www.unodc.org/documents/Advocacy-Section/ES_-_Ciberdelito_y_COVID-19_spanish.pdf

Verma, A. (2021, January 10). Gender, power, and resistance: the diversity in feminism. *IPleaders*. https://blog.ipleaders.in/gender-power-resistance-diversity-feminism/#:~:text=Gender%20resistant%20feminisms%20focus%20on

Verma, M., Haq, F., & Rai, G. (2018). Social media a tool of cyber feminism activism. *International Journal of Research Culture Society*, *2*(2), 488–497. https://ijrcs.org/wp-content/uploads/201802093.pdf

Women, U. N. (2020). *Online and ICT-facilitated violence against women and girls during COVID-19*. https://www.unwomen.org/sites/default/files/Headquarters/Attachments/Sections/Library/Publications/2020/Brief-Online-and-ICT-facilitated-violence-against-women-and-girls-during-COVID-19-en.pdf

Women, U. N. (2022). *Frequently asked questions: Tech-facilitated gender-based violence*. https://www.unwomen.org/en/what-we-do/ending-violence-against-women/faqs/tech-facilitated-gender-based-violence#:~:text=TF%20GBV%20can%20also%20exacerbate

Women, U. N. (2023). *Global Database on Violence Against Women*. https://evaw-global-database.unwomen.org/en

Women's Media Center (WMC). (n.d.). *Online Abuse 101*. Retrieved May 29, 2023, from https://womensmediacenter.com/speech-project/online-abuse-101/

World Economic Forum. (2022). *Global Gender Gap Report 2022*. https://reports.weforum.org/globalgender-gap-report-2022

World Wide Web Foundation. (2020, November 25). *The impact of online gender-based violence on women in public life*. https://webfoundation.org/2020/11/the-impact-of-online-gender-based-violence-on-women-in-public-life/

KEY TERMS AND DEFINITIONS

Cyberfeminism: Cyberfeminism is a movement that addresses the intersection of gender, technology, and the internet. It seeks to challenge gender inequalities in digital spaces and promote equal opportunities for women. By advocating for access, representation, and empowerment, cyberfeminism aims to create a more inclusive and equitable online environment.

Embodiment: Embodiment in cyberfeminism recognizes the real-world impacts of gender-based violence in digital spaces, emphasizing the need to validate survivors' experiences and prioritize their well-being. It highlights the importance of creating supportive and inclusive online environments that acknowledge the emotional toll of online harassment and violence.

Grassroots Activism: Grassroots activism in cyberfeminism involves community-driven initiatives to address gender-based issues in digital spaces. Activists at the local level raise awareness, create networks, and mobilize communities to challenge online harassment, promote inclusivity, and advocate for change. They work collectively to empower marginalized voices, dismantle discriminatory practices, and create equitable digital environments.

Intersectionality: Intersectionality in cyber feminism recognizes and analyzes how multiple forms of oppression intersect and interact in digital spaces. It acknowledges that individuals' experiences of gender-based violence and discrimination are shaped by the intersections of their race, class, sexuality, ability, and other social identities. By considering these intersecting factors, cyber feminism aims to challenge power dynamics, promote inclusivity, and advocate for equitable digital environments that address the diverse experiences and vulnerabilities of women from marginalized communities.

Online Gender-Based Violence (OGBV) or Technology-Facilitated Gender-Based Violence (TF GBV): OGBV or TF GBV refers to acts of violence, harassment, and discrimination targeting individuals based on their gender in digital spaces. It includes cyberbullying, trolling, revenge porn, stalking, and hate speech. OGBV or TF GBV negatively affects victims' well-being and perpetuates gender inequalities. Addressing OGBVor TF GBV requires awareness, digital literacy, policies, victim support, and accountability for perpetrators. Creating a safe and inclusive online environment is crucial for gender equality and respect.

Resistance: Resistance in cyberfeminism involves challenging power structures, promoting change, and empowering individuals and communities in digital spaces. It aims to counter gender-based violence and inequality through diverse strategies, advocating for accountability and amplifying marginalized voices. By fostering collective action and reshaping societal norms, cyberfeminism strives for a more equitable and just online environment.

Chapter 9
Neuropsychological Impact of Cyber Victimisation in Females

Asmita Gaur
https://orcid.org/0000-0002-2744-2904
Maastricht University, The Netherlands

Smriti Maini
https://orcid.org/0000-0001-8947-6897
IILM Institute for Higher Education, India

ABSTRACT

Cyber victimization is a phenomenon where people are subjected to cyber bullying through online harassment, exposure to unsolicited sexual content, and hurtful comments. This phenomenon is said to induce embarrassment, traumatic experiences, and in severe cases, psychopathological cascades. Social withdrawal, shame, and social anxiety are commonly witnessed in victims of cyber bullying. According to previous research and substantiated theories, women are more commonly the victims of online abuse. In such a scenario, a discussion regarding clear definition of cyber victimization, social media addiction processes, prevalence of gender differences, and effects of cyber victimization is important. This chapter aims to review all these relevant topics and discuss neuropsychological mechanisms underlying these processes.

INTRODUCTION

A female in her late adolescent years went through an agonizing experience online where she was bullied based on her appearance and identity, publicly being regularly taunted and was constantly told to commit suicide. Fortunately, the girl shared about her experiences with concerned authorities and sought help in the right time. (A Personal anecdote shared by a victim of cyber bullying.)

A young adult, university going student was subjected to online hate and exposed to revengeful and unwanted sexual content after rejecting a classmate's romantic proposal. She was bombarded with hateful abusive names after rejecting the boy's advances and was character shamed by her peers subsequently.

DOI: 10.4018/978-1-6684-8893-5.ch009

The girl faced severe post-traumatic stress and social anxiety after the incident but slowly after seeking psychological help, recovered and today works as a successful PhD candidate at a renowned university. She describes her experiences as embarrassing and guilt inducing when she recalls her past trauma. (A Personal anecdote shared by victim of cyber bullying.)

Such experiences induce deep psychological impact on the victim's psyche and life. In recent times with increased engagement in digital platforms, the risk of being cyber victimized gets invariably high. Social media platforms allow users to provide personal information to their audience which raises the likelihood of being exploited. The term *cyber victimization* refers to encountering violent conduct or behavior through technology for communication and information, including the internet, video games, and mobile phones (Wright & Wachs, 2020). Cyber victimization involves the victims being subjected to sexual solicitation and approaches, harassment, bullying, and unwanted exposure to sexual content (Finkelhor et al, 2005), because of such experience's trauma, embarrassment and guilt can be induced in the victim. It effects a person's self-concept, self-esteem in a profound manner. In this chapter we'd explain sub themes important in context of psychological effects of cyber victimization and its neurological underpinnings. We have used the term neuropsychological to explain certain phenomena instead of solely neurological as both underpinnings work together to create certain behaviours as reactions to traumatic events like being a victim of cyber bullying.

DEFINING CYBER VICTIMIZATION

Cyber-victimization is defined as the harm suffered due to being a victim of cyberbullying including frequent undesirable, detrimental, abusing, and/or threatening interactions using electronic communication medium. (Corcoran et al., 2015). Being the target of offensive messages, harsh comments, embarrassing images, and threats via electronic messaging or social media are examples of cybervictimization. It is projected that between 9% and 22% of college students will become victims of cybercrime at some point (Sargent et al., 2016). Cyber victimization therefore can cause extreme distress in the lives of the individuals enduring cyber bullying. Online sextortion, non-consensual forwarding of sexts, and revenge porn are other types of online harassment that are frequently assessed to be distinct types of online abuse but could additionally be categorized as online sexual harassment (Buchanan & Mahoney, 2021). Such experiences are rooted in various gender differences to be discussed further in chapter.

SOCIAL MEDIA AS A "DIGITAL DRUG"

Nowadays, social media can be equated to a digitalized drug. The term "social media addiction" entails three key characteristics: (a) being excessively concerned about one's social media presence, (b) being propelled by a strong desire to use social media, and (c) spending so much time and effort on social media that it negatively impacts other facets of life, such as social interactions, job or school, relationships, and general wellbeing (Andreassen & Pallesen, 2014). Adverse consequences are observed, including addiction, which is characterized by a need to be noticed, mood swings, spending too much time on social media, withholding oneself from their environment, and engaging in interpersonal confrontations. Social media and other communication platforms are considered as an addictive platform due its permanence in availability, communication with no definite patterns of synchronicity and ease in usage, which is usually mediated by rewards. Reward can be observed of being composed of two separate parts: a 'liking' and 'wanting'. The enjoyable or pleasurable experience is what the 'liking' component involves, whereas the 'wanting' entails stimulating or reinforcement-based characteristics. Any form of stimulus is said to be reinforcing when an individual behaves in a manner to maximize receiving the stimulus. In the case of social media, various likes, comments full of praise, friends and follow requests act as reinforcers.

According to Meshi et al. (2015), various reward processing units of the brain, ventromedial prefrontal cortex (VMPFC), ventral striatum (VS), and ventral tegmental area (VTA) together comprising of the reward processing network are activated when encountering these reinforcers. Various likes, friend requests, comments posted on social media sites (Facebook, Instagram, Snapchat, etc.) activate this system. It is not a one-way process concerning oneself but also reading other people's postings might generate reward activity because obtaining insights about others life, stimulates curiosity (Arnone et al., 2011), an emotional response connected with ventral striatal activity (Gruber et al., 2014). Curiosity further feeds the need to be present on social media and enhances prolonged usage by reinforcing the behaviour. This has a role in shaping a growing individual's identity as well.

People are often interested in scrolling through social media pages, which coincides with co-construction theory. This theory postulates that people's identities are formed simultaneously and in similar fashion in both online and offline worlds. Firstly, due to social media's omnipresent natures allows individuals to keep a tab on everyone's life, even if they are not physical present around them. Secondly, it provides a unique opportunity to form identities, self-explore in the case of adolescents (Gottman & Mettetal, 1986). For adults it substantiates existing identities by providing similar interests based on posts through digital algorithms. This algorithmic data tracking nature of the social media sites are also responsible for social media addiction in some manner. If one engages himself in watching a particular video or liking a certain post, the algorithm will ensure to post similar content to the persons feed to higher engagement by the user. These algorithmic data tracking mechanisms are professionally created by technologists and the data is further studied by social media networking companies to boost their business by prolonged engagement.

Presence of Women on Social Media: What Are the Gender Differences and Why Do They Prevail?

Certain gender similarities and differences do exist when it comes to prolonged presence on social media. A study conducted by Lin and Wang (2020) demonstrated that men and women place equal value on social presence and desire to engage with others on SNSs, but women prefer to act in social and people-oriented situations, focusing more on interpersonal connections, and hence value social ties and commitment on SNSs more than males. Social role theory was the foundation of authors research agenda which postulates that due to differing societal and cultural expectations, men and women fulfill different social roles that have an impact on their social conduct. Further the findings reveal that compared to men, women place a considerably higher value on privacy risk when forming attitudes toward information sharing as men are more assertive according to social role theory (Lin & Wang 2020). The behaviour manifested in online settings are also different for males and females. Women typically post more images and stories, appear differently than men by emphasizing more on social interactions and interpersonal relations (Tifferet and Vilnai, 2014). Women also display higher levels of emotional expression on social media than men do (Tifferet and Vilnai, 2016) which further inflates their self-esteem and other predictors of positive development.

The need of self-esteem is crucial and if this need is not satisfied in the physical world, one will attempt to fulfill it in cyberspace. As Abraham Maslow postulates in theory of needs, human beings have basic need for acceptance, respect, and sense of belonging in their environments. Utilization of social media would cater to satisfy one's desire for respect by creating a sense of self and identity that is accepted, respected, and plays a part in the online world (Aransih et al., 2018). A cross sectional study conducted by Lynch et al., 1999 aimed to investigate adolescent self-esteem and gender. The results postulated that large gender differences prevailed in self-esteem mediated by body image, media influences and emotional expression. Girls displayed lower levels of self-esteem and negative body image as compared to boys. Self-esteem can also be boosted due to social support present on social media. A meta-analysis study conducted by Tifferet (2020) investigating gender difference in social support on networking sites concluded that women tend to give more social support with visible significant difference, but modest differences were observed in terms of receiving social support. According to personality assessments, women score greater on agreeableness than men. Trust, generosity, consideration, and empathy are characteristics of an agreeable person, as are other personality trait. Given that agreeableness is associated with more social support seeking and giving behaviours (Tifferet, 2020). As such evidence exist, previous theories have tried to postulate inherent differences between males and females.

By envisioning several characteristics that potentially separate males and females, Terman and Miles (1936) constructed a theoretical framework for understanding masculinity and femininity. Such a paradigm proposed gender as a single dimension, with femininity and masculinity at two opposites ends. The masculine aspect is made up of functional personality traits including individuality, self-affirmation, taking risks, social dominance, and aggression. On the other hand, the dimension of femininity is represented through expressive qualities, such as warmth, sensitivity, and compassion. It is therefore regarded that among adolescent boys and girls, victimization is linked to feminine attributes (Navarro et al., 2011). A study by Wright and Wachs (2020) demonstrated that the highest rates of cyber victimization were reported by teenagers who were inclined towards more feminine features. Another study reported that peer aggression and problematic use of SNS were highly associated with males except relational reactive dimension (Martínez-Ferrer, 2018). Women also consume more aesthetically focused social media platforms than men do (Lenhart, 2015).

EFFECTS OF CYBER VICTIMIZATION

Cyber victimization irrespective of gender can produce devastating effects for the individual. Since in traditionalistic setting, women's value in the social sphere is tied to their social image, the impact cyber harassment brings might be regarded as more devastating and emotionally damaging in the case of women. Victimization patterns may also differ among cultures as cultural conditioning and culture specific expectations may differ across the globe (Zhou et al., 2013). In more eastern cultures there is much prevalent tolerance for boys' aggressive behaviours whereas women are reprimanded for being impolite or forceful and are criticized for initiating sexual interactions or sharing intimate photos even from peers (Marret and Choo, 2017). Because of these societal expectations, women are particularly susceptible to being negatively impacted by cyber bullying.

Cyberbullying may not be a fundamentally distinct behavior from traditional bullying, but rather a new medium for verbal and interpersonal hostility (Cornell & Limber, 2015) and because of the continuity between online and offline social lives, co-construction theory suggests that cyber aggression should hurt as much as face-to-face hostility. Girls may be more likely than boys to dwell on or talk about feelings of inadequacy or exclusion with friends, which could heighten feelings of sadness, if they are distressed by what they see on social media and therefore may ruminate more (Rose, 2002). Gender differences also prevail when it comes to emotional impact of online sexual harassment (OSH). Powell and Henry (2019) discovered that 11.6% of women assessed online sexual assault as highly disturbing, compared to just 5.7% of males, and that men considered OSH less distressing than women. Women also rated explicit picture sharing and unsolicited joking as more disturbing than males. (Buchanan & Mahoney, 2021).

Psychopathology can also be induced due to greater exposure to cyber victimization. Another study conducted by Zhao and Yao (2021) investigating relationship, bullying, victimization and suicidal ideation, found that only among females, relational and cyber bullying victimization had a mediating influence on suicide thoughts. Additionally, females had higher rates of suicide ideation than boys had of cyberbullying victimization and depressed symptoms (Zhao & Yao 2021). Another study by Kaloeti et al., (2021), found that women except for school avoidance, which was not gender-related, girls were more likely to experience the onset of anxiety. Girls were shown to have higher rates of social anxiety, panic disorder, generalized anxiety disorder, and separation anxiety disorder than boys (Kaloeti et al., 2021). Cyberbullying is associated with a variety of adjustment issues, such as symptoms of depression and disruptive conduct (Campbell et al., 2020).

Another specific type of cyber victimization involves psychological intimate partner violence (IPV) characterized by threats to break up the relationship, unsubstantiated accusations of infidelity, and persistent location inquiries etc. A study conducted by Sargent et al., 2016 investigating association between psychological IPV, cyber victimization and mental health outcomes demonstrated that psychological IPV and cyber victimization were connected, both of which led specifically to depressive symptoms, suicidal thoughts, while only cyber victimization specifically contributed to antisocial behavior (Sargent et., 2016). A study conducted by Kim et al., (2020) reveals that cyber victimization was linked to an elevated risk of suicide and association with school mediated this correlation by lowering the likelihood of reporting suicidal behavior among kids who were cyberbullying victims. Another study conducted by Bonnano and Hymel (2013) investigated associations among cyber bullying and internalizing difficulties. The findings showed that, in addition to typical types of bullying (physical, verbal, and relational), engagement in cyberbullying as a victim contributed specifically to the prediction of both symptoms of depression and suicidal ideation (Bonnano & Hymel, 2013).

Alcohol abuse as resultant of cyber victimization is also prevalent. A study conducted by Selkie et al., (2015) investigated prevalence of alcohol abuse in female college going students who have been perpetrated to cyber victimization. The findings suggest that female college students are just as vulnerable to the damaging effects of cyberbullying on their mental health as younger teenagers. It is possible that individuals who had been subjected to cyberbullying in college had also been subjected to cyberbullying or other forms of bullying in earlier years may be one explanation. Another study conducted by Mitchell et al., 2007 demonstrated that depressive symptomology, substance abuse and victimization were associated significantly with each other.

Importance of Interpersonal Relationships in Women's Lives

What Happens During Disruption?

Interpersonal relationships include family, social, work, friends, acquaintances, religious, intimate relationships. As postulated earlier in the chapter, women majorly use social media to connect with existing personal relations through messages and chatting, form new interpersonal relations and practice networking. Women also find social networking sites as a safer resort to meet new people than real life. Interpersonal interactions often depend significantly on how she displays herself in both the online and offline worlds, especially in traditionalistic communities where women's self-image is seen as a major determinant of her social acceptance. When someone is the victim of cyberbullying, especially when it involves online sexual harassment, there are significant repercussions in westernized communities as well. Females subjected to online sexual harassment are often taunted, looked down upon and secluded leading to social withdrawal, social anxiety and post trauma where psychopathological traits of depressive symptoms and suicide ideation are natural to occur. But what follows when cyberbullying damages their interpersonal relationships? According to a study by Alonsoe and Coe (2001), dearth in social support characteristics must be taken into consideration when examining the relationship between social support and health since they may contribute to the worsening of menstrual pain symptoms. Attachment disruption is also found as a responsible precipitating factor in anorexia nervosa and bulimia nervosa disorders in female patients (O'Kearney, 1996). Currently extremely less research prevails which aims to investigates the impact of cyber victimization on individual's interpersonal relationships, a niche area of enquiry where research gap exists.

Neuropsychological Mechanisms Underlying Traumatic Events

Every action an individual takes is mediated by brain mechanisms. Traumatic events specially including being emotionally hurt, mentally affected by certain events involve underlying neuropsychological mechanisms. We don't use 'neurological' as a nomenclature to define these mechanisms as we are not going to discuss about them in separation to psychological consequences. Both neurological and psychological underpinnings work hand in hand to produce physical, emotional, and behavioural responses in an individual. When people experience traumatic events, they might react to them in a numerous way. They are conscious of dangers to their security, integrity, and wellness. They could go through an instance of intense emotion. They could feel a physical increase in autonomic arousal. They may engage passively by accepting the situation and blaming themselves, or proactively by engaging in conflict with others (Wilson & Li, 2011). The term traumatic stress response (TSR) refers to an adjustment in the neurochemical cascade that generally reacts to psychological stress by maintaining homeostasis and permitting continue along the developmental trajectory supplied by the typical expected environment (Wilson & Li).

Glucocorticoids and other neurological chemicals are released in different parts of the brain when the physiological stress response is activated (Gunnar and Quevedo, 2007). The brain is especially sensitive to this during adolescence as according to dual systems model, cognitive control systems is being formed in a linear fashion. This formation of cognitive control system is further substantiated in future with time, but experiencing traumatic events like cyber bulling can disrupt the flow of an adolescent's healthy neurological growth. According to Yehuda and LeDoux (2007), hippocampal disruption is also likely linked to post-traumatic processing difficulties, in which the person is unable to discriminate between safe and harmful circumstances, leading to an increased reaction to trauma-related stimuli. A system known as the hypothalamus-pituitary-adrenal axis (HPA-axis) is crucial to the stress response. The HPA-axis' primary role is to evaluate threat, start a neuroendocrine cascade that initiates behavioural reaction, and cease that cascade when the threat is no longer there (Bevans et al., 2005). Following a stressor, elevated catecholamines stimulate the hypothalamus, starting the neuroendocrine cascade in the HPA-axis. The hypothalamus releases corticotrophin-releasing factor (CRF) in response to stimulation which is essential to the stress response. By raising arousal, vigilance, focus, and readiness—factors that when combined can lead to anxious behavior, which improves brain function. Additionally, CRF from the hypothalamus stimulates the pituitary to create ACTH. The adrenal glands are subsequently stimulated by pituitary ACTH to create the glucocorticoids namely cortisol and corticosterone. Cortisol is the first of these two glucocorticoids to trigger a behavioral response (Disseth, 2005). Prefrontal cortex which is supposed to develop until young adulthood is also susceptible to aberrations due to traumatic events. In the hippocampus and prefrontal cortex, respectively, cell loss and delayed myelination create anatomical damage that may result in functional deficiencies in memory and spatial processing, attention, and executive functioning.

Psychopathological consequences are also witnessed when it comes to traumatic cyber events like depression. Nolen-Hoeksema (1990) discovered that males were more prone to engage in a distracting activity, such as sports, whereas women were more inclined to ruminate while depressed. Problems in emotion regulation have been linked to alcohol consumption disorder, borderline personality disorder, eating disorders, and anxiety and depression disorders (Polivy & Herman 2002). In Post-traumatic stress disorders, the superior temporal gyrus in children with PTSD had more grey matter volume than white matter volume, which means the rise in volume was not proportionate to what would be expected for normal functioning, according to MRI studies (De bellis et al., 2002). The hippocampus is also shown to be smaller as compared to healthy cohorts (Turley et al., 2012).

Possible Solutions for Cyber Victimization.

Despite the possibility of being a cyber victim persists, there are procedures that may be taken to stop this terrible phenomenon. An adequate help must be provided to cyber victimized individuals through help of psychotherapists and legal teams wherever necessary, though prevention is better than cure should be the outlook of institutions and responsible agencies. Psychoeducation of especially younger students both females and males are a must where impacts of cyber victimization are adequately discussed. Psychoeducation aims to encourage prevention, give insight into the phenomena, and ensure that victims and their family members have a basic understanding of the same, while ensuring crisis management and suicide prevention activities (Singh and Arora, 2020). Psychoeducation not only educates people about tackling such cases but also makes them conscious about taking personal steps to be safe. Assertiveness is another key life skill that should be promoted in both genders specially females. According to Alberti and Emmons (1986), assertiveness occurs when a person expresses his or her rights, views, and feelings without rejecting the rights of others. Seeking adequate help and speaking out when faced with such situations should be encouraged which is only possible if adequate trust is built between stakeholders, concerned authorities and people themselves. Women specially are targets of victim shaming and even character shaming when faced with such situations. Assertiveness in men is broadly accepted, which should be promoted while teaching them to be respectful and responsible towards society.

According to previous research best positive developmental outcomes are present for men when they are exposed to civic responsibility, civic engagement, and activities outside classroom, whereas females' positive developmental outcomes are observed when they maintain healthy interpersonal relationships with family and peers and creating a secure environment (Veenstra & Wijnen, 2022). Taking steps for creating healthy developmental outcomes for our youth is extremely important to safeguard them and make them responsible citizens. Regular counselling sessions at schools and university level is a must with promotion of mental wellbeing. Cyber victims often socially withdraw themselves therefore reaching out if seeing any signs of untimely absence from work or class is also important. Sometimes reaching out and making the person feel safe is also a steppingstone to ensure their wellbeing. Parents must work on developing strong, trustworthy connections with their children for them to stand for themselves, and to achieve the most efficient developmental outcomes.

On the other hand, for existing victims several therapeutic techniques may be found beneficial like cognitive behavioural therapy, aiming to mold existing cognitive patterns that may include several cognitive distortions, guilt inducing feelings and further lead to secluding behaviour, social withdrawal. Cognitive behavioural therapy taps on both thinking patterns and behavioural mechanisms involved together. Rational emotive therapy can also be used in mild cases where the individual facing deep feelings can be tackled through emotions being targeted. Other techniques may involve promoting healthy self-reflection through Socratic questioning, calming techniques like grounding and better emotion handling through personalized exercises.

CONCLUSION

Cybervictimization may have a severe negative impact on mental health, and victims may experience trauma that causes their self-concept to become unstable. Psychopathology might arise from such cases with post-traumatic stress disorder, social anxiety, depression, generalized anxiety being common disorders. Feelings of guilt and remorse, self-blaming tendencies are also common. In several cases it has been observed that the personal relationships of women are affected due to such cases and affected interpersonal relationships might further sabotage the persons wellbeing. HPA axis is the first neurological response when a person is met with challenging and stress inducing circumstances. Prefrontal cortex and hypothalamus are also sensitive to damage specially in younger cohorts. Therefore, it is important to maintain positive developmental outcomes for each gender under an essence of prevention is better than cure. Though cognitive behavioural therapy and rational emotive therapy may act as best action plans in ensuring a victim's mental wellbeing in therapeutic setting.

REFERENCES

Alberti, R. E., & Emmons, M. L. (1986). Your Perfect Right. A Manual for Assertiveness Trainers. Impact.

Alonso, C., & Coe, C. L. (2001). Disruptions of social relationships accentuate the association between emotional distress and menstrual pain in young women. *Health Psychology*, *20*(6), 411–416. doi:10.1037/0278-6133.20.6.411 PMID:11714182

Andreassen, S.C., & Pallesen, S. (2014). Social network site addiction-An overview. *Current Pharmaceutical Design, 20*(25), 4053-4061.

Arnone, M. P., Small, R. V., Chauncey, S. A., & McKenna, H. P. (2011). Curiosity, interest and engagement in technology-pervasive learning environments: A new research agenda. *Educational Technology Research and Development, 59*(2), 181–198. doi:10.100711423-011-9190-9

Bevans, K., Cerbone, A. B., & Overstreet, S. (2005). Advances and future directions in the study of children's neurobiological responses to trauma and violence exposure. *Journal of Interpersonal Violence, 20*(4), 418–425. doi:10.1177/0886260504269484 PMID:15722496

Bonanno, R. A., & Hymel, S. (2013). Cyber bullying and internalizing difficulties: Above and beyond the impact of traditional forms of bullying. *Journal of Youth and Adolescence, 42*(5), 685–697. doi:10.100710964-013-9937-1 PMID:23512485

Buchanan, N., & Mahoney, A. (2022). Development of a scale measuring online sexual harassment: Examining gender differences and the emotional impact of sexual harassment victimization online. *Legal and Criminological Psychology, 27*(1), 63–81. doi:10.1111/lcrp.12197

Campbell, M., Spears, B., Slee, P., Butler, D., & Kift, S. (2012). Victims' perceptions of traditional and cyberbullying, and the psychosocial correlates of their victimization. *Emotional & Behavioural Difficulties, 17*(3-4), 389–401. doi:10.1080/13632752.2012.704316

Cooper, S., Estes, R. J., Giardino, A., Kellogg, N., & Vieth, V. (2005). *Medical, legal & social science aspects of child sexual exploitation: A comprehensive review of pornography, prostitution, and Internet crimes*. GW Medical.

Cornell, D., & Limber, S. P. (2015). Law and policy on the concept of bullying at school. *The American Psychologist, 70*(4), 333–343. doi:10.1037/a0038558 PMID:25961314

De Bellis, M. D., Keshavan, M. S., Shifflett, H., Iyengar, S., Beers, S. R., Hall, J., & Moritz, G. (2002). Brain structures in pediatric maltreatment-related posttraumatic stress disorder: A sociodemographically matched study. *Biological Psychiatry, 52*(11), 1066–1078. doi:10.1016/S0006-3223(02)01459-2 PMID:12460690

Diseth, T. H. (2005). Dissociation in children and adolescents as reaction to trauma–an overview of conceptual issues and neurobiological factors. *Nordic Journal of Psychiatry, 59*(2), 79–91. doi:10.1080/08039480510022963 PMID:16195104

Finkelhor, D., Mitchell, K. J., & Wolak, J. (2005). Online victimization: What youth tell us. *Medical, legal, and social science aspects of child sexual exploitation: A comprehensive review of pornography, prostitution, and Internet crimes, 1*, 437-467.

Gottman, J., & Mettetal, G. (1986). Speculations about social and affective development: Friendship and acquaintanceship through adolescence. In J. M. Gottman & J. G. Parker (Eds.), *Conversations with friends: Speculations on affective development* (pp. 192–237). Cambridge University Press.

Gruber, M. J., Gelman, B. D., & Ranganath, C. (2014). States of curiosity modulate hippocam- pus-dependent learning via the dopaminergic circuit. *Neuron*, *84*(2), 486–496. doi:10.1016/j.neuron.2014.08.060 PMID:25284006

Kaloeti, D. V. S., Manalu, R., Kristiana, I. F., & Bidzan, M. (2021). The role of social media use in peer bullying victimization and onset of anxiety among Indonesian elementary school children. *Frontiers in Psychology*, *12*, 635725. doi:10.3389/fpsyg.2021.635725 PMID:33995192

Kim, J., Walsh, E., Pike, K., & Thompson, E. A. (2020). Cyberbullying and victimization and youth suicide risk: The buffering effects of school connectedness. *The Journal of School Nursing: the Official Publication of the National Association of School Nurses*, *36*(4), 251–257. doi:10.1177/1059840518824395 PMID:30665324

Lin, X., & Wang, X. (2020). Examining gender differences in people's information-sharing decisions on social networking sites. *International Journal of Information Management*, *50*, 45–56. doi:10.1016/j.ijinfomgt.2019.05.004

Marret, M. J., & Choo, W. Y. (2017). Factors associated with online victimisation among Malaysian adolescents who use social networking sites: A cross-sectional study. *BMJ Open*, *7*(6), e014959. doi:10.1136/bmjopen-2016-014959 PMID:28667209

Martínez-Ferrer, B., Moreno, D., & Musitu, G. (2018). Are adolescents engaged in the problematic use of social networking sites more involved in peer aggression and victimization? *Frontiers in Psychology*, *9*, 801. doi:10.3389/fpsyg.2018.00801 PMID:29896139

Meshi, D., Tamir, D. I., & Heekeren, H. R. (2015). The emerging neuroscience of social media. *Trends in Cognitive Sciences*, *19*(12), 771–782. doi:10.1016/j.tics.2015.09.004 PMID:26578288

Mitchell, K. J., Ybarra, M., & Finkelhor, D. (2007). The relative importance of online victimization in understanding depression, delinquency, and substance use. *Child Maltreatment*, *12*(4), 314–324. doi:10.1177/1077559507305996 PMID:17954938

Morrow, J., & Nolen-Hoeksema, S. (1990). Effects of responses to depression on the remediation of depressive affect. *Journal of Personality and Social Psychology*, *58*(3), 519–527. doi:10.1037/0022-3514.58.3.519 PMID:2324941

Navarro, R., Larranaga, E., & Yubero, S. (2011). S. Bullying-victimization problems and aggressive tendencies in Spanish secondary school students: The role of gender stereotypical traits. *Social Psychology of Education*, *14*(4), 457–473. doi:10.100711218-011-9163-1

O'Kearney, R. (1996). Attachment disruption in anorexia nervosa and bulimia nervosa: A review of theory and empirical research. *International Journal of Eating Disorders*, *20*(2), 115–127. doi:10.1002/(SICI)1098-108X(199609)20:2<115::AID-EAT1>3.0.CO;2-J PMID:8863063

Polce-Lynch, M., Myers, B. J., Kliewer, W., & Kilmartin, C. (2001). Adolescent self-esteem and gender: Exploring relations to sexual harassment, body image, media influence, and emotional expression. *Journal of Youth and Adolescence*, *30*(2), 225–244. doi:10.1023/A:1010397809136

Polivy, J., & Herman, C. P. (2002). Causes of eating disorders. *Annual Review of Psychology*, *53*(1), 187–213. doi:10.1146/annurev.psych.53.100901.135103 PMID:11752484

Rose, A. J. (2002). Co-rumination in the friendships of girls and boys. *Child Development*, *73*(6), 1830–1843. doi:10.1111/1467-8624.00509 PMID:12487497

Sargent, K. S., Krauss, A., Jouriles, E. N., & McDonald, R. (2016). Cyber victimization, psychological intimate partner violence, and problematic mental health outcomes among first-year college students. *Cyberpsychology, Behavior, and Social Networking*, *19*(9), 545–550. doi:10.1089/cyber.2016.0115 PMID:27548623

Sarkhel, S., Singh, O. P., & Arora, M. (2020). Clinical practice guidelines for psychoeducation in psychiatric disorders general principles of psychoeducation. *Indian Journal of Psychiatry*, *62*(8, Suppl 2), S319. doi:10.4103/psychiatry.IndianJPsychiatry_780_19 PMID:32055073

Terman, L. M., & Miles, C. C. (1936). *Sex and Personality*. McGraw-Hill.

Tifferet, S. (2020). Gender differences in social support on social network sites: A meta-analysis. *Cyberpsychology, Behavior, and Social Networking*, *23*(4), 199–209. doi:10.1089/cyber.2019.0516 PMID:32096662

Tifferet, S., & Vilnai-Yavetz, I. (2014). Gender differences in Facebook self-presentation: An international randomized study. *Computers in Human Behavior*, *35*, 388–399. doi:10.1016/j.chb.2014.03.016

Tifferet, S., & Vilnai-Yavetz, I. (2018). Self-presentation in LinkedIn portraits: Common features, gender, and occupational differences. *Computers in Human Behavior*, *80*, 33–48. doi:10.1016/j.chb.2017.10.013

Turley, M. R., & Obrzut, J. E. (2012). Neuropsychological effects of posttraumatic stress disorder in children and adolescents. *Canadian Journal of School Psychology*, *27*(2), 166–182. doi:10.1177/0829573512440420

Underwood, M. K., & Ehrenreich, S. E. (2017). The power and the pain of adolescents' digital communication: Cyber victimization and the perils of lurking. *The American Psychologist*, *72*(2), 144–158. doi:10.1037/a0040429 PMID:28221066

Veenstra, R., & Laninga-Wijnen, L. (2022). Peer network studies and interventions in adolescence. *Current Opinion in Psychology*, *44*, 157–163. doi:10.1016/j.copsyc.2021.09.015 PMID:34662775

Wilson, K. R., Hansen, D. J., & Li, M. (2011). The traumatic stress response in child maltreatment and resultant neuropsychological effects. *Aggression and Violent Behavior*, *16*(2), 87–97. doi:10.1016/j.avb.2010.12.007

Wright, M. F., & Wachs, S. (2020). Adolescents' cyber victimization: The influence of technologies, gender, and gender stereotype traits. *International Journal of Environmental Research and Public Health*, *17*(4), 1293. doi:10.3390/ijerph17041293 PMID:32079366

Zhao, R., & Yao, X. (2022). The relationship between bullying victimization and suicidal ideation among Chinese adolescents: The role of depressive symptoms and gender differences. *Journal of School Violence*, *21*(1), 60–80. doi:10.1080/15388220.2021.1985327

Zhou, Z., Tang, H., Tian, Y., Wei, H., Zhang, F., & Morrison, C. M. (2013). Cyberbullying and its risk factors among Chinese high school students. *School Psychology International*, *34*(6), 630–647. doi:10.1177/0143034313479692

Chapter 10

Cybersecurity Oversight and Board Diversity: The Disclosure Paradigm

Manjula Shukla
SSSVS Government PG College, Chunar, India

Piyush Pandey
AMPG College, Varanasi, India

ABSTRACT

The study aims to determine how board diversity affects cybersecurity information disclosure for financial companies listed on S&P BSE 150. To create a CSD scorecard, the authors rely on past studies as well as SEC guidelines. The empirical research is based on data from 30 financial companies that were listed in India between 2013 and 2022. Panel data estimation technique was used to examine the connection between board diversity and CSD. The results demonstrate that CSD in Indian financial companies is in its infancy. CSD and independence diversity are significantly and favourably related. Gender diversity has no effect on CSD. Additionally, having an IT specialist on board considerably raises CSD levels and moderates the association between independence diversity and CSD, but does not successfully moderate the association between gender diversity and CSD. This study contributes to the literature through empirical evidence on the extent of CSD practises, relationship between board diversity and CSD, and the importance of an IT specialist on the board in defining CSD practises.

1. INTRODUCTION

A constant advancement in technology has brought about an era of internet-based transactions, mesh computing, data analytics and computerized methods, which have become an inherent part of the working system of businesses. Although information technology has proved to be a boon, it comes with a myriad of complexities, threats, and cybersecurity risks incidental to companies (SEC, 2018).

DOI: 10.4018/978-1-6684-8893-5.ch010

The Kotak Committee in 2017, heightened the role of the risk management committee and added cybersecurity to its purview. RBI in its recent circular mandated organizing training programs for the board of directors (B of D) of Indian banks to familiarize them and broaden their understanding of cybersecurity. The 2022 report of IBM Security Data Breach declares that for the financial year 2022, on average the data breach cost in India increased by 6.6 percent as of the financial year 2021 and reached ₹ 17.5 crores. In the year 2021, the major cybersecurity incidents pertained to compromised confidential information and unauthorized access. In a cyberattack case by Air India, the data files of millions of customers were leaked. In another instance, a data leak of the personal information of customers was witnessed from Domino's India's database (Chin, 2023). The major cybersecurity regulations currently administered in India are The Information Technology Act of 2000, which is the first cybersecurity law of India, NCS Policy, 2013, NCS Strategy, 2020, IT Rules, 2021, etc. CERT-In, NCIIPC, CRAT, SEBI, IRDAI, TRAI, DoT, etc. are the main cybersecurity regulatory bodies of India. In a ruling on a special petition of 2021, the Supreme Court of India declared that data theft and cyber-attacks are a crime under the IT Act of 2000 and the IPC. However, as the IPC is more than 150 years old, the IT Act, of 2000 is regarded as the prime cybercrime regulation in India (Chin, 2023).

Proper disclosures about the key aspects and functioning of a corporation are central to maintaining the public's confidence in the company. Companies have a continuous duty to promptly disclose information that investors would consider in making investment choices, including developments relating to a company's internal dynamics or that could otherwise have a bearing on the share price. The regulating agencies have frequently modified the mandatory disclosure standards for Indian corporations. However, the disclosures on cybersecurity have not been labelled as mandatory disclosure. Indian businesses are free to disclose cybersecurity issues as they see fit. The SEC 2011 proposed guidelines and regulations regarding cybersecurity disclosures by publicly traded companies in the USA. The regulations require companies to report cybersecurity incidents within a few hours of their occurrence through Form 8-K. The firms need to make periodic disclosures regarding the policies and procedures undertaken by the company to tackle and manage cybersecurity incidents, the role, expertise and oversight of the management and B of D in understanding and implementing cybersecurity functions, and make necessary cybersecurity disclosures in the annual report of the company through Form 10-K (Morse et al., 2018). There are currently no legislations in India requiring corporations to disclose cyber-risks in their annual reports. In a recent report by Yagnik, et al. (2022) there are relatively fewer disclosures in the annual reports of Indian companies on the topic of cyber-security, which indicates that this issue receives inappropriate attention from stakeholders.

The B of D, as per the agency hypothesis, act as the shareholders' agents. and as such, it is their responsibility to protect the shareholders' interests. The directors would take care to ensure that shareholders and other interested parties were informed of pertinent facts to do this. The value of diversity in management has long been appreciated since it allows for the inclusion of unique perspectives, diversity of thought, stakeholder representation, competitive advantage, inclusion of necessary skills, etc.

Several prior studies have investigated the effect of board diversity on various types of disclosures, which include GHG disclosure (Barg et al., 2022; Liao et al., 2015; Tingbani et al., 2020;), CSR disclosure (Ibrahim & Hanefah, 2016; Muttakin et al., 2015; Rao & Tilt, 2016), risk information disclosure (Bravo, 2018; Saggar et al., 2022), IC disclosure (Anifowose et al., 2017; Mooneeapen et al., 2022; Vitolla et al., 2020), carbon disclosure (Ben-Amar et al., 2017; Elleuch, 2022; Kılıç & Kuzey, 2019), etc. However, as per the researcher's knowledge, there is a narrow stream of research focusing on the impact of board attributes on cybersecurity disclosures and the area of research is still in its infancy (Heroux & Fortin, 2022; Mazumdar & Hossain, 2023)

Considering the postulations of the agency theory and stakeholder theory, the current study attempts to investigate the potential impact of board diversity on the degree of cybersecurity disclosures made by the financial sector-listed companies of India. The present study intends to examine the extent of cybersecurity-related disclosures made in the annual reports of sample financial services companies. The study further extends to observing the influence of board diversity on the level of cybersecurity disclosure. Board diversity is measured as the share of independent board members and female board members. Moreover, the study analyses whether the presence of directors having qualifications in the area of IT possibly moderates the association between board diversity and CSD.

2. REVIEW OF LITERATURE AND HYPOTHESES DEVELOPMENT

2.1 Growth of Cybersecurity Disclosure in the Global Sphere

The prime difficulties in cybersecurity are international in scope. Because of the way that technology has permeated every aspect of human life and the extraordinary levels of innovation and interdependence that have resulted, cybersecurity cannot be regarded as a technical problem or a distinct area of policy. Consumers today have a greater reliance on technology. Businesses must now maintain key consumer data in their database due to the unprecedented rise in e-commerce platforms and transactions. If not prevented with vigilant cyber-security technologies, this raises the potential for data leaks and improper usage. To reduce cyberthreats globally, a variety of cybersecurity laws and regulations have been drafted, including the Budapest Convention, the first international convention on cybercrimes, which was signed in 2001.

Companies are also advised to divulge information regarding cybersecurity risks and measures taken by them to the public in a systematic and timely manner through mandatory and voluntary disclosures in their annual reports. Increased cybersecurity disclosure practices are advocated for by academics, researchers, and regulators who focus on and investigate cybersecurity challenges. Campbell et al., (2014) explain that when a company faces higher incidences of risk, they tend to publish more information on risk factors. Additionally, they focus more of their disclosures on outlining the dangers they confront. On the other hand, Kravet and Muslu (2013) argue that industry-level characteristics and risks rather than firm-specific ones impact the amount of risk disclosed by the companies.

The governments of the United States and Canada have advocated for corporations to disclose risk-related information, and as a result, there are greater cybersecurity disclosures in US and Canadian corporate annual reports. Despite the absence of any applicable regulations, businesses in Latin America have gradually begun disclosing information about cybersecurity in their annual reports. The disclosures are provided along with risk management disclosures, and financial sector companies excel at it (SEC, 2018). A rise in these disclosures in the context of cybersecurity by the corporations listed on international stock exchanges could be linked to the SEC's recommendations (DCF & SEC, 2011). The guidelines were made available to publicly traded corporations in 2018, and the first sanctions were imposed in 2021 (SEC, 2021; SEC, 2021).

The GDPR and the NIS in the European context mandate that publicly traded corporations publish cyber incidents and cyber-attacks in the proper format. There are no laws in place that require corporations to disclose cybersecurity events in their annual reports, but the GDPR and NIS legislation that requires such disclosure may encourage board members to do so (Eijlelenboom & Nieuwesteeg, 2021).

It is unclear how board membership and corporate governance affect risk disclosure practices, as the limited literature confines itself to disclosures related to finance, social responsibility, and the environment. It is crucial to research the association between different components of corporate governance and other areas of corporate disclosure (Bravo, 2018; Camélia & Nadia, 2022). The focus of earlier research on cybersecurity disclosures has been on US-based companies' disclosure practices (Amir et al., 2018; Berkman et al., 2018; Ettredge et al., 2018). Studies concentrating on cybersecurity disclosures by Indian companies are scarce.

2.2 Board Diversity and Disclosure

The public is paying closer attention to the decisions made and the makeup of the boards of directors of business organizations as a result of historical and contemporary examples of corporate governance failure in multinational and domestic enterprises (Bear et. al., 2010; Jain & Jamali, 2016). Scholars define board diversity as the compositional variability of a company's B of D. This compositional heterogeneity may be based on demographic factors or may be observed (Issa et al., 2021; Katmon et al., 2019). A wide range of benefits is reportedly provided by board diversity to an organization, including a broader spectrum of perspectives (Cox, 1991), higher-quality decisions (Kang et al., 2007), a greater competitive advantage in terms of inventiveness and novelty (Cox, 1991), improved problem-solving, and a variety of proficiencies and capabilities (Anderson et al., 2011), among others. Several theories have provided the basis for analyzing the linkage concerning board diversity and disclosure practices of concern. According to the legitimacy theory, businesses make voluntary disclosures to legitimize their actions to enhance their reputation, goodwill, and brand image (Cho & Patten, 2007). One of the most popular theories is agency theory, which holds that board diversity tends to increase the independence and efficacy of the board, allowing the directors to better supervise and regulate the administration's opportunistic behavior more effectively (Jensen, 1988).

According to Freeman's (1984) stakeholder theory, a company operates in a larger social system that includes not just the shareholders but also other people and organizations including consumers, employees, society, the government, etc. The management of an organization has obligations not just to the shareholders but also to other associated parties, who are collectively referred to as a business's stakeholders (Hill & Jones, 1992). Therefore, by the stakeholder theory, a corporation's management ought to take action to safeguard the interests of all its stakeholders.

According to the resource dependence theory, a certain organization needs certain resources to operate, and each organization is reliant on the other for these resources. In a nutshell, the theory describes the connections between a company and outside resources. The B of D works to establish ties between the organization and outside resources. Additionally, the directors themselves are a valuable source of expertise that they bring with them (Hillman & Dalziel, 2003). This idea offers a foundation for figuring out the make-up and organization of the corporate board. The long-term growth and development of the organization are made possible by a professional and well-organized board. The resource dependence theory, according to Carter et al. (2010), presents more specific theoretical explanations for board diversity.

The current study has been built on the outline of the agency theory and resource dependence theory to clarify how board diversity affects the scale of cybersecurity disclosure by companies.

2.3 Board Diversity and Cybersecurity Disclosure

Cybersecurity has been elevated to a top concern for management and board members due to the significant influence it has on a company's operations, value, and financial performance. The board members are expected to actively participate in controlling and addressing cybersecurity risks and concerns within their organization as part of their oversight duties (Radu & Smaili, 2022; Simon et al., 2021). Few studies concentrate on how board structure affects cybersecurity disclosure (CSD), even though board composition has been identified by prior research as a determining factor of the level of voluntary disclosures (Mazumder & Hossain, 2022). Through prompt, sufficient, and meaningful voluntary disclosure of pertinent information, an efficient and effective board seeks to reduce asymmetry in information between management and stakeholders.

In line with the premise of the agency theory, independent directors have little to no personal conflict of interest and no fiduciary duty to the corporation. Due to this, they can make decisions without any intervention from management, which allows for fairness and objectivity (Fama & Jensen, 1983). They reduce agency conflict and information asymmetry (Linsley & Shrives, 2006), improve company transparency and maximize disclosure (Kolsi, 2017). The independent board members are more inclined to better openness and demand better accountability from management since they must uphold and sustain their name and goodwill in the industry.

In a similar vein, independent directors are better sources of talents, different experience, social networking, supervisory abilities, etc., as per the resource dependence hypothesis, which has a material impact on how corporations make decisions (Hillman & Dalziel, 2003; Pfeffer & Salancik, 2003). Because they have up-to-date knowledge of the sector, independent directors are expected to increase firms' transparency by implementing fresh, pertinent disclosure procedures (Mazumder & Hossain, 2022). Several previous studies viz. Lopes and Rodrigues (2007); Lajili (2009); Oliveira et al., (2011); Alkurdi et al., (2019) have found a significant and positive impact of independent directors on board on the disclosure of risk elements. The study uses the term "independence diversity" to refer to the proportion of independent directors on the board (Bin Khidmat et al., 2020). The study's first hypothesis, supported by the evidence from earlier research and the aforementioned theoretical postulations, is:

H_1: There exists a significant positive relationship between independence diversity on board and cybersecurity disclosure in the financial firms in India.

The term "gender diversity" refers to the quantity or share of female directors who serve on corporate boards. According to earlier research, women directors are shown to be more dedicated, effective monitors, autonomous, conscientious, and capable of effectively addressing the agency problem when evaluated in the context of agency theory (Cabedo & Tirado, 2004). Female directors put in a lot of effort to get their companies ethically up to par (Baker et al. 2020). They are also less self-centered. They significantly lessen information asymmetry and increase transparency in the company since they are better at developing trust and demonstrating leadership than their male counterparts (Abad et al., 2017; Srinidhi et al., 2011). As a result, it stands to reason that organizations with a better share of female directors would increase cybersecurity disclosure. According to the resource dependence hypothesis, having female board members gives you access to a wider range of perspectives, unique resources, and advantageous connections. In terms of leadership, innovative attitude, risk-taking ability, knowledge and experience, personality, communication style, diversity of view and prospects, etc., they differ from their male counterparts (Radu & Smaili, 2022; Saggar & Singh, 2017). In earlier studies on gender diversity, it was discovered that female directors were more adept than male directors at recognizing, managing, and communicating risk (Saggar & Singh, 2017; Schubert, 2006; Slovic et al., 1997). Thus, it is reasonable to anticipate that increasing the number of female directors on the board will significantly improve CSD.

H_2: There exists a significant positive relationship between gender diversity on board and cybersecurity disclosure in financial firms in India.

Cybersecurity breaches are substantially less frequent in businesses where corporate leaders have IT competence, according to a study by Kwon et al., (2013). Based on these findings, Higgs et al., (2016) infer the conclusion that the engagement of an IT expert at the board level has a major impact on the cybersecurity aspect of information technology risk. Putting the appropriate personnel and technological resources in place is a duty of supervision vested in the board of directors for the organization's cybersecurity efforts (Crabb, 2018). According to Lipton (2017), internal auditors should be selected who have the time and experience to concentrate on lowering the corporation's cybersecurity risk. For an organization, cybersecurity has taken on strategic importance, thus the directors need to understand the technical aspects of cybersecurity to deal with the problems (Rothrock et al., 2018). To effectively supervise the cybersecurity governance parts of the organization, Bonime-Blanc and Tonello (2017) advise that at least one cybersecurity or IT expert be recruited to the B of D. The board of directors' decisions fall under the category of "participative decision making," and while no one director can directly influence the board's final decision (Graewe, 2021; Scott, 2019), they can have an indirect impact on how the board deliberates as a whole and express their opinions. Therefore, it is logical to assume that the presence of a director with information technology expertise has the potential to positively affect the board members' cybersecurity disclosure decisions by equipping them with the necessary knowledge about cybersecurity aspects. Based on the findings and recommendations of prior studies, the study hypothesizes that:

H_3: The presence of an information technology expert on the board of directors significantly and positively moderates the relationship between board diversity and cybersecurity disclosure in financial firms in India.

3. RESEARCH DESIGN

3.1 Sample Selection and Data Collection

The financial companies listed on the S&P BSE 150 in the year 2022 made up our initial sample. We omitted companies whose annual reports were completely unavailable for the study period, which ran from the FY 2012–2013 to the FY 2021–2022, or whose corporate governance data was unavailable. With this constraint in place, our final sample, which covered the years 2013 through 2022, comprised 30 financial institutions and a total of 300 firm-year observations. Since none of the databases contain the necessary information for cybersecurity disclosure, content analysis was utilized to extract CSD data from the banks' annual reports. The corporate governance part of the annual reports was accessed for information on independent directors, women directors, and the presence of an IT expert on the board.

3.2 Variable Description

A. **Dependent Variable:** *Cybersecurity Disclosure (CSD):* To determine the volume of cybersecurity disclosures, we employed the approach of content analysis. Prior research on voluntary disclosure has made substantial use of content analysis (Dennis et al., 2015; Guthrie et al., 2004; Islam, 2020; Kamath, 2008; Neifar & Jarboui, 2018). Both automated and manual methods can be used for content analysis. We chose the manual method of content analysis because it allows us to more accurately assess and pinpoint certain themes in the reports' textual content, even if the automated content analysis could analyse enormous amounts of data while saving time.

To assess the level of CSD reporting in the firm's annual report, a checklist comprising 20 items was developed for this study. We carried out several steps to create a suitable checklist for the CSD reporting. To begin with, the categories and elements were taken from the SEC's Form 10-K, Form 8-K and Regulation S-K guidance on cybersecurity disclosures and were adopted from previous studies viz. Ravishankar et al., (2019), Seets et al., (2018) and Seets & Niemann (2022). Second, all of the items listed in the SEC rules were initially taken into consideration for the disclosure checklist. Third, to be more accurate, it was confirmed that the checklist is appropriate for Indian organizations by comparing the chosen items with the country's cybersecurity reporting laws, such as the IT Act, 2000, CERT-In, IT Rules, 2021, etc. Fourth, the checklist was updated as a result of a thorough examination of the annual reports of Indian financial companies to compare and identify the components and trends of cybersecurity disclosures made by Indian businesses. The number of items in the checklist was restricted to 20 basic indicators because the extent of CSD by Indian companies is still in its infancy and it is a voluntary category of disclosure. The items were sub-categorized into 4 categories according to the nature of the information disclosed viz. (i) board oversight (ii) cybersecurity risk and strategy (iii) risk management and (iv) measurement of risk. Table 5 in Appendix I lists the 20 fundamental indicators that we use to construct our CSD scorecard.

The presence or absence of a certain cybersecurity-related disclosure item in the company's annual report is assessed using an unweighted disclosure scorecard. Various keywords were used to search for cybersecurity-related disclosures in annual reports, as Indian companies do not reserve a separate section in the annual reports for cybersecurity-related disclosures. Selection of keywords was based on the nature of cyber-details required to be disclosed as per SEC guidance and IT rules of India. A disclosure item's existence received a score of 1, and its absence received a value of 0. The CSD index is calculated by dividing the actual score provided to a corporation by the 20-point maximum disclosure score. If a corporation earns a score of 15, for instance, its real score is 15 and the CSD index is 15/20, which is equivalent to 0.75.

$$CSD_i = \frac{\sum \frac{ni}{t=1} X_{ki}}{n_i}$$

Where, CSD_i = CSD disclosure index of the ith firm, n_i = maximum score that can be obtained by the ith firm (n = 20) and $X_{ki} = 1$ if the ith firm has disclosed k^{th} item and 0 if not disclosed. Therefore, $0 \leq X_{ki} \leq 1$.

The details pertaining to the item selection from various cybersecurity rules in US and India, and the keywords used by the authors while searching for various cybersecurity disclosures made by the companies have been depicted in Table 5 in Appendix I.

B. **Independent Variables:** *Independence Diversity and Gender Diversity:* We considered two facets of board-level diversity, namely independence diversity and gender diversity, to assess the impact of board diversity on the amount of cybersecurity disclosure. The proportion of a company's overall independent directors to all of its directors in a given year has been used to measure independence diversity (INDP). Similar to this, the proportion of a company's overall female directors to all of its directors in a given year has been used to measure gender diversity (WOD). Blau's Index of Diversity (WOD_BLAU) was also employed to gauge the degree of gender diversity on the board because the proportion of female directors across all firms throughout the study period was less than 0.5. The formula for Blau's Index is , where P represents the proportion of directors in a particular category (there are two categories: male directors and female directors), and i is the total number of categories (Blau, 1977).
C. **Control Variables:** There are additional factors that could potentially have a substantial impact on the CSD, as per the results of previous literature, that were incorporated into the model as control variables. Level of disclosure could be affected by firm-specific variables viz. firm size (SIZE) (Elfeky, 2017; Ettredge et al., 2011; Karim et al., 2013), firm age (AGE) (Elberry & Hussainey, 2020; Jiao, 2011; Maryana & Carolina, 2021), leverage (LEVERAGE) (Elisabeth & Utami, 2021; Khlifi & Bouri, 2010), sector the firm belongs to (SECTOR) viz. public sector or private sector, and the presence or absence of CEO duality (CEOD) (Gul & Leung, 2004; Lassoued & Khanchel, 2023). Furthermore, we include an additional control variable viz. presence or absence of an information technology expert on board (ITEXP), which is a dichotomous variable and was also employed as a moderating variable between the relationship between board diversity and cybersecurity disclosure.

3.3 Method

The study's hypotheses have been investigated using multiple regression analysis. The study has employed panel data estimation methods because the data are longitudinal. Fixed effects (FE) and random effects (RE) estimators are the two basal techniques for estimating panel data. However, because the FE estimation technique applies a time-demeaning procedure to the data, time-invariant variables cannot be employed in the model (Battaglia & Gallo, 2015). We opted for the random effects estimator for the investigation since one of our variables, SECTOR, was a time-invariant variable. Additionally, the random effects model was appropriate for the study because we aim to draw general conclusions about the study population rather than focus on individual specific effects (Schaeck & Ihák, 2007) and because the random effects estimator tends to reduce the factor of endogeneity to some extent (De, 2012). Stationarity of the variables is a requisite factor before the application of any econometric technique, thus Levin-Lin-Chu and Harris-Tzavalis test of stationarity was applied. Cluster-robust standard errors were employed using the company as the cluster variable to account for the potential effects of heteroscedasticity and autocorrelation in the models.

3.4 Model Specification

The following is the mathematical notation of the econometric model used to examine the association between board diversity and CSD.:

$$CSD_{it} = \alpha_0 + \Sigma\, \beta_n \text{ Board Diversity}_{nit}$$

$$+\Sigma\, \delta_k CV_{kit} + \gamma Z_i + \psi_i + \varepsilon_{it} \quad (1)$$

Where,

CSD_{it}: CSD index of financial firm i for the fiscal year t,
α_0: The intercept of the regression equation,
β : Coefficient for independent variable Board Diversity $_{nit}$,
δ_k: Coefficients for the control variables CV $_{kit}$,
γ: Coefficient for the time-invariant observed variable,
ψ_i: The unobserved heterogeneity in the model,
ε_{it}: The error term of the model,
i = 30; t = 10; n = 2; k = 5

The notation 'Board Diversity' in the model (1) measures the proportion of independent directors (INDP) and the proportion of female directors (WOD and WOD_BLAU) on the board of the ith firm for the tth year. The model's k control variables are collectively represented by CV. Z_i represents the time-invariant observed variable SECTOR.

The following is the mathematical notation of the econometric model used to examine the possible moderating effect of ITEXP on the association between board diversity and CSD.:

$$CSD_{it} = \alpha_0 + \Sigma\, \beta_n \text{ Board Diversity}_{nit}$$

$$+ \Sigma\, ¥_n \text{ Board Diversity}_{nit} * ITEXP_{it}$$

$$+\Sigma\, \delta_k CV_{kit} + \gamma Z_i + \psi_i + \varepsilon_{it} \quad (2)$$

Where,

CSD_{it}: CSD index of financial firm i for the fiscal year t,
α_0: The intercept of the regression equation,
β : Coefficient for independent variable Board Diversity $_{nit}$
¥ : Coefficient for the interaction effect between Board Diversity $_{nit}$ and ITEXP $_{it}$
δ_k: Coefficients for the control variables CV $_{kit}$,
γ: Coefficient for the time-invariant observed variable,
ψ_i: The unobserved heterogeneity in the model,
ε_{it}: The error term of the model,
i = 30; t = 10; n = 3; k = 5

Table 1. Unit Root Tests of Stationarity

Variables	Levin-Lin-Chu		Harris-Tzavalis	
	Adjusted t[I (0)]	p-Value	z[I (0)]	p-Value
CSD	-4.333	0.000	-4.060	0.000
INDP	-6.128	0.000	-6.047	0.000
WOD	-11.594	0.000	-4.604	0.000
WOD_BLAU	-13.098	0.000	-4.912	0.000
SIZE	-9.959	0.000	-4.733	0.000
AGE	-26.150	0.000	-5.750	0.000
LEVERAGE	-8.031	0.000	-4.212	0.000

Table 2. Descriptive Statistics

Variables	x̄	SD	Min	Max
CSD	4.573	3.277	0.000	18.000
INDP	0.488	0.012	0.166	0.800
WOD	0.088	0.121	0.000	0.333
WOD_BLAU	0.154	0.025	0.000	0.444
SIZE	7.194	0.757	4.272	8.697
AGE	1.575	0.318	0.698	2.103
LEVERAGE	5.172	3.179	0.000	31.830
ITEXP	-	-	0	1
CEOD	-	-	0	1
SECTOR	-	-	0	1

Table 3. Variance inflation factor (VIF) and tolerance values

Variables	MODEL 1 (IV: INDP)		MODEL 2 (IV: WOD)		MODEL 3 (IV: WOD_BLAU)		MODEL 4 (INTERACTION: INDP*ITEXP)		MODEL 5 (INTERACTION: WOD*ITEXP)		MODEL 6(Interaction: WOD_ BLAU*ITEXP)	
	VIF	1/VIF	VIF	1/VIF	VIF	1/VIF	VIF	1/VIF	VIF	1/VIF	VIF	1/VIF
INDP	1.23	0.814	-	-	-	-	1.74	0.575	-	-	-	-
WOD	-	-	1.10	0.908	-	-	-	-	1.89	0.530	-	-
WOD_ BLAU	-	-	-	-	1.11	0.902	-	-	-	-	1.76	0.569
SIZE	1.28	0.781	1.28	0.782	1.28	0.781	1.28	0.779	1.29	0.777	1.29	0.775
AGE	1.24	0.803	1.24	0.805	1.24	0.805	1.25	0.800	1.25	0.800	1.25	0.801
LEVERAGE	1.26	0.792	1.34	0.746	1.34	0.746	1.27	0.789	1.34	0.746	1.34	0.745
ITEXP	1.07	0.933	1.09	0.920	1.09	0.919	1.07	0.932	1.11	0.903	1.12	0.895
CEOD	1.15	0.867	1.14	0.874	1.14	0.874	1.15	0.867	1.16	0.864	1.16	0.863
SECTOR	1.44	0.695	1.28	0.781	1.29	0.777	1.44	0.695	1.29	0.775	1.29	0.773

Figure 1. Cybersecurity-related disclosure by Indian financial companies

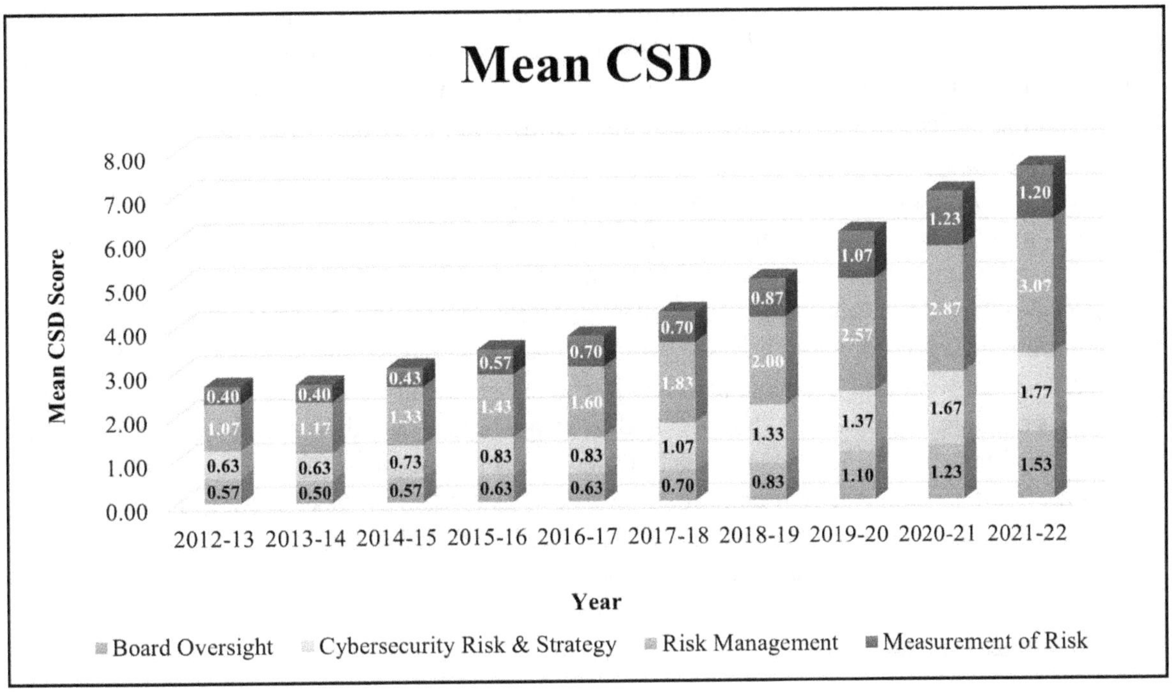

The notation 'Board Diversity' in the model (2) measures the proportion of independent directors (INDP) and the proportion of female directors (WOD and WOD_BLAU) on the board of the ith firm for the tth year. Board Diversity* ITEXP is the interaction variable (INDP*ITEXP, WOD*ITEXP and WOD_BLAU*ITEXP) between variables measuring board diversity and ITEXP. The model's k control variables are collectively represented by CV. Z_i represents the time-invariant observed variable SECTOR.

4. RESULTS AND DISCUSSION

4.1. Univariate Analysis

Table 2 displays the descriptive statistics for the study's dependent and independent variables. The CSD score ranges from 0 to 18, with a mean of 4.573, indicating low disclosure of cybersecurity-related information by Indian financial companies during the study period. However, Figure 1 shows that from FY 2012–13 to FY 2021–22, the sample companies' average disclosure score increased steadily. The average CSD score increased by more than 2.5 times throughout the study, indicating that management is becoming increasingly aware of cybersecurity disclosures. As can be seen from the figure, the companies disclosed comparatively more information regarding cybersecurity risk management efforts done by them followed by providing statements on cybersecurity risk and strategy in operation within the company. With a minimum of 0.166 and a maximum of 0.800, the average proportion of independent directors on boards of sample companies is 0.488. This indicates that, on average, less than 50% of the board of the sample financial companies are independent directors. According to the mean for gender diversity

(WOD), men make up the majority of the sample companies' boards, with women directors making up only 8% on average. In addition, the minimum proportion of women on boards (0.000) reveals that female directors are absent on the boards of some Indian financial companies. A director with expertise in information technology was present on the board in 126 out of the 300 firm-year cases studied, or 42% of the total, indicating that the practice of appointing an IT specialist to the board is still relatively new in Indian financial institutions.

To check for the issue of multicollinearity in the study models, we used the technique of VIF and Tolerance values. Table 3 shows the results of multicollinearity tests on the different models of the study. Models 1, 2 and 3 include the main independent variables of the study along with the control variables. The VIF values for all the independent variables in the three models are less than 3 and the tolerance values are more than 0.1, depicting lack of multicollinearity in the models (Hair et al., 2019). The moderation analysis between the main independent variables of the study and the presence of IT experts (ITEXP) has been done through models 4, 5 and 6. To avoid the potential problem of multicollinearity between the primary independent variables and the interaction term, all the independent variables in models 4, 5, and 6 were mean-centered (Aiken & West, 1991). As the results suggest, the VIF values for all the independent variables in models 4, 5 and 6 are less than 3 and tolerance values are more than 0.1, showing a lack of multicollinearity in the models.

4.2 Multivariate Analysis

The results of the Levin-Lin-Chu test and Harris-Tzavalis test of unit root stationarity as depicted in Table 1 show that all the variables were stationary at level (I(0)). The lag selection for the unit root test was done through the automatic lag selection based on the AIC and SIC. The results suggested a lag selection of 1 for all the variables. Moreover, as a common practice, a lag of 1 is considered adequate for annual data (Song et al., 2003; Liu, 2022). Table 4 lists the random effects estimation results. The choice of the random effects estimator over the OLS estimator was based on the results of the Breusch-Pagan LM test. As shown in Table 4, the random effects estimator is a more reliable and effective estimator than the OLS estimator for the data and models of the study, as shown by the significant results of the LM test for all six of the study's models. Table 4 lists the results of the regression analysis of board diversity variables on cybersecurity disclosure scores of Indian financial companies. As stated in hypothesis 1 (H_1), a financial firm having higher independence diversity will disclose significantly higher cybersecurity information annually.

In Model 1, the results of the association between the proportion of independent directors on board (INDP) and CSD have been reported. The results in Table 6 show a significantly positive effect of independence diversity on CSD ($\beta = 6.470$, $z = 2.95$). Therefore, the first null hypothesis of the study stands rejected. On a B of D with 10 directors, adding 1 more independent director would increase the CSD by 10% of 6.470, or 0.647. These results substantiate the suppositions of agency theory and resource dependence theory. These results corroborate the findings of Héroux and Fortin (2022) and Mazumder and Hossain (2022) of board independence having a significant and positive association with cybersecurity disclosures. Moreover, the results also depict that the presence of an IT expert on board (ITEXP) will result in a better and higher cybersecurity disclosure by the company ($\beta = 0.457$, $z = 2.29$).

As stated in hypothesis 2 (H_2), a financial firm having higher gender diversity will disclose significantly higher cybersecurity information annually. In Model 2 and Model 3, the results of regression estimation of CSD on gender diversity (WOD and WOD_BLAU) have been reported. The results in

Table 4. Random effects regression of CSD on board diversity

Variables	MODEL 1(β, z-Score)	MODEL 2(β, z-Score)	MODEL 3(β, z-Score)	MODEL 4(β, z-Score)	MODEL 5(β, z-score)	MODEL 6(β, z-score)
INDP	6.470 (2.95)**	-	-	5.313 (2.29)*	-	-
WOD	-	2.218 (0.69)	-	-	2.408 (0.785)	-
WOD_BLAU	-	-	1.313 (0.65)	-	-	2.956 (1.39)
SIZE	0.854 (2.10)*	0.910 (2.18)*	0.908 (2.17)*	0.918 (2.19)*	0.883 (2.15)*	0.877 (2.13)*
AGE	4.138 (2.20)*	3.892 (2.09)*	3.892 (2.09)*	3.298 (2.06)*	4.139 (2.18)*	4.128 (2.17)*
LEVERAGE	0.076 (0.88)	0.080 (0.93)	0.081 (0.94)	0.078 (0.89)	0.080 (0.94)	0.081 (0.95)
ITEXP	0.457 (2.29)*	0.447 (2.13)*	0.448 (2.13)*	0.465 (2.18)*	0.504 (2.09)*	0.509 (2.09)*
CEOD	-0.914 (-1.27)	-0.899 (-1.24)	-0.894 (-1.23)	-0.917 (-1.24)	-0.828 (-1.13)	-0.828 (-1.12)
SECTOR	0.431 (2.10)*	0.492 (2.58)**	0.486 (2.43)*	0.464 (2.22)*	0.487 (2.41)*	0.492 (2.42)*
INDP*ITEXP	-	-	-	7.597 (2.99)**	-	-
WOD*ITEXP	-	-	-	-	2.046 (1.68)	-
WOD_BLAU*ITEXP	-	-	-	-	-	2.870 (1.47)
Constant	-7.537 (-1.86)	-8.828 (-2.04)*	-8.818 (-2.03)*	4.410 (4.23)***	4.466 (4.11)***	4.460 (4.10)***
No. of Observations	300	300	300	300	300	300
Wald test (χ^2, p-value)	20.13 (0.005)	19.98 (0.005)	20.14 (0.005)	20.92 (0.007)	27.70 (0.000)	27.40 (0.000)
R-square	0.7789	0.7677	0.7638	0.8289	0.7500	0.7361
LM test (χ^2, p-value)	219.47 (0.000)	209.19 (0.000)	209.92 (0.000)	207.07 (0.000)	211.01 (0.000)	211.51(0.000)
OLS / RE	RE	RE	RE	RE	RE	RE

*Significant at 0.5 level **Significant at 0.1 level ***Significant at 0.01 level

Table 6 show an insignificant effect of gender diversity on CSD (β = 2.218, z = 0.69; β = 1.313, z = 0.65). Therefore, we fail to reject the second null hypothesis of the study. These findings run counter to the assumptions of both resource dependence theory and agency theory. These results corroborate with the findings of Radu and Smaili (2022) of board gender diversity having an insignificant association with cybersecurity disclosures. The insignificant association between gender diversity and CSD in the case of Indian financial firms could be attributed to the fact of unsatisfactory representation of women directors on the boards of sample companies. As per the regulations of SEBI in February 2014, the listed companies in India were mandated to appoint at least one female director on the board by October 2014. However, as the data suggests, the financial listed firms of India have failed to comply with the regulations in a strict sense. A complete absence of women directors on board could be witnessed in many financial companies, years after the passing of the SEBI regulation. Moreover, in the majority of the cases, only a single woman director was appointed on the board which depicts tokenism. Konrad et al., (2008) claimed that gender diversity would have a significant effect when more than one women director is appointed on board. Torchia et al., (2011) assert that a 'critical mass' of women directors is needed on board for gender diversity to show its positive impact, and the critical mass is 3 or more women directors. Radu and Smaili (2022) declare that gender diversity can have a significant impact on

CSD only in cases where 3 or more women directors are present on the board. The Indian financial firms did not once reach the critical mass of 3 women directors on board during the study period of 10 years.

Model 4 depicts the moderation effect of the presence of an IT expert director on board (ITEXP) on the association between independence diversity (INDP) and CSD. The results show that the presence of an IT expert on board positively and significantly moderates the relationship between independence diversity and CSD ($\beta = 7.597$, $z = 2.99$). This implies that although independent directors are capable of positively affecting CSD, the presence of an IT expert would act as a catalyst to the process. As the coefficient of the interaction term shows, when an IT expert director is present on the board, a 10 percent increase in the proportion of independent directors on the board would increase CSD by 10 percent of 7.597 i.e., 0.759, which is higher than the level of impact asserted on CSD by independent directors acting alone (0.647). However, even if the main effect of independence diversity reduces with the addition of the interaction term ($\beta = 5.313$, $z = 2.29$), the effect is still significant.

Model 5 and Model 6 depict the moderation effect of the presence of an IT expert director on board (ITEXP) on the association between gender diversity (WOD and WOD_BLAU) and CSD. The results show that the presence of an IT expert on board does not significantly moderate the relationship between gender diversity and CSD ($\beta = 2.046$, $z = 1.68$; $\beta = 2.870$, $z = 1.47$). This implies that even with the presence of an IT expert on board, the women directors fail to positively affect CSD. As the results reveal a significant and positive moderation effect of IT experts on CSD in the case of independence diversity but the same fails to moderate the association between gender diversity and CSD, we conclude that the third hypothesis (H_3) of the study is partially accepted.

5. CONCLUSION

The present study intends to assess the level of cybersecurity-related disclosures made in the annual reports and investigate the potential impact of board diversity on the volume of cybersecurity disclosures made by Indian financial sector companies. The study also examines whether the presence of directors with expertise in IT may act as a moderator of the association between board diversity and disclosure level.

The results show that Indian financial firms' level of cybersecurity disclosure is still in its infancy. Our findings about independence diversity on board is in line with the postulations of agency theory and resource dependence theory. As they act in the best interests of the stakeholders, they have a positive influence on the CSD, to reduce the information asymmetry between the company and its stakeholders. However, board diversity when measured by gender has no impact on the level of CSD. Furthermore, the presence of an IT expert on board has a significant and positive direct effect on the level of CSD and also positively and significantly moderates the relationship between independence diversity and CSD. However, it fails to show any possible moderating effect on the relationship between gender diversity and CSD, possibly because of the absence of any direct significant association between gender diversity and CSD.

Considering the study's findings, this study offers practical implications for various stakeholder groups on how boardroom diversity in Indian financial firms may promote cybersecurity disclosure. Given this situation, it should come as no surprise that gender diversity in Indian financial firms has little effect on the level of CSD because women make up such a small percentage of board members in comparison to men. A single woman's presence on board will have no discernible impact on the amount of cybersecurity disclosure. In this vein, our study recommends that authorities encourage the inclusion of more women in boardrooms. Additionally, laws must be passed that make the appointment of at least 3 female directors to the boards a requirement. Furthermore, as the results point out, having IT professionals on the board can have a beneficial impact on the extent of CSD, so Indian policymakers and regulators must create legislation requiring the nomination of directors with IT expertise to the boards of Indian enterprises. In March 2022, the SEC ordered public corporations in the United States to declare whether their boards include individuals with expertise in cybersecurity. Regulations requiring mandatory rather than voluntary cybersecurity disclosures are required due to the low level of CSD by Indian financial companies.

Numerous limitations in the present study could serve as possible areas of investigation in further studies. First, our study focuses on only two aspects of board diversity viz. independence diversity and gender diversity due to the non-availability of requisite data. Inclusion of other diversity aspects viz. age diversity, national diversity, and ethnic diversity could be done by future studies depending on the data availability. Second, we assume a linear association between board diversity variables and CSD. A non-linear approach to the same could bring out different results. Third, we used a dichotomous and unweighted approach to the CSD index, whereas a weighted approach to the same would provide weights to different categories of CSD based on their importance. Lastly, the study has been conducted on only 30 financial firms for 10 years. An increase in sample size and period of the study could bring out more robust results.

REFERENCES

Abad, D., Lucas-Pérez, M. E., Minguez-Vera, A., & Yagüe, J. (2017). Does gender diversity on corporate boards reduce information asymmetry in equity markets? *Business Research Quarterly*, *20*(3), 192–205. doi:10.1016/j.brq.2017.04.001

Aiken, L. S., & West, S. G. (1991). Multiple regression: Testing and interpreting interactions. Sage Publications, Inc.

Alkurdi, A., Hussainey, K., Tahat, Y., & Aladwan, M. (2019). The Impact of Corporate Governance on Risk Disclosure: Jordanian Evidence. *Academy of Accounting and Financial Studies Journal, 23*(1).

Amir, E., Levi, S., & Livne, T. (2018). Do firms underreport information on cyber-attacks? Evidence from capital markets. *Review of Accounting Studies*, *23*(3), 1177–1206. doi:10.100711142-018-9452-4

Anderson, R. C., Reeb, D. M., Upadhyay, A., & Zhao, W. (2011). The economics of director heterogeneity. *Financial Management*, *40*(1), 5–38. doi:10.1111/j.1755-053X.2010.01133.x

Anifowose, M., Abdul Rashid, H. M., & Annuar, H. A. (2017). Intellectual capital disclosure and corporate market value: Does board diversity matter? *Journal of Accounting in Emerging Economies*, *7*(3), 369–398. doi:10.1108/JAEE-06-2015-0048

BargJ. A.DrobetzW.GhoulS. E.GuedhamiO.SchroderH. (2022, March 10). Board ancestral diversity and voluntary greenhouse gas emission disclosure. doi:10.2139/ssrn.3998920

Bear, S., Rahman, N., & Post, C. (2010). The impact of board diversity and gender composition on corporate social responsibility and firm reputation. *Journal of Business Ethics, 97*(2), 207–221. doi:10.100710551-010-0505-2

Ben-Amar, W., Chang, M., & Mcllkenny, P. (2017). Board gender diversity and corporate response to sustainability initiatives: Evidence from the carbon disclosure project. *Journal of Business Ethics, 142*(2), 369–383. doi:10.100710551-015-2759-1

Bendovschi, A. (2015). Cyber-attacks-trends, patterns and security countermeasures. *Procedia Economics and Finance, 28*, 24–31. doi:10.1016/S2212-5671(15)01077-1

Berkman, H., Jona, J., Lee, G., & Soderstrom, N. (2018). Cybersecurity awareness and market valuations. *Journal of Accounting and Public Policy, 37*(6), 508–526. doi:10.1016/j.jaccpubpol.2018.10.003

Bin Khidmat, W., Ayub Khan, M., & Ullah, H. (2020). The Effect of Board Diversity on Firm Performance: Evidence from Chinese L isted Companies. *Indian Journal of Corporate Governance, 13*(1), 9–33. doi:10.1177/0974686220923793

Blau, P. M. (1977). *Inequality and Heterogeneity: A Primitive Theory of Social Structure*. Free Press.

Bonime-Blanc, A., & Tonello, M. (2017, January 12). A Strategic Cyber-Roadmap for the Board. *The Harvard Law School Forum on Corporate Governance*. https://corpgov.law.harvard.edu/2017/01/12/a-strategic-cyber-roadmap-for-the-board/

Bravo, F. (2018). Does board diversity matter in the disclosure process? An analysis of the association between diversity and the disclosure of information on risks. *International Journal of Disclosure and Governance, 15*(2), 104–114. doi:10.105741310-018-0040-4

Cabedo, J. D., & Tirado, J. M. (2004). The disclosure of risk in financial statements. *Accounting Forum, 28*(2), 181–200. doi:10.1016/j.accfor.2003.10.002

Camélia, R., & Nadia, S. (2022). Board gender diversity and corporate response to cyber risk: Evidence from cybersecurity related disclosure. *Journal of Business Ethics, 177*(2), 351–374. doi:10.100710551-020-04717-9

Campbell, J. L., Chen, H., Dhaliwal, D. S., Lu, H. M., & Steele, L. B. (2014). The information content of mandatory risk factor disclosures in corporate filings. *Review of Accounting Studies, 19*(1), 394–455. doi:10.100711142-013-9258-3

Carter, D. A., D'Souza, F., Simkins, B. J., & Simpson, W. G. (2010). The gender and ethnic diversity of US boards and board committees and firm financial performance. *Corporate Governance, 18*(5), 396–414. doi:10.1111/j.1467-8683.2010.00809.x

Chin, K. (2023, March 2). *Top cybersecurity regulations in India [Updated 2023]*. Retrieved from UpGuard: https://www.upguard.com/blog/cybersecurity-regulations-india

Cho, C. H., & Patten, D. M. (2007). The role of environmental disclosures as tools of legitimacy: A research note. *Accounting, Organizations and Society, 32*(7/8), 639–647. doi:10.1016/j.aos.2006.09.009

Cox, T. J. Jr. (1991). The multicultural organization. *The Academy of Management Perspectives*, *5*(2), 34–47. doi:10.5465/ame.1991.4274675

Dennis, P., Connole, H., & Kraut, M. (2015). *The efficacy of voluntary disclosure: A study of water disclosures by mining companies using the global reporting initiative framework*. Academic Press.

Eijlelenboom, E. V., & Nieuwesteeg, B. F. (2021). An analysis of cybersecurity in Dutch annual reports of listed companies. *Computer Law & Security Report*, *40*, 105513. Advance online publication. doi:10.1016/j.clsr.2020.105513

Elberry, N., & Hussainey, K. (2020). Does corporate investment efficiency affect corporate disclosure practices? *Journal of Applied Accounting Research*, *21*(2), 309–327. doi:10.1108/JAAR-03-2019-0045

Elfeky, M. I. (2017). The extent of voluntary disclosure and its determinants in emerging markets: Evidence from Egypt. *The Journal of Finance and Data Science*, *3*(1), 45–59. doi:10.1016/j.jfds.2017.09.005

Elisabeth, A., & Utami, W. (2021, May 6). The Effect of Good Corporate Governance, Leverage and Company Profile on Risk Disclosure. *Proceedings of the 1st MICOSS Mercu Buana International Conference on Social Sciences, MICOSS 2020*. https://eudl.eu/doi/10.4108/eai.28-9-2020.2307512

Elleuch, F. L. (2022). Corporate board diversity and carbon disclosure: Evidence from France. *Accounting Research Journal*, *35*(6), 721–736. doi:10.1108/ARJ-12-2021-0350

Ettredge, M., Guo, F., & Li, Y. (2018). Trade secrets and cyber security breaches. *Journal of Accounting and Public Policy*, *37*(6), 564–585. doi:10.1016/j.jaccpubpol.2018.10.006

Ettredge, M., Johnstone, K., Stone, M., & Wang, Q. (2011). The effects of firm size, corporate governance quality, and bad news on disclosure compliance. *Review of Accounting Studies*, *16*(4), 866–889. doi:10.100711142-011-9153-8

Fama, E. F., & Jensen, M. C. (1983). Separation of Ownership and Control. *The Journal of Law & Economics*, *26*(2), 301–325. doi:10.1086/467037

Forum, W. E. (2019, October 1). *Cyberattacks and fiscal crises top list of business risks in 2019*. Retrieved from World Economic Forum: https://www.weforum.org/press/2019/10/cyberattacks-and-fiscal-crises-top-list-of-business-risks-in-2019/

Freeman, R. E. (1984). *Strategic Management: A Stakeholder Approach*. Cambridge University Press.

Gamerschlag, R., Möller, K., & Verbeeten, F. (2011). Determinants of voluntary CSR disclosure: Empirical evidence from Germany. *Review of Managerial Science*, *5*(2), 233–262. doi:10.100711846-010-0052-3

Graewe, D. (2021). *Advisory Boards in Medium-Sized Companies: An International Comparison*. Walter de Gruyter GmbH & Co KG. doi:10.1515/9783110666182

Gul, F. A., & Leung, S. (2004). Board leadership, outside directors' expertise and voluntary corporate disclosures. *Journal of Accounting and Public Policy*, *23*(5), 351–379. doi:10.1016/j.jaccpubpol.2004.07.001

Guthrie, J., Petty, R., Yongvanich, K., & Ricceri, F. (2004). Using content analysis as a research method to inquire into intellectual capital reporting. *Journal of Intellectual Capital*, *5*(2), 282–293. doi:10.1108/14691930410533704

Hair, J. F., Risher, J. J., Sarstedt, M., & Ringle, C. M. (2019). When to use and how to report the results of PLS-SEM. *European Business Review, 31*(1), 2–24. doi:10.1108/EBR-11-2018-0203

Héroux, S., & Fortin, A. (2022). Board of directors' attributes and aspects of cybersecurity disclosure. *The Journal of Management and Governance*. Advance online publication. doi:10.100710997-022-09660-7

HiggsJ. L.PinskerR. E.SmithT. J.YoungG. (2016). The Relationship between Board-Level Technology Committees and Reported Security Breaches. doi:10.2308/isys-51402

Hill, C. W., & Jones, T. M. (1992). Stakeholder-agency theory. *Journal of Management Studies, 29*(2), 131–154. doi:10.1111/j.1467-6486.1992.tb00657.x

Hillman, A. J., & Dalziel, T. (2003). Boards of Directors and Firm Performance: Integrating Agency and Resource Dependence Perspectives. *Academy of Management Review, 28*(3), 383–396. doi:10.5465/amr.2003.10196729

Ibrahim, A. H., & Hanefah, M. M. (2016). Board diversity and corporate social responsibility in Jordan. *Journal of Financial Reporting and Accounting, 14*(2), 279–298. doi:10.1108/JFRA-06-2015-0065

Islam, M. (2020). Investigating the relationship between integrated reporting and firm performance in a voluntary disclosure regime: Insights from Bangladesh. *Asian Journal of Accounting Research, 6*(2), 228–245. doi:10.1108/AJAR-06-2020-0039

Issa, A., Zaid, M. A., Hanaysha, J. R., & Gull, A. A. (2021). An examination of board diversity and corporate social responsibility disclosure: Evidence from banking sector in the Arabian Gulf countries. *International Journal of Accounting and Information Management, 30*(1), 22–46. doi:10.1108/IJAIM-07-2021-0137

Ivashkovskaya, I., & Adamu, M. U. (2021). Corporate governance and risk disclosure in emerging countries. *Journal of Corporate Finance Research, 15*(4), 5–16.

Jain, M., & Jamali, D. (2016). Looking inside the black box: The effect of corporate governance on corporate social responsibility. *Corporate Governance, 24*(3), 253–273. doi:10.1111/corg.12154

Jensen, M. C. (1988). Takeovers: Their causes and consequences. *The Journal of Economic Perspectives, 2*(1), 21–48. doi:10.1257/jep.2.1.21

Jiao, Y. (2011). Corporate Disclosure, Market Valuation, and Firm Performance. *Financial Management, 40*(3), 647–676. doi:10.1111/j.1755-053X.2011.01156.x

Kamath, B. (2008). Intellectual capital disclosure in India: Content analysis of "TecK" firms. *Journal of Human Resource Costing & Accounting, 12*(3), 213–224. doi:10.1108/14013380810919859

Kang, H., Cheng, M., & Gray, S. J. (2007). Corporate governance and board composition: Diversity and independence of Australian boards. *Corporate Governance, 15*(2), 194–207. doi:10.1111/j.1467-8683.2007.00554.x

Karim, K., Pinsker, R., & Robin, A. (2013). Firm size and the voluntary disclosure of nonfinancial information by private versus public firm managers. *Managerial Auditing Journal, 28.* Advance online publication. doi:10.1108/MAJ-01-2013-0800

Katmon, N., Mohamad, Z. Z., Norwani, N. M., & Faroogue, A. (2019). Comprehensive board diversity and quality of corporate social responsibility disclosure: Evidence from an emerging market. *Journal of Business Ethics, 157*(2), 447–481. doi:10.100710551-017-3672-6

Khlifi, F., & Bouri, A. (2010). Corporate disclosure and firm characteristics: A puzzling relationship. *Journal of Accounting. Business & Management, 17*, 62–89.

Kılıç, M., & Kuzey, C. (2019). The effect of corporate governance on carbon emission disclosures: Evidence from Turkey. *International Journal of Climate Change Strategies and Management, 11*(1), 35–53. doi:10.1108/IJCCSM-07-2017-0144

Kolsi, M. (2017). The Determinants of Corporate Voluntary Disclosure Policy: Evidence from Abu Dhabi Securities Exchange (ADX). *Journal of Accounting in Emerging Economies*, 7(2), 249–265. Advance online publication. doi:10.1108/JAEE-12-2015-0089

Konrad, A., Kramer, V., & Erkut, S. (2008). Critical Mass: The Impact of Three or More Women on Corporate Boards. *Organizational Dynamics, 37*(2), 145–164. doi:10.1016/j.orgdyn.2008.02.005

Kravet, T., & Muslu, V. (2013). Textual risk disclosures and investors' risk perceptions. *Review of Accounting Studies, 18*(4), 1088–1122. doi:10.100711142-013-9228-9

Kwon, J., Ulmer, J. R., & Wang, T. (2013). The Association between Top Management Involvement and Compensation and Information Security Breaches. *Journal of Information Systems, 27*(1), 219–236. doi:10.2308/isys-50339

Lajili, K. (2009). Corporate Risk Disclosure and Corporate Governance. *Journal of Risk and Financial Management, 2*(1), 1. Advance online publication. doi:10.3390/jrfm2010094

Lassoued, N., & Khanchel, I. (2023). Voluntary CSR disclosure and CEO narcissism: The moderating role of CEO duality and board gender diversity. *Review of Managerial Science, 17*(3), 1075–1123. doi:10.100711846-022-00555-3

Liao, L., Luo, L., & Tang, Q. (2015). Gender diversity, board independence, environmental committee and greenhouse gas disclosure. *The British Accounting Review, 47*(4), 409–424. doi:10.1016/j.bar.2014.01.002

Linsley, P. M., & Shrives, P. J. (2006). Risk reporting: A study of risk disclosures in the annual reports of UK companies. *The British Accounting Review, 38*(4), 387–404. doi:10.1016/j.bar.2006.05.002

Lipton, M. (2017, February 15). Risk Management and the board of directors. *The Harvard Law School Forum on Corporate Governance*. https://corpgov.law.harvard.edu/2017/02/15/risk-management-and-the-board-of-directors-4/

Liu, A. L. (2022). The autoregressive distributed lag model. In Econometric Modelling and Forecasting of Tourism Demand. Routledge.

Lopes, P. T., & Rodrigues, L. L. (2007). Accounting for financial instruments: An analysis of the determinants of disclosure in the Portuguese stock exchange. *The International Journal of Accounting, 42*(1), 25–56. doi:10.1016/j.intacc.2006.12.002

Maryana, M., & Carolina, Y. (2021). The Impact of Firm Size, Leverage, Firm Age, Media Visibility and Profitability on Sustainability Report Disclosure. *Jurnal Keuangan Dan Perbankan*, *25*(1). Advance online publication. doi:10.26905/jkdp.v25i1.4941

Mazumder, M. M. M., & Hossain, D. M. (2022). Voluntary cybersecurity disclosure in the banking industry of Bangladesh: Does board composition matter? *Journal of Accounting in Emerging Economies*, *13*(2), 217–239. doi:10.1108/JAEE-07-2021-0237

Mooneeapen, O., Abhayawansa, S., Ramdhony, D., & Atchia, Z. (2022). New insights into the nexus between board characteristics and intellectual capital disclosure: The case of the emerging economy of Mauritius. *Journal of Accounting in Emerging Economies*, *12*(1), 29–51. doi:10.1108/JAEE-12-2020-0322

Morse, E. A., Raval, V., & Wingender, J. R. (2018). SEC cybersecurity guidelines: Insight into the utility of risk factor disclosures for investors. *Business Lawyer*, *73*, 1–34.

Muttakin, M. B., Khan, A., & Subramaniam, N. (2015). Firm characteristics, board diversity and corporate social responsibility: Evidence from Bangladesh. *Pacific Accounting Review*, *27*(3), 353–372. doi:10.1108/PAR-01-2013-0007

Neifar, S., & Jarboui, A. (2018). Corporate governance and operational risk voluntary disclosure: Evidence from Islamic banks. *Research in International Business and Finance*, *46*, 43–54. doi:10.1016/j.ribaf.2017.09.006

Oliveira, J., Lima Rodrigues, L., & Craig, R. (2011). Risk-related disclosures by non-finance companies: Portuguese practices and disclosure characteristics. *Managerial Auditing Journal*, *26*(9), 817–839. doi:10.1108/02686901111171466

Pfeffer, J., & Salancik, G. R. (2003). *The External Control of Organizations: A Resource Dependence Perspective*. Stanford University Press.

Radu, C., & Smaili, N. (2022). Board Gender Diversity and Corporate Response to Cyber Risk: Evidence from Cybersecurity Related Disclosure. *Journal of Business Ethics*, *177*(2), 351–374. doi:10.100710551-020-04717-9

Rao, K., & Tilt, C. (2016). Board diversity and CSR reporting: An Australian study. *Meditari Accountancy Research*, *24*(2), 182–210. doi:10.1108/MEDAR-08-2015-0052

Ravindra, M. J. P. & S. (n.d.). *Management Principles and Applications (For Sem.- 3rd, Utkal University, Odisha)*. Vikas Publishing House.

Ravishankar, V., Boni, B. V., & Karananou, A. (n.d.). *Engaging on cyber security: Results of the PRI collaborative engagement 2017-2019*. PRI. Retrieved 25 May 2023, from https://www.unpri.org/cyber-security/engaging-on-cyber-security-results-of-the-pri-collaborative-engagement-2017-2019/5680.article

Rothrock, R. A., Kaplan, J., & van Oord, F. (2018). The board's role in managing cybersecurity risks. *MIT Sloan Management Review*, *59*, 12–15.

Saggar, R., Arora, N., & Singh, B. (2022). Gender diversity in corporate boardrooms and risk disclosure: Indian evidence. *Gender in Management*, *37*(2), 182–201. doi:10.1108/GM-06-2020-0174

Saggar, R., & Singh, B. (2017). Corporate governance and risk reporting: Indian evidence. *Managerial Auditing Journal*, *32*(4/5), 378–405. doi:10.1108/MAJ-03-2016-1341

Schubert, R. (2006). Analyzing and managing risks – on the importance of gender differences in risk attitudes. *Managerial Finance*, *32*(9), 706–715. doi:10.1108/03074350610681925

Scott, P. (2019). *Introduction to Management Accounting*. Oxford University Press.

SEC. (2018). *Commission statement and guidance on public company cybersecurity disclosures*. Security Exchange Commission. Retrieved from https://www.sec.gov/rules/interp/2018/33-10459.pdf

SEC. (2021a, August 30). *SEC Announces Three Actions Charging Deficient Cybersecurity Procedures*. Retrieved from US Securities and Exchange Commission: https://www.sec.gov/news/press-release/2021-169

SEC. (2021b, June 15). *SEC Charges Issuer With Cybersecurity Disclosure Controls Failures*. Retrieved from US Securities and Exchange Commission: https://www.sec.gov/news/press-release/2021-102

SEC cybersecurity disclosure: A how-to guide. (2018, July 9). IFLR. https://www.iflr.com/article/2a63bsmabqyzreejoirk0/sec-cybersecurity-disclosure-a-how-to-guide

Seets, C., Brorsen, L., & Klemash, S. (2018, October 21). Cybersecurity Disclosure Benchmarking. *The Harvard Law School Forum on Corporate Governance*. https://corpgov.law.harvard.edu/2018/10/21/cybersecurity-disclosure-benchmarking/

Seets, C., & Niemann, P. (2022, October 2). How cyber governance and disclosures are closing the gaps in 2022. *The Harvard Law School Forum on Corporate Governance*. https://corpgov.law.harvard.edu/2022/10/02/how-cyber-governance-and-disclosures-are-closing-the-gaps-in-2022/

Simon, D., Sweeney, J., Rosenfeld, R., & Mohan, V. (2021, July 25). SEC Increasingly Turns Focus Toward Strength of Cyber Risk Disclosures. *The Harvard Law School Forum on Corporate Governance*. https://corpgov.law.harvard.edu/2021/07/25/sec-increasingly-turns-focus-toward-strength-of-cyber-risk-disclosures/

Slovic, P., Malmfors, T., Mertz, C. K., Neil, N., & Purchase, I. F. (1997). Evaluating chemical risks: Results of a survey of the British Toxicology Society. *Human and Experimental Toxicology*, *16*(6), 289–304. doi:10.1177/096032719701600601 PMID:9219024

Song, H., Witt, S. F., & Jensen, T. C. (2003). Tourism forecasting: Accuracy of alternative econometric models. *International Journal of Forecasting*, *19*(1), 123–141. doi:10.1016/S0169-2070(01)00134-0

Srinidhi, B., Gul, F. A., & Tsui, J. (2011). Female Directors and Earnings Quality*. *Contemporary Accounting Research*, *28*(5), 1610–1644. doi:10.1111/j.1911-3846.2011.01071.x

Tingbani, I., Chithambo, L., Tauringana, V., & Papanikolaou, N. (2020). Board gender diversity, environmental committee and greenhouse gas voluntary disclosures. *Business Strategy and the Environment*, *29*(6), 2194–2210. doi:10.1002/bse.2495

Torchia, M., Calabrò, A., & Huse, M. (2011). Women Directors on Corporate Boards: From Tokenism to Critical Mass. *Journal of Business Ethics*, *102*(2), 299–317. doi:10.100710551-011-0815-z

Vitolla, F., Raimo, N., Marrone, A., & Rubino, M. (2020). The role of board of directors in intellectual capital disclosure after the advent of integrated reporting. *Corporate Social Responsibility and Environmental Management*, *27*(5), 2188–2200. doi:10.1002/csr.1957

Yagnik, B., Kaushal, D., Ballabh, M., Gupta, R., Gayal, S., & Sengupta, V. (2022). *Our take - Navigating the cyber-pass*. Pricewaterhouse Coopers Private Limited.

APPENDIX I

Table 5. Cybersecurity disclosure index

Cybersecurity Disclosure Category
I. BOARD OVERSIGHT
1. Disclosure of board oversight approach
2. Disclosure of oversight by board-level committees
3. Disclosure of cybersecurity qualifications and experience of board members
4. Disclosure of management's cybersecurity reporting structure to board or committees.
5. Disclosure of management's cybersecurity reporting frequency to board or committees.
II. STATEMENT ON CYBERSECURITY RISK AND STRATEGY
1. Disclosure of strategy-focused cybersecurity statement.
2. Disclosure of cybersecurity being a topic in shareholder engagement conversations.
3. Disclosure statement declaring cybersecurity as a risk factor.
4. Disclosure statement declaring data privacy as a risk factor.
III. RISK MANAGEMENT
1. Disclosure regarding efforts to mitigate cybersecurity risk.
2. Disclosure regarding education and training to mitigate cybersecurity risk.
3. Disclosure of engagement or collaboration with outside security community.
4. Disclosure regarding appointment of external independent advisor for cybersecurity.
5. Disclosure regarding engagement of board with external independent advisor
6. Disclosure regarding attestation provided by external independent advisor
7. Disclosure regarding maintenance of a level of cybersecurity insurance.
8. Disclosure regarding inclusion of cybersecurity in executive compensation consideration
IV. MEASUREMENT OF RISK
1. Disclosure of quantity / scale of attacks and incidents detected and resolved
2. Disclosure of resources expended to resolve the attacks or incidents
3. Disclosure of maintaining compliance with regulatory requirements or practices

Chapter 11
Semiotic Violence and Gender in Digital Spaces

Soumya Sankar Ghosh
School of Advanced Sciences and Languages (SASL), VIT Bhopal University, India

ABSTRACT

Various definitions of violence exist, ranging from those that only consider physical assaults to those that also take into account sexual assault, psychological abuse, and economic exploitation. Both genders are discursively represented in their heterogeneity. (The feminine is frequently portrayed as a commodity, while the masculine is frequently portrayed as weak and pathological.) What is more important, though, is the understanding that there are specific types of gender violence that target women and utilize sexist language and images to harm and oppress them. This incident is categorized in the study as semiotic violence. Women are not the only ones who may experience this type of assault; anybody can. Even though it is the most pervasive, covert, and despised kind of violence committed against a person, it is generally ignored. The main goal of this study on semiotic violence is to improve understanding of this kind of violence.

1. INTRODUCTION

On May 18, 2016, Maneka Gandhi, the Minister for Women and Child Development in India, expressed her opinion that the issue of online harassment and abuse of Indian citizens ought to be addressed with the same level of gravity as physical violence. The rationale behind the Indian Government's resolute decision to undertake such severe measures is easily conceivable. As per a report by India Today, which references Amnesty International, from March to May in the year 2019, nearly one million abusive mentions were directed towards 95 female politicians on Twitter. Of these mentions, one in every five was found to be misogynistic in nature. According to Adrian Lovett, the executive director of the World Wide Web Foundation, there has been a global increase in gender-based online violence in both developed and developing nations. This report corroborates his claims. The author proceeds to assert that digital violence based on gender has a significant impact on the political engagement of women, as young women, in particular, are deterred by the prevalence of online harassment. The assertion made by

DOI: 10.4018/978-1-6684-8893-5.ch011

Adrian is reinforced by the findings of Amnesty International's 2018 report, which revealed that 7% of the tweets directed towards 323 female politicians from the United States and Britain were characterized by unpleasant or abusive language. Several female politicians in the United Kingdom have opted out of participating in the upcoming 2019 general elections as a result of the online harassment they have received. Currently, it would be fallacious to hold the belief that cyber violence is exclusively confined to the realm of politics. Pasricha's (2021) study highlights eight notable cases that occurred since 2012, where Indian women from diverse professions faced harassment for expressing their views on social media platforms such as Facebook or Twitter. The recent incident in West Bengal, wherein a university professor was dismissed from her position based on an Instagram post, has the potential to bring about a significant revision to the existing list. The truth is, the list never finishes.

Pasricha's research highlights the challenge faced by women in comprehending the violent nature of the attacks they encounter on social media platforms. Women tend to block or dismiss such attacks rather than reporting them, which forms the basis of the current study. The current article aligns with Pasricha's assertion that the absence of action by women against digital abuse can be attributed to factors such as lack of knowledge, inadequate education, and limited comprehension of their legal entitlements. However, the research suggests that there may be certain linguistic factors influencing the situation. The paper categorizes this as an instance of semiotic violence. The utilization of semiotic instruments is employed to inflict harm, humiliation, and subjugation upon individuals. This form of violence is not limited to women, as individuals of all genders can be subjected to it. Semiotic violence is a form of violence that is frequently overlooked, yet it is the most widespread, concealed, and disparaged type of violence directed towards an individual. Moreover, it is a constituent of a broader spectrum of violent behaviours. The employment of a mechanism within social processes that curtails the complete and equitable involvement of women and transgender individuals is a practice that undermines both gender parity and democratic principles. The primary objective of this study, which focuses on semiotic violence, is to enhance comprehension of this type of violence. It is more widespread and fluid in nature, as it subtly infiltrates our socio-cultural milieu and is often disregarded as a form of gender-based violence due to our lack of knowledge. The following illustration from a grammar textbook for a second grade can provide greater clarity (Sameeran 2016):

Upon initial observation, the depicted figure exhibits a seemingly simplistic nature. However, after further scrutiny, certain intricacies become apparent, necessitating our careful consideration. Upon careful examination of the occupational distribution between genders, it becomes evident that the female gender has been predominantly associated with only one profession, namely, teaching. However, men have been afforded the advantage of pursuing careers in domains such as medicine, engineering, and science. Historically, teaching has been perceived as a profession that aligns with the feminine gender role, as women have been socialized to assume the primary responsibility for managing domestic affairs. In contemporary times, female educators are consistently preferred over their counterparts in the private industry. The aforementioned figure serves as a replication of this social concept. If we follow this line of reasoning, we will see that the image is also seeking to create some traditions surrounding women's clothing; a teacher will wear a saree, a mischievous child's clothes are a t-shirt and pants, etc.

The present study adopts a perspective that regards signs as products of social construction, rather than as authentic and unmediated reflections of the external reality. The aforementioned constructions often accentuate the perspectives and encounters of advantaged factions owing to power dynamics, in which dominant factions perceive themselves as the norm and classify others as the exception (Barthes 1957). Fig. 1 accurately depicts the information being conveyed. The utilization of words and images is

Figure 1. Projection of gender in the school curriculum (Sameeran 2016)

significant in the establishment and sustenance of social hierarchies. Consequently, the act of dismantling signs can serve as a potent tool in the exposure and resistance of oppressive and privileged establishments (Chandler, 2017). The concept of semiotic violence holds relevance at this particular level.

A comprehensive understanding of the expansion of gender within the semiosphere is imperative before further exploration of the subject of semiotic violence. Henceforth, we shall endeavour to comprehend this concept initially in Section 2.

2. LITERATURE REVIEW: THE CONSTRUCTION OF GENDER SEMIOSPHERE

Semiotics is an academic discipline that concerns itself with the analysis of language's signalling systems, which may take the form of an index, an icon, or a symbol. As per Chandler's (2017) exposition, semiotics encompasses the examination of entities that represent something beyond their literal meaning, alongside the colloquially termed "signs." The author proceeds to assert that semiotics allows for the representation of signs through various means such as verbal language, visual depictions, auditory stimuli, physical movements, and tangible items. According to Eco's (1976) perspective, semiotics is the scholarly investigation of any entity that may be interpreted as a sign. In contemporary times, the field of semiotics is not examined in a vacuum due to its focus on the construction of meanings and representation of reality.

Conversely, gender is conveyed through a diverse range of physical indicators, such as attire, nonverbal behaviours, and linguistic features such as intonation. The degree of control and recognition of semiotic presentations varies among individuals. Individuals who self-identify as transgender, intersex, or gender variant and do not conform to binary gender categories often exhibit a heightened level of self-awareness regarding their gender identity and expression. Borba and Osterman (2007) utilize the concept of "an embodiment" to denote the active engagement of individuals in their gender identity.

Embodiment is defined as the process by which individuals are marked with sociopolitically relevant cultural gender and sexuality indicators.

2.1 Gender Identity and Construction in a Social Realm

Late modernity, defined as a post-traditional milieu where media of all kinds take an integral part in identity fabrication and where social structures are expanded, is linked to the theoretical discussion regarding identity (Giddens, 2000). People's sense of self and their emotions have been impacted by late modernity. The advent of quasi-interaction, an umbrella term defined by the potential of its reception in a new context, has significantly affected the creation of oneself due to shifts in temporal and spatial conceptions (Thompson 1998). This entails shaping how individuals perceive themselves and their surroundings in spatial-temporal reception contexts that differ significantly from production contexts everywhere. Since contemporary society is mostly moulded by quasi-interaction in the sphere of media, fundamentalist characteristics in regard to gender need to be problematic. Various institutions, like the family, religious community, and classroom, have long-established and enforced gendered roles. These conventional identities have given way to more fluid hybrid ones as a result of the international connections brought about by migration.

When compared to other identities, such as the feminine identity established in print and electronic media, Talbot (1998) argues that the *mother* identity now co-exists. Magalhaes (2005) argues that the interplay between verbal and visual texts is responsible for the construction of gender identities in dynamic and social processes. Two more paradigms were added to his definition of texts: (i) the semiotic component of practice (Haliday and Hasan, 1989) and (ii) a discursive contribution intended to be adopted in a different context (Chouliaraki and Fairclough, 1999). Different texts are appropriated, quoted, or re-contextualized not only directly but also implicitly in the realm of marketing and digital space, which has given rise to a new domain of textual changes. Since then, gendered spaces have been implicitly constructed, violated, and re-constructed.

With this connection when we are particularly looking into the construction of the word *feminism*, we will see that it is often defined as the *womanness of a woman*. Gender, as stated by (Litosseliti, 2006), may be enacted, tracked, and expressed. Further femininities and masculinities are created as a result of the societal establishment of gender. Mills (1995, 2005) contrasts the traditional image of womanhood with the contemporary one, arguing that traditional femininity focused on outward beauty at the expense of intellectual capacity, whereas contemporary womanhood encompasses a spectrum of conventional behaviour that may be ironized and toyed with. In our society, feminism is typically conceptualized and viewed as something that exists solely inside an individual's inner circle. Due to the changes that have occurred in the last two decades in regard to the positions of women in the public sphere, it is becoming increasingly difficult to maintain the stereotypical markers of femininity, such as compassion, concern for physical looks, emotional excess, and ineptitude with regards to non-domestic tasks. Women's evolving roles, including increased social mobility and the freedom to make their own choices about marriage, divorce, and having children, have had far-reaching effects on how society views women generally.

Hence, the pertinent questions are: (i) How has the newly evolved concept of womanhood been portrayed in the digital space? (ii) When it comes to the discourse norms of cyberspace, what kind of power dynamic defines gender roles? and (iii) Is it the imbalance of power in the virtual world that leads to semiotic aggression? Answering these problems requires a firm grasp of gender as it relates to the semiosphere, an idea first proposed by Lotamn (1990). This will allow us to comprehend the elements that are crucial in initiating semiotic violence in cyberspace.

2.2 Gender Semiosphere in a Digital Space: A Semiosphere Within a Semiosphere

Lotman introduced the idea of the semiosphere as a prolongation of Vernadsky's (1926) biosphere concept, drawing an analogy between the two. Based on Lotman (1990), the biosphere encompasses all living matter and serves as the essential condition for the perpetuation of life. In contrast, the semiosphere refers to the semiotic space that is indispensable for the existence and operation of languages. This space possesses pre-existing qualities and consistently interacts with various languages (Lotman 1990). The concept of Lotman's semiosphere pertains to a highly intangible and frequently non-locatable cognitive realm. The interpretation of Lotman's semiosphere as a metaphorical space has been observed by Nöth (2006), However, it should be noted that the author himself refutes the notion of his semiosphere concept being metaphorical. Lotman appears to be attempting to distinguish clearly between models and metaphors while also arguing semiotic space as a form of the model and not a "mere metaphor." Notwithstanding Lotman's assertion to the contrary, his depictions of the semiosphere contain a plethora of spatial analogies. According to Lotman (1990: 123), a semiosphere refers to a spatial domain that envelops us during the act of communication or speech. The concept being referred to is a demarcated area, which may not necessarily have a physical presence. This boundary can be intangible, such as the perceived divide between allies and adversaries, the economically disadvantaged and the affluent, or the domestic sphere and the enchanted forest in fictional narratives (1977 [1970]: 229–30). The locations inside of it are the consequence of cultural values being metaphorically projected onto geographic space. With this idea of semiosphere, the current paper will now look into the construction of gender semiosphere within the cyber-spatial or digital-spatial semiosphere domain.

2.2.1 Digital-Spatial Semiosphere

As evidence that it provides practical tools for comprehending twenty-first-century digital space, the semiotic theory previously mentioned has inspired academics in cyberspace and online culture. According to Santaella (2010), cyberspace possesses attributes of connectivity, mobility, and ubiquity, thereby qualifying it as a semiosphere. While extending this idea, Ibrus (2010: 90), in his semiotic analysis consider the "Web semiosphere" as a domain that is shaped by power imbalances and a dynamic of centre-periphery. At the core of this semiotic realm, the author perceives the influential "infrastructure enablers" who possess the ability to dictate the structure of web content on a global scale. If the dominant providers are considered the focal point, the less prominent providers may emerge as the most popular areas of the digital communication sphere. The emergence of these cores in the semiosphere may lead to their dominance and the consequent establishment of a system characterised by perpetual shifts in societal power asymmetries, which aligns with Lotman's prophesied shift of cultural periphery towards the centre, while the centre is concurrently displaced towards the periphery (Lotman 1990: 141).

The legal and contractual frameworks that safeguard conflicting economic interests serve to distinctly delineate the boundaries among service providers. However, the boundaries among internet users lack such clear demarcation. Internet users exhibit a level of resistance towards the purported authority of knowledge, information, and entertainment hubs. Instead, they actively engage in creating and disseminating knowledge and innovative content. The internet can be regarded as a self-organizing domain of communal knowledge, functioning as a decentralized and independent entity that generates collective intelligence (Santaella, 2007: 182). Like other semiotic spaces, Lotman's perspective suggests that the web space is characterized by being intersected by multiple boundaries (Lotman, 1990, p. 140). This implies that the existence of various boundaries and peripheries also encompasses a diversity of centres. Santaella (2007) notes, that the semiosphere boundaries of digital space have become malleable and the areas they aim to contain have become amorphous. The present semiotic scenario diverges from Lotman's semiotic space model, which featured a central point, a periphery, and a boundary. Lotman's semiotic dynamics, as applied to the semiosphere, are also evident in the semiotic processes occurring in cyberspace. The digital sphere is a semiotic sphere that has the capacity to self-organize, self-describe, and self-regulate following the traditional conceptualization of the semiosphere (Lotman, 1990: 134). It emerges as a continuous state of interaction with other semiospheres, undergoing a perpetual process of self-transformation that leads to a continuous expansion of signs and culture.

The above text presents a common configuration of the semiosphere in the realm of cyberspace or digital space. When considering gender within the semiotic space in question, it is apparent that the concept of gender is intertwined with the prevailing social hierarchy. Consequently, individuals are frequently prompted to fulfil their societal obligations within their respective communities. The interplay between the social order and digital-spatial semiosphere can be understood as a reciprocal relationship, wherein each entity serves as a reflection of the other. Specifically, the social order functions as a mirror that portrays the digital-spatial semiosphere, while the latter serves as a mirror of the former, representing its image. Therefore, it is crucial for us to comprehend the gender construction within the digital-spatial semiosphere conceptualization, which is essentially a semiosphere constructed within another semiosphere.

2.2.2 Gender Semiosphere

The semiosphere notion offers the theoretical depth and richness necessary to conjure the dimension and idea to construct the gender-semiosphere domain. The study of digital-spatial semiosphere texts adheres to Fairclough's three dimensions of depiction, elucidation, and clarification, as outlined in his works (Fairclough 1989;1992). The texts, in the said domain, are utilized in the construction of gender identities. The aforementioned elements serve as substantiation for elucidating and explicating the dialogue as discursive occurrences of collective customs (Chouliaraki and Fairclough 1999). Upon close examination, it becomes apparent that within the digital realm, the concept of femininity has predominantly been portrayed as either maternal or sexual in nature. Two identities have been historically constructed. Therefore, the notion of a gender semiosphere has been formulated positing that women are reliant on men and are primarily expected to fulfil men's desires. It is evident that the conceptualization of gender semiosphere elicits semiotic violence, both overtly and covertly.

This idea, further, enables the extant body of work to evolve and adapt to accommodate novel concepts and shifting gender patterns. The establishment of an iconic relationship between indigenous content and extrapolated contemporary content within a semiotic framework necessitates the application of structural semiotics. In order to gain a comprehensive understanding of the gender semiosphere, the present study will adopt Fairclough's (1999) framework to examine the textual and semiotic features of digital discourse. The framework in question primarily relies on four foundational elements, namely: (i) semiotic factors, (ii) vocabulary, (iii) coherence, (iv) modality, and (v) intertextuality.

Semiotic Factors- The primary focus of these factors pertains to the methodologies employed in the analysis of textual representations of gender identities, including their sartorial expressions and associated bodily concerns. In visual genres like digital commercials, Kress and van Leeuwen (1996) contend that verbal and visual players might switch roles. They further assert that the participants exhibit heterogeneity. Verbal participants refer to written text segments, whose semantic coherence is derived from their semiotic features. The work in question references semiotic elements such as images, abstract concepts, written language, and alphabetical characters. Comprehending such texts primarily hinges on comprehending the visual semiotic tools employed to unify disparate components into a cohesive entity, or a textual unit.

Vocabulary- It places particular emphasis on lexical selections, preferred word choices, and the attribution of new meanings to words in rephrasing and new lexical creations, as discussed in the works of Mey (1985) and Halliday (1978). Furthermore, it is crucial to take into account whether there is an endeavour to investigate lexical units about a particular semantic domain during the act of over-wording, which denotes the range of methods utilized to express a single meaning (Fairclough, 1992). Hence, the process of word formation leads to the construction of novel meanings and the codification of fresh lexical entities.

Coherence- In the realm of digital communication, the linking of clauses and periods serves to generate a specific rhetorical style that is intended to incite a desire to engage with the promoted content. This study will focus on cohesive devices such as references, ellipses, conjunctions, and lexical items.

Intertextuality- The aforementioned term can be categorized into interdiscursivity, which pertains to the relationship between the discourse types or genres utilized in the text, correspondence to said discourse types or genres, and manifest intertextuality. Intertextuality is regarded by Fairclough (1992) as a realm that lies at the intersection of discourse practice and text. The objective of intertextuality is to precisely identify the other texts that are utilized in the formation of the text under scrutiny. The primary objective is to comprehend the historical association of the voices that embody specific social groups and identities within the realm of the digital sphere under examination. Kristeva (1994) posits that intertextuality can be categorized into two distinct dimensions. a) The concept of horizontal intertextuality pertains to the antecedent and subsequent texts of a given literary work. b) Vertical intertextuality involves the historical correlation that exists between a text and other literary works that are situated within its immediate or remote social milieu. The aforementioned text underscores the heterogeneous and frequently paradoxical components and strands that contribute to its composition, thereby elucidating the equivocal nature of textual works. The source cited is Fairclough's work from 1992.

Based on this framework, the proposed approach would facilitate the integration of the gender semiosphere by accommodating the evolution of the current globalized platform-based sign system and the repositioning of the pre-existing semiosphere. These measures are imperative for the consolidation of the foreseeable sign system. The figure extracted from Żurawicka's (2015) work holds significant value in its depiction of gender within a semiotic square.

Żurawicka (2015) challenges the notion that moccasins represent masculinity and stilettos represent femininity within the gender binary system of Polish culture, as the term "gender" encompasses more than just these two concepts by the semiotic square's logic. Therefore, we must direct our attention towards the semi-symbolic system that pertains to non-masculinity and non-femininity, which is comprised of various cultural contexts, colours, languages, music, and other related components. Nevertheless, a cursory examination of the vast body of cultural material highlights the necessity for caution when addressing the topic. Each of the four categories possesses a profound symbolic significance, albeit subject

Figure 2. Masculinity and femininity in today's culture (Żurawicka's 2015)

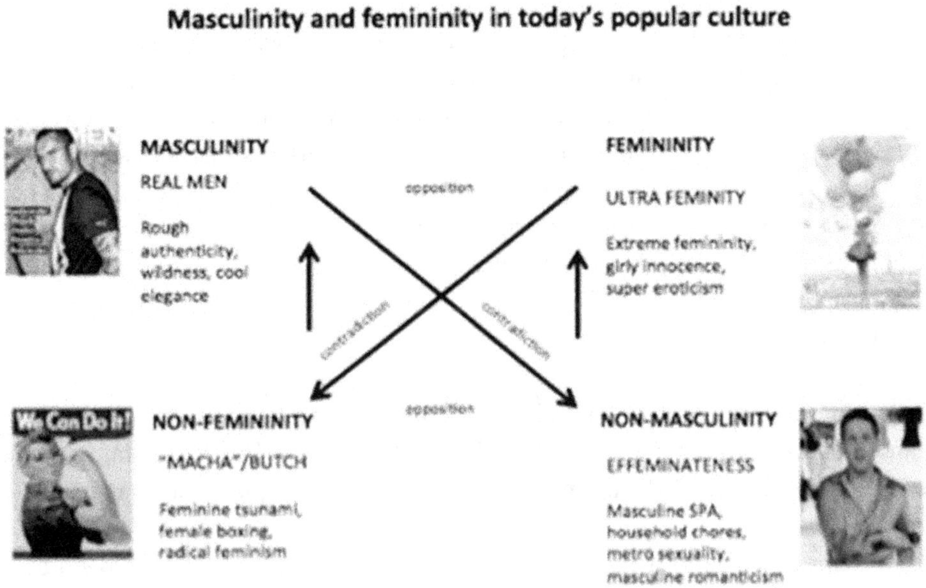

to perpetual fluctuations. Hence, the process of allocating distinct indicators to each gender necessitates a momentary cessation of time and the careful curation of prime illustrations.

The notion suggested by Żurawicka (2015) is depicted in Figure 2. This concept employs traits such as sincerity, feistiness, nostalgia for a mediaeval era of chivalry, cool elegance, and colours such as black, graphite, or grey to represent the "masculine" gender. The gender commonly denoted as "feminine" is distinguished by vivid hues, motifs, emblems, and representations that are linked with a female's sensuousness, eroticism, and charm, along with a girl's purity or a woman's ambivalence. The non-masculine gender category is inclusive of the notion of effeminacy or masculinity that integrates feminine traits. The semiotics and iconography attributed to males are indicative of their inclination towards romanticism and metrosexuality. Examples of male physicality depicted in a feminine manner and instances where men take on female roles serve as indicative of non-masculine characteristics. The semiotic square delineates the construct of non-femininity as a composite of femininity and complementary masculine attributes. The utilization of assertive women and depictions of women possessing masculine traits such as physical fitness, rationality, composure, and self-discipline as symbolic representations is a manifestation of the concept of feminism taken to an extreme.

The focus of this study mostly revolves around the gender square and the gender semiosphere, both of which have been previously investigated and recognized as fundamental ideas. This article delves into the framework of semiotic violence, which serves as the central subject of investigation in the latter portion of the discussion. Before moving on, it is crucial to understand the research methodology employed in the present study, since it represents an integral component of the inquiry.

3. RESEARCH METHODOLOGY

This study aims to investigate the role of social media pictures and memes in instigating semiotic gender violence. In order to assess the implementation in this particular instance, the content analysis methodology has been utilized. An in-depth analysis of the effects of memes and images on viewers is the primary goal of this study, which also looks at the possibility that such effects may be negative. Moreover, the study also emphasizes the utilization of exploratory qualitative analysis on pre-existing secondary data obtained from online platforms. These platforms provide individuals with the opportunity to access their social media profiles, browse through articles and news sources, and interact with user-generated comments related to the subject matter. This research has created the methodology for its investigation in a subsequent manner:

a. Data Collection: The research will entail the acquisition of a heterogeneous array of social media photos and memes from a range of sites, including Facebook, Twitter, Instagram, and Reddit. To achieve a complete dataset, a combination of qualitative and quantitative methodologies will be employed.
b. Sampling Technique: A stratified random sampling technique will be employed to select images and memes from different categories, topics, and user demographics to ensure a representative sample.
c. Data Source Verification: The authenticity and credibility of the collected data will be verified to avoid misinformation and ensure the validity of the findings.

The examination of the gathered data using both qualitative and quantitative methodologies yields useful insights into their influence, importance, and cultural significance.

3.1 Qualitative Analysis

The process of qualitative analysis entails the interpretation of the content and context of data to comprehend their fundamental significance and symbolism. The current research project investigates the following dimensions:

(i) Themes and Topics: The identification of reoccurring themes and subjects enables researchers to unveil the societal challenges, events, or cultural references that are mirrored and amplified through memes and illustrations. The project aims to investigate the mechanisms via which semiotic violence is elicited and its associations with individuals utilizing social media platforms.
(ii) Context and Intent: Upon analysis of the visual and written elements, it becomes evident that memes and images used in digital space utilize a combination of pictures, text, and font styles to communicate their meanings. Furthermore, gaining knowledge about the inception and intended communication of those facilitates the comprehension of its dissemination and uptake on various social media platforms.

The adoption of a qualitative methodology in the present study facilitates the acquisition of full comprehension of the gathered data. This study offers a comprehensive analysis of the cultural context and semio-semantic significance of memes and pictures inside the digital space. However, it is critical to note that the current work's scope may be constrained in its capacity to thoroughly analyze the wide range of social media photos and memes, and it is likely to only take into account memes and images that were well-liked at the time the data was being gathered.

4. THE FRAMEWORK OF SEMIOTIC VIOLENCE

The micro-level or individual-level perspective is employed in explanations of violence against women that centre on traits that individuals possess. It offers theoretical frameworks for understanding violence against women, including social learning theory, psychopathology, psychological and physiological explanations, resource theory, and exchange theory. The social learning theory is a widely accepted explanatory framework for violence against women. It posits that individuals acquire behavioural patterns through the observation and experience of violent acts. The psychopathological perspective posits that violence perpetrated against women may be attributed to the presence of a personality disorder or mental illness in the perpetrator, which may impede their ability to adhere to typical inhibitions against violent conduct. According to biological and physiological theories, violence perpetrated against women can be attributed to the process of natural selection. These theories posit that men, who are biologically inclined to maximize their reproductive success, may resort to non-consensual sexual acts when faced with challenges in securing willing female partners. Researchers have identified alcohol as a common contributing factor to violent acts perpetrated against women. Following exchange theory, individuals are perceived as exhibiting specific behaviours to receive a reward or avoid punishment. Within this framework, it is plausible to interpret men's violence against women as a strategy employed by men to uphold their social status. The theory of resource allocation is positioned within the exchange theory paradigm, which posits that men resort to violent means to assert dominance over women in familial relationships when alternative methods of influence are unavailable. Unlike micro-level theories, macro-level or sociocultural theories centre on the social and cultural factors that contribute to the likelihood of violence against women. Several macro-oriented theories can be categorized as explanations for violence against women. The factors under consideration encompass societal tolerance towards violent behaviour, the influence of patriarchal or feminist ideologies, a subculture that promotes violent conduct, and structural stress.

Sociocultural theories have endeavoured to incorporate social structural and family processes while examining the impact of social location, including social class, education, and income, on violence against women. In contemporary times, the inclination in theoretical advancement concerning violence perpetrated against women has shifted towards the creation of multidimensional theories that incorporate social structural factors and individual characteristics.

The paper's various theories demonstrate that gender hierarchies are reinforced and justified through reflexive and unconscious means of structural, political, and cultural violence. Upon examining semiotic violence, it becomes apparent that this framework has predominantly remained concealed. The statement advocates for a re-examination of women's experiences to determine if current typologies are all-encompassing in capturing the various tactics utilized to inflict harm, delegitimize, and marginalize women in their overall life trajectory. Theoretical work in feminist studies that proposes a spectrum of violence perpetrated against women emphasizes the importance of identifying a comprehensive range of violent acts. This is crucial because acts of gender violence are interconnected and can overlap, thereby influencing and strengthening one another (Kelly, 1988). Feminist activism must excavate and label these acts that undermine human dignity. This process is also essential for the development of novel terminologies that can articulate and legitimize women's encounters.

According to semiotic analysis, lexical items as well as images could be valuable tools for maintaining the status quo. Semiotic violence, as a generic notion, refers to the infliction of harm, punishment, and subjugation on women through the exploitation and reinforcement of gender inequality through the use of words, pictures, and, occasionally, body language. The public significance of these crimes, which are committed against specific women but aim to convey the idea that all women are unworthy, is one of their distinguishing characteristics. By utilizing semiotic resources to denigrate other oppressed groups, acts can take on greater resonance and result in intersectional expressions of violence.

Semiotic analysis, drawing from the fields of philosophy of language and philosophy of art and aesthetics, aims to interpret words and images as texts. This approach offers a valuable understanding of the interpretive frameworks that shape and direct human perceptions of the external world (Chandler 2017). As per the assertions of Charles Peirce (1994), the entirety of the human experience is subject to mediation by signs, the impact of which on the structuring of cognitive processes remains imperceptible and involuntary. According to Ferdinand Saussure ([1959] 2001), the objective of the analysis is to identify fundamental units of meaning and patterns that can facilitate the clarification of these interpretive frameworks.

This study, pertaining to feminist research, posits that signs are products of social construction rather than mere reflections of objective reality. The prevalence of power dynamics often results in the prioritization of the viewpoints and encounters of advantaged factions. This is exemplified by the occurrence of exnomination, in which dominant groups perceive themselves as the unmarked standard and classify others as the marked classification (Barthes 1957). The act of deconstructing signs can serve as a vital means of exposing and contesting systems of privilege and oppression, as words and images play a significant role in the establishment and perpetuation of social hierarchies (Chandler 2017).

The utilization of semiotic analysis, in conjunction with theories pertaining to structural, cultural, and symbolic violence, posits that verbal and visual representations can serve as significant means for upholding the existing societal order. According to Kate Manne, the psychic threat that powerful women pose can be reduced using imaginative takedowns, such as vilification, demonization, belittlement, humiliation, mockery, lampooning, shunning, and shaming, rather than physical ones. This insight is discussed in her work published in 2018. The public often tends to trivialize such attacks, even though the harms caused by words and images are significant. Furthermore, women may be accused of being excessively sensitive in such situations.

The dynamics referred to by Krook (2022) are denoted as "semiotic violence against women." Semiotic violence is a broad notion that involves utilizing language, imagery, and, in certain instances, nonverbal cues to harm, regulate, and oppress women, thereby perpetuating gender disparities. In the realm of politics, the term is specifically utilized to denote the use of semiotic resources to deprive women of their political rights. A salient characteristic of these actions is their conspicuousness in the public sphere: although directed towards specific women, they aim to convey the notion that women collectively lack merit. Acts can acquire greater significance by applying semiotic resources to disparage other marginalized communities, resulting in the emergence of intersectional forms of violence.

The occurrence of semiotic violence is not a recent development. The proliferation of harmful depictions has been greatly facilitated by recent technological advancements, resulting in the normalization of such tropes as they are disseminated to wider and potentially worldwide audiences. Online communities that allow users to remain anonymous play a significant role in creating and disseminating digitally altered visual media. Additionally, these communities provide a shield of anonymity for those who engage in such activities, as noted by Citron (2014). According to Emma Jane's (2017) observations, the internet is not the originator of sexism, but it is significantly intensifying its impact in ways that have not been witnessed before.

With this understanding of semiotic violence in place, now we will see how it gets triggered in the digital space.

5. DATA ANALYSIS: SEMIOTIC VIOLENCE IN DIGITAL SPACE

In 1965, Saussure introduced a semiotic dyad comprising a signifier and a signified. The signifier refers to concrete components such as lines or background, while the signified pertains to an abstract concept within an individual's cognition. Chandler (2017) posits that the differentiation between the signifier and the signified can also be explicated in relation to form and content. In order to achieve a comprehensive comprehension of the signifier and the signified, a specific signifier/signified combination must be accompanied by additional signals, rather than existing in isolation. Saussure introduced a semiotic paradigm that is "structural" in nature in his theoretical framework.

To conduct a semiotic analysis of memes or images, available in the digital-spatial semiosphere, it is necessary to scrutinize their external characteristics and forms as they function as signs. Of particular interest is how the memetic components, in conjunction with the societal conventions and shared encounters they represent, manifest an additional phenomenon. Consider the following:

Digital advertisements, which aim to promote goods and services, incorporate an analysis of societal attitudes in order to effectively engage potential consumers. Due to the fact that a significant portion of their intended audiences belongs to these groups, they tailor their approach to align with the prevailing moral standards and principles of the majority. During the course of their actions, they reiterate unfavourable principles and standardize rigid, male-dominated standards. *Imperial Blue* has a collection of promotional materials categorized under the heading "Men will be Men" which is a perfect example in this juncture of discussion. Figure 3 can be located not only on the organization's website but also on its official account. The advertisement features a group of three individuals, comprising two males and a female, who are situated within a lift. The female is depicted as being engaged in a phone conversa-

Figure 3. Digital advertisement: Imperial Blue

Figure 4. Projection of gender in memes (Instance 1)

Figure 5. Projection of gender in memes (Instance 2)

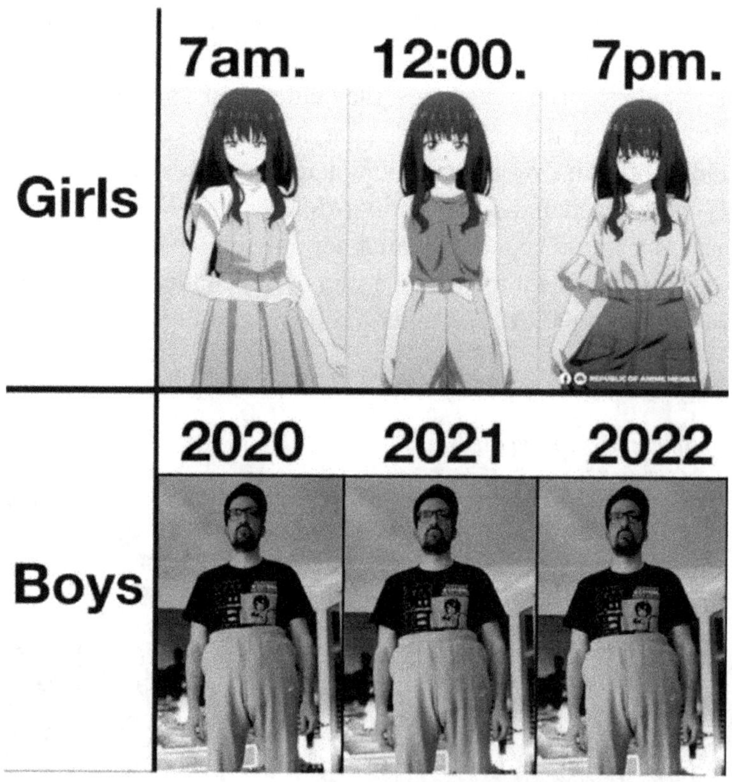

tion, while the males are portrayed as standing still and attempting to conceal their physical discomfort by holding their breath in anticipation of the lift's descent. Upon the woman's departure from the lift, they exhale, thereby enabling the abdomen to revert to its normal state. The aforementioned matter is devoid of any profanity, however, it does overtly exhibit content that disparages the human physique and employs the catchphrase "Men will be Men" to bolster its stance.

Likewise, the image depicted in Figure 4 subtly perpetuates the prevalent stereotype that women possess an inherent inclination towards materialism, and are susceptible to the allure of consumer goods and shopping.

This discussion can further be supported by the following figure as well:

Upon examining this meme or image, it becomes apparent that it reinforces established societal expectations by presupposing that women are inherently demanding. Women are frequently subjected to objectification and stereotyping based on their clothing or fashion choices, rather than being evaluated based on their abilities or qualifications. In contrast, there is a prevailing portrayal of men as pragmatic individuals who prioritize their obligations over their attire and dietary choices.

6. SEMIOTIC MODELLING

Items, colours, and shapes are used particularly as elements of advertisement design in the semiotic study displayed above (Figure 3). A thorough semiotic investigation, however, should go beyond the previously mentioned details and, if at all possible, attempt to comprehend the context.

Table 1. Semiotic analysis of Figures 3, 4, and 5

<table>
<tr><td rowspan="9">Semiotic Interpretation of Figure 3</td><td></td><td></td><th>Signifiers of Figure 3</th><th>Signified of Figure 3</th><th>Semiotic Violence</th></tr>
<tr><td rowspan="2">Body Presence/posture</td><td>Male</td><td>The abdominal region undergoes a retraction while the remaining portion of the body suspends respiration.</td><td>It is advisable to maintain a presentable and physically fit appearance when in the company of women.</td><td rowspan="2">Gender stereotyping pertains to the projection of societal norms and expectations regarding the roles and behaviours of men and women.</td></tr>
<tr><td>Female</td><td>whole body in a relaxed posture.</td><td>fit, smart and confident.</td></tr>
<tr><td rowspan="2">Body type</td><td>Male</td><td>Fat</td><td rowspan="2">In society, an individual's physical appearance is often evaluated based on their body shape and size.</td><td rowspan="2">The act of body shaming and the perpetuation of misogynistic ideals are concepts that objectify individuals regardless of gender.</td></tr>
<tr><td>Female</td><td>Slim</td></tr>
<tr><td rowspan="2">Dress type</td><td>Male</td><td>Sweater in check and formal</td><td>Mid-aged men</td><td rowspan="2">The age-old concept of 'mid-life crisis' has been observed to particularly objectify males.</td></tr>
<tr><td>Female</td><td>Saree</td><td>Traditionalism</td></tr>
<tr><td rowspan="2">Colour of the dress</td><td>Male</td><td>Dull colour</td><td>Dull life</td><td rowspan="2">The act of objectifying women is often associated with the colour pink, which is commonly associated with delicacy and femininity.</td></tr>
<tr><td>Female</td><td>Bright pink</td><td>Vibrant life</td></tr>
</table>

continued on following page

Table 1. Continued

			Signifiers of Figure 4	**Signified of Figure 4**	**Semiotic Violence**
Semiotic Interpretation of Figure 4	Body type	Female	Slim	In society, an individual's physical appearance is often evaluated based on their body shape and size.	The act of body shaming and the perpetuation of misogynistic ideals are concepts that objectify individuals regardless of gender.
	Foreground Element		Lots of shopping boxes in the hands of a female model	Women's love for shopping.	Gender stereotypes posit that women possess an inherent inclination towards materialism, and are susceptible to the influence of material possessions and shopping.
	Colour prominence		Red	Categorize something for a special purpose, in this case, 'sale'.	Demitting the projection of women.
			Signifiers of Figure 5	**Signified of Figure 5**	**Semiotic Violence**
Semiotic Interpretation of Figure 5	Body type	Male	Fat	It is a commonly held societal assumption that men who are not well-groomed or who have excess body weight or poor physical fitness are deemed acceptable. It is widely accepted that women are expected to possess a slender physique, maintain physical fitness, and exhibit well-groomed appearances without question.	The act of body shaming and the perpetuation of misogynistic ideals are concepts that objectify individuals regardless of gender.
		Female	Slim		
	Dress and time	Male	A black T-shirt and grey pyjama over a constant period.	It is commonly believed that men are less concerned about their attire. In contrast, females tend to exhibit greater interest in their attire.	The portrayal of women as high-maintenance spendthrifts is a form of objectification.
		Female	Contemporary attire undergoes frequent alterations.		
	Colour of the dress	Male	Black and Grey	Dull life	The phenomenon of associating masculinity with black and grey hues, while femininity is often linked with red, green, and pink, commonly associated with delicacy and femininity, can be seen as a form of objectification.
		Female	Bright colours	Vibrant life	

The paper's analysis highlights that the portrayal of individuals influences the construction of social representations. The composition of the images showcased in this context pertains to contemporary social practices, delving into novel approaches to objectifying individuals based on their gender. The aforementioned projections are frequently intertwined with traditional methods through specific ideological mechanisms, which are conveyed through discursive, textual, and semiotic elements. These elements include intertextuality/interdiscursivity, modality, vocabulary, cohesion, and semiotic features such as photographs, colour, body posture, and body shape. As previously posited, gender identities can exhibit both a degree of rigidity and adaptability. The semiotic violence that is inherent in language and is inflicted upon the bodies of women, despite its seemingly immutable nature, has the potential to be further transformed within the digital realm. The resolution of this issue is contingent upon individuals, regardless of their gender identities, actively participating in political activism aimed at combatting discrimination. This activism must be conducted through the use of symbolic tools that are capable of effecting change within institutions that perpetuate systems of oppression.

CONCLUSION

The present investigation on gender-based violence, utilizing semiotic analysis of images and memes within the digital semiosphere, posits that conventional gender identities persist alongside novel depictions of both males and females. Moreover, it demonstrates that within digital media, certain elements that may appear innocuous to the naked eye perpetuate gender bias in their portrayal of femininity and masculinity. However, our analysis indicates that individuals, regardless of gender, have their identities constructed by advertising through a combination of various lifestyles and fragments of discourse technologies. These technologies serve to ideologically position individuals to embrace identity transformations to integrate into consumer communities within the global digital marketplace.

Despite its predictable and methodical expressions, semiotic violence has become normalized to obscure it from the wider populace. This study posits the existence of semiotic violence within the realm of gender projection, drawing upon social media content and research from various semiotic fields. The present paper expounds upon each subtype of every mode, employing illustrative examples to demonstrate the utilization of language and imagery in the act of opposing, excluding, and debasing gender.

REFERENCES

Barthes, R. (1957). *Mythologies.* Paris: Les Lettres nouvelles.

Borba, R., & Osterman, A. (2007). Do bodies matter? Travestis' embodiment of (trans)gender identity through the manipulation of the Brazilian Portuguese grammatical gender system. *Gender and Language, 1*(1), 131–147. doi:10.1558/genl.2007.1.1.131

Chandler, D. (2017). *Semiotics: The Basis* (3rd ed.). Routledge.

Chouliaraki, L., & Fairclough, N. (1999). *Discourse in Late Modernity: Rethinking Critical Analysis.* Edinburgh University Press.

Citron, D. K. (2014). *Hate Crimes in Cyberspace.* Harvard University Press. doi:10.4159/harvard.9780674735613

Eco, U. (1976). *A theory of semiotics.* Indiana University Press. doi:10.1007/978-1-349-15849-2

Essien-Eyo, A., & Ottoh, B. (2011). Semiotics of cartoon in two Nigerian newspapers: the guardian and the punch. *LWATI: Journal of Contemporary Research, 8*(3), 79-90.

Fairclough, N. (1989). *Language and Power*. Longman.

Fairclough, N. (1992). *Discourse and Social Change*. Polity Press.

Fairclough, N. (1995). *Media Discourse*. Edward Arnold.

Fairclough, N. (1999). Linguistic and Intertextual Analysis within Discourse Analysis. In The Discourse Reader (pp. 183-211). Academic Press.

Fairclough, N. (2000). *New Labor, New Language*. Routledge.

Giddens, A. (2000). *Mundo em Descontmle*. Academic Press.

Haliday, M. (1978). *Language as Social Semiotic: The Social Interpretation of Language and Meaning*. Edward Arnold.

Halliday, M., & Hasan, R. (1989). *Language Context and Text: Aspects of Language in a Social-Semiotic Perspective* (2nd ed.). Oxford University Press.

Jane, E. (2017). Misogyny Online: A Short (and Brutish) History. *Sage (Atlanta, Ga.)*. Advance online publication. doi:10.4135/9781473916029

Kelly, L. (1988). *Surviving Sexual Violence*. University of Minnesota Press.

Kress, G., & van Leeuwen, T. (1996). *Reading Images: The Grammar of Visual Design*. Routledge.

Kristeva, J. (1994). *On Yury Lotman* (Vol. 109). Publications of the Modern Language Association.

Krook, M. (2022). Semiotic Violence against Women: Theorizing Harms against Female Politicians. *Signs (Chicago, Ill.)*, *47*(2), 371–397. doi:10.1086/716642

Litosseliti, L. (2006). *Gender and Language: Theory and Practice*. Hodder Arnold.

Lotman, Y. (1990). *Universe of the Mind*. Indiana University Press.

Magalhaes, I. (2005). Critical Discourse Analysis and the Semiotic Construction on Gender Identities. *DELTA. Documentação de Estudos em Lingüística Teórica e Aplicada*, ●●●, 179–205. doi:10.1590/S0102-44502005000300011

Matsuda, M. J., III. C. R., Delgado, R., & Crenshaw, K. W. (1993). Words That Wound: Critical Race Theory, Assaultive Speech, and the First Amendment. Westview.

Mey, J. (1985). *Whose Language: A Study in Linguistic Pragmatics*. John Benjamin Publishing Company. doi:10.1075/pbcs.3

Mills, S. (1995). *Feminist Stylistics*. Routledge.

Mills, S. (2005). *Discourse*. Routledge.

Pasricha, J. (2021, August). *"Violence" Online in India: Cybercrimes Against Women and Minorities on Social Media.* Retrieved January 25, 2023, from Feminism India: https://feminisminindia.com/wp-content/uploads/2021/08/Cyberviolence-Against-Women-in-India_Research-Report_FII.pdf

Pierce, C. S. (1994). Peirce on Signs: Writings on Semiotic. In J. Hoopes (Ed.). University of North Carolina Press.

Reuters. (2020, January 23). *India Today*. Retrieved February 1, 2023, from https://www.indiatoday.in/india/story/women-politicians-abused-social-media-amnesty-study-1639432-2020-01-23

Sameeran, P. (2016). *Arrow Perfect Grammar Class 2*. Arrow Publications Private Limited.

Saussure, F. (1959). *Course in General Linguistics*. Columbia University Press.

Talbot, M. (1998). *Language and Gender*. Polity Press.

Thompson, J. (1998). *A Midia e a Modernidade: Uma Teoria Social da Midia*. Academic Press.

Vernadsky, V. (1926). Biosfera. Leningrad.

Żurawicka, M. (2015, July). *Research World*. Retrieved December 2022, from https://archive.research-world.com/semiotics-of-brand-gender-what-gender-is-your-brand/

Chapter 12
Cyberbullying:
A Rapidly Growing Social Cancer

Mayuri Pathak
CMR University, Bangalore, India

ABSTRACT

The internet is directly proportional to the influence it has on society. Although contacting others has become quite simple with the internet, it has its own disadvantages. Privacy invasion, internet abuse, cyberbullying, and many more negative effects are just a few of its downsides. The purpose of this chapter is to provide a succinct analysis of the notion of cyberbullying. Not every internet user in the digital world identifies what they encounter as cyberbullying since it seems to be becoming more commonplace. Finding solutions to problems becomes challenging if the cause of the issue cannot be located. To have an in-depth understanding of the issue, it is essential to first define cyberbullying and examine its characteristics. This chapter attempts to understand cyberbullying in its many forms and causes in addition to examining people's, especially youths', idea on this deadly phenomenon that is rapidly growing.

INTRODUCTION

Today's general public is dependent on the Internet, which has developed into a daily requirement. The impact of the internet on society is inversely correlated. The internet has made it relatively easy to communicate with people, but it also has drawbacks. Once upon a time, defying societal expectations by standing up to bullies was considered a heroic act. The scenery is less bare-bones today with the entry of cyberbullying. At any time of day, teenagers are required to put up with peer bullying online, sometimes without even knowing who is doing it. Youth throughout the world are facing serious health issues as a result of the widespread use of digital gadgets, and this issue extends beyond school grounds. Cyberbullying is the use of an internet platform to harass, threaten, denigrate, or embarrass another person. Bullying data indicate that victims are more likely to commit suicide as a result of cyberbullying in the most severe situations. Just a few of its drawbacks include privacy invasion, online abuse, and several other unfavourable outcomes. According to this definition, cyberbullying is conventional bullying with the addition of modern communication technology. Its aggressive behaviour is what gives it its hostile

DOI: 10.4018/978-1-6684-8893-5.ch012

quality. Although we might debate the extent to which criminals are aware of the gravity of their actions, the purpose relates to the degree of knowledge of injuring others. It is challenging to determine whether a cyberbullying assault was intended or a response because of its indirect nature. In addition, according to some writers, cyberbullying may spread widely or be imitated by others if it meets the conditions for recurrence and regularly creates an imbalance of power, even if it originates from a single individual act. Since it appears to be getting more prevalent, not every internet user in the digital world recognises what they experience as cyberbullying. If the root of the problem cannot be identified, finding remedies becomes difficult. So, the most important requisite in today's digital world is to not only recognise the issue but work on understanding it in-depth and find accurate solutions to it. The focus of this chapter is to offer a brief study of the concept of cyberbullying, its consequences, ways of prevention, its gender-related viewpoint, and so on.

Compared to other kinds of bullying, cyberbullying is more likely to go undetected by parents and authorities. The reason for this is that victims believe they must learn how to handle it on their own, and they also worry that if they notify their parents, their access to the internet would be restricted or discontinued. This brand-new kind of bullying—cyberbullying—follows youngsters from the school corridors to their homes. When they check their e-mail or cell phone first thing in the morning and continue until they turn off their computer or mobile phone at night, many cyberbullying victims are being harassed.

Bullying and cyberbullying have numerous distinctions, even though they are frequently compared in terms of form and approach, which can make the latter even more harmful. In the first case, the targets might not be aware of the bully's identity or motivation. Using anonymous email addresses or fictitious screen identities, the cyberbully can hide their identity behind a computer or phone. Second, a cyberbully's unpleasant activities are contagious, meaning that with a few keystrokes or touchscreen impressions, a sizable number of individuals can be engaged in the victimisation or at least learn about the occurrence. Therefore, it appears that there is an endless supply of prospective victims, criminals, and witnesses/bystanders. Third, as cyberbullying may be carried out from a distance and the bully need not be aware of the target's prompt retaliation, it is frequently simpler to be cruel using technology. Because they are shielded from the victim's reaction, some teenagers may fail to realise the significant hurt they are causing. However, many people lack the technological know-how to monitor what teenagers are doing online, despite the fact that parents and educators are doing a better job of supervising children at home and in school. As a consequence, it's possible to overlook a victim's experiences and fail to stop a bully in their tracks. Even if bullies are discovered, many adults are unprepared to respond in an appropriate way.

With the increasing number of students utilising and fully embracing internet interaction, cyberbullying is becoming a bigger concern. They do this for a variety of reasons, including their academic work, staying in touch with their friends, playing games, learning about famous people, sharing their digital creations, and many more. It is not unexpected that some young people have chosen to utilise technology to be spiteful or threatening towards others given how much of their lives now revolve around online communication tools. Teenagers are vulnerable to victimisation all the time since they are always linked to technology. Moreover, it is also simpler to be hostile when typing than when speaking to someone in person as per human psychology.

As mentioned by Charles E. Notar (2013) in CyberBullying: A Review of the Literature, a total of 137 participants took part in the Wong-Lo and Bullock study (2011). Of these 137 participants, 62 were adolescents and 75 were parents; 90% of the adolescents said they had either been victims of cyberbullying or witnessed it. Additionally, 50% of the victims did not know the attacker, and 70% of the victims had experienced cyberbullying once to twice in the previous month. 89% of the parent participants said they were familiar of cyberbullying-related concerns, and 89% said they did not know whether or not their kid has experienced cyberbullying. The findings of this study provide some credence to other studies that have highlighted the connection between cyberbullying and more conventional forms of bullying. It should be highlighted that there is not a significant degree of conventional and cyberbullying overlap. This finding leads to the conclusion that, despite certain similarities between conventional bullying and cyberbullying, the latter appears to be characterised by its own distinctive traits.[1]

Moreover, parents appear to be generally aware of cyberbullying as a kind of aggressive behaviour involving ICT according to earlier study (Mesch, 2009). Nevertheless, people frequently accept stereotypes about the victim and the offender that, according to relevant scientific results, is incorrect, skewed, or oversimplified because they lack adequate information. It may be claimed that although parents are unsure of how to conceptualise cyberbullying, they generally feel it is a significant issue that their children frequently face and that a victim will not lie. However, the scenarios is quite different.

Cyberbullying and Teenagers

Teenage cyberbullying has elevated to the level of a global public health problem, thus it merits more research. The current research on the impact of cyberbullying on adolescent health is reviewed in this article, along with recommendations for further study. According to an analysis of the available data, cyberbullying endangers the health and well-being of teenagers. Numerous correlational research has shown a clear connection between teenage engagement in cyberbullying and detrimental health indicators. Teenagers who experience cyberbullying report more severe bodily symptoms, anxiety, loneliness, and depression symptoms. Personal traits are mostly the cause of cyberbullying. Online bullying, which occurs when people abuse others for nefarious, hegemonic, retaliatory, or amusing reasons, is the key contributing cause. Independent of the status of present victimisation, prior research, and data indicate that moral disengagement has a comparable impact on bullying perpetration for those who are most involved. This makes it one of the factors contributing to bullying. Since most cyberbullying occurs in an anonymous setting, it is simple for bullies to abuse anybody online while hiding their genuine identities. A variety of factors have been shown to have a role in someone becoming a cyberbully. Narcissism, in which people emphasise their interpersonal connections over social position and authority, is, in fact, another cause of cyberbullying.

Even if the number of incidents varies throughout the globe, cyberbullying is a worldwide burning issue. Some of the instances as per different statistical data of different reputed websites, including Statista, Cyberbullying Research Center, and SDG,[2] belonging to various countries and institutions are the following: 1) Bullying in mobile gaming has happened to 34 percent of British teenagers, 2) In the United States, 15 percent of kids claim to have experienced cyberbullying, 3) Since COVID-19 happened, 75 percent of Romanian students say they experience cyberbullying less frequently. 4) Cyberbullying victims in Myanmar were made fun of for having problems paying attention and comprehending lectures, 5) Male teenagers are more likely than female adolescents to report cyberbullying offenders in Taiwan, Hong Kong, and Mainland China.[3]

Cyberbullying perpetrators are more likely to admit to abusing drugs, acting aggressively, and engaging in delinquent behaviour. Cyberbullying and teenage relationships have been discovered to be affected by mediating/moderating mechanisms. In the digital world, a lot of people even think that there is minimal probability of detection, identification, and even penalty on the Internet. On the whole, the Internet has been a good thing because it has truly opened up the entire globe to consumers who access it on a variety of devices. Despite this, some children feel free to communicate or publish whatever they want online due to the problems previously mentioned, without taking into account the fact that this behaviour can hurt others and can result in severe psychological and emotional traumas.

This new public realm, online communication, has both benefits and drawbacks for humanity. When the internet first entered society, it wrought havoc, of which cyberbullying is only a minor part. Contrarily, this is not meant to discount all the positive effects it has produced. Communication has altered as a result of the value of information being shared globally without regard to time or geographic constraints. That brings with it the advocacy of individuals battling to address this behaviour and who have committed themselves to further mental health. To educate any prospective law that tackles the issue, it is essential to document how this generation is impacted by a new domain of communication and what the consequence will be. In order to solve new difficulties, it will be difficult to avoid studying these new trends. Bullying has many different subtypes, and as society is always changing, cyberbullying will probably develop into a brand-new problem in the future. However, this issue may be diminished and perhaps even help save or enhance the lives of people with diligence, tenacity, and awareness of mental health. Prevention, education, or a combination of the two may be used to achieve this. This is why it's important to acknowledge the issue.

Online crimes may come after or come before those that are committed offline. As cyberbullying has far-reaching effects on its victims, who suffer from intrusions of their privacy as well as emotional and psychological suffering, impairment to their professional prospects, and withdrawal from public discourse, it also represents an infringement of the freedom of expression, the right to equal participation in public life, and the right to a private and family life from the standpoint of human rights. Thus it is also clear that cyberbullying poses the greatest danger to equality and safety from violence and prejudice. In addition, it is no surprise that the places where kids gather the most frequently are the places where cyberbullying happens most frequently across a range of venues and mediums in cyberspace. As a result of the fact that many youngsters initially hung out in chat rooms, that is where the majority of abuse occurred. Most young people nowadays are attracted to social media platforms like Instagram, Snapchat, and Twitter as well as video-sharing websites like YouTube in recent years. More instances of cyberbullying in certain settings have been reported as a result of this development. An environment where hate and harm are conveyed can also be created using voice chat, text chat, and messaging on phones or tablets.

Relation Between Cyberbullying and Gender

The performance of gender, cyberbullying, and cyber victimization all have intricate, nuanced relationships. Cyberbullying, especially in the case of women and girls, may occur instantly, spread swiftly, and be savage due to the nearly unrestricted access individuals have to internet communications. Besides, the teachings that women and girls acquire about being female frequently have an impact on how they see themselves, how confident they feel, how they relate to others, and how they seek approval. Girls who feel uncertain about their standing in the world are more open or susceptible to criticism. Cyberbullies and online predators prey on this weakness in order to abuse and oppress women and girls.

One of the instances where a 12-year-old girl takes her own life due to cyberbullying was reported in The New York Times on Sep 13, 2013, under the heading "Girl's Suicide Points to Rise in Apps Used by Cyberbullies" by Lizette Alvarez. The death of Rebecca Ann Sedwick, "after being maligned, threatened and taunted online, mostly through a new collection of texting and photo-sharing cell-phone applications" raises concerns regarding the prevalence and appeal of these applications and websites among kids, as well as the capacity of parents to monitor their kids' online connections.4

One issue with studies on cyberbullying is that it frequently makes excessively generic statements about its impact on teenagers or adults. Researchers who generalise neglect crucial concerns that are tied to particular ages as well as gender. Additionally, the majority of studies on cyberbullying is quantitative, concentrating on the quantity of encounters rather than the nature of the events. It is necessary to talk about people who are victims of cyberbullying.

In order to comprehend and address the problem of gender-based cyberbullying, we must accept that violence against women and girls, whether it occurs offline or online, is the most extreme instance of discrimination based on gender. Sexual assault, domestic abuse, other forms of physical, emotional, or financial violence as well as cyberbullying all stem from the same patriarchal structure.

A worldwide occurrence, cyberbullying is a major reason behind victimisation of women and the objectification of women as a result of technological innovation. Even though India is one of the few countries to pass and execute legislation to prevent cybercrimes, any particular provisions involving cybercrime against women are yet unaddressed. The lack of respect for women in modern culture is a major factor in why cybercrimes against women are still tolerated in India, as well as the fact that many individuals find it difficult to accept that simply posting on social media is now considered a criminal.

Cyberbullying Statistics

In India, 83% of children between the ages of 10 and 14 own a smartphone, which is 7% higher than the global average of 76%. Due to the significant security gap between parents and children, this increases the likelihood of being exposed to internet hazards. In addition, 22% of Indian children reported experiencing cyberbullying at some point, which is significantly higher than the global average of 17%, despite the fact that parental concern is often minimal.[5]

According to a poll done by the neighbourhood social media platform LocalCircles, more than 40% of urban Indian parents acknowledge their 9–17-year-old children are addicted to films, games, and social media. However, parents acknowledge that they are partly or entirely to blame for this "addiction" that is now blatantly apparent in youngsters. The majority of respondents—about 31%—said that kids were learning via play. Nearly 28% of them claimed that giving kids access to electronics sooner than they ought to have was what caused the addiction, while 26% blamed online activities connected to school. As a part of SMM's YOLO (Youth Online Learning Organization) initiative, the Institute of Governance, Policies & Politics (IGPP) in collaboration with Social Media Matters and Youth Online Learning Organisation (Yolo), has performed a survey on "Patterns of Internet Usage Among Youths In India." The survey includes many elements linked to inclination, pattern, susceptibility, and awareness connected to internet usage. According to this research, 85% of non-adult users who are Indian youth have access to cellphones. The majority of them spend five hours every day online, and 80% acknowledged using social media. More young people are watching videos on OTT sites outside YouTube. However, there is a dearth of knowledge regarding safety and privacy controls on internet platforms.[6]

Literature Review

The present study has been conducted by an ethical researcher. The prevalence and intensity of cyberbullying are clearly identified in the literature review. Additionally, the literature review outlines several types of cyberbullying among the youth that engage in victims. As cyberbullying is a relatively recent phenomenon, there may be limits to the study due to the fact that many studies have already been published on the subject.

In *Cyberbullying: Bullying in the Digital Age,* Robin M. Kowalski, Susan P. Limber, Patricia W. Agatston mentions that the main aim of writing the book is to assist adults in gaining the information and skills necessary to be real resources for children in preventing and dealing with cyberbullying incidents rather than being seen as obstacles, which is regrettably a common perspective of young people. (Kowalski et al., 2016) It is a prime necessity to educate parents, educators and community organizations about the growing problem of cyberbullying, and empower them to prevent this new form of bullying from becoming a regular experience for youth navigating the internet and other technological tools.

Published in *Current Issues in Middle Level Education*, the article 'Cyberbullying: Victimization Through Electronic Means' written by Gahan Bailey describe various forms of cyberbullying, a portrayal of victims and offenders, prevention programs, and policy implications for school districts with a detailed analysis of several research works carried on understanding and defining cyberbullying. "The literature reveals that cyberbullying, bullying by electronic means, is a reality affecting our youth in negative, serious, and disturbing ways. Although most of the cyberbullying takes place off school grounds, school districts are distressed as they are compelled to create policy addressing this form of 21st Century bullying. Keeping our youth safe at school when involved in off-campus electronic bullying and aggressive behaviors is central to the policies school districts must develop" (Bailey 2013, p.6).

Charisse L Nixon in the well-researched article *Current perspectives: the impact of cyberbullying on adolescent health* discusses the impact of cyberbullying on the health of the adolescent victims referring to several correlational studies that demonstrates a cogent relationship between adolescents' involvement in cyberbullying and negative health indices. Teenagers who experience cyberbullying report more severe bodily symptoms, anxiety, loneliness, and depressed symptoms. Cyberbully perpetrators are more likely to admit to abusing drugs, acting aggressively, and engaging in delinquent behaviour. It has been discovered that mediating/moderating mechanisms have an impact on how cyberbullying and adolescent health are related. To further comprehend the long-term implications of cyberbullying on adolescent health, more longitudinal research is required (Nixon, 2014).

In *Cyberbullying: Approaches, Consequences and Interventions*, Lucy R. Betts gives a detailed idea on cyberbullying, the debates related to it, its unique nature, its prevalence, the consequences of this rising crime, and most importantly its prevention. The author discusses the rising danger of suicides related to cyberbullying cases. "Researchers', educational practitioners', and parents' interest in cyberbullying can be attributed to the many consequences associated with involvement in face-to-face bullying and cyberbullying. However, perhaps the greatest catalyst for society's interest in cyberbullying is the many well-documented cases of 'cyberbullycide.' Cyberbullycide is the term used to describe a case where a young person has committed suicide, and one of the causes of their actions is attributed to cyberbullying and negative experiences in the digital world" (Betts, 2016, p. 3).

Cyberbullying: A Deadly Trend edited by The New York Times Editorial Staff (2019) is an anthology on cyberbullying incidents of some of the serious cyberbullying cases that took place in the USA, including some high-profile cases, evolution of technology, the need for parenting and proper education on cyberbullying and its consequences. It is divided into 5 chapters, each dealing with different notions of cyberbullying. "Privacy issues that were until recently restricted to celebrities now concern the most anonymous among us. The result has been a kind of Information Age vertigo. Sadly, young people are the most deeply impacted. Many young parents and educators feel helpless in the face of these developments, caught between encouraging children and young adults to immerse themselves in the many benefits of technological innovation, and trying to protect them from the profound damage this same innovation makes possible" (p. 7).

From the literature on cyberbullying, it is quite evident that cybercrimes lack a moral foundation in society and are thus ignored. This gets us to the most crucial section, where individuals must progress socially, respect others' rights, and comprehend what is considered a crime. The general public has to learn to appreciate each other and to respect other people's privacy. Only if young children are taught to appreciate others from an early age can all of this be accomplished. As a result, altering the educational system is a crucial component of any strategy to combat cybercrime against women in India. Stricter punitive measures are also necessary. People, government, NGOs, and other groups need to work together for this change since it cannot come from one section of society alone.

RESEARCH METHODOLOGY

The research methodology of this study consisted of a survey of the perceptions of the samples on cyberbullying. Through survey, a researcher can investigate social psychological phenomena using samples that are representative of the population that will be the subject of generalisations. These benefits of survey research make it an important tool in the toolbox of methodological tools available to social psychologists. Researchers can triangulate across measurements and methodologies by including this methodology into a comprehensive programme of study, which provides more convincing evidence of social psychological phenomena than any other methodological approach can.[7]

The questions for this survey were provided by the author herself, and it was sent out to the samples using the author's email system. Participants were guaranteed the confidentiality of their replies on the survey instrument, and the responses provided to the authors were anonymous. The return rate was 77.5%, with 31 valid replies.

The samples selected randomly belong to the age range of 18 to 25 years, most of whom are pursuing their formal education. As an unprejudiced portion of a population is chosen in a simple random sampling, every person in the population has a precisely equal probability of getting chosen using this method of sampling. Since it only includes one random selection and requires minimal prior population knowledge, this method is the easiest of all the probability sampling techniques. Any research conducted on this sample should have high internal and external validity since it incorporates randomization, which also reduces the likelihood of biases like sampling bias and selection bias.

In this chapter, the author tries to examine the knowledge of the samples on cyberbullying and their awareness level. As cyberbullying is a growing phenomenon in the digital world, it is necessary to know how the youth—the most vulnerable group—takes cyberbullying as, knowing their ideas is very important to protect them. The results of this research will be analysed in light of the prevalence of cyberbullying and the issue's seriousness or lack thereof, as determined by the perspectives of the populations being studied (young).

Objectives of the Study

The primary objectives of the study are:

1) To understand the necessity of focusing on the topic of cyberbullying.
2) To raise awareness among elders and kids about the deadly consequences of this new horrendous phenomenon—cyberbullying.
3) To have a basic idea on the impact of cyberbullying on the youth.

DISCUSSION

In the present research, out of the 31 respondents, 17 (55%) are female and 14 (45%) are male. The respondents were asked if they know about cyberbullying to which 26 of them (83.9%) replied positively and 5 of them (16.1%) replied that they don't have any idea on cyberbullying. (Table 1) The second question asked if they have ever experienced cyberbullying, to which 21 respondents (70%) said 'yes' and the other 9 (30%) said 'no,' 1 respondent didn't answer the question (Table 2). The third question was about the impact of cyberbullying on them, to which 18 respondents (60%) replied with a 'yes' and 12 respondents (40%) replied 'no,' 1 respondent refrained from answering this specific question (Table 3). The fourth question was trickier compared to the rest so only 28 of 31 respondents responded; it was about the impact of social media on cyberbullying. 25 of them (89.3%) think that social media does have an impact on cyberbullying whereas the other 3 (10.7%) denies the fact (Table 4). The fifth question was if the impact of cyberbullying remains limited to the mental and psychological condition of the victim or it reaches to the extent of physical harm. 28 of the participants responded to this question: 19 respondents (67.9%) think that cyberbullying has a direct impact on the mental and psychological condition; the other 9 respondents (32.1%) think it causes physical harm to the cyberbullying victim (Table 5).

It is a general consensus that the rape culture has a significant rise due to the increased cyber-culture, so the researcher thought of confirming it in the survey and added a question related to this matter in the questionnaire. 28 of 31 participants responded to this question: 19 of them (67.9%) think that the increase in rape is directly proportional to the increased cyber-culture, whereas the remaining 9 (32.1%) respondents disagree to the fact (Table 6). It is usually believed that the traditional bullies are likely to carry out cyberbullying as well. Based on that thought, the researcher thought of asking the participants about their idea on traditional bullies engaging in cyberbullying, to which 22 (78.6%) respondents responded in a 'yes' and 6 (21.4%) responded in a 'no.' (Table 7) The other 3 participants refrained from answering to this question.

As cyberbullying is quite a serious crime in the present digital world, knowledge on the implementation of specific laws and understanding of them is very trivial. Accordingly, the researcher has added a question on the implementation of legal rules and laws to prevent cyberbullying and punish cyberbullies. To this question, the options given were agree, neutral, and disagree. 28 participants responded to this question out of which 27 (96.4%) selected 'agree' whereas 1 (3.6%) selected 'neutral,' none of them 'disagree'd to the implementation of laws to punish cyberbullies. (Table 8)

The researcher observed a much unexpected response in the next question which is related to their relation to the bullies that victimize them. The options given were 'someone you know,' 'relatives,' 'school/collegemates,' and 'others.' There were 25 responses to the query, out of which majority 13 (52%) responded as 'others,' 4 (16%) marked 'school/collegemates,' 3 (12%) mentioned 'relatives,' and 5 (20%) selected 'someone you know.' (Table 9)

For the question related to the cyberbullies' age, most respondents 16 (72.7%) mentioned that the cyberbullies who victimized them are older than the victims while 6 respondents (27.3%) selected the 'younger' option (Table 10). The final question was a subjective one: 'What do you think are the measures that should be taken to diminish matters of cyberbullying?' This question had various types of replies; the most common pointed out need was raising awareness, controlling the amount of gadget usage by parents, and implementation of laws related to cyberbullying.

From the survey, it is clearly visible that the respondents' ideas on cyberbullying is very limited, which points toward the fact that their innocence level is quite high. This innocence can lead to serious consequences in the future. Though they have faced cyberbullying to a certain extent, yet they are unaware of its devastation. They were even hesitating to reply to most of the questions due to the fear of getting recognised. Inspite of being literate, they are so uneducated in this field that they are yet to know the deadly results of cyberbullying; by the time they realise it, it will be too late to the extent of lose of human lives.

Moreover, since the majority of relevant studies were published within the past 20 years, research on cyberbullying may be regarded as being relatively new. As a result, there is currently no agreement among researchers investigating cyberbullying about fundamental questions relating to its conceptualization and the research approach that should be used. Furthermore, a comparable assessment of the relative empirical evidence for cyberbullying is that the lack of understanding about procedures that can protect their children has been observed to make parents particularly sensitive to cyberbullying and very concerned (Tokunaga, 2010).

SUGGESTIONS AND RECOMMENDATIONS

In order to communicate about any experiences they have online (or off) that upset or make them uncomfortable, youth should first establish a connection with an adult they trust (a parent, teacher, or someone else). Teenagers should, wherever possible, ignore mild name-calling or taunting and refrain from retaliating against bullies because doing so could just fuel the situation. Additionally, they should utilise the account and privacy options available in each network, app, and device to manage who may get in touch with them, engage with them, and view their online information. This can drastically lower their likelihood of being a victim.

While it is clear that much more study must be done on cyberbullying, both researchers and participants must agree on a specific description and a thorough understanding of the phenomenon. Keeping any documentation of cyberbullying for presentation to an adult who can assist with the problem is of great help to prevent cyberbullying cases. If victims of cyberbullying are able to keep a diary or journal of the dates, times, and incidents of the online abuse, it may also assist in verifying what was happening and who initiated it, during an inquiry. You can also send this information to the specific website or business that acts as the setting or conduit for the cyberbullying. Young people ought to take the time to report any harassment, threats, impersonation, or other issues they come across or encounter, and should keep in mind that doing so will ensure that their identity is protected to the fullest degree possible under the law.

Moreover, the involvement of onlookers is very important. Cyberbullying witnesses typically do not want to get involved due to the inconvenience and issues they worry it may cause them, but they frequently understand that what they are seeing is wrong and should stop. Bystanders, on the other hand, are actively promoting the behaviour by doing nothing. People believe that bystanders may significantly improve the situation for targets, who frequently feel powerless and hopeless and need someone to come to their rescue, by actively stepping up—in that instant or soon after. Anyone watching should record what they see and when. They should also step in when they feel safe doing so, and then speak with a responsible adult afterward.

Cyberbullying's immediate and long-term consequences are still being investigated, and there is growing agreement that they are detrimental. According to many research done on this area, those who experience online bullying are more likely to hurt themselves. Cyberbullying results in low self-esteem and intensely unpleasant feelings. Being the target of cyberbullying carries the danger of having suicidal thoughts or really trying to kill oneself.

As cyberbullying is a result of the interactions and choices made by a number of social actors within a dynamic, interactive framework of society as a whole, rather than just being a private offence between people, the barriers to effective management of cyberbullying include unclear topics of responsibility for prevention and control, a patchwork of legal protections, a low priority given to special documents, and a lack of specialised legal rules. Additionally, as there are now a variety of rules and regulations controlling cyberbullying, it is crucial to look into the legislative framework of special laws in order to effectively regulate it going forward. All social groups must work together, however, in the meantime

Fast-moving technological advancements have made cyberbullying an ever-evolving, dynamic problem. It is crucial that research in this area receives the attention it deserves and maintains pace with the rapidly evolving state of technology. In the Indian context, more research is necessary to fully understand the repercussions of cyberbullying, according to the materials that have been obtained so far. First off, qualitative study in particular would provide light on young people's real-life interactions with the digital world. Next, in order to examine the issue of digital dangers across different age groups and social subgroups, nationally representative surveys are required. This will help the society better comprehend the local complexities involved and emphasise the severity of the issue in India. When preparing preventative interventions, they must be taken into consideration. It is also necessary to perform longitudinal studies to examine the immediate and long-term effects of digital risk on adolescent development and health. Last but not least, participatory research should be used to create or modify contextually appropriate treatments.

The development of multiple-level therapies that are theoretically sound and contextually aware is necessary, including programmes that target kids, parents, teachers, and the school setting. It is crucial to take into account both the cultural dynamics and the availability of resources when adopting preventative treatments created elsewhere.

Impressive results from the current study can add to the body of knowledge on cyberbullying. But one should note that it has several limitations: First, the most recent types of cyberbullying, such as happy slapping and sexting, were not included in the list of cyberbullying forms. The study also did not fully examine potential disparities in the severity rankings of various kinds of cyberbullying in relation to other factors that were looked at, such as gender and age. The researcher has randomly selected the samples and casually asked the questions on the topic cyberbullying, and did not apply the various formulae and process of calculating the results. Moreover, the sample selected is quite small for such a serious and important topic. The reasons that underlie the disparities discovered in the present study may be highlighted by a qualitative method that examines various variables related to cyberbullying. Despite these limitations, the present resrach provided important information on the basics of cyberbullying, and by doing so it laid the groundwork for challenging future research projects in a sector where many issues remain unanswered.

Need of the Hour

Cyberbullying might devastate the real world if nothing is done to stop it. In light of the significant mental distress that bullying causes in children, who are frequently the victims, policymakers should speak with psychologists before enacting laws to stop cyberbullying. In addition to cyberbullying, other cybercrimes occur across the country that calls for separate rules. If laws are not swiftly passed, the victims will experience more misery. All organisations should be instructed by laws on how to exercise their First Amendment rights to free speech. People should also be better informed about the security measures in place online and the legal options open to them if their rights are violated, both online and offline.

REFERENCES

Bailey, G. (2013). Cyberbullying: Victimization Through Electronic Means. *Current Issues in Middle Level Education, 18*(1), 1–7.

Barlett, C., & Coyne, S. M. (2014). A meta-analysis of sex differences in cyber-bullying behavior: The moderating role of age. *Aggressive Behavior, 40*(5), 474–488. doi:10.1002/ab.21555 PMID:25098968

Betts, L. R. (2016). *Cyberbullying: Approaches, Consequences and Interventions*. Macmillan Publishers Ltd. doi:10.1057/978-1-137-50009-0

Charisse, L. (2014). Current perspectives: The impact of cyberbullying on adolescent health. *Adolescent Health, Medicine and Therapeutics, 5*, 143–158. doi:10.2147/AHMT.S36456 PMID:25177157

Cross, D., Li, Q., Smith, P. K., & Monks, H. (2012). Understanding and preventing cyberbullying: Where have we been and where should we be going? In Q. Li, D. Cross, & P. K. Smith (Eds.), *Cyberbullying in the global playground: Research from international perspectives* (pp. 287–305). Wiley Blackwell. doi:10.1002/9781119954484.ch14

Gradinger, P., Strohmeier, D., & Spiel, C. (2009). Traditional bullying and cyberbullying: Identification of risk groups for adjustment problems. *Zeitschrift für Psychologie. Zeitschrift für Psychologie mit Zeitschrift für Angewandte Psychologie, 217*(4), 205–213. doi:10.1027/0044-3409.217.4.205

Hinduja, S., & Patchin, J. W. (2014). *Cyberbullying Identification, Prevention, and Response*. Cyberbullying Research Center. www.cyberbullying.us

Kowalski, R. M., Limber, S. P., & Agatston, P. W. (2012). *Cyberbullying: Bullying in the Digital Age*. Blackwell Publishing Ltd.

Mahagan, C. A. (2016). Cyberbullying: Feminine Vulnerability in Anonymous Spaces. *Dissenting Voices, 5*, 25–40.

Menesini, E., & Nocentini, A. (2009). Cyberbullying Definition and Measurement. *Zeitschrift für Psychologie mit Zeitschrift für Angewandte Psychologie, 217*(4), 230–232. doi:10.1027/0044-3409.217.4.230

Mesch, G. S. (2009). Parental mediation, online activities and cyberbullying. *Cyberpsychology & Behavior, 12*(4), 387–393. doi:10.1089/cpb.2009.0068 PMID:19630583

Molluzzo, J. C., Lawler, J., & Manneh, J. (2013). A Comprehensive Survey on Cyberbullying Perceptions at a Major Metropolitan University – Faculty Perspectives. *Information Systems Education Journal, 11*(3), 15-34. https://files.eric.ed.gov/fulltext/EJ1145042.pdf

Nixon, C. L. (2014). Current perspectives: The impact of cyberbullying on adolescent health. *Adolescent Health, Medicine and Therapeutics, 5*, 143–158. doi:10.2147/AHMT.S36456 PMID:25177157

Pasricha, J. (2016). *Violence Online in India: Cybercrimes Against Women and Minorities on Social Media*. https://www.comminit.com/content/violence-online-india-cybercrimes-against-women-and-minorities-social-media

Tang, S. (2023). Gender Perspectives on Cyberbullying in Different Countries for Comparison. *Journal of Education, Humanities and Social Sciences, 7*. https://www.researchgate.net/publication/367536292_Gender_Perspectives_on_Cyberbullying_in_Different_Countries_for_Comparison

The New York Times Editorial Staff. (2019). Cyberbullying: A Deadly Trend. New York: The Rosen Publishing Group, Inc.

Tokunaga, R. S. (2010). Following you home from school: A critical review and synthesis on research on cyber bullying victimization. *Computers in Human Behavior, 26*(3), 277–287. doi:10.1016/j.chb.2009.11.014

ENDNOTES

1. https://files.eric.ed.gov/fulltext/EJ1053975.pdf
2. http://uis.unesco.org/en/news/new-sdg-4-data-bullying
3. https://www.pandasecurity.com/en/mediacenter/family-safety/cyberbullying-statistics/
4. https://www.nytimes.com/2013/09/14/us/suicide-of-girl-after-bullying-raises-worries-on-web-sites.html
5. https://indianexpress.com/article/technology/tech-news-technology/indian-children-have-the-highest-online-risk-exposuremcafees-2022-connected-family-7915324/
6. https://www.socialmediamatters.in/patterns-of-internet-usage-among-youths-in-india
7. https://web.stanford.edu/dept/communication/faculty/krosnick/Survey_Research.pdf

APPENDIX

Tables portraying the received responses

Questions	YES (%)	NO (%)
1. Do you know about cyberbullying?	**83.90%**	**16.10%**
2. Have you ever experienced cyberbullying?	**70%**	**30%**
3. Do you think cyberbullying has had an impact on you?	**60%**	**40%**
4. Does Social Media play a significant role in cyberbullying?	**89.30%**	**10.70%**
5. Is the impact of cyberbullying limited to only the mental and psychological condition of the victim or it reaches to the extent of physical harm?	**67.90%**	**32.10%**
6. Do you think that the rape culture has a significant rise due to the increased cyber-culture?	**67.90%**	**32.10%**
7. Do you think the ones who are engaged in traditional bullying are also likely to engage in cyberbullying?	**78.60%**	**21.40%**

Question	Agree	Neutral	Disagree
8. Should specific laws be implemented to prevent cyberbullying and punish cyberbullies?	**96.40%**	**3.60%**	**0**

Question	Someone You Know	Relatives	School/Collegemates	Others
9. If you have ever experienced the horror of cyberbullying, who are usually the bullies that victimize you?	**20%**	**16%**	**12%**	**52%**

Question	OLDER	YOUNGER
10. Are the bullies older than you or younger than you?	**72.7%**	**27.3%**

Chapter 13
A Discussion on the Current Situation of Cybersecurity and the Upcoming Wave of Cyberattacks

Sonal Jain
School of Social, Financial, and Human Sciences, KIIT University, Bhubaneswar, India

ABSTRACT

Cyber-feminism is a concept that has emerged in response to the increasing use of technology and the internet in our daily lives. At its core, cyber-feminism is about challenging the gender biases that exist in the technology industry and ensuring that women have equal access to technology and digital spaces. The chapter covers the history of cyber-feminism, including key thinkers and activists who have contributed to its development. The chapter discusses strategies for staying safe online, including the importance of digital literacy and education. This chapter explores the role of cyber-feminism in the digital space through a case study approach. Specifically, it examines the impact of the #MeToo Movement, the Women's March, and the story of Malala Yousafzai. By highlighting the successes and challenges of cyber-feminist movements, this chapter offers insights into how we can work towards a more inclusive and feminist digital future. The chapter provides a unique and original perspective on the topic of Cyber-feminism. While existing literature on the subject tends to focus on theoretical discussions, this chapter employs a case study methodology to examine the impact of Cyber-feminism on real-world events such as the #MeToo Movement, Women's March, and the story of Malala Yousafzai. This approach provides a deeper understanding of the practical applications of Cyber-feminism and how it can affect change in society. Furthermore, the chapter highlights the potential impact that Cyber-feminism can have in promoting gender equality in the digital space and beyond. By analyzing the key issues of Cyber-feminism and offering potential solutions, the chapter adds significant value by providing actionable insights for those interested in promoting gender equality.

DOI: 10.4018/978-1-6684-8893-5.ch013

INTRODUCTION

In recent years, the digital space has become an integral part of our daily lives, shaping how we interact with each other, access information, and conduct business. With the growth of digital technology, the concept of cyber-feminism has emerged, and it has become increasingly relevant in our society today. Cyber-feminism is a term that refers to the intersection of feminism and digital technology, and it focuses on how women can use digital technology to promote gender equality and challenge patriarchy (Starcevic & Aboujaoude, 2015). According to Wall (Wall & David S., 2005, p. 79), *"crimes that are mediated by networked computers and not just related to computers"* are considered to be cybercrimes. Computer viruses, Internet fraud or scams, identity theft, stock manipulation or securities fraud, cyber-stalking or cyber-harassment, and computer hacking are all examples of cybercrime. In 2011, one third of the world's population, or about 2.3 billion people, had access to the internet, and by 2018 that number had increased to 4 billion (Kemp, 2018). Additionally, 45% of these internet users are under the age of 25, and 60% of them are from developing nations (Kshetri, 2010). Cybercrime has become more prevalent in developing economies as a result of the internet's quick spread and the digitalization of commercial activity and hence underscores the urgency to address the impact of cybercrime. Some estimates claim that in recent years, the global cybercrime sector has been generating US$1 trillion annually (Kshetri, 2010). International discourses have changed as a result of the significant roles that developing world-based criminals are playing in the criminal value chain of the cyberworld. According to Kaspersky Labs (Kshetri, 2010), developing nations produced seven of the top ten countries for producing trojans meant to steal passwords in 2009, accounting for 92% of all such trojans globally. The utilization of hardware and software, broadband connections, the pool of cybercriminal expertise, the availability of employment prospects, and the spread of security products are all economic elements that are changing in developing nations (Al-Shalan, 2006). The statistics on the increasing number of internet users, particularly in developing nations, highlights the growing vulnerability of women to cybercrime. As more women gain access to the digital space, there is a higher likelihood of them encountering cyber threats, making it imperative to address gender-specific risks and ensure the protection of women in the online environment.

This chapter explores cyber-feminism's role in the digital space, promoting women's empowerment, security, and gender equality. It focus on issues like online harassment, cyber-bullying, and the gender gap in digital skills. Strategies for women's online safety and using digital technology for advocacy are examined. The chapter covers cyber-feminism's history, online activism, and its intersection with cybersecurity and privacy. It highlights the impact of social media on promoting positive change and managing online communities. This chapter aims to empower women in the digital world through cyber-feminism.

DEFINING CYBER-FEMINISM

Cyber-feminism is a term that has emerged in recent years to describe the intersection of feminism and digital technology. It is rooted in the belief that the digital world can be a space for women to challenge patriarchy, advocate for their rights, and promote gender equality. As stated by (Wilkinson & Kitzinger, 2013), "cyber-feminism is a movement that recognizes the role of digital technology in shaping gender identities and seeks to use this technology to empower women and challenge traditional gender roles".

Cyber-feminism encompasses a range of practices, from online activism and advocacy to digital storytelling and social media campaigns. According to (Wajcman, 2006), "cyber-feminism involves the use of digital technology to challenge patriarchal structures and promote social change". Cyber-feminists seek to create a more inclusive and equitable digital space, one that is free from harassment and discrimination, and that allows women to fully participate in public discourse. Through the lens of cyber-feminism, we can explore issues such as online harassment, cyber-bullying, and the gender gap in digital skills and access, and work towards creating a more just and equitable digital world.

In addition, cyber-feminism is also concerned with issues of privacy and security in the digital space. As highlighted by (Schwarz et al., 2020), "cyber-feminism acknowledges the risks that women face in the digital world, including online harassment, stalking, and doxing, and seeks to empower women to navigate these threats safely and confidently". Cyber-feminists recognize that the digital space can be a double-edged sword, offering opportunities for empowerment and advocacy, but also presenting risks and challenges for women's safety and well-being. Therefore, they advocate for the development of digital literacy and education to promote cyber-security awareness and enable women to take control of their digital lives. Through their activism and advocacy, cyber-feminists are working towards creating a more inclusive and equitable digital space that promotes gender equality and empowers women to participate fully in public life.

CYBER-FEMINISM: AN OVERVIEW AND ITS HISTORY IN BRIEF

Cyber-feminism is a concept that emerged in the 1990s, with the widespread adoption of the internet and other digital technologies. At its core, cyber-feminism is concerned with the ways in which technology intersects with gender, and the potential for these intersections to either perpetuate or challenge existing gender hierarchies. One of the key early figures in the development of cyber-feminism was Donna Haraway, whose 1985 essay "A Cyborg Manifesto" argued for a reconceptualization of the relationship between humans and machines (Thrift, 2006). Haraway's vision of the cyborg as a hybrid entity that challenges the boundaries between nature and culture has been influential in shaping the ways in which cyber-feminists think about technology and gender. Another important figure in the development of cyber-feminism is Sadie Plant, whose 1997 book "Zeroes + Ones: Digital Women and the New Technoculture" argued for the potential of digital technologies to enable women to transcend traditional gender roles and to create new forms of identity and community (Plant, 1995a). Plant's work was important in highlighting the ways in which digital technologies could be used to empower women and to challenge gender hierarchies. In more recent years, cyber-feminism has been associated with a range of online activism, including the #MeToo movement and the Women's March. These movements have used social media and other digital technologies to organize and mobilize women around issues of gender equality, highlighting the potential for technology to facilitate feminist activism and to give voice to marginalized groups. Overall, the history of cyber-feminism is a complex and multifaceted one, shaped by a diverse range of thinkers and activists. While cyber-feminism has made significant contributions to our understanding of the relationship between technology and gender, there is still much work to be done in terms of addressing the ways in which technology can perpetuate gender inequalities and in developing strategies for using technology to promote gender justice.

CYBER-FEMINISM IS AT PLAY IN THE CONTEMPORARY ERA

Putting cyber-feminism into practice involves taking action to address the systemic inequalities and injustices that women face in the digital space. This can include advocating for policy changes, promoting education and awareness, and engaging in online activism and community-building. It also involves recognizing the diversity of women's experiences in the digital space, and the intersecting factors that shape those experiences, including race, ethnicity, class, sexuality, and ability.

Cyber-feminism is a dynamic field that encompasses a range of practices, from online activism to digital storytelling to social media campaigns. Today, feminist movements are using digital tools to create and spread messages of empowerment, inclusivity, and resistance across the globe. One way in which cyber-feminism is practiced is through online activism, which includes protests, petitions, and other forms of collective action. For instance, the #MeToo movement, which began as a hashtag on social media, quickly spread and led to significant changes in the way that sexual harassment and assault are addressed in many industries. Similarly, the Women's March, which took place both online and offline, brought millions of people together in support of gender equality and human rights Another way in which cyber-feminism is practiced is through digital storytelling, which allows individuals to share their personal experiences and perspectives in a public forum. This can take many forms, from blogs and podcasts to videos and visual art. Through digital storytelling, women and other marginalized groups can challenge dominant narratives and speak their own truths. Social media campaigns are also a powerful tool for cyber-feminists, allowing them to reach a broad audience and engage in conversation with others. For instance, the #SayHerName campaign, which aims to bring attention to the stories of black women who have been victims of police violence, has gained significant traction on social media platforms. Additionally, campaigns such as #FreeTheNipple and #BodyPositive promote body positivity and challenge traditional beauty standards. Cyber-feminism is a multifaceted field that is constantly evolving as new digital technologies and practices emerge. Its practitioners are using digital tools to challenge the status quo, amplify marginalized voices, and create a more just and inclusive world.

CYBER-FEMINISM AND ITS INTERSECTION WITH ISSUES OF CYBER-SECURITY AND PRIVACY

Cyber-feminism, as a movement, is concerned with issues of gender and technology. One area of intersection with this movement is the issue of cyber-security and privacy. The digital space can be a hostile environment for women, and their personal information can be compromised through cyber-stalking, cyber-bullying, and other forms of online harassment. Cyber-feminism recognizes the importance of addressing these issues and advocates for the creation of safer digital spaces for women. One approach taken by cyber-feminists is to raise awareness of the importance of online privacy and to educate women on how to protect themselves. This includes strategies such as using strong passwords, encrypting data, and using privacy settings on social media platforms (Carrington, 2014). Cyber-feminists also work to challenge the dominant narratives around cyber-security and privacy, which often reinforce gendered stereotypes and perpetuate victim-blaming. In addition to personal security, cyber-feminists are also concerned with broader issues of privacy, particularly as they relate to government surveillance and corporate data mining. They recognize that women's privacy rights are often ignored or marginalized in these contexts, and advocate for policies and practices that respect and protect women's rights to privacy in the digital realm (Lopez et al., 2019). Cyber-feminism's intersection with cyber-security and privacy highlights the importance of addressing gendered power dynamics in the digital space. By advocating for women's safety and privacy online, cyber-feminists seek to create a more equitable and just digital world.

THREATS THAT WOMEN FACE IN THE DIGITAL SPACE AND SUGGESTED STRATEGIES FOR STAYING SAFE ONLINE

As more and more women continue to occupy online spaces, they also face an increasing number of online threats such as cyberstalking, online harassment, revenge porn, doxing, and trolling. These digital threats can have real-life consequences and impact women's psychological well-being, personal safety, and professional lives. To stay safe online, women can take various strategies including using strong passwords, enabling two-factor authentication, regularly updating their software and antivirus programs, limiting personal information online, and using a virtual private network (VPN). Additionally, women can use social media tools such as privacy settings, blocking and reporting features, and muting to manage and control their online presence. However, these strategies alone may not be enough to fully protect women from online threats. In response to the issue, feminist organizations and activists have developed various campaigns and initiatives aimed at combating online harassment, including Hollaback, #MeToo, and Stop Online Violence Against Women (Chang, 2011). These initiatives promote awareness about online harassment, create supportive communities, and advocate for policy changes to hold perpetrators accountable. Furthermore, it is important to recognize the intersectionality of online threats, as women of color, trans women, and other marginalized groups often face disproportionately higher rates of online harassment and violence. Cyber-feminism must strive to address these intersectional issues and create inclusive online spaces where all women can thrive and stay safe.

The exploration of cyber fraud related to females, examining their roles as victims or culprits, is a significant topic in cyber-feminism. It must be approached with care to avoid victim-blaming and gender biases. Presenting females solely as victims or culprits may reinforce gender binaries. Acknowledging that cyber fraud is not solely gender-specific is essential. By addressing underlying factors and recognizing women's agency, the discourse can enhance our understanding of cyber-feminism and foster a safer digital environment for all.

ROLE OF DIGITAL LITERACY AND EDUCATION IN PROMOTING CYBER-SECURITY AWARENESS

Digital literacy and education play a crucial role in empowering women to take control of their digital lives and promoting cyber-security awareness. By providing women with the tools and knowledge to navigate the digital space safely, they can reduce their risk of being targeted by cyber-criminals and abusers. Digital literacy initiatives can include programs that teach basic computer skills, social media etiquette, and online privacy practices. These programs can also provide information on how to report and block online abuse, as well as how to seek support from relevant authorities and organizations. In addition to these educational initiatives, it is important to address the systemic issues that contribute to gender-based violence and harassment online (Martin & Rice, 2012). This can involve advocating for stronger legal protections for women who experience online abuse, as well as working with technology companies to create safer online environments. It is also important to challenge harmful gender stereotypes and social norms that perpetuate violence against women, both online and offline (Yuliana, 2022). By promoting digital literacy and education, we can empower women to take control of their digital lives and reduce the risks they face online. This is a crucial step in promoting gender equality and ensuring that women can participate fully in the digital world without fear of harassment or violence.

THE IMPACT OF SOCIAL MEDIA TO PROMOTE POSITIVE SOCIAL CHANGE

Social media has become a ubiquitous aspect of modern life, with billions of people around the world using platforms like Facebook, Twitter, and Instagram to connect with others, share information and experiences, and express themselves. In recent years, social media has also emerged as a powerful tool for promoting positive social change, with movements like #MeToo and Black Lives Matter leveraging online platforms to raise awareness about issues of gender-based violence and systemic racism (Lee et al., 2017). However, social media also presents a number of challenges, particularly when it comes to managing online communities and ensuring that all voices are heard. Cyberbullying, harassment, and hate speech are all too common on social media, and these phenomena can have a chilling effect on the ability of individuals to engage in meaningful online discourse. In addition, there are concerns about the role that social media companies play in shaping public discourse, with some critics arguing that these platforms have too much power to control what users see and hear (Al-Saggaf & Simmons, 2015). Despite these challenges, social media remains a powerful tool for promoting positive social change, particularly when it comes to issues related to gender, race, and social justice. By leveraging the power of digital networks and online communities, activists and advocates can amplify their voices and reach audiences that might not otherwise be accessible (Gupta et al., 2013). Moreover, by promoting digital literacy and education, it is possible to empower individuals to take control of their online lives, and to promote greater awareness about issues of online safety, security, and privacy.

CURRENT GAP IN LITERATURE

The current literature on cyber-feminism has several gaps that need to be addressed. One of the significant gaps is the limited attention given to the intersectional experiences of women in the digital space. Most studies on cyber-feminism have focused on white women's experiences and failed to address the unique challenges and experiences faced by women of color, LGBTQ+ women, and women from marginalized communities. Another gap in the literature is the lack of focus on the role of technology in perpetuating gender inequality in the digital space (Dean, 2010a). While some studies have examined the ways in which women use technology to challenge patriarchal norms, few have focused on how technology itself perpetuates gender inequality and reinforces existing power dynamics. Moreover, there is a need to examine the role of cyber-feminism in challenging broader societal issues such as neoliberalism and capitalism (Martinez-Pecino & Durán, 2019). While some studies have examined the relationship between cyber-feminism and these issues, more research is needed to fully understand how cyber-feminism can contribute to larger social justice movements. Additionally, there is a need to explore the impact of cyber-feminism beyond the digital space (Elsadda, 2010). While cyber-feminism has had a significant impact on online discourse, it is essential to examine its potential for creating change in offline spaces.

Finally, there is a need to explore the role of cyber-feminism in promoting global gender equality (Coward, 1980). While some studies have examined the impact of cyber-feminism in specific regions, there is a need to examine how cyber-feminism can be used to promote gender equality on a global scale.

THE MULTIPLE ROLE OF CYBER-FEMINISM WITHIN THE DIGITAL SPACE

Cyber-feminism plays multiple roles within the digital space, and its impact can be felt in many areas. As highlighted by (Yin & Sun, 2021), cyber-feminism is concerned with issues of representation, access, and participation in the digital world. Cyber-feminists have been instrumental in challenging the underrepresentation of women in technology and promoting initiatives that increase access to digital technologies for women. They have also been vocal advocates for greater diversity and inclusion in the tech industry and have called for more representation of women and minorities in tech leadership positions. Additionally, cyber-feminism has been central to efforts to combat online harassment and violence against women in the digital space. Cyber-feminists have developed strategies for responding to and preventing online harassment and have also been active in promoting legal and policy changes to address this issue. Finally, cyber-feminism has been a powerful force for promoting digital literacy and education for women, equipping them with the tools and knowledge necessary to navigate the digital world safely and confidently. As noted by (Schuster, 2013), "cyber-feminism offers a valuable perspective on the multiple ways in which gender and technology intersect and can be an effective force for promoting greater equality and empowerment for women in the digital age". However, the effectiveness of cyber-feminism in promoting gender equality in the digital space is not without its challenges. One of the main challenges is the persistence of structural inequalities and power relations that shape women's experiences in the digital world. As noted by (Carrington, 2014), "despite the gains made by cyber-feminism, there remain significant structural barriers that prevent women from achieving full equality in the digital space". These barriers include unequal access to digital technologies, the underrepresentation of women in the tech industry, and the persistence of online harassment and violence against women. Additionally, cyber-feminism must also contend with the ways in which digital technologies themselves can reinforce gendered norms and stereotypes. As argued by (Starcevic & Aboujaoude, 2015), "digital technologies can sometimes be used to perpetuate gendered power relations, reproducing existing social hierarchies in new and insidious ways". In this context, cyber-feminism must be vigilant and adaptive, responding to the changing technological landscape and the evolving ways in which gender is constructed and negotiated in the digital space. Ultimately, the success of cyber-feminism in promoting gender equality in the digital age will depend on its ability to navigate these challenges and remain responsive to the needs and experiences of women in the digital world. In sum, cyber-feminism's multiple roles in the digital space make it a powerful force for promoting gender equality and challenging patriarchal structures in the digital age.

METHODOLOGY

The chapter seeks to explore how cyber-feminism can empower women to navigate the digital space and protect themselves against online threats, while also challenging patriarchal structures and promoting gender equality. By examining the various roles of cyber-feminism and their impact on women's well-being and awareness of cyber security, the chapter aims to contribute to the growing body of literature on gender and technology, and to promote greater understanding and engagement around issues of cyber security and online safety.

Case study methodology is a valuable research approach for exploring complex phenomena in their real-life context, particularly when the boundaries between the phenomenon and context are blurred, and when multiple perspectives and factors are involved. In the context of the chapter titled "Understanding Cyber-feminism and its roles in the digital space", case studies provide a useful method for examining the roles of cyber-feminism within the digital space, as they allow for an in-depth analysis of specific examples that illustrate the concepts and issues being discussed (Stake, 1978). One of the main advantages of using case study methodology is that it allows for a rich and detailed analysis of a phenomenon or event, including its historical, social, cultural, and political context(Sandelowski, 2011). This depth of analysis enables researchers to identify and explore the multiple factors and perspectives that shape the phenomenon, and to develop a nuanced understanding of its complexities and dynamics. Case studies also provide a means of triangulation, allowing researchers to compare and contrast different cases to identify patterns, similarities, and differences. Furthermore, case studies provide a flexible and adaptive research approach, allowing researchers to adjust their research design and methods based on the emerging findings and the specific needs of the research question (Patton & Appelbaum, 2003). They also provide opportunities for collaboration and engagement with stakeholders, including the communities and individuals being studied, allowing for a more participatory and ethical research process. The use of case study methodology in this chapter on cyber-feminism in the digital space offers a robust and comprehensive means of examining the various roles of cyber-feminism and their impact on women's well-being and awareness of cyber security. The case studies provide concrete examples of cyber-feminism in action, enabling the research to move beyond theoretical discussions and to explore the practical implications of cyber-feminism for women's lives and experiences.

EXAMPLES OF CASE STUDIES ABOUT THE ROLES OF CYBER-FEMINISM WITHIN THE DIGITAL SPACE

Case Study 1: #MeToo Movement

One of the most notable examples of cyber-feminism in action is the #MeToo movement, which emerged in 2017 in response to widespread allegations of sexual harassment and assault in Hollywood and other industries. The movement quickly spread through social media, with women sharing their own stories of harassment and abuse using the hashtag #MeToo. The movement was widely hailed as a powerful example of cyber-feminism, with its ability to amplify the voices of women who had been silenced for too long (Fileborn & Loney-Howes, 2019). The #MeToo movement demonstrates the ways in which cyber-feminism can challenge patriarchal structures and amplify marginalized voices in the digital space. By providing a platform for women to share their stories and connect with others who have had similar experiences, the movement helped to break down the isolation and shame that often accompanies experiences of sexual harassment and assault (Kaufman et al., 2021). Additionally, the movement helped to hold powerful men accountable for their actions, with many high-profile figures facing consequences for their behavior as a result of the movement. The #MeToo movement also highlights some of the challenges and limitations of cyber-feminism in practice. As noted by (Kaufman et al., 2021), "the #MeToo movement has been criticized for its reliance on social media platforms that are controlled by large corporations with their own interests and priorities". Additionally, the movement has faced criticism for its lack of intersectionality, with some voices arguing that the movement has primarily focused on the experiences of white, middle-class women and has overlooked the experiences of marginalized groups (Brown & Battle, 2019). The #MeToo movement serves as a powerful case study for understanding the multiple roles of cyber-feminism in the digital space. While the movement has faced criticism and challenges, it remains a powerful example of the ways in which digital technologies can be used to promote gender equality and challenge patriarchal structures. By providing a platform for marginalized voices and amplifying the experiences of those who have been silenced for too long, cyber-feminism has the potential to promote greater equality and empowerment for women in the digital age.

Case Study 2: Women's March

Another notable example of cyber-feminism in action is the Women's March, which took place in January 2017 in response to the election of President Donald Trump in the United States. The Women's March was a global event, with millions of women marching in cities around the world to demand gender equality and protest the policies of the new administration. The Women's March demonstrates the power of cyber-feminism to mobilize large-scale collective action in the digital age. The movement was organized largely through social media, with organizers using platforms like Facebook and Twitter to spread the word and coordinate logistics. Additionally, the movement relied heavily on digital technologies to amplify its message and connect with supporters around the world. By leveraging the power of digital technologies to mobilize a global movement for gender equality, cyber-feminism played a significant role in the Women's March. However, the Women's March also highlights some of the challenges and limitations of cyber-feminism in practice. As noted by (McDuffie & Ames, 2021), "the Women's March faced criticism for its lack of inclusivity and its failure to adequately address issues of intersectionality". Additionally, the movement has faced challenges in sustaining its momentum and translating its online activism into concrete political gains. The Women's March serves as a powerful case study for understanding the multiple roles of cyber-feminism in the digital space. While the movement has faced criticism and challenges, it remains a powerful example of the ways in which digital technologies can be used to promote gender equality and challenge patriarchal structures (Silverstein, 2019). By mobilizing a global movement for gender equality through the power of social media and digital technologies, cyber-feminism has the potential to catalyze real change in the digital age.

Case Study 3: Malala Yousafzai

Malala Yousafzai is a prominent example of how cyber-feminism can empower women and girls to challenge gender inequality and patriarchal structures in the digital age. Malala is a Pakistani activist for female education and the youngest Nobel Prize laureate. In 2012, at the age of 15, she was targeted by the Taliban for her activism and shot in the head while riding a bus to school. Malala survived the attack and had since become a global advocate for girls' education and women's rights (Sattar et al., 2021). Malala's story highlights the role of digital technologies in amplifying the voices of marginalized groups and enabling them to challenge oppressive systems. In the aftermath of the attack, Malala became a global symbol of resilience and resistance against patriarchal violence. Her story was shared widely on social media, and she used digital platforms to continue her activism and advocate for girls' education around the world (Kross, 2021). Furthermore, the Malala Fund, founded by Malala and her father, has leveraged digital technologies to support girls' education around the world. The fund uses online platforms to raise awareness about the importance of girls' education and to connect with supporters and donors. By using digital technologies to build a global network of advocates for girls' education, the Malala Fund represents a powerful example of cyber-feminism in practice (Kross, 2021). The case of Malala Yousafzai adds value to the chapter by demonstrating the multiple roles of cyber-feminism in empowering women and girls to challenge patriarchal structures and promote gender equality. Malala's story illustrates how digital technologies can be used to amplify the voices of marginalized groups, connect with supporters around the world, and catalyze real change. By highlighting the ways in which cyber-feminism can be used to challenge patriarchy and support marginalized groups, the case of Malala Yousafzai serves as a powerful example of the potential of cyber-feminism in the digital age.

CRITIQUING OF CYBER-FEMINISM

While cyber-feminism offers many opportunities for promoting gender equality and challenging patriarchal structures in the digital space, it has also been subject to critique. One critique of cyber-feminism is that it can be overly focused on individual empowerment and fail to address larger structural inequalities. As argued by (Kruschek, 2019), "cyber-feminism may offer opportunities for individual women to assert themselves in the digital world, but it does not necessarily address broader issues of social inequality and power relations". In addition, cyber-feminism has been criticized for its narrow focus on gender issues and its failure to address issues of race, class, and sexuality in the digital space. As noted by (Starr, 2016), "cyber-feminism risks reproducing the same exclusions and hierarchies that it seeks to challenge, by focusing too narrowly on gender issues and ignoring the intersections of race, class, and sexuality in the digital world". Moreover, some have argued that cyber-feminism's emphasis on individual empowerment may also mask the systemic issues that prevent women from achieving full equality in the digital space. Despite these critiques, cyber-feminism remains a powerful tool for promoting gender equality and challenging patriarchal structures in the digital age, and its impact should continue to be studied and evaluated critically. Furthermore, some scholars have also pointed out that cyber-feminism can sometimes reinforce binary gender norms and essentialize the experiences of women in the digital space. As noted by (Dean, 2010b), "cyber-feminism can sometimes reproduce essentialist notions of gender identity and fails to recognize the diversity of experiences and perspectives among women in the digital world". This critique suggests that cyber-feminism must be attentive to the ways in which gender identity is constructed and negotiated in the digital space and must be open to diverse perspectives and experiences. Additionally, the emphasis on individual empowerment and self-reliance in cyber-feminism can obscure the structural issues and systemic inequalities that shape women's experiences in the digital space. As highlighted by (Plant, 1995b), "cyber-feminism may provide tools for individual women to navigate the digital world, but it does not necessarily address the larger systemic issues that limit women's participation and access to digital technologies". Therefore, while cyber-feminism offers a valuable perspective on gender and technology, it must be critically evaluated and nuanced to address the complex issues that women face in the digital age.

Cyber-feminism has become a major topic of discussion in recent years, as feminist scholars have started exploring the intersection of gender, technology, and the digital space. Cyber-feminism is a movement that emerged in the 1990s as a response to the lack of women's representation and participation in the technology sector. Since then, cyber-feminism has evolved to include the examination of the ways in which gender, race, class, sexuality, and other identities intersect with digital technologies. In this article, I will critically discuss the issues of cyber-feminism and its roles in the digital space.

One of the main issues of cyber-feminism is the notion of a gender digital divide. This divide refers to the disparity in access to and use of digital technologies between men and women. Studies have shown that women are underrepresented in the technology sector and are less likely to have access to digital technologies. This divide can have significant consequences on women's economic, political, and social opportunities. In their article, "The Gender Digital Divide in Developing Countries," (Chang, 2011) discuss how the gender digital divide can impact women's access to education, healthcare, and employment opportunities. Another issue of cyber-feminism is the problem of online harassment and violence. Women are disproportionately targeted for online abuse, harassment, and violence. This can lead to women's silencing and exclusion from online spaces. A study by (Pew Research Centre, 2021) found that 41% of women have been subjected to online harassment, compared to 17% of men. The problem of online harassment has become a major concern for cyber-feminists, who argue for the need to create safer online spaces for women.

Furthermore, cyber-feminists have also criticized the ways in which digital technologies reproduce gendered and sexist norms. Digital technologies are not neutral and can reinforce and amplify social inequalities. In her article, "Feminist Approaches to Media Literacy," (Wajcman, 2006) discusses how media literacy can be used to challenge gendered norms and stereotypes perpetuated by digital technologies.

Roles of Cyber-Feminism in the Digital Space

Despite these issues, cyber-feminism has played a crucial role in promoting gender equality in the digital space. Cyber-feminists have been at the forefront of advocating for women's representation and participation in the technology sector. They have also called for the creation of safer online spaces for women and have worked towards the development of policies and tools to combat online harassment and violence (Lopez et al., 2019). Additionally, cyber-feminists have raised awareness about the ways in which digital technologies can reinforce gendered norms and stereotypes and have advocated for the need to develop media literacy programs to challenge these norms.

CONCLUSION: FUTURE DIRECTIONS FOR RESEARCH IN CYBERFEMINISM

The chapter challenges oversimplified and polarizing ways of thinking about gender and virtual spaces that limit cyberfeminist efforts to achieve greater online gender equality. These false binaries include ideas such as online vs. offline, cyberfeminism vs. non-cyberfeminism, and utopian vs. dystopian views of cyberspace. Other false dichotomies relate to empowerment vs. vulnerability, privacy vs. self-disclosure, and victimhood vs. blameworthiness. By examining these dichotomies more closely, it becomes clear that girls' virtual experiences are complex and diverse. The aim of the volume is to continue breaking down these polarized ways of thinking in order to facilitate more productive discussions and work towards common goals of reducing virtual gender inequality and increasing girls' and young women's online agency.

To achieve greater online gender equality, future cyberfeminist efforts need to move beyond micro-level discussions and punitive policy initiatives and shift towards collective macro-level action that involves wider social engagement. This could include educational or family-based initiatives that promote media literacy and respect for all genders. It's important to avoid patriarchal and neo-liberal discourses that blame girls for being susceptible to online abuse and instead focus on promoting a culture of empowerment and agency. These discourses perpetuate harmful gender stereotypes and contribute to the notion that girls are responsible for protecting themselves from victimization online. Instead, cyberfeminist initiatives should aim to promote self-expression for girls in virtual spaces and challenge harmful beliefs that blame victims of online abuse.

To move past problematic discourses, cyberfeminists must challenge prevailing media representations of gender and societal expectations that dictate accepted standards for online femininity. This can be achieved by deconstructing these narratives on a larger scale to challenge normative standards of online gender performance, critique online spaces and current policies for entrenching sexist narratives. The experiences and perceptions of marginalized groups such as non-heterosexual, trans, and racialized girls should also be included in future cyberfeminist initiatives to promote intersectional insights and increase girls' online agency. It is important to solicit girls' own perceptions and experiences to ensure that they have a voice in discussions on gender and virtual space. This approach will move beyond patriarchal binary thought, promote gender "e-quality," and help construct virtual spaces that better reflect diverse perspectives.

REFERENCES

Al-Saggaf, Y., & Simmons, P. (2015). Social media in Saudi Arabia: Exploring its use during two natural disasters. *Technological Forecasting and Social Change*, *95*, 3–15. doi:10.1016/j.techfore.2014.08.013

Al-Shalan, A. (2006). *Cyber-Crime Fear and Victimization: An Analysis of a National Cyber-Crime Fear and Victimization*. Mississippi State University. https://scholarsjunction.msstate.edu/td

Brown, S. E. V., & Battle, J. S. (2019). Ostracizing targets of workplace sexual harassment before and after the #MeToo movement. *Equality, Diversity and Inclusion*, *39*(1), 53–67. doi:10.1108/EDI-09-2018-0162

Carrington, K. (2014). *Feminism and Global Justice*. Routledge., doi:10.4324/9781315748368

Chang, J. (2011). Cyberspace and Reconstruction of Women's Identity. *Trans-Humanities Journal*, *4*(2), 125–149. doi:10.1353/trh.2011.0018

Coward, R. (1980). "This Novel Changes Lives": Are Women's Novels Feminist Novels? A Response to Rebecca O'Rourke's Article 'Summer Reading.'. *Feminist Review*, *5*(1), 53–64. doi:10.1057/fr.1980.12

Dean, J. (2010). Feminism in the Papers. *Feminist Media Studies*, *10*(4), 391–407. doi:10.1080/14680777.2010.514112

Elsadda, H. (2010). Arab Women Bloggers: The Emergence of Literary Counterpublics. *Middle East Journal of Culture and Communication*, *3*(3), 312–332. doi:10.1163/187398610X538678

Fileborn, B., & Loney-Howes, R. (2019). Introduction: Mapping the Emergence of #MeToo. In #MeToo and the Politics of Social Change (pp. 1–18). Springer International Publishing. doi:10.1007/978-3-030-15213-0_1

Gupta, A., Tyagi, M., & Sharma, D. (2013). Use of Social Media Marketing in Healthcare. *Journal of Health Management*, *15*(2), 293–302. doi:10.1177/0972063413489058

Kaufman, M. R., Dey, D., Crainiceanu, C., & Dredze, M. (2021). #MeToo and Google Inquiries Into Sexual Violence: A Hashtag Campaign Can Sustain Information Seeking. *Journal of Interpersonal Violence*, *36*(19–20), 9857–9867. doi:10.1177/0886260519868197 PMID:31441695

Kemp, S. (2018). *Digital in 2018: World's Internet Users Pass the 4 Billion Mark*. https://wearesocial.com/blog/2018/01/global-digital-report-2018

Kross, E. (2021). *Talking to Yourself*. Character Lab Tips. doi:10.53776/tips-talking-to-yourself

Kruschek, G. (2019). Stigma in the Comments Section: Feminist and Anti-Feminist Discussions Online. *Computers and Composition*, *54*, 102515. doi:10.1016/j.compcom.2019.102515

Kshetri, N. (2010). Diffusion and effects of cyber-crime in developing economies. *Third World Quarterly*, *31*(7), 1057–1079. doi:10.1080/01436597.2010.518752

Lee, F. L. F., Chen, H.-T., & Chan, M. (2017). Social media use and university students' participation in a large-scale protest campaign: The case of Hong Kong's Umbrella Movement. *Telematics and Informatics*, *34*(2), 457–469. doi:10.1016/j.tele.2016.08.005

Lopez, K. J., Muldoon, M. L., & McKeown, J. K. L. (2019). One Day of #Feminism: Twitter as a Complex Digital Arena for Wielding, Shielding, and Trolling talk on Feminism. *Leisure Sciences*, *41*(3), 203–220. doi:10.1080/01490400.2018.1448022

Martin, N., & Rice, J. (2012). Children's cyber-safety and protection in Australia: An analysis of community stakeholder views. *Crime Prevention and Community Safety*, *14*(3), 165–181. doi:10.1057/cpcs.2012.4

Martinez-Pecino, R., & Durán, M. (2019). I Love You but I Cyberbully You: The Role of Hostile Sexism. *Journal of Interpersonal Violence*, *34*(4), 812–825. doi:10.1177/0886260516645817 PMID:27118344

McDuffie, K., & Ames, M. (2021). Archiving affect and activism: Hashtag feminism and structures of feeling in Women's March tweets. *First Monday*. Advance online publication. doi:10.5210/fm.v26i2.10317

Patton, E., & Appelbaum, S. H. (2003). The case for case studies in management research. *Management Research News*, *26*(5), 60–71. doi:10.1108/01409170310783484

Pew Research Centre. (2021). *The State of Online Harassment*. Author.

Plant, S. (1995). The Future Looms: Weaving Women and Cybernetics. *Body & Society*, *1*(3–4), 45–64. doi:10.1177/1357034X95001003003

Sandelowski, M. (2011). "Casing" the research case study. *Research in Nursing & Health*, *34*(2), 153–159. doi:10.1002/nur.20421 PMID:21381044

Sattar, G., Safeer, A. K., Pasha, M. I., Furqan, K. M. Y., & Riaz, N. (2021). Stereotypical ideologies towards women: Feminist poststructuralist discourse analysis of Malala Yousafzai's political speeches. *Humanities & Social Sciences Reviews*, *9*(3), 1245–1257. doi:10.18510/hssr.2021.93123

Schuster, J. (2013). Invisible feminists? Social media and young women's political participation. *Political Science (Wellington, N.Z.)*, *65*(1), 8–24. doi:10.1177/0032318713486474

Schwarz, M., Scherrer, A., Hohmann, C., Heiberg, J., Brugger, A., & Nuñez-Jimenez, A. (2020). COVID-19 and the academy: It is time for going digital. *Energy Research & Social Science*, *68*, 101684. doi:10.1016/j.erss.2020.101684 PMID:32839703

Silverstein, S. (2019). Women's March Colloquy - On Sirens and Lamp Posts: Sound, Space, and Affective Politics. *Music and Politics*, *13*(1). Advance online publication. doi:10.3998/mp.9460447.0013.103

Stake, R. E. (1978). The Case Study Method in Social Inquiry. *Educational Researcher*, *7*(2), 5–8. doi:10.3102/0013189X007002005

Starcevic, V., & Aboujaoude, E. (2015). Cyberchondria, cyberbullying, cybersuicide, cybersex: "new" psychopathologies for the 21st century? *World Psychiatry; Official Journal of the World Psychiatric Association (WPA)*, *14*(1), 97–100. doi:10.1002/wps.20195 PMID:25655165

Starr, M. (2016). Beyond Machine Dreams: Zen, Cyber-, and Transnational Feminisms in Ruth Ozeki's *A Tale for the Time Being*. *Meridians (Middletown, Conn.)*, *13*(2), 99–122. doi:10.2979/meridians.13.2.06

Thrift, N. (2006). Donna Haraway's Dreams. *Theory, Culture & Society*, *23*(7–8), 189–195. doi:10.1177/0263276406069231

Wajcman, J. (2006). Review: Wajcman Confronts Cyberfeminism. *Social Studies of Science*, *36*(2), 321–327. doi:10.1177/0306312706058828

Wall, & David S. (2005). The Internet as a Conduit for Criminal Activity. In *Information Technology and the Criminal Justice System* (pp. 77–98). Sage Publications.

Wilkinson, S., & Kitzinger, C. (2013). Representing Our Own Experience. *Psychology of Women Quarterly*, *37*(2), 251–255. doi:10.1177/0361684313483111

Yin, S., & Sun, Y. (2021). Intersectional digital feminism: Assessing the participation politics and impact of the MeToo movement in China. *Feminist Media Studies*, *21*(7), 1176–1192. doi:10.1080/14680777.2020.1837908

Yuliana, Y. (2022). The importance of cyber-security awareness for children. *Lampung Journal of International Law*, *4*(1), 41–48. doi:10.25041/lajil.v3i2.2526

Chapter 14
Media:
The Crux of Gender Violence

Pragyan Mohanty
Kalinga Institute of Social Sciences, India

Rasmita Tripathy
https://orcid.org/0000-0003-2260-4465
Kalinga Institute of Social Sciences, India

ABSTRACT

Gender, viewed differently throughout history, is influenced by media. Media's reach and influence on society, particularly regarding women, can be both positive and negative. Restrictive portrayals of women perpetuate gender-based violence, and media's role in this is concerning. However, media can also be a powerful tool to raise awareness, sensitize people, and promote gender equality. Grassroots efforts, especially in developing countries like India, can benefit from media interventions to inform and uplift marginalized groups. Violence against women, including trafficking and sexual abuse, remains prevalent, highlighting the need for media to address these issues responsibly. Media should be gender-sensitive, trained, and aware of the impact it can have on society. It can challenge stereotypes, showcase strong female role models, and contribute to ending gender inequality. However, media must also avoid sensationalizing sensitive stories and misrepresenting victims. By promoting equality and respect, the media industry can play a pivotal role in shaping perceptions of women.

I. INTRODUCTION

Gender is an ever-changing word having different connotations from ancient to contemporary times, a word viewed from different lenses by different generations. And these lenses have taken a very aggressive and edifying way in the form of media. As contemporary times revolve around the system generated by media. Media has evolved and continues to evolve taking into its fold every encompassable entity. Especially in contemporary times, the role of media is interlinked with every single soul and psyche. Its effect is far-reaching and its consequences have become inconsequential. The effect media has on a

DOI: 10.4018/978-1-6684-8893-5.ch014

particular gender that is the feminine gender is described as challenging as the view on women keeps changing as it is completely dependent upon the role of women as portrayed in media. This role is mostly confined to certain restricted views and ideologies on women which the waves of feminism have been trying to eradicate from society. These restricted views of women have become a challenge for women as it entangles them in a web of expected roles of either the goddess or the witch having a very thin line showing the normal persona of a woman. And media has become the feeding ground for gender-based violence by having a fixed notion of the role women play in society and if she deviates, she becomes a soft target for gender-based violence within the family or the society. The gender perspective harboured by the media is often misleading and tends to be dangerous. And the scope to harness such types of violence is the myriad media systems that have spread across the globe and have become perhaps the new age messiah.

The impact of media on gender can be a boon or a bane depending on the gender-friendly perception in general and the gender-censored perception in particular be it at an international or grassroots level. The positive side of media on women can be multidimensional and can be used to highlight and sensitize people regarding a myriad of issues surrounding women from every sphere. It is especially crucial at the grass root level as awareness generation, especially in a developing country where the tribals, the rural and the urban poor are left out from the mainstream and are not oriented about welfare measures, plans and policies and are not at all gender oriented. Thus, sensitization measures especially at the grass root areas where the tribal populace is completely cut off from any gender mainstreaming initiatives and as India especially Odisha has a rich tribal culture and several PVTGs, special initiatives should be undertaken to improve their condition and what better way than media to orient them on several proposal and efforts undertaken at centre and state level for their upliftment.

Gender-specific programs in various areas like entrepreneurship, education, skill enhancement, family planning and gender budgeting can be implemented within the target group easily by the proper media intervention. As most people are not aware of the various welfare measures for them. An important area that remains grey is violence against women in our country where the capital Delhi remains the most unsafe place for a woman in the global count. Gender-specific violence against women results in trafficking, sexual assault and abuse, girl child abuse, rape, dowry, sexual harassment at the workplace, acid throwing, and female infanticide to name a few.

Other horrendous acts such as incest are also dominant in our tradition-bound country which makes us question the role of media. It is perhaps adding fuel to the fire as globalization has opened many doors the various use of media and technology has resulted in cybercrimes that take gendered violence to a new level of menace surrounding our society and making this place an unsafe haven for women. Gender violence does not limit itself to only women but has also risen against transgenders in acts of violence and abuse. Gender violence many times is the result of gender inequality which is visible in every sphere and is extremely pronounced among women and the transgender communities. Through a workshop held by UN Women, 21 Georgian journalists received training on gender-sensitive reporting and how to cover violence against women in the media. Media should be gender sensitive as well as trained and properly sensitized while handling issues dealing with gender. According to a study of gender stereotypes in Georgian media, the majority of journalists lack awareness of gender issues and stereotypical attitudes dominate coverage of women's issues. During the training, journalists produced survivors' stories on domestic violence for an interactive exhibit and performance.

According to the Beijing platform: media plays an important role in perpetuating and challenging social norms that condone discrimination or violence against women. It can objectify women but also showcase strong women leaders and protagonists who can become role models for their audience. Media many times to sensationalize a story and misinterprets an issue of domestic violence or rape whereas these types of sensitive stories should be checked before telecasting. Media should protect women through proper reporting especially while portraying women as the vulnerable victim and many types type casting them in a role-specific way. This limits women's roles and type casts their potential. Evidence shows that violence against women is much more likely to occur when power, opportunities and resources are not shared equally between men and women in society, and when women are not valued and respected as much as men. The media industry can address gender inequality, challenge dominant gender stereotypes and work to end disrespect towards women, as a sector.

When we take mass media as indices of women's development or a crux in women's development, we have to carefully consider communication. The recent increase in the participation of women in the education and employment sector is due to communication and the impact of media. The impact of media has been felt in all walks of life be it sex ratio, awareness generation regarding acts and policies, growth in literacy, tribal women's empowerment issues, Reproductive health and sexual wellness, gender sensitization and many more. In terms of awareness generation focusing on the inclusion of women in every sphere free from the patriarchal mindset plays a key role in negating all kinds of marginalization that women face in public and private spaces. This type of wholistic arising of women as a subjugated race is possible only through a clean and unbiased media involvement and action. In developing countries such as India media as an instrument for positive change is not properly implemented as the portrayal of women is many times underplayed and sectionalized events especially relating to violence against women, telecast, broadcast, reels or print leave women more exposed leading to an increase in crimes against women as these events are often hyped and further leaves women more vulnerable. The goal of media exposure is not to glorify or degrade but to present facts in a clear and unbiased way for information and awareness generation.

The stereotypical image of women seldom graces them with a headline or prime-time coverage unless it's on issues of social or sexual orientation. Empowering issues highlighting women's true potential gets much less TRP perhaps as they are less sensational in nature. In a study conducted by the Media Advocacy Group viz. "Violence against Women: Media Coverage and Representation". The Media Advocacy Group made the following recommendations on reporting violence against women. (i) Media needs to take an extended, broader view of crimes against women. It has to be instrumental in conducting a social audit on factors responsible for increasing crimes, particularly against women and children, including indifferent investigative procedures, miscarriage of justice, and growing social impunity of the perpetrators of crime. (ii) It also has to be instrumental in creating an awareness among civil society of the causes and nature of the crime itself, and of the preventive measures. (iii) When treating these issues, media has to be extremely factual and empirical. The study also stated that the only regulation that governs sensitive reporting on this issue is that the rape victim's name should not be disclosed. But many cases disregard these guidelines and focus on how sensational a story gets without much focus on the effect on women or guidelines issues. A ray of hope may be hoped for after the Press Council has in consultation with the UNDP and the activists of the field redrawn the guidelines for media reportage that find a place in the souvenir that is to be shortly released (Cott, 1986).

II. OBJECTIVE OF THE STUDY

(i) To identify the crux that leads to gender-based violence as a result of media
(ii) To identify the various sources of media and their effect on crimes against women

III. REVIEW OF LITERATURE

Cyber feminism is a new age quandary for many and has to be explored in its true sense to initiate proper action which will help in highlighting the positives and negating the negatives. Hence converting the crux in media will not lead to any more cybercrimes against women. The few books explored in this context can perhaps shed some light on this issue.

CYBER-FEMINISM INDEX edited by Mindy Seu (Pierce & Russell, 2022) critiques the past and brings forth the future in terms of the struggle against male domination in cyberspace. It offers a very helpful insight into the era of life online and tries to evaluate the kaleidoscope of associations of real life and reel life and focuses on the attempt that has been made to dissuade women through cybercrimes.

GLITCH FEMINISM: A Manifesto by Legacy Russel Brooklyn (Russell, 2020) talks of the techno-cultural promise and the latent radicalism of the internet in the early days. How it blazed through and increased the sense of freedom as well as control in the hands of man. This book talks about the age-old mindset of blocking women automatically even in the area of technology.

CYBERFEMINISM edited by Susan Hawthorne and Renate Klein (Hawthorne & Klein, 1999) is a collection of writings from feminists of international repute from broad disciplines of multimedia games production, Virtual reality creation, program development and electronic product, data delivery, educational multi-media and many more fields.

EGIRLS, ECITIZENS by Jane Bailey and Valerie Steeves (Steeves & Bailey, 2015) is a great work focusing on the reality of private space a sense of identity and equality in a digitally censored era and the experiences of girls and young women.

In the article REVISITING CYBERFEMINISM (Paasonen, 2011), she discussed the attraction of cyberfeminism and poses some tentative explanations for its appeal fading and for cyberfeminist activities being channelled into other networks and practised under different names.

IV. DISCUSSION

A. Cyberfeminism: A Right-Based Approach

Approaches towards cyberfeminism can be multiple but at least two approaches can be focused on. One is to clear this patriarchal space on the internet and technological aspect as the term techno-savvy is for all and not a particular gender and the other most important to make women visible and focus on gender issues with a feminist backdrop. Social media is a powerful tool and cyberfeminism if propagated properly can raise relevant issues and information rather than be a breeding ground for women being in an unsafe space and hence subjected to indecent exposure and cybercrimes against women.

An example of cyberfeminism can be traced back to June 2009 uprising following Iran's presidential election that sparked the immediate scattering of its women's rights leaders across the globe. Activists living in exile took their activities online to pursue on-the-ground projects, initiating online campaigns and raising feminist awareness. In the Gulf countries, the protest that followed the Arab Spring, which began on 17 December 2010 and continued till December 2012 against the authoritarian regimes in West Asia and North Africa, saw largescale use of social media by activists who strongly protested against the suppression of Arab women and their rights. Following the 2012 Nirbhaya rape, the anti-rape movement in India launched a new feminist politics that embodied a rights-based discourse of gender in a way that had not been seriously taken up by the mainstream Indian Women's Movement. Many experts view that this feminist discourse was connected to a global vocabulary of rights facilitated, to a large extent, using the Internet. In the Iran anti-hijab row, social media has been flooded with women chopping off their hair and burning veils, encouraging each other to join the movement against the forceful imposition of wearing a Hijab. Women posting on social media with the campaign hashtag #notocompulsoryhijab have attracted reactionary tweets accusing them of being anti-Islam and anti-society. Women who use their social media accounts to reject the hijab are often met with sexist attacks and threats that attempt to shame and silence them. In Pakistan, several feminist movements including Women's Democratic Front (WDF) and Women Action Forum have taken shape largely by claiming their space and encouraging others to do so as well on social media. These movements have set the online debate on society's set rights and wrongs, which have helped people develop their independent perspectives. (*Outlook India*, 2023)

Through cyberfeminism women all over the world with the help of social media tools such as Twitter, Facebook, Instagram and many more have maintained a camaraderie to voice the right opinion and fight against and for each other to overthrow autocracy in any sphere and stop violence against women.

B. Feminism in the Digital Era

In the ever-evolving landscape of technology, the involvement of women has historically been overshadowed by patriarchal impositions and the deeply entrenched subjugation of women. The media, in its various forms, has often perpetuated the perils faced by women, sensationalizing events and narratives that further marginalize them. However, despite the obstacles, women have taken a remarkable leap into the realm of cyber pursuits, carving a path for themselves in the digital world. This transition, while met with hostility, holds the potential for transformative empowerment. It is imperative that the media recognizes its role in shedding light on real issues faced by women and refrains from sensationalism, thereby advocating for meaningful change.

The media's influence cannot be understated, particularly when it comes to highlighting the challenges that disproportionately affect women. Poverty's impact on women, for instance, is an issue often sidelined or inadequately covered. Consider the case of Shanti Devi from a remote village in Jharkhand, India. Shanti Devi's story, while not an isolated incident, underscores the stark reality of impoverished women who lack access to basic necessities. Her struggle to provide for her family amidst a cycle of destitution serves as a stark reminder of the urgency to address economic disparities.

Similarly, the prevailing dowry-related deaths in societies across the globe demand media attention beyond mere sensationalism. The tragic story of Aisha, a young woman from Pakistan, highlights the harrowing consequences of dowry-related violence. Her untimely demise due to dowry demands and subsequent abuse paints a grim picture of the underlying gender inequalities that persist. The media can play a pivotal role in dismantling such practices by amplifying the voices of victims and advocating for stricter legal measures.

Sex ratio imbalances, another critical issue, have far-reaching implications for societies. In regions like Uttar Pradesh, India, the skewed sex ratios due to gender-based discrimination have given rise to a host of socio-cultural challenges. Media outlets have the responsibility to delve into the root causes of this disparity and foster conversations that promote gender equality, rather than merely sensationalizing the statistics.

HIV and its disproportionate impact on women are yet another facet that requires the media's earnest attention. The story of Maria, an HIV-positive woman in sub-Saharan Africa, encapsulates the struggles of countless women who face stigma and discrimination due to their health status. The media can help counteract this prejudice by disseminating accurate information, promoting awareness, and advocating for comprehensive healthcare services for affected women.

Maternal mortality rates, unwed motherhood, and instances of incest are grim realities that women navigate silently. The media's role in unravelling these issues is pivotal, as evidenced by the story of Sarah in a conservative society. Sarah's ordeal of concealing her unwed pregnancy, battling societal judgment, and seeking limited support exemplifies the urgency of addressing these concerns openly. By shedding light on such stories, the media can push for de-stigmatization, thereby offering solace and support to women grappling with similar challenges.

While the media has a responsibility to raise awareness about these pressing issues, it must also celebrate the triumphs and opportunities that women have carved out for themselves. Highlighting women's achievements in various domains, such as career advancements, entrepreneurship, and leadership roles, can inspire future generations and shatter glass ceilings. The media should act as a catalyst for change, advocating for legal aid, counselling services, daycare facilities, and women-friendly public transport to create an environment conducive to women's growth and empowerment.

A study conducted across diverse regions in India—Jharkhand, Chhattisgarh, Uttarakhand, Uttar Pradesh, and Jammu and Kashmir—revealed an alarming trend in media coverage. Only a mere 5% of women-related issues were given prominence in prominent newspapers, with a mere 8% making it to the front page. The remaining stories were relegated to interior pages, reflecting the continued lack of priority for women's development issues. Television serials, although often centred around women characters, often perpetuated harmful stereotypes, depicting them as either tormentors or victims. This skewed portrayal not only fails to reflect reality but also contributes to reinforcing detrimental gender norms.

The National Commission for Women's call for amending the Indecent Representation of Women (Prohibition) Act, 1986, to include new technologies and media forms like MMS and electronic media is a step in the right direction. By addressing media portrayals that perpetuate stereotypes, society can take a collective stride towards dismantling deeply ingrained biases.

Cyberfeminism offers a powerful means to bridge the gap between women and technology. The media plays a pivotal role in this transformation, by spotlighting issues that affect women's lives while avoiding sensationalism. By focusing on substantive topics such as poverty's impact, dowry-related deaths, sex ratio imbalances, HIV, and the multitude of challenges women face, the media can inspire change and advocate for improved policies. Additionally, the media should celebrate women's achievements and promote opportunities, thereby fostering a more inclusive and equitable digital world. Through these concerted efforts, the media can transcend its role as a mere observer and become an active force in safeguarding women's rights and empowering them in the digital age. (*Indian Printer & Publisher*, n.d.)

Thus, the media has an important role to play to safeguard women and not just merely report some events relating to women. (*Outlook India Magazine Online- Read News India, Latest News Analysis, World, Sports, Entertainment | Best Online Magazine India*, n.d.)

V. CONCLUSION

Be it the portrayal of women in media or cyberfeminism today's techno world is often used to the disadvantage of women or to portray women in a negative light... the sexism women face has also seeped into this cyber world. All this can change by several factors like pluralistic media, stringent policy framework, Gender sensitization workshops, and educating the young masses to be free from stereotypical thinking. By incorporating certain factors women's role and portrayal in media and cyberspace can be holistic and evolved. The portrayal of women by media needs to be less glamorous and more basic and real. The real stories should be showcased without sensationalizing them for TRP purposes. Be it mass media or cyberspace in contemporary times we need to be responsible while using it and while subjecting others to information. As the information needs to be unbiased and clear and should have a concurrent effect on everybody and should not negate a person's capabilities based on biases of any kind be it gender bias, casteism, classism or based on someone's sexual orientation. Women have been facing the wrath of role expectation from every sphere and it's the same in this cyberspace many times. It is challenging for women to stay afloat in this sea of expectation and exploitation. Thus, it is imperative to take stringent measures on both legal and policy frameworks and make cyberspace safe and developed without any preconceptions or misconceptions relating to gender.

REFERENCES

Cott, N. F. (1986). *What is Feminism?* Pantheon Books.

Hawthorne, S., & Klein, R. (1999). *Cyberfeminism: Connectivity, Critique and Creativity*. Spinifex Press.

Indian Printer & Publisher. (n.d.). Retrieved June 3, 2023, from https://indianprinterpublisher.com/

Outlook India: Best Online Magazine India, Latest News, Story. (2023, May 23). Https://Www.Outlookindia.Com/. https://www.outlookindia.com

Outlook India Magazine Online- Read News India, Latest News Analysis, World, Sports, Entertainment | Best Online Magazine India. (n.d.). Https://Www.Outlookindia.Com/. Retrieved June 3, 2023, from https://www.outlookindia.com

Paasonen, S. (2011). *Revisiting cyberfeminism. 36*(3), 335–352. doi:10.1515/comm.2011.017

Pierce, J., & Russell, L. (2022). *Cyberfeminism Index*. Inventory Press.

Russell, L. (2020). *Glitch Feminism: A Manifesto*. Verso Books.

Steeves, V., & Bailey, J. (2015). *EGirls, ECitizens: Putting Technology, Theory and Policy into Dialogue with Girls' and Young Women's Voices*. University of Ottawa Press.

Chapter 15
Gendered Harassment and Bias in Online Gaming: Experiences of Female Gamers

Archana Parashar
Indian Institute of Management, Raipur, India

S. Niranjana Varma
Tata Institute of Social Sciences, Hyderabad, India

ABSTRACT

The chapter provides an overview of the history of online gaming, highlighting its evolution from the early days of home video games to the emergence of online gaming communities and the rise of eSports. It also explores the gender dynamics within the gaming industry, discussing the challenges and discrimination faced by female gamers and the efforts to create a more inclusive gaming environment. The chapter further examines women's roles as players, game designers, objects of the male gaze, and viewers in the gaming industry, emphasising women's increasing participation and contributions in various capacities. It discusses women's representation in games and objectification's impact on female gamers. Additionally, it touches on the importance of diversity and inclusivity in the gaming industry and the role of online gaming as a social platform. The chapter also attempts to address the gendered themes in popular online games and the potential for alternative gaming experiences to challenge traditional notions of gender in gaming.

1. INTRODUCTION

1.1. The Evolution of Online Gaming and the Importance of Gender Inclusivity

In recent years, online gaming has undergone an extraordinary surge in popularity, establishing itself as a global phenomenon that captivates a diverse player base through a myriad of gaming experiences. What initially began as a simple pastime has since matured into a comprehensive industry, encompass-

DOI: 10.4018/978-1-6684-8893-5.ch015

ing not only game production but also promotional activities and the orchestration of online gaming tournaments, among other endeavours. The expansive landscape of online gaming is home to various platforms, notable ones including Steam, Xbox Live, PlayStation Network, and Nintendo Switch Online. Within these platforms, a wide spectrum of gaming services is offered, ranging from game distribution and multiplayer functionality to cross-platform compatibility, socialisation features, and player incentives. Adding another layer of engagement, players frequently live stream their gaming sessions on platforms like YouTube and Twitch, thus opening new avenues for interaction and even potential monetisation. The accessibility and utilisation of these platforms experienced an unprecedented upswing during the Covid-19 lockdown period, as individuals – including those not professionally engaged in gaming – turned to online gaming for solace and connectivity from the confines of their residences.

1.2. Platforms and Their Proliferation

The online gaming universe, characterised by an extensive array of platforms, has bestowed upon itself the status of a diverse ecosystem that caters to a global gaming community. Noteworthy platforms, including but not limited to Steam, Xbox Live, PlayStation Network, and Nintendo Switch Online, have emerged as significant platforms for various gaming services. These encompass multifaceted functions such as game distribution, cross-platform compatibility, social interaction features, and rewards systems that attract more players. It is also pertinent to acknowledge the surge in streaming platforms like YouTube and Twitch, providing players with an innovative medium for engaging their audience, thereby also holding the potential for financial gain. As the gaming ecosystem diversifies further, it is imperative to acknowledge additional dimensions contributing to its complexity and dynamism.

The surge of mobile gaming, fuelled by the universality of smartphones and tablets, has democratised gaming even further, making it accessible to a wider audience. Additionally, the advent of cloud gaming services, exemplified by Google Stadia and Xbox Cloud Gaming, has begun to reshape how games are experienced, erasing the barriers of hardware limitations. Social integration is another vital facet, with platforms seamlessly embedding social features that foster connections among players, enabling them to forge communities and share their gaming escapades effortlessly. Moreover, virtual reality (VR) and augmented reality (AR) platforms, such as Oculus and Microsoft's HoloLens, have shattered conventional boundaries, immersing players in realms that blur the lines between the real and the digital. E-sports, yet another advancement, and competitive gaming platforms have emerged as integral components of the gaming sphere, transforming it into a global spectacle that draws enthusiasts from across the world.

1.3. The Pandemic's Catalyst

The landscape of online gaming underwent a significant transformation due to the Covid-19 pandemic. Lockdown measures imposed during the pandemic led to an unparalleled surge in the use of online gaming platforms. These platforms served not only as sources of entertainment but also as avenues for social interaction, extending beyond traditional gaming circles. The pandemic-induced lockdowns brought about a remarkable shift in how online gaming was embraced, blurring the boundaries between recreational and professional gaming realms. This transition underscored the vital role of online gaming in fostering entertainment and social engagement during times of isolation.

1.4. Gender Dynamics in Online Gaming

Online gaming serves as a diverse realm, catering to a spectrum of motivations, including entertainment, stress relief, financial gains, and personal achievements. However, it is crucial to recognise that female gamers frequently face gender-based harassment and bias, which significantly impact their interactions within these digital spaces. The female video gaming community grew by 19% last year, according to data commissioned by Google. Google and Niko partners say that women comprise 40-45% of the Asian gaming population. Despite the increasing presence of female gamers, gendered harassment and bias remain pervasive in online gaming. Despite the notable expansion of the female gaming community, the pervasive nature of gendered harassment continues to cast a long shadow over the online gaming landscape. This reality emphasises the urgent need to place a greater emphasis on amplifying the voices and narratives of women within this space. Doing so can foster a more inclusive and equitable gaming culture, paving the way for a gaming environment where all individuals can participate and flourish without the hindrance of bias or harassment.

The issue of gendered harassment and bias in online gaming has gradually ascended the ladder of scholarly, activist, and industry concern. Research within academia has spotlighted the prevalence of verbal abuse, sexual objectification, and exclusionary practices that disproportionately affect female gamers. These circumstances incubate a toxic gaming environment, reinforcing and normalising sexist stereotypes. To holistically understand the experiences of female gamers, it is crucial to recognise the intricate intersectional nature of these encounters. Factors like race, ethnicity, sexual orientation, and socio-economic status converge with gender, forging distinct challenges and experiences for women hailing from diverse backgrounds. Exploring the interplay of these multifaceted identities will lay the groundwork for comprehensive strategies and interventions catering to female gamers' distinct needs.

This chapter thus aims to shed light on women's unique challenges within online gaming communities, examining the harassment and discrimination they encounter. By delving into the underlying causes and consequences of gendered harassment, we can gain a deeper understanding of the experiences and perspectives of female gamers. By examining women's pervasive issues within the online gaming realm and analysing the perpetuation and reinforcement of gender biases within the gaming industry, this chapter aims to contribute to a deeper understanding of gendered harassment and bias in online gaming. Through this exploration, we can work towards fostering a more inclusive and equitable gaming environment for all players.

2. REVIEW OF LITERATURE

This section presents a comprehensive review of existing literature, offering insights into the diverse dimensions of gendered harassment and bias in online gaming. Through an exploration of academic studies, activist discourse, and industry reports, this review aims to contextualise the issues, shed light on the prevailing dynamics, and lay the foundation for understanding the unique challenges faced by female gamers in digital spaces.

2.1. The Prevalence of Gendered Harassment and Bias

The prevalence of gendered harassment and bias within online gaming communities is a concerning phenomenon underscored by many research studies and reports. These investigations consistently shed light on the disturbing extent to which female gamers encounter various forms of mistreatment, including but not limited to verbal abuse, sexual objectification, exclusionary practices, and explicit online threats (Patrick W. Galbraith, 2017). Research has documented instances where derogatory language and demeaning comments are directed at women, creating a hostile environment that undermines their ability to engage in gaming without fear or discomfort (Dietz, T. L., 1998; Jesse Fox, Wai Yen Tang, 2014; Kirsten Mettler, 2023; Patrick W. Galbraith, 2017). Moreover, the objectification of female characters and players persists as a deeply rooted issue, perpetuating harmful stereotypes and diminishing the potential for authentic and equitable experiences. Exclusionary practices manifest through gatekeeping and targeted isolation, inhibiting female gamers' opportunities for meaningful participation and collaboration (Matthew Johnson, 2015). The alarming prevalence of online threats, ranging from explicit messages to doxing and stalking, further amplifies the urgency of addressing gendered harassment and bias (Stephanie Boluk and Patrick Lemieu, 2017). The 2020 Female Gamer Survey by Bryter reveals that approximately 58.0% of female gamers have encountered various forms of mistreatment from male gamers during online play, with 28.0% enduring instances of sexual harassment (Jenny McBean, 2022; Mariela Bustos-Ortega, Hugo Carretero-Dios, and Mónica Romero-Sánchez, 2023). This harassment often manifests as objectifying remarks or alarming threats of a sexual or violent nature. Statistical data and illustrative examples collectively underscore the pervasive nature of these issues, urging a comprehensive understanding of the complexities involved and a dedicated commitment to fostering a safer and more inclusive digital gaming environment.

2.2. Intersectionality in Gaming Experiences

The concept of intersectionality is a crucial lens to comprehend the multifaceted experiences of female gamers within the online gaming landscape. This perspective highlights the interconnected nature of various identity markers and how they converge to shape distinctive challenges and opportunities. Factors such as race, ethnicity, sexual orientation, socio-economic status, and disability intersect with gender, giving rise to nuanced experiences that are far from monolithic (Gabriela T. Richard and Kishonna L. Gray, 2018). The experiences of women in online gaming are not uniform, and the intersectionality framework underscores that these experiences are shaped by the convergence of different social identities. A woman's experience in online gaming can be profoundly influenced by her racial background as she navigates the interplay between gender bias and racial stereotypes. For example, in their paper, Gabriela T. Richard and Kishonna L. Gray talk about how the default image of a gamer is associated with white males, overshadowing the presence and perspectives of marginalised groups. To address these disparities, the authors advocate for the application of transformative frameworks like Black Cyberfeminism and Inclusive Communities of Practice. These frameworks, they suggest, offer valuable insights to comprehend and tackle these intricate challenges. Similarly, a queer woman may face unique forms of harassment that stem from both her gender and sexual orientation. Research has shown how games perpetrate homophobic and transphobic content online games (Adrienne Shaw and Elizaveta Friesem, 2016). The literature presents an array of examples and research findings that illuminate the intricate interplay of these identities, offering insights into how various aspects of a person's identity combine to produce complex and often contradictory experiences within the gaming realm.

2.3. Impact on Mental Health and Well-Being

The psychological ramifications of gendered harassment and bias against female gamers constitute a critical aspect of the discourse. Studies have probed into this area, revealing the impact of such mistreatment on the mental health and overall well-being of women engaged in online gaming. These studies underline how the cumulative effect of enduring gendered harassment can culminate in elevated stress levels, heightened anxiety, bouts of depression, and diminished self-esteem. The consistent exposure to derogatory comments, objectification, and exclusionary behaviour within gaming communities manifests as a persistent source of psychological distress (Dietz, T. L., 1998). Cases of direct physical violence were also uncovered by researchers (Monit Khanna, 2021).

3. GAPS AND OBJECTIVES

The review of the literature underscores the urgency of addressing gendered harassment and bias within the online gaming domain. Despite the comprehensive insights provided by existing studies, several gaps persist that warrant further exploration. While studies have discussed the extent of harassment, fewer have delved into the socio-psychological factors that contribute to the perpetration of such behaviour by male gamers. Intersectionality is recognised as a pivotal concept; more in-depth research is needed to explore how these intersecting identities influence and interact within the gaming context. The review also highlights that there's not much research about how ongoing harassment based on gender affects how female gamers see themselves and how they interact with others outside of the gaming world. It is also important to note that limited attention has been given to the effectiveness of current interventions and strategies in mitigating gendered harassment and fostering inclusive gaming environments.

The comprehensive exploration of the gendered dynamics within the gaming landscape has led to the identification of several crucial objectives. These objectives seek to shed light on the history, representation, experiences, and challenges of women in the gaming industry, offering a multifaceted perspective that contributes to the ongoing dialogue on gender equality and inclusivity. Building upon the insights from the reviewed literature, this chapter aims to address these gaps and achieve the following objectives:

3.1. Understanding Perpetration Mechanisms

Investigate the underlying socio-psychological mechanisms that lead to the perpetuation of gendered harassment by male gamers, shedding light on factors such as anonymity, social norms, and power dynamics that contribute to such behaviour.

3.2. Exploring Intersectionality Dynamics

Examine in-depth how the interplay of various identity markers such as race, ethnicity, sexual orientation, and disability with gender shapes the unique experiences of women from diverse backgrounds in online gaming communities.

3.3. Understanding Historical Evolution

The history of online gaming is intricately tied to the evolution of entertainment and technology. By examining the historical progression from early home video games to contemporary online platforms, this chapter aims to explore how gender dynamics have shaped and continue to influence the gaming landscape. Through this understanding, the chapter seeks to contextualise the current challenges faced by women in the industry.

3.4. Recognising Women's Diverse Roles

The diverse roles that women occupy within the gaming industry constitute a significant aspect of this chapter's objectives. By highlighting the contributions of women as players, game designers, objects of the female gaze, viewers, and professionals, this section aims to dismantle the notion of a monolithic gaming experience. It aims to demonstrate how women's involvement enriches the gaming culture, challenges stereotypes, and fosters a more inclusive environment for all participants. Addressing Gendered Preferences

3.5. Addressing Gendered Preferences

Exploring the concept of gendered preferences in online gaming is another key objective. This section aims to delve into the complex interplay between gaming themes, personal preferences, societal expectations, and individual motivations. By examining the prevalence of violent themes and the emergence of alternative gaming experiences, this chapter seeks to uncover the nuanced motivations behind women's engagement with different types of games and how gaming can serve as a liberating space.

3.6. Confronting Gendered Violence

The objective of addressing gendered violence within the gaming industry is pivotal to fostering a safer and more inclusive environment. By investigating the various forms of gendered violence, such as sexist comments, harassment, stalking, and the hyper-sexualization of avatars, this chapter seeks to raise awareness about the pervasive nature of these issues. Additionally, it aims to emphasise the consequences of gendered violence on mental health, well-being, and professional opportunities for women in gaming.

3.7. Advocating for Change

Central to the objectives of this chapter is advocating for meaningful change within the gaming industry. By highlighting the experiences of women gamers, designers, viewers, and professionals, this section aims to contribute to a broader discourse on gender equality and representation. It seeks to inspire actions that address the existing disparities, challenge harmful stereotypes, and create a more inclusive and welcoming gaming culture for all participants.

4. DISCUSSION

4.1. History of Online Gaming

The history of video games can be traced back to the introduction of home video games in the 1970s, marking the beginning of a transformative era in entertainment (Angela Bassey Hjelpdahl, 2020). At its inception, gaming was a novel addition to the leisure activities available, capturing the curiosity of individuals who eagerly began exploring this emerging medium. However, the early games lacked the addictive nature and sophistication characteristic of today's gaming landscape (Jesse Fox, Wai Yen Tang, 2014). As the industry progressed and games like Zelda and Mario emerged in the 1990s, video games slowly gained the attention of adults and children, eventually becoming an integral part of popular culture. As video games evolved and moved beyond solitary experiences, gaming communities began to form, acting as hubs where gamers could connect, share experiences, and engage in multiplayer interactions. These communities paved the way for online gaming platforms, further transforming the gaming landscape. Within these communities, gendered dynamics started to shape the experiences of female gamers, influencing their interactions, opportunities, and challenges. While exploring the evolution of video games, it is imperative to delve into the gender dynamics that have shaped the gaming landscape over time. The gaming history reveals a predominantly male-dominated industry, with the experiences of female gamers often marginalised and underrepresented. The emergence of gaming communities in the aftermath of the 1990s provides a focal point for examining the gendered trends within online gaming.

Gaming communities have been traditionally male-dominated, with the prototype of a white man. Masculine discourse and ideologies are integral to the gaming domain (Saralyn McKinnon-Crowley, 2020). For example, Saralyn McKinnon-Crowley, in her scholarly personal narrative of her gaming experiences in the *Magic* gaming community, talks about a universal 'bro-code' that all the players follow knowingly or unknowingly, showing the masculine culture of such gaming communities. These communities often reflect traditional gender norms and reinforce stereotypes, creating an environment where female gamers may face challenges and biases (Phiona Martin, Antoni Barnard, 2013). Studies have investigated the roots and manifestations of gendered harassment and discrimination in online gaming. Research also emphasises the role of social norms and stereotypes in perpetuating such discriminatory behaviour. Traditional gender roles and expectations often influence the treatment of female gamers, leading to their exclusion, objectification, and marginalisation within gaming communities. Understanding the experiences of female gamers in this context is crucial for recognising the existing disparities and working towards a more inclusive gaming environment. Examining the gendered trends within online gaming communities sheds light on female gamers' unique challenges. It is essential to acknowledge that gender disparities are not inherent to gaming itself but rather arise from the broader social structures and norms that influence interactions within gaming spaces.

With the advancement of technology and the internet, gaming communities have undergone a transformation, giving rise to the phenomenon of eSports. eSports refers to the competitive playing and spectatorship of video games in online spaces. It has gained immense popularity, with millions of players and viewers engaging in various eSports titles. Games such as Call of Duty, Rocket League, Valorant, Fortnite, Overwatch, Counter-Strike, Dota 2, and League of Legends have emerged as prominent eSports, attracting a large player base and garnering substantial viewership on streaming platforms (Seth E. Jenny,, R. Douglas Manning, Margaret C. Keiper, Tracy W. Olrich, 2017). The rise of eSports has led to a paradigm shift in how video games are perceived, with a growing acceptance of eSports as a legitimate form of sport and its players as skilled athletes. This shift in perception can be seen in popular culture, where eSports events are now broadcasted on mainstream television channels, and eSports players are celebrated for their achievements. For example, in 2018, ESPN, a prominent sports network, aired the Overwatch League Grand Finals, showcasing the growing recognition of eSports within traditional sports media (Stefanie Fogel, 2018). Additionally, eSports tournaments attract massive audiences, with live events filling arenas and stadiums around the world. For instance, the League of Legends World Championship recorded over 100 million unique viewers for its 2020 grand finals (KEVIN WEBB, 2019). These examples demonstrate the increasing prominence and cultural acceptance of eSports.

Online gaming today has become a social platform, enabling players to communicate, collaborate, and build communities. The development of virtual reality (VR) and augmented reality (AR) technologies has added a new dimension to online gaming experiences, allowing players to immerse themselves in virtual worlds and interact with their environments in unprecedented ways. This immersive aspect of online gaming can potentially create a sense of presence and social connection among players, transcending geographical boundaries. In terms of monetisation models, online gaming has undergone significant changes. Traditional models, such as one-time game software purchases, have expanded to include free-to-play games supported by in-game purchases and microtransactions. This shift has created new revenue streams for game developers, allowing players to access and enjoy games without upfront costs.

As an extension of the contemporary patriarchal structures present in our society, the most modern gaming industry also absorbs patriarchal values and has evolved over time. With broader access, there are many women gamers in the industry, but their experiences are not always pleasant. The patriarchal nature of society, characterised by unequal power dynamics and gender stereotypes, seeps into the gaming industry, impacting the experiences of women gamers. Despite the increasing number of women involved in gaming, they often face gender discrimination, stereotypes, and harassment.

4.2. Women in the Gaming Industry

The gaming industry has evolved significantly over the years, with women playing diverse roles and contributing in various capacities. Women are actively involved as players, game designers, objects of the female gaze, and viewers of game streaming.

4.2.1. Women as Players

The presence of women as players in the gaming community has witnessed significant growth in recent years, challenging enduring stereotypes and the perception of gaming as a male-dominated activity. Women have increasingly embraced gaming as a form of entertainment, self-expression, and social interaction, leading to a rise in the number of female gamers worldwide. This shift is reflected in statistics and reports, such as the 'Think with Google APAC – Play like a Girl' report released in 2021, highlighting women's increasing participation in gaming. According to the report, 18 per cent of all gamers across different age groups are female, with India specifically showing that 48 per cent of smartphone gamers are women. These figures indicate that women actively engage with games, regardless of their location or cultural background.

The growing popularity of mobile gaming has played a significant role in attracting female players. Mobile games offer accessibility, convenience, and a wide variety of genres and experiences that appeal to diverse audiences. Women find enjoyment in casual games, puzzle games, role-playing games, and many other genres, exploring the vast array of gaming experiences available.

Online gaming platforms, such as Twitch and YouTube Gaming, have also provided opportunities for women to connect, collaborate, and compete with other players worldwide. Female players form friendships, join gaming communities, and engage in team-based activities, breaking down barriers and challenging the notion that gaming is a solitary pursuit. Online communities, such as The PMS Clan, GirlGamers subreddit, Twitch Women, Frag Dolls, and Women in Games International (WIGI), offer spaces and platforms for women in gaming to connect, share experiences, and find support. These communities not only provide a sense of belonging but also foster empowerment and representation within the gaming industry.

The increasing visibility of women in the gaming industry has played a crucial role in inspiring more women to become players. Female streamers, content creators, and professional gamers have emerged as role models, showcasing their skills, passion, and achievements in the gaming world. Personalities like Imane "Pokimane" Anys, Kathleen "Loserfruit" Belsten, Sejal "Sejal Kumar" Kumar, and Sasha "Scarlett" Hostyn have gained popularity and success in their respective fields, serving as inspirational figures for aspiring female gamers. Their presence challenges stereotypes and reinforces the idea that gaming is inclusive and for everyone, regardless of gender.

The presence of women as players in the gaming industry has grown significantly, defying stereotypes and contributing to the diversity and inclusivity of the gaming community. The rising number of female gamers, supported by online communities and inspired by influential female streamers, content creators, and professional gamers, reflects a positive shift in the industry. This progress empowers women and enriches the gaming experience for players of all genders, promoting a more vibrant and inclusive gaming culture.

4.2.2. Women as Designers

Women game designers are making significant strides in the gaming industry, leaving an indelible mark on the medium. Their creative vision and storytelling abilities have helped shape the industry by pushing boundaries and introducing fresh perspectives. By challenging stereotypes and traditional gender roles, these designers have opened doors to more diverse narratives and gameplay experiences that resonate with players of all genders.

Prominent female game developers such as Brenda Romero, Rebecca Ann Heineman, Judy Tyrer, Brianna Wu, and Jane Ng have shared their experiences and insights in the book "Women in Game Development: Breaking the Glass Level-Cap" by Patricia Hernandez (Jennifer Brandes Hepler (Ed.), 2007). Through this book, they shed light on the common issues faced by women in the industry.

One prevalent issue these designers discuss is the pervasive gender stereotyping that women encounter. Assumptions about women's technical skills, creative abilities, and suitability for specific roles can hinder their progress and contribute to a lack of recognition. By defying these stereotypes, female game designers challenge societal norms and pave the way for greater inclusivity. The lack of representation is another concern raised by these designers. Both in terms of female developers and female characters in games, there is a need for more diverse and realistic portrayals. By advocating for better representation, women game designers strive to create more inclusive experiences that reflect the diversity of players. Patriarchal workplace culture and harassment are significant barriers women face in the industry. The toxic and hostile work environments they encounter can impede their professional growth and well-being. Addressing these issues and fostering safer and more inclusive spaces where women can thrive and contribute their talents is crucial.

Despite the progress made, women still need to be represented in game development roles. Efforts to encourage and support women in pursuing careers in game design are vital to ensuring diverse perspectives in the industry. Mentorship programs, networking opportunities, and initiatives that promote equality and fair treatment are essential for nurturing the talent and potential of women game designers. Women game designers make remarkable contributions to the gaming industry, challenging stereotypes and reshaping the medium with their unique perspectives. The narratives shared by prominent female game developers emphasise the need to address gender stereotyping, lack of representation, patriarchal workplace culture, and harassment. Efforts to encourage and support women in game design are crucial for achieving a more diverse and inclusive industry that benefits from their creative vision and storytelling prowess.

4.2.3. Women as Objects of Male Gaze

The portrayal of women as objects of the female gaze in gaming has sparked considerable discussion and critique. This phenomenon refers to the representation of female characters primarily designed to cater to the heterosexual male gaze, often resulting in their objectification and sexualisation. Numerous quantitative studies conducted over the years have consistently highlighted the trend of representing women as hypersexualised objects of the male gaze (Dietz, T. L., 1998; Downs, E. & Smith, S.L., 2010). Critics argue that the objectification of women in gaming perpetuates harmful stereotypes and reinforces gender inequalities. By reducing female characters to mere objects, reinforces traditional gender roles and restricts their representation to narrow and limited stereotypes. Women are frequently depicted as passive, sexualised beings, reinforcing the notion that their worth lies primarily in their physical appearance and desirability. This perpetuation of stereotypes undermines the progress towards gender equality and contributes to the marginalisation of women within the gaming industry.

Objectification of women in gaming has a direct impact on the self-perception of women gamers. Constant exposure to unrealistic and sexualised representations can lead to feelings of inadequacy, body image issues, and the internalisation of harmful beauty standards. This can result in a negative gaming experience for women and girls, further alienating them from the medium. It also implicitly reinforces patriarchal power dynamics in the gaming industry. By catering primarily to the heterosexual male audience, the industry perpetuates an exclusionary environment and contributes to the marginalisation of women. This imbalance of power and representation limits diversity and inhibits the industry's ability to create inclusive and welcoming spaces for all gamers.

4.2.4. Women as Viewers

The rise of game streaming platforms has opened new opportunities for women to engage as viewers, content creators, and influencers in the gaming community. Women viewers are an integral part of online gaming communities that cater to the needs of women. Unlike the traditional 'gaming brotherhood,' these spaces are more inclusive and help form a sisterhood among female gamers. Community building by women streamers and viewers is crucial in fostering supportive and inclusive gaming communities. They share their unique perspectives and experiences, bringing diverse viewpoints to the table. This creates an environment that welcomes individuals from all backgrounds and helps marginalised groups feel a sense of belonging and representation within the gaming community. Previously, gaming communities may have felt exclusionary or dominated by a specific demographic, but the presence of women viewers and streamers helps break down those barriers.

Women content creators are playing a significant role in reshaping the gaming industry. Through their streaming channels and content creation efforts, they provide diverse and relatable content that appeals to a wide range of audiences. This allows women to connect with one another, find role models, and challenge existing gender norms in gaming. By showcasing their skills and passion, women content creators encourage more women to actively participate and break free from the stereotypes and barriers that may have limited their involvement in the past. For example, Pokimane, a popular Twitch streamer, is known for her engaging personality and diverse content. She has created a space that is not only inclusive but also supportive of marginalised individuals. Pokimane's channel serves as an inspiring example of how women content creators can contribute to the growth of supportive and inclusive gaming communities. Her presence and influence have helped redefine the gaming industry, providing a platform where women can connect, share their experiences, and challenge existing norms.

4.2.5. Women as Game Developers

Gender-based exclusion and the lack of diversity within the digital games industry have been the focus of extensive scholarly research spanning many years. Women encounter difficulties accessing game-related education and training programs, being underrepresented and facing adverse treatment. This trend continues into employment, where women may be confined to lower-level positions, encountering discrimination and inequity(Johanna Weststar and Legault Marie-Josée, 2018). Initially, approaches inadvertently perpetuated stereotypical gender preferences. However, feminist frameworks have since illuminated the profound influence of play spaces and expertise development on gendered play patterns. Even though more and more women are playing games and popular games are reaching a wider audience, the number of women involved in creating digital games is still minimal. The ways that gender roles are seen, influenced by post-feminism and neoliberalism, limit the opportunities for women to be part of the industry (Alison Harvey & Stephanie Fisher, 2015). Women within the digital games industry have played an indispensable role in championing diversity and unsettling the existing status quo. Their prominence and advocacy have spurred dialogues about sexism, harassment, and the underlying inequities within the industry's structure. Prominent female game developers, such as Brenda Romero, Rebecca Ann Heineman, Judy Tyrer, Brianna Wu, and Jane Ng, have made significant contributions to the industry. Their works have pushed boundaries, shattered stereotypes, and paved the way for future generations of women game developers.

4.3. Gendered Preferences in Online Gaming

The world of online gaming is heavily influenced by themes rooted in Western war scenarios, masculinity, and a thirst for violent gameplay. One potential explanation for this phenomenon lies in the concept of gender performativity, as theorised by Judith Butler(Judith Butler, 1990). However, it is essential to recognise that gender preferences are not fixed or deterministic, and individuals often defy stereotypical notions imposed upon them by society. Looking into the complexities surrounding gendered preferences in gaming, examining the dominant themes in popular online games, and the emergence of alternative gaming experiences for women will help us understand the motivations behind women's engagement with violent games and the potential role of gaming as a liberating space beyond societal expectations.

The prevalence of war scenarios, themes of violence, and a focus on traditional notions of masculinity in popular online games cannot be overlooked. Titles such as Call of Duty, Battlefield, and Grand Theft Auto consistently top the charts in terms of sales and player engagement (Enrico Gandolfia and Mariacristina Sciannamblob, 2019). These games often depict hypermasculine protagonists engaged in intense combat, reinforcing the perception that gaming is primarily a male-dominated activity. The influence of corporate interests, which capitalise on gender divisions based on stereotypical notions, cannot be ignored, as these themes have proven successful in capturing the attention and financial investment of a significant portion of the gaming market. Despite the prevalence of masculine themes, the gaming industry has recognised the diversity of its audience and begun developing alternative gaming experiences catering specifically to women. Games like Stardoll, The Sims Social, and Diva Chix offer more feminine and less violent themes, allowing players to engage in activities such as fashion design, socialising, and virtual representation. These games acknowledge the existence of a substantial female gaming population and seek to provide them with gaming experiences that align with their interests. While some may argue that such categorisation reinforces gender stereotypes, it is essential to consider that these games offer a choice and an opportunity for women to engage with gaming on their own terms. It is crucial to recognise that women's participation in gaming extends beyond the confines of games specifically tailored for them. Many women engage in and enjoy violent games online, despite the societal expectations surrounding their behaviour. These gaming spaces provide a unique outlet for women to explore and express facets of their identity that may be restricted in their everyday lives. Contrary to gender performativity, where individuals conform to societal expectations of their assigned gender, gaming allows individuals to break free from traditional gender roles and explore a range of experiences that go beyond the expectations imposed upon them.

Research conducted by Sam Schelfhout1, Matthew T. Bowers1, & and Y. Andrew Hao (2021) supports this notion, revealing that women are drawn to violent online games as a means of venting their frustrations and engaging in activities that may not be acceptable or accessible in their real lives. The virtual gaming space offers them the freedom to be whomever they want to be, transcending the limitations imposed by gender performativity. In these virtual worlds, women can embody powerful, skilled characters who defy traditional gender roles and challenge the notion that gaming is solely a male domain.

The desire for competition, social interaction, and the thrill of gameplay may also drive women's participation in violent games. The adrenaline rush and sense of achievement experienced through intense gaming sessions are not limited by gender. Women, like men, seek excitement, challenge, and the opportunity to showcase their skills in the gaming arena. By participating in violent games, women are able to shatter stereotypes and demonstrate their capabilities, dispelling the notion that their interests are solely confined to traditionally feminine pursuits.

It is important to note that gendered preferences in gaming are not fixed or universal. Individuals possess diverse interests and motivations, transcending the narrow boundaries of gendered categorisations. While it is true that certain themes and game genres may be more popular among one gender, these preferences should not be treated as absolutes. Men may enjoy fashion-oriented games, and women may find a thrill in action-packed shooters. The gaming community is a diverse and evolving space, embracing individuals from all walks of life, regardless of their gender identity.

4.4. Gendered Violence in the Gaming Industry and its Consequences

The gaming industry is not immune to the presence of gendered violence, which poses a pervasive issue with far-reaching consequences. Within this industry, women who participate as players and professionals encounter a multitude of forms of harassment and abuse, spanning from the utterance of sexist comments and slurs to instances of stalking and even physical violence. The violence is not limited to real-life individuals alone; female avatars and game developers also face gendered violence.

4.4.1. Forms of Gendered Violence

4.4.1.1. Sexist Comments and Slurs

Sexist comments and slurs are pervasive in the gaming community, creating an atmosphere that is hostile and unwelcoming for women. Whether playing online multiplayer games, participating in gaming forums, or streaming content, women often encounter a constant stream of derogatory remarks. These comments not only undermine their skills and abilities but also reinforce harmful gender stereotypes, perpetuating the idea that gaming is primarily a male domain. The cumulative effect of this verbal abuse is an inherently exclusionary environment, making it difficult for women to feel safe and comfortable while engaging in their passion for gaming. One of the significant impacts of sexist comments and slurs on women in gaming is the detrimental effect on their mental health(Kirsten Mettler, 2023). The constant exposure to derogatory remarks can lead to feelings of anxiety, depression, and low self-esteem. Women may experience a sense of isolation and alienation as they are reminded of their gender at every turn, often in disparaging and dehumanising ways. This toxic environment can erode their enjoyment of the gaming experience and, in severe cases, lead to them abandoning their gaming pursuits altogether. While it is true that both male and female gamers may encounter sexist comments and slurs, it is necessary to acknowledge the unique experiences faced by women due to their historical marginalisation and oppression(Kirsten Mettler, 2023). The gaming industry has been predominantly male-dominated, with female gamers frequently facing scepticism, gatekeeping, and outright discrimination. Consequently, women bear the brunt of gendered violence in gaming, with research indicating that they experience higher levels of harassment compared to their male counterparts. This disparity in intensity further reinforces the need to address and challenge the prevalence of sexist comments and slurs within the gaming community.

4.4.1.2. Stalking and Harassment

Women in the gaming industry often find themselves subjected to stalking and harassment, which takes a toll on their well-being. The online nature of gaming platforms provides perpetrators with the means to track and intimidate their targets, leading to distressing experiences. In some cases, the harassment can escalate to the point where victims fear for their personal safety, compelling them to withdraw from gaming communities or even abandon their aspirations within the industry altogether. Tragically, there have been instances where the consequences of gendered violence have been fatal. For example, in 2021, Sol Oliveira Bueno da Silva, a female Call of Duty player in Brazil, was brutally murdered by a fellow male player (Monit Khanna, 2021). Such extreme cases highlight the severity of the issue and the urgent need for action.

The most extreme consequence of gendered violence in the gaming industry is the loss of life itself. The tragic case of Sol Oliveira Bueno da Silva serves as a stark reminder of the potential dangers faced by female players. This horrific event not only highlights the vulnerability of women in the gaming community but also exposes the urgent need for measures to prevent such tragedies from occurring in the future. The loss of life due to gendered violence is a devastating outcome that demands attention and action to ensure the safety of all individuals involved in gaming. Beyond the loss of life, gendered violence in gaming has significant psychological consequences for its victims. Women who experience stalking, harassment, and other forms of abuse often suffer from heightened levels of anxiety, stress, and depression. The constant fear and emotional distress can have long-lasting effects on their mental well-being, leading to diminished self-esteem, self-doubt, and even the development of psychological disorders. The psychological impact of gendered violence hinders women's ability to fully engage in gaming, enjoy the experience, and pursue their passions within the industry. It also has implications for women seeking careers within the gaming industry. The hostile environment created by harassment and abuse hampers their professional development and opportunities. Women may face limited access to networking, mentorship, and career advancement, hindering their progress and stifling their potential. The consequences of gendered violence in the industry lead to the loss of talented individuals, perpetuating the cycle of gender imbalance and reinforcing the dominance of males in the gaming sector. The prevalence of violence thus leads to the underrepresentation and stereotyping of females in the industry.

4.4.1.3. Gendered Violence Towards Avatars

Female avatars, particularly in violent games, often fall victim to hyper-sexualisation, serving the purpose of catering to the male gaze. Stereotypically, video games have been created with a male audience in mind, resulting in female avatars that conform to idealised and sexualised standards (Carina Assunção, 2016). One example of this could be in video games, where the portrayal of female characters with exaggerated physical features, revealing clothing, and provocative poses. These avatars often embody the stereotypical image of a hypersexualised female character, designed to cater to the male gaze and fulfil the fantasies of male players. Another example can be found in open-world games or role-playing games (RPGs), where players can customise their avatars. While these games offer the freedom to choose a female avatar, the options available often prioritise sexualised designs. Customisation features may include an array of revealing outfits, unrealistic body proportions, and limited choices that perpetuate narrow beauty standards.

This perpetuates the objectification of women within the gaming industry and reinforces harmful gender stereotypes. Despite the growing inclusivity in modern games, where players can choose avatars of different genders or non-binary identities, it is important to note that proper representation and equal treatment remain lacking.

The consequences of this include; female players who assume the role of these hypersexualised avatars may experience a sense of discomfort, objectification, and alienation. By perpetuating harmful stereotypes and reducing female characters to objects of desire or targets of violence, the gaming industry perpetuates a culture of inequality and exclusion. This not only affects the gaming experience of female players but also contributes to an overall environment that is hostile and unwelcoming to women. The normalisation of mistreatment towards female avatars can have a broader impact on society's perception of women. When virtual spaces reflect and reinforce gendered violence, it becomes harder to challenge and change real-world attitudes and behaviours. The portrayal of female avatars as objects to be controlled or abused contributes to the persistence of gender inequality in society, both within and beyond the gaming community.

5. POLICY IMPLICATIONS

Creating an inclusive and diverse gaming industry requires deliberate efforts and thoughtful policies that address the challenges faced by women in various roles within the field. The insights from examining women's roles as players, designers, objects of gaze, and viewers provide valuable guidance for shaping policies that promote equity, representation, and empowerment. Here are some key policy implications to consider:

5.1. Psychoeducational Interventions

Studies suggest that specialised psychoeducational interventions using ICTs (Information and Communication Technologies) are required to reduce sexism and other negative attitudes(María Aranda, Marta García-Domingo, Beatriz Montes-Berges, and Virginia Fuentes, 2022). These interventions can help increase awareness of gender-based cyber violence and promote critical thinking about online content. For example, workshops or online courses can be designed to educate young people about the different forms of online gender violence, the impact it has on individuals and society, and strategies to prevent and address such violence. It can help increase awareness of gender-based cyberviolence and promote critical thinking about online content.

5.2. Promoting Gender Diversity in Education

To increase the representation of women in game development, educational institutions should prioritise gender diversity in technology and design programs. Offering scholarships, mentorship programs, and outreach initiatives targeting young girls can encourage them to explore careers in game design and technology-related fields. Educational institutions and industry training programs should also aim to integrate content highlighting the importance of gender diversity, respectful representation, and avoiding harmful stereotypes. This can contribute to a more informed and conscious game development workforce.

5.3. Videogames and Sociological Thinking

Sam Han (2013), in his research, argues that video games should be brought to the forefront of sociological thinking. Han contends that policymakers must acknowledge the inherent social essence of gaming and view it through a sociological lens. By doing so, a more comprehensive comprehension of the profound influence of video games on individuals and society can be attained. This approach highlights gaming's communal nature and potential to shape social dynamics. By recognising video games as a sociocultural phenomenon, researchers can explore how gaming interacts with broader contexts and influences behaviour and perceptions.

5.4. Supporting Diversity in Tech Initiatives

It is important to endorse and foster initiatives and partnerships that strive to enhance diversity within the tech industry. Notable examples like Project Include, the Hidden Genius Project, Code 2040, and Black Girls Code exemplify these efforts (Gabriela T. Richard, 2017). These initiatives centre on facilitating entry, skill development, and mentorship for women and underrepresented ethnic minorities in areas like coding, computing, and creative innovation. Policies can play a pivotal role in cultivating a more inclusive and equitable tech ecosystem by endorsing such initiatives.

5.5. Future Research Directions

Looking ahead, there is ample potential for continued investigation and examination within gaming. These forthcoming directions of research hold the promise of providing a more profound understanding, ultimately influencing a gaming industry that is more diverse and inclusive in its representation.

One crucial avenue for research lies in developing inclusive game design principles. By examining how game mechanics, narratives, and character portrayals can be crafted to cater to a wider spectrum of genders, researchers can help guide game developers in creating more diverse and welcoming gameplay experiences. Collaborating with female and marginalised game designers can enrich this understanding, fostering the creation of games that resonate with a broader audience. Mentorship programs have shown promise in encouraging women to pursue careers in game development. However, delving into the long-term effects of such initiatives can provide valuable insights. Research that explores the impact of mentorship on career trajectories, job satisfaction, and retention rates of women in the industry can inform the development of more effective and impactful mentorship programs.

Queer game studies also emerge as a pivotal area for future exploration. Examining the portrayal of LGBTQ+ characters, narratives, and relationships within games, along with the impact of such representation on players, can provide insights into the evolving landscape of inclusivity and diversity in the gaming world. As the gaming industry strives for a more inclusive future, understanding the evolution of workplace culture is imperative. Research that investigates the efficacy of diversity and inclusion policies, the role of allyship in fostering inclusive environments, and the strategies companies employ to address issues of sexism, harassment, and discrimination can guide the ongoing journey toward industry-wide inclusivity.

By embarking on these research directions, scholars and industry professionals can work collaboratively to foster a more nuanced understanding of gender dynamics in gaming. This understanding, in turn, can contribute to a more diverse, inclusive, and vibrant gaming landscape that celebrates and welcomes individuals of all genders and identities.

6. CONCLUSION

In the ever-evolving digital gaming realm, the intricate interplay between gender, representation, and inclusivity continues to shape the landscape. This chapter has delved into various facets of this multifaceted relationship, shedding light on the roles and challenges that women encounter as players, developers, and cultural agents within the gaming industry. The journey through gender dynamics in gaming reveals a complex tapestry of progress, struggles, and opportunities that intersect with larger societal currents.

As the gaming industry moves forward, the importance of recognising and addressing gender disparities cannot be overstated. The industry has begun to shift from the flourishing presence of female players challenging stereotypes to the growing influence of women as game developers pushing the boundaries of creativity. The emergence of grassroots initiatives, the power of high-profile advocates, and the potential of queer game studies all contribute to the trajectory toward a more diverse and inclusive gaming environment. However, this journey is far from complete. Future research directions in this chapter underscore the need for continued exploration and action, guiding the industry toward a future where gender diversity and equitable representation are not just aspirations but fundamental pillars of the gaming world. By embracing these insights, industry stakeholders and scholars can work together to foster an inclusive space where gamers of all genders and backgrounds can thrive, express themselves, and shape the gaming universe for generations to come.

REFERENCES

Aranda, M., García-Domingo, M., Montes-Berges, B., & Fuentes, V. (2022). Variables Contributing to the Awareness of Online Gendered Violence: Focus on Observers. SAGE Publications, 8(4).

Assunção, C. (2016). "No Girls on the Internet": The Experience of Female Gamers in the Masculine Space of Violent Gaming. *Press Start*. http://press-start.gla.ac.uk

Boluk, S., & Lemieu, P. (2017). Breaking the Metagame Feminist Spoilsports and Magic Circle Jerks. In *Metagaming* (pp. 275–290). University of Minnesota Press. doi:10.5749/j.ctt1n2ttjx.9

Bustos-Ortega, M., Carretero-Dios, H., & Romero-Sánchez, M. (2023). Sexist Attitudes in Online Video Gaming: Development and Validation of the Sexism Against Women Gamers Scale in Spanish and English. *Psychology of Women Quarterly*, *47*(3), 320–342. Advance online publication. doi:10.1177/03616843231162837

Butler, J. (1990). *Gender Trouble*. Routledge.

Dietz, T. L. (1998). An examination of violence and gender role portrayals in video games: Implications for gender socialization and aggressive behaviour. *Sex Roles*, *38*(5–6), 425–442. doi:10.1023/A:1018709905920

Downs, E. & Smith, S.L. (2010). Keeping abreast of hypersexuality: A video game character content analysis. *Sex Roles, 62*(11–12), 721–733.

Fogel, S. (2018, July 11). ESPN, Disney, ABC Airing Overwatch League. *VARIETY*. https://variety.com/2018/gaming/news/espn-disney-abc-overwatch-league-1202870413/

Fox & Tang. (2014). *Sexism in Online Video Games: The Role of Conformity to Masculine Norms and Social Dominance Orientation.* doi:10.1016/j.chb.2013.07.014

Galbraith, P. W. (2017). Adult Computer Games and the Ethics of Imaginary Violence: Responding to Gamergate from Japan. *University of Hawai'i Press on Behalf of International Institute of Gender and Media*, *52*(1), 67–88. doi:10.1353/jwj.2017.0012

Gandolfia, E., & Sciannamblob, M. (2019). Unfolding female quiet in wargames: Gender bias in Metal Gear Solid V: The Phantom Pain from representation to gameplay. *Feminist Media Studies*, *19*(3), 331–347. Advance online publication. doi:10.1080/14680777.2018.1467476

Han, S. (2013). Ethnographies of the Videogame: Gender, Narrative and Praxis byHelen Thornham. *American Sociological Association*, *42*(1), 112–114.

Harvey & Fisher. (2015). *"Everyone Can Make Games!": The post-feminist context of women in digital game production.* doi:10.1080/14680777.2014.958867

Hepler, J. B. (Ed.). (2007). *Women in Game Development Breaking the Glass Level-Cap*. CRC Press.

HjelpdahlA. B. (2020). *Online Gaming: A Successful Life? The Influence of Gaming on Development.* University of South-Eastern Norway Faculty of Health and Social Sciences. doi:10.13140/RG.2.2.34362.41922

Jenny, S. E., Manning, R. D., Keiper, M. C., & Olrich, T. W. (2017). Athletes: Where eSports Fit Within the Definition of "Sport." *Quest*, *69*(1), 1–18. Advance online publication. doi:10.1080/00336297.2016.1144517

Johnson, M. (2015). Digital Literacy and Digital Citizenship: Approaches to Girls' Online Experiences. In *EGirls, eCitizens*. University of Ottawa Press. https://www.jstor.org/stable/j.ctt15nmj7f.17

Khanna, M. (2021, February 24). Female Call Of Duty Player Murdered By Fellow Gamer In Brazil. *The Time of India*. https://www.indiatimes.com/technology/news/female-call-of-duty-player-murdered-by-fellow-gamer-in-brazil-535018.html

Martin, P., & Barnard, A. (2013). The experience of women in male-dominated occupations: A constructivist grounded theory inquiry. *SA Journal of Industrial Psychology*, *39*(2). Advance online publication. doi:10.4102ajip.v39i2.1099

McBean, J. (2022). *Bryter's Female Gamer Survey* [Infographic]. Bryter Research. https://www.womeningames.org/wp-content/uploads/2021/03/Bryter-Female-Gamers-Survey-2020-12.11.20-SHORT-no-quotes.pdf

McKinnon-Crowley, S. (2020). Fighting Gendered Battles: On Being a Woman in a Contemporary Gaming Community. *Journal of Contemporary Ethnography*, *49*(1), 118–142. doi:10.1177/0891241619864405

Mettler, K. (2023). *Let Her Play, A report on gender-based violence in video games*. Stanford University.

Richard, G. T. (2017). *Video Games, Gender, Diversity, and Learning as Cultural Practice: Implications for Equitable Learning and Computing Participation Through Games.* Educational Technology Publications. *Inc.*

Richard, G. T., & Gray, K. L. (2018). Gendered Play, Racialized Reality: Black Cyberfeminism, Inclusive Communities of Practice, and the Intersections of Learning, Socialization, and Resilience in Online Gaming. *Frontiers*, *39*(1), 112–148. doi:10.1353/fro.2018.a690812

Schelfhout, Bowers, & Hao. (2021). *Balancing Gender Identity and Gamer Identity: Gender Issues Faced by Wang 'BaiZe' Xinyu at the 2017 Hearthstone Summer Championship.* Sage Publications, Ltd. doi:10.1177/1555412019866348

Shaw, A., & Friesem, E. (2016). Where Is the Queerness in Games? Types of Lesbian, Gay, Bisexual, Transgender, and Queer Content in Digital Games. *International Journal of Communication.* https://www.semanticscholar.org/paper/Where-is-the-Queerness-in-Games%3A-Types-of-Lesbian%2C-Shaw-Friesem/9c68711e2af254ffc625f0616f94007b139aad3c

Webb. (2019, December 18). More than 100 million people watched the "League of Legends" World Championship, cementing its place as the most popular esport. *Business Insider.* https://www.businessinsider.in/tech/news/more-than-100-million-people-watched-the-league-of-legends-world-championship-cementing-its-place-as-the-most-popular-esport/articleshow/72875445.cms

Weststar, J., & Marie-Josée, L. (2018). Women's Experiences on the Path to a Career in Game Development. In *Feminism in Play* (pp. 105–123). ResearchGate. doi:10.1007/978-3-319-90539-6_7

Chapter 16
Educating Women on Cyberfeminism:
A Solution-Oriented Approach to Cybercrime

B. Balunkeswari
KIIT University, India

Deepanjali Mishra
KIIT University, India

ABSTRACT

Cyberfeminism is one that makes the relationship between cyberspace, information and communication technology, and the internet in general. Living in the 21st century we still haven't been able to do justice in giving parity to women as a gender in cyberspace. Hence empowering women for their emancipation in this platform has become the need of the hour. Women are having to face the brunt of such blatant misuse of the cyberspace. There is an intrinsic relation of cyber security with gender violence. Women have been at the receiving end of the stick facing the brunt of gender discrimination even in the virtual world where their extortion and harassment is seen often in opposition to the pledge of the internet for neutrality and equality. Hence, a solution-oriented approach is the need of the hour as has been elucidated in the chapter, connecting the dots and linking every other issue in cyber security to master the art of living in the digital space, deriving optimum output from the same without being masqueraded by the pretentious elements with ulterior motives.

INTRODUCTION

With the 21st century moving towards a more digitized space, exchange of information and messages through various digital platforms has become easier and faster, thus building connections with different people, transcending geographical and spatial boundaries. This also means circulation of legit information for people to no longer undermine women in the digital space as they have been doing till date.

DOI: 10.4018/978-1-6684-8893-5.ch016

Technology has always been perceived as masculine even in history as it was believed to be something that men were good at and understood better, thus obscuring all the developments and innovations by women in the field of technology including the creation and development of computer as well in which their contributions have been marginalized. Hence empowering women for their emancipation in this platform has become the need of the hour. There is a concept of masculinization in which technology is considered as masculine and that is the general belief and hence women are compared to tech-savvy men. According to research the Internet is falling out of women users because of cyber harassment, cyber bullying and cyber teasing. With services like online payments (including Universal Payment Interface (UPI) in every other transaction (in India)), digital banking, digital media, IOT (Internet of Things) on the rise, there is IPV (Intimate Partner Violence), revenge porn (non-consensual sharing of intimate photos), rape videos, morphed images, child pornography etc acting conspicuously to its detriment.

The COVID-19 pandemic has rendered a lot many people jobless and with this there has been a marked increase in criminal activities on the Internet that needs serious acknowledgement. People have resorted to scam calls and messages for siphoning money and through other methods of social engineering to befool the naivest to invest money in the name of Ponzi schemes. It has been found that women, especially housewives are being trapped in numbers because of lack of technical know-how in certain cases and lack of exposure in most.

Cyberbullying is on the rise and women are the majority stakeholders to be on the rough end of the stick and hence cyberbullying and cyber teasing have to be taken seriously because they are one of the major reasons for spoiling the mental state and mind-set of women who surf the internet for some kind of solace in search of equality if not opportunity which unfortunately is still a farfetched idea. Cyberbullying however is very less talked about and its existence, a lesser known fact. People have a tendency of trolling and shaming others on social media in the quest to look smart while demeaning and undermining the mental, physical and emotional state of the recipient. There cannot be a check on conversations owing to the freedom of free speech and expression but definitely on certain verbatim through the intelligent and resourceful use of machine learning and artificial intelligence. They have been cat called, body shamed and constantly reminded of their position in the society which promised them a level playing field, if not anything else, at the least.

LITERATURE REVIEW

The convergence of cyberfeminism and cybercrime presents a distinct and urgent challenge in the digital age. Cybercrime encompasses a wide range of illicit activities, such as hacking, online harassment, identity theft, and cyberbullying. Unfortunately, women bear a disproportionate brunt of cybercrime, experiencing gender-based violence and harassment in online spaces. To effectively tackle this issue, it is imperative to adopt a proactive approach that empowers women through cyberfeminism and education. This literature review delves into existing research and insights concerning the education of women on cyberfeminism, aiming to combat cybercrime and promote digital empowerment. Numerous studies have shed light on the gendered nature of cybercrime victimization. Women are more vulnerable to online harassment, revenge porn, stalking, and other forms of gender-based digital violence. Scholars emphasize the need for targeted interventions to address these disparities effectively.

Cyberfeminism, a contemporary feminist theory, explores the interplay between gender, technology, and society. It encourages women to actively participate in digital spaces and advocate for their rights.

This literature review explores the historical development of cyberfeminism, highlighting its potential to challenge patriarchal structures and foster inclusivity (Toto & Scarinci, 2021).

Education plays a pivotal role in empowering women to protect themselves from cybercrime and actively engage in online environments. Research indicates that cyberfeminist education enhances digital literacy, raises awareness about online risks, and instills confidence in women's ability to navigate the digital world safely. Numerous organizations and initiatives offer technology and online safety training specifically designed for women. These programs aim to bridge the digital gender gap, equipping women with knowledge and skills to mitigate cybercrime risks and advocate for digital rights.

Social media platforms can serve as spaces for empowerment and platforms for cybercrime perpetration. Researchers have explored how social media can promote cyberfeminism and positive online behaviors while addressing issues like cyberbullying and online harassment.

Critics of cybercrime policies emphasize the importance of addressing systemic gender biases and misogyny. Policymakers must consider the unique challenges women face in digital spaces and develop more inclusive and equitable measures to combat cybercrime effectively.

Case studies of successful cyberfeminist initiatives and educational programs offer valuable insights into effective strategies for combating cybercrime. These examples can provide guidance for designing new interventions and approaches. Therefore, this literature review underscores the need for a solution-oriented approach to address cybercrime's gendered impact on women. By embracing cyberfeminism and providing targeted education and training, women can be empowered to navigate digital spaces safely and advocate for their rights online. Policymakers, educators, and technology providers must collaborate to foster an inclusive and secure digital environment for everyone. This review lays the foundation for further research and policy development in this crucial domain.

As time has passed by, cybercrime has been on the rise and hence it has made women more vulnerable to their already debilitated position in the digital space. The respective cybercrimes are the ones that have been elucidated in detail to understand their relationship with women and the nuance of the same to better the situation of women in the cyberspace and to make them aware and vigilant regarding the same. In this paper few of them are discussed in details.

TFIPV (Technology Facilitated Intimate Partner Violence)

There has been a 420% marked increase in IPV w.r.t cyberspace according to a UK Home Office report by the researchers at the University's Institute of Cyber Security for Society (ICSS) (Miller, 2022). Understanding the behavioral pattern of a friend on social media and accessing their passwords through guesswork and other methods of deceptive techniques to win over the trust of partners and luring them into a trap where there is no looking back for the victim. Perpetrators are constantly and consistently looking forward for gaps in security to breach, exploit and extort the most naïve and hence it is very important for frontline responders to assess the technologies used and the perspective of the perpetrators to catch hold of their ulterior motives in the nascent stage. TFIPV is a serious domestic abuse, however it does not fall under the Domestic Violence Act and hence immediate cognizance of the same needs to be taken without further ado. Blind faith and belief in one's partner leads to dire consequences if the other person has covert motives to access personal data and use it as a revenge (most of the times leading to revenge porn) later if things turn awry between the two people in future. This also shows that one form of Cyber-violence leads to another kind (as shown in the Fig.1) and culminates into a vicious cycle knitted by a web of deceit, lies and bad faith that does not bode or auger well for any of the partners involved

Table 1.

Issues	Cybersecurity Initiatives
Virus (1990s)	Antivirus Firewalls
Worms (2000)	Intrusion detection and prevention
Botnets (2000s- present)	Data Leakage Mitigation (DLP), Application-ware firewalls, SIM (Security Information Management)
APT (Advanced Persistent Threat) Insiders(2000s-Present)	Network Flow Analysis

resulting in heartbreaks, clearly leading to toxicity in relationships and making it very difficult for the victim to ever be able to believe people without having second thoughts about them. Self-awareness hence is a must where people need to keep their personal documents, photos and videos etc. protected and secured. Self-awareness government schemes should also be launched to make people have a better technical know-how of their day-to-day activities on the internet and to let them know as to how vulnerable and susceptible their activities may turn out to be if they are not vigilant enough.

EVOLUTION OF CYBERSECURITY

Revenge Porn

Revenge Porn is a grave version of sextortion, a portmanteau or Franken word for 'sexual' and 'extortion' which is the non-consensual sharing of photos or videos while sextortion basically being the threat of sharing photos whether they are actually shared or not. With the advancement of social media and with farrago of platforms having come up for exchange of conversations through texts, emoticons, photos and videos, extortion through photos and videos with explicit content being shared in these platforms has become very common. Various dating applications and social media platforms will always try to be better in a competitive world where each one of them is striving to be the best but that should not make users take things lightly while operating and using these applications for sharing personal documents, photos and videos. The most vital element of sextortion is the use of blackmail and the power exerted by the offender on their partner, coercing their compliance into a certain action which in itself is a greater crime (Reid, 2023). Such activities have become the new normal and have resulted in the suppression of voices that have not been able to free themselves from the shackles of toxicity and such people normally make the headlines of news dailies for having given up their lives, trying to save the so-called image and repute of their families. Revenge porn does not only happen locally or with people who have prior acquaintances but also occurs on a large scale transnationally as well (Bates, 2017). Such activities have been promulgated by dating applications and platforms where the initial acquaintance is mostly through sharing of photos, even with the prior knowledge of the other person being miles apart or time zones apart. Such has been the fad or the trend that the conscious of the layman has taken a backseat. Therefore, such people need to understand that the sharing of such intimate details may lead to morphed images being created and being used in rape videos as well. Legislations for the same are also very tricky as establishing precedent for 'no consent' becomes very difficult as these are intricate matters that have a very delicate line of action through which matters have occurred in real time and to showcase the same in the form of proof in the court of law, however right one may be becomes an arduous task. We also need to make ourselves aware of these nefarious activities on the rise and take steps to educate the younger ones to not fall into such traps and be able to make optimum use of the resources available to them.

Cyberbullying

Cyberbullying although very less talked about, is a lesser-known fact anyways. Trolling and shaming people in name of fame and attention projects a very parochial mindset and because of no stern legislation for Cyberbullying so to speak there is undue advantage taken on the internet in the name of freedom of speech and expression. It can have psychological effects on the recipient mostly because of the anonymous nature of messaging and because it's done in an open platform where people from all spheres and aspects of life are associated. The quest to maintain a social image, although one may be diametrically opposite to it in reality helps them be a pretentious form of themselves that acts to their detriment when they are not able to fulfill their expectations even on their social media platform. This creates a sense of low morale and low self-esteem often leading to depression and anxiety. Bullies in real life can be avoided but then cyber bullies are everywhere because every other person is on the internet and therefore is connected to the world of social media in one way or the other. The act of undermining or demeaning someone becomes a convention so much so that it tends to have a pernicious influence on the youth of today often resulting in heated exchange of words and culminating into a war of words till the point in time where there are too many against a single entity trying to prove their point and make a statement and thus singling out, isolating and secluding that one person who ends up having an existential crisis. All this results in the imbalance of the mental, physical and emotional state of the person at the receiving end of the stick. Therefore, putting a check on the same may not be possible as filtering out every conversation would not be practical but then the scrutiny of certain verbatims through the intelligent use of machine learning and artificial intelligence can definitely go a long way in solving the current problem at hand.

Cyber-Violence Against Women

There is an intrinsic relation between cybersecurity and gender violence. Women have been facing the brunt of gender discrimination including their extortion and harassment in the virtual world where there were expectations of a level playing field but turned out be no different than the real world. They have been catcalled and slut shamed exacerbating their already poor condition in the society. There is multifarious violence against women in the cyber world such as those of sexual harassment, revenge porn, online solicitation, rape threats, gender-based hate speech, unsolicited nude images, doxing etc. Most of it is seen in cases of misogynists who target those women who are feminists and try and blackmail them from taking an unrelenting stand to further their own cause. Technology should have always acted as a facilitator and been gender neutral at the least but then it is technology that has rather made the access to political knowledge and avenues for civic management limited in the case of women which speaks volumes of the ingrained mindset and mentality and hence only showing that the same issue that women face offline have only been reified and manifested online. There are classical examples of women who have single handedly taken up such causes to fight for their entire sex and de-fang and dodge all the criticisms hurled at them but then there must be support from the technology front as well otherwise the holier than thou attitude of the society will keep shoving responsibilities on women while the world watches in silence (Kumar, 2019). Amongst all this that has been happening, the individual responsibility is a priority when it comes to Technology Facilitated Gendered Violence (TFGV) as there are numerous ways of preventing such mishaps or violence for women on the internet if precautionary measures for the same are taken like that of desisting social media use, filtering unsolicited content and abuse through privacy settings and simply blocking. At the same time community responsibility cannot be ignored, one that starts with educating the young mass and policing the elderly as and when required so that the essence of a civilized society is perpetuated.

It is clear hence from the aforementioned cybercrimes that we need to be a step ahead by educating women through various learning programs that are going to help women steer their way successfully through the world of cyberspace. For this we need to understand the perception of people towards gender on the internet. There is also a concept of cyberutopia where women have to leave their bodies behind while coming on to the Internet. These are somehow or the other placing women at a disadvantageous position from the start and hence not being weighed correctly on the beam balance. The narrative can however change if more and more women are inducted into the highest positions for the development and policy making of technologies and set an example for the youth thus making a statement in the global forefront of their capabilities and hence announcing their rights on various platforms including social media.

CONCLUSION

The access to communication technologies can help women improve their condition manifolds by bringing in better ways of working. Women generally do not have equal access to public resources as men do. Many western nations have gone through a transition to find the significance of communication technologies through a technologically enabled population. Hence, women will be found to be on the disadvantaged side if not too much is done for them to feel comfortable with the public access points being made more female-friendly and hence women being placed on equal footing with their male counterparts. Women conferences are being organized by various governments to bring them close to each other's problem and hence looking for solutions to counteract their already deteriorating situation in their respective societies. This not only paves the way for women to lead in the future but also helps change the mindset of men who have always felt that patriarchy and male dominance is then only option left for them moving forward. Although opportunities are slowly being provided to women on the internet there are other barriers that are also putting them at the backfoot an done amongst them is the language barrier. Language often happens to be a barrier for those originating from different countries and hence mediation of the real time issues and struggles are missed when coming together on the digital space because of communication issues. Women are also being encouraged in politics these days as previously that sector was believed to be absolutely for the male gender. Various political campaigns over twitter and various social media handles have helped encourage and empower several women to put forth their ideas and viewpoints to cater to the general public and hence garner support in their favor.

The progress of women is generally hindered by the prejudices existing in the society like the internet being more of a platform for men to utilize and further their interests. Women have been looked down upon when it comes to technology and their ability to adapt to newer technologies. During COVID times as well when all the classes were to be online, and everything had been shifted to the virtual world there was a lot of chaos regarding online classes and the belief was that the male teachers would adapt and gel well with technology while the female teachers would not. Generally, there is a belief that a male professor is more qualified and a better teacher than his female counterpart. Even in the films and web series' the female leads are paid much less compared to their male counterpart as a result making them realize the harsh reality of the world that they live in. Strategically there being a greater number of male users on the internet than women are also because of the socio-economic status. Because education, job status and income are required for internet access as a result count of men is more than women. Hence technical skills need to be provided to women and opportunities as well for women to be independent and to be equally placed in the society even in the cyberspace. Therefore, better financial support from the government towards women for their education on communication technologies will help augment their access to the internet and their usage.

We are still in the nascent stages of discovering possibilities for feminist use on the Internet. But that does not mean that the ones already discovered have to undermine the position of women in anyway. All that they expect is similar treatment to men and parity in the work that they are performing, mostly coming out of their comfort zones to prove to the world that they are much more than society's myopic vision of their future.

REFERENCES

Bates, S. (2017). Revenge Porn and Mental Health: A Qualitative Analysis of the Mental Health Effects of Revenge Porn on Female Survivors. *Feminist Criminology, 12*(1), 22–42.

Gamble, S. (Ed.). (2004). *The Routledge Companion to Feminism and Post-feminism.* Routledge. doi:10.4324/9780203011010

Miller, O. (2022). *Technology Facilitated Intimate Partner Violence Surged during Covid-19 Pandemic.* University of Kent, News Centre.

Mohanty, J. R., & Samantaray, S. (2017). Cyberfeminism: Unleashing women's power through technology. *Rupkatha Journal on Interdisciplinary Studies in Humanities*, *9*(2), 328–336. doi:10.21659/rupkatha.v9n2.33

Reid, S. (2023). *Dealing with Revenge Porn and "Sextortion"*. helpGuide.org

Sanjeev, P. (2019). Cyber Crime Against Women: Right to Privacy and Other Issues. *Journal of Legal Studies and Research, 5*(5).

Toto, G. A., & Scarinci, A. (2021). Cyberfeminism: A relationship between cyberspace, technology, and the Internet. Elementa. *Intersections Between Philosophy, Epistemology and Empirical Perspectives, 1*(1-2), 135–151.

Chapter 17
Cyber Crime in India:
An Indian Perspective

Ritu Pareek
https://orcid.org/0000-0002-8124-0561
Birla Institute of Technology, Mesra, Jaipur, India

ABSTRACT

The increasing use of digital technologies and the internet has provided immense opportunities for communication, information sharing, and social interaction. However, alongside these benefits, the cyber world has also become a platform for the perpetration of offences against women. This chapter investigates the problem of violations and crimes targeting women in the cyber world, with particular emphasis on India. It explores the various forms of cyber offence women face, the underlying factors contributing to such crime, and the legal and policy framework in India. The chapter also highlights the challenges in addressing cyber offences against women and proposes strategies for prevention and support.

1. INTRODUCTION

The advent of digital technologies and the widespread use of the internet have revolutionized the way people communicate, access information, and engage in social interactions. Every day, millions of men and women utilize the internet as a platform for expressing their ideas freely without restrictions. These advancements have undoubtedly brought numerous benefits and advantages to society, but they have also given rise to a dark side of the cyber world, marked by offenses and crimes specifically targeted against women. As women increasingly embrace digital platforms for personal, professional, and social interactions, they are also facing unprecedented risks and vulnerabilities online. This research paper delves into the pressing issue of cyber offenses and crimes against women, focusing particularly on the context of India. Cyber-crime against women encompasses a broad range of offenses, from online harassment and cyber stalking to revenge porn, sextortion, and online grooming. Perpetrators exploit the anonymity and distance provided by the internet to target and victimize women, making it crucial to address these issues from an Indian perspective.

DOI: 10.4018/978-1-6684-8893-5.ch017

The paper aims to comprehensively explore the various forms of cyber offense faced by women in the digital realm. These offenses encompass a wide range of activities, including but not limited to cyber harassment, cyber stalking, revenge pornography, online bullying, identity theft, and online fraud. This research paper also aims to shed light on the prevalent forms of cyber-crime against women in India, the underlying factors contributing to such crimes, the impact on victims and society at large, and the existing legal and policy framework to combat these offenses.

The key areas of focus in the paper include:

1. Types of Cyber Crimes Against Women: This section will explore the various forms of cyber-crime targeting women, such as online harassment, cyber bullying, dozing, morphed images, and non-consensual distribution of intimate content. Real-life examples and statistics will help illustrate the gravity of the problem.
2. Factors Contributing to Cyber Crime Against Women: Understanding the social, cultural, and technological factors that contribute to the perpetration of cyber-crimes against women is crucial for devising effective prevention and intervention strategies.
3. Impact on Women and Society: Cybercrime not only violates an individual's privacy and dignity but also has broader implications for gender equality and women's participation in the digital world. This section will delve into the psychological, emotional, and professional consequences experienced by victims.
4. Challenges in Reporting and Prosecution: Many cases of cybercrime against women go unreported due to fear of social stigma, lack of awareness, or mistrust in the legal system. This section will examine the obstacles hindering reporting and the difficulties in prosecuting offenders.
5. Legal and Policy Measures: An analysis of the existing laws and policies in India aimed at addressing cyber-crimes against women will be provided. This will include an assessment of the effectiveness of these measures and potential gaps in the legal framework.
6. Support and Awareness Initiatives: Highlighting the efforts made by government agencies, NGOs, and civil society in raising awareness about cyber safety for women and providing support to victims will be an integral part of this study.
7. International Comparisons: A comparative analysis of how other countries are tackling cyber-crime against women will provide valuable insights and potential best practices for India.

By shedding light on the pressing issue of cybercrime against women in India, this research paper aims to contribute to the collective efforts of policymakers, law enforcement agencies, and civil society to create a safer and more inclusive digital environment for women in the country. By examining these different forms, the study seeks to shed light on the gravity and extent of the problem faced by women in cyberspace. Furthermore, this research endeavors to unravel the underlying factors that contribute to the perpetration of cyber offenses against women. These factors can be multifaceted, stemming from deeply ingrained societal norms, gender inequalities, cultural biases, and technological vulnerabilities. By understanding these root causes, the paper seeks to provide insights into the complex dynamics that fuel cyber offenses targeting women. In addition, the study examines the existing legal and policy framework in India to address cyber offenses against women.

It analyzes relevant laws, such as the Information Technology Act, the Indian Penal Code, and other legislations, to assess their effectiveness in combating cyber-crimes. Furthermore, the research investigates the implementation and enforcement challenges faced by law enforcement agencies and the judiciary in dealing with cyber offenses against women. The paper also highlights the hurdles and limitations in effectively addressing cyber offenses against women in India. These challenges include inadequate reporting mechanisms, lack of awareness and education, social stigma, and the rapidly evolving nature of technology. By recognizing these barriers, the study aims to foster and enhance a deeper understanding of the systemic issues that hinder the prevention and prosecution of cyber-crimes against women. Lastly, this research proposes strategies and interventions to prevent cyber offenses against women and provide support to the victims. These strategies encompass a multi-faceted approach, involving legal reforms, awareness campaigns, capacity building for law enforcement agencies, collaboration between government and non-governmental organizations, and the promotion of digital literacy and online safety education.

By outlining these recommendations, the paper seeks to contribute to the ongoing efforts to combat cyber offenses against women in India and beyond. In this manner, the research paper critically examines the problem of cyber offenses and crimes against women, particularly in the context of India. It provides a comprehensive analysis of the various forms of cyber offense faced by women, explores the contributing factors, evaluates the legal and policy framework, identifies the challenges, and proposes strategies for prevention and support. It is hoped that this research will raise awareness not only among victims but also among people in general, inform policy decisions, and pave the way for a safer and more inclusive digital environment for women.

2. BACKGROUND AND SIGNIFICANCE OF THE ISSUE

The issue of offenses against women is not limited to physical boundaries but has expanded into the digital realm, becoming a pervasive global problem. With the rapid advancement of technology and the widespread use of the internet, the cyber world has become a platform for various forms of offenses against women. As Garima Tiwari explains, cybercrime encompasses illegal activities related to computer systems or networks, including the possession, dissemination, and distribution of information (Tiwari, 2014:8). This research paper aims to comprehend and tackle the issue of offenses against women in the cyber world, with a specific focus on India.

In January 2021, an accusation surfaced regarding a significant data breach involving 150 million Indian records, purportedly up for sale. The government denied these allegations, with the center asserting that there was no such data leakage. However, in response to the situation, the Computer Emergency Response Team - India (CERT-IN) initiated an investigation, collaborating with international IT experts to thoroughly examine the matter. The IT Minister made a public announcement, informing the public about these developments (Aryan). Surprisingly, the Dhantia village cyber gang case emerged, involving a staggering scam of Rs. 300 crores. The mastermind behind this criminal operation was Jamshed Khan, the son of a rickshaw puller. Jamshed, along with other families residing in the village near Bareilly, Uttar Pradesh, whose primary occupations were embroidery and farming, managed to amass wealth by deceitfully swindling people primarily from Jharkhand. Their modus operandi involved luring victims with attractive offers and subsequently hacking into their bank accounts.

Over the past years, India has experienced a notable surge in internet penetration and smartphone usage, leading to an increasing number of women venturing into the digital realm. The growth of information communication technologies (ICT) and social networking sites has played a significant role in fostering economic and social development (Al-Jenaibi, 2016; Backe et al., 2018; van der Gaag, 2010). While the internet has brought forth new avenues for empowerment and engagement, it has also exposed women to distinct risks and vulnerabilities. The rise of cyber offenses targeting women has become an urgent concern that requires attention from policymakers, law enforcement agencies, and society.

The significance of this issue stems from its profound impact on women's lives and their fundamental rights. Cyber offenses encompass a range of abusive behaviors, including online harassment, cyber bullying, revenge porn, and digital stalking. As noted by Shruti Bist, women are often subjected to cybercrimes such as cyber harassment, online stalking, cyber pornography, cyber defamation, matrimonial fraud, and more, which not only violate their privacy and dignity but also have detrimental effects on their mental and emotional well-being (Bist, 2020:9). Furthermore, cyber offenses can hinder women's participation in the digital world, limiting their access to education, employment opportunities, and social engagement.

Addressing offence against women in the cyber world is crucial for several reasons. First, it aligns with the global movement to promote gender equality and protect women's rights. Recognizing and combating cyber offence is an essential step towards creating a safe and inclusive digital environment that allows women to fully exercise their rights and freedoms. Second, cyber offence has significant socioeconomic implications. Debarati points out that there is a prevalent belief that women in India are highly susceptible targets on the internet and digital communication technology, primarily due to their gender and the objectification of women's images as pornographic material (Halder, 2017:5). It can lead to reduced productivity, loss of employment, and financial insecurity for women who become victims. Moreover, it perpetuates a climate of fear and intimidation, discouraging women from actively participating in online spaces and hindering their socioeconomic empowerment.

Third, addressing this issue requires a comprehensive approach that encompasses legal, social, and technological dimensions. It involves strengthening legislation and enforcement mechanisms, raising awareness, promoting digital literacy, and providing support services for victims. Cyberspace represents a novel frontier dominated by machines, serving as a realm for information exchange and various activities. When computers or networks are utilized as the means, tools, or objectives for criminal endeavors, this category is termed as Cybercrime (Desai, 2007). By tackling cyber offence against women, India can set an example for other countries and contribute to the global fight against gender-based offence in the digital sphere. Overall, the background and significance of the issue of offence beside females in the virtual domain, with a special focus on India, lie in the urgent need to protect women's rights, ensure their safety online, and foster a digital ecosystem that promotes equality, inclusivity, and respect for all individuals. By understanding the underlying factors, exploring the legal framework, and proposing effective strategies, this research paper aims to contribute to the efforts aimed at eradicating cyber offence against women and creating a more equitable digital future.

3. SCOPE OF THE RESEARCH

The research focuses specifically on crime against women in the cyber world within the context of India. The primary objective of this research is to offer a comprehensive comprehension of the diverse manifestations of cyber offenses experienced by women in India. It aims to explore the underlying factors that contribute to such offenses, assess the existing legal and policy framework, analyze the prevalence and consequences of cyber offenses, and identify the challenges involved as well as potential strategies for prevention and support.

3.1 Objectives of the Research

- To identify and examine the forms of cyber offence faced by women in India, including online harassment, cyber bullying, revenge porn, digital stalking, and other related behaviors.
- To analyze the factors contributing to cyber offence against women, such as gender inequality, digital divide, anonymity in the online environment, lack of awareness, and cultural and social factors specific to India.
- To explore the legal and policy framework in India concerning cyber offence against women, including relevant legislation, amendments, guidelines, and initiatives taken by government agencies.
- To evaluate the prevalence and impact of cyber offenses against women in India. This will be achieved by analyzing reported cases, statistical data, and existing studies that shed light on the psychological, emotional, and socio-economic consequences of such offenses.
- To identify and discuss the challenges faced in addressing cyber offence against women in India, including under reporting, social stigma, enforcement issues, jurisdictional complexities, and technological advancements.
- To propose strategies for prevention and support, including the strengthening of legal frameworks, awareness campaigns, digital literacy programs, empowerment initiatives, collaboration between stakeholders, and the provision of comprehensive support services for victims.
- To provide insights and recommendations for policymakers, law enforcement agencies, civil society organizations, and other stakeholders involved in combating cyber offence against women in India.

The research aims to contribute to the existing knowledge and understanding of offence against women in the cyber world, with a specific focus on India. By exploring the scope outlined above and achieving the objectives, this research seeks to generate actionable insights and recommendations that can inform policy decisions, advocacy efforts, and practical interventions to address cyber offence against women and create a safer and more inclusive digital environment in India.

3.2 Methodology

Literature Review: A thorough review of existing literature, research studies, academic papers, reports, and relevant publications will be conducted. This will provide a foundation for understanding the conceptual framework, theories, and previous research related to offence against women in the cyber world, specifically focusing on India. The literature review will help identify gaps in knowledge and inform the research design.

Data Sources: The research will draw data from various secondary sources, including academic journals and research papers on crime against women in the cyber world. Government reports, policy documents, and legal frameworks related to cyber-crime and women's rights in India are also used as an important tool of research. At the same time, reports and publications from NGOs and international organizations working on gender-based offence and digital rights are also taken into consideration.

Figure 1. Cyber crimes against women from 2017-20

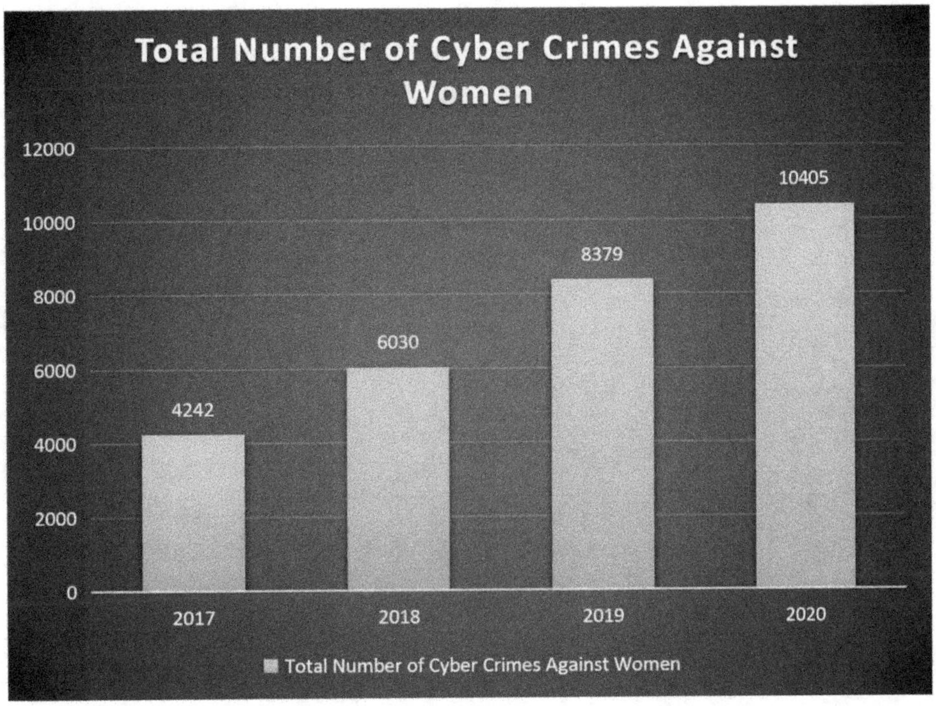

4. FORMS OF CYBER OFFENCE AGAINST WOMEN

Online harassment and abuse include sending threatening or derogatory messages through email, social media platforms, or online forums. It also includes engaging in persistent and unwanted online communication, often with the intent to intimidate, humiliate, or degrade women. Posting defamatory content or spreading rumors with the purpose of damaging a woman's reputation also falls under this category.

Cyber bullying and trolling refer to targeting women with repeated, hostile, or offensive online messages or comments while sharing personal information or spreading false rumors to provoke emotional distress and to deliberate attempts to shame or embarrass women publicly.

Non-consensual Sharing of Intimate Images (Revenge Porn) refer to posting or sharing explicit or private images or videos of women without their consent. It also includes distributing intimate content to shame, humiliate, or exert control over women and threatening to share or blackmailing women with their private images.

Digital stalking is Engaging in persistent, unwanted online surveillance or monitoring of women's activities, sending constant messages, emails, or comments, causing fear and psychological distress, and using geolocation or tracking tools to monitor women's physical movements.

Online Grooming and sexual exploitation are manipulating and building trust with women online, often with the intention of engaging them in sexual activities or exploiting them, coercing women into sharing explicit content or engaging in sexually explicit conversations and exploiting the vulnerability of women, especially young girls, for sexual purposes.

Figure 2. Reported cyber-crime against women according to NCRB 2019

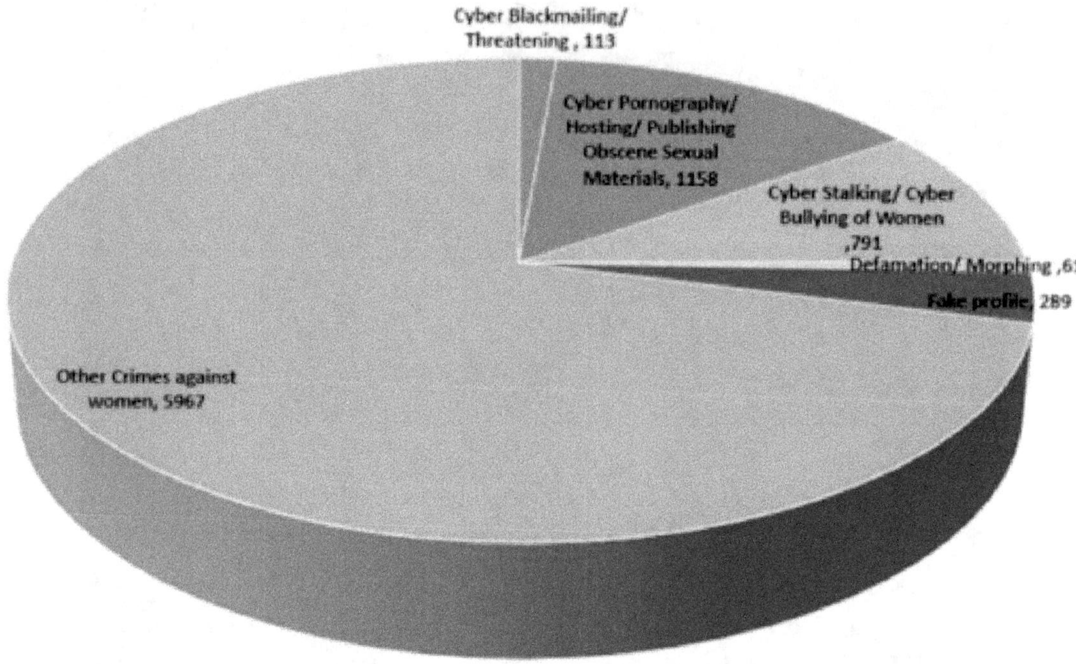

Identity theft and impersonation implies stealing personal information and using it to create fake profiles or accounts impersonating women, misrepresenting women online to defraud or deceive others and using stolen identities to engage in illegal activities, tarnishing the reputation of women.

Online Hate Speech and Misogyny is engaging in online hate speech targeting women based on their gender, ethnicity, or other personal attributes. It also includes spreading misogyny, sexism, and discriminatory ideologies through online platforms and participating in online communities that promote offence, harassment, or discrimination against women.

These forms of cyber offence against women can have severe emotional, psychological, and social consequences. They infringe upon women's privacy, safety, and well-being, limiting their ability to freely express themselves and participate in the digital world. Understanding these forms of cyber offence is crucial for developing effective strategies to prevent and address the issue, ensuring a safer and more inclusive cyber space for women in India.

As per the latest available data, it is evident that there is a significant underreporting of cybercrimes against women in India. With a formal population of around 58 crores as per the 2011 census, the reported cases of cybercrimes, which amount to less than 10,000, paint a stark picture of the scale of underreporting in the country. The categorization of these cybercrimes further emphasizes the lack of recognition of cybercrimes against women as a distinct category.

Out of the reported 8,379 cases, approximately 71% (5,967 cases) fall under the category of "other crimes against women." This indicates that even at the reporting level, cybercrimes specifically targeting women have not been adequately recognized or classified. This highlights the need for a more comprehensive understanding of the unique challenges faced by women in the cyber world and the development of specific mechanisms to address these issues.

The National Commission for Women and Children plays a crucial role in facilitating the reporting of cybercrimes against women. Through its dedicated portal, it not only enables the reporting of such crimes but also monitors the progress of police investigations. However, it is important to recognize that cybercrimes targeting women are increasing, as reported by various news sources. The Ministry of Home Affairs (MHA) takes proactive measures by collaborating with states and union territories, urging them to expedite the resolution of cybercrime cases concerning women and children and emphasizing the gravity of the issue.

Recognizing the need to tackle cybercrimes against women, the MHA launched the Cybercrime Prevention against Women and Children (CCPWC) Scheme in 2009. The scheme focuses on multiple directions, including online cybercrime reporting through a central citizen portal, establishment of a national cyber forensic laboratory for forensic analysis, capacity building of law enforcement agencies, prosecutors, judiciary, and other stakeholders involved in detection and investigation, research, and development in collaboration with renowned academic institutions, and creating awareness to prevent cybercrimes against women.

These efforts indicate the growing recognition of the need for comprehensive measures to address cyber-crimes against women in India. However, there is still a long way to go in terms of strengthening the legal framework, enhancing law enforcement capabilities, promoting research and awareness, and fostering a safe and inclusive cyber environment for women.

5. FACTORS CONTRIBUTING TO CYBER CRIME AGAINST WOMEN IN INDIA

According to Awadhesh Kumar Singh, the term "Crime Against Women" refers to the direct or indirect physical or mental cruelty inflicted upon women. Crimes that specifically target women, with women being the sole victims, are categorized as Crimes Against Women (Singh 2012:2). In the context of cyber-crime against women in India, several factors contribute to its occurrence. Some of these factors include:

Gender Inequality: Deep-rooted gender inequality in society contributes to cyber offence against women. Patriarchal norms and attitudes that perpetuate discrimination, objectification, and control over women translate into the online space, leading to harassment, abuse, and other forms of cyber offence.

Digital Divide: The digital divide, characterized by unequal access to technology and internet connectivity, exacerbates cyber offence against women. Limited access to digital resources and skills among women can make them more vulnerable to online abuse and exploitation.

Anonymity and Impersonation: The anonymity provided by the online environment enables perpetrators to engage in cyber offence against women without fear of identification or consequences. The ease of creating fake profiles and impersonating others facilitates harassment, stalking, and deception.

Lack of Awareness and Digital Literacy: Insufficient awareness and digital literacy among women contribute to their vulnerability. Many women may not be aware of their rights, the potential risks in the online world, or how to protect themselves from cyber offence. This lack of knowledge increases their susceptibility to online threats.

Social and Cultural Factors: Social and cultural factors influence the prevalence of cyber offence against women in India. Deep-seated norms, stereotypes, and attitudes that devalue women, objectify them, or restrict their agency can manifest in the form of cyber offence. For example, revenge porn and slut-shaming are often rooted in societal judgments about women's sexuality.

Online Hate and Misogyny: The existence of online spaces that promote hate speech, misogyny, and gender-based discrimination contributes to cyber offence against women. Extremist ideologies, online hate groups, and platforms that facilitate the spread of harmful content contribute to an environment conducive to harassment and abuse.

Technological Advancements: While technology brings numerous benefits, it also poses challenges regarding cyber offence against women. Advancements in digital tools and platforms provide perpetrators with new means to carry out acts of offence and harassment, making it essential to continually adapt prevention and response strategies.

Inadequate Legal Framework: The absence of comprehensive legislation specifically addressing cyber offence against women hampers effective redressal. The legal framework may lack clarity, fail to keep pace with technological advancements, or face challenges in implementation and enforcement.

These factors collectively contribute to the growth and persistence of cyber offence against women in India. Addressing these underlying factors requires a multi-faceted approach, including legal reforms, awareness campaigns, capacity-building programs, and efforts to challenge gender stereotypes and promote gender equality. By addressing these factors, India can create a safer and more inclusive online environment for women, ensuring their fundamental rights and well-being are protected.

6. LEGAL AND POLICY FRAMEWORK IN INDIA

India has acknowledged the importance of addressing offenses against women in the cyber world and has implemented various legal and policy measures to ensure protection and justice for the victims. As highlighted by Aruna Goel, there is a need to review, sensitize, and strengthen law drafting technologies and enforcement mechanisms, including the police, judiciary, and other relevant components, in order to bring about a change in this situation (Goel, 2006:6). The following key aspects form the foundation of the legal and policy framework in India:

In India, the Information Technology Act, 2000 serves as the primary legislation governing cyber-related offenses. This act, amended in 2008, encompasses a broad range of cyber-crimes, including offenses such as hacking, identity theft, and cyber stalking, which are also applicable to offenses against women in the cyber world.

However, it is important to note that Section 66A of the Information Technology Act, which criminalized online communication causing annoyance, inconvenience, or insult, was declared unconstitutional by the Supreme Court of India in 2015. The court deemed it vague and in violation of the freedom of speech and expression, thus safeguarding these fundamental rights.

In addition to the Information Technology Act, the Sexual Harassment of Women at Workplace (Prevention, Prohibition, and Redressal) Act, 2013 provides a legal framework to address sexual harassment in both physical and virtual workplaces. This act mandates the establishment of Internal Complaints Committees (ICCs) within organizations, which are responsible for receiving and addressing complaints of sexual harassment, including incidents occurring in the cyber world.

In India, the primary legislation governing cyber-related offenses is the Information Technology Act, 2000. This act, amended in 2008, covers a wide range of cyber-crimes, including hacking, identity theft, and cyber stalking, as well as offenses against women in the cyber world.

However, Section 66A of the Information Technology Act, which criminalized online communication that caused annoyance, inconvenience, or insult, was declared unconstitutional by the Supreme Court of India in 2015. The court ruled that it was vague and violated free speech and expression, thereby protecting these fundamental rights.

In addition to the Information Technology Act, the Sexual Harassment of Women at Workplace (Prevention, Prohibition, and Redressal) Act of 2013 provides a remedy for sexual harassment in the workplace.

Legal Aid and Support Services: Organizations and helplines, such as the National Commission for Women (NCW) and the Women Helpline (181), provide legal aid, counseling, and support services to victims of offence against women in the cyber world.

While India has made progress in establishing a legal and policy framework to address offence against women in the cyber world, challenges remain. As stated by Karnika Seth, "In order to combat rising cybercrimes against women in India, greater cyber awareness is required and conscious proactive reporting of such incidents to law enforcement" (Seth 2018:54). The implementation and enforcement of existing laws, capacity building of law enforcement agencies, raising awareness among women about their rights and available support systems, and adapting the legal framework to address emerging forms of cyber offence are areas that require further attention and improvement.

7. PREVALENCE AND IMPACT OF CYBER OFFENCE AGAINST WOMEN IN INDIA

The prevalence of cyber offenses against women in India is a serious concern, as it has significant social, psychological, and emotional impacts on the victims. The following key aspects highlight the prevalence and impact of cyber offenses against women in India:

1. Prevalence:
    a. High Incidence: Cybercrime against women is widespread in India, affecting women from various age groups, socio-economic backgrounds, and geographical locations. Incidents such as online harassment, cyberbullying, revenge porn, and stalking are frequently reported.
    b. Underreporting: Many incidents of cyber offenses go unreported due to factors such as social stigma, fear of retaliation, lack of awareness about legal remedies, and a lack of trust in the response mechanisms. Underreporting contributes to the underestimation of the true prevalence of cyber offenses.
2. Psychological and Emotional Impact:
    a. Psychological Trauma: Victims of cyber offence often experience psychological trauma, including anxiety, depression, post-traumatic stress disorder (PTSD), and suicidal tendencies. The constant fear, humiliation, and invasion of privacy inflicted through online platforms can have long-lasting effects on a woman's mental well-being.
    b. Emotional Distress: Cybercrime can cause significant emotional distress, leading to a loss of self-esteem, social isolation, and feelings of powerlessness. The public nature of online attacks exacerbates the emotional impact, as victims often face public shaming and humiliation.
3. Social Impact:
    a. Reputational Damage: Cyber offence can severely damage a woman's reputation and personal life. False allegations, revenge porn, and character assassination through online platforms can

lead to social ostracization, strained relationships, and difficulty in personal and professional pursuits.

   b. Restricted Participation: Women who have experienced cyber offence may become hesitant to participate actively in the digital world, limiting their online presence and engagement. This curtails their access to opportunities, resources, and social connections available in cyber space.

4. Economic Consequences:
   a. Professional Implications: Cyber offence can have adverse effects on a woman's professional life. Online harassment, cyber bullying, or false accusations can harm her career prospects, limit job opportunities, and create a hostile work environment.
   b. Financial Losses: In some cases, cyber offence can result in financial losses, such as unauthorized access to bank accounts, fraudulent activities, or online scams. These financial implications further exacerbate the negative impact on women's lives.
5. Implications on Freedom of Expression:
   a. Self-Censorship: Fear of cyber offence can lead to self-censorship among women, inhibiting their freedom of expression and inhibiting their ability to participate in online discussions, share opinions, or advocate for their rights.
   b. Chilling Effect: The prevalence of cyber offence creates a chilling effect on women's voices, suppressing their ability to engage in public discourse and contribute to social, political, and cultural conversations.

Gaining a comprehensive understanding of the prevalence and impact of cyber offenses against women in India is of utmost importance for policymakers, law enforcement agencies, and civil society organizations. It enables them to develop effective strategies and interventions to address this pressing issue. As highlighted by Shobhana Jeet, the effects of cyber offenses go beyond individual victims, impacting the broader society and creating an environment where women no longer feel safe. To combat cyber offenses against women, several key steps are crucial. Empowering women with knowledge about online safety, enhancing digital literacy, and promoting awareness are essential to enable them to protect themselves in the digital realm. Strengthening legal frameworks and ensuring their effective implementation will serve as a deterrent and provide avenues for justice for victims. Additionally, fostering a culture of online safety, where respect and accountability are upheld, will contribute to creating a secure and inclusive digital space for women in India.

8. CASES HIGHLIGHTING THE INCIDENTS OF OFFENCE AGAINST WOMEN IN THE CYBER WORLD, SPECIFICALLY IN THE CONTEXT OF INDIA

JNU Morphing Case: In 2017, a disturbing incident took place at Jawaharlal Nehru University (JNU) in Delhi. Private photographs of female students were manipulated and morphed to create explicit images, which were then shared on various social media platforms without their consent. The victims faced severe emotional distress, humiliation, and reputational damage. This case brought significant attention to the issue of non-consensual distribution of intimate images, commonly referred to as revenge porn. It emphasized the pressing need for stronger legal measures to effectively combat this form of cyber offense. The incident underscored the importance of addressing and preventing the unauthorized sharing of intimate images, safeguarding the privacy and dignity of individuals. It serves as a catalyst for urgent action to strengthen legal frameworks and develop robust strategies to tackle this alarming issue in the digital realm.

Priya Anand Case: Priya Anand, a renowned Indian journalist, became a target of online harassment and cyberbullying after she exposed a high-profile sexual harassment case. She received countless abusive messages, threats, and derogatory comments on social media platforms. The relentless online attacks not only affected her mental well-being but also had a chilling effect on her ability to carry out her professional duties. This case underscores the challenges faced by women who speak out against injustice and the urgent need for effective support systems and legal safeguards to protect them from cyber offence.

Acid Attack Survivor Case: In 2016, a young acid attack survivor faced further victimization in the cyber world. Her photographs were widely circulated on social media platforms accompanied by derogatory comments, further exacerbating her trauma. This case sheds light on the intersection of physical offence and cyber offence, highlighting how online platforms can be used as tools for humiliation, intimidation, and perpetuating harm. It underscores the urgent need for comprehensive legal measures and support systems to address the unique vulnerabilities faced by survivors of gender-based offence in the cyber realm.

Indecent Representation of Women Case: Instances have emerged where women's images have been misused or manipulated in inappropriate ways on the internet. These images have been used in online advertisements, fake profiles, or pornographic materials without the consent of the individuals involved. Such incidents showcase the objectification of women and the non-consensual use of their images, further contributing to their vulnerability in the cyber world. This case highlights the need for stringent laws and enforcement mechanisms to tackle the unauthorized use and exploitation of women's images online.

These case studies serve as powerful examples of the various forms of offence against women in the cyber world and emphasize the urgent need for robust legal frameworks, awareness campaigns, and support systems to address and prevent such incidents. It is crucial to respect the privacy and anonymity of the individuals involved and handle these case studies with sensitivity and discretion when discussing them on public forums.

9. CHALLENGES IN ADDRESSING CYBER OFFENCE AGAINST WOMEN

Addressing cyber offence against women in India is a complex and multifaceted challenge. Several factors contribute to the difficulties encountered in effectively combating this issue. The following are key challenges faced in addressing cyber offence against women in India:

Under reporting and Lack of Awareness: Numerous incidents of cyber offense remain unreported for several reasons, including social stigma, fear of retaliation, and limited awareness regarding available support systems and legal remedies. Victims may not identify certain behaviors as cyber offenses or may underestimate the gravity of the situation, resulting in underreporting. This underreporting phenomenon highlights the need to address these barriers and enhance awareness among individuals, ensuring they recognize and report cyber offenses promptly. By fostering a supportive environment, educating the public, and promoting accessible support mechanisms, victims can be encouraged to come forward, seek help, and initiate necessary actions against cyber offenses.

Jurisdictional Issues: Cyber-crimes often transcend geographical boundaries, making it challenging to determine the jurisdiction for investigation and prosecution. Lack of international cooperation and coordination hampers the investigation and apprehension of perpetrators operating from other countries.

Technological Advancements: Rapid advancements in technology create new avenues for cyber offence, challenging law enforcement agencies to keep pace with evolving tactics and techniques used by perpetrators. Encryption and anonymity tools employed by offenders can make it difficult to trace and identify them, hindering the investigation process.

Limited Digital Literacy: Limited digital literacy among women poses challenges in recognizing and effectively responding to cyber offence. Lack of knowledge about online safety practices, privacy settings, and reporting mechanisms can make women more vulnerable to cyber-crimes.

Lack of Gender Sensitization: Deep-rooted societal attitudes, norms, and biases contribute to a culture of victim-blaming and trivialization of cyber offence against women. Insufficient gender sensitization among law enforcement agencies, judiciary, and the public can hinder effective response and support for victims.

Inadequate Legal Framework: The existing legal framework in India may not fully address the specific nuances of cyber offence against women. Laws might lack clarity, require updates to incorporate emerging forms of cyber offence, or face challenges in implementation and enforcement.

Capacity Building: Law enforcement agencies may lack adequate training, resources, and expertise in handling cyber-crimes, including cyber offence against women. Building capacity among relevant stakeholders is crucial to ensure effective investigation, prosecution, and support services for victims.

Online Platforms and Privacy Concerns: Social media platforms, messaging apps, and other online platforms play a significant role in cyber offence against women. Balancing the need for user privacy and protection with the responsibility of platforms to prevent and address cyber offence poses challenges in terms of policies, reporting mechanisms, and accountability.

Addressing these challenges requires a comprehensive and multi-pronged approach. Efforts should focus on raising awareness, promoting digital literacy, strengthening the legal framework, enhancing cooperation between stakeholders, and fostering a supportive environment for victims to come forward and seek justice. By addressing these challenges, India can work towards creating a safer and more inclusive cyber space for women, free from the scourge of cyber offence.

10. STRATEGIES FOR PREVENTION AND SUPPORT

Prevention and support are critical components in addressing cyber offence against women in India. Implementing effective strategies can help prevent such incidents and provide support to victims. The following are key strategies for prevention and support:

Awareness and Education: Promote awareness campaigns targeting women, men, and society at large about cyber offence, its impact, and available support systems. Conducting digital literacy programs to enhance knowledge of online safety, privacy settings, and responsible online behavior can prove to be a helpful tool. By engaging educational institutions, community organizations, and online platforms in spreading awareness and educating users about the risks and preventive measures will create awareness among everyone.

Strengthening Legal Framework: It has been a requisite of the time to review and update existing laws to encompass emerging forms of cyber offence against women. It will ensure clarity and effectiveness in legislation, enabling swift investigation, prosecution, and appropriate punishment for offenders. By establishing specialized cyber-crime units and train law enforcement agencies to handle cases related to cyber offence against women will enhance the confidence not only in cyber victims but also among public.

Reporting Mechanisms and Support Systems: It is very necessary to establish user-friendly reporting mechanisms, both online and offline, that enable victims to report incidents of cyber offence. At the same time developing support systems, helplines, and counseling services to provide immediate assistance and emotional support to victims is also required. By collaborating with NGOs, women's organizations, and support groups to offer comprehensive support services, including legal aid and counseling can also be of immense importance.

Collaboration and Cooperation: Foster collaboration between law enforcement agencies, government bodies, technology companies, and civil society organizations to combat cyber offence against women. Another step which can be taken is to encourage platforms to implement stronger measures for user safety, including reporting mechanisms, content moderation, and privacy settings. By enhancing international cooperation to address cross-border cyber-crimes and to ensure the extradition of offenders is also important.

Capacity Building: Conduct regular training programs for law enforcement agencies, judiciary, and other relevant stakeholders on cyber-crime investigation and victim support. Enhancing the technical skills of investigators and prosecutors to effectively handle digital evidence and cyber forensic techniques and to collaborate with academic institutions to develop specialized courses on cyber law and cyber-crime investigation.

Empowerment and Support for Victims: For this it is vital to promote a victim-centered approach, ensuring confidentiality, empathy, and non-judgmental support for victims. It is equally important to provide comprehensive legal aid, counseling, and rehabilitation services to help victims overcome the trauma of cyber offence and to encourage victim participation in the legal process and provide them with information about their rights, options, and available resources.

Research and Data Collection: Research studies need to be encouraged to understand the prevalence, impact, and emerging trends of cyber offence against women in India. It will foster collaboration between academia, government agencies, and NGOs to collect data, analyze trends, and evaluate the effectiveness of interventions. These research findings can be utilized to inform policy development, enhance preventive measures, and address the specific needs of victims.

By implementing these strategies, India can make significant progress in preventing cyber offence against women and providing effective support to victims. Creating a safe and inclusive cyber space requires the collective efforts of government bodies, law enforcement agencies, technology companies, civil society organizations, and the public. As mentioned by Sujata Bali, "It can safely be concluded that reporting cyber-crimes against women in India need a victim perspective approach" (Bali 2023:54).

11. RESULTS AND DISCUSSION

The escalating number of crimes against women is a significant concern for any state, but the advent of cyber-crimes adds an additional layer of complexity. Cyber criminals exploit the anonymity provided by the digital realm, allowing them to assume false identities and engage in illegal activities. Addressing this issue requires concerted efforts from the government, particularly in the realm of Internet Service Providers (ISPs), who possess crucial data related to users' online activities. To effectively counter cybercrimes, it is imperative for the government to impose stricter laws and regulations on ISPs. These laws should mandate ISPs to maintain comprehensive records of all data accessed by users while surfing the internet. By ensuring that ISPs retain this data securely, law enforcement agencies can have access to valuable information when investigating criminal activities.

The government should collaborate with ISPs to implement a robust reporting system. ISPs should be required to report any suspicious activities they come across to the relevant authorities promptly. This proactive approach will aid in identifying and curbing potential crimes in their early stages, preventing further harm, and protecting potential victims. Moreover, raising awareness and educating users about cybersecurity best practices is vital. The government, in partnership with ISPs and other stakeholders, should conduct public awareness campaigns to inform individuals about the risks of cybercrimes and ways to safeguard themselves while using digital platforms.

The rising prevalence of crimes against women, especially in the digital realm, demands immediate action. By enacting stricter laws on ISPs, promoting reporting mechanisms, and prioritizing awareness and education, the government can take crucial steps towards curbing cybercrimes and ensuring a safer online environment for all citizens, particularly women.

12. FINDINGS

It is evident from the research paper that the cyber harassment via email and cyber stalking are the predominant cyber-crimes targeting women in India. As a result of these and other forms of cyber-crimes against women, the respondents highlight numerous challenges faced by the victims. It is also clear that a surge in cyber-crimes against women, attributed to various factors. Among the significant contributing factors are the easy accessibility of the internet and the allure of browsing without adequate knowledge, leading to a rise in cyber-crimes against women.

It is apparent that most of the women victims of cyber-crimes faced various challenges, including mental disturbances, marital problems, and difficulties in marriage arrangements. These cyber-crimes have adverse effects on the social life of the women affected. It is also highlighted that, a significant deficiency in the Indian IT Act of 2000 and 2008 is the lack of specific provisions addressing cyber-crimes against women and children. Women victims' hesitation and shyness play a crucial role in preventing the reporting of cyber-crimes against women. Additionally, factors such as fear of defamation and mistakes committed by the victims also contribute to under-reporting.

The insights provided in the paper shed light on the complexities surrounding cyber-crimes against women. Addressing these issues requires a comprehensive approach, including the improvement of legislation, raising awareness, and creating a supportive environment that encourages women to report such crimes without fear of stigma or repercussions.

CONCLUSION

The matter of offense against women in the cyber world is a pressing concern that demands immediate attention. This research paper has provided insights into the context, importance, extent, and aims of the study. It has outlined the methodology, data sources, and significant findings concerning offense against women in the cyber world, with a specific focus on India. By examining these aspects, the paper contributes to a better understanding of the issue and sets the foundation for addressing and mitigating cyber offenses targeting women effectively.

The prevalence of cyber offence against women in India is alarming, with various forms such as online harassment, cyber bullying, revenge porn, stalking, and identity theft. These acts not only cause immediate harm but also have long-lasting psychological, emotional, social, and economic impacts on the victims. The research has highlighted the factors contributing to cyber offence against women, including gender inequality, patriarchal attitudes, digital gender divide, and lack of awareness and education. The legal and policy framework in India plays a crucial role in addressing cyber offence against women, and several initiatives have been taken to strengthen legislation, establish reporting mechanisms, and provide support services. However, challenges persist, including under reporting, jurisdictional issues, technological advancements, limited digital literacy, and gender insensitivity. Overcoming these challenges requires collaborative efforts, capacity building, and a victim-centered approach.

The research paper has presented strategies for prevention and support, emphasizing the importance of awareness and education, strengthening the legal framework, establishing reporting mechanisms and support systems, fostering collaboration and cooperation, building capacity, and empowering and supporting victims. These strategies aim to create a safer and more inclusive cyber space for women, where their rights are protected, and they can actively participate without fear of offence.

In conclusion, addressing offence against women in the cyber world requires a comprehensive approach that combines legal measures, technological solutions, educational initiatives, and societal change. It is essential for all stakeholders, including government bodies, law enforcement agencies, technology companies, civil society organizations, and the public, to work together to prevent cyber offence, support victims, and create an environment that respects and upholds the rights and dignity of women in the digital realm. By taking concerted action, India can pave the way for a safer and more gender-equal cyber space, ultimately contributing to the overall empowerment and well-being of women.

REFERENCES

Al-Jenaibi, B. (2016). The Twitter revolution in the Gulf countries. *Journal of Creative Communications*, *11*(1), 61–83. doi:10.1177/0973258616630217

Aryan, A., & Raghavan, P. (n.d.). *Post reports of Co Win leak, IT Min asks CERT 1In to probe.* https://indianexpress.com/article/business /economy/post-reports-of-coin-leak-it min-asks-cert-in-to- probe-7355150/

Bali, S. (2023). *Cyber Crime Against Women in India: How can the Law and Technology Help the Victims.* Unleashing the Art of Digital Forensics. Taylor & Francis Publication.

Bist, S. (2020). *Cyber Crime Against Women in India-Investigative and Legislative Challenges*. Wordshrew Press.

Cybercrime-Descriptive Portrayal of Crimes against Women in India. (n.d.). https://www.legalserviceindia.com/legal/article-5858-cybercrime-descriptive-portrayal-of-crimes-against women-in-india.html

Debarati, H., & Jaishankar, K. (2016). *Cyber Crime Against Women in India*. Sage Publications.

Desai, M., & Jaishankar, K. (2007). *Cyber Stalking-Victimization of Girl Student: An Empirical Study*. Academic Press.

Goel, A. (2006). *Violence and Protective Measures for Women Development and Empowerment*. Deep & Deep Publications.

Jeet, S. (2012). Cyber-crimes against women in India: Information Technology Act, 2000. *Elixir Criminal Law*, *47*, 8891–8895.

Marturana, F., Tacconi, S., & Italiano, G. F. (2013). Cybercrime and Cloud Forensics: Applications for Investigation Processes. Academic Press.

Park, J. (2012). Cyber Crime: Concepts, Methodologies, Tools, and Applications. Academic Press.

Schell, B. H., & Melnychuk, J. (2011). Corporate Hacking and Technology-Driven Crime: Social Dynamics and Implications. Academic Press.

Seth, K. (2018). *Cyber Crime Against Women*. Published in New Delhi.

Singh, K. A., & Choudhary, J. (2012). *Violence against Women and Children-Issues and Concerns*. Serials Publications.

Tiwari, G. (2014). *Understanding Laws Cyber Laws & Cyber Crimes*. Lexis Nexis Publication.

Chapter 18
Can Hashtags Promote Body Acceptance?
A Content Analysis Study of Cyber-Feminism on Social Media

Cassia Liandra Carvalho
University of Aveiro, Portugal

Belem Barbosa
https://orcid.org/0000-0002-4057-360X
University of Porto, Portugal

ABSTRACT

Th chapter presents an empirical study on a Brazilian cyber-activism movement on Instagram associated with the hashtag #CorpoLivre (#FreeBody in Portuguese). This movement, which was established in 2018, has published more than 3,000 posts and has over 400,000 followers, disseminates anti-fatphobia and real body discourses, and promotes a positive relationship between women and their bodies beyond traditional beauty standards. The study analyses the posts made by the feminist movement on Instagram in December 2022, with a sample size of 101 posts. The study adopted the framework developed by Khurana and Knight for the analysis, which enables the classification of the sample posts in terms of message appeal, orientation, engagement, popularity, and image characteristics. This framework was used to examine the relationship between content characteristics and engagement. Additionally, the study includes a content analysis of the posts' comments, specifically evaluating the valence (positive, negative, or neutral) to assess the effectiveness of the characteristics of the posts.

INTRODUCTION

The recent decades have seen a significant transformation in the way citizens access information, communicate, and interact with one another, owing to the revolution in information and communication

DOI: 10.4018/978-1-6684-8893-5.ch018

technologies. This trend of digitalization has had a profound impact on all aspects of society, including business, peer interaction, and activist movements. Social networking sites (SNS) have emerged as a crucial tool for the articulation of feminist movements in the current era. These sites are widely used by a large segment of the population, facilitate social interaction, and are therefore considered fundamental for activist mobilization (Drüeke & Zobl, 2016). Activist groups use SNS to organize, engage in debate, articulate their causes, and plan actions.

Despite social media frequently facing criticism for promoting violence against women through means such as bullying and perpetuating unrealistic female stereotypes, they can also serve as a platform for informing, motivating, and empowering women. For instance, although digital platforms commonly exhibit fatphobia, feminist individuals and groups generate and distribute content to endorse authentic depictions of women and campaign for body positivity. However, the significance of social media as a tool for cyber-feminism remains under-researched. While there is a growing body of literature concerning fatphobia, there exists a scarcity of research that explores the ways in which social media can be utilized for educating society and empowering women. To address this gap, this chapter aims to answer the following research question: What are the characteristics of social media content that effectively promote body acceptance?

This chapter presents an empirical study on a Brazilian cyber-activism movement on Instagram associated with the hashtag #CorpoLivre (#FreeBody in Portuguese). This movement, which was established in 2018, has published more than 3,000 posts and has over 400,000 followers. It disseminates anti-fatphobia and real body discourses, and promotes a positive relationship between women and their bodies beyond traditional beauty standards. The study analyses the posts made by the feminist movement on Instagram in December 2022, with a sample size of 92 posts. The study adopted the framework developed by Khurana and Knight (2021) for the analysis, which enables the classification of the sample posts in terms of message appeal, orientation, engagement, popularity, and image characteristics. This framework was used to examine the relationship between content characteristics and engagement. Additionally, the study includes a content analysis of the posts' comments, specifically evaluating the valence (positive, negative, or neutral) to further assess the effectiveness of the characteristics of the posts.

This chapter makes several contributions to the field. Firstly, it helps to understand feminist cyber-activism on Instagram in relation to body acceptance, aesthetic body pressure, and fatphobia. Secondly, it provides valuable insights on a popular hashtag in Brazil. Thirdly, it identifies strategies recommended for cyber-activism. And overall, it gives a contribution to women in their ongoing efforts to combat aesthetic violence and foster self-esteem by providing indications on the means to develop positive social consciousness.

The following section presents the literature review that formed the basis of the empirical study also included in these pages.

Cyberfeminism on Social Media

Since the emergence of social networking sites (SNS), feminists have been working to diversify their messages and generate new discussions (Wang & Driscoll, 2019) while occupying digital spaces as a form of power. Of all the available channels, social platforms have been at the forefront of public dialogues promoting awareness and change (Baker & Ryalls, 2016; PettyJohn et al., 2018). Activists combat sexism, patriarchy, and other forms of domination, and stimulate male behavior change (Hardaker

& McGlashan, 2016). It is their role to take the conversation from the web and occupy offline spaces (Rivers, 2017a, 2017b) creating protests, marches, and acts in support of the common goal: women. SNS have played a significant role in many feminist digital movements. The new generation of activists believes that alternative spaces can be more effective in engaging social projects (Keller, 2012, 2017). Facebook, Instagram, and Twitter have become the stage for great demonstrations and discussions about sexism (Baer, 2016), misogyny (Ging & Siapera, 2018) and sexual harassment (Retallack et al., 2016; Thompson, 2018). The body has also become an important topic in cyberfeminism. Women's collectives increasingly discuss fatphobia (Gurrieri, 2013; Puhakka, 2021) and aesthetic pressure on social media. Feminist groups sustain their presence in social networks and increase their influence by connecting other causes and other people's stories. Feminist groups sustain their presence in social networks and increase their influence by connecting with other causes and sharing other people's stories. Cyberfeminism highlights that women must learn how power and knowledge are incorporated into the internet and how they can interrupt and change a culture that attacks them (Oyosoro et al., 2022).

Feminist movements have found in online media a way to intersect the different struggles of women, forming true communities within "cyberfeminism" (Escosteguy, 2019; Varela, 2019; Viana, 2019).). It was in this space that the questioning of the female body standard gained strength. Stigmatized, judged, and excluded bodies share their realities on the internet: users come together to denounce fatphobic comments and practices, criticize aesthetic pressure, and, above all, create a support network. Matich, Ashman e Parsons (2019) argue that the exposure of the female body can be used as a mechanism of activism to question the construction of femininity presented in capitalist-patriarchal society. In the same vein, the present research analyzes the use of the hashtag #corpolivre (meaning "free body" in Portuguese) in Brazil as a means to defend the diversity of the female body and challenge the established idealized standard. Many groups have used hashtags as a strategy to expand the debate, making engagement easier for feminists to plan for social change.

Feminist Hashtags on Body Acceptance

The use of hashtags has significantly increased the power of feminist discourse (Clark, 2016; Linabary et al., 2019; Mishra, 2020; Myles, 2019; Williams, 2015). Not only do hashtags play the role of subject categorizers (Salazar, 2017), they also enable greater engagement since they are themselves messages of activism. Girls and women are increasingly using technology to protest and voice their complaints against violence, harassment, sexism, and body shaming (Cooper, n.d.; Mendes et al., 2019; Winderman, 2019). In recent years, many hashtags have emerged with the aim of raising awareness of real problems experienced by women (Drüeke & Zobl, 2016). For instance, #YesAllWoman (Rodino-colocino, 2014; Thrift, 2014) and #PrimeiroAssédio (meaning #FirstHarassment in Portuguese language) are some of the pluralized social media campaigns that have emphasized minority discourses. Hashtags usually represent events that serve as a gateway to understanding more complex scenarios about structural inequalities through short but convincing narratives. With many shares, campaigns with hashtags are intended to raise awareness about problems and facilitate broad discussions of solutions (Bijker & Bijsterveld, 2000; Hynnä & Kyrölä, 2019; Towns, 2016). Popular feminism used in hashtag campaigns is important to pluralize the message and give voice to the non-privileged, as noted by Sarah (Banet-Weiser, 2018). As Bowles Eagle (2015) argues, it aims to break the silence that often occurs due to the assumption of problems being part of the culture. According to Bennett and Segerberg, (2012, p.742), "compared to the protests and conventional social movements of identifiable organizations and with members leading the common under-banner mobilizations, hashtag activism is more personalized, and digitally mediated, more widely used."

Feminist hashtags play an important role in creating a digital space where women with shared opinions can unite and make visible the experiences and challenges they face, contributing to social change and the empowerment of women (Chen et al., 2018; Kangere et al., 2017). This virtual space is crucial for promoting social justice and providing a platform for collective action (Franklin, 2016). However, it is also important for activists to overcome online and offline struggles and tensions in order to achieve their goals. Hashtags can serve as a multiplier agent, allowing more women to recognize and share the message, thereby strengthening activism. Currently, a range of feminist activism inundate social media, addressing body acceptance and the pressure women face worldwide to conform to idealized standards of beauty.

Feminist hashtags for body acceptance such as #amesuascurvas, #ameuseucorpo, #foradopadrão, #corpãoquerido, #meucorpodeverão, #positividadecorporal, and #bodypositive have surpassed 6 million uses, according to Instagram (Statista, 2022). These hashtags are usually accompanied by images that reflect real bodies and more loving texts in relation to the aesthetic pressure experienced by women. According to Rodgers et al., (2021), social media has played a fundamental role in the process of body acceptance. Bombak et al. (2019) explain that cultural body acceptance is directly linked to diversity and inclusion with important narratives about gender representation, sexual variety, racial and ethnic variety, as well as body type (fat, thin, tall, short, etc.).

Fat activism, also known in Brazil as "gordoativismo," is a movement that seeks to fight for social inclusion and combat stigmas and prejudices against larger bodies. Plus size is another movement that emerged in the market to include women who wear larger sizes. The object of this study (#corpolivre) defends the break of the feminine aesthetic paradigm, molded by the capitalist structure, which uses all media to introject the idealized and unrealistic feminine body standard. It can be considered a banner for the body acceptance movement, either by combating subjective violence or objectively welcoming all body types.

Starting with the feminist fat acceptance movement that emerged in the late 1960s and early 1970s in Canada and the United States, the primary body acceptance movement, Body Positive, was created in response to the idealized appearance promoted in mainstream media (Afful & Ricciardelli, 2015; Cohen et al., 2019) The movement advocates for the promotion of a positive body image. Brathwaite and DeAndrea, (2022) state that Body Positive aims to promote bodies that are not historically admired or accepted by society and that posts featuring women with bodies different from those traditionally considered standard bodies can be perceived as true and realistic.

Fat acceptance emerged in the 1960s as a response to weight discrimination and stigma directed towards larger adults, aiming to create an alternative discourse on obesity

(Cooper, 2008). Currently referred to as Fat Activism, fat empowerment, or fatphobia, it refers to the aversion to fat and people who are overweight, treating them badly, belittling, or making the overweight person feel inferior. Women have suffered a lot from fatphobic discourses (Matacin & Simone, 2019) on social media, besides being flooded by campaigns that value the thin body (Taylor et al., 2016).

Content Marketing

Content Marketing is a marketing strategy focused on engaging with a target audience and growing a network of clients through the creation of relevant and valuable content (Holliman & Rowley, 2014; Koiso-Kanttila, 2004). It is a way to create a positive perception of a brand and generate more business. In recent years, content marketing has gained strength by focusing on creating content that meets the needs and preferences of the audience (Ho et al., 2020). The result of a strategic content marketing approach is the generation of authority in the market on a particular topic, with content that solves consumer problems and pains.

Content creation has also extended to social media. The number of active users worldwide approached the 5 billion mark in January 2022 (DataReportal, 2022). representing almost 63% of the world's population. Adapted to the limitations of each network, there are several strategies to attract more customers and even educate the target audience. Paul Clifford, (2016) explains in his book that the first step to an effective strategy is to define what you want to say and to whom. From this first step, it becomes easier to prepare the message structure, generate content, and monitor results. With a good social media strategy, there are advantages such as improving brand visibility, generating notoriety on the subject, and influencing customer purchasing decisions.

METHOD

The main aim of this chapter is to identify the characteristics of social media content that effectively promote body acceptance. Despite the relevant contributions in the literature of cyberfeminism, feminist hashtags, and content marketing that flourish in the literature, the significance of social media as a tool for cyber-feminism remains under-researched and there exists a scarcity of research that explores the ways in which social media can be utilized for educating society and empowering women. To address this gap, an empirical quantitative study was conducted following the framework developed by Khurana and Knight (2021). The Brazilian cyber-activism movement on Instagram associated with the hashtag #CorpoLivre (#FreeBody in Portuguese) was chosen due to the fact tht this is an established movement with more than 3,000 posts published between 2018 and 2022, and counting with 400,000 followers. It disseminates anti-fatphobia and real body discourses, and promotes a positive relationship between women and their bodies beyond traditional beauty standards.

Framework of Analysis

The framework presented by Khurana and Knight, (2021) offers four categories for content analysis: message appeal, message orientation, engagement, and popularity. Each category has been further divided into subcategories to facilitate a more comprehensive analysis, as follows:

Message Appeal: Messages are analyzed as emotional or informative. Rietveld et al. (2020) found that "emotional appeals influence customer engagement more than informative appeals for both visual and textual modalities" (p. 36).

Table 1. Framework of analysis adopted by this study

Category	Description	Subcategory
Message appeal	"Emotional appeals influence customer engagement more than informative appeals for both visual and textual modalities." (Rietveld et al., 2020, p. 36)	• Emotional • Informative • Mixed
Engagement	"SNS consumer-brand engagement was operationalized at three levels, namely, low/conative (likes), medium/affective (share) and high/cognitive (comments)." (Yousaf et al., 2021)	• Low • Medium • High
Message orientation (image)	"Image-based features of Instagram visual content affect the digital user's perception of such content and consequently his/her level of engagement with the image" (Valentini et al., 2018)	• Human body • Human face • Scenery • Drawing
Popularity	"in raising EG were image quality, day and time of post, user tags, and type of image" (Purba et al., 2021)	• Weekday • Hashtag

Source: The authors

Message Orientation: Analysis models refer to low orientation, which leads to likes; medium orientation, which leads to shares; and high orientation, which leads to comments. Yousaf et al. (2021) operationalized SNS consumer-brand engagement at three levels: low/conative (likes), medium/affective (share), and high/cognitive (comments).

Engagement: Research has shown that images are responsible for users' engagement on social media platforms. Valentini et al. (2018) noted that "image-based features of Instagram visual content affect the digital user's perception of such content and, consequently, his/her level of engagement with the image" (p. 11).

Popularity: The popularity of a post is also linked to the quality of the image, the day and time of posting, and the associated hashtags. Purba et al. (2021) found that "the factors that were found to be effective in raising EG were image quality, day and time of post, user tags, and type of image" (p. 32).

Table 1 describes in more detail the analysis framework used in this study.

This study collected data by analyzing the Brazilian Instagram page @corpolivre, examining a sample of 92 posts made during the month of December. Engagement information, such as the number of likes and comments, was retrieved from Instagram. The posts were then coded independently by two researchers according to categories, including message orientation and message appeal, based on the framework utilized in the study. Additionally, the study included a content analysis of the posts' comments, specifically evaluating the valence (positive, negative, or neutral) to further assess the effectiveness of the characteristics of the posts. During the coding process, the two researchers were blinded to each other's coding to minimize potential biases. Any discrepancies in the coding were resolved through discussions and consensus, and the intercoder reliability was assessed using Cohen's kappa coefficient. The high level of agreement between the coders demonstrated the reliability of the coding process. The rigorous coding process ensured the accuracy and reliability of the study's findings.

Sample's Characteristics

The sample consists of 92 posts, and there are no missing data. The majority of the posts (75%) include video as their media format, followed by carousel (21%), and photo (4%). In terms of content, most posts (61%) have an emotional appeal, while 39% are predominantly informative. Regarding the images used, the human body is the most commonly featured (57%), followed by the human face (21%) and drawing (21%). The sample is evenly distributed across weekdays, with an average of 13 posts per weekday, with the highest number of posts (17) being published on Saturdays and the lowest number (9) on Sundays. Finally, the majority of posts include 1 (48%) or 2 (32%) hashtags.

Data Analysis Techniques

The Kruskal-Wallis test was selected as a nonparametric alternative to one-way ANOVA to test for statistical differences across the categories of each independent variable by comparing the medians across three or more independent groups. This test is appropriate when the data do not meet the normality assumption and is suitable for testing the statistically significant differences among post categories. Results will be presented and discussed in the following sections.

Data-driven content analysis was performed on both the posts and their comments. This approach to analyzing textual data is popular in social science research due to its effectiveness in handling large amounts of data collected from social media and other online platforms. The process involves collecting text-based data, such as posts or comments, and analyzing it for patterns, themes, and trends. Data-driven content analysis, in conjunction with quantitative analysis, provides a more comprehensive understanding of the data, helping to reveal patterns and insights that may not be immediately apparent through traditional qualitative methods.

FINDINGS

As presented in Table 2, the posts published by @movimentocorpolivre exhibited substantial variations with respect to media format, message appeal, and message orientation. Videos, messages with emotional appeal, and a more general message orientation (scenario) were found to have a greater ability to generate comments. Furthermore, posts made on Wednesdays received a higher average number of comments. Emotional posts also tended to generate more likes from users. However, photos were found to have a higher average number of likes, with images of the human body receiving the most likes compared to other message orientations of the images. Wednesdays also recorded a higher average number of likes.

It is worth noting that the number of hashtags used also exhibited considerable variation among posts. The movement posted regularly on every weekday, with slightly fewer posts made on Sundays. In regards to the day of the week for publishing and the shared hashtags, Purba et al. (2021) found that content generation occurred mostly on Saturdays and regarding the hashtags used, most posts only utilized one: #corpolivre. The utilized hashtag has become a "battle cry" for promoting content related to body acceptance. The discursive power of feminist hashtags is essential for activism around women's causes, given the ways in which discourse intersects with everyday life for women (Clark, 2016). #Corpolivre represents much more than just a hashtag; it also carries an important reflection on beauty standards that greatly affect the confidence and self-esteem of hundreds of women.

Table 2. Comments and likes per post characteristics

	Sample		Comments		Likes	
	Posts	**Percent**	**Total**	**Average**	**Total**	**Average**
Media format	92	100%				
Video	69	75%	9232	133.8	503992	7304.2
Photo	4	4%	134	33.5	36779	9194.8
Carousel	19	21%	962	50.6	26422	1390.6
Message appeal	92	100%				
Informative	36	39%	3176	88.2	151539	4209.4
Emotional	56	61%	7152	127.7	415654	7422.4
Message orientation	92	100%				
Human body	52	57%	7448	143.2	416194	8003.7
Human face	19	21%	1825	96.1	97785	5146.6
Scenario	2	2%	702	351.0	11791	5895.5
Drawing	19	21%	353	18.6	41423	2180.2
Day of the week	92	100%				
Monday	15	16%	996	66.4	58494	3899.6
Tuesday	12	13%	1865	155.4	95725	7977.1
Wednesday	12	13%	2345	195.4	99522	8293.5
Thursday	15	16%	1360	90.7	74149	4943.3
Friday	12	13%	742	61.8	41481	3456.8
Saturday	17	18%	1932	113.6	123702	7276.6
Sunday	9	10%	1088	120.9	74120	8235.6
Hashtags	92	100%				
0	5	5%	503	100.6	48814	9762.8
1	44	48%	5192	118.0	328131	7457.5
2	29	32%	3481	120.0	129961	4481.4
3	8	9%	248	31.0	22124	2765.5
4	3	3%	612	204.0	24258	8086.0
6	1	1%	15	15.0	778	778.0
7	2	2%	277	138.5	13127	6563.5

Source: The authors

A Closer Look on User Engagement

This section provides a more in-depth analysis of the study's results, highlighting statistically significant differences in engagement related to the characteristics of the posts, such as message orientation and appeal. Furthermore, the study presents an exploration of the content analysis of the posts and comments.

Media Format

The majority of posts in the sample consisted of videos (75%), while some posts were photos or carousels. Despite the unbalanced sample, a Kruskal-Wallis test was conducted to identify differences in the ability of different media types to generate likes and comments. The results showed statistically significant differences in the number of likes ($H(2, N = 92) = 30.500$, $p < 0.001$) and comments ($H(2, N = 92) = 29.007$, $p < 0.001$) across media types. Post-hoc tests revealed that carousels had a significantly lower ability to generate likes compared to posts featuring images or videos. Additionally, carousels had a significant lower ability to generate comments when compared with video.

Therefore, it can be concluded that carousels are significantly less effective in generating likes and comments than videos. It should be noted that the number of posts featuring other types of media (i.e., photos) was very small ($n = 4$), and therefore no statistically significant differences were identified in the post-hoc tests. However, it is worth mentioning that, on average, photo posts generated the highest average number of likes and the lowest average number of comments among all media types considered.

According to Yousaf et al. (2021), public engagement is measured through likes, comments, and shares. Each action indicates the level of audience involvement with the content, with sharing being a high level of engagement that demonstrates people's commitment to the content to the extent of reposting it. The most liked content in the data collection was posts aligned with the group's purpose that addressed the societal pressures for a perfect body. For instance, @movimentocorpolivre shared a video that received 18,008 likes and 165 comments, indicating high engagement (Yousaf et al., 2021). The video was presented to the public with the following call to action:

@movimentocorpolivre: Your body is NOT an accessory that should be molded according to trends. Come here and I'll explain why!

The video discusses current fashion trends and issues a warning about the return of 90s-style clothing that promotes extreme thinness. The content creator, Lara Cunha, shares that she developed bulimia and anorexia during that decade due to aesthetic standards and the pressure to be thin. She concludes by emphasizing the importance of body acceptance and healthy living.

In the comments section, women shared their experiences and testimonies about how they have mistreated themselves to fit into a certain clothing size and conform to the standards set by the fashion industry.

@[USER1]: Don't pay too much attention to the skinny women in the media, it's just a disservice. Our bodies have different shapes and they are important, but what's most important is what they carry inside!

@[USER2]: I wish I could feel free in my body, but as a nutritionist, I feel judged and at risk of having a failed career if I don't lose the weight I gained in the last 2 years 😭 I just wanted to be a fat person in peace.

Hence, in the comments section, users aim to raise awareness among other women that all bodies are beautiful, contrary to what the fashion industry preaches. Linabary et al. (2019) explain that feminist activism aims to challenge and criticize the internal dynamics of feminist experiences and understand the patriarchal power in the social construction of femininity. The engagement generated by @movimentocorpolivre not only demonstrates high levels of engagement, but also highlights the co-creation and user collaboration that these types of posts generate.

In the study, it is observed that videos generate higher engagement and are the most utilized format by the profile. According to Holliman & Rowley, (2014) content generation enhances engagement and provides opportunities for further connection with the audience, which is evident in the study of the @ movimentocorpolivre profile. Another significant aspect of video content generation is the identification of the target audience, particularly in this profile, which focuses on body acceptance and body positivity, an effective strategy (Paul Clifford, 2016) for connecting with the audience.

Appeal

A Kruskal-Wallis test was conducted to examine the differences in total likes per post between emotional and informative posts. The results revealed a statistically significant difference between the rank totals of emotional (Mdn = 54.21) and informative (Mdn = 34.50) posts, $H(1, N = 92) = 11.945$, $p = 0.001$.

The analysis of total comments per post also revealed a statistically significant difference between emotional (Mdn = 52.03) and informative (Mdn = 37.90) posts, $H(1, N = 92) = 6.132$, $p = 0.013$, suggesting that the emotional appeal is more likely to attract higher levels of engagement than the informative appeal.

Hence, this study found that emotional posts received significantly more likes and comments than informative posts. These findings suggest that emotional appeals are more effective in engaging Instagram users and generating higher levels of social media engagement.

Indeed, this the @movimentocorpolivre profile has invested heavily in messages with emotional appeal to reinforce its purpose. Rietveld et al. (2020) confirm that emotional appeals are more effective in customer engagement. This is because emotions are essential in brand connection, and the more the brand's beliefs resemble those of the consumer, the better the relationship and engagement. Emotional appeals encourage favorable brand associations, create meaningful connections with consumers, and encourage their loyalty (Ashley & Tuten, 2015; Bülbül Menon, 2010).

In one example, the singer Iza talks about her experience as a teenager, recalling beauty standards for white and black women during her adolescence and comparing them to her body type and people's reactions to it. This post received 7,473 likes:

@movimentocorpolivre: "Who has never hoped to appear on the list of the prettiest girls in school, right? With @iza, it was no different! Press play and see when she started to perceive racism in her life."

In another example, influencer @rafamologni discusses the changes her body has undergone over the years, the phases of life, and the lack of self-compassion and self-love. This post received 5,515 likes:

@movimentocorpolivre: "The truth is that we are hardly satisfied with the body we have in the present, right? It's super important that, besides being kinder to ourselves, we recognize our history and understand that the changes our bodies have undergone are part of it all! Let's love ourselves? - #CorpoLivre via @rafamologni"

Both examples contain feminist emotional messages. This is in line with the literature that shows that feminist emotional content generates high engagement rates and credibility for brands (Baer, 2016;

Sternadori & Abitbol, 2019) and helps break gender barriers through positive messages. Emotional appeals are also important in the construction of cyberfeminism, which uses social media to share feminist causes and fight for equity (Rivers, 2017a, 2017b).

The audience has positively responded to content that creates an intimate and authentic experience, while also exercising humor and empathy. Hence, content generation strategies that consider the audience's preferences and align closely with consumer tastes generate engagement and foster loyalty (Paul Clifford, 2016). It is concluded that content generation that leaves an emotional impact on the audience directly influences the brand's reputation and value.

Message Orientation (Image)

The Kruskal-Wallis test was used to analyze the differences in image types regarding their ability to generate likes, and a statistically significant difference was found among the three categories, $H(3, N = 92) = 30.173$, $p < 0.001$. Post-hoc pairwise comparisons, adjusted by Bonferroni approach to control for multiple tests, revealed that posts with drawings had a significantly different number of likes compared to those with human body or human face images, whereas the other image categories did not show significant differences.

Similarly, the Kruskal-Wallis test was used to analyze the differences in media types regarding their ability to generate comments, and a statistically significant difference was found among the three categories, $H(3, N = 92) = 34.476$, $p < 0.001$. Post-hoc pairwise comparisons adjusted by Bonferroni approach showed similar results as for likes, highlighting significant differences between posts featuring drawings compared to human face or human body images.

Hence, it can be concluded that the type of image used in Instagram posts significantly affects their ability to generate likes and comments. Specifically, posts featuring drawings had a significantly different level of engagement compared to those featuring human body or human face images. However, no significant differences were found in the ability of images showing human body or human face to generate user engagement. As the number of posts featuring a scenario was rare in the sample, no conclusions can be drawn regarding this type of image.

The message orientation is also a crucial factor to be analyzed in understanding the effectiveness of messages aimed at promoting body acceptance.

The @movimentocorpolivre profile predominantly utilizes videos in which content creators showcase their bodies, ranging from swimwear to tight and loose-fitting clothing. The @movimentocorpolivre advocates that beauty ideals imposed by media and the beauty industry are often unattainable, and that beauty lies in a normal body. According to Valentini et al. (2018), when the user has a connection to the generated image, there is higher engagement. The profile uses images of fat people with messages aimed at deconstructing standards and promoting self-love.

@movimentocorpolivre: The message is clear! We will have a body free summer! @marinabtkoo is a goddess! #CorpoLivre #summerbody #plussize #playgroundvivi - 6,488 likes.

In the video, content creator Marina (@marinabtkoo) is wearing a tiger print bikini and dancing to music. The image of the black woman's body, with its imperfections, fat, and curly hair, is a way to bring representation and generate a connection with other women who identify with this body shape. In the comments, women praise the content creator and talk about their own bodies. They recognize the beauty of the other woman in a bikini and encourage each other to have new experiences.

@[USER3]: And here I am, feeling ashamed of my body, wanting to wear a one-piece swimsuit. You are so beautiful

@[USER4]: What a beautiful woman!

In general, the data indicate that social media engagement is higher when there are images of natural bodies. The three posts with the highest number of comments are videos featuring individuals in intimate clothing depicting situations that fat people face:

@movimentocorpolivre: "Why is it so difficult for people to accept that we, LGBTQIAP+ people, are free and love living our freedom? For others, when we explore our creativity and our most varied versions, we are going against God. But what kind of God sows hatred?" #corpolivre #lgbt - 555 comments, 11,900 likes

@movimentocorpolivre: "Why do people insist on using our body as an agenda? My body is not public and doesn't need your opinion for anything! Comment 'me' if someone has ever talked about your body!" #corpolivre - 466 comments, 15,300 likes

@movimentocorpolivre: "This one is for those who have always been curious about how much I weigh. Stay tuned until the end!" #corpolivre - 465 comments, 19,500 likes

Natural bodies are well received by the audience, who engage in spreading the message and interacting with the content. Bombak et al. (2019) explain that messages about diverse bodies, such as those produced by the @movimentocorpolivre profile, are necessary to promote body acceptance and enable others to learn about different bodies from their own. Posts featuring fat bodies generate more participation and engagement, as well as providing representation for others who experience similar issues. The position expressed shows a more caring outlook towards one's own characteristics without caring about standards. This is reinforced by the comments of users and the feelings and emotions that they share:

@[USER 3]: The worst is when you tell the store that you don't feel represented, and they don't care.

@[USER 4]: I finally found my style in recent years, and it's liberating! Wearing what I find beautiful, rather than hiding my body, is the best feeling ever.

@[USER 5]: I suffered from this every day to the point where I stopped going out because of it.

The profile @movimentocorpolivre utilizes social media as a communication platform due to its proximity and engagement with its audience. Through social media, the profile interacts and builds strong relationships with its followers. Content marketing encourages a conversation between the brand and users to initiate and maintain an interesting, healthy, and long-lasting relationship for both parties (Koiso-Kanttila, 2004), which is precisely what the profile achieves with its posts: it encourages the audience to engage in dialogue about important topics in the construction of body positivity - self-acceptance, fatphobia, and the impact of the perfect body portrayed in the media. In line with what is proposed by Clifford (2016), the profile employs an effective strategy with its followers: it maintains consistent communications, aligns with trends, is data-driven, and audience-focused. Another important aspect of the strategy is the storytelling that generates identification and engagement.

The Role of Hashtag #corpolivre

Feminist hashtags are a major aggregator of women's stories, where they come together to fight for a purpose (Winderman, 2019). Women find a safe space in the hashtag to fight against beauty standards and share their stories, as a form of therapy. In this hashtag, they share courage, fears, and stories about their relationship with the mirror.

@[USER6]: Hi Isa, I've been following you for a short time and you're helping me a lot to accept myself after gaining 10kg... after all, it's what we have now, so let's live this present ♡

@[USER7]: It's very cool to hear that. After my second pregnancy, I spent years not facing a mirror! I'm coming back little by little with love! 😍

In addition, the images used alongside the content create identification and sorority among many women. They interact with each other by supporting and encouraging self-acceptance. Not comparing themselves to other women, reflecting on what they consume on social media, and valuing their own qualities are some of the main rules among the comments of women who value body positivity on the profile.

@[USER8]: I hated my facial hair for a long time until I found out that everyone has it. It's unbelievable what the media does to our heads.

Quality content creates engagement, which reflects the value and notoriety of the brand (Holliman & Rowley, 2014). The @movimentocorpolivre Qual profile shares content where people have a positive relationship with their bodies and do not compare themselves to beauty standards imposed by the beauty industry. In other words, the posts encourage women to share self-acceptance and their uniqueness, generating high levels of sharing, likes, and comments on the profile.

SOLUTIONS AND RECOMMENDATIONS

The hashtag #CorpoLivre emerged when Alexandra Gurgel decided to address a common concern among women: their bodies. As a result of her action, a profile with over 400,000 followers hungry for content featuring real bodies was created. Currently, the success of the profile lies in the development of content with self-acceptance as the main protagonist. The posts display women who do not conform to society's imposed beauty standards, but who love themselves and are aware that there are parts of their bodies that they may not like as much, but they choose to accept them instead of hating them. The content is constructed with a highly emotional appeal combined with informative posts that demystify questions and issues related to the body. The messaging type is highly engaging, as the posts are liked, commented on, and shared. The message orientation alternates between body images and facial images. Finally, the hashtag #corpolivre has solidified as a movement that brings together women's main body concerns and their testimonials on how they have overcome them and learned to love themselves. The women who participate in the movement aim to use their voice to stand against impossible beauty standards and have earned their space in the media, empowering other women.

The Body Positive trend emerges to challenge the societal beauty standards and encourage people to love their bodies as they are. Women's collectives aiming to generate greater engagement on social media in favor of body diversity must keep in mind that content generation should be aligned with a clear message of body acceptance. These women's groups seeking to create digital marketing strategies centered around body positivity must understand that connecting with the audience involves a basic formula that encompasses emotional messages, videos, and addressing important themes in the discourse promoting different body types.

To increase engagement, it is important for these female groups to engage in direct conversations about the topic and encourage comments from other women on their posts. Girls who also invest in this narrative should be aware of the significance of the theme and understanding the target audience. Sharing true stories and showcasing that perfect bodies do not exist are essential in constructing a digital image.

Brands that aim to amplify this theme in their posts need to first align themselves with the purpose of body positivity. Additionally, they should use individuals sharing their stories and encouraging the audience to demystify the beauty standards imposed by the media. People who showcase their diverse bodies, imperfections, and are happy and comfortable discussing the topic are crucial. Videos also play a key role in constructing an authentic narrative of body positivity. Listening to people talking about their stories, showing their bodies, and sharing their experiences fosters audience identification with the brand. Engagement through comments and hashtags is also of utmost importance for brands to gain a digital presence.

Digital content generation has posed a significant challenge for the market. Captivating the audience, fostering loyalty, and generating audience commitment are complex steps to achieve. There has been a tremendous shift in the message conveyed when discussing beauty in recent years. Social standards are being questioned by influencers and brands, and people have begun to understand that beauty lies in healthy bodies. Social media plays a significant role in driving this change and can propel further steps in this thematic area.

Diversifying body positivity and body acceptance, teaching the appreciation of individual diversity, and respecting different perspectives and ways of being are crucial in this construction. Another important aspect is always opening a dialogue with the audience. In addition to speaking, it is also essential to listen to what others think about the topic.

FUTURE RESEARCH DIRECTIONS

This study presents a preliminary investigation into the factors that influence engagement on body acceptance communication through social media. The findings suggest that videos play a critical role in driving engagement. Future research could build on these results by compiling a set of videos and conducting a more comprehensive analysis of their characteristics and engagement metrics. Storyboard and storytelling strategies are particularly relevant for furthering our understanding of how they foster engagement.

The study's limitations also provide interesting cues for future research. Data was limited to one feminist movement centered on one Instagram hashtag, and the sample size was relatively small. Therefore, examining the content of other hashtags related to self-acceptance and body positivity can provide a better understanding of the broader conversation surrounding these topics. Given that the findings may not be generalizable to other platforms or populations, future research should approach different hashtags that succeed in other regions, compare different cultures and movements, and explore the possible integration of other social media platforms with different features for user engagement, namely TikTok. Given the exponential growth of TikTok adoption among younger generations, it represents a relevant platform for future studies on the engagement of young women with feminist movements.

Finally, the study did not investigate the potential impact of external factors, such as current events or societal trends, on engagement levels. Given the relevance of real-time marketing as a social media marketing strategy, exploring trendy topics is also critical for future research.

CONCLUSION

After decades of extreme thinness inundating the media, TV soap operas, movies, and music videos, today there is more talk about the beauty of real bodies and self-love, self-compassion, and body acceptance. The study shows that the @movimentocorpolivre profile creates a permanent campaign with speeches that deconstruct old beauty standards. The women who are part of this community are active spokeswomen in sharing this purpose. The hashtag #corpolivre has a deep meaning in cyberfeminism. Drüeke & Zobl (2016) explain that a feminist protest is connected to a feminist cause and goes beyond digital spheres and becomes a movement. The same occurs with the profile, which created a movement of women who fight for the awareness and liberation of fat bodies. The hashtag brings together this content and unites women who fight against the discrimination of fat women. Mishra (2020) explains that women increasingly occupy social media and use feminist hashtags to express their ideas related to gender and everything that affects this atmosphere, such as their bodies.

Through images of human bodies, content with a focus on emotions, and the hashtag #corpolivre, this profile navigates social networks with an important discussion for today's society, seeking to disseminate the discourse of body acceptance and self-esteem. The content creators of the profile aim to question and propose an important reflection on beauty standards and people's experiences with aesthetic pressure, thus building a new social culture that accepts differences. The result of this process is the high levels of engagement through likes, comments, and content sharing.

To be successful in their narrative and connection with other women, it is clear that the profile needs to expose human bodies in different forms and show the digital community that a fat woman can wear whatever she wants. Brathwaite & DeAndrea (2022) assert that body acceptance movements on social media challenge traditional ideals of appearance and encourage increased representation and normalization of normal bodies. The analyzed posts have formats of diverse women's bodies and discuss how external aesthetic judgments affect people's self-image perception.

REFERENCES

Afful, A. A., & Ricciardelli, R. (2015). Shaping the online fat acceptance movement: Talking about body image and beauty standards. *Journal of Gender Studies*, *24*(4), 453–472. doi:10.1080/09589236.2015.1028523

Baer, H. (2016). Redoing feminism: Digital activism, body politics, and neoliberalism. *Feminist Media Studies*, *16*(1), 17–34. doi:10.1080/14680777.2015.1093070

Baker & Ryalls. (2016). Technologizing feminist pedagogy: Using blog activism in the gender studies classroom. *Feminist Teacher, 25*(1), 23. doi:10.5406/femteacher.25.1.0023

Banet-Weiser, S. (2018). Empowered: Popular feminism and popular misogyny. In Feminist Media Studies (Vol. 19, Issue 8). Duke University Press. doi:10.1080/14680777.2019.1685190

Bennett, W. L., & Segerberg, A. (2012). The logic of connective action: Digital media and the personalization of contentious politics. *Information Communication and Society*, *15*(5), 739–768. doi:10.1080/1369118X.2012.670661

Bijker, W. E., & Bijsterveld, K. (2000). Women walking through plans: Technology, democracy, and gender identity. *Technology and Culture*, *41*(3), 485–515. doi:10.1353/tech.2000.0091

Bombak, A. E., Meadows, A., & Billette, J. (2019). Fat acceptance 101: Midwestern American women's perspective on cultural body acceptance. *Health Sociology Review*, *28*(2), 194–208. doi:10.1080/14461242.2019.1604150

Bowles Eagle, R. (2015). Loitering, lingering, hashtagging: Women reclaiming public space via #Boardthebus, #Stopstreetharassment, and the #Everydaysexism project. *Feminist Media Studies*, *15*(2), 350–353. doi:10.1080/14680777.2015.1008748

Brathwaite, K. N., & DeAndrea, D. C. (2022). BoPopriation: How self-promotion and corporate commodification can undermine the body positivity (BoPo) movement on Instagram. *Communication Monographs*, *89*(1), 25–46. doi:10.1080/03637751.2021.1925939

Chen, G. M., Pain, P., & Barner, B. (2018). "Hashtag Feminism": Activism or Slacktivism? In D. Harp, J. Loke, & I. Bachman (Eds.), *Feminist Approaches to Media Theory and Research* (pp. 197–218). Palgrave Macmillan. doi:10.1007/978-3-319-90838-0_14

Clark, R. (2016). "Hope in a hashtag": The discursive activism of #WhyIStayed. *Feminist Media Studies*, *16*(5), 788–804. doi:10.1080/14680777.2016.1138235

Clifford, P. (2016). *Content Marketing*. John Wiley & Sons, Inc.

Cohen, R., Irwin, L., Newton-John, T., & Slater, A. (2019). #bodypositivity: A content analysis of body positive accounts on Instagram. *Body Image*, *29*, 47–57. doi:10.1016/j.bodyim.2019.02.007 PMID:30831334

Cooper, C. (2008). *What's Fat Activism?* https://www.ul.ie/sociology/docstore/workingpapers/wp2008-02.pdf

Cooper, C. (2011). Fat Lib: How Fat Activism Expands the Obesity Debate. In Debating Obesity (Vol. 1, pp. 164–191). Palgrave Macmillan.

DataReportal. (2022). *Global Digital Insights*. https://datareportal.com/

Drüeke, R., & Zobl, E. (2016). Online feminist protest against sexism: The German-language hashtag #aufschrei. *Feminist Media Studies*, *16*(1), 35–54. doi:10.1080/14680777.2015.1093071

Escosteguy, A. C. (2019). Mídia e questões de gênero no Brasil: pesquisa, categorias e feminismos. *XXVIII Encontro Anual Da Compós*. www.compos.org.brwww.compos.org.br/anais_encontros.php

Franklin, C. A. (2016). Sorority affiliation and sexual assault victimization: Assessing vulnerability using path analysis. *Violence Against Women*, *22*(8), 895–922. doi:10.1177/1077801215614971 PMID:26597086

Ging, D., & Siapera, E. (2018). Special issue on online misogyny. *Feminist Media Studies*, *18*(4), 515–524. doi:10.1080/14680777.2018.1447345

Gurrieri, L. (2013). Stocky bodies: Fat visual activism. *Fat Studies*, *2*(2), 197–209. doi:10.1080/21604851.2013.779554

Hardaker, C., & McGlashan, M. (2016). "Real men don't hate women": Twitter rape threats and group identity. *Journal of Pragmatics*, *91*, 80–93. doi:10.1016/j.pragma.2015.11.005

Ho, J., Pang, C., & Choy, C. (2020). Content marketing capability building: A conceptual framework. *Journal of Research in Interactive Marketing*, *14*(1), 133–151. doi:10.1108/JRIM-06-2018-0082

Holliman, G., & Rowley, J. (2014). Business to business digital content marketing: Marketers' perceptions of best practice. *Journal of Research in Interactive Marketing*, *8*(4), 269–293. doi:10.1108/JRIM-02-2014-0013

Hynnä, K., & Kyrölä, K. (2019). "Feel in Your Body": Fat Activist Affects in Blogs. *Social Media + Society*, *5*(4). Advance online publication. doi:10.1177/2056305119879983

Kangere, M., Kemitare, J., & Michau, L. (2017). Hashtag activism: Popularizing feminist analysis of violence against women in the Horn, East and Southern Africa. *Feminist Media Studies*, *17*(5), 899–902. doi:10.1080/14680777.2017.1350526

Keller, J. (2012). Virtual feminisms: Girls' blogging communities, feminist activism, and participatory politics. *Information Communication and Society*, *15*(3), 429–447. doi:10.1080/1369118X.2011.642890

Keller, J. (2017). Making activism accessible: Exploring girls' blogs as sites of contemporary feminist activism. In Girlhood and the Politics of Place (pp. 261–278). doi:10.2307/j.ctt14jxn16.20

Khurana, P., & Knight, T. (2021). Content Analysis of Athletic Brand Posts on Instagram. *Proceedings of the New York State Communication Association*.

Koiso-Kanttila, N. (2004). Digital Content Marketing: A Literature Synthesis. *Journal of Marketing Management*, *20*(1–2), 45–65. doi:10.1362/026725704773041122

Linabary, J. R., Corple, D. J., & Cooky, C. (2019). Feminist activism in digital space: Postfeminist contradictions in #WhyIStayed. *New Media & Society*, 1–22. doi:10.1177/1461444819884635

Matich, M., Ashman, R., & Parsons, E. (2019). #freethenipple–digital activism and embodiment in the contemporary feminist movement. *Consumption Markets & Culture*, *22*(4), 337–362. doi:10.1080/10253866.2018.1512240

Mendes, K., Ringrose, J., & Keller, J. (2019). *Digital feminist activism: Girls and women fight back against rape culture.* OUP USA. https://digitalfeministcollective.net/

Mishra, S. (2020). From # MeToo to # MeTooIndia : News Domestication in Indian English Language Newspaper. *Journalism Studies*, *21*(5), 1–19. doi:10.1080/1461670X.2019.1709882

Myles, D. (2019). Anne goes rogue for abortion rights!: Hashtag feminism and the polyphonic nature of activist discourse. *New Media & Society*, *21*(2), 507–527. doi:10.1177/1461444818800242

Oyosoro, F. I., Okafor, C. I., & Aigbe, R. (2022). The #EndSARS protest and Black cyberfeminism: A study of the Feminist Coalition and the rise of cyber-feminist ideologies in Nigeria. *Gender, Technology and Development*, *26*(3), 485–502. Advance online publication. doi:10.1080/09718524.2022.2144099

PettyJohn, M. E., Muzzey, F. K., Maas, M. K., & McCauley, H. L. (2018). #HowIWillChange: Engaging Men and Boys in the #MeToo Movement. *Psychology of Men & Masculinity*, (October). Advance online publication. doi:10.1037/men0000186

Puhakka, A. (2021). Sofie's World: Resistance toward the Thin Ideal in Sofie Hagen's Fat Activist Online Content. In Appearance as Capital: The Normative Regulation of Aesthetic Capital Accumulation and Conversion (pp. 135–148). Emerald Group Publishing Ltd. doi:10.1108/978-1-80043-708-120210009

Purba, K. R., Asirvatham, D., & Murugesan, R. K. (2021). Instagram post popularity trend analysis and prediction using hashtag, image assessment, and user history features. *The International Arab Journal of Information Technology*, *18*(1), 85–94. doi:10.34028/iajit/18/1/10

Retallack, H., Ringrose, J., & Lawrence, E. (2016). "Fuck Your Body Image": Teen girls' Twitter and Instagram feminism in and around school. *Learning Bodies - Perspectives on Children and Young People, 2*, 85–103. doi:10.2307/j.ctv62hhgr

Rietveld, R., van Dolen, W., Mazloom, M., & Worring, M. (2020). What You Feel, Is What You Like Influence of Message Appeals on Customer Engagement on Instagram. *Journal of Interactive Marketing*, *49*(1), 20–53. doi:10.1016/j.intmar.2019.06.003

Rivers, N. (2017a). Celebrity Feminists: Selling Feminism or Feminism Selling Out? In Postfeminism(s) and the Arrival of the Fourth Wave: Turning Tides (pp. 1–162). doi:10.1007/978-3-319-59812-3

Rivers, N. (2017b). New Media, New Feminism? In Postfeminism(s) and the Arrival of the Fourth Wave: Turning Tides (pp. 107–131). doi:10.1007/978-3-319-59812-3

Rodgers, R. F., Paxton, S. J., & Wertheim, E. H. (2021). Take idealized bodies out of the picture: A scoping review of social media content aiming to protect and promote positive body image. In *Body Image* (Vol. 38, pp. 10–36). Elsevier Ltd. doi:10.1016/j.bodyim.2021.03.009

Rodino-colocino, M. (2014). #YesAllWomen: Intersectional Mobilization Against Sexual Assault is Radical (Again). *Feminist Media Studies*, *14*(6), 1113–1115. doi:10.1080/14680777.2014.975475

Salazar, E. (2017). Hashtags 2.0 - An annotated history of the hashtag and a window to its future. *Revista ICONO14 Revista Científica de Comunicación y Tecnologías Emergentes, 15*(2), 16. doi:10.7195/ri14.v15i2.1091

Statista. (2022, January 18). *Instagram users worldwide 2022*. Statista.

Taylor, J., Johnston, J., & Whitehead, K. (2016). A Corporation in feminist clothing? Young women discuss the Dove real beaut campaign. *Critical Sociology*, *42*(1), 123–144. doi:10.1177/0896920513501355

Thompson, L. (2018). "I can be your tinder nightmare": Harassment and misogyny in the online sexual marketplace. *Feminism & Psychology*, *28*(1), 69–89. doi:10.1177/0959353517720226

Thrift, S. C. (2014). #YesAllWomen as feminist meme event. *Feminist Media Studies*, *14*(6), 1090–1092. doi:10.1080/14680777.2014.975421

Towns, A. R. (2016). Geographies of Pain: #SayHerName and the fear of black women's mobility. *Women's Studies in Communication*, *39*(2), 122–126. doi:10.1080/07491409.2016.1176807

Valentini, C., Romenti, S., Murtarelli, G., & Pizzetti, M. (2018). Digital visual engagement: Influencing purchase intentions on Instagram. *Journal of Communication Management (London)*, *22*(4), 362–381. doi:10.1108/JCOM-01-2018-0005

Varela, N. (2019). *Feminismo 4.0. La cuarta ola*. Ediciones B.

Viana, G. de C. S. (2019). *Ciberfeminismo e a (in) visibilidade da mulher negra youtuber*. Universidade Federal do Rio Grande do Norte.

Wang, B., & Driscoll, C. (2019). Chinese feminists on social media: Articulating different voices, building strategic alliances. *Continuum (Perth)*, *33*(1), 1–15. doi:10.1080/10304312.2018.1532492

Williams, S. (2015). Digital defense: Black feminists resist violence with hashtag activism. *Feminist Media Studies*, *15*(2), 341–344. doi:10.1080/14680777.2015.1008744

Winderman, E. (2019). Anger's volumes: Rhetorics of amplification and aggregation in #MeToo. *Women's Studies in Communication*, *42*(3), 327–346. doi:10.1080/07491409.2019.1632234

Yousaf, A., Amin, I., Jaziri, D., & Mishra, A. (2021). Effect of message orientation/vividness on consumer engagement for travel brands on social networking sites. *Journal of Product and Brand Management*, *30*(1), 44–57. doi:10.1108/JPBM-08-2019-2546

Chapter 19
A Study of Cyber Threats on Physical and Mental Health With Special Reference to Pandemic Times

Sanju Choudhary
University of Rajasthan, India

Vishva Chaudhary
https://orcid.org/0000-0003-3180-6448
University of Rajasthan, India

Vijendra Singh Meel
Samsung India, India

ABSTRACT

Cyber security has always been critical for safeguarding sensitive information, but in recent years, its impact on physical health has become increasingly apparent. The need for cyber security has become more critical in the digital age, as cyber threats have become more sophisticated and pervasive. As healthcare becomes increasingly digitized, the need for robust cyber security measures has become more important than ever. Cyber-attacks on healthcare systems can have devastating consequences on patient care, as the loss of crucial patient information can lead to delays or errors in medical treatment. Moreover, the pandemic has accelerated the shift to remote healthcare and telemedicine, leading to an increase in cyber-attacks on personal devices used for medical purposes, such as laptops and smartphones. These attacks can compromise personal health data, leading to delayed or ineffective medical treatment.

DOI: 10.4018/978-1-6684-8893-5.ch019

INTRODUCTION

The COVID-19 proved to be a global crises. These pandemic times literally ravaged the psyche of the people. It proved to be more than a disease. It deeply impacted us at unconscious and subconscious levels of our brains and evoked rage, violence, exclusion, panic, paranoid suspiciousness. People responded to the pandemic in different ways and at different levels in their own specific ways. The cure of the disease became worse than the disease itself. People even today are limping back to a semblance of normalcy. The disease was not only a health crises but also a humanitarian crises. It had severe and far fetching repercussions for health systems throughout the globe. Countless people died, or lost their livelihood. The heath sector too was disturbed in various ways and technology became the greatest support as never before. As in recent years technology has brought revolutionary changes in the lives of human beings. This was very well felt during the pandemic times. Technology, though has simplified the lives of human being but the sad part of the story is that technology itself is in danger of cyber threats. In today's digital age, cyber security has increasingly become crucial for individuals and organizations to protect their sensitive information from cyber threats. However, the impact of cyber security on physical health is often overlooked. The paper will explore the relationship between cyber security and physical health, highlighting the potential consequences of cyber-attacks on personal health and wellbeing.

Cyber security and physical health refer to the potential impact of cyber-attacks on an individual's physical health and wellbeing. With the increasing dependence on technology in healthcare, cyber-attacks on healthcare systems can potentially put patients' health at risk. Cyber-attacks on medical devices such as pacemakers or insulin pumps can be life-threatening if compromised. The rise of remote healthcare due to the COVID-19 pandemic has also increased the risk of cyber- attacks on personal devices used for healthcare purposes, potentially exposing personal health information and compromising the effectiveness of medical treatment. Moreover, the rise of remote healthcare and telemedicine due to the COVID-19 pandemic has increased the risk of cyber-attacks on personal devices used for healthcare purposes. Cyber-attacks on personal devices used for healthcare, such as smartphones or laptops, can potentially expose personal health information and compromise the effectiveness of medical treatment, it is essential to understand the relationship between cyber security and physical health to prevent potential harm and ensure the safety and security of healthcare systems, devices, and personal health information. The relationship between cyber security and physical health refers to the potential impact of cyber-attacks on an individual's physical health and wellbeing. With the increasing dependence on technology in healthcare, cyber-attacks on healthcare systems can potentially put patients' health at risk. For example, a cyber-attack on a hospital's network may result in the loss of critical patient information, leading to delays or errors in medical treatment. In addition, cyber-attacks can also target medical devices such as pacemakers or insulin pumps, which can be life-threatening if compromised.

Cyber Security and Its Need in the Present Digital Era

Cyber security has always been critical for safeguarding sensitive information, but in recent years, its impact on physical and mental health has become increasingly apparent. In the recent times we have a "tsunami of connectedness" which has become a challenge for each one of us. The need for cyber security has become more critical in the digital age, as cyber threats have become more sophisticated and pervasive. As healthcare becomes increasingly digitized, the need for robust cyber security measures has become more important than ever. Cyber-attacks on healthcare systems can have devastating consequences on patient care, as the loss of crucial patient information can lead to delays or errors in medical treatment. Moreover, the pandemic has accelerated the shift to remote healthcare and telemedicine, leading to an increase in cyber-attacks on personal devices used for medical purposes, such as laptops and smartphones. These attacks can compromise personal health data, leading to delayed or ineffective medical treatment. Furthermore, the growing use of *Internet of Things* (IoT) devices in healthcare, such as wearable health monitors, may lead to additional security risks that need to be addressed to ensure patient safety. Thus, it is imperative to continuously evaluate and enhance cyber security measures to prevent potential harm and safeguard the physical health and well-being of individuals.

There are several reasons why cyber security is essential in healthcare.

Firstly, cyber-attacks can lead to the loss or theft of critical patient information, resulting in delays or errors in medical treatment, which can cause serious harm or even loss of life. *Secondly,* cyber-attacks can target medical devices such as pacemakers or insulin pumps, compromising patients' health and wellbeing. *Thirdly*, the COVID-19 pandemic has led to an increase in remote healthcare, which increases the risk of cyber-attacks on personal devices used for healthcare purposes, exposing personal health information.

The physical safety of patients is also at risk when cyber security is compromised. In 2017, the *WannaCry ransomware* attack impacted healthcare systems worldwide, causing widespread disruption to patient care (Jun Li & et al., 2023). The attack highlighted the vulnerability of healthcare systems to cyber-attacks, as patient care was severely impacted by the loss of access to vital patient data. In another example, the *Triton malware attack in 2018* targeted an industrial facility in the Middle East, causing a shutdown of critical safety systems and resulting in physical damage to the facility. These incidents demonstrate that cyber-attacks can have real-world, physical consequences, and highlight the need for robust cyber security measures in healthcare systems and medical devices (Myung, J. W., & Hong, S., 2019).

The consequences of cyber-attacks can be severe and long-lasting and crucial for individuals and organizations ranging from financial loss to reputational damage and, in extreme cases, physical harm. Beyond healthcare, cyber-attacks on critical infrastructure such as power grids, transportation systems, and water treatment plants can have far-reaching and potentially devastating consequences. For instance, a cyber-attack on a power grid could result in blackouts and cause harm to people who rely on electricity for medical treatment or other essential services. Moreover, cyber-attacks can also impact mental health, causing anxiety, stress, and other psychological effects. Individuals who have been victims of cyber-attacks may experience a sense of violation or loss of control, leading to feelings of distress or even trauma. The psychological impact of cyber-attacks on individuals and communities can be significant and long-lasting and can have serious implications. For instance, Cyber-attacks on healthcare systems can compromise medical treatment and jeopardize patient safety, as it happened in the recent ransom ware attack on *Ireland's National Health Service*. The consequences of these attacks can be severe and long-lasting, leading to both physical and mental health issues. (McGorry, P., Bates, T., & Birchwood, M., 2013).

Internet of Things (IoT) and Physical Health

The increasing usage of *Internet of Things (*IoT) devices in the healthcare industry, the potential attack surface has grown immensely. We have become more vulnerable to cyber-attacks. To address these challenges, it is essential to prioritize cyber security measures to ensure the safety and security of sensitive information and critical infrastructure. This includes raising awareness about the importance of cyber security, developing and implementing robust cyber security policies and procedures, and investing in cyber security technologies. In addition to addressing cyber security risks and vulnerabilities, it is also crucial to have a robust incident response plan in place to mitigate the impact of cyber-attacks. An incident response plan should include procedures for detecting, containing, and eradicating cyber threats, as well as communication protocols for notifying stakeholders, including employees, customers, and regulators, of the incident. Effective incident response planning can help minimize the damage caused by cyber-attacks and enable organizations to recover more quickly. Ultimately, by taking a comprehensive and proactive approach to cyber security, we can help ensure the safety and security of our digital infrastructure, physical health, and well-being.

The rapid advancement of technology has made it possible to achieve significant progress in various fields, including medicine and finance. However, this progress has also paved the way for the increase in cyber-attacks, making cyber security a crucial aspect of modern-day living. A cyber-attack is a malicious attempt to gain unauthorized access to computers, networks, and data systems with the aim of stealing, disrupting or destroying sensitive information. Cyber criminals may employ several techniques such as malware, phishing, and ransom ware to accomplish their goals.

With the increasing use of the Internet of Things (IoT) in healthcare, the potential implications of cyber security on physical health are significant. Connected medical devices, such as those used to monitor patients remotely and transmit health data to healthcare providers in real-time, may be vulnerable to cyber-attacks. If such devices are compromised, patients could face life-threatening situations, as cybercriminals could control or manipulate devices, leading to incorrect dosages or complete shutdown. Moreover, attacks on a hospital's network or electronic health record system may result in patient data being stolen, altered, or deleted, compromising patient care and confidentiality. The impact of cyber-attacks can be devastating. It can disrupt business operations, leading to financial losses and damaging reputations. Additionally, it can jeopardize personal and sensitive information, including credit card data, social security numbers, and medical records, resulting in identity theft and other forms of fraudulent activities.

While cyber security is often seen as a purely technical issue, it is critical to recognize that it has significant implications for public health and safety. Cyber security breaches in healthcare can have far-reaching consequences beyond individual patient harm, such as public health emergencies or widespread public panic. For example, a cyber-attack on a hospital network could result in the loss of crucial medical data, creating confusion among healthcare providers and delaying critical medical treatments. In addition, compromised medical devices could lead to widespread health emergencies or even fatalities. As such, healthcare institutions and policymakers must take cyber security seriously and invest in the necessary resources to ensure the safety and security of patients' health and well-being. By doing so, we can help safeguard our digital infrastructure and protect public health from the increasingly complex and sophisticated cyber threats of the modern era.

Technology and Cyber-Attacks and Cyber Security

The use of technology in the healthcare industry has increased to improve patient care, but it has also made the industry vulnerable to cyber-attacks that can have severe consequences on patient health and safety. Hence, it is critical for the healthcare industry to give utmost importance to cyber security to protect patients' personal health information and prevent potential harm. Moreover, as the healthcare industry continues to embrace innovative technology, such as wearable devices and remote patient monitoring systems, the need for robust cyber security measures becomes more urgent. Failing to address cyber security concerns can result in significant harm to patients, such as the unauthorized access or manipulation of personal medical records or medical devices.

The threat of cyber-attacks on medical devices is particularly concerning, as compromised devices can have life-threatening implications. Medical devices like insulin pumps and pacemakers are increasingly connected to the internet and can be remotely accessed by healthcare providers for monitoring and adjusting treatment. However, this connectivity also makes them vulnerable to cyber-attacks. In 2019, the *US Food and Drug Administration* (FDA) issued a warning about a vulnerability in certain insulin pumps that could potentially be exploited by attackers. The vulnerability could allow attackers to remotely control the pump and deliver incorrect doses of insulin, which can be life-threatening for patients (Davis, A. A., & Patel, V. G., 2019).

The healthcare industry's growing dependence on technology has made it vulnerable to cyber-attacks, which can have severe consequences for patient health and well-being. Cyber-attacks targeting healthcare systems may lead to the loss or theft of critical patient information, resulting in delays or errors in medical treatment that can be harmful or fatal in some cases. Additionally, cyber-attacks may target medical devices such as pacemakers or insulin pumps, which can jeopardize patients' health and well-being. The COVID-19 pandemic's increase in remote healthcare has also raised the risk of cyber-attacks on personal devices used for healthcare, potentially exposing personal health information and compromising medical treatment effectiveness. Therefore, it is essential to prioritize cyber security measures to ensure the safety of individuals and communities. This includes training healthcare staff on the importance of cyber security and providing them with the necessary resources to identify and respond to potential threats. By doing so, we can ensure that healthcare systems, devices, and personal health data remain secure, and that patients' physical and mental well-being are protected. Therefore, prioritizing cyber security measures is critical for healthcare organizations to protect against cyber-attacks and ensure patient safety.

Case Studies of Cyber-Attacks on Healthcare Industry

The healthcare industry has experienced several notable cyber-attacks in recent years that have had serious implications for patient health and wellbeing. The following are some examples:

The Wanna Cry Ransomware Attack: In 2017, multiple hospitals and healthcare organizations in the UK were impacted by the WannaCry ransomware attack, which caused considerable disruptions to patient care. The attack encrypted computer files and demanded payment of a ransom in exchange for the decryption key (Mohurle, S., & Patil, M.,2017).

The University of Vermont Health Network attack: In 2020, the University of Vermont Health Network experienced a ransomware attack that affected their electronic medical record system, resulting in significant disruptions to patient care. Additionally, the attackers stole patient data, including Social Security numbers and medical histories (Stokes, A. M., 2022).

The Med Star Health attack: In 2016, the MedStar Health network, which operates over 250 outpatient clinics and ten hospitals in the Washington DC area, was targeted by a ransom ware attack that impacted the organization's electronic medical record system and led to major disruptions to patient care (Gordon, W. J., Fairhall, A., & Landman, A.,2017).

The Finnish psychotherapy centre attack: In 2020, a psychotherapy centre in Finland was impacted by a ransom ware attack that led to the theft of sensitive patient data, including mental health information. The attackers demanded payment of a ransom to prevent publishing the data online (Prime, H., Wade, M., & Browne, D. T., 2020).

These instances illustrate the severe consequences of cyber-attacks on the health measures to safeguard patient health and wellbeing.

Personal Cyber Security Practices for Physical and Mental Health

The increasing use of technology in healthcare has highlighted the importance of personal cyber security practices for physical health. Cyber-attacks on personal devices used for healthcare purposes, such as smartphones or laptops, can compromise the effectiveness of medical treatment and expose sensitive personal health information. For instance, if an individual's medical device is hacked, an attacker can manipulate the device's settings and cause harm to the user. Similarly, if personal health information is stolen, it can be used for fraudulent activities or identity theft, causing financial and emotional distress. Therefore, it is essential to comprehend the link between cyber security and physical health and take appropriate measures to safeguard healthcare systems, devices, and personal health information.

One of the most critical step in protecting personal health information is using strong passwords and keeping software up-to-date. Strong passwords with a mix of letters, numbers, and symbols can prevent attackers from accessing personal information. Additionally, keeping software up-to-date with the latest security patches and updates can close vulnerabilities that attackers can exploit. Moreover, avoiding suspicious links or emails can prevent phishing attacks, which are commonly used to steal personal information. Personal devices used for healthcare should also be encrypted and have remote wiping capabilities in case of theft or loss.

In addition to personal cyber security practices, healthcare organizations and device manufacturers should also prioritize cyber security to ensure patient safety. This includes conducting regular security audits, implementing multi-factor authentication, and using encryption to protect sensitive data. Device manufacturers should also design medical devices with security in mind and provide regular security updates to prevent vulnerabilities from being exploited. Healthcare professionals should be trained on cyber security best practices and understand the risks of cyber-attacks on healthcare systems and medical devices.

Future Implications and of Cyber Security on Physical Health

Considering the increasing reliance on technology in healthcare, the future implications of cyber security on physical health are significant. The evolving integration of technology into healthcare systems means that the risk of cyber-attacks will continue to rise. One potential implication is the emergence of new types of cyber threats, such as attacks on AI systems and deep fake technology's use to manipulate medical records or images, which can lead to misdiagnosis or delayed treatment, thus impacting physical health.

Another potential implication is the growing use of internet-connected medical devices, which can be vulnerable to cyber-attacks. These devices, such as insulin pumps or pacemakers, are critical for patients' health, and if compromised, can be life-threatening. As the number of these devices continues to increase, the risk of cyber-attacks targeting them also increases.

Additionally, the COVID-19 pandemic has accelerated the shift towards telemedicine and remote healthcare, making personal devices like smartphones and laptops a fundamental part of healthcare delivery. However, this shift also makes them potential targets for cyber-attacks, which can compromise medical treatment's effectiveness and expose personal health information.

To mitigate the potential implications of cyber security threats on physical health it has become an urgent need for organizations and individuals to prioritize cyber security in health care systems and personal devices. We need to implement robust security measures that are continuously updated to prevent any potential cyber threats. This includes regularly updating software and security protocols, training staff to identify and respond to potential threats, and conducting regular security audits. These measures include implementing encryption, multi-factor authentication, and intrusion detection systems to safeguard against unauthorized access and data breaches. It is crucial to ensure that medical devices are adequately tested and evaluated for security vulnerabilities before they are used on patients. Healthcare providers should prioritize the security of connected medical devices to ensure patient safety and confidentiality.

CONCLUSION

By prioritizing cyber security in healthcare, organizations can safeguard patient health and wellbeing, maintain trust in the healthcare system, and protect their reputation. By doing so, we can ensure the safety and security of healthcare systems, devices, and personal health information, reducing the potential impact of cyber security on physical health in the future.

In today's digital age, personal cyber security practices are critical for safeguarding both physical and mental health. Here are some recommended best practices to follow:

Ensure your devices and software are up to date: Keep your devices and software up to date by regularly applying the latest security patches to prevent known vulnerabilities.

Use strong and unique passwords: Generate strong passwords that are unique to each account and use a password manager to store them securely.

Enable two-factor authentication: Enhance security by enabling two-factor authentication, which requires a second form of verification in addition to a password.

Be cautious with public Wi-Fi: Public Wi-Fi networks can be insecure, so use a virtual private network (VPN) to encrypt your internet traffic when accessing public Wi-Fi.

Be wary of phishing scams: Stay vigilant of phishing scams, which can trick you into giving away sensitive information. Be cautious of unsolicited emails and avoid clicking on suspicious links or downloading attachments from unknown sources.

Limit personal information online: Be mindful of the personal information you share online and check your privacy settings on social media platforms to limit the amount of information you share publicly.

Take care of your mental health: Digital devices and social media can negatively affect mental health, so limit your screen time and engage in activities that promote mental well-being, such as meditation or exercise. Seek professional help if needed.

By adopting these personal cyber security practices, one can protect oneself against cyber threats and promote both physical and mental well-being in the digital age.

REFERENCES

Bailey, J. (2014). "Sexualized online bullying" through an equality lens: Missed opportunity in AB v. Bragg? *McGill Law Journal. Revue de Droit de McGill*, *59*(3), 709–737. doi:10.7202/1025142ar

Davis, A. A., & Patel, V. G. (2019). The role of PD-L1 expression as a predictive biomarker: An analysis of all US Food and Drug Administration (FDA) approvals of immune checkpoint inhibitors. *Journal for Immunotherapy of Cancer*, *7*(1), 1–8. doi:10.118640425-019-0768-9 PMID:31655605

Gordon, W. J., Fairhall, A., & Landman, A. (2017). Threats to information security—Public health implications. *The New England Journal of Medicine*, *377*(8), 707–709. doi:10.1056/NEJMp1707212 PMID:28700269

Li, J., Niu, J., Qian, X., & Liu, Y. (2023). Real-Time Ransomware Detection Method Based on TextGCN. In *2023 6th International Conference on Artificial Intelligence and Big Data (ICAIBD)* (pp. 535-541). IEEE. 10.1109/ICAIBD57115.2023.10206378

McGorry, P., Bates, T., & Birchwood, M. (2013). Designing youth mental health services for the 21st century: Examples from Australia, Ireland and the UK. *The British Journal of Psychiatry*, *202*(54), 30–35. doi:10.1192/bjp.bp.112.119214 PMID:23288499

Mohurle, S., & Patil, M. (2017). A brief study of wannacry threat: Ransomware attack 2017. *International Journal of Advanced Research in Computer Science, 8*(5), 1938-1940.

Myung, J. W., & Hong, S. (2019). ICS malware Triton attack and countermeasures. *Int. J. Emerg. Multidiscip. Res*, *3*, 13–17.

Prime, H., Wade, M., & Browne, D. T. (2020). Risk and resilience in family well-being during the COVID-19 pandemic. *The American Psychologist*, *75*(5), 631–643. doi:10.1037/amp0000660 PMID:32437181

Rathi, S., & Chaudhary, V. (2023). Effect of Eye Yoga and Mindful Relaxation Practices on Management of Digital Eye Strain in a Tertiary Care Hospital: A Comparative Interventional Study. *Journal for ReAttach Therapy and Developmental Diversities*, *6*(8s), 40–44.

Stokes, A. M. (2022). Disruption of Library Services Due to Hospital Cyberattack: A Case Study. *Medical Reference Services Quarterly*, *41*(2), 204–212. doi:10.1080/02763869.2022.2054198 PMID:35511424

Chapter 20
A Study of Social Media and Cyber Bullying:
Addressing a Growing Problem

Anil Kumar Saraswat
Samsung India Electronics, New Delhi, India

Vijendra Singh Meel
Samsung India Electronics, New Delhi, India

ABSTRACT

The use of social media has become increasingly prevalent over the past decade, with platforms such as Facebook, Twitter, and Instagram boasting billions of active users. Social media platforms provide users with a variety of ways to connect with others, including the ability to share photos, videos, and messages in real-time. However, this increased connectivity has also led to a rise in cyber-bullying. Cyber-bullying refers to the use of electronic devices and technology, such as social media platforms, to harass, intimidate, or embarrass others. Cyber-bullying can take many forms, including spreading rumors, making threats, and posting hurtful or humiliating comments or images. Unlike traditional forms of bullying, cyber-bullying can occur 24/7, and the anonymity afforded by social media platforms can make it difficult to identify perpetrators.

INTRODUCTION

Cyber-bullying is the deliberate and repeated use of electronic devices to harm, intimidate, or harass an individual or group. It can manifest in various forms, such as sending threatening messages, spreading rumours, sharing private information, impersonating others, or posting hurtful comments, images, or videos online. The impact of cyber-bullying on victims can be severe and enduring. Victims of cyber-bullying often experience emotional distress, anxiety, depression, lowered self-esteem, and social isolation. The persistent harassment and humiliation can have detrimental effects on their mental health, well-being, and overall quality of life. "Cyber-bullying can also disrupt victims' academic or professional

DOI: 10.4018/978-1-6684-8893-5.ch020

performance, relationships, and daily activities (Dehue et al., 2018). In some cases, it has even resulted in "serious consequences, such as self-harm, suicide, or other forms of self-destructive behaviour" (Walrave & Heirman, 2011).

The anonymity and detachment provided by social media platforms can amplify the impact of cyber-bullying, as perpetrators may feel empowered to engage in harmful behaviour without facing immediate consequences (Mesch, 2009). Furthermore, the viral nature of social media can lead to the rapid spread of cyber-bullying, involving a wider audience in witnessing and participating in the harassment. It is crucial to acknowledge the significant impact of cyber-bullying on victims and take proactive measures to prevent and address this harmful behaviour effectively. The present chapter attempts to define and explore varied dimensions and impact of cyber bullying in the present times. The paper is divided into various sections to discuss the concepts and evaluate the impact and suggest solutions to combat this very critical issue.

Cyber-bullying can have profound psychological and emotional effects on victims, leading to a range of negative outcomes that may persist long after the bullying has stopped. Among the most common impacts of cyber-bullying on victims are feelings of anxiety, depression, low self-esteem, and social isolation. Research has shown that "victims of cyber-bullying are at an increased risk of developing anxiety and depression, which can be debilitating and negatively impact their quality of life" (Jackson, 2011). Additionally, cyber-bullying can erode a victim's sense of self-worth, leading to feelings of inadequacy and self-doubt, and negatively affect their relationships with others. Victims may also feel isolated and excluded from social groups, leading to feelings of loneliness and further exacerbating the negative effects of the bullying. Physical symptoms, such as headaches, stomach-aches, and sleep disturbances, may also result from the stress and anxiety caused by the bullying. In severe cases, cyber-bullying can even lead to suicidal ideation and self-harm. Victims may feel trapped and helpless, with no escape from the bullying, leading to feelings of hopelessness and despair. It is essential to recognize the severity of these impacts and to work towards preventing cyber-bullying to ensure the safety and wellbeing of individuals online.

Cyber-bullying refers to the use of electronic devices and technology, such as social media platforms, to harass, intimidate, or embarrass others. Cyber-bullying can take many forms, including spreading rumours, making threats, and posting hurtful or humiliating comments or images. Unlike traditional forms of bullying, cyber-bullying can occur 24/7, and the anonymity afforded by social media platforms can make it difficult to identify perpetrators.

One factor contributing to the rise of cyber-bullying is the ease of access to social media platforms. Many young people have access to smartphones and other electronic devices, which can make it easier for them to engage in cyber-bullying. Additionally, social media platforms provide a wider audience for cyber-bullying, as messages and images can be shared with a large number of people instantaneously.

Another factor contributing to the rise of cyber-bullying is the lack of consequences for perpetrators. Because social media platforms are often viewed as separate from the real world, some individuals may feel emboldened to engage in cyber-bullying without fear of repercussions. Additionally, the anonymity afforded by social media platforms can make it difficult to identify perpetrators, which can make it challenging to hold them accountable for their actions.

Section One: Understanding Cyber-Bullying on Social Media

Understanding cyber-bullying on social media goes beyond recognizing its various forms, motivations, and dynamics. Berthaud J has rightly opined that "It involves a comprehensive understanding of the risk factors, vulnerability of victims, and the severe impact it can have on them" (Berthaud & Smith, n.d.). Additionally, recognizing the legal and ethical implications of cyber-bullying is crucial. Here are some key aspects to consider:

Forms of cyber-bullying: Cyber-bullying on social media can manifest in different ways and forms including sending threatening messages, sharing private information, spreading rumors, impersonating others, or posting hurtful comments, images, or videos. It occurs on various platforms like Facebook, Twitter, Instagram, Snapchat, and others.

Motivation behind cyber-bullying: Cyber-bullies engage in such behavior for various reasons, such as seeking power and control, attention or validation, revenge, boredom, jealousy, or prejudice etc. Understanding the underlying motivations is important in addressing the root causes of cyber-bullying (Jones et al., 2011).

Dynamics of cyber-bullying: Cyber-bullying often involves an imbalance of power, where the perpetrator seeks to intimidate or harm a victim who may be perceived as vulnerable or different. The anonymity and detachment provided by social media can embolden cyber-bullies, and the viral nature of social media can amplify the impact of cyber-bullying, spreading it to a wider audience.

Risk factors and vulnerability: Certain individuals may be more vulnerable to cyber-bullying, such as those with a history of bullying, low self-esteem, lack of social support, or mental health issues. Understanding the risk factors and vulnerability can aid in identifying and supporting potential victims of cyber-bullying.

Section Two: Explanation of How Social Media Platforms Are Used to Facilitate Cyber-Bullying

Social media platforms have become prevalent avenues for cyber-bullying due to their widespread usage and the convenience of communication they offer. These are a few ways in which social media platforms are utilized to facilitate cyber-bullying:

Direct messages: Cyber-bullies can leverage direct messages on social media platforms to send threatening or derogatory messages to their victims. These private channels permit them to intimidate or harass their victims without others being aware of the content of the messages.

Public posts: Cyber-bullies can employ public posts on social media platforms to spread rumors, share embarrassing information, or post hurtful comments, images, or videos about their victims. These public posts are visible to a wide audience, and the viral nature of social media can lead to the rapid dissemination of bullying content.

Fake accounts or impersonation: Cyber-bullies may create fake accounts on social media platforms to impersonate others and engage in bullying behavior causing emotional distress and harm.

Cyberbullying groups or communities: Some social media platforms allow the creation of groups or communities where like-minded individuals can gather. Cyber-bullies can form groups or communities to collectively target and harass their victims. They can share harmful content, coordinate attacks, or amplify bullying behavior through these groups.

Cyberbullying through comments and replies: Cyber-bullies can use comments and replies on social media platforms to post hurtful or derogatory comments about their victims' posts or profiles. They can also engage in "pile-on" behavior, where multiple individuals join in on the bullying by adding negative comments or replies to the victim's posts, amplifying the harassment.

Cyberbullying through sharing and tagging: Cyber-bullies can also exploit the sharing and tagging features on social media platforms to spread harmful content about their victims. They can share embarrassing information, images, or videos and tag the victim, making the content visible to a wider audience and causing embarrassment and distress.

It is crucial to recognize that social media platforms can be misused as a means to facilitate cyber-bullying. The anonymity, ease of communication, and viral nature of social media can embolden cyber-bullies to engage in harmful behavior. It is imperative to take appropriate measures to prevent and address cyber-bullying effectively on social media platforms.

Section Three: The Scope of the Problem

Examination of research and statistics related to the prevalence of cyber-bullying on social media:

Research has also revealed that the prevalence of cyber-bullying on social media varies by age and gender. Adolescents and young adults are found to be more vulnerable to cyber-bullying compared to older age groups, and females are more likely to be victims, while males may be more likely to engage in cyber-bullying behaviour. The impact of cyber-bullying on mental health is well-documented, with research indicating that victims of cyber-bullying are at an increased risk of experiencing depression, anxiety, and other mental health issues. Cyber-bullying can also lead to decreased self-esteem, increased social isolation, and even suicidal ideation, underscoring the serious consequences.

It is important to note that cyber-bullying on social media may be significantly underreported, as many victims feel hesitant or fearful of reporting incidents. This can result in an inaccurate representation of the true prevalence of the issue. Different types of cyber-bullying occur on social media, including harassment, public shaming, rumour spreading, impersonation, and more, as discussed in previous responses, according to research findings. Efforts to prevent cyber-bullying on social media have also been explored in studies, with interventions such as increased awareness, education, and supportive school and community environments shown to be effective in mitigating the prevalence of cyber-bullying.

Research and statistics shed a good deal of light on the extent of cyber-bullying on social media, revealing concerning frequencies of this phenomenon. Numerous studies have been conducted to understand the scope and impact of cyber-bullying, and the findings provide valuable insights into its prevalence. Globally, a survey conducted by Ipsos MORI in 28 countries found that 25% of young people aged 18-24 reported experiencing cyber-bullying on social media, indicating that it is a widespread issue affecting individuals worldwide. Similarly, national surveys in various countries, such as a study by the National Institutes of Health in the United States, have shown significant rates of cyber-bullying among middle and high school students, with social media being a common platform for such incidents.

Section Four: Analysis of the Legal and Ethical Implications of Cyber-Bullying on Social Media Platforms

Cyber-bullying can have severe *legal consequences*, especially when it involves harassment, threats, or hate speech. "The severity of the offense can result in civil or criminal charges, including fines, imprisonment, or both" (Hinduja & Patchin, 2008). Social media platforms can also be held accountable if they fail to take adequate measures to address cyber-bullying on their platforms or violate users' privacy rights. In some countries, such as the United States, the Communications Decency Act provides legal immunity to social media platforms regarding user-generated content. However, "this immunity is not absolute, and platforms may still be held liable for certain types of content, such as child pornography or copyright infringement" (Mishna et al., 2009).

Social media platforms have an *ethical obligation* to ensure a safe and supportive environment for their users. They must develop policies and practices that adhere to ethical standards and values, including respect for human dignity, privacy, and freedom of expression. Additionally, social media platforms must consider the potential impact of their policies and practices on marginalized groups and take appropriate measures to reduce the harm caused by cyber-bullying. Ethical considerations also extend to the use of algorithms and other technologies that can exacerbate cyber-bullying on social media platforms. Platforms must ensure that their use of technology is in line with ethical principles and does not contribute to the spread of harmful content.

Section Five: Approaches to Address Cyber-Bullying on Social Media

Cyber-bullying is a complex and pervasive issue that requires a multifaceted approach to combat it effectively. Various approaches can be utilized to combat this problem. Some of the approaches include:

Education and Awareness: Educating people, especially young people, about cyber-bullying can be an effective approach. This can be done through classroom education, workshops, and online resources that promote responsible online behavior and digital citizenship.

Reporting Mechanisms: Social media platforms can implement reporting mechanisms that enable users to report instances of cyber-bullying. Bauman has cited that "Reports can be reviewed by trained moderators who can take necessary action, such as removing the offending content or banning the responsible user" (Holladay, 2011).

Moderation and Enforcement: Employing moderators responsible for monitoring user-generated content and enforcing community guidelines can help to prevent and control cyber-bullying. Moderators can remove content that violates guidelines or ban users who repeatedly engage in cyber-bullying.

Empowering Bystanders: Bystanders can play a vital role in combating cyber-bullying by reporting instances of cyber-bullying and supporting victims. Social media platforms can encourage bystanders to report incidents and provide resources to empower them to take action.

Counseling and Support: Victims of cyber-bullying may require counseling and support to cope with the emotional and psychological impact of the bullying. Social media platforms can partner with mental health organizations to provide resources and support to victims.

Examination of the Effectiveness of Each Approach and the Challenges Associated With Implementation

To combat cyber-bullying effectively, a multi-faceted approach is necessary, and each approach has its strengths and weaknesses, which depends on various factors. Let's examine the effectiveness and challenges associated with implementing each approach:

Education and Awareness: Educating individuals about cyber-bullying is a proactive approach that can help prevent cyber-bullying. But, "it requires resources like trained educators, appropriate materials, and funding" (Trolley, n.d.). Moreover, it can be challenging to reach the intended audience, particularly when cyber-bullying occurs outside of the school or workplace.

Reporting Mechanisms: Reporting mechanisms provide victims and bystanders with a means to report instances of cyber-bullying, which can lead to the removal of offending content or consequences for the bully. However, it can be difficult to manage and review large volumes of reports effectively. Additionally, some bullies may create new accounts or use anonymous profiles to avoid being identified, making it difficult to take action.

Moderation and Enforcement: Moderation and enforcement involve the use of trained moderators responsible for monitoring user-generated content and enforcing community guidelines. However, it can be resource-intensive, particularly for large social media platforms. Moderators must be well-trained to identify cyber-bullying, which can be difficult in cases where the bullying is subtle or disguised.

Empowering Bystanders: Empowering bystanders involves encouraging individuals to speak out against cyber-bullying and support victims. Humphrey and Symes (2010) stated "students with exceptionalities are bullied at all grade levels, as well as in and away from school. Students with exceptionalities may be bullied directly or indirectly It can create a culture of support and accountability"(Humphrey and Symes 82) But, encouraging bystanders to report requires trust in reporting mechanisms, which can be difficult to establish. Additionally, bystanders may face retaliation from bullies, which can discourage them from speaking out.

Counseling and Support: Counseling and support provide victims of cyber-bullying with resources and support to cope with the emotional and psychological impact of the bullying. It can be effective in helping victims recover from the trauma of cyber-bullying. But, victims may be reluctant to seek help, and providing counseling and support can be resource-intensive and require trained professionals.

Case Studies and Examples of Best Practices

There are various successful approaches that can be taken to address cyber-bullying on social media. Here are some examples of best practices and case studies:

Instagram's Hidden Words: To reduce cyber-bullying on the platform, Instagram has implemented "Hidden Words," which filters out offensive words and phrases from comments. By automatically preventing offensive comments from being posted, the feature has been successful in reducing bullying comments by 40% in early test" (Mesch, 2009).

Twitter's Safety Centre: Twitter's Safety Centre empowers users to take action to protect themselves from cyber-bullying by providing them with resources and information about reporting abusive behavior, managing privacy and security settings, and blocking or muting users.

Snapchat's Support for Mental Health: Snapchat recognizes the emotional impact of cyber-bullying on victims and has partnered with organizations like Crisis Text Line and the National Eating Disorders Association to provide resources and support for mental health issues.

TikTok's Community Guidelines: TikTok's community guidelines outline rules against cyber-bullying and harassment and are enforced by moderators who remove content that violates the guidelines. By creating a safe and positive environment on the platform, cyber-bullying is deterred.

The #BeStrong Anti-Bullying Campaign: The #BeStrong campaign, launched by anti-bullying organization Ditch the Label and promoted by celebrities like Paris Hilton and Liam Payne, raises awareness about cyber-bullying and encourages individuals to take action to combat it. The campaign provides victims with resources such as a bullying helpline and an online support community. It has been successful in providing support and resources to victims and raising awareness about cyber-bullying (Miller & Hufstedler, 2009).

Analysis of the Factors That Contributed to the Success of These Approaches

Collaborations and partnerships are a common factor in successful approaches to addressing cyber-bullying on social media. For instance, Snapchat's collaboration with Crisis Text Line and the National Eating Disorders Association provides users with resources and support for mental health issues. These partnerships ensure that users have access to necessary resources and support to cope with cyber-bullying.

Empowerment and education are also crucial in successful approaches to addressing cyber-bullying. Platforms that focus on empowering users with the knowledge and tools to combat cyber-bullying can make a significant impact. For instance, Twitter's Safety Center provides resources and information on how to stay safe on the platform. Instagram's "Hidden Words" feature automatically filters out offensive words and phrases in comments, empowering users to protect themselves. By educating users and giving them the power to protect themselves, these platforms can help prevent cyber-bullying.

Effective moderation is another essential factor in reducing cyber-bullying. Platforms like TikTok use moderation techniques to monitor user-generated content and enforce community guidelines that deter cyber-bullying. TikTok's community guidelines outline rules against cyber-bullying and harassment, and moderators are responsible for removing content that violates the guidelines. Effective moderation helps create a safe and positive environment on the platform.

Public awareness and support campaigns can make a significant difference in combating cyber-bullying. The #Be Strong campaign, launched by the anti-bullying organization Ditch the Label and promoted by celebrities like Paris Hilton and Liam Payne, is an example of a successful public awareness campaign. Such campaigns raise "awareness about cyber-bullying and provide resources and support to victims, reducing the stigma associated with cyber-bullying and encouraging individuals to speak out against it" (Cowie & Colliety, 2010).

In this chapter, the successful approaches to combatting cyber-bullying on social media were discussed with examples of best practices and case studies. The effectiveness of these approaches was attributed to several factors, including partnerships between social media platforms and organizations specializing in mental health, anti-bullying, and digital safety; empowering users with knowledge and tools to combat cyber-bullying; effective moderation techniques to monitor user-generated content and enforce community guidelines; and public awareness campaigns that raise awareness about cyber-bullying and provide resources and support to victims. The chapter emphasized the need for a multi-faceted approach to prevent, educate, and support victims of cyber-bullying, ultimately creating a safer and more positive environment on social media platforms.

REFERENCES

Bhat, C., Suniti, C., Shih-Hua, L., & Jamie, A. (2010). Addressing cyber bullying's media literacy. *New Horizons in Education*, *58*(3), 34–43.

Cowie, H., & Colliety, P. (2010). Cyberbullying: Sanctions or sensitivity? *Pastoral Care in Education, 28*(4), 261–268. doi:10.1080/02643944.2010.528017

Dehue, F., Bolman, C., & Völlink, T. (2008). Cyberbullying: Youngsters' experiences and parental perception. *Cyberpsychology & Behavior, 11*(2), 217–223. doi:10.1089/cpb.2007.0008

Hinduja, S., & Patchin, J. W. (2008). Cyberbullying: An exploratory analysis of factors related to offending and victimization. *Deviant Behavior, 29*(2), 129–156. doi:10.1080/01639620701457816

Holladay, J. (2011). Cyberbullying. *Education Digest, 76*(5), 4–9.

Humphrey, N., & Symes, W. (2010). A Review of the Literature spectrum disorders (ASDs) in mainstream schools: A qualitative study. *Journal of Research in Special Educational Needs, 10*(2), 82. doi:10.1111/j.1471-3802.2010.01146.x

Jackson, C. (2011). Your students love social media ... and so can you. *Teaching Tolerance, 39*, 38–41.

Jones, S. E., Manstead, A. S. R., & Livingstone, A. G. (2011). Ganging up or sticking together? Group processes and children's responses to text-message bullying. *British Journal of Psychology, 102*(1), 71–96. doi:10.1348/000712610X502826

Menesini, E., Nocentini, A., Palladino, B. E., Frisén, A., Berne, S., Ortega-Ruiz, R., Calmaestra, J., Scheithauer, H., Schultze-Krumbholz, A., Luik, P., Naruskov, K., Blaya, C., Berthaud, J., & Smith, P. K. (2012). Cyberbullying definition among adolescents: A comparison across six European countries. *Cyberpsychology, Behavior, and Social Networking, 15*(9), 455–463. doi:10.1089/cyber.2012.0040

Mesch, G. S. (2009). Parental mediation, online activities, and cyberbullying. *Cyberpsychology & Behavior, 12*(4), 387–393. doi:10.1089/cpb.2009.0068

Miller, J. D., & Hufstedler, S. M. (2009). *Cyberbullying knows no borders*. Australian Teacher Education Association, Paper presented at the Annual Conference of the Australian Teacher Education Association (ATEA) (Albury, Jun 28-Jul 1, 2009). (ED524610).

Mishna, F., Saini, M., & Solomon, S. (2009). Ongoing and online: Children and youth's perceptions of cyber bullying. *Children and Youth Services Review, 31*(12), 43. doi:10.1016/j.childyouth.2009.05.004

Walrave, M., & Heirman, W. (2011). Cyberbullying: Predicting victimisation and perpetration. *Children & Society, 25*(1), 59–72. doi:10.1111/j.1099-0860.2009.00260.x

Chapter 21
Technologized Sexism:
Controlling (Re)presentation of Women's Bodies Through Selfies

Pratham Prakash Parekh
https://orcid.org/0000-0002-6358-0677
Nirma University, India

ABSTRACT

Digital revolution experienced by the human race has made great impact on presentation of bodies and self. Observing the (re)presentation of self in the social constructed phenomenon of 'selfie' through sociological lens opens up gate for variety of conceptual and theoretical perspectives. The study aims to make inquiry in complex interplay among body, technology, and social control reflected in selfie. For this purpose, the study employs Netnography techniques along with thematic analysis under frameworks like dramaturgy, sociosemiotic, and dialectic to explore and describe sociologically relevant theories to grasp novel avenues of social control and (re)presentation of women's bodies through selfie. The chapter intend to develop space for further sociological research that enables the perception of selfies not only as socially constructed phenomenon but also a tool for social control over (re)presentation of self and objectification women bodies in cyberspace.

1. INTRODUCTION

The digital revolution has dramatically impacted how people present themselves and their bodies. Examining the presentation of 'self' through the concept of "selfies" in a sociological context reveals a variety of theoretical perspectives. The concept of selfies is observed as a part of a new culture evolved because of social media. This new culture has unique ways in which it influences sexism. People taking and posting selfies on social media are often mocked, shamed, or seen as objects of sexist content.

The chapter examines the complex relationship between the body, technology, and social control as reflected in selfies. The study employs techniques like Netnography and thematic analysis under

DOI: 10.4018/978-1-6684-8893-5.ch021

frameworks like dramaturgy, sociosemiotics, and dialectics to explore and describe relevant sociological strands to grasp the novel avenues of social control and re-presentation of women's bodies through selfies.

The aim of the chapter is to highlight vacuum for further sociological research that sees selfies not only as a socially constructed phenomenon but also as a tool for social control over the presentation of self and the objectification of women's bodies in cyberspace. Studying technologised sexism through sociology provides a critical and nuanced understanding of the ways in which technology and society are intertwined and reinforces the sociocultural implications of technological advancements.

Technologised sexism uses technology to perpetuate the objectification and sexualisation of women. This may take many forms, including the production and distribution of pornographic images and videos, the creation of virtual female characters that are overly sexualised, and the use of social media to spread and amplify sexist and degrading messages. These technologies contribute to the normalisation of sexist attitudes and beliefs, and they profoundly impact how women are perceived and treated in society. Technologised sexism sometimes results in online harassment and cyberstalking, which are often directed towards women. The anonymity and accessibility of the internet make it easier for ill-intend users to engage in these types of behaviours, and the impact on the victims might be devastating. These technologies are often used to spread false and damaging information about women, intimidate and threaten them, and stalk and monitor their online activities.

Sociology serves as an essential discipline in studying technologised sexism because it helps to understand how social, cultural, and political forces shape technology and its uses. In other words, technology and its uses are not neutral but are instead influenced by the power dynamics that exist in society. Sociology also helps to analyse how these ideologies and beliefs are perpetuated through technology and the consequences of these perpetuations for women and society. For instance, the study of technologised sexism through sociology potentially reveals the ways in which social media platforms and the algorithms used on these platforms are used to manipulate people's perception of themselves and others and the impact this has on gender and body image. From a philosophical perspective, studying technologised sexism helps uncover the underlying ideologies and beliefs that inform how technology is used to perpetuate and reinforce sexism. For instance, in the context of social media and selfies, how women's bodies are represented, objectified, and consumed can be seen as a manifestation of more prominent patriarchal and sexist ideologies that shape the way society views women and their bodies. In sociology and history, technologised sexism is a relatively new concept that has arisen with the proliferation of technology in recent years. However, its roots can be traced back to earlier forms of sexism and gender-based violence that have existed throughout history.

1.1. History of Technologized Self and Sexism

The history of selfies can be traced back to the earliest days of photography, and it is a reflection of the evolving technology and cultural attitudes towards self-portraiture. While some scholars have criticised selfies as a symbol of vanity and self-obsession, they have also been embraced as a means of self-expression and communication. The selfie represents a new form of visual culture that is rapidly changing and adapting to new technologies and platforms. A selfie is technically a self-portrait picture captured with a smartphone or camera and shared on social media or internet platforms. The term "selfie" was first used in 2002 and has since become a ubiquitous aspect of modern digital culture. At the same time, the act of taking a selfie may seem like a recent phenomenon; the history of self-portraits can be traced back to the earliest days of photography.

One of the earliest recorded selfies was taken in 1839 by American photographer and chemist Robert Cornelius. Cornelius took a self-portrait by setting up his camera, running into the frame, and exposing the image. This marked the beginning of a lengthy history of self-portraiture in photography, which continued to evolve and expand as new technologies were developed.

In the early 20th century, self-portraits were often taken with large format cameras, and artists and photographers primarily used them to explore their own identity and creativity. With the advent of smaller and more portable cameras in the 1950s and 1960s, self-portraits became more accessible and widespread. The Polaroid camera, in particular, was instrumental in popularising the practice of taking self-portraits, as it allowed users to take instant photos and see the results immediately.

With the rise of digital and web technologies in the late 1990s and early 2000s, self-portraits became even more accessible and widespread. The term 'selfie', as used in it contemporary connotations can be traced back to 2004 when Flickr, a social media platform, used the word 'selfie' to label digital pictures of an individual (Shah & Tewari, 2016). The introduction of the front-facing camera on smartphones in 2010 marked a major turning point, as it made it possible for users to take selfies without using a mirror or asking someone else to take a picture. Along with this, the rise of platforms such as Instagram, Snapchat, and Facebook further fuelled the popularity of selfies, as users could easily share their self-portraits with friends and followers. Google (2016) reported 24 billion selfies on the Google photo platform, and 93 million selfies are captured by Android devices daily.

Based on sociological theorisations, one can perceive the 'selfie' as a social fact that presents communally socialised ways of portraying self through social media, the internet and digital mobile devices where such social fact has its roots in coercive power that exercises control over particular individual (Durkheim, 2016). As a social rite/practice, a selfie can be considered a meaning-creating process of re-presentation of self-produced within the realm of interpersonal relations that governs power dynamics between the "object" of looking and gazing "subject" (Pham, 2015). Scholars like Sontag (2001) considered photography as a widely accepted social rite as a defence against anxiety or a tool of power. Though Sontag criticised photographic culture, her logic interprets photography as a social rite.

On the other hand, the history of technologised sexism is a reflection of more significant societal attitudes towards gender and power dynamics, and it is a major issue that must be addressed in order to create a more equitable and just society through a deeper understanding of how technology has been used to perpetuate and reinforce sexism. Technologised sexism refers to the use of technology to perpetuate and reinforce sexist attitudes, beliefs, and practices. It encompasses a wide range of issues and phenomena, including online harassment, cyberstalking, digital dating violence, and the sexualisation and objectification of women through various forms of media and entertainment. It is a reflection of more significant societal attitudes towards gender and power dynamics.

One of the earliest examples of technologised sexism can be found in the use of early forms of communication technology, such as telegraphs and telephones, to harass and intimidate women. For example, in the late 19th and early 20th centuries, women who worked as telephone operators were often subjected to vulgar and harassing messages from male customers. This early form of technologised sexism set the stage for the ways in which technology would be used to perpetrate gender-based violence and harassment in the years to come.

With the advent of the internet in the late 20th century, technologised sexism became even more widespread and accessible. The anonymity and accessibility of the internet made it easier for perpetrators to engage in online harassment and cyberstalking, and the impact on the victims became more devastating. The rise of social media platforms and online forums in the early 2000s further amplified the reach and impact of technologised sexism, as users could quickly spread false and damaging information about women, harass and intimidate them, and stalk and monitor their online activities.

In addition to online harassment and cyberstalking, technologised sexism is also found in how women's bodies are sexualised and objectified through various forms of media and entertainment. This includes the production and distribution of pornographic images and videos, the creation of virtual female characters that are overly sexualised, and the use of social media to spread and amplify sexist and degrading messages. These technologies contribute to the normalisation of sexist attitudes and beliefs, and they profoundly impact how women are perceived and treated in society.

1.2. Power Dynamics Related to Technologised Sexism

The power dynamics involved in technologised sexism are complex and multifaceted, and they reflect more extensive patterns of gender inequality and oppression in society. The power dynamics involved in technologised sexism are complex and multifaceted, reflecting larger patterns of gender inequality and oppression in society. Understanding these power dynamics is crucial to address and combat technologised sexism effectively.

One key power dynamic involved in technologised sexism is the unequal distribution of power and control between men and women. Men are often in positions of power and control in technology and media industries, and they use this power to create and distribute sexist and degrading images, messages, and content. This creates a cultural environment in which women are objectified and sexualised, and it reinforces patriarchal attitudes that perceive women as inferior and exist solely for the pleasure of men. Another power dynamic involved in technologised sexism is the ways in which technology is used to reinforce traditional gender roles and stereotypes. For example, the sexualisation of women in video games, movies, and other forms of media perpetuates the idea that women are only valued for their appearance and sexual availability. This reinforces patriarchal notions of femininity and reinforces the idea that women are passive and submissive, and it creates a cultural environment in which women are oppressed and discriminated against. A third power dynamic involved in technologised sexism is the anonymity and accessibility of technology, which makes it easier for perpetrators to engage in online harassment and cyberstalking. The anonymity of the internet provides perpetrators with a shield of protection and makes it difficult for victims to seek justice and hold perpetrators accountable. This reinforces patterns of gender-based violence and harassment, and it creates a hostile online environment in which women are targeted and subjected to abusive and degrading messages and images.

Foucault's theory also suggests that those in positions of authority do not necessarily exercise power and control explicitly. However, instead, they are diffused throughout society and exercised through a variety of mechanisms. In the context of technologised sexism on social media, individuals can exercise power and control by creating and distributing sexist and degrading images and messages and through their participation in online communities that perpetuate harmful attitudes and beliefs. The power and control are exercised through a variety of mechanisms, including social norms, cultural values, and institutional practices. In the context of technologised sexism on social media, these mechanisms include the norms and values prioritising men over women, the lack of gender-sensitive laws and regulations, and the absence of effective mechanisms for addressing online harassment and cyberstalking.

1.3. Culturally Promoted Technologised Sexism (Indian Context)

Culturally promoted technologised sexism on social media refers to the ways in which sexist attitudes and practices are perpetuated and reinforced through technology in India. This phenomenon results from larger cultural norms and beliefs in India that perpetuate gender inequality and objectification of women. Social media platforms play a significant role in perpetuating and amplifying these harmful attitudes. Individuals immerse themselves in such a self-objectifying culture and gradually internalise this perspective, learning to see value in themselves based on social validations (Fox & Vendemia, 2016). According to such cultural (re)making of body image is the prime force of self (re) presentation for fulfilling others' expectations. The major argument comes from Jesse Fox and Margaret Rooney (2015), that people are socialised within such sexual objectifying culture, forcing them to internalise body objectification. Following such proposition, many feminist scholars viewed the power dynamics of technologised sexism where selfies are observed as a tool for extending sexist ideas, patriarchal constraints and maintenance of objectification of female bodies.

In India, cultural norms and beliefs surrounding gender often prioritise men over women, and this leads to women being subjected to sexist and degrading messages, images, and treatment on social media. This is articulated in many forms, including online harassment, cyberstalking, and distributing pornographic images and videos. These cultural attitudes towards women are often exacerbated by the lack of gender-sensitive laws and regulations in India, which makes it difficult for women to seek justice and hold perpetrators accountable for their actions.

Another way culturally promoted technologised sexism is evident on social media in India is through how women's bodies are objectified and sexualised. This takes many forms, including creating and distributing sexist and degrading images and messages and using social media to spread and amplify harmful and damaging content. This objectification of women reinforces patriarchal attitudes that view women as inferior and exist solely for the pleasure of men. It creates a cultural environment in which women are oppressed and discriminated against.

The widespread use of social media in India has created new avenues for the reinforcement of traditional gender roles and stereotypes. This is visible in the ways in which women are often portrayed in advertisements and other forms of media, where they are often sexualised and portrayed as passive and submissive. This reinforces patriarchal norms and reinforces the idea that women are only valued for their appearance and sexual availability.

2. IMPACT OF SEXUAL OBJECTIFICATION OF WOMEN'S BODIES ON SOCIAL MEDIA

The adaptation of the 'selfie' by human society is not immune to the societal constraints and taboos that come with it. A wealth of literature in journalism explores feelings of guilt associated with not uploading selfies. People often justify their behaviour by linking it to specific events, locations, or even irony. This widespread practice of taking, uploading, and sharing selfies is rooted in culture and social control.

A significant part of social control over selfies has been exerted by the technology used for self-portraiture, such as digital cameras, front-facing mobile cameras, and social media platforms. The evolution of technology, specifically digital technology, has made the art of self-portrayal more accessible and popular. Some sociologists argue that these technological advancements have the potential to liberate art and humanity from their dependence on labour. The selfie manifests its form of rationality that significantly impacts human lives.

The rise of social media and its widespread use has brought new opportunities and challenges in the representation and objectification of bodies. In particular, the increasing prevalence of sexual objectification of women's bodies on social media has become a significant concern. Women's bodies are often objectified through sexually suggestive or explicit images, videos, and comments. This type of objectification contributes to the degradation and dehumanisation of women and reinforces patriarchal and sexist ideologies.

Impact of sexual objectification of women's bodies on social media has a range of negative impacts on women's physical and mental health, self-esteem, and body image. For example, exposure to sexually suggestive or explicit images of women's bodies leads to decreased self-esteem and body satisfaction and increased anxiety and depression. Women who experience sexual objectification on social media may also feel pressured to conform to unrealistic beauty standards, leading to a mental health condition that involves a persistent and intense preoccupation with perceived flaws. People with Body Dysmorphic[1] Disorder (BDD) experience significant distress and impairment in their daily lives because of their distorted beliefs about their appearance.

One of the ways in which sexual objectification of women's bodies on social media can contribute to body dysmorphia It is by exposing women to unrealistic beauty standards and ideals. Women who see sexually suggestive or explicit images of women's bodies may feel pressure to conform to these standards, leading to negative body image and feelings of inadequacy. This triggers or worsens symptoms of BDD, including repetitive checking, comparing, and grooming behaviours and a strong desire to hide or alter perceived flaws. Sexual objectification of women's bodies on social media significantly impacts women's mental health and well-being and can contribute to the development and maintenance of body dysmorphia. Addressing this issue requires a multifaceted approach that promotes positive body image and self-esteem and reduces exposure to unrealistic beauty standards and sexually objectifying content.

Sexual objectification on social media also contributes to the reinforcement of patriarchal and sexist ideologies. Women's bodies are often depicted as objects for male pleasure and consumption, perpetuating the notion that women exist solely for the pleasure and benefit of men. This type of objectification leads to normalising violence (emotional & mental) against women and perpetuating unfair gender norms and stereotypes. It is important to address the issue of sexual objectification of women's bodies on social media by taking a multifaceted approach that addresses the underlying causes.

The selfie has become a ubiquitous form of self-expression and self-representation in the digital age. However, the cultural significance and impact of the selfie have been widely debated, with some people viewing it as a mere fad or trend, while others consider it as just another type of digital photography.

Nishant Shah (2015) explored the issue of "slut shaming", where women who take and share sexually suggestive or explicit selfies are criticised and shamed, to demonstrate how the phenomenon of selfie-shaming produces new forms of control and visibility over women's bodies online. Using the case of #GamerGate, a controversial online movement focused on the gaming industry; the chapter shows how the issue of women's consent and agency online goes beyond cases of revenge and non-consensual pornography to encompass broader social, cultural and technological dimensions. Drawing on theories and concepts from software studies, cyber-feminism, and digital cultures, the author argues for an expansion of the analysis of women's problems of consent and agency online to encompass the complex interplay of body, technology, control, and regulation associated with the phenomenon of selfie shaming and the subsequent processes of "slut shaming." Such an approach offers a more nuanced and comprehensive understanding of the implications of the selfie for women's bodies and how technology and culture shape and regulate online visibility and representation.

Alicia Eler's (2017) work, "The Selfie Generation", provides insights into the topic of selfies and their place in social media. The author argues that selfies are a form of personal branding in the digital age and more than just a picture. She examines the impact of selfies and social media on people's lives, including the blurring of physical and digital lives, privacy, consent, ownership, and authenticity. Eler also addresses the issues of sexism and double standards faced by women who take selfies, exposing themselves to criticism and judgment. The book presents the selfie as a paradox that serves as a tool for self-empowerment and a symbol of surveillance culture. "The Selfie Generation" offers an insight into how social media has changed the way people connect, communicate and present themselves to the world.

Katrin Tiidenberg (2017) argued against the view that taking and sharing "sexy selfies" is a source of shame and dismissible in both mass media and academic discourse. The author has spent five years studying a community of "sexy selfie" enthusiasts on Tumblr and argues that these selfies bring both personal satisfaction and political empowerment to women. The author presents an analysis of empirical data and ethnographic analysis to show that these selfies create subject positions that fall between postfeminist self-objectification and the joyless rejection of neoliberal sexiness. The author uses visual, textual, and hypertextual data to support the argument, including photographs, captions, comments, hashtags, and interviews from 2011 to 2015 relating to two female bloggers.

2.1. Using Technologized Sexism for Empowerment

Women are utilizing technology to address and challenge sexism in various ways. Feminist scholars argues that technology has been used to control both nature and women, leading to the devaluation of women's roles and contributions (Rakow,1986). For instance, in the field of journalism, women journalists working in technology, particularly the video gaming industry, have experienced online harassment and sexist abuse. They have responded by changing their working practices and sometimes disguising their identity to avoid abuse (Catherine, 2018). Some feminist scholars suggest that the way to challenge the male monopoly of technology is to have more women in technology, as they bring unique skills and perspectives (Aschauer, 1999). Shulamith Firestone, a foundational feminist thinker, envisioned a future where technology would eliminate sexism by freeing women from childbirth and dismantling the patriarchal nuclear family(Halbert, 2004). Women are utilizing technology to expose and resist sexism, but more research and action are needed to create substantive changes in gender relations and technological practices (Hanton, 2015). Women are using social media activism to respond to sexism, but they often face gendered criticisms that can silence them. Tweeting about sexism have in present times served as a form of collective action and enhance women's well-being (Foster, Tassone, & Matheson, 2021) However, the effects of sexist hashtags on social media may lead to increased sexism and negative evaluations of women (Fox, Cruz, & Lee, 2015). But it is not meant to be generalized. For instance, In the Middle East, women have turned to unconventional media such as Facebook, Twitter, and YouTube to combat discrimination and inequality in their societies (Ezeh, Chukwuma, & Okanume, 2017). social media many times serves as a platform for women to raise awareness, mobilize, and advocate for their rights, leading to empowerment and the marginalization of inequality in society (Shata, & Seelig, 2021).

Social media has the potential to amplify women's voices, promote gender equality, and facilitate positive change in various aspects of women's lives. Social media has emerged as a powerful tool for promoting and empowering women. It has the potential to raise awareness about women's health issues and bridge the gap between grassroots activism and policy-making processes (Corsini, Luc, & Antonoff, 2021). Also, social media platforms provide a platform for women entrepreneurs to discuss challenges, mobilize attention towards women's rights, and encourage government commitments to gender equality(Kumari, 2020) The utilization of social media has been found to have a direct contribution to empowering women in pursuing business and promoting their economic welfare and social well-being(Rasul, Hoque, & Arefin, 2020).

3. TECHNOLOGISED SEXISM, SELFIE, AND SOCIOLOGY

The act of sharing a selfie is not just an individual act but also a social one. It is shaped by an individual's relationships with others, social institutions, and larger social structures. The presence of an individual on social media is derived from the identity they create through information stored digitally, which can force individuals to engage in "identity work" to maintain a specific image in the eyes of others (Snow & Anderson, 1987).

Well-known sociologists, such as Erving Goffman (1979) and C.H. Cooley (1918), have theorised about the role of impression management in shaping self-presentation and the construction of identity. Goffman's theory of impression management emphasises the importance of presenting oneself in a manner that meets the expectations of others, while Cooley's theory of "crafting self" highlights the influence of society in shaping an individual's self-image. These theories provide a micro-sociological perspective on the social processes of selfie-taking and sharing in the context of self-presentation and the construction of identity.

Technologised sexism is a manifestation of the patriarchal power structures that pervade over society. Next part of the chapter explore how the dramaturgical, socio-semiotic, and dialectical approaches provide a deeper understanding of technologised sexism on social media. The dramaturgical, socio-semiotic, and dialectical approaches provide a robust framework for understanding technologised sexism on social media. By considering the ways in which gender performance, symbolic meanings, and power structures interact on these platforms, one can gain a deeper understanding of the challenges faced in creating more inclusive and equitable online environments. Radical feminists evidently have used such perceptions to challenge and disrupt the patriarchal power structures that perpetuate technologised sexism and work towards a more just and equitable world for all women.

4. THEORETICAL LENSES TO PERCEIVE SELFIE AS TECHNOLOGIZED SELF

Selfies can be studied through a variety of theoretical lenses, but the dramaturgical framework is particularly relevant in a sociological context. According to this framework, selfies are seen as a manifestation of the subjectivity, self-representation, and performativity of the self in line with societal expectations. The central concern of this approach is how the selfie culture influences our understanding of the self. The dramaturgical approach offers a rich perspective on the cultural and societal forces that shape the production and interpretation of selfies. However, it is essential also to consider the intersections with feminist perspectives and how these cultural norms and expectations are resisted and subverted through selfies.

Looking at selfies through a dramaturgical lens highlights the relationship between self-presentation on the internet and the public-private divide. Scholars such as Walsh Baker (2017) have drawn on the classical arguments of Goffman (2021) to argue that selfies exacerbate the transformation of social life from public to private. The face is seen as an image of the defined through socially approved attributes and claims a positive social value. The face carries meaning and reflects a person's involvement in a specific situation, serving as a critical resource in constructing the self. Thus, selfies add value to communication and interaction rituals by offering an opportunity for the producer to redefine their self through the face or facial expressions. It is impossible to separate selfies from online expectations and the pressure to present oneself acceptably. The digital world has made it inevitable for individuals to interact and create boundaries using symbols, such as keyboards (Markham, 2016). Another aspect of the dramaturgical approach is the production of body images (Dutta et al., 2018), which are closely tied to selfies as they perform and produce the self.

Selfies are also seen as a platform for the proclaimed "I am here", as theorised by Lilie Chouliaraki (2017). This performance contains subjective, existential, and locative dimensions, with the arrival of self-signifying survival. The selfie democratises self-representation, making the self the protagonist of every selfie through performing the self within space and time and with materials and networked existence. Self-representation through dramaturgy is also manifested through self-objectification, where individuals view and evaluate themselves based on societal standards of appearance (Rollero & Piccoli, 2017). This reinforces the objectification of the self and has been linked to behaviours such as narcissism, psychopathy, body dissatisfaction, and idealised beauty standards. Some scholars argue that this reinforces a cultural (re)making of the body image driven by fulfilling others' expectations.

However, from a feminist perspective, this focus on appearance and the objectification of the self is seen as perpetuating patriarchal norms and expectations for women. Feminist scholars have pointed out that these standards often reflect and reinforce societal norms for women to be thin, conventionally attractive, and sexually appealing. The emphasis on appearance leads to the internalisation of these expectations and contributes to body image concerns, low self-esteem, and the sexualisation of women. Despite this, some argue that selfies are also seen as a form of resistance and empowerment, allowing individuals, particularly women, to reclaim control over their image and present a different version of themselves. In this sense, selfies are seen as a tool for subverting traditional beauty standards and promoting body positivity and self-expression.

The dramaturgical approach views social interactions as performances, with individuals playing different roles in front of different audiences. On social media, this approach highlights how individuals perform gender to meet expectations and fit into prescribed roles. For example, women are often expected or pressurized to present a hyper-feminine and sexualised image of themselves online, while men are encouraged to present a macho and dominant image. This reinforces traditional gender norms and the idea that women's worth is based on appearance.

The socio-semiotic approach focuses on how meaning is constructed through symbols and signs. In the context of social media, this approach highlights how sexist messages are encoded into the language, images, and symbols used on these platforms. For example, the widespread use of gendered emoji, such as the high-heeled shoe emoji used to indicate femininity, reinforces traditional gender norms and reinforces the idea that women should be concerned with their appearance. The socio-semiotic approach also highlights how language is used to reinforce sexist attitudes, such as through the use of gendered slurs or language that infantilises or dismisses women.

The dialectical approach, on the other hand, views technology as a double-edged sword. While it provides new opportunities for challenging sexist attitudes and behaviours, it can reinforce existing power structures and perpetuate existing inequalities. In the context of social media, this approach would highlight how online harassment and cyberbullying target women and amplify their experiences of sexism. For example, the prevalence of hate speech and misogynistic content on social media contributes to a hostile online environment for women, making it difficult for them to engage in online discussions or express their opinions.

It then becomes crucial to understand how technology and social media perpetuate technologised sexism. Drawing on the dramaturgical, socio-semiotic, and dialectical approaches, it becomes clear how patriarchal power structures are encoded into social media's language, images, and symbols by challenging these structures and advocating for more inclusive and respectful online environments.

The mass production of images and videos of women on social media are used to create a particular narrative about women and femininity, perpetuating the patriarchal notion that women exist for the sexual gratification of men. The proliferation of sexualised images and videos of women on social media also contributes to the normalisation of violence against women. It reinforces the belief that women are inherently inferior to men. The commodification of women on internet and social is a prevalent phenomenon. Women's experiences in the outdoors are often subject to critique and judgment, with social media platforms like Instagram and Facebook playing a significant role in portraying women in specific ways (Muljadji, Sekarningrum, & Muhammad, 2017). Moreover, social media platforms has led to an increased commodification of women in social realms that were previously outside of economic markets (Gray, et., 2018). Everyday Internet users are shaping themselves into social media microcelebrities known as "Influencers," who capitalize on their followers by inserting advertisements for products and services through their personal narratives (Bolin, 2018). Social media coverage often exploits women as objects, treating them as biological satisfiers and subjecting them to harassment and marginalization(Abidin, 2016). The commodification of women's bodies through the sale of sexualised images and videos is a form of exploitation that reinforces the patriarchal notion that women are inferior and exist solely for the pleasure of men. The societal norms and cultural representations perpetrating this objectification are based on patriarchal values and reinforce the belief that men are superior to women. This reinforces the oppression of women and contributes to the maintenance of patriarchal structures and power imbalances.

4.1. Socio-Semiotic Approach: Selfie as Communication

The study of the selfie through the socio-semiotic approach provides a comprehensive understanding of the inter-subjectivity and communicative structure inherent in taking selfies and the meaning-making processes associated with it. Language plays a crucial role in connecting humans, and the language of culture defines every social role in society. These social roles are not exclusive, and individuals have multiple roles defined by the language of culture.

From a socio-semiotic perspective, taking a selfie is a meaning-making process that involves the formation of social relationships online. In this sense, selfies serve as a new language expressing social relations formation. According to Zhao and Zappavigna (2018), selfies are unique from other forms of photography due to their potential to create and share a variety of perspectives among creators and viewers. This unique communicative language allows creators to narrate their stories and re-imagine themselves as part of society. Moreover, the act of taking a selfie represents the technologisation of the self, where the materiality of the self informs its identity (Wargo, 2017). Identity formation is not an isolated process and occurs within a relationship network or culture. In this sense, selfies serve as a tool for identity formation within social networks.

The meanings generated by selfies from a socio-semiotic viewpoint are an essential study area. Semiotic systems are organised around three functions: ideation (an individual's understanding of culture), interpersonal (actions that facilitate social relationships), and textual (the actual communication process among individuals) (Urban, 1981). Selfies can be considered as a visual message that operates in all three functions, as the self in a selfie represents an understanding of culture (ideation), enacts social relations (interpersonal), and provides textual information (textual) within the image.

The sexual objectification of women on social media is a complex issue that requires a critical examination of the sociocultural norms and expectations that underpin it. By using a Socio-Semiotic approach, it is possible to understand how images, messages, and symbols contribute to the sexual objectification of women on social media and the impact this has on women's experiences and well-being. Addressing this issue requires a comprehensive examination of the patriarchal structures perpetuating gender-based violence and a commitment to creating a more equitable society.

The Socio-Semiotic approach is used to understand the sexual objectification of women on social media. This approach is concerned with the relationship between signs and symbols and the social and cultural meanings attached to them. In social media, images and messages are used to convey specific meanings and attitudes, and how women are represented on these platforms has a significant impact on their experiences and well-being.

The sexual objectification of women on social media is a form of gender-based violence that perpetuates the objectification and dehumanisation of women. This is achieved through images, videos, and texts that present women as objects for male pleasure and satisfaction rather than autonomous beings with agency and dignity. The sociocultural norms and expectations of beauty and femininity, which prioritise women's physical appearance and judge their worth based on their sexual appeal, are heavily reinforced on social media. This leads to the creation of unrealistic beauty standards that are impossible to meet and reinforces harmful gender norms that view women as passive sexual objects.

4.2. Dialectical Approach: Selfie as a Struggle

The dialectical approach highlights the complex and dynamic nature of the relationship between social media, technology, and the sexual objectification of women. While technology and social media have perpetuated techno-sexism and sexual objectification, they also provide a platform for resistance and agency for women. An ongoing process of synthesis and antithesis is necessary to reconcile these conflicting forces and create a more inclusive and equitable digital world. The dialectical approach provides a nuanced understanding of the complex and dynamic relationship between social media, technology, and the sexual objectification of women. This approach recognises the multiple and conflicting forces at play and seeks to reconcile them through an ongoing process of synthesis and antithesis.

Sexual objectification of women has been a long-standing issue in society, and the advent of social media has further exacerbated the problem. Social media platforms often highlight and reinforce traditional beauty standards, leading to a culture of sexual objectification, where women's bodies are reduced to mere objects for male consumption. The pervasive presence of sexualised images and content on social media has normalised the objectification of women and led to a culture of techno-sexism.

These platforms' algorithmic and commercial nature perpetuates the technologised sexism on social media. Algorithms promote content that generates maximum engagement, which often includes sexualised images and videos of women. The commodification of women's bodies on social media, through advertisements and influencer marketing, further perpetuates the sexual objectification of women. However, the dialectical approach also recognises the agency and resistance of women in this process. Women are not passive objects but active agents challenging and subverting traditional beauty standards and patriarchal norms. The rise of feminist and body-positive movements on social media exemplifies this resistance. Women are using social media to reclaim their bodies and challenge the sexual objectification of women by promoting diverse representations of bodies and beauty.

Feminist movements and the body-positive movement on social media are examples of resistance against traditional beauty standards and patriarchal norms that perpetuate the objectification of women's bodies. These movements use social media to challenge the narrow definition of beauty and promote body diversity and self-acceptance. These movements often face opposition and resistance from those who seek to maintain traditional beauty standards and patriarchal norms. The rise of counter-movements, such as the "fitspiration" trend, which promotes a narrow definition of beauty and body ideals, is an example of this resistance. The dialectical approach highlights the complex and dynamic relationship between feminist movements, the body-positive movement, and social media. While these movements use social media to challenge traditional beauty standards and patriarchal norms, they also face limitations and opposition. An ongoing process of synthesis and antithesis is necessary to reconcile these conflicting forces and create a more inclusive and equitable digital world.

5. FINAL REMARKS

The history of selfies dates back to 1839, when Robert Cornelius took a self-portrait with his camera. With the advent of smaller and more portable cameras, self-portraits became more accessible and widespread, and the rise of digital technology and social media platforms like Instagram, Snapchat and Facebook fuelled its popularity. Technologised sexism refers to the use of technology to perpetuate sexist attitudes and is rooted in more significant societal attitudes toward gender and power dynamics. Early forms of communication technology, like telegraphs and telephones, were used to harass women. With the advent of the internet, technologised sexism became even more widespread with the rise of social media platforms and online forums. Technologised sexism also includes the sexualisation and objectification of women's bodies through media and entertainment, contributing to the normalisation of sexist attitudes.

The sexual objectification of women's bodies on social media reinforces patriarchal and sexist ideologies, depicting women as objects for male pleasure and consumption. This led to normalising violence against women and perpetuating harmful gender norms. Addressing this issue requires a multidisciplinary approach to grasp underlying causes and promote "*positive*" representations of women's bodies. A selfie is a form of self-expression and representation in the digital age. However, its cultural significance and impact are, to date, debated, with some viewing it as a trend and others as just another type of digital photography.

The chapter has employed a sociological lens to capture the new regimes of social control and visualisation of women's bodies through selfies and the impact of technology on sexuality, gender and body image. Technologised sexism in the present day is manifested in objectification, sexualisation, and online harassment of women. Sociological theories appropriately analyse the perpetuation of such conditions and the consequences for women and society; they also capture the interplay between technology and social control exercised over sexism and (re) the presentation of self.

Addressing technologised sexism requires an understanding of power dynamics. Technologised sexism is a complex issue that reflects more extensive patterns of gender inequality and oppression in society. It involves the unequal distribution of power and control between men and women in technology and media industries, reinforcement of traditional gender roles and stereotypes, and the anonymity of technology enabling online harassment and cyberstalking. Foucault's theory suggests that power and control are diffused throughout society and exercised through a variety of mechanisms, such as social norms, cultural values, and institutional practices (Bevir, 1999). Culturally promoted technologised sexism is evidently present in India, where sexist attitudes and practices are now perpetuated and reinforced through technology. This is due to cultural norms and beliefs that prioritise men over women, resulting in the objectification and sexualisation of women over social media platforms. This has taken the form of online harassment, cyberstalking, and boosting the distribution of pornographic content. The lack of gender-sensitive laws and regulations in India makes it difficult for women to seek justice and fairness over visualising their bodies. Women's bodies are objectified and sexualised, reinforcing patriarchal values and creating a cultural ecosystem of oppression and discrimination. Social media also reinforces traditional gender roles and stereotypes, where women are portrayed as passive, submissive and valued only for their appearance and sexual availability.

Cultural and social pressures and their embodiment influence the practice of taking and uploading selfies on social media. Technology has made self-portrayal more accessible and popular. However, the widespread adaptation of social media has led to the increased sexual objectification of women's bodies. In some cases, this objectification has resulted in negative impacts on women's physical and mental health, self-esteem, and body image, including decreased self-esteem and increased anxiety, depression, and body dysmorphia. Addressing this issue requires promoting positive body image, reducing exposure to unrealistic beauty standards, and sexually objectifying content.

Taking and sharing selfies is shaped by social relationships, institutions, and structures that are grasped through theoretical lenses of self-presentation and identity construction. The dramaturgical framework views selfies as a manifestation of the self's subjectivity and performativity in line with societal expectations. The production of body images through selfies reinforces objectification. It perpetuates patriarchal norms, but from a feminist perspective, selfies are also a form of resistance and empowerment for women to reclaim control over their image and subvert traditional beauty standards.

Technologised sexism refers to perpetuating sexist attitudes and behaviours through technology, specifically social media. Three approaches, the dramaturgical, socio-semiotic, and dialectical, provide insight into this phenomenon and the patriarchal power structures that drive it. The dramaturgical approach highlights the performance of gender on social media and reinforces traditional gender norms. The socio-semiotic approach examines the symbols and language used on social media to encode sexist messages and reinforce sexist attitudes. The dialectical approach views technology as both a challenge and reinforcement of sexist attitudes and behaviours and highlights the adverse effects of online harassment and cyberbullying on women. These approaches are used to challenge and disrupt patriarchal power structures and work towards a more inclusive and equitable "online" environment.

Selfies are analysed through a dramaturgical framework, which examines how societal expectations shape self-representation and performativity in self-portraits. This approach highlights the connection between self-presentation online and the public-private divide and emphasises the role of facial expressions and body images in constructing the self. The dramaturgical perceptions also highlight the pressure to conform to societal norms in self-presentation, which can lead to self-objectification and reinforce patriarchal beauty standards. However, some feminist scholars argue that selfies can also be a form of resistance and empowerment, allowing individuals to subvert traditional beauty standards and promote body positivity and self-expression.

Studying selfies from a socio-semiotic perspective provides insight into the social relationships and meaning-making processes associated with taking selfies. Language and culture define social roles and influence identity formation, and selfies serve as a new language that articulates these processes. The act of taking a selfie represents the technologisation of self, and the meanings generated by selfies are influenced by ideation (culture), interpersonal (social relationships), and textual (communication) functions. Selfies are perceived as a visual message that operates in all three functions: representing cultural understanding, enacting social relations, and providing textual information.

The dialectical approach examines the complex relationship between social media, technology, and the sexual objectification of women. While technology and social media contribute to the objectification of women, they also provide a platform for resistance and agency. The approach recognises the multiple and conflicting forces at play and seeks to reconcile them through ongoing synthesis and antithesis. Algorithms and commodification perpetuate the normalisation of sexual objectification on social media, but women are challenging traditional beauty standards and patriarchal norms through movements like feminist and body-positive activism. These movements use social media as a platform for resistance but face opposition and limitations and require ongoing synthesis and antithesis to create a more equitable digital world.

By applying sociological theories and frameworks, one gains a deeper understanding of the underlying causes of technologised sexism and works towards a more equitable and just society in which technology empowers women and promotes gender equality. The sexual objectification of women's bodies on social media is not just a technological problem but also a manifestation of larger societal attitudes toward gender and power dynamics. Addressing this issue requires a multi-dimensional approach, considering the complex interplay between technology, cultural norms, and power dynamics. This issue was analysed through various sociological theories such as feminist theory, social constructivism, and the theory of power and control by Michel Foucault. Foucault's theory of power and control suggests that power is diffused throughout society and is exercised through various mechanisms, including social norms, cultural values, and institutional practices. In the context of technologised sexism, power dynamics play a crucial role in perpetuating sexist attitudes and behaviours through technology and media. The sexual objectification of women's bodies on social media is a manifestation of patriarchal and sexist ideologies, which depict women as objects for male pleasure and consumption.

The sexual objectification of women's bodies on social media is a manifestation of more prominent patriarchal and sexist ideologies that depict women as objects for male pleasure and consumption. The widespread use of social media has contributed to the perpetuation of technologised sexism, leading to the normalisation of violence against women and the perpetuation of harmful gender norms. Addressing this issue requires a multifaceted approach, addressing underlying causes and promoting positive representations of women's bodies. Cultural and social pressures influence the practice of taking and sharing selfies and reinforce objectification and patriarchal norms. However, from a feminist perspective, selfies can also be a form of resistance and empowerment for women to reclaim control over their image and subvert traditional beauty standards. The study of technologised sexism through sociological theories and techniques provides a fresh perception of the interplay between technology and social control, manifested through the negative impacts of online harassment and cyberbullying on women. Addressing technologised sexism requires understanding power dynamics and creating a more equitable and inclusive cyberspace, and this further opens up new avenues for multi-disciplinary research.

REFERENCES

Abidin, C. (2016). *Please subscribe!: Influencers, social media, and the commodification of everyday life* [Doctoral dissertation, University of Western Australia].

Aschauer, A. B. (1999). Tinkering with technological skill: An examination of the gendered uses of technologies. *Computers and Composition, 16*(1), 7–23. doi:10.1016/S8755-4615(99)80003-6

Baker, S. A., & Walsh, M. J. (2018). 'Good Morning Fitfam': Top posts, hashtags and gender display on Instagram. *New Media & Society, 20*(12), 4553–4570. doi:10.1177/1461444818777514

Bevir, M. (1999). Foucault, power, and institutions. *Political Studies, 47*(2), 345–359. doi:10.1111/1467-9248.00204

Bolin, G. (2018). Media use and the extended commodification of the lifeworld. *Technologies of labour and the politics of contradiction*, 235-252.

Catherine, A. (2018). They Go for Gender First. *Journalism Practice, 12*(7), 850–869.

Chouliaraki, L. (2017). Symbolic bordering: The self-representation of migrants and refugees in digital news. *Popular Communication, 15*(2), 78–94. doi:10.1080/15405702.2017.1281415

Cooley, C. H. (1918). *Social process*. Scribner's.

Corsini, E. M., Luc, J. G., & Antonoff, M. B. (2021). Women in thoracic surgery: Social media and the value of mentorship. *Journal of Thoracic Disease, 13*(1), 464–472. doi:10.21037/jtd.2020.04.11

Durkheim, E. (2016). The rules of the sociological method. In *Social Theory Re-Wired* (pp. 10–15). Routledge.

Dutta, E., Sharma, P., Shah, N., Bharati, A., Sonavane, S., & Desousa, A. (2018). Attitude toward selfie taking and its relation to body image and narcissism in medical students. *Indian Journal of Psychological Medicine, 40*(1), 17–21. doi:10.4103/IJPSYM.IJPSYM_169_17

Eler, A. (2017). *The selfie generation: How our self-images are changingchange our notions of privacy, Sex, consent, and culture*. Simon and Schuster.

Ezeh, N. C., Chukwuma, N. A., & Okanume, O. B. (2017). Internet and women selfempowerment: Opportunities, strategies, and challenges. *International Journal of Social Sciences and Humanities Review, 17*(1), 203–212.

Foster, M. D., Tassone, A., & Matheson, K. (2021). Tweeting about sexism motivates further activism: A social identity perspective. *British Journal of Social Psychology, 60*(3), 741–764. doi:10.1111/bjso.12431

Fox, J., Cruz, C., & Lee, J. Y. (2015). Perpetuating online sexism offline: Anonymity, interactivity, and the effects of sexist hashtags on social media. *Computers in Human Behavior, 52*, 436–442. doi:10.1016/j.chb.2015.06.024

Fox, J., & Rooney, M. C. (2015). The Dark Triad and trait self-objectification as predictors of men'smen's use and self-presentation behaviorsbehaviours on social networking sites. *Personality and Individual Differences, 76*, 161–165. doi:10.1016/j.paid.2014.12.017

Fox, J., & Vendemia, M. A. (2016). Selective self-presentation and social comparison through photographs on social networking sites. *Cyberpsychology, behaviorbehaviour, and social networking, 19*(10), 593-600.

Goffman, E. (1979). *Gender advertisements*.

Goffman, E. (2021). *The presentation of self in everyday life*. Anchor.

Google. (2016, May 27). *Google Photos: One year, 200 million users, and a whole lot of selfies*. Google. https://blog.google/products/photos/google-photos-one-year-200-million/

Gray, T., Norton, C., Breault-Hood, J., Christie, B., & Taylor, N. (2018). Curating a public self: Exploring social media images of women in the outdoors. *Journal of Outdoor Recreation, Education, and Leadership, 10*(2), 153–170. doi:10.18666/JOREL-2018-V10-I2-8191

Halbert, D. (2004). Shulamith Firestone: Radical feminism and visions of the information society. *Information Communication and Society, 7*(1), 115–135. doi:10.1080/1369118042000208933

Hanton, P. B. (2015). *The lack of women in technology: The role culture and sexism play*.

Karwowski, M., & Brzeski, A. (2017). Selfies and the (creative) self: A diary study. *Frontiers in Psychology, 8*, 172. doi:10.3389/fpsyg.2017.00172

Kumari, M. (2020). Social media and women empowerment. *Int. J. Sci. Technol. Res, 9*(3), 626–629.

Lobinger, K., & Brantner, C. (2015). In the eye of the beholder: Subjective views on the authenticity of selfies. *International Journal of Communication, 9*, 1848-1860.

Luppicini, R. (Ed.). (2012). *Handbook of Research on Technoself: Identity in a Technological Society: Identity in a Technological Society*. IGI Global.

Marcuse, H. (2013). *One-dimensional man: Studies in the ideology of advanced industrial society*. Routledge. doi:10.4324/9780203995211

Markham, A. (2016). The dramaturgy of digital experience. In *The Drama of Social Life* (pp. 297–312). Routledge.

Muljadji, Y., Sekarningrum, B., & Muhammad, R. (2017). The Commodification of Religious Clothes Through The Social Media: The Identity Crisis on Youth Muslim Female in Urban Indonesia. *Romanian Journal of Journalism & Communication/Revista Romana De Jurnalism Si Comunicare-RRJC, 12*.

Pham, M. H. T. (2015). "I click and post and breathe, waiting for others to see what I see": On# FeministSelfies, outfit photos, and networked vanity. *Fashion Theory, 19*(2), 221–241. doi:10.2752/175174115X14168357992436

Rakow, L. F. (1986). *Feminist Approaches to Technology: Implications for Communications Scholarship*.

Rasul, T., Hoque, M. R., & Arefin, M. S. (2020). Social media for web-communities of female entrepreneurs: A PRISMA-compliant exploration. *International Journal of Web Based Communities, 16*(4), 396–409. doi:10.1504/IJWBC.2020.111379

Rollero, C., & De Piccoli, N. (2017). Self-objectification and personal values. An exploratory study. *Frontiers in Psychology, 8*, 1055. doi:10.3389/fpsyg.2017.01055

Shah, N. (2015). The selfie and the slut: Bodies, technology and public shame. *Economic and Political Weekly*, 86–93.

Shah, R., & Tewari, R. (2016). Demystifying 'selfie': A rampant social media activity. *Behaviour & Information Technology, 35*(10), 864–871. doi:10.1080/0144929X.2016.1201693

Shata, A., & Seelig, M. I. (2021). The Dragonfly Effect: Analysis of the Social Media Women's Empowerment Campaign. *Journal of Creative Communications, 16*(3), 331–346. doi:10.1177/09732586211036551

Snow, D. A., & Anderson, L. (1987). Identity work among the homeless: The verbal construction and avowal of personal identities. *American Journal of Sociology, 92*(6), 1336–1371. doi:10.1086/228668

Sontag, S. (2001). *On photography* (Vol. 48). Macmillan.

Tiidenberg, K. (2017). "Nude selfies til I die"–making of 'sexy'in selfies. In *Sex in the Digital Age* (pp. 78–88). Routledge. doi:10.4324/9781315446240-8

Urban, G. (1981). *Language as Social Semiotic: The Social Interpretation of Language and Meaning.*

Walsh, M. J., & Baker, S. A. (2017). The selfie and the transformation of the public-private distinction. *Information Communication and Society, 20*(8), 1185–1203. doi:10.1080/1369118X.2016.1220969

Warfield, K. (2016). Making the cut: An agential realist examination of selfies and touch. *Social Media + Society, 2*(2), 2056305116641706. doi:10.1177/2056305116641706

Wargo, J. M. (2017). "Every selfie tells a story…": LGBTQ youth lifestreams and new media narratives as connective identity texts. *New Media & Society, 19*(4), 560–578. doi:10.1177/1461444815612447

Zhao, S., & Zappavigna, M. (2018). Beyond the self: Intersubjectivity and the social semiotic interpretation of the self. *New Media & Society, 20*(5), 1735–1754. doi:10.1177/1461444817706074

ENDNOTE

1 It is important to note that body dysmorphia is a complex and multifaceted condition and that a range of psychological, biological, and environmental factors influence its development and expression. However, research suggests that exposure to sexually objectifying content on social media may contribute to developing and maintaining BDD symptoms.

Chapter 22
Understanding Cyber-Feminism and Its Roles in the Digital Space

Anushka Lydia Issac
https://orcid.org/0000-0002-1493-1047
Westford University College, UAE

ABSTRACT

Cyber-feminism is a concept that has emerged in response to the increasing use of technology and the internet in our daily lives. At its core, cyber-feminism is about challenging the gender biases that exist in the technology industry and ensuring that women have equal access to technology and digital spaces. The chapter covers the history of cyber-feminism, including key thinkers and activists who have contributed to its development. The chapter discusses strategies for staying safe online, including the importance of digital literacy and education. This chapter explores the role of cyber-feminism in the digital space through a case study approach. Specifically, it examines the impact of the #MeToo Movement, the Women's March, and the story of Malala Yousafzai. By highlighting the successes and challenges of cyber-feminist movements, this chapter offers insights into how we can work towards a more inclusive and feminist digital future.

SECTION ONE: INTRODUCTION

In recent years, the digital space has become an integral part of our daily lives, shaping how we interact with each other, access information, and conduct business. With the growth of digital technology, the concept of cyber-feminism has emerged, and it has become increasingly relevant in our society today. Cyber-feminism is a term that refers to the intersection of feminism and digital technology, and it focuses on how women can use digital technology to promote gender equality and challenge patriarchy (Starcevic & Aboujaoude, 2015). According to Wall (Wall & David S., 2005, p. 79), *"crimes that are mediated by networked computers and not just related to computers"* are considered to be cybercrimes. Computer viruses, Internet fraud or scams, identity theft, stock manipulation or securities fraud, cyber-stalking

DOI: 10.4018/978-1-6684-8893-5.ch022

or cyber-harassment, and computer hacking are all examples of cybercrime. In 2011, one third of the world's population, or about 2.3 billion people, had access to the internet, and by 2018 that number had increased to 4 billion (Kemp, 2018). Additionally, 45% of these internet users are under the age of 25, and 60% of them are from developing nations (Kshetri, 2010). Cybercrime has become more prevalent in developing economies as a result of the internet's quick spread and the digitalization of commercial activity and hence underscores the urgency to address the impact of cybercrime. Some estimates claim that in recent years, the global cybercrime sector has been generating US$1 trillion annually (Kshetri, 2010). International discourses have changed as a result of the significant roles that developing world-based criminals are playing in the criminal value chain of the cyberworld. According to Kaspersky Labs (Kshetri, 2010), developing nations produced seven of the top ten countries for producing trojans meant to steal passwords in 2009, accounting for 92% of all such trojans globally. The utilization of hardware and software, broadband connections, the pool of cybercriminal expertise, the availability of employment prospects, and the spread of security products are all economic elements that are changing in developing nations (Al-Shalan, 2006). The statistics on the increasing number of internet users, particularly in developing nations, highlights the growing vulnerability of women to cybercrime. As more women gain access to the digital space, there is a higher likelihood of them encountering cyber threats, making it imperative to address gender-specific risks and ensure the protection of women in the online environment.

This chapter explores cyber-feminism's role in the digital space, promoting women's empowerment, security, and gender equality. It focus on issues like online harassment, cyber-bullying, and the gender gap in digital skills. Strategies for women's online safety and using digital technology for advocacy are examined. The chapter covers cyber-feminism's history, online activism, and its intersection with cybersecurity and privacy. It highlights the impact of social media on promoting positive change and managing online communities. This chapter aims to empower women in the digital world through cyber-feminism.

Defining Cyber-Feminism

Cyber-feminism is a term that has emerged in recent years to describe the intersection of feminism and digital technology. It is rooted in the belief that the digital world can be a space for women to challenge patriarchy, advocate for their rights, and promote gender equality. As stated by (Wilkinson & Kitzinger, 2013), "cyber-feminism is a movement that recognizes the role of digital technology in shaping gender identities and seeks to use this technology to empower women and challenge traditional gender roles". Cyber-feminism encompasses a range of practices, from online activism and advocacy to digital storytelling and social media campaigns. According to (Wajcman, 2006), "cyber-feminism involves the use of digital technology to challenge patriarchal structures and promote social change". Cyber-feminists seek to create a more inclusive and equitable digital space, one that is free from harassment and discrimination, and that allows women to fully participate in public discourse. Through the lens of cyber-feminism, we can explore issues such as online harassment, cyber-bullying, and the gender gap in digital skills and access, and work towards creating a more just and equitable digital world.

In addition, cyber-feminism is also concerned with issues of privacy and security in the digital space. As highlighted by (Schwarz et al., 2020), "cyber-feminism acknowledges the risks that women face in the digital world, including online harassment, stalking, and doxing, and seeks to empower women to navigate these threats safely and confidently". Cyber-feminists recognize that the digital space can be a double-edged sword, offering opportunities for empowerment and advocacy, but also presenting risks and challenges for women's safety and well-being. Therefore, they advocate for the development of digital literacy and education to promote cyber-security awareness and enable women to take control of their digital lives. Through their activism and advocacy, cyber-feminists are working towards creating a more inclusive and equitable digital space that promotes gender equality and empowers women to participate fully in public life.

Cyber-Feminism: An Overview and Its History in Brief

Cyber-feminism is a concept that emerged in the 1990s, with the widespread adoption of the internet and other digital technologies. At its core, cyber-feminism is concerned with the ways in which technology intersects with gender, and the potential for these intersections to either perpetuate or challenge existing gender hierarchies. One of the key early figures in the development of cyber-feminism was Donna Haraway, whose 1985 essay "A Cyborg Manifesto" argued for a reconceptualization of the relationship between humans and machines (Thrift, 2006). Haraway's vision of the cyborg as a hybrid entity that challenges the boundaries between nature and culture has been influential in shaping the ways in which cyber-feminists think about technology and gender. Another important figure in the development of cyber-feminism is Sadie Plant, whose 1997 book "Zeroes + Ones: Digital Women and the New Technoculture" argued for the potential of digital technologies to enable women to transcend traditional gender roles and to create new forms of identity and community (Plant, 1995a). Plant's work was important in highlighting the ways in which digital technologies could be used to empower women and to challenge gender hierarchies. In more recent years, cyber-feminism has been associated with a range of online activism, including the #MeToo movement and the Women's March. These movements have used social media and other digital technologies to organize and mobilize women around issues of gender equality, highlighting the potential for technology to facilitate feminist activism and to give voice to marginalized groups. Overall, the history of cyber-feminism is a complex and multifaceted one, shaped by a diverse range of thinkers and activists. While cyber-feminism has made significant contributions to our understanding of the relationship between technology and gender, there is still much work to be done in terms of addressing the ways in which technology can perpetuate gender inequalities and in developing strategies for using technology to promote gender justice.

Cyber-Feminism Is at Play in the Contemporary Era

Putting cyber-feminism into practice involves taking action to address the systemic inequalities and injustices that women face in the digital space. This can include advocating for policy changes, promoting education and awareness, and engaging in online activism and community-building. It also involves recognizing the diversity of women's experiences in the digital space, and the intersecting factors that shape those experiences, including race, ethnicity, class, sexuality, and ability.

Cyber-feminism is a dynamic field that encompasses a range of practices, from online activism to digital storytelling to social media campaigns. Today, feminist movements are using digital tools to create and spread messages of empowerment, inclusivity, and resistance across the globe. One way in which cyber-feminism is practiced is through online activism, which includes protests, petitions, and other forms of collective action. For instance, the #MeToo movement, which began as a hashtag on social media, quickly spread and led to significant changes in the way that sexual harassment and assault are addressed in many industries. Similarly, the Women's March, which took place both online and offline, brought millions of people together in support of gender equality and human rights Another way in which cyber-feminism is practiced is through digital storytelling, which allows individuals to share their personal experiences and perspectives in a public forum. This can take many forms, from blogs and podcasts to videos and visual art. Through digital storytelling, women and other marginalized groups can challenge dominant narratives and speak their own truths. Social media campaigns are also a powerful tool for cyber-feminists, allowing them to reach a broad audience and engage in conversation with others. For instance, the #SayHerName campaign, which aims to bring attention to the stories of black women who have been victims of police violence, has gained significant traction on social media platforms. Additionally, campaigns such as #FreeTheNipple and #BodyPositive promote body positivity and challenge traditional beauty standards. Cyber-feminism is a multifaceted field that is constantly evolving as new digital technologies and practices emerge. Its practitioners are using digital tools to challenge the status quo, amplify marginalized voices, and create a more just and inclusive world.

Cyber-Feminism and Its Intersection With Issues of Cyber-Security And Privacy

Cyber-feminism, as a movement, is concerned with issues of gender and technology. One area of intersection with this movement is the issue of cyber-security and privacy. The digital space can be a hostile environment for women, and their personal information can be compromised through cyber-stalking, cyber-bullying, and other forms of online harassment. Cyber-feminism recognizes the importance of addressing these issues and advocates for the creation of safer digital spaces for women. One approach taken by cyber-feminists is to raise awareness of the importance of online privacy and to educate women on how to protect themselves. This includes strategies such as using strong passwords, encrypting data, and using privacy settings on social media platforms (Carrington, 2014). Cyber-feminists also work to challenge the dominant narratives around cyber-security and privacy, which often reinforce gendered stereotypes and perpetuate victim-blaming. In addition to personal security, cyber-feminists are also concerned with broader issues of privacy, particularly as they relate to government surveillance and corporate data mining. They recognize that women's privacy rights are often ignored or marginalized in these contexts, and advocate for policies and practices that respect and protect women's rights to privacy in the digital realm (Lopez et al., 2019). Cyber-feminism's intersection with cyber-security and privacy highlights the importance of addressing gendered power dynamics in the digital space. By advocating for women's safety and privacy online, cyber-feminists seek to create a more equitable and just digital world.

Threats That Women Face in the Digital Space and Suggested Strategies for Staying Safe Online

As more and more women continue to occupy online spaces, they also face an increasing number of online threats such as cyberstalking, online harassment, revenge porn, doxing, and trolling. These digital threats can have real-life consequences and impact women's psychological well-being, personal safety, and professional lives. To stay safe online, women can take various strategies including using strong passwords, enabling two-factor authentication, regularly updating their software and antivirus programs, limiting personal information online, and using a virtual private network (VPN). Additionally, women can use social media tools such as privacy settings, blocking and reporting features, and muting to manage and control their online presence. However, these strategies alone may not be enough to fully protect women from online threats. In response to the issue, feminist organizations and activists have developed various campaigns and initiatives aimed at combating online harassment, including Hollaback, #MeToo, and Stop Online Violence Against Women (Chang, 2011). These initiatives promote awareness about online harassment, create supportive communities, and advocate for policy changes to hold perpetrators accountable. Furthermore, it is important to recognize the intersectionality of online threats, as women of color, trans women, and other marginalized groups often face disproportionately higher rates of online harassment and violence. Cyber-feminism must strive to address these intersectional issues and create inclusive online spaces where all women can thrive and stay safe.

The exploration of cyber fraud related to females, examining their roles as victims or culprits, is a significant topic in cyber-feminism. It must be approached with care to avoid victim-blaming and gender biases. Presenting females solely as victims or culprits may reinforce gender binaries. Acknowledging that cyber fraud is not solely gender-specific is essential. By addressing underlying factors and recognizing women's agency, the discourse can enhance our understanding of cyber-feminism and foster a safer digital environment for all.

Role of Digital Literacy and Education in Promoting Cyber-Security Awareness

Digital literacy and education play a crucial role in empowering women to take control of their digital lives and promoting cyber-security awareness. By providing women with the tools and knowledge to navigate the digital space safely, they can reduce their risk of being targeted by cyber-criminals and abusers. Digital literacy initiatives can include programs that teach basic computer skills, social media etiquette, and online privacy practices. These programs can also provide information on how to report and block online abuse, as well as how to seek support from relevant authorities and organizations. In addition to these educational initiatives, it is important to address the systemic issues that contribute to gender-based violence and harassment online (Martin & Rice, 2012). This can involve advocating for stronger legal protections for women who experience online abuse, as well as working with technology companies to create safer online environments. It is also important to challenge harmful gender stereotypes and social norms that perpetuate violence against women, both online and offline (Yuliana, 2022). By promoting digital literacy and education, we can empower women to take control of their digital lives and reduce the risks they face online. This is a crucial step in promoting gender equality and ensuring that women can participate fully in the digital world without fear of harassment or violence.

The Impact of Social Media to Promote Positive Social Change

Social media has become a ubiquitous aspect of modern life, with billions of people around the world using platforms like Facebook, Twitter, and Instagram to connect with others, share information and experiences, and express themselves. In recent years, social media has also emerged as a powerful tool for promoting positive social change, with movements like #MeToo and Black Lives Matter leveraging online platforms to raise awareness about issues of gender-based violence and systemic racism (Lee et al., 2017). However, social media also presents a number of challenges, particularly when it comes to managing online communities and ensuring that all voices are heard. Cyberbullying, harassment, and hate speech are all too common on social media, and these phenomena can have a chilling effect on the ability of individuals to engage in meaningful online discourse. In addition, there are concerns about the role that social media companies play in shaping public discourse, with some critics arguing that these platforms have too much power to control what users see and hear (Al-Saggaf & Simmons, 2015). Despite these challenges, social media remains a powerful tool for promoting positive social change, particularly when it comes to issues related to gender, race, and social justice. By leveraging the power of digital networks and online communities, activists and advocates can amplify their voices and reach audiences that might not otherwise be accessible (Gupta et al., 2013). Moreover, by promoting digital literacy and education, it is possible to empower individuals to take control of their online lives, and to promote greater awareness about issues of online safety, security, and privacy.

Current Gap in Literature

The current literature on cyber-feminism has several gaps that need to be addressed. One of the significant gaps is the limited attention given to the intersectional experiences of women in the digital space. Most studies on cyber-feminism have focused on white women's experiences and failed to address the unique challenges and experiences faced by women of color, LGBTQ+ women, and women from marginalized communities. Another gap in the literature is the lack of focus on the role of technology in perpetuating gender inequality in the digital space (Dean, 2010a). While some studies have examined the ways in which women use technology to challenge patriarchal norms, few have focused on how technology itself perpetuates gender inequality and reinforces existing power dynamics. Moreover, there is a need to examine the role of cyber-feminism in challenging broader societal issues such as neoliberalism and capitalism (Martinez-Pecino & Durán, 2019). While some studies have examined the relationship between cyber-feminism and these issues, more research is needed to fully understand how cyber-feminism can contribute to larger social justice movements. Additionally, there is a need to explore the impact of cyber-feminism beyond the digital space (Elsadda, 2010). While cyber-feminism has had a significant impact on online discourse, it is essential to examine its potential for creating change in offline spaces. Finally, there is a need to explore the role of cyber-feminism in promoting global gender equality (Coward, 1980). While some studies have examined the impact of cyber-feminism in specific regions, there is a need to examine how cyber-feminism can be used to promote gender equality on a global scale.

The Multiple Role of Cyber-Feminism Within the Digital Space

Cyber-feminism plays multiple roles within the digital space, and its impact can be felt in many areas. As highlighted by (Yin & Sun, 2021), cyber-feminism is concerned with issues of representation, access, and participation in the digital world. Cyber-feminists have been instrumental in challenging the underrepresentation of women in technology and promoting initiatives that increase access to digital technologies for women. They have also been vocal advocates for greater diversity and inclusion in the tech industry and have called for more representation of women and minorities in tech leadership positions. Additionally, cyber-feminism has been central to efforts to combat online harassment and violence against women in the digital space. Cyber-feminists have developed strategies for responding to and preventing online harassment and have also been active in promoting legal and policy changes to address this issue. Finally, cyber-feminism has been a powerful force for promoting digital literacy and education for women, equipping them with the tools and knowledge necessary to navigate the digital world safely and confidently. As noted by (Schuster, 2013), "cyber-feminism offers a valuable perspective on the multiple ways in which gender and technology intersect and can be an effective force for promoting greater equality and empowerment for women in the digital age". However, the effectiveness of cyber-feminism in promoting gender equality in the digital space is not without its challenges. One of the main challenges is the persistence of structural inequalities and power relations that shape women's experiences in the digital world. As noted by (Carrington, 2014), "despite the gains made by cyber-feminism, there remain significant structural barriers that prevent women from achieving full equality in the digital space". These barriers include unequal access to digital technologies, the underrepresentation of women in the tech industry, and the persistence of online harassment and violence against women. Additionally, cyber-feminism must also contend with the ways in which digital technologies themselves can reinforce gendered norms and stereotypes. As argued by (Starcevic & Aboujaoude, 2015), "digital technologies can sometimes be used to perpetuate gendered power relations, reproducing existing social hierarchies in new and insidious ways". In this context, cyber-feminism must be vigilant and adaptive, responding to the changing technological landscape and the evolving ways in which gender is constructed and negotiated in the digital space. Ultimately, the success of cyber-feminism in promoting gender equality in the digital age will depend on its ability to navigate these challenges and remain responsive to the needs and experiences of women in the digital world. In sum, cyber-feminism's multiple roles in the digital space make it a powerful force for promoting gender equality and challenging patriarchal structures in the digital age.

METHODOLOGY

The chapter seeks to explore how cyber-feminism can empower women to navigate the digital space and protect themselves against online threats, while also challenging patriarchal structures and promoting gender equality. By examining the various roles of cyber-feminism and their impact on women's well-being and awareness of cyber security, the chapter aims to contribute to the growing body of literature on gender and technology, and to promote greater understanding and engagement around issues of cyber security and online safety.

Case study methodology is a valuable research approach for exploring complex phenomena in their real-life context, particularly when the boundaries between the phenomenon and context are blurred, and when multiple perspectives and factors are involved. In the context of the chapter titled "Understanding Cyber-feminism and its roles in the digital space", case studies provide a useful method for examining the roles of cyber-feminism within the digital space, as they allow for an in-depth analysis of specific examples that illustrate the concepts and issues being discussed (Stake, 1978). One of the main advantages of using case study methodology is that it allows for a rich and detailed analysis of a phenomenon or event, including its historical, social, cultural, and political context(Sandelowski, 2011). This depth of analysis enables researchers to identify and explore the multiple factors and perspectives that shape the phenomenon, and to develop a nuanced understanding of its complexities and dynamics. Case studies also provide a means of triangulation, allowing researchers to compare and contrast different cases to identify patterns, similarities, and differences. Furthermore, case studies provide a flexible and adaptive research approach, allowing researchers to adjust their research design and methods based on the emerging findings and the specific needs of the research question (Patton & Appelbaum, 2003). They also provide opportunities for collaboration and engagement with stakeholders, including the communities and individuals being studied, allowing for a more participatory and ethical research process. The use of case study methodology in this chapter on cyber-feminism in the digital space offers a robust and comprehensive means of examining the various roles of cyber-feminism and their impact on women's well-being and awareness of cyber security. The case studies provide concrete examples of cyber-feminism in action, enabling the research to move beyond theoretical discussions and to explore the practical implications of cyber-feminism for women's lives and experiences.

Examples of Case Studies About the Roles of Cyber-Feminism Within the Digital Space

Case Study One: #MeToo Movement

One of the most notable examples of cyber-feminism in action is the #MeToo movement, which emerged in 2017 in response to widespread allegations of sexual harassment and assault in Hollywood and other industries. The movement quickly spread through social media, with women sharing their own stories of harassment and abuse using the hashtag #MeToo. The movement was widely hailed as a powerful example of cyber-feminism, with its ability to amplify the voices of women who had been silenced for too long (Fileborn & Loney-Howes, 2019). The #MeToo movement demonstrates the ways in which cyber-feminism can challenge patriarchal structures and amplify marginalized voices in the digital space. By providing a platform for women to share their stories and connect with others who have had similar experiences, the movement helped to break down the isolation and shame that often accompanies experiences of sexual harassment and assault (Kaufman et al., 2021). Additionally, the movement helped to hold powerful men accountable for their actions, with many high-profile figures facing consequences for their behavior as a result of the movement. The #MeToo movement also highlights some of the challenges and limitations of cyber-feminism in practice. As noted by (Kaufman et al., 2021), "the #MeToo movement has been criticized for its reliance on social media platforms that are controlled by large corporations with their own interests and priorities". Additionally, the movement has faced criticism for its lack of intersectionality, with some voices arguing that the movement has primarily focused on the experiences of white, middle-class women and has overlooked the experiences of marginalized groups (Brown & Battle, 2019). The #MeToo movement serves as a powerful case study for understanding the multiple roles of cyber-feminism in the digital space. While the movement has faced criticism and challenges, it remains a powerful example of the ways in which digital technologies can be used to promote gender equality and challenge patriarchal structures. By providing a platform for marginalized voices and amplifying the experiences of those who have been silenced for too long, cyber-feminism has the potential to promote greater equality and empowerment for women in the digital age.

Case Study Two: Women's March

Another notable example of cyber-feminism in action is the Women's March, which took place in January 2017 in response to the election of President Donald Trump in the United States. The Women's March was a global event, with millions of women marching in cities around the world to demand gender equality and protest the policies of the new administration. The Women's March demonstrates the power of cyber-feminism to mobilize large-scale collective action in the digital age. The movement was organized largely through social media, with organizers using platforms like Facebook and Twitter to spread the word and coordinate logistics. Additionally, the movement relied heavily on digital technologies to amplify its message and connect with supporters around the world. By leveraging the power of digital technologies to mobilize a global movement for gender equality, cyber-feminism played a significant role in the Women's March. However, the Women's March also highlights some of the challenges and limitations of cyber-feminism in practice. As noted by (McDuffie & Ames, 2021), "the Women's March faced criticism for its lack of inclusivity and its failure to adequately address issues of intersectionality". Additionally, the movement has faced challenges in sustaining its momentum and translating its online activism into concrete political gains. The Women's March serves as a powerful case study for understanding the multiple roles of cyber-feminism in the digital space. While the movement has faced criticism and challenges, it remains a powerful example of the ways in which digital technologies can be used to promote gender equality and challenge patriarchal structures (Silverstein, 2019). By mobilizing a global movement for gender equality through the power of social media and digital technologies, cyber-feminism has the potential to catalyze real change in the digital age.

Case Study Three: Malala Yousafzai

Malala Yousafzai is a prominent example of how cyber-feminism can empower women and girls to challenge gender inequality and patriarchal structures in the digital age. Malala is a Pakistani activist for female education and the youngest Nobel Prize laureate. In 2012, at the age of 15, she was targeted by the Taliban for her activism and shot in the head while riding a bus to school. Malala survived the attack and had since become a global advocate for girls' education and women's rights (Sattar et al., 2021). Malala's story highlights the role of digital technologies in amplifying the voices of marginalized groups and enabling them to challenge oppressive systems. In the aftermath of the attack, Malala became a global symbol of resilience and resistance against patriarchal violence. Her story was shared widely on social media, and she used digital platforms to continue her activism and advocate for girls' education around the world (Kross, 2021). Furthermore, the Malala Fund, founded by Malala and her father, has leveraged digital technologies to support girls' education around the world. The fund uses online platforms to raise awareness about the importance of girls' education and to connect with supporters and donors. By using digital technologies to build a global network of advocates for girls' education, the Malala Fund represents a powerful example of cyber-feminism in practice (Kross, 2021). The case of Malala Yousafzai adds value to the chapter by demonstrating the multiple roles of cyber-feminism in empowering women and girls to challenge patriarchal structures and promote gender equality. Malala's story illustrates how digital technologies can be used to amplify the voices of marginalized groups, connect with supporters around the world, and catalyze real change. By highlighting the ways in which cyber-feminism can be used to challenge patriarchy and support marginalized groups, the case of Malala Yousafzai serves as a powerful example of the potential of cyber-feminism in the digital age.

Critiquing of Cyber-Feminism

While cyber-feminism offers many opportunities for promoting gender equality and challenging patriarchal structures in the digital space, it has also been subject to critique. One critique of cyber-feminism is that it can be overly focused on individual empowerment and fail to address larger structural inequalities. As argued by (Kruschek, 2019), "cyber-feminism may offer opportunities for individual women to assert themselves in the digital world, but it does not necessarily address broader issues of social inequality and power relations". In addition, cyber-feminism has been criticized for its narrow focus on gender issues and its failure to address issues of race, class, and sexuality in the digital space. As noted by (Starr, 2016), "cyber-feminism risks reproducing the same exclusions and hierarchies that it seeks to challenge, by focusing too narrowly on gender issues and ignoring the intersections of race, class, and sexuality in the digital world". Moreover, some have argued that cyber-feminism's emphasis on individual empowerment may also mask the systemic issues that prevent women from achieving full equality in the digital space. Despite these critiques, cyber-feminism remains a powerful tool for promoting gender equality and challenging patriarchal structures in the digital age, and its impact should continue to be studied and evaluated critically. Furthermore, some scholars have also pointed out that cyber-feminism can sometimes reinforce binary gender norms and essentialize the experiences of women in the digital space. As noted by (Dean, 2010b), "cyber-feminism can sometimes reproduce essentialist notions of gender identity and fails to recognize the diversity of experiences and perspectives among women in the digital world". This critique suggests that cyber-feminism must be attentive to the ways in which gender identity is constructed and negotiated in the digital space and must be open to diverse perspectives and experiences. Additionally, the emphasis on individual empowerment and self-reliance in cyber-feminism can obscure the structural issues and systemic inequalities that shape women's experiences in the digital space. As highlighted by (Plant, 1995b), "cyber-feminism may provide tools for individual women to navigate the digital world, but it does not necessarily address the larger systemic issues that limit women's participation and access to digital technologies". Therefore, while cyber-feminism offers a valuable perspective on gender and technology, it must be critically evaluated and nuanced to address the complex issues that women face in the digital age.

Cyber-feminism has become a major topic of discussion in recent years, as feminist scholars have started exploring the intersection of gender, technology, and the digital space. Cyber-feminism is a movement that emerged in the 1990s as a response to the lack of women's representation and participation in the technology sector. Since then, cyber-feminism has evolved to include the examination of the ways in which gender, race, class, sexuality, and other identities intersect with digital technologies. In this article, I will critically discuss the issues of cyber-feminism and its roles in the digital space.

One of the main issues of cyber-feminism is the notion of a gender digital divide. This divide refers to the disparity in access to and use of digital technologies between men and women. Studies have shown that women are underrepresented in the technology sector and are less likely to have access to digital technologies. This divide can have significant consequences on women's economic, political, and social opportunities. In their article, "The Gender Digital Divide in Developing Countries," (Chang, 2011) discuss how the gender digital divide can impact women's access to education, healthcare, and employment opportunities. Another issue of cyber-feminism is the problem of online harassment and violence. Women are disproportionately targeted for online abuse, harassment, and violence. This can lead to women's silencing and exclusion from online spaces. A study by (Pew Research Centre, 2021) found that 41% of women have been subjected to online harassment, compared to 17% of men. The problem of online harassment has become a major concern for cyber-feminists, who argue for the need to create safer online spaces for women.

Furthermore, cyber-feminists have also criticized the ways in which digital technologies reproduce gendered and sexist norms. Digital technologies are not neutral and can reinforce and amplify social inequalities. In her article, "Feminist Approaches to Media Literacy," (Wajcman, 2006) discusses how media literacy can be used to challenge gendered norms and stereotypes perpetuated by digital technologies.

Roles of Cyber-feminism in the digital space

Despite these issues, cyber-feminism has played a crucial role in promoting gender equality in the digital space. Cyber-feminists have been at the forefront of advocating for women's representation and participation in the technology sector. They have also called for the creation of safer online spaces for women and have worked towards the development of policies and tools to combat online harassment and violence (Lopez et al., 2019). Additionally, cyber-feminists have raised awareness about the ways in which digital technologies can reinforce gendered norms and stereotypes and have advocated for the need to develop media literacy programs to challenge these norms.

CONCLUSION: FUTURE DIRECTIONS FOR RESEARCH IN CYBERFEMINISM

The chapter challenges oversimplified and polarizing ways of thinking about gender and virtual spaces that limit cyberfeminist efforts to achieve greater online gender equality. These false binaries include ideas such as online vs. offline, cyberfeminism vs. non-cyberfeminism, and utopian vs. dystopian views of cyberspace. Other false dichotomies relate to empowerment vs. vulnerability, privacy vs. self-disclosure, and victimhood vs. blameworthiness. By examining these dichotomies more closely, it becomes clear that girls' virtual experiences are complex and diverse. The aim of the volume is to continue breaking down these polarized ways of thinking in order to facilitate more productive discussions and work towards common goals of reducing virtual gender inequality and increasing girls' and young women's online agency.

To achieve greater online gender equality, future cyberfeminist efforts need to move beyond micro-level discussions and punitive policy initiatives and shift towards collective macro-level action that involves wider social engagement. This could include educational or family-based initiatives that promote media literacy and respect for all genders. It's important to avoid patriarchal and neo-liberal discourses that blame girls for being susceptible to online abuse and instead focus on promoting a culture of empowerment and agency. These discourses perpetuate harmful gender stereotypes and contribute to the notion that girls are responsible for protecting themselves from victimization online. Instead, cyberfeminist initiatives should aim to promote self-expression for girls in virtual spaces and challenge harmful beliefs that blame victims of online abuse.

To move past problematic discourses, cyberfeminists must challenge prevailing media representations of gender and societal expectations that dictate accepted standards for online femininity. This can be achieved by deconstructing these narratives on a larger scale to challenge normative standards of online gender performance, critique online spaces and current policies for entrenching sexist narratives. The experiences and perceptions of marginalized groups such as non-heterosexual, trans, and racialized girls should also be included in future cyberfeminist initiatives to promote intersectional insights and increase girls' online agency. It is important to solicit girls' own perceptions and experiences to ensure that they have a voice in discussions on gender and virtual space. This approach will move beyond patriarchal binary thought, promote gender "e-quality," and help construct virtual spaces that better reflect diverse perspectives.

REFERENCES

Al-Saggaf, Y., & Simmons, P. (2015). Social media in Saudi Arabia: Exploring its use during two natural disasters. *Technological Forecasting and Social Change*, *95*, 3–15. doi:10.1016/j.techfore.2014.08.013

Al-Shalan, A. (2006). *Cyber-Crime Fear and Victimization: An Analysis of a National Cyber-Crime Fear and Victimization* Mississippi State University. https://scholarsjunction.msstate.edu/td

Brown, S. E. V., & Battle, J. S. (2019). Ostracizing targets of workplace sexual harassment before and after the #MeToo movement. *Equality, Diversity and Inclusion*, *39*(1), 53–67. doi:10.1108/EDI-09-2018-0162

Carrington, K. (2014). *Feminism and Global Justice*. Routledge. doi:10.4324/9781315748368

Chang, J. (2011). Cyberspace and Reconstruction of Women's Identity. *Trans-Humanities Journal*, *4*(2), 125–149. doi:10.1353/trh.2011.0018

Coward, R. (1980). "This Novel Changes Lives": Are Women's Novels Feminist Novels? A Response to Rebecca O'Rourke's Article 'Summer Reading.'. *Feminist Review*, *5*(1), 53–64. doi:10.1057/fr.1980.12

Dean, J. (2010). Feminism in the Papers. *Feminist Media Studies*, *10*(4), 391–407. doi:10.1080/14680777.2010.514112

Elsadda, H. (2010). Arab Women Bloggers: The Emergence of Literary Counterpublics. *Middle East Journal of Culture and Communication*, *3*(3), 312–332. doi:10.1163/187398610X538678

Fileborn, B., & Loney-Howes, R. (2019). Introduction: Mapping the Emergence of #MeToo. In #MeToo and the Politics of Social Change (pp. 1–18). Springer International Publishing. doi:10.1007/978-3-030-15213-0_1

Gupta, A., Tyagi, M., & Sharma, D. (2013). Use of Social Media Marketing in Healthcare. *Journal of Health Management*, *15*(2), 293–302. doi:10.1177/0972063413489058

Kaufman, M. R., Dey, D., Crainiceanu, C., & Dredze, M. (2021). #MeToo and Google Inquiries Into Sexual Violence: A Hashtag Campaign Can Sustain Information Seeking. *Journal of Interpersonal Violence*, *36*(19–20), 9857–9867. doi:10.1177/0886260519868197

Kemp, S. (2018). *Digital in 2018: World's Internet Users Pass the 4 Billion Mark*. We Are Social. https://wearesocial.com/blog/2018/01/ global-digital-report-2018

Kross, E. (2021). *Talking to Yourself*. Character Lab Tips. doi:10.53776/tips-talking-to-yourself

Kruschek, G. (2019). Stigma in the Comments Section: Feminist and Anti-Feminist Discussions Online. *Computers and Composition*, *54*, 102515. doi:10.1016/j.compcom.2019.102515

Kshetri, N. (2010). Diffusion and effects of cyber-crime in developing economies. *Third World Quarterly*, *31*(7), 1057–1079. doi:10.1080/01436597.2010.518752

Lee, F. L. F., Chen, H.-T., & Chan, M. (2017). Social media use and university students' participation in a large-scale protest campaign: The case of Hong Kong's Umbrella Movement. *Telematics and Informatics*, *34*(2), 457–469. doi:10.1016/j.tele.2016.08.005

Lopez, K. J., Muldoon, M. L., & McKeown, J. K. L. (2019). One Day of #Feminism: Twitter as a Complex Digital Arena for Wielding, Shielding, and Trolling talk on Feminism. *Leisure Sciences*, *41*(3), 203–220. doi:10.1080/01490400.2018.1448022

Martin, N., & Rice, J. (2012). Children's cyber-safety and protection in Australia: An analysis of community stakeholder views. *Crime Prevention and Community Safety*, *14*(3), 165–181. doi:10.1057/cpcs.2012.4

Martinez-Pecino, R., & Durán, M. (2019). I Love You but I Cyberbully You: The Role of Hostile Sexism. *Journal of Interpersonal Violence*, *34*(4), 812–825. doi:10.1177/0886260516645817

McDuffie, K., & Ames, M. (2021). Archiving affect and activism: Hashtag feminism and structures of feeling in Women's March tweets. *First Monday*. doi:10.5210/fm.v26i2.10317

Patton, E., & Appelbaum, S. H. (2003). The case for case studies in management research. *Management Research News*, *26*(5), 60–71. doi:10.1108/01409170310783484

Pew Research Centre. (2021). *The State of Online Harassment*. Pew Research Center.

Plant, S. (1995a). The Future Looms: Weaving Women and Cybernetics. *Body & Society*, *1*(3–4), 45–64. doi:10.1177/1357034X95001003003

Plant, S. (1995b). The Future Looms: Weaving Women and Cybernetics. *Body & Society*, *1*(3–4), 45–64. doi:10.1177/1357034X95001003003

Sandelowski, M. (2011). "Casing" the research case study. *Research in Nursing & Health*, *34*(2), 153–159. doi:10.1002/nur.20421

Sattar, G., Safeer, A. K., Pasha, M. I., Furqan, K. M. Y., & Riaz, N. (2021). Stereotypical ideologies towards women: Feminist poststructuralist discourse analysis of malala yousafzai's political speeches. *Humanities & Social Sciences Reviews*, *9*(3), 1245–1257. doi:10.18510/hssr.2021.93123

Schuster, J. (2013). Invisible feminists? Social media and young women's political participation. *Political Science (Wellington, N.Z.)*, *65*(1), 8–24. doi:10.1177/0032318713486474

Schwarz, M., Scherrer, A., Hohmann, C., Heiberg, J., Brugger, A., & Nuñez-Jimenez, A. (2020). COVID-19 and the academy: It is time for going digital. *Energy Research & Social Science*, *68*, 101684. doi:10.1016/j.erss.2020.101684

Silverstein, S. (2019). Women's March Colloquy - On Sirens and Lamp Posts: Sound, Space, and Affective Politics. *Music and Politics*, *13*(1). doi:10.3998/mp.9460447.0013.103

Stake, R. E. (1978). The Case Study Method in Social Inquiry. *Educational Researcher*, *7*(2), 5–8. doi:10.3102/0013189X007002005

Starcevic, V., & Aboujaoude, E. (2015). Cyberchondria, cyberbullying, cybersuicide, cybersex: "new" psychopathologies for the 21st century? *World Psychiatry; Official Journal of the World Psychiatric Association (WPA)*, *14*(1), 97–100. doi:10.1002/wps.20195

Starr, M. (2016). Beyond Machine Dreams: Zen, Cyber-, and Transnational Feminisms in Ruth Ozeki's *A Tale for the Time Being*. *Meridians (Middletown, Conn.)*, *13*(2), 99–122. doi:10.2979/meridians.13.2.06

Thrift, N. (2006). Donna Haraway's Dreams. *Theory, Culture & Society*, *23*(7–8), 189–195. doi:10.1177/0263276406069231

Wajcman, J. (2006). Review: Wajcman Confronts Cyberfeminism. *Social Studies of Science*, *36*(2), 321–327. https://www.jstor.org/stable/25474445. doi:10.1177/0306312706058828

Wall, & David S. (2005). The Internet as a Conduit for Criminal Activity. In April Pattavina (Ed.), *Information Technology and the Criminal Justice System* (pp. 77–98). Sage Publications.

Wilkinson, S., & Kitzinger, C. (2013). Representing Our Own Experience. *Psychology of Women Quarterly*, *37*(2), 251–255. doi:10.1177/0361684313483111

Yin, S., & Sun, Y. (2021). Intersectional digital feminism: Assessing the participation politics and impact of the MeToo movement in China. *Feminist Media Studies*, *21*(7), 1176–1192. doi:10.1080/14680777.2020.1837908

Yuliana, Y. (2022). The importance of cyber-security awareness for children. *Lampung Journal of International Law*, *4*(1), 41–48. doi:10.25041/lajil.v3i2.2526

Chapter 23
Exploring Operation of Gender in the Virtual Space

Rajni Nair
Usha Mittlal Institute of Technology, SNDT Women's University, India

ABSTRACT

We find ourselves inhabiting a world that has been brought closer together by the vast reach and influence of the world wide web. The interconnectedness provided by the internet offers access to information, connectivity, anonymity, and power, unlike any other medium. It is therefore crucial to recognize that the apparent anonymity of the internet conceals a multitude of secrets and layers of information, making it a more public medium than one might initially perceive. Engaging in the exploration and use (exploitation) of this virtual realm exposes us to numerous perils and dangers. The idealistic notion that the virtual realm would transcend physical markers such as age, gender, class, caste, and race, and not be defining factors of individual existence, remains uncertain. This chapter aims to examine how the internet simultaneously acts as a liberating and entrapping force, becoming a new arena for reinforcing existing gender inequalities.

INTRODUCTION

The cyber world has been hailed as a realm which would dissolve markers of corporeal existence like age, gender, class, caste, race etc. The argument being that as these markers which polarize are indiscernible in the virtual world they will lose their salience and we would have a utopian space where an individual can float free of all these restricting markers. However, the reality is far from removed. In Zeros and Ones: Digital Women and the New Technoculture (1997), Sadie Plant implies that dual roles still prevail in the new seamless boundless cyberspace: zeroes and ones are at the core of new digital technologies where she sees '1' as the man and '0' as the woman, the '0-ther' or nothing.

There is no denying the fact that the internet seems to be leaving an indelible mark on the warp and weft of our social interactions and systems by subverting prevalent norms and rules. The flux we are witnessing in the digital space can be harnessed into a productive space that can be used to mark a departure from traditional norms that define social power; however, the current reality seems to be far

DOI: 10.4018/978-1-6684-8893-5.ch023

removed. According to Nielsen's India Internet Report 2023, India had over 700 million active internet users aged 2 years and above as of December 2022. Of these, rural India accounted for 425 million users, which was almost 44% higher than the number of active internet users in urban areas, with 295 million users. Female active internet users as per the report grew by 27%, whereas male users increased by around 18%. Nearly 90% of internet users were daily users. There were over 450 million smartphone users in the country, with video watching and video calling being the top two online activities. Facebook users in India have crossed the 240-million mark, becoming the largest audience country for the social media giant. You tube, Instagram and Whatsapp are the other platforms frequented by users in India. On an average people spend 6-8 hours on the Internet in a day and most log on to one of their favorite platforms every two to three minutes in a day.

It is obvious by the above facts that the virtual space is slowly emerging as an extension of reality. In fact the boundaries between what can be perceived as real and what now constitutes the virtual is constantly blurring. What with artificial intelligence and intruding algorithms percolating into our daily life and existence. Smart devices have now become extensions of the human selves and almost every citizen who owns a smartphone is not a netizen. Women are increasingly participating in social networking and other related activities on social media where they are constantly interacting with other netizens who carry the markers of their gender identity to the virtual space. Oftentimes carrying prejudices and misogyny too. This is evident in the multifarious instances of cyberbullying, slut shaming and other related discrimination women and people identifying to other marginalized groups face on social media. An attempt thus needs to be made to understand how gender roles and misogynist practices percolate to the social media platforms and whether users of social media are aware of the choices they are making and the dangers that lurk in social media.

REVIEW OF LITERATURE

Researchers who have explored the operation of gender on social media suggest presentation and representation of self on social media as "identity performance" (boyd and Ellison, 2007; Buckingham, 2008; Liu, 2007; Westlake, 2008; Cover, 2012). The process of identity construction and management of gender on social media can be explored by deliberation on the ideas of sociologists like Erving Goffman, who have spoken about the 'performance of self in everyday life'. Social media profiles, posts, stories and statuses, especially the selfies can be looked at as conscious and reflective performances and representations of the self for designated audiences. These representations are constructed to give specific impressions about the self and surge narratives about one's life, identity and choices (boyd, 2008). This is similar to how one presents oneselves to one's audience through speech, dressing and so on. In the online sphere often these representations or expressions of the self elicit name-calling or insults which can be referred to as *networked harassment*, in which an individual is harassed by a group of people connected by social media; and more nebulous interpersonal situations in which at least one participant strategically labels an incident or set of incidents as "harassment" although it may not meet evaluative criteria as such (Marwick, 2021). Online harassment is more common for women and nonbinary people, particularly women of color, queer women, and women in the public eye (Barton & Storm, 2014; Krook, 2017; Lenhart et al., 2016). These studies also reveal that harassment is often used to police women's online behavior and may have a debilitating effect on women's participation in the public sphere both online and offline. As a result, scholars deploy terms like "online hate," "e-bile," "gender trolling," and "online misogyny" to connect online behavior such as "revenge porn" and digitally enabled sexual violence to structural sexism and violence against women (Banet-Weiser & Miltner, 2016 ; Citron, 2014; Eikren & Ingram-Waters, 2016). However, while most of this research argues that online harassment is caused by misogyny, there exist no explanatory models of *why* misogyny results in networked harassment. Most of the research in this domain speaks about the extension of prevailing gender norms and discrimination from the real to the online and newer forms of gender based discrimination in the online sphere that have emerged due to the anonymity offered by the virtual sphere.

METHODOLOGY

To understand how aware the users are of the tools they use on a daily basis and how deep is their understanding of the dangers that lurk in cyberspace and the agencies they can approach in case they fall prey to cybercrime, a survey was conducted. An online questionnaire was created and the link was shared with respondents. The method used to decide on the respondents was snowballing. Out of the 253 respondents, 190 were in the age group of 18-25 having a background in science and technology, residing in Mumbai and were either college students or professionals working in the field of computer science and technology, 34 were in the age group of 25-35 and 33 above 35. All of them obviously used a smartphone and claimed to be well versed in technology. All of them accessed the internet numerous times in a day and use both mobile and Wifi data, paid and free to access the internet. In addition, semi structured interviews were conducted with 30 respondents who fall in the same demographic category. Along with this a detailed textual analysis of the social media platforms like Facebook, Instagram, Twitter, blogs by women and women dominant groups on social media handles was conducted.

RESULTS

The response to the question as to why they used the internet was interesting, 245 (93.5%) respondents said they use the internet for information, for professional purposes (141- 53%) and to make friends (85 – 32.5%). Which means the assumption that the majority of people use the internet to network or for entertainment; to pass time is not the reason why these individuals use the internet. The interviews revealed that though logging on to the internet and checking their Facebook, Instagram, Twitter and LinkedIn accounts has become almost akin to addiction for most of the respondents, they did not do it only for entertainment. Most of the respondents did it out of FOMO while a few claimed that they actually found a lot of interesting stuff on the internet which helped them deal with their day-to-day lives as students and professionals in Mumbai city in a better manner. As Zomato would help them decide which restaurant to go to, which not to and what to order from where on line. They also enjoyed posting their experiences and pictures on Zomato to help others out with their food preferences. An app like Twitter was generally accessed to gain insight about what celebrities had to say about a particular event or just to explore their creative side, the fact that one could make profound statements and comments in less than 140 characters found appeal with the generation which survives on all things instant. A few said that reading a witty to the point twitter post was much more informative than reading 'hopelessly lengthy and boring articles' in the newspaper.

The interviews also revealed that many don't think about existence without social media platforms and tend to overlook harassment faced or at the most report or block the perpetrators account. Textual analysis of the social media platforms revealed that these spaces were frequented by men and women alike, women faced hate, trolling and abuse more than men. In the case of celebrities and social media influencers, hate comments seem to abound the messages made to posts by women, so also sexually motivated comments and hate in comparison to those directed towards their male counterparts. Women also tend to focus more on issues related to empowerment and refashioning of selves in their blogs and posts in comparison to men.

DISCUSSION

Many of the respondents and almost all of the people interviewed used the internet to unleash their creative potential. Photography as a passion was taken up to click and post meaningful pictures with comments on Instagram and Facebook pages created to give vent to the artistic calling in terms of writing on social issues to writing poems and even composing songs and recording covers to be uploaded on you tube and linked to their social media accounts. Almost all had a chosen list of sites, apps and internet celebrities they religiously followed. Internet celebrities enjoy more popularity and followers than some of our real life celebrities. Poet Rupi kaur seemed to be a hot favorite with her Instagram account. Rupi kaur has about 1.8 million followers and about 507 posts to her credit on Instagram. Rupi Kaur's 2015 Instagram post picturing her lying in bed with her clothes and sheets stained with a small amount of menstrual blood catapulted her into instant headlines. This picture was banned by Instagram. Kaur did not take this lying down, she in fact fought back by bringing to light the hypocrisy of the site which allowed pictures of "objectified" and "pornified" women but had pulled out her post. Followers flocked to her, cheering her on as she added, "I will not apologize for not feeding the ego and pride of misogynist society that will have my body in underwear but not be okay with a small leak." Instagram was forced to back out. Insults and death threats were launched at Kaur, but her followers on Instagram grew seven times over. Kaur is more of a spoken word artist and is perceived to be too aggressive or uncomfortable. Kaur's short poems continues to churn out simple, raw lines as short visual poems dealing with topics such as rape, domestic violence and alcoholism. Her poems are usually accompanied by a startling image. Kaur prefers to call her poetry 'design poetry' – poems based on the spoken word where what is usually under the wraps in society is voiced using simple pictorial language and images.

Kaur is not alone in this endeavor, there are many others who explore the anonymity and creative canvas offered by the internet to explore their creativity and find voice and agency as women. Kaur has collaborated with Carlota Guerrero, a 26-year-old photographer and art director whose body of work can be described as a visual celebration of the female body. Guerrero usually captures nature- flowers, snow beds, trees leaves and women, usually nude. In an interview, she stated her endeavor is to separate sexuality from nudity and establish a new way of living the relationship with our bodies.

Both women shot to fame using social media as the platform to explore themselves, and their art and gain visibility and agency. The reason behind quoting the above example is to highlight how women are reclaiming cyberspace and finding agency. The internet and especially social media is changing the very nature of what can be considered text. Writing today does not require paper and printing. This truly can be called the age of the 'non-text' where writing is a purely an electronic experience with the doing away of the need and importance of printing. It is the writer's force of ideas and means of presentation using the visual medium which gets visibility and reach with the interference of the publishing house. With the doing away of printing a new relationship is established between the artist and the audience. In the virtual world, a little-known or unknown artist publishes alongside a veritable literary celebrity. The hierarchical structures set up by the patriarchal world seem to be diminishing by the way and women are gaining not just a voice but a platform to talk about and discuss issues which were earlier taboo.

Two other platforms used by women as a cathartic experience are blogs and the groups formed on social media platforms. Many of the women interviewed either had a blog or page of their own on social media sites. Pressures of the family and society at times forced them to be away from some of the creative expressions that they really wanted to pursue. The anonymity of the cyber space provides them with a platform which they can explore and exploit to their advantage. For most women blogs or blogging acts like a mental visit to the gym where they give a creative outlet to themselves and use their latent talent to either find agency and voice in a system that is otherwise famous for gagging their voices and individuality. One finds the presence of many online women's groups which act as soul sharing mediums for women. Women share their deepest aspirations, hopes and dreams, fears and tribulations with other like minded women and aim to find solace in other like-minded women and their thoughts and opinions. Women's groups have helped many terminally ill and depressed women overcome their ailments and find agency and creative outlet. These groups also provide newly married women and young mothers with a platform to express their doubts about the new roles assigned to them and discuss questions that they could possibly have reservations about sharing. The suggestions and advice given by other women help them deal with specific problems encountered as most women who participate in these discussions are not really known to each other, hence the feeling that the advice is third person and unbiased.

With the unprecedented rise in the use of the internet, the instances of crime using the internet is also spreading its vicious tentacles far and wide. Cybercrime has become a global phenomenon with women and children becoming easy targets to the perpetrators of these crimes. Cyber stalking, cyber bullying, harassment via social media, morphing and message spoofing are examples of crimes being perpetrated on the internet. Most women find themselves easy targets of stalkers and bullies on the internet. These people create fake social media accounts to befriend women and children and get easy access to private information, pictures and other personal details. The anonymity that social media offers and the ability of social media to give a creative and emotional outlet to people especially women who do not necessarily enjoy these freedoms burdened by their societal roles and expectations makes women and children 'put themselves out' on social media. New age social media apps like snap chat prove to be especially dangerous because participation in these apps means posting through pictures. These pictures most of the time end up being too personal or sexual in nature. Women place a lot of trust on their friends on these platforms and believe the images and text they share in confidence will not be shared or misused by their so called social media friends but the reality is far from removed. Most reported cases of cyberbullying happen between close friends and relatives. In recent times there has been a spurt in the circulation of rape videos and other acts of physical and sexual abuse. People shoot these videos and circulate them causing a lot of psychological trauma to the women involved.

Another cause of concern is the use of the mobile phone as a security vault. Most people use mobile phones to store and record information, text, images and other private and confidential information as people used to maintain a personal diary in the past. The assurance that most people have is that the mobile has a password which will keep their information safe. But most phones can be easily unlocked by software experts and information stored on the cell phones be easily snooped around by the multiple apps whom we unknowingly authorize and grant access to our personal information when we accept the terms and conditions of the apps we install on our phones and on other platforms of the internet without reading them of understanding the ramifications of our actions.

We need to understand that crime is not new to humankind but cybercrime is and the legal system and we are users of the internet are still underprepared to understand the onslaught of cyber crime. Women are easy targets in the cyber world and the nature of cyber crime changes with the gender of the victim. Cyber Bullying, stalking, morphing slut Shaming, flaming and doxing are forms of cyber crimes that are used extensively on the internet against women in particular. The survey and the interviews revealed 75% women have experienced cyber bullying and stalking in some form. Slut shaming and flaming are two other forms of cyber crime that are extensively being used against women and to silence them. As any keen observer of the internet would notice that most women celebrities are usually either slut shamed or bullied for every act of theirs. Example an actress who puts on weight post pregnancy or wears revealing clothes or expresses her frank opinions about issues is trolled, bullied and slut shamed to silence. Many women celebrities have either reduced or refrain from posting and commenting on social networking sites. One is forced to point out that the leaps that technology has made in the cyber world should have enabled women to sense a feeling of equality and safety in the cyber realm but the reality is that the cyber realm had created its own forms of gendered identities and crime. The crux of the matter being that there is a credibility gap between the promises of Virtual Reality and cyberspace and the quality of what it delivers. The new technological frontier seems to be intensifying the gender-gap and increasing the polarization between the sexes. We seem to be back to the war metaphor, but its location is the real world, not the hyperspace of abstract masculinity. And its protagonists are no computer images, but the real social agents of postindustrial urban landscapes.

In spite of the existing misogyny and hate and even cyber crime,being the undeniable reality of how gender and dominant and marginalized groups operate on the internet. Women and people prescribing to other marginalized gender groups have still formed ways of connecting with each other and forming gated online communities of sisterhood where questions related to gender and voice are discussed and raised. Where gender based solidarities and bonds are forged. No doubt the internet seems to be extending gender based misogyny. But it is also emerging as a 'counterpublics' for women and other marginalized gender groups to voice agency.

CONCLUSION

The question one needs to deliberate on is that when Donna Haraway (Haraway 1997) envisioned the Cyborg, "The cyborg is a kind of disassembled and reassembled, postmodern collective and personal self." a self which feminists must code. She envisioned a platform for women which would enable them to be themselves. With the boundaries of gender being blurred and the vision of a cyborg existence, she thought that she would want to be more of a 'cyborg' than a 'goddess' in cyberspace. The question remains: have we been able to create such a realm in cyberspace? To quote Rosser (Rosse r2004), "Cyberfeminism can be a critique of equality in cyberspace, challenge the gender stereotype in cyberspace, examine the gender relationship in cyberspace, examine the collaboration between human and technology, and examine the relationship between women and technology and more. For examples: the innovation of internet has a huge impact on women's lives (Like how the innovation of telephone bought women security from crime and no longer being isolated from geographical constraint), the idea of digital life has been introduced to all users of the internet; but is this new technology liberating or oppressing women?

In this sense, we can think of this innovation once again freeing women from time and space constraints which enable them to become active users on the web. On the other hand, this innovation can possibly oppress women by encouraging cybersex, pornography or prostitution which ultimately makes them more vulnerable. Therefore, Cyberfeminism is the approach to examine these matters." The need of the hour is to critically examine and interrogate gender in cyberspace. The interrogation must happen both at the level of law and at the level of society. We need to re-examine the ways by which women have been subjected to oppression and violence on the internet. While we do this we need to also applaud and celebrate the ways in which women are reclaiming their identity and existence in cyberspace.

There seems to be a lot of ignorance about existing laws related to cyber crime. Policy decisions at the state level related to the internet and operations on it need to be relook at on a timely basis to include new and diverse forms of crimes and hate that are creeping in into cyberspace. For crime and hate based crime and even misogyny is not a new phenomenon. What has changed in the space where it operates. And that has made these issues more pertinent. Interventions at the policy level are required to streamline these issues. Only time will tell whether we have been able to make optimum and good use of the immense possibilities offered to us by the internet.

REFERENCES

Abidin, C. (2015). Communicative Intimacies: Influencers and Perceived Interconnectedness. *Ada: A Journal of Gender, New Media & Technology, 8*. https://adanewmedia.org/2015/11/issue8-abidin/

Banet-Weiser, S., & Miltner, K. M. (2016). # MasculinitySoFragile: Culture, structure, and networked misogyny. *Feminist Media Studies, 16*(1), 171–174. doi:10.1080/14680777.2016.1120490

Barton, A., & Storm, H. (2014). *Violence and harassment against women in the news media: A global picture*. International Women's Media Foundation. https://www.iwmf.org/our-research/journalist-safety/violence-and-harassment-against-women-in-the-news-media-a-global-picture/

Boyd, D. (2014). *It's Complicated: The Social Lives of Networked Teens*. New Haven; London: Yale University Press.

Boyd, D. & Ellison, N. (2007). Social network sites: Definition, history and scholarship. *Journal of Computer-Mediated Communication, 13*(1), 210–230.

Boyd, D. (2008). Why youth (heart) social network sites: The role of networked publics in teenage social life. In D. Buckingham (ed.), *Youth, Identity, and Digital Media* (pp. 119–142). Cambridge, MA: MIT Press.

Buckingham, D. (Ed.). (2008). *Youth, Identity, and Digital Media*. MIT Press.

Butler, J. (1990). *Gender Trouble: Feminism and the Subversion of Identity*. Routledge.

Butler, J. (1993). *Bodies That Matter: On the Discursive Limits of "Sex*. Routledge.

Butler, J. (2005). *Giving an Account of Oneself*. Fordham.University Press. doi:10.5422/fso/9780823225033.001.0001

Citron, D. (2014). *Hate crimes in cyberspace*. Harvard University Press. doi:10.4159/harvard.9780674735613

Cover, R. (2012a). Performing and undoing identity online: Social networking, identity theories and the incompatibility of online profiles and friendship regimes. *Convergence (London)*, *18*(2), 177–193. doi:10.1177/1354856511433684

Eikren, E., & Ingram-Waters, M. (2016). Dismantling "you get what you deserve": Toward a feminist sociology of revenge porn. *Ada: A Journal of Gender, New Media, and Technology*, *10*. https://adanewmedia.org/2016/10/issue10-eikren-ingramwaters/

Frosh, P. (2015). The Gestural Image: The Selfie, Photography Theory, and Kinesthetic Sociability. *International Journal of Communication*, *9*(Feature), 1607–1628. https://doi.org/ doi:1932–8036/2015FEA0002

Goffman, E. (1969). *The Presentation of Self in Everyday Life*. Allen Lane.

Goffman, E. (1979). *Gender Advertisements*. Harper & Row.

Haraway, D. (1997). *Modest_Witness@Second_Millennium. FemaleMan©_Meets_OncoMouse™: Feminism and Technoscience*. Routledge.

Krook, M. L. (2017). Violence against women in politics. *Journal of Democracy*, *28*(1), 74–88. doi:10.1353/jod.2017.0007

Lenhart, A., Ybarra, M. L., Zickuhr, K., & Price-Feeney, M. (2016). *Online harassment, digital abuse, and cyberstalking in America*. Data & Society Research Institute.

Liu, H. (2007). Social network profiles as "taste performances.". *Journal of Computer-Mediated Communication*, *13*(1), 252–275. doi:10.1111/j.1083-6101.2007.00395.x

Lövheim, M. (2013). Negotiating Empathic Communication. *Feminist Media Studies*, *13*(4), 613–628. doi:10.1080/14680777.2012.659672

Luckman, S. (1999). (En)gendering the Digital Body: Feminism and the Internet. *Hecate*, *25*(2), 36–48.

Marwick, A. (2013). *Status Update: Celebrity, Publicity, and Branding in the Social Media Age*. Yale University Press.

Munster, A. (1999). Is There Postlife After Postfeminism? Tropes of Technics and Life in Cyberfeminism. *Australian Feminist Studies*, *14*(29), 119–131. doi:10.1080/08164649993371

Nielsen. (2022, June 27). *Nielsen's Bharat 2.0 Study reveals a 45% growth in Active Internet Users in rural India since 2019*. Nielsen. https://www.nielsen.com/news-center/2022/nielsens-bharat-2-0-study-reveals-a-45-growth-in-active-internet-users-in-rural-india-since-2019/

Plant, S. (1997, January 27). Babes in the Net. *New Statesman & Society*, p. 28.

Rosser, S. V. (2004). *The science glass ceiling: Academic women scientists and the struggle to succeed*. Psychology Press.

Senft, T. M. (2008). *Camgirls: Celebrity and Community in the Age of Social Networks*. Peter Lang.

Spender, D. (1995). *Nattering on the Net: Women, Power and Cyberspace*. Spinifex Press.

Tripathi, V. (2014). Cyber Laws India. *Cyber Laws India.* http://www.cyberlawsindia.net/

Westlake, E. J. (2008). Friend me if you Facebook: Generation Y and performative surveillance. *The Drama Review*, *52*(4), 21–40. doi:10.1162/dram.2008.52.4.21

Chapter 24
Messaging App Using Flutter

Sreelalitha Talluri
Vignan Bharathi Institute of Engineering and Technology, India

G. Vaishnavi
Vignan Bharathi Institute of Technology, India

G. Naidu
Vignan Bharathi Institute of Technology, India

D. Shiva
Vignan Bharathi Institute of Technology, India

ABSTRACT

The aim of this project is to build a real-time messaging app using modern technologies. Unlike most chat apps available in the market, the present system will focus on developers and will try to increase their productivity are coding and archive view. The main features of the project are completely open source. The users will be able to dig into the code to learn what happens after the scenes or contribute to the source code. It was therefore within this intent to write pure codes, which could be measured by following the most popular patterns and principles of each language and relevant libraries. The main objective of this project is going to build an application through which Instant mobile app and web applications are used for communication between the users. The applications initiate message sending via internet, making it free of cost for the users. Sending messages can be in the form of a text message or it can be a voice call.

INTRODUCTION

In today's world, information and telecommunication technologies have triggered drastic development in our educational field. Teaching and learning methods in the field have shifted from the traditional face-to-face to digital learning atmosphere that resists the need for common time and geographical distances. The widespread of technology such as smartphones, iPads, tablets and personal computers among students in academic and institutions of learning, together with the possibility and ability of the Internet

DOI: 10.4018/978-1-6684-8893-5.ch024

and instant messaging tools have influenced communication, as well as learning (Ling, 2016). pecifically, students use technology tools to improve their language and academic achievement (Yin, 2016).

Messaging apps now have more global users than traditional social networks which means they will play an increasingly important role in the distribution of digital journalism in the future. Drawing upon interviews and case studies, it was identified a number of opportunities and challenges for organizations using or hoping to use messaging apps for news. The project main focus is to devise a successful messaging app strategy, publishers must understand regional strongholds, user demographics and popular features of each app. After the early days of social media, before which a proliferation of services (some with regional strengths) led to intense competition for user attention, we expect to see some eventual consolidation among chat apps.

LITERATURE SURVEY

Overview of Existing System

The collaboration and communication are the foundation of building a successful work environment and culture. There are an array of ways for team members to communicate, and today's modern professional doesn't want to be inundated with emails. Emails require a title and lengthy paragraphs, and aren't well suited for quick back-and-forth conversations. Team messaging apps simplify business communications.

Drawbacks of existing system:

Productivity issues with instant messengers
Security issues with instant messengers
Ineffective tool for mass communication
Problematic system for archiving

PROPOSED SYSTEM

The proposed system of a messaging application using flutter is a messaging system that is responsible for transferring data from one application to another so that the applications can focus on data without getting bogged down on data transmission and sharing. Distributed messaging is based on the concept of reliable message queuing. An Internet messaging platform is any system on the Internet that exchanges messages for the purpose of human communications. Messaging platforms are considered one of few key Internet infrastructure elements. Another big benefit of messaging apps is that they can be used to enhance verbal communication with customers. They can be used to quickly provide further clarification or information to prevent a breakdown in communications, thereby offering a major efficiency boost.

Advantages of proposed system:

Real-Time Communication
Task Management Features & Mobile Apps
Eliminate Unproductive Meeting Time
Increased Productivity & Easier Project Management

File Storage and Sharing
Automatic Reporting Features

Online Chat Request (Mittal, 2020)

In this paper, a detail study on saving the security and protection of the talk application is discussed. This portrayed a lot of prerequisites for making secure talk and actualize it by utilizing present day strategies and lightweight for giving velocity and great assurance to its customers. Using the XSalsa20 calculation is perfect for cell phones in view of its high security, superior and keeps up battery life. Customers can be sure that no one can peruse their messages, regardless of whether the cell phone arrives at wrong hands cannot enter to the application and cannot get to the information put away locally. There is in every case some spot for improvements in any product application, anyway great and proficient the application might be. At this moment, it is managed just by texting between the friends. In future the application may add more features to incorporate a few highlights, for

Voice informing.
Gathering calling.
Live spilling.
Messages auto erase after a given time.
Customized message tunes.

IJEAT (Gayathri & Kalieswari, 2020)

The latest development of the Internet has brought the world into our hands. Everything happens through internet from passing information to purchasing something. Internet made the world as small circle. This project is also based on internet. This paper shows the importance of chat application in day-to-day life and its impact in technological world. This project is to develop a chat system based on Java multithreading and network concept. The application allows people to transfer messages both in private and public way. It also enables the feature of sharing resources like files, images, videos, etc. This online system is developed to interact or chat with one another on the Internet. It is much more reliable and secure than other traditional systems available. Java, multi-threading and client-server concept were used to develop the web based chat application. This application is developed with proper architecture for future enhancement. It can be deployed in all private organizations like Colleges, IT parks, etc.

ICSET (Henriyan et al., 2016)

The chat app provides a better and more flexible chat system. It was developed with the latest technology in the way of providing a reliable system. The main advantage of the system is instant messaging, real-world communication, added security, group chat, etc. This application may find the best demand in the market for most organizations that aim to have independent applications.This research paper contains that the chat app should be a real-time forum and multi-site for use by many users. The programming language used to build project was the Dart and google firebase server with a clear framework and MongoDB website.

Use of Whatsapp for English Language Proficiency Among B.ED. Trainees (Ramakrishnan, 2017)

The median and mode values for the B.Ed. trainees on use of WhatsApp for development of English Language proficiency are 146 and 141 respectively. The highest score is 183 and the lowest score is 11. The mean value obtained is

143.98 with standard deviation of 20.63. It is well above the theoretical mean of 95. It is proved from the data that the B.Ed. students are using WhatsApp more for development of English Language proficiency than expected.

There is no significant difference in use of WhatsApp for development of English language proficiency among B.Ed. students in terms of Gender.

A Systematic Review on Mobile Instant Messaging as a Collaborative Tool for Language Learning (Sivabalan & Ali, 2019)

The analysis of the systematic review of the topic revealed that the use of mobile instant messaging as a collaborative learning tool in education had positive impact on teaching and learning activities. WhatsApp was identified the most used tool in teaching and learning due to its versatility (Hamad, 2017; Mistar & Embi, 2016; Centikaya, 2017; Statista, 2016; Church & de Oliveira, 2013). WhatsApp had made communication in lessons a success, helped teachers in exploiting its benefits (Malecela, 2016; Yin 2016) hence, was considered as a perfect collaborative learning tool. In general, most of the students in the reviewed studies used are WhatsApp, Telegram, Line, WeChat and etc., because they considered instant mobile

Design and Implementation of Web Based Real Time Chat Interfacing Server (Henriyan & Subiyanti, 2017)

The analysis of the systematic review of the topic revealed that the chat application is a feature or a program on the Internet to communicate directly among Internet users who are online or who were equally using the internet. Chat applications allow users to communicate even though from a great distance. Therefore, this chat application must be real-time and multi-platform to be used by many users. The development of information and communication technologies are rapidly making one of the reasons for Indonesia, especially Bandung to develop this chat application. That's because Indonesia does not always rely on outsiders. It is important for Indonesia to develop this chat application for themselves. This chat application in the manufacture begins with the collection of relevant data that will be displayed in the web and mobile versions. The programming language used to build server is Node.js with express framework and MongoDB database. The research revealed that the chat application built with Node.js, Socket.io, and MongoDB is running in real time very well with a speed less than one second (6 times faster) than the chat application built with PHP and MySQL. So it can be ascertained if data more than 200 chat, Node.js, Socket.io and MongoDB will have a speed 1200 faster than PHP and MySQL.

CONCLUSION

In the present days instant messaging is widely used. It provides a way to real time chatting and communication. It is easy to use and gives fast instant response. The messaging application is free of cost and the client can manage all the lists of contacts. Although, it has some disadvantages too. It has security risks and privacy concerns. Instant messaging has very bright future. Instant messaging is a whole new world of communication. It is fastest and latest form raising of business communications overall the globe. It is a quick communication channel to deliver short messages. It enables employees to communicate privately and quickly with each other. Online Messaging apps are those apps which allow one to send and receive a message instantly. It is the fastest and latest solution for raising business communications overall the globe. The application consists of many elements of multi media as text, audio, video, image and many file sharing methods.A messaging app is most secured and safe application for communication. The application which is being developed consists of various features involved in various applications for example video chat, payments, bitmoji's, storis, file sharing and security etc. The messaging app can be innovatively good for the present world.

REFERENCES

Adelore, O. (2017). Using WhatApp mobile application as tutorial delivery tool for advanced level learners in adult literacy programmes: Lessons. *AJPSSI*, *20*(1), 131–139.

Ajid, L. H., Reni, R., Yunita, D. U., & Dwi, S. (2018). The use of WhatsApp in collaborative learning to improve English teaching and learning process. *International Journal of Research Studies in Educational Technology*, *7*(May), 29–35.

Henriyan, D., Subiyanti, D., Fauzian, R., Anggraini, D., & Aziz, M. (2016). *Design and implementation of web based real time chat interfacing server*. IEEE. https://ieeexplore.ieee.org/document/7849628

Bamane, A., Bhoyar, P., Dugar, A., & Antony, L. (2023). Enhanced Chat Application. *Global Journals*. https://globaljournals.org/GJCST_Volume12/2-Enhanced-Chat-Application

Hamad, M. M. (2017). Using WhatsApp to enhance students' learning of English language "Experience to Share.". *Higher Education Studies*, *7*(4), 74. doi:10.5539/hes.v7n4p74

Kim, H., Lee, M., & Kim, M. (2014). Effects of mobile instant messaging on collaborative learning processes and outcomes: The case of South Korea. *Journal of Educational Technology & Society*, *17*(2), 31–42.

Le, H., Janssen, J., & Wubbels, T. (2018). Collaborative learning practices: Teacher and student perceived obstacles to effective student collaboration. *Cambridge Journal of Education*, *48*(1), 103–122. doi:10.1080/0305764X.2016.1259389

Odia, O. U. (2016). *A Study of University Students' Perceptions and Usage Behaviour of Mobile Media Technologies in Nigeria*. University of Leicester.

Ramakrishnan, N. (2017). Use of Whatsapp for English language proficiency. *International Journal of Research*, *5*, 1–6.

Sutikno, T., Handayani, L., Stiawan, D., Riyadi, M. A., & Subroto, I. M. I. (2016). WhatsApp, Viber and Telegram: Which is the best for instant messaging? *Iranian Journal of Electrical and Computer Engineering*, *6*(3), 909–914.

Ta'amneh, A. (2017). The Effect of Using "Whats App Messenger" in learning English language among university students. *International Journal of Humanities and Applied Social Science*, *2*(2), 15–22.

Turay, P., Jr. (2016). *Are messaging apps considered social media?* LinkedIn. https://www.linkedin.com/pulse/messaging-apps- considered-social-media-peter-tur ay-jrc.

Verheijen, A. J. P., & Spooren, W. P. M. S. (2017). *The impact of WhatsApp on Dutch youths' school writing*.

Yavuz, F. (2016). Do smartphones spur or deter learning: A Whatsapp case study. *International Journal of Educational Sciences*, *15*(3), 408–415. doi:10.1080/09751122.2016.11890551

Yeboah, J., & Ewur, G. D. (2014). The impact of Whatsapp messenger usage on students' performance in tertiary institutions in Ghana. *Journal of Education and Practice*, *5*(6), 157–164.

Zarei, R., Darani, L. H., & Golestan, A. A. (2017). Effect of Telegram application on Iranian advanced EFL learners' vocabulary knowledge and attitude. *International Journal of Foreign Language Teaching and Research*, *5*(20), 9.

Chapter 25
Comprehensive Analysis of the Artificial Intelligence Approaches for Detecting Misogynistic Mixed-Code Online Content in South Asian Countries:
A Review

Sargam Yadav
https://orcid.org/0000-0001-8115-6741
Dundalk Institute of Technology, Ireland

Abhishek Kaushik
https://orcid.org/0000-0002-3329-1807
Dundalk Institute of Technology, Ireland

Surbhi Sharma
Institute of Dental Science, Jammu, India

ABSTRACT

The rise of social media has drastically altered several aspects of daily life and businesses. With all its advantages, the anonymity and lack of accountability social media provides encourages unsavoury individuals to spread hate. Hate targeted towards a particular group, such as women, can have a silencing effect and discourage them from participating in online discourse. In this chapter, the authors review recent studies and toolkits that attempt to tackle the issue of hate speech on online platforms using natural language processing (NLP) techniques. Challenges and shared tasks that are regularly conducted to advance the current state-of-the-art in hate speech detection in English and other under-resourced languages are also reviewed. The comprehensive survey suggests that despite the recent increase in interest in the problem of filtering online hate speech, the field is still in its infancy, specifically the problem of misogyny identification in under-resourced languages.

DOI: 10.4018/978-1-6684-8893-5.ch025

Figure 1. Example of a hateful statement

> Real question is do feminist liberal bigots understand that different rules for men/women is sexism

INTRODUCTION

Hate speech refers to disparaging speech that targets people based on factors such as race, religion, gender, sexual orientation, etc. Although social media has greatly boosted connectivity and communication, it has also provided a new medium for individuals who want to spread hate (Djuric et al., 2015) and misinformation, and facilitate trolling (Cheng et al., 2017) and cyber-bullying (Moreno et al., 2019). The volume of content posted online daily makes it difficult to manually moderate and remove such content. There has been an increasing amount of interest for automatic hate speech detection amongst NLP researchers. Social media platforms have become the epicenter of communication, networking, and gaining visibility. As most businesses have migrated online and political discourses are being conducted on social media, targeting hate towards a group of individuals can have a devastating impact on their continued participation. The United Nations Human Rights Council states that human rights in the offline world also apply online (*Amnesty Decoders - Troll Patrol India*, 2021), and social media companies must respect human rights where they operate (*Guiding Principles on Business and Human Rights Implementing the United Nations "Protect, Respect and Remedy" Framework*, 2011). Thus, the responsibility of ensuring a safe environment for all users falls on the platforms.

One generally agreed upon definition of hate speech is "any communication that disparages a target group of people based on some characteristic such as race, colour, ethnicity, gender, sexual orientation, nationality, religion, or other characteristic" (Nockleyby, 2000). Figure 1 shows an example of hate speech on the basis of gender.

According to (Feinberg & Robey, 2009), cyberbullying can be defined as "sending or posting harmful or cruel text or images using the internet or other digital communication devices. It can involve stalking, threats, harassment, impersonation, humiliation, trickery, and exclusion." Thus, cyberbullying is generalized abuse as opposed to hate speech, which is abuse directed towards a unique, non-controllable attribute of a group of people such as race and gender (*Ditch The Label 2016 | Brandwatch*, 2016). Hate speech detection is a challenging task, as it is highly contextual and subjective. The research in the field is still very nascent. Very few studies have tackled misogyny identification solely (Fersini, Rosso, et al., 2018), with the number being even lower for under-resourced and code-switched languages (Mandl et al., 2021).

India serves one of the largest user bases of social media platforms, with an approximate 450 million YouTube (*YouTube Users by Country 2022 | Statista*, 2022) users and 23 million Twitter (*Countries with Most Twitter Users 2022 | Statista*, 2022) users as of 2022. A large portion of content posted online in India combines some features of the native languages with English through code-mixing. For example, 'Hinglish', a portmanteau of English and Hindi, consists of English words, as well as Hindi words written in the Roman script rather than Devanagari script. For example, the hateful statement "Look ye politicians suvar jaise baithe rahte hain sirf money ke liye kaam karte hain. They don't care about public" in Hinglish translates to "Look these politicians are sitting like pigs and they only work for money. They don't care about public." in English (Sreelakshmi et al., 2020). Currently, Twitter's hateful conduct policy is as follows: "You may not promote violence against or directly attack or threaten other people based on race, ethnicity, national origin, caste, sexual orientation, gender, gender identity, religious affiliation, age, disability, or serious disease. We also do not allow accounts whose primary purpose is inciting harm towards others based on these categories" (*Twitter's Policy on Hateful Conduct | Twitter Help*, 2023). However, these guidelines are not easily enforceable due to the volume of content and lack of moderation. Also, the reporting process for hateful content in not transparent and many users find it inadequate for filtering hateful messages (*Toxic Twitter - The Reporting Process - Amnesty International*, 2018). Therefore, more effective measures for countering online abuse must be explored and put in place.

Several instances of online hate speech have unfortunately permeated to the real world and resulted in hate crimes. Women are at a higher risk of being victims of domestic abuse, with every 1 in 3 women worldwide being subjected to some form of abuse (*What We Do: Ending Violence against Women | UN Women – Headquarters*, 2023). Repeated online abuse can have a gateway affect and result in real-world murders (Chan, 2016). Individuals have also committed suicide due to persistent cyberbullying (Yousif, 2022) (*Young Woman Killed Herself After Being Made To Feel Insecure By Facebook Trolls*, 2022). Therefore, a system for automatically filtering such hateful content is pertinent to ensure equal participation. Certain legislatures are also in the process of classifying online hate speech towards women and other protected categories as a hate crime (*Hate Crime - Law Commission*, 2021).

Models trained for hate speech classification may learn some biases from the datasets (Attanasio et al., 2022). For example, a model for misogynistic hate speech detection can perform well by simply looking at the word "woman" and classifying it as positive for hate speech. It is important to ensure that hate speech classifiers are filtering content based on plausible explanations. Explainable Artificial Intelligence (XAI) (Gunning et al., 2019) is an important technique to ensure model fairness and interpretability. It allows us to understand and interpret the decisions made by black-box machine learning and deep learning models. Examples of XAI tools include Local Interpretable Model Agnostic Explanations (LIME) (Ribeiro et al., 2016), and Shapely Additive Explanations (SHAP) (Lundberg & Lee, 2017).

In this chapter, the authors will analyze the various publicly available datasets for hate speech detection, the current state of the art machine learning and deep learning models, and the limitations and future scope for multilingual code-mixed text. A special focus has been placed on studies done specifically on misogynistic hate speech. The rest of the chapter is structured as follows: Section 2 describes the motivation behind conducting this study. In section 3, the recent literature on state-of-the-art and explainable models for automatic hate speech detection in English and other languages is reviewed, along with the welfare reports that have been published by human rights organizations across the world. Section 4 discusses the various shared tasks and challenges that are regularly held to advance the state-of-the-art in hate speech detection, along with the best approaches in each task. Section 5 discusses the limitations that currently impede the development of an automated approach to counter online hate speech. Section 6 provides a conclusion to the work, along with the future steps to be taken.

MOTIVATION

Social media has proliferated many aspects of everyday life. With this exposure, also comes the risk of harassment and abuse. Twitter and other social media platforms were expected to provide a platform for free expressions for everyone, especially marginalized communities and minorities. However, due to perceived anonymity, lack of regulations, and content monitoring, it has become a toxic place for several communities (*Toxic Twitter - The Solution - Amnesty International*, 2018). The current guidelines in place to prevent harassment by social media companies are not adequate (*Toxic Twitter - The Solution - Amnesty International*, 2018). Online abuse can have an adverse psychological impact on the target individual and can lead to them taking drastic measures. It can also impact the target community. For example, misogynistic hate speech can deter the participation of women in important political and social discourse online and urge them to stay off the platforms, thereby silencing their voices and opinion (*What We Do: Ending Violence against Women | UN Women – Headquarters*, 2023) (*Amnesty Decoders - Troll Patrol India*, 2021). Instances of online hate speech have also permeated into the real world resulting in hate crimes and marginalization of certain groups. Considering these events, it is of paramount importance that social media platforms implement automated toolkits that filter out abusive and hateful content, in addition to user reports and manual content moderation. The motivation of this study is to highlight the lack of multilingual corpora for misogynistic hate speech in code-switched Indian languages, highlight the limitations of previous work in the area, and serve as a base for future researchers.

LITERATURE REVIEW

In this section, the relevant literature on artificial intelligence toolkits and welfare reports on the topic of combating hate speech have been discussed.

Welfare Reports

Several welfare reports have been published based on studies and surveys conducted in the past decade that attempt to analyze the impact of online hate speech throughout the world.

"The First 100 Days of COVID-19 In Asia and the Pacific: a Gender Lens" is a report by UN Women (*The First 100 Days of the COVID-19 Outbreak in Asia and the Pacific | UN Women – Asia-Pacific*, 2020) that discusses how the socio-economic impact of the pandemic was disproportionately worse for women and girls. The pandemic increased the strain on women's financial positions because of the increase in the pay gap, cases of intimate partner violence due to them being confined with their abusers (Hingorani, 2020) (*Ending Violence Is Our Business: Workplace Responses to Intimate Partner Violence in Asia and the Pacific | UN Women – Asia-Pacific*, 2019) (Nortajuddin, 2020), and greater unemployment rates due to jobs with limited protection. Cyber-harassment can be traumatizing, and in combination with lack of access to devices and internet, can prevent more women from developing technical skills and pursuing a career in tech fields (*Issue Paper: Asia-Pacific Bureau Gender - Internet Society*, 2017). The impact was worse for marginalized communities amongst women such as religious and ethnics minorities, women with disabilities, members of the LGBT community, and migrant workers.

The "Social Media Monitoring on COVID-19 and Misogyny in Asia and the Pacific" report by UN Women (*Social Media Monitoring on COVID-19 and Misogyny in Asia and the Pacific | UN Women – Asia-Pacific*, 2020) is based on the research done by Mythos Labs for UN Women Regional Office for Asia and the Pacific. During the COVID-19 pandemic lockdowns, the volume of misogynistic Facebook posts and user interaction on these posts increased by 168% in India, Sri Lanka, and Malaysia compared to the previous year. In India and Indonesia, there was a spike in misogynistic profanities, misogynistic narratives, as well as organizations promoting misogynistic hashtags like "men going their own way", "men's rights", etc.

The Troll Patrol India was a project undertaken by Amnesty International (*Amnesty Decoders - Troll Patrol India*, 2021) that aimed to expose the online harassment directed towards women politicians in India during the 2019 General Elections of India. During March to May 2019, 114,716 tweets mentioning 95 Indian women politicians were 'Decoded' with the help of 1912 volunteers from 82 countries. The common language choice for decoders was English. 'Decoding' involved labelling the tweets as 'Problematic', 'Abusive', or None. If a tweet was found to be 'Abusive', it could be further categorized to contain any of the following types of abuse: Sexism or misogyny, Racism, Homophobia or Transphobia, Ethnic or religious slur, Caste slur, Physical threats, Sexual threats, and other. Additional labelling was done identify the part of the tweet that was offensive (Text, Video, Image, Other attachment).

The project discovered that out of all the tweets sent to the 95 politicians, 10.5% were problematic and 3.3% were abusive. Indian women politicians were also subjected to a higher level of abuse (13.8%) as compared to UK and USA women politicians (7.1%) according to a similar study (*Amnesty Decoders - Troll Patrol*, 2021). The level of abuse was higher for women who were more active on Twitter, Muslim women who received 94.1% more ethnic and religious slurs than others, politicians from marginalized castes who received 59% more caste-based abuse, and women belonging to political parties other than the Bharatiya Janata Party, who received 56.7% more problematic or abusive tweets. Additionally, politicians who lost the election received 24.6% more problematic or abusive tweets, and unmarried women received 40.6% more abusive tweets and 31% more problematic tweets.

Almost 20% of women have been a victim of doxing according Amnesty International's online poll in USA. Doxing refers to posting personal details and intimate pictures without consent of the subject. Moreover, 10% of women in the USA and 8% in the UK have had their sexual and private images without their consent (Dhrodia, 2017). The harassment can become targeted due to the nature of social media. An infamous example of this instance is 'Gamergate', which was the targeted harassment of games developer Zoe Quinn and other women in the gaming industry on multiple social platforms (Vineyard, 2014). The women targeted faced relentless abuse and received threats of rape, torture, and murder. Online abuse can also be a tool of current or former domestic partners to cause further harassment (*Toxic Twitter - Women's Experiences of Violence and Abuse on Twitter - Amnesty International*, 2018) (Dhrodia, 2017). According to research on domestic online abuse by the Women's Aid organization in the UK, 85% of victims responded that they received online abuse from a partner or ex-partner, which was part of a pattern of abuse that continued offline (*Online and Digital Abuse - Women's Aid*, 2022). A survey conducted by the National Network to End Domestic Violence organization in US found that 97% of domestic abuse programs report that technology was used by abusers to harass and stalk victims (*Recognizing and Combating Technology-Facilitated Abuse - NNEDV*, 2016). Such persistent abuse can have adverse psychological impacts such as lack of sleep, increased anxiety, a decreased sense of safety and well-being, panic attacks, sense of powerlessness, and symptoms of PTSD (*Toxic Twitter - The Psychological Harms of Violence and Abuse Against Women Online - Amnesty International*, 2018).

Artificial Intelligence Toolkits for Hate Speech Detection

Due to the increase in popularity of online forums in the recent years, research into making the online space safe and abuse free has picked up pace. Current state-of-the-art machine learning and deep learning approaches have given excellent performance in hate speech detection for English and other languages. Google and Jigsaw developed the 'Perspective' tool (*Perspective API*, 2021) that provides a toxicity score from 0 to 100 with the help of machine learning models. The tool accommodates several languages such as Arabic, Hindi, German, etc.

Machine learning (Bishop & Nasrabadi, 2006) is a branch of artificial intelligence that allows computer systems to learn to perform tasks using statistical models and algorithms by drawing inferences and learning patterns from data. Deep learning (Goodfellow et al., 2016) is a subset of machine learning that makes use of complex neural networks to mimic the human brain. As compared to machine learning, deep learning models require more training data, longer training time, and lesser human intervention. They learn complex correlations from the data and generally provide higher accuracy than machine learning models. NLP is a branch of Artificial intelligence that allows computer systems to understand and process human language (Bird et al., 2009). NLP utilizes computational linguistics, machine learning, and deep learning models to understand languages.

Bidirectional Encoder Representations from Transformers (BERT) (Devlin et al., 2018) is a Transformer-based pre-trained language representation model that learns deep bidirectional representations from text and gives state-of-the-art performance on various NLP tasks such as question answering, text classification, etc. Recurrent Neural Networks (RNN) (Rumelhart et al., 1985) are a type of artificial neural network that considers previous inputs when calculating the output at a certain step. As compared to a feed-forward network, the information in RNN cycles through a loop, allowing it to better deal with sequential data. Long short-term memory (LSTM) (Hochreiter & Schmidhuber, 1997) is a type of RNN and is good at handling sequential data and processing long-term dependencies in text. It improves upon RNNs by solving the vanishing gradient problem, which is the loss if information in a neural network over long periods.

Hatebase is an online repository of regionalized and multilingual hate speech data (*Hatebase*, 2023). Figure 2 displays the vocabulary of hate speech, which is divided according to the following categories:

Figure 2. Classification according to Hatebase

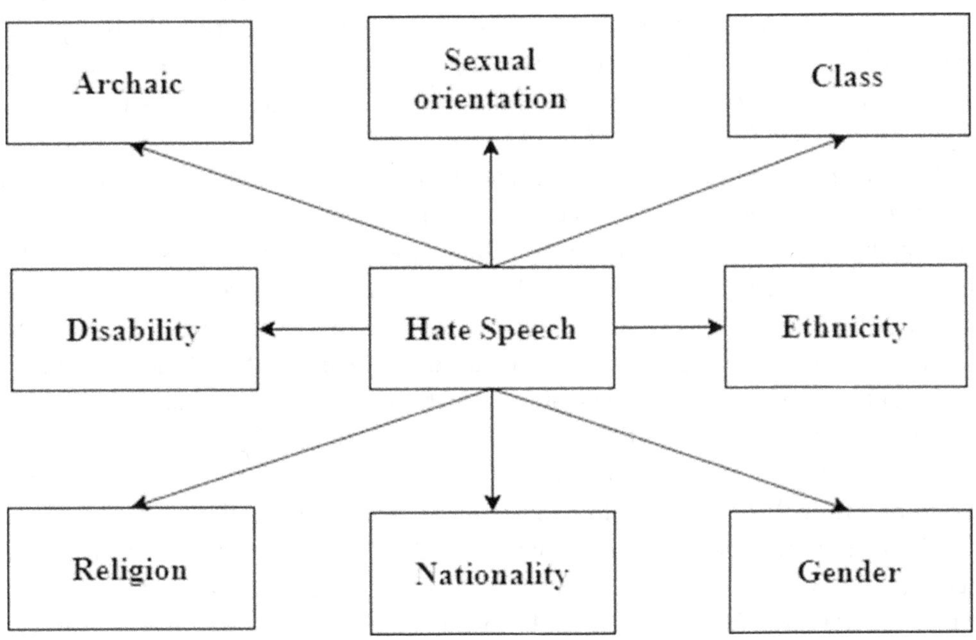

archaic, class, disability, ethnicity, gender, nationality, religion, and sexual orientation. Examples of each target are as follows:

- **Ethnicity:** Hate based on race and ethnicity. For example, "Poor white kids being forced to treat apes and parasites as their equals." (de Gibert et al., 2018). In this example, terms such as 'apes' and 'parasites' have been used to refer to children with darker skin colors and assert that they are inferior to "white kids".
- **Religion:** "Are Muslims, in general a nuisance to be tolerated by the rest of the world ? #SaveBengal #DoctorsFightBack #DoctorsStrike #MamtaBanerjee" (Mandl et al., 2019). In this example, negative stereotypes are attributed to all Muslims.
- **Nationality:** "Sick barstewards! This is what happens when we put up the refugees welcome signs! They not only rape our wives or girlfriends, our daughters but our ruddy mothers too!! https://t.co/XAYLr6FjNk" (Basile et al., 2019). This statement attacks all immigrants and wrongly implies that they are all rapists.
- **Disability:** "People with cerebral palsy are subhuman and shouldn't be seen in public". This statement dehumanizes and degrades people with disabilities and asserts that they don't have the right to be in public.
- **Gender:** "@chirag785790094 Apki galti nahi hai Sarkar bhi gender terrorists se itna darti hai ki wife ke domestic violence ko report karne ki bajay ""family problem"" bolti hai taki koi law gender terrorism par n banana pare #bycottmarriage #notmyCJI #marriagestrike #SupremeCourtOfIndia @scofind https://t.co/9Ku2rhjHFz". In this statement, it is implied that laws for protecting domestic violence are biased towards women and the government is unwilling to change these laws due to "gender terrorists".

(Mathur, Ratn Shah, et al., 2018) present the Hindi-English Offensive Tweet (HEOT) dataset, consisting of 3679 Hinglish tweets divided into three classes: non-offensive (1414), abusive (1942) and hate speech (323). A convolutional neural network (CNN) model was first trained on a much larger English dataset, and transfer learning was subsequently performed on the HEOT dataset. This approach achieved a good accuracy of 83.90% and F1-score of 0.714. (Bhattacharya et al., 2020) present a dataset of over 25,000 YouTube comments for aggression and misogyny identification in Indian English, Hindi, and Indian Bangla. The comments were tagged at two levels: Aggression (overtly aggressive, covertly aggressive, and non-aggressive) and Misogyny (gendered and non-gendered). To establish a baseline for misogyny detection, a Support Vector Machine (SVM) classifier was trained on a subset of the original dataset. The highest F1 score achieved for Hindi, Bangla, and English was 0.87, 0.89, and 0.93, using 3-, 5-, and 2-character n-grams respectively. (Bohra et al., 2018a) composed a dataset of 4575 tweets in code-mixed Hindi-English and annotated into normal and hate speech categories. Highest classification accuracy of 71.7% is achieved using SVM classifier and a combination of the following features in a vector: character n-grams, word n-grams, punctuation, negation words and hate lexicon. (Waseem & Hovy, 2016) provide an annotated dataset of 16,914 tweets (3,383 sexist, 1,972 racist, 11,559 neither) based on critical race theory. Extra-linguistic features such as gender of user, location, length of tweet, along with character n-grams, are analyzed for classification using a Logistic Regression classifier. Character bi- to fourgrams and gender information gives the highest F1 score of 73.89 out of all the feature combinations. (Banerjee et al., 2020) investigate the performance of an ensemble of 4 Transformer-based pre-trained models, namely BERT, RoBERTa, DistilBERT, and XLNet. The ensemble model was created using

Bootstrap aggregation and hard voting was used to determine classification results. Word embeddings with a word-level CNN were also studied for comparison. The dataset consists of 4575 Hindi-English code-mixed tweets manually annotated as hate speech and non-hate speech. The results show that XLNet attained the highest Macro Average Recall, Macro Average F1 score, Weighted Average Recall, Weighted Average F1 score and accuracy with the scores of 0.66, 0.67, 0.73, 0.71, and 0.73, respectively.

(Mathur, Sawhney, et al., 2018) experimented with a multi-input multi-channel transfer learning-based model to detect hateful content in the Hinglish Offensive Tweet (HOT) dataset, which consists of 3189 tweets labelled as Non-Offensive, Abusive, and Hate-Inducing. Pre-processing, transliteration, and translation was performed on the tweets, so that transfer learning could be performed using a model pre-trained on the English Offensive Tweet (EOT) dataset. Two types of features were considered for the models: word embeddings (Glove, Twitter word2vec, FastText), and secondary features (profanity vector, sentiment score, linguistic inquiry and word count features). Both CNN and LSTM models are trained concurrently. The best Macro-F1 achieved are 0.895 by using the Twitter word2vec, FastText, and all secondary features. (Biradar et al., 2022) applied the Transformer-based Interpreter and Feature extraction model on Deep Neural Network (TIF-DNN) approach to the dataset in (Bohra et al., 2018b). The proposed model is made of three layers: the interpretation layer, the feature extraction layer, and the classification layer. The tweets are first converted into Hindi in Devanagari script, and then feature extraction is performed using mBERT. Final classification is performed using traditional machine learning classifiers and later through DNN based models. The TIF-DNN model provides the best scores with an accuracy of 73%, F1-Hate score of 56, and F1-Non-Hate score of 78. Translating the tweets into monolingual data thus improved performance. mBERT outperforms IndicBERT model, which is a multilingual ALBERT model pre-trained on 12 Indian languages. (Kamble & Joshi, 2018) conducted a similar study to classify mix-code Hindi and English data for hate speech and observed that domain-specific embeddings improve the F-score when implementing deep learning models.

EXPLAINABLE HATE SPEECH CLASSIFIERS

(Karim et al., 2020) performed a study to detect hate speech in the under-resourced South Asian language Bengali using ensemble BERT variants. A total of 8087 comments were divided into the following categories: political, personal, geopolitical, and religious hate. An ensemble of BERT-based models (Bangla BERT base, Multilingual BERT cased, Multilingual BERT base, XLM-RoBERTa) out-performed baseline Deep Neural Networks (Conv-LSTM) and ML algorithms. For local explainability, the most and least relevant words are highlighted through sensitivity analysis and layer-wise relevance propagation on the Conv-LSTM baseline model. Model explainability is also computed through faithfulness w.r.t comprehensiveness and sufficiency using ERASER. XLM-RoBERTa achieves the best scores on faithfulness, suggesting that models which score highest on other metrics (accuracy, F1 score), may not also perform best on explainability metrics.

The HateXplain (Mathew et al., 2020) dataset is a benchmark for hate speech detection and includes human rationale as a perspective to classification. It includes 20,148 posts from Twitter and Gab, which are annotated from 3 perspectives: classification into hate, offensive, and normal, identification of the target community, and the rationale used to classify a text into one of the 3 categories. Models that score high on explainability metrics are based on human rationale for training and were shown to reduce unintended bias. (Attanasio et al., 2022) performed a benchmark study on explainability approaches for misogyny detection using BERT model in English and Italian. Out of the various post-hoc feature attribution methods tested, SHAP and Sample-And-Occlusion (SOC) (Jin et al., 2019) provide plausible and faithful explanations. (Vijayaraghavan et al., 2021) present a deep neural network that receives multi-modal input and considers the socio-cultural context when performing hate speech classification. Interpretability of the model was analyzed using the attention scores.

SHARED TASKS

Shared tasks and challenges are regularly held for hate speech detection in different languages to promote further research in the area. The annotation process for hate speech datasets varies greatly. Usually, native speakers who are also social media users are selected for the process. Annotators can be experts (Guest et al., 2021), non-experts (Mandl et al., 2019), or crowd-workers (Pavlopoulos et al., 2021). Hate speech is highly subjective and contextual, which can cause a high degree of variation in the class assignments. The annotator's decision may be affected by personal bias, world knowledge, geographic location, language proficiency, etc.

The Hate speech and Offensive Content Identification (HASOC) challenge is conducted to identify hate content from online posts in English and Indo-Aryan languages. It is divided into 2 subtasks: Task A: classification into Hate and Not Offensive, Task B: fine-grained classification into Hate speech, Offensive, and Profanity. The HASOC subtrack at FIRE 2021 was conducted in English, Hindi, and Marathi tweets (Mandl et al., 2021). The highest macro-F1 scores achieved for Task A were 0.8215 in English, 0.7797 in Hindi, 0.9144 in Marathi, through transformer-based classification techniques. The HASOC 2020 challenge (Mandl et al., 2020) presented the same two classification subtasks for Hindi, German, and English. For task A, the macro-F1 scores achieved are 0.51, 0.53 and 0.52 for English, Hindi, and German, respectively. For task B, the best macro-F1 scores achieved are 0.26, 0.33 and 0.29 for English, Hindi, and German. The HASOC 2019 (Mandl et al., 2019) consisted of a binary classification and 3 fine-grained classification subtasks. For the binary classification task, the best Macro-F1 scores for English, Hindi, and German were 0.78, 0.81, and 0.61, respectively. For the fine-grained classification subtasks, identification of the type of hate and the target of hate is also considered.

Figure 3. Classification according to AMI shared task IberEval

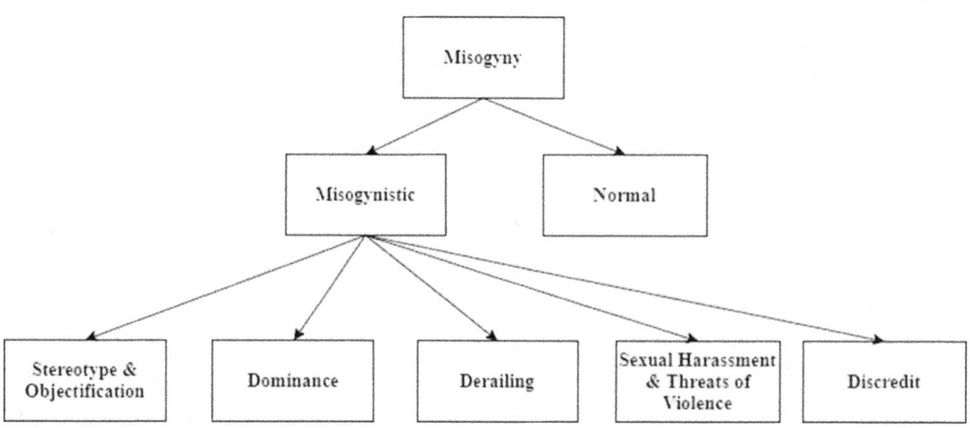

The Automatic misogyny identification (AMI) shared task at Evalita 2018 (Fersini, Nozza, et al., 2018) was based on Italian and English tweets and consisted of two subtasks: Subtask A on misogyny identification and Subtask B on misogynistic behaviour categorization and target classification. The dataset consisted of 10,000 tweets for each language. The labels for misogynistic behavior were Stereotype & Objectification, Dominance, Derailing, Sexual Harassment & Threats of Violence, and Discredit. The targets can be 'Active' or 'Passive'. Figure 3 displays the categorization of misogynistic behavior. Descriptions and examples of each category are listed as follows:

- **Stereotype & Objectification:** A widely held but fixed and oversimplified image or idea of a woman; description of women's physical appeal and/or comparisons to narrow standards. For example, "Women are good only into the kitchen..#makemeasandwich".
- **Dominance:** To assert the superiority of men over women to highlight gender inequality. For example, "Women are inferior to men..so shut up please!"
- **Derailing:** To justify woman abuse, rejecting male responsibility. For example, "@yesallwomen wearing a tiny skirt is "asking for it". Your teasing a (hard working, taxes paying) dog with a bone. That's cruel. #YesAllMen"
- **Sexual Harassment & Threats of Violence:** To describe actions as sexual advances, requests for sexual favours, harassment of a sexual nature; intent to physically assert power over women through threats of violence. For example, "Stupid bi**ch I'll put you down on the floor and I'll rape you! You should be scared!"
- **Discredit:** Slurring over women with no other larger intention. For example, "@AsiaArgento brainless fuc**ing bi**ch"

The AMI task at IberEval 2018 (Fersini, Rosso, et al., 2018) was based on Spanish and English and consisted of the same two subtasks that were used in Evalita 2018 (Fersini, Nozza, et al., 2018). For subtask A, the highest accuracy achieved was 0.9132 for English using SVM trained with a combination of stylistic, structural, and lexical features (i.e., Hashtag Presence, Link Presence, Swear Word Count, Swear Word Presence, Sexist Slurs Presence and Woman-related Words Presence). For Spanish, the highest accuracy achieved was 0.8146 by two approaches. The first approach was based on Bag of Word, Bag of Hashtags, Bag of Emojis, Sexist Slurs Presence, Woman Word Presence, count of negative stereotypes words and count of hate words and slurs beyond stereotypes. The second approach used a TF-IDF representation of words obtained after a pre-processing step focused on maintaining specific hashtags. For subtask B, the highest macro average F-Measure achieved was 0.4424 for English using SVM trained with a combination of lexicons concerning sexuality, profanity, femininity and human body. For Spanish, the highest macro average F-measure obtained was 0.4461 by exploiting SVM trained with Bag of Word, Bag of Hashtags, Bag of Emojis, Sexist Slurs Presence and Woman Word Presence. Again, the results for subtask-B were relatively low due to under-representation of misogynistic behavior category of 'Derailing'.

The AMI task at Evalita (2020) (Fersini et al., 2020) shared task was conducted in Italian and consisted of two subtasks: Subtask A: Misogyny and Aggressive Behavior Identification and Subtask B: Unbiased Misogyny Identification. Subtask B attempts to measure model fairness when classifying sentences with identity terms that might indicate misogyny such as 'girlfriend' and 'wife'. Further analysis of the results shows that identifying misogyny was simple, but aggression identification was challenging, probably because of the subjectivity of aggressiveness in the dataset. Also, domain-dependent debiasing methods can increase fairness in models. The findings suggest that more data should be collected on different types of misogynistic behavior to improve model performance.

The HatEval task was conducted in SemEval 2019 to detect hate speech towards women and immigrants in Spanish and English (Basile et al., 2019). The dataset consisted of 19,600 tweets. There were a total of 13,000 English tweets and 6,600 Spanish tweets, and 9,091 tweets about immigrants and 10,509 about women. The classification subtasks are as follows: Subtask-A (Hate Speech), and Subtask-B (Target and Aggressiveness). For Subtask A in English, the highest macro F1-score achieved was 0.651, obtained by training a SVM model with RBF kernel on the data and exploiting sentence embeddings from Google's Universal Sentence Encoder as features. For subtask A in Spanish, the highest macro-F1 score obtained was 0.73 using linear SVM. For subtask B in English, the highest Exact Match Ratio (EMR) achieved was 0.570, using a SVM model combining standard lexical and syntactic features with specific features for capturing offensive language by exploiting external lexicons. For subtask B in Spanish, the best EMR result was 0.705 with a word-based representation by training a combination of Logistic Regression, Multinomial Naive Bayes, Classifiers Chain and Majority Voting on the provided dataset. Pre-processing steps included removal of HTML tags, punctuation marks and special characters, conversion of slang and short forms into correct English words and stemming. TF and TF-IDF were applied for feature engineering. The results indicate that it is easier to predict the presence of hate speech than the aggressiveness and targets.

The OffensEval task at International Workshop on Semantic Evaluation-2019 (SemEval) (Zampieri et al., 2019b) was based on the Offensive Language Identification Dataset (OLID) (Zampieri et al., 2019a), which consists of over 14,000 English tweets. It was divided into 3 subtasks: subtask A: Offensive language identification (Offensive and Not Offensive), subtask B: Automatic categorization of offense types (Untargeted and targeted insults), and subtask C: Offense target identification (individual, group, other). For subtask A, the highest macro-F1 score achieved was 82.9%, using a BERT-base-uncased with default parameters, a maximum sentence length of 64 and 2 training epochs. For subtask B, the highest f1-score achieved was 75.5%, using a rule-based approach with a keyword filter based on a Twitter language behavior list, which included strings such as hashtags and signs. For subtask C, the best macro-F1 score achieved was 66% using BERT and pre-trained word embeddings based on GloVe.

The First Shared Task on Aggression Identification was organized as part of the First Workshop on Trolling, Aggression and Cyberbullying (TRAC - 1) at COLING 2018 (Kumar et al., 2018). The task was to classify the comments into the following categories: Overtly Aggressive, Covertly Aggressive, and Non-aggressive. The training and development dataset consisted of 12,000 and 3,000 Facebook posts and comments, respectively, in Hindi and English each. The testing set consisted of 916 English comments and 970 Hindi comments. A surprise test set consisting of 1,257 English tweets and 1,194 Hindi tweets was also provided. The dataset had some inconsistencies. Along with Roman and Devanagari script in Hindi, some instances of mix-code were also included. Also, a few comments in German were included. The best system obtained a weighted F-score of 0.64 for both Hindi and English on the Facebook test sets, while the best scores on the surprise set were 0.60 and 0.50 for English and Hindi respectively.

The Second shared task on Aggression Identification organized with the TRAC-2 workshop at LREC-2020 was conducted on a dataset of approximately 6000 YouTube comments each in Bengali, Hindi, and English (Kumar et al., 2020). It featured two subtasks: subtask A: Aggression identification (overtly aggressive, covertly aggressive, and non-aggressive), and subtask B: Gendered aggression identification (gendered or non-gendered). For subtask A, the best weighted F-score was 0.82 for Bengali, 0.80 for English and 0.81 for Hindi. For subtask B, the best weighted F-score obtained was approximately 0.93

for Bengali, 0.87 for English and 0.87 for Hindi. The best performing system uses multiple fine-tuned BERT models, based on bootstrap aggregating. The results indicate that identifying the type of aggression is still a challenging task.

LIMITATIONS

In this section, we discuss the limitations and challenges that are currently encountered by studies in hate speech detection:

- **Dataset annotation:** The availability of a robust annotated dataset is essential for training machine learning and deep learning models. The standard practice for assigning annotators is recruiting researchers in the field or crowd-sourcing the process (Basile et al., 2019), which are both time-consuming and costly. Detailed instructions are important for reliable annotation (Ross et al., 2017). Since the nature of hate speech is highly contextual and varies geographically, achieving a high inter-annotator agreement is difficult. The annotation process can be very vague and can result in low agreement scores (Schmidt & Wiegand, 2017). The personal biases and knowledge of the annotator can greatly influence their decisions (Waseem, 2016). Throughout the annotation process, it is also mentally taxing to sift through volumes of hateful content and annotate it. Annotations guidelines can be tricky and must be clearly defined (de Gibert et al., 2018).
- **Context:** Instances of hate speech do not always include profanity, making it more difficult for machine learning algorithms to detect it. Language is highly nuanced and constantly evolving, and it is very important to understand the context in which a comment is made to determine if it is hateful or not (Watanabe et al., 2018) (Schmidt & Wiegand, 2017). Also, the presence of sarcasm, humor, and irony can also confuse the model and result in incorrect classifications (Frenda, 2018). The model may require additional world knowledge to understand the context (Wiegand et al., 2018) (Schmidt & Wiegand, 2017). Noise can also be introduced into the model through common misspellings, substitution of a single character, and use of homophones to evade the classifier (Warner & Hirschberg, 2012). Use of certain profane words such as the 'Nigga', 'bitch', etc., may indicate hate speech, but can also be used within the target communities without any hateful sentiments. The user posting the comment should be kept in mind before classifying a statement as hateful.
- **Lack of datasets:** In the past few years, several shared tasks have been organized for utilizing machine learning to detect hate speech. Efforts to identify various types of offensive and hateful content have been made in several languages such as English, Italian (Fersini, Rosso, et al., 2018), Hindi, and Bengali (Mandl et al., 2021). However, the number of datasets released from these shared tasks have still not facilitated enough research in the area. Several approaches still have difficulty in fine-grained classification of abusive content. Datasets that focus specifically on detection of misogyny are limited to English. There is a great need to develop automated systems to prevent such online abuse in multilingual and code-switched settings.
- **Explainability:** Very few studies reviewed in this survey have implemented XAI techniques to understand model behavior. There has been some effort regarding criminalizing online hate speech. Such an effort can only be successful if the model decisions are trustworthy and unbiased. XAI techniques can provide human-readable and interpretable explanations of model decisions.

Thus, it can greatly assist in assuring legal liability, preventing the prosecution of innocent users, and protecting freedom of speech (de Smedt et al., 2018).

- **Under-resourced languages:** Code-switched languages, such as Hinglish, lack grammatical structure (Lal et al., 2019), informal transliteration (Singh et al., 2018) and inconsistent syntactic rules. Also, there is no consistent spelling for most code-switched words, and variations are very common (Mathur, Ratn Shah, et al., 2018). These factors can make it more complex for NLP tools to understand the language and detect hate speech.
- **Lower number of positive samples:** In real-world scenarios, the number of instances of hate speech or offensive language are relatively low compared to non-offensive content (Schmidt & Wiegand, 2017). This results in imbalanced datasets, as the data is skewed towards one class. The models need to be trained and calibrated as such, so that they can more sensitively detect instances of the minority class.
- **Bias:** AI systems are prone to develop and show certain biases, which can be introduced during dataset curation, feature engineering, and model training. Word embeddings such as Word2Vec are biased and contain gender stereotypes (Bolukbasi et al., 2016). A model may predict that a sentence is misogynous simply due to the presence of certain identity terms such as 'women', which were present in several positive instances of the misogynous class in the training set (Nozza et al., 2019).

CONCLUSION AND FUTURE WORK

In this review study, we have surveyed the recent and relevant work for hate speech detection. We explored the current state-of-the-art machine learning and deep learning models and toolkits that have been used in recent studies for detecting offensive and hateful language in various online platforms such as Facebook, Twitter, etc. The analysis done in the study suggests that AI tools, specifically deep neural networks, perform well in detecting hate speech towards various target groups on the basis of gender, nationality, ethnicity, and more. Shared tasks such as HASOC, Evalita, TRAC, etc., encourage teams from around the world to collaborate and advance the state-of-the-art hate speech detection. However, the field is still in its infancy as most of the studies conducted and datasets available have been limited to English and do not focus specifically on a particular target such as women. Very few datasets are available in code-switched and under resourced languages. The current measures in place for reporting and filtering such content are currently lackluster.

The future scope of this study is to create robust datasets for hate speech detection in low-resource and code-switched languages. It is important to select annotators with the relevant social sciences background or training for labeling the instances in the dataset, as hate speech is highly contextual. It is also important to develop modeling techniques that can handle fine-grained classification more appropriately in the context of hate speech detection. The inclusion of XAI tools, such as LIME and SHAP, into the machine learning and deep learning models also needs to be explored to increase the trust that is placed in model decisions.

REFERENCES

Amnesty Decoders. (2021). *Troll Patrol*. Amnesty International. https://decoders.amnesty.org/projects/troll-patrol

Amnesty Decoders. (2021). *Troll Patrol India*. Amnesty International. https://decoders.amnesty.org/projects/troll-patrol-india

Attanasio, G., Nozza, D., Pastor, E., Hovy, D., & Associates. (2022). Benchmarking post-hoc interpretability approaches for transformer-based misogyny detection. *Proceedings of NLP Power! The First Workshop on Efficient Benchmarking in NLP*. ACL Anthology. 10.18653/v1/2022.nlppower-1.11

Banerjee, S., Raja Chakravarthi, B., & McCrae, J. P. (2020). Comparison of Pretrained Embeddings to Identify Hate Speech in Indian Code-Mixed Text. *Proceedings - IEEE 2020 2nd International Conference on Advances in Computing, Communication Control and Networking, ICACCCN 2020*, (pp. 21–25). IEEE. 10.1109/ICACCCN51052.2020.9362731

Basile, V., Bosco, C., Fersini, E., Nozza, D., Patti, V., Pardo, F. M. R., Rosso, P., & Sanguinetti, M. (2019). Semeval-2019 task 5: Multilingual detection of hate speech against immigrants and women in twitter. *Proceedings of the 13th International Workshop on Semantic Evaluation*, (pp. 54–63). ACL Anthology. 10.18653/v1/S19-2007

Bhattacharya, S., Singh, S., Kumar, R., Bansal, A., Bhagat, A., Dawer, Y., Lahiri, B., & Kr Ojha, A. (2020). *Developing a Multilingual Annotated Corpus of Misogyny and Aggression*. Kaggle. http://bit.ly/2FhLMVz

Biradar, S., Saumya, S., & chauhan, A. (2022). Fighting hate speech from bilingual hinglish speaker's perspective, a transformer- and translation-based approach. *Social Network Analysis and Mining*, *12*(1), 87. doi:10.100713278-022-00920-w PMID:35911486

Bird, S., Klein, E., & Loper, E. (2009). *Natural language processing with Python: analyzing text with the natural language toolkit*. O'Reilly Media, Inc.

Bishop, C. M., & Nasrabadi, N. M. (2006). Pattern recognition and machine learning (Vol. 4, Issue 4). Springer.

Bohra, A., Vijay, D., Singh, V., Akhtar, S. S., & Shrivastava, M. (2018a). *A Dataset of Hindi-English Code-Mixed Social Media Text for Hate Speech Detection*. Github. https://github.com/deepanshu1995/HateSpeech-Hindi-

Bohra, A., Vijay, D., Singh, V., Akhtar, S. S., & Shrivastava, M. (2018b). *A Dataset of Hindi-English Code-Mixed Social Media Text for Hate Speech Detection*. https://github.com/deepanshu1995/HateSpeech-Hindi-

Bolukbasi, T., Chang, K.-W., Zou, J. Y., Saligrama, V., & Kalai, A. T. (2016). Man is to computer programmer as woman is to homemaker? debiasing word embeddings. *Advances in Neural Information Processing Systems*, 29.

Chan, S. (2016). Right-Wing Extremist Convicted of Murdering Jo Cox, a U.K. Lawmaker. *The New York Times.* https://www.nytimes.com/2016/11/23/world/europe/thomas-mair-convicted-murder-jo-cox.html

Cheng, J., Bernstein, M., Danescu-Niculescu-mizil, C., & Leskovec, J. (2017). Anyone can become a troll: Causes of trolling behavior in online discussions. *Proceedings of the ACM Conference on Computer Supported Cooperative Work, CSCW*, (pp. 1217–1230). ACM. 10.1145/2998181.2998213

Countries with most Twitter users 2022. (2022). Statista. https://www.statista.com/statistics/242606/number-of-active-twitter-users-in-selected-countries/

de GibertO.PerezN.García-PablosA.CuadrosM. (2018). *Hate Speech Dataset from a White Supremacy Forum.* https://arxiv.org/abs/1809.04444 doi:10.18653/v1/W18-5102

de Smedt, T., Jaki, S., Kotzé, E., Saoud, L., Gwóźdź, M., de Pauw, G., & Daelemans, W. (2018). *Multilingual Cross-domain Perspectives on Online Hate Speech.* OHCHR. https://www.ohchr.org/EN/ProfessionalInterest/Pages/CCPR.aspx

DevlinJ.ChangM.-W.LeeK.ToutanovaK. (2018). *BERT: Pre-training of Deep Bidirectional Transformers for Language Understanding.* https://arxiv.org/abs/1810.04805

Dhrodia, A. (2017, November 20). Unsocial Media: The Real Toll of Online Abuse against Women. *Medium.* https://medium.com/amnesty-insights/unsocial-media-the-real-toll-of-online-abuse-against-women-37134ddab3f4

Ditch The Label 2016. (2016). Brandwatch. https://www.brandwatch.com/reports/cyberbullying-2016/

Djuric, N., Zhou, J., Morris, R., Grbovic, M., Radosavljevic, V., & Bhamidipati, N. (2015). Hate speech detection with comment embeddings. *WWW 2015 Companion - Proceedings of the 24th International Conference on World Wide Web*, 29–30. 10.1145/2740908.2742760

Ending Violence is Our Business: Workplace Responses to Intimate Partner Violence in Asia and the Pacific. (2019). UN Women – Asia-Pacific. https://asiapacific.unwomen.org/en/digital-library/publications/2019/10/workplace-responses-to-intimate-partner-violence

Feinberg, T., & Robey, N. (2009). Cyberbullying. *Education Digest, 74*(7), 26.

Fersini, E., Nozza, D., & Rosso, P. (2018). *Overview of the Evalita 2018 Task on Automatic Misogyny Identification (AMI).* Future Eight. https://figure-eight.com/

Fersini, E., Nozza, D., & Rosso, P. (2020). *AMI @ EVALITA2020: Automatic Misogyny Identification.*

Fersini, E., Rosso, P., & Anzovino, M. (2018). *Overview of the Task on Automatic Misogyny Identification at IberEval 2018.* Figure Eight. https://figure-eight.com/

Frenda, S. (2018). *The role of sarcasm in hate speech. A multilingual perspective.* QCRI. https://alt.qcri.org/semeval2019/index

Goodfellow, I., Bengio, Y., & Courville, A. (2016). *Deep learning.* MIT press.

Guest, E., Vidgen, B., Sastry, N., Tyson, G., & Margetts, H. (2021). *An Expert Annotated Dataset for the Detection of Online Misogyny.* Github. https://github.com/ellamguest/

OHCHR. (2011). *Guiding Principles on Business and Human rights Implementing the United Nations "Protect, Respect and Remedy" Framework.* OHCHR. https://www.ohchr.org/Documents/Publications/GuidingPrinciplesBusinessHR_EN.pdf

Gunning, D., Stefik, M., Choi, J., Miller, T., Stumpf, S., & Yang, G. Z. (2019). XAI-Explainable artificial intelligence. *Science Robotics*, *4*(37), eaay7120. doi:10.1126cirobotics.aay7120 PMID:33137719

Hate Crime - Law Commission. (2021). Lawcom. https://www.lawcom.gov.uk/project/hate-crime/

Hatebase. (2023). *Home.* Hatebase. https://hatebase.org/

Hingorani, S. (2020, March 26). *Commentary: Isolated with your abuser? Why family violence seems to be on the rise during COVID-19 outbreak.* CNA. https://www.channelnewsasia.com/commentary/coronavirus-covid-19-family-violence-abuse-women-self-isolation-1324466

Hochreiter, S., & Schmidhuber, J. (1997). Long short-term memory. *Neural Computation*, *9*(8), 1735–1780. doi:10.1162/neco.1997.9.8.1735 PMID:9377276

Internet Society. (2017). *Issue Paper: Asia-Pacific Bureau Gender.* Internet Society. https://www.internetsociety.org/wp-content/uploads/2017/08/APAC-Issue-Papers-Gender_0.pdf

Jin, X., Wei, Z., Du, J., Xue, X., & Ren, X. (2019). Towards hierarchical importance attribution: Explaining compositional semantics for neural sequence models. *ArXiv Preprint ArXiv:1911.06194.*

KambleS.JoshiA. (2018). *Hate Speech Detection from Code-mixed Hindi-English Tweets Using Deep Learning Models.* https://arxiv.org/abs/1811.05145

Karim, Md. R., Dey, S. K., Islam, T., Sarker, S., Menon, M. H., Hossain, K., Chakravarthi, B. R., Hossain, Md. A., & Decker, S. (2020). *DeepHateExplainer: Explainable Hate Speech Detection in Under-resourced Bengali Language.* https://arxiv.org/abs/2012.14353

Kumar, R., Ojha, A. K., Malmasi, S., & Zampieri, M. (2018). *Benchmarking Aggression Identification in Social Media.* CodaLab. https://competitions.codalab.org/

Kumar, R., Ojha, A. K., Malmasi, S., & Zampieri, M. (2020). *Evaluating Aggression Identification in Social Media.* CodaLab. https://competitions.codalab.org/

Lal, Y. K., Kumar, V., Dhar, M., Shrivastava, M., & Koehn, P. (2019). De-mixing sentiment from code-mixed text. *Proceedings of the 57th Annual Meeting of the Association for Computational Linguistics: Student Research Workshop*, (pp. 371–377). ACL. 10.18653/v1/P19-2052

Lundberg, S. M., & Lee, S.-I. (2017). A unified approach to interpreting model predictions. *Advances in Neural Information Processing Systems*, 30.

Mandl, T., Modha, S., Majumder, P., Patel, D., Dave, M., Mandlia, C., & Patel, A. (2019). Overview of the hasoc track at fire 2019: Hate speech and offensive content identification in indo-european languages. *Proceedings of the 11th Forum for Information Retrieval Evaluation*, (pp. 14–17). IEEE. 10.1145/3368567.3368584

Mandl, T., Modha, S., Shahi, G. K., Kumar Jaiswal, A., Nandini, D., Patel, D., & Schäfer, J. (2020). *Overview of the HASOC track at FIRE 2020: Hate Speech and Offensive Content Identification in Indo-European Languages under Creative Commons License Attribution 4.0 International (CC BY 4.0)*. CEUR. http://ceur-ws.org

Mandl, T., Modha, S., Shahi, G. K., Madhu, H., Satapara, S., Schäfer, J., Ranasinghe, T., Zampieri, M., Nandini, D., Kumar Jaiswal, A., & Zampieri, M. (2021). *Overview of the HASOC Subtrack at FIRE 2021: Hate Speech and Offensive Content Identification in English and Indo-Aryan Languages under Creative Commons License Attribution 4.0 International (CC BY 4.0)*. CEUR. http://ceur-ws.org

MathewB.SahaP.YimamS.M.BiemannC.GoyalP.MukherjeeA. (2020). *HateXplain: A Benchmark Dataset for Explainable Hate Speech Detection*. https://arxiv.org/abs/2012.10289

Mathur, P., Ratn Shah, R., Sawhney, R., & Mahata, D. (2018). *Detecting Offensive Tweets in Hindi-English Code-Switched Language*. Github. www.github.com/pmathur5k10/

Moreno, M. A., Gower, A. D., Brittain, H., & Vaillancourt, T. (2019). Applying Natural Language Processing to Evaluate News Media Coverage of Bullying and Cyberbullying. *Prevention Science*, *20*(8), 1274–1283. doi:10.100711121-019-01029-x PMID:31414277

Nockleyby, J. (2000). *'Hate speech in Encyclopedia of the American Constitution*. Electron. J. Acad. Spec. Libr.

Nortajuddin, A. (2020, March 30). Virus Lockdown Causing Rise In Domestic Abuse. *The ASEAN Post*. https://theaseanpost.com/article/virus-lockdown-causing-rise-domestic-abuse

Nozza, D., Volpetti, C., & Fersini, E. (2019). Unintended bias in misogyny detection. *Proceedings - 2019 IEEE/WIC/ACM International Conference on Web Intelligence, WI 2019*, 149–155. 10.1145/3350546.3352512

Women's Aid. (2022). *Online and digital abuse*. Women's Aid. https://www.womensaid.org.uk/information-support/what-is-domestic-abuse/online-safety/

Pavlopoulos, J., Sorensen, J., Laugier, L., & Androutsopoulos, I. (2021). SemEval-2021 Task 5: Toxic Spans Detection. *Proceedings of the 15th International Workshop on Semantic Evaluation (SemEval-2021)*, (pp. 59–69). ACL. 10.18653/v1/2021.semeval-1.6

Perspective API. (2021). *Home*. Perspective API. https://perspectiveapi.com/

Recognizing and Combating Technology-Facilitated Abuse. (2016, October 13). NNEDV. https://nnedv.org/latest_update/combating-technology-facilitated-abuse/

Ribeiro, M. T., Singh, S., & Guestrin, C. (2016). "Why should i trust you?" Explaining the predictions of any classifier. *Proceedings of the 22nd ACM SIGKDD International Conference on Knowledge Discovery and Data Mining*, (pp. 1135–1144). ACM. 10.1145/2939672.2939778

RossB.RistM.CarbonellG.CabreraB.KurowskyN.WojatzkiM. (2017). *Measuring the Reliability of Hate Speech Annotations: The Case of the European Refugee Crisis*. doi:10.17185/duepublico/42132

Rumelhart, D. E., Hinton, G. E., & Williams, R. J. (1985). *Learning internal representations by error propagation*.

Schmidt, A., & Wiegand, M. (2017). *A Survey on Hate Speech Detection using Natural Language Processing*. Wikipedia. https://en.wikipedia.org/wiki/List_

Singh, R., Choudhary, N., & Shrivastava, M. (2018). Automatic normalization of word variations in code-mixed social media text. *ArXiv Preprint ArXiv:1804.00804*.

UN Women – Asia-Pacific. (2020). *Social Media Monitoring on COVID-19 and Misogyny in Asia and the Pacific*. UN. https://asiapacific.unwomen.org/en/digital-library/publications/2020/10/ap-social-media-monitoring-on-covid-19-and-misogyny-in-asia-and-the-pacific

Sreelakshmi, K., Premjith, B., & Soman, K. P. (2020). Detection of Hate Speech Text in Hindi-English Code-mixed Data. *Procedia Computer Science*, *171*, 737–744. doi:10.1016/j.procs.2020.04.080

UN Women – Asia-Pacific. (2020). *The First 100 Days of the COVID-19 Outbreak in Asia and the Pacific.* UN. https://asiapacific.unwomen.org/en/digital-library/publications/2020/04/the-first-100-days-of-the-covid-19-outbreak-in-asia-and-the-pacific

Amnesty International. (2018). *Toxic Twitter - The Psychological Harms of Violence and Abuse Against Women Online.* Amnesty International. https://www.amnesty.org/en/latest/news/2018/03/online-violence-against-women-chapter-6-6/

Amnesty International. (2018). *Toxic Twitter - The Reporting Process.* Amnesty International. https://www.amnesty.org/en/latest/news/2018/03/online-violence-against-women-chapter-4-4/

Amnesty International. (2018). *Toxic Twitter - The Solution - Amnesty International.* (2018). https://www.amnesty.org/en/latest/news/2018/03/online-violence-against-women-chapter-8-8/

Amnesty International. (2018). *Toxic Twitter - Women's Experiences of Violence and Abuse on Twitter.* Amnesty International. https://www.amnesty.org/en/latest/news/2018/03/online-violence-against-women-chapter-3-2/

Twitter's policy on hateful conduct. (2023). Twitter. https://help.twitter.com/en/rules-and-policies/hateful-conduct-policy

VijayaraghavanP.LarochelleH.RoyD. (2021). *Interpretable Multi-Modal Hate Speech Detection*. https://arxiv.org/abs/2103.01616

Vineyard, J. (2014, October 16). You Don't Need to Care About Video Games to Care About Gamergate. *Vulture.* https://www.vulture.com/2014/10/why-you-should-care-about-gamergate.html

Warner, W., & Hirschberg, J. (2012). *Detecting Hate Speech on the World Wide Web*. Yahoo. http://info.yahoo.com/legal/us/yahoo/utos/utos-173.html

Waseem, Z. (2016). *Are You a Racist or Am I Seeing Things? Annotator Influence on Hate Speech Detection on Twitter*. Spacy. www.spacy.io

Waseem, Z., & Hovy, D. (2016). *Hateful Symbols or Hateful People? Predictive Features for Hate Speech Detection on Twitter*. Github. https://github.com/zeerakw/hatespeech

Watanabe, H., Bouazizi, M., & Ohtsuki, T. (2018). Hate Speech on Twitter: A Pragmatic Approach to Collect Hateful and Offensive Expressions and Perform Hate Speech Detection. *IEEE Access : Practical Innovations, Open Solutions*, *6*, 13825–13835. doi:10.1109/ACCESS.2018.2806394

What we do: Ending violence against women. (2023). UN Women – Headquarters. https://www.unwomen.org/en/what-we-do/ending-violence-against-women

Wiegand, M., Siegel, M., & Ruppenhofer, J. (2018). *Overview of the GermEval 2018 Shared Task on the Identification of Offensive Language*. Kaggle. https://www.kaggle.com/c/

Cybersmile. (2022). Young Woman Killed Herself After Being Made To Feel Insecure By Facebook Trolls. *CyberSmile.* https://www.cybersmile.org/news/young-woman-killed-herself-after-being-made-to-feel-insecure-by-facebook-trolls

Yousif, N. (2022, October 15). *Amanda Todd: Dutchman sentenced for fatal cyber-stalking - BBC News.* BBC News, Toronto. https://www.bbc.com/news/world-us-canada-63218797

YouTube users by country 2022. (2022). Statista. https://www.statista.com/statistics/280685/number-of-monthly-unique-youtube-users/

Zampieri, M., Malmasi, S., Nakov, P., Rosenthal, S., Farra, N., & Kumar, R. (2019a). *Predicting the Type and Target of Offensive Posts in Social Media.* Association for Computational Linguistics. http://bit.ly/2FhLMVz

Zampieri, M., Malmasi, S., Nakov, P., Rosenthal, S., Farra, N., & Kumar, R. (2019b). *SemEval-2019 Task 6: Identifying and Categorizing Offensive Language in Social Media (OffensEval).* https://competitions.codalab.org/

Chapter 26
Exploring Motivations, Impact, and Coping Mechanisms of Post-Dating on Female Dating App Users

S. Shantharaju
https://orcid.org/0000-0003-2663-7176
CHRIST University (Deemed), India

Banik Aishwarya
CHRIST University (Deemed), India

ABSTRACT

Online dating apps are a popular platform for forming new connections. Generally, a virtual acquaintance intensifies between the users, eventually converting it into an offline relationship. Despite the anonymity of users being a prime motivation to initiate a conversation, it does pose challenges, including mental health issues and sexual abuse. There are increasing reports of privacy violations, extortions, cyberstalking, and sexual assaults connected with dating apps. While people in a relationship decide to set boundaries to avoid each other, both users go through an uncomfortable phase. Unless both parties mutually share the responsibility, the relationship issues are not sorted out without going through an abusive phase. One person's separation anxiety might become a physical manifestation, including virtual and physical assaults. The current study relies on focus group discussions to understand post-dating app manifestations and its impact on female dating app users. The study involves respondents mostly exposed to online dating.

DOI: 10.4018/978-1-6684-8893-5.ch026

INTRODUCTION

Dating is part of urban culture, and it expanded with technological intervention. The app-based dating matches made the process of finding easier. There are both positive and negative aspects of dating apps, and incidentally, it is the female gender which is more vulnerable to exploitation. Abundant literature points to the significant impact of dating apps on young adults, predominantly female users. Most dating apps are used out of boredom, peer pressure, seeking causal relationships, and loneliness. Once users get matched, they would develop their casual acquaintances into severe relationships without even considering the post-dating repercussions. The current study focuses on understanding the impact of a person's post-dating experiences and attempts to discover the coping mechanisms of exploitation. The study focuses on understanding the abuses and the mental trauma female dating app users (FDAU) go through in the entire process. The repercussions of such actions and understanding the motive and effects are necessary. At the same time, we study the online dating phenomenon and its lasting impact when one faces abuse through such a platform.

Dating App Experiences

Many dating apps exist, but Tinder is one of the most well-known, with more than 10.5 million users globally (Anon, n.d.-b). For many, it is a convenient way to connect and find potential partners. However, the rise of dating apps has also brought various issues related to safety, privacy, and cultural norms to light. Numerous studies have shown sexting as a standard practice between individuals in romantic relationships and exchanging private pictures. Such a digital footprint has challenges and could lead to risky cyber behaviour. There are hazards associated with dating apps, including problematic relationships and becoming the object of antisocial behaviour, such as sexual harassment or abuse (Castro & Barrada, 2020a). Vulnerable groups, such as women and sexual minorities, are particularly concerned about the perils associated with dating apps (Castro & Barrada, 2020a; Ilakkuvan et al., 2019).

Most of the time, location-based dating applications let users establish individual profiles. For instance, members of Tinder upload images and a brief biography (or "bio") about themselves. By using parameters like GPS location, age, and gender, users may browse through the profiles of others. Users can then swipe left or right to discard or like a profile. Once two users have liked each other's profiles, they are considered a match and can begin messaging on the app (Kaakinen et al., 2018).

The potential dysfunctions that Internet usage might suggest in a person's life are highlighted by problematic Internet use (Caplan, 2002). The chance of displaying poor self-regulation increases with a preference for online social connection and mood control through the Internet, which has several detrimental effects on the person's life (Gámez-Guadix et al., 2013). The prevalence rates reported by epidemiological research (Jennings et al., 2023) show this condition's clinical and societal significance, which worsens as people age (Panova & Carbonell, 2018). Although other studies (Cebollero-Salinas et al., 2022) find no differences, more problematic Internet use has been seen in females (Panova & Carbonell, 2018).

Social Platforms, Validation, and Risky Behaviour

In recent years, dating apps have gained immense popularity among the youth. With the increasing penetration of smartphones and affordable internet, dating apps have become part of the urban lifestyle. As the peer pressure increases, one tends to have to use the medium to get validated (Ren and Wang 2022).

In the current scenario, validation plays a vital role in one's self-image. External validation can stimulate the exploration of different aspects of oneself, good or bad. It can lead to taking actions that can have a temporary or permanent effect that is not always healthy but can be scarring (Lenton-Brym et al. 2021). Although the literature on teen dating violence and abuse has increased significantly over the past 20 years, recent technological developments (such as social networking and cell phone texting) have given those who engage in dating violence new tools to harass, control, and abuse their partners. However, little is known about the characteristics of cyberdating abuse, how frequently it affects young people, and how it relates to other types of dating violence (Toma 2022). How young people handle their information and interactions online affects the overall quality of online connections (Sánchez, Muñoz-Fernández, and Ortega-Ruíz 2015). These management techniques are crucial in determining whether ODA usage promotes healthy social interactions or results in disputes and misuse. Teenagers' abilities to safely manage internet conversation and information sharing vary significantly from person to person (Stanton and Campbell 2014). Adolescents engage in various risky online behaviours, such as sharing personal information with strangers online or looking for new friends online, which, per prior research may expose adolescents to potentially harmful interactions. Young individuals frequently engage in such behaviours when using ODA (Castro and Barrada 2020).

Sexting and Cyber Abuse

Many studies correlate cyber practice and its harmful physical manifestations. Suppose Cyberbullying has shown a higher degree of association with problematic Internet use (PIU) (Cebollero-Salinas et al., 2022). In that case, cyber dating abuse victimisation tends to be associated with sexting and PIU (Madigan et al., 2018). A step ahead, cyberdating abuse could perpetuate aggression and cyberbullying (Zweig et al., 2013) and victimisation. Fewer studies have connected possible mental health concerns, digital practice, and post-dating manifestations, including coping mechanisms. The current study attempts to study the post-dating manifestations of female participants' experiences.

BACKGROUND

There is a correlation between how youth interact with the world around them and their virtual indulgence. Today's young people may locate and begin contact with prospective love interests and romantic partners via various dating websites and mobile applications made available by the widespread use of smartphones (Sumter et al., 2017). Online dating services (ODAs) have grown significantly over the past ten years (Lee & Kim, 2020), and they are now a typical aspect of people's life all over the world (Castro & Barrada, 2020a). These applications are used by teenagers as well, although they are more popular among young adults (Castro and Barrada, 2020a; Sánchez et al., 2015; Sumter et al., 2017)

Young, Vulnerable, and Impact of the Post-Dating Phase

Young people value developing strong peer connections (Steinberg & Morris, 2001); developing romantic relationships with a stronger feeling of commitment quickly becomes essential for many (Shulman & Connolly, 2013). Accepting peers and nearby and age-specific circumstances can impact a young person's love decisions (Shulman & Connolly, 2013). Studies indicate higher levels of violence among teens in dating relationships (Castro & Barrada, 2020b). Studies on high school students across different cultures have produced various estimates for the number of young people who experience dating violence. The American agency's Biennial Youth Risk Behavior Surveys found considerable violence among school students while dating. These school students (grades 9-12) have reported being hit or physically hurt. According to the survey, increased violence has increased since 1999 (Clayton et al., 2023).

Zweig et al. (2013) and Draucker and Martsolf (2010) conducted a qualitative study with 56 participants to examine the role of electronic communications in dating violence and abuse. Their study emphasises the variety of ways that young people can abuse their partners through technology. They discovered eight specific ways that partners interacted electronically, the last six of which were connected to abusive, violent, or controlling behaviours: Relationship-building, non-aggressive communication, fighting, keeping track of a partner's whereabouts or controlling their activities, emotional aggression towards a partner, seeking assistance during a violent episode, cutting off a partner's access to oneself by not returning calls, texts, or other technological contacts, and re-establishing contact after a violent episode are all examples. This study revealed examples of cyber abuse, including a guy who hacked into his partner's Facebook account, read every message she had ever sent or received, and then forced her to explain each to him. Another instance involves one partner developing a website others may submit with similarly vile remarks against their ex-partner. Based on this research, we can observe that people may abuse and dominate their relationship partners in various ways. Calling names, insulting via text and phone, explicit requests, distributing false information online, and sharing humiliating images or videos are common forms of violence (Levesque et al., 2016; Martsolf et al., 2012).

This viewpoint shows that teenagers' ODA usage indicates a dangerous online lifestyle. Online behaviours that increase the likelihood of victimisation include unsafe and maybe irresponsible dating and information-sharing practices. These online behaviours and lifestyles also help to explain why some people experience online. For instance, a study by Choi et al. (2016) shows how Asian cyberbullying victimisation was associated with dangerous online lifestyle, leisure, and social networking activities (Choi et al., 2016).

Online Victimisation and Forms of Abuse

Women using dating apps may be more vulnerable to various risks, including harassment, stalking, and violence, due to societal norms, gender power dynamics, and online anonymity (Burke et al., 2011; Wang et al., 2017). Some dating apps may have inadequate safety measures, leaving women vulnerable to potential harm or exploitation. This includes concerns about meeting strangers, sharing personal information, or encountering dangerous individuals (Burke et al., 2011; Wang et al., 2017).

Women's experiences with dating apps can impact their emotional well-being. Negative interactions, such as ghosting or rejection, can lead to disappointment and self-doubt (Alexopoulos et al., 2020). Women may encounter instances of catfishing, where individuals create fake profiles or misrepresent themselves on dating apps. This deception can lead to emotional manipulation and disappointment (Abbasi, 2018). In a particular relationship, dating violence is frequently interpreted to include a variety of abusive behaviours, including physical, sexual, psychological, and emotional abuse (Anon, n.d.-a; Levesque et al., 2016).

Although there is some overlap between online harassment and cyberbullying (Kaakinen et al. 2018, 2021), harassment is more specific and encompasses all types of online victimisation. In addition to peer-to-peer interactions, it also encompasses adult and random stranger harassment. Receiving non-consensual content (such as images or videos) with sexual content, risk factors like frequent use of social media and sharing personal information online, and a lack of self-control (Kaakinen et al., 2021), threats or blackmail (such as the pressure to publish sexual content about someone), or pressure to engage in sexual activities (on or offline) are examples of typical forms of online sexual harassment.

METHODS

Research Questions

1. To explore the post-dating experience of female users concerning abuses of any form.
2. Understanding setting and breaching of boundaries in online dating setup.
3. Exploring coping mechanisms of the post-dating phase by female users.
4. Exploring the usage pattern and general experience of dating apps.

Research Design Study

This study utilizes a qualitative research design, explicitly employing focus group discussions to gain insights into the dating app experience. Focus groups provide an interactive platform for participants to express their perspectives, share experiences, and engage in group discussions.

Primarily, the study intended to create as many groups as possible from diverse backgrounds to conduct focus group discussions. As the group dynamics prompt the participants to open up comfortably, focus groups result in unbiased patterns and themes. Despite being challenged to reach out to dating app users, the study intends to include respondents from the student community to working professionals. The author effectively utilized primary contacts to reach out to respondents. Such respondents should have been part of at least one dating app and should have dated someone matched through the app. However, they need not be the victims of the app. The dominant pattern observed has been documented systematically through the themes presented in the further section.

Sampling Techniques

Convenience sampling is employed to recruit participants who meet the age criteria (20-28 years) and should have used at least one dating app. After the first group's discussion was documented, a snowball technique was employed to recruit more participants through the participating members. Potential participants are selected based on their accessibility and willingness to participate in the study. Discussions are conducted when at least more than three participants agree to come at the same time, either to a virtual space or a physical space.

Participants

Participants for the research include young adults aged 20 to 28 who have used dating apps. The study includes 20 participants, divided into five focus groups of 4 to 5 members, depending on their availability.

Data Collection

FGD topic guide: The focus group discussions are conducted in a suitable and comfortable environment, ensuring privacy and minimal distractions using an audio recorder and google meet. Each focus group session is audio-recorded. The focus group discussion was conducted between 21st April 2023 to 21st May 2023.

A comprehensive discussion guide is developed to facilitate the focus group discussions. The guide includes open-ended questions related to the dating app experience, forms of abuse encountered, personality traits exhibited, problems faced, and coping mechanisms employed. The guide encouraged participants to share their personal experiences and insights.

Limitations of the Study

1. **Critical data collection method:** Using focus group discussions as the primary data collection method presents inherent limitations. While focus groups allow for interactive discussions and the exploration of diverse perspectives, they may capture individual experiences in a different level of detail than one-on-one interviews. Certain participants may have felt more comfortable sharing their experiences in a more private setting, which was not accommodated by the group setting of focus groups.
2. **Unavailability of participants:** The selection of participants for the study has been challenging due to their unavailability or lack of interest. Participants may have had conflicting schedules or other commitments that limited their ability to participate in the focus group discussions. The limitation could introduce selection bias and impact the representativeness of the findings.
3. **Reluctance to share personal stories:** Some participants may have been hesitant or unwilling to openly share their personal dating app experiences, especially if it involved sensitive or negative encounters. The reluctance may have limited the depth and breadth of the data collected, potentially resulting in a complete understanding of the dating app experiences within the target population.
4. **Time management between participants:** Managing time effectively during the focus group discussions may have been challenging, particularly when coordinating a group of individuals with different schedules and availability. The varied time constraints of participants may have limited the duration of each focus group session, potentially affecting the depth of the discussions and the comprehension exploration of relevant topics.
5. **Sample Size and Generalizability:** The study's sample size, which included 20 participants divided into five focus groups, may limit the generalizability of the findings to the broader population of young adults aged 20 to 28. The small sample size and potential self-selection bias due to convenience sampling may restrict the study's external validity.
6. **Social desirability bias:** Due to the sensitive nature of discussing dating app experiences, participants may have been inclined to present themselves in a more socially desirable light or withhold

certain information. This social desirability bias may have influenced the responses provided, potentially leading to an incomplete understanding of the actual experiences and challenges faced by participants.

7. **Potential Homogeneity of the Sample:** Convenience sampling and the limited sample size may have resulted in a relatively homogeneous sample regarding demographic characteristics, experiences, and perspectives. This homogeneity could restrict the generalizability of the findings to a more diverse population.

RESULTS AND ANALYSIS

See Table 1.

Table 1. Results and analysis

Group	No. of Participants	Dating app usage in year	Occupation	Motive to use ODA	Forms of abuse	Coping mechanisms	Post dating impact
1	4	<1 year	Student	• Exploration, friends, peer pressure • New to city, Building connections • Romantic relationship	• Emotional abuse, physical abuse, coercive control • Bad touch, no consent, boundary violation • Emotional manipulation • Appearing shirtless or encouraging to be romantic • Inappropriate touch • Groping • Kissing without notice • Stalking • Unannounced visits • Digging on the past, suspicious personality • Forcing to visit his house/ sexual advances and gestures • Trust issues and multiple dating	• Scared to talk, Feel social isolation • Not confident to go out during late night	• Deleted the app • Avoiding contact • Physical confrontation • More cautious to meet in person • Meeting a stranger only with friends or in group • Informing friends before meeting and arranging a call every half an hour. • Thorough background checks up • Not sharing the residence location • Afraid of public scene

continued on following page

Table 1. Continued

Group	No. of Participants	Dating app usage in year	Occupation	Motive to use ODA	Forms of abuse	Coping mechanisms	Post dating impact
2	4	<1 year	Working professionals	• hectic life • wanted to socialize • physical needs	• Physical abuse, sexual assault • Drunk and don't remember what all happened • Stalking	• seeking help from friends • Police complaint • Professional help	• Feel vulnerable • Guilty • Depression • Social isolation • Fear of sharing • Loneliness
3	5	<1 year	Students	• physical intimacy • friendship	• Disappeared after involved physically • Ghosting • Emotional abuse • Blackmail • Self-harming and sharing photos and videos of it • Sexual assault, emotional manipulation • Forcing to consume alcohol and smoke • Inviting friends to join	• Blocking the contact • Professional help • Careful usage of the app • Longer and multiple telephonic conversations before meeting physically	• Anxiety • Depression • Social fear • Guilty and regretful
4	3	>1 year	Working	• Exploring the app, Boredom, new to city • Companionship	• Threating to end relationship • Forced to travel to strange places	• Uninstallation app • Talking to family members	• Broke financially • Emotional trauma
5	4	<1year	Students		• Forcing to sleep with another man • Physical assault and insulting conversation	• More conscious • Not deceived by the profile or the words • Working on self-care • Not using apps to find relationships • Support from family	• Emotional trauma • Disappointment and skeptical

Motivation for Using Dating Apps

There are varied motivations to use dating apps, including exploring dating apps to look for serious romantic relationships. Many first-time dating app users have tried the app out of boredom, curiosity to explore, monotonous life, companionship, physical needs, peer pressure, and curiosity. Many participants hail from cities other than their current employment or studying city. As new people in an unknown city, they felt the need for a friend or companion. Out of 20 participants from five groups, 12 were students, and eight were young working professionals. More than half of them have tried Tinder, followed by Bumble. Interestingly, people who have tried other apps, including Instagram and Facebook, have found a match indirectly.

Dating App User: Novice vs. Cautious User

Various kinds of misconduct on dating apps exist, from inviting sexual gestures to physical sexual abuse. In many cases, the boy tends to lure the girl, assuming that she also needs a lustful relationship. If girls have explored dating apps for various reasons, from curiosity to real connections, the boys have believed that the app exists only for sexual hookups. Most first-time dating app users have avoided further escalation of their dating relationship or uninstalled the app. Those who exchanged phone numbers have had online and offline stalking experiences. In a couple of cases, girls took the risk of visiting their date's residences and were forced to have nonconsensual sexual advances. In a few cases, those who indulged in a sexual act have quickly discovered that their dates were either dating multiple girls at a time or just disappeared after a while. Such experiences have turned novice dating app users into pessimistic individuals with suspicions about the people around them. More importantly, they feel guilty about using dating apps and accepting the app matches without proper background checks.

In the case of those who did not uninstall, they have learned mindful usage methods. They do not prefer to meet a boy immediately after they find a match. They have taken ample time to investigate the authenticity of the person they have matched with and have chosen a safe public place to meet. They tended to alert their friends about this dating schedule and arrange a friendly intervention through telephone conversations to update them about their safety. More importantly, they have learnt that physical intimacy might put them in a spot of guilt unless it is a genuine connection.

Physical Intimacy and Complexity of a Relationship

Despite most respondents not going through trauma, those who sustained their relationships for longer with the person they matched with tend to have higher reports concerning abuse. Within a month or two, the girls had realised their partner's disloyalty, including cheating, emotional manipulation, and physical abuse. For this statistically small number of respondents (5 out of 20), the physical involvement with the person they have matched with made them vulnerable as they tend to believe the other person. Many of them were suspicious of their partners in the initial period. However, they gave the benefit of the doubt despite having considerable evidence. These women were encouraged to consume alcohol and smoke. When girls confronted their partners about trust concerns, they were made to believe it was only in the boy's past relationship. At some point, either girls realised they were being manipulated, or the boys stopped seeing them. In either case, these relationships were never sustained beyond a year.

All five of these women sought professional help, and one respondent was still seeing a therapist during these interviews.

In two cases out of 20, a police complaint had to be registered with the help of friends when the relationship had reached the stage of physical abuse to avoid further escalation. Though the matter did not reach the court, securing themselves was an essential step. In seven out of 20 cases, men tried to stalk/ghost the girls online or offline. The initial tone of the request turned into an abusive phase over telephonic conversations, despite blocking the numbers. Two respondents had to change their residences as the men they were dating were following them.

Post Dating Impact

A common experience for most of the negatively impacted dating app users was that they tend to have experienced general depression, and 20% of first-time dating app users have experienced clinical depression. They had to seek mental health professional support, and some of these clinically depressed former dating app users are experiencing social anxiety and guilt even after years. Due to horrible experiences, they had, from forceful groping to physical assault, they are finding it difficult to cope with any relationships. Many dating app users could never find a connection and feel comfortable being single. The forms of deception, Emotional manipulation, gaslighting and discovery of their parallel relationships have made the woman dating app users feel they were victims and easily vulnerable individuals. This has affected their general confidence and communication abilities, especially in the case of cross-gender conversations.

According to all the groups, the dating boys/men were given a positive initial impression initially and offered to have a dinner or lunch date. Many boys had highly manipulated images that may not resonate with their appearances. Quickly they discovered that the boundaries are very fluid for boys/men, unlike women. Boundary violations, inappropriate touch, and vocal response was common experience. The boys did not want to take anything slowly. They did not want to take things slowly and assumed that a dinner date was an invitation to consume a woman. Despite making it clear, frequent and unwanted visits to the girl's residence were a typical pattern following verbal abuse and a tendency to create a public obscene.

Coping Mechanisms

Most dating app users have taken a step to uninstall the apps. A small number, primarily working professionals, had installed the apps after a few months and were more careful in choosing their dates. Their previous experiences left them with a permanent suspicion of not believing a person by the online profile they put up in public. They are not easily deceived by looking at a profile. They tend to check the profile's history on other social media platforms.

As a common practice, women tend to share their experiences (negative) with their friends and roommates who have used dating apps. In a way, their peers have acted as their mentors. They needed to share these experiences as they could not normalize the trauma they were going through. They were mentored by their friends, who supported their aspirations.

In two cases, the dating app users had to open up to their family members as they had dated for longer. In one case, after eight months of dating, the boy suddenly vanished, leaving the girl puzzled and depressed. She also realized she was financially exploited and suffered severe depressive phases. The girl had to rely on family members as the relationship had paralyzed her day-to-day functioning.

For her, getting back to her parents helped sustain her emotional balance, and it took months for her to resume normal functions.

FINDINGS AND DISCUSSION

Several common patterns, comparisons, and similarities can be observed in the scenarios described above. Firstly, each interview involves an initial attraction and connection between the individuals who meet through dating apps. Whether it is shared interests, enjoyable conversations, or a sense of anticipation, these factors contribute to developing a relationship or a hopeful expectation for one. A common thread observed can be the social alienation felt by urban migrants irrespective of their profession. However, a recurring theme in these stories is misrepresentation and deception. Some individuals on dating apps portray themselves inaccurately by using outdated or edited profile pictures or providing false information. This deception leads to disappointment, mistrust, and feelings of being deceived when the actual appearance or characteristics of the person do not align with what was initially presented.

Boundary violations and non-consensual actions are prevalent in many of these stories. One person may cross the boundaries of the other, engaging in unwanted physical advances, pressuring for intimacy, or even resorting to physical violence. These actions violate personal boundaries and demonstrate a lack of respect and consent, perpetuating a harmful and abusive dynamic. The emotional and psychological impact on the victims in these stories is significant. As a result of the abusive behaviour they encounter, individuals may experience a range of distressing emotions, such as guilt, regret, fear, or confusion. These negative experiences can harm their mental well-being and self-esteem, potentially leading to a decline in overall psychological health.

Furthermore, some stories mention the long-lasting effects of abuse, such as trauma or emotional scars. These individuals may carry the emotional burden of past experiences, impacting their future relationships and overall quality of life. In response to this abuse, some individuals seek professional help to cope with their trauma. In contrast, others confide in their friends and family for support, emphasizing the importance of seeking assistance and building a support network. These stories' common patterns, comparisons, and similarities involve an initial attraction and connection, followed by misrepresentation and deception, boundary violations and non-consensual actions, emotional and psychological impact, and the subsequent need for support and healing. These patterns highlight the prevalence and damaging effects of abusive behaviour within the context of dating apps, emphasizing the significance of fostering healthy and respectful relationships.

Personality, Distress, and Abuse

There are many familiar personality traits found in the focus group discussions. The most prominent being "Neuroticism". It refers to the tendency to experience negative emotions such as anxiety, depression, and insecurity. In this case, 20 participants exhibited higher levels of neuroticism. Individuals high in neuroticism may be more susceptible to experiencing emotional distress and vulnerability when faced with cyber abuse. They may be more likely to internalize negative experiences, leading to a decline in their mental well-being and self-esteem. This could make them more prone to the adverse effects of cyber dating and more impacted by abusive behaviour.

Secondly, Agreeableness reflects an individual's tendency to be cooperative, compassionate, and considerate of others. With 12 participants exhibiting higher levels of Agreeableness, these individuals may have a greater desire for harmonious relationships and may be more accommodating of others' needs and desires. This trait may make them more susceptible to manipulation or mistreatment in cyber dating situations, as they may be more inclined to prioritize the well-being of their partners over their own.

Third, Extraversion refers to the degree of sociability, assertiveness, and outgoingness of individuals. With 9 participants displaying higher levels of extraversion, they may actively seek social interactions and engage in more outgoing behaviour. While extraversion can be a positive trait, in the context of cyber dating abuse, these individuals may be more at risk of encountering abusive individuals who exploit their Openness and friendliness. Fourth, Openness reflects a person's inclination towards being imaginative, curious, and open to new experiences. In this case, 9 participants displayed higher levels of Openness. While Openness can be beneficial in fostering meaningful connections and personal growth, individuals high in Openness may also be more susceptible to manipulation or deception in cyber-dating. Their Openness may lead them to overlook red flags or give others the benefit of the doubt, making them more vulnerable to cyber abuse.

Fifth, Conscientiousness represents traits such as organization, responsibility, and self-discipline. With only 4 participants displaying higher levels of Conscientiousness, individuals with a strong sense of responsibility and self-discipline may be less likely to engage in risky online behaviour or tolerate abusive situations. Their Conscientiousness may act as a protective factor, reducing their likelihood of becoming victims of cyber abuse.

Moreover, lastly, Introversion refers to a preference for quieter, more solitary activities and a reduced need for external stimulation. With 7 participants displaying introverted tendencies, these individuals may be more cautious and selective in their online interactions. Introverts may engage in more thoughtful and careful communication, potentially reducing their exposure to cyber abuse. However, it is essential to note that Introversion alone does not guarantee protection against cyber abuse, as anyone can become a victim regardless of their personality traits. The mentioned personality traits can impact individuals' cyber dating experiences and vulnerability to cyber abuse. While traits like neuroticism, Agreeableness, Extraversion, Openness, and Introversion can influence individuals' behaviours and tendencies, it is important to recognize that no personality trait alone determines whether someone will experience cyber abuse. Cyber abuse can happen to anyone, and building awareness, setting boundaries, and practising safe online behaviours are crucial for protecting oneself from cyber-dating.

Common Personality Traits

Based on the case mentioned above studies, some common personality traits exhibited by the victims include: trusting and hopeful; empathetic and compassionate; self-doubt and low self-esteem; reluctance to make a scene or confront; vulnerability and emotional investment. Women who approach dating apps with trust and optimism may be more susceptible to manipulation and deception. Abusers can exploit this trust to establish a connection and then exploit the victim's vulnerability. They display empathy and compassion and may be more likely to give abusive partners the benefit of the doubt or excuse their behaviour. This can prolong their exposure to mistreatment and make it difficult to recognize and address the abuse.

Women with self-doubt and low self-esteem may be more inclined to tolerate abusive behaviour as they may believe they do not deserve better treatment. This can make them more vulnerable to staying in toxic relationships or accepting mistreatment. They are hesitant to confront abusive partners or make a scene due to societal expectations of women to be polite, accommodating, or avoid conflict. This reluctance can enable the abuser to continue their behaviour unchecked.

Women seeking love, companionship, and emotional connection may be more willing to overlook red flags or tolerate mistreatment to achieve their desired relationships. This desire for connection can make them more vulnerable to manipulation and mistreatment. They become more emotionally invested in relationships developed through dating apps and may be more susceptible to manipulation. Abusers can exploit this emotional investment to exert control or harm their victims.

CONCLUSION

Unfortunately, abuse against women through dating apps has been an enduring issue throughout their history and shows no signs of abating. This form of mistreatment has persisted across generations, affecting countless women worldwide. Despite advancements in technology and social awareness, the proliferation of dating apps has created new avenues for abuse, perpetuating a cycle that seems difficult to break.

The prevalence of abuse against women on dating apps manifests in various insidious forms, perpetuating a cycle of mistreatment and harm. Emotional abuse, characterized by manipulation, control, and undermining of self-worth, leaves lasting scars on victims' mental and emotional well-being. Although less common, physical abuse poses a grave threat to women's safety, often resulting in physical harm, injuries, and even fatalities. Verbal abuse, including insults, demeaning language, and threats, inflicts deep emotional wounds, erodes self-esteem, and perpetuates a toxic environment. Catfishing, where individuals create fake identities to deceive and exploit others, plays with victims' emotions, leading to feelings of betrayal, trust issues, and even financial losses. Boundary violations occur when personal boundaries and consent are disregarded, ranging from unwarranted advances to unwanted sexual contact, causing significant distress and violating autonomy. Cheating, a betrayal of trust within a relationship, erodes emotional security and self-confidence and can lead to a profound sense of betrayal. Stalking, both online and offline, involves persistent and intrusive behaviours that instil fear, invade privacy, and compromise personal safety. Gaslighting, a manipulative tactic that distorts reality, undermines victims' perceptions, leaving them confused, doubting their sanity, and questioning their own experiences.

Each form of abuse highlights the dire need for awareness, education, and advocacy to combat the deeply rooted issues that persist on dating apps. Empowering women with knowledge regarding these abusive tactics, promoting healthy relationship dynamics, and strengthening support systems are essential steps towards breaking the cycle of abuse.

The various personality traits exhibited by victims of cyberdating abuse shed light on the factors contributing to their vulnerability and experiences in online dating. The victims' trust, hope, empathy, compassion, self-doubt, low self-esteem, reluctance to confront, desire for love and companionship, resilience, self-reflection, increased caution, vulnerability, and emotional investment all play significant roles in shaping their interactions and responses to abusive behaviour. These traits can make women particularly susceptible to cyber dating abuse due to societal and cultural dynamics that have influenced their dating behaviour for ages. Traditional gender roles and expectations often burden women to be accommodating, polite, and nurturing, making it challenging for them to assert themselves or recognize abusive behaviour. Women's desire for love, companionship, and emotional connection can also make them more vulnerable to manipulation and mistreatment, as they may be willing to overlook red flags or tolerate abusive actions to pursue these desired relationships.

Furthermore, the emergence of online dating platforms introduces a new dimension to dating behaviour, where individuals with different personalities and intentions can easily interact and connect. The anonymity and distance dating apps can amplify individuals' personality traits' positive and negative aspects. Abusers can exploit women's trust, empathy, and emotional investment, leading to an increased risk of cyber dating abuse.

Recognizing these personality traits and their impact on women's dating behaviour is crucial for addressing and preventing cyber dating abuse. Educating individuals about healthy relationship dynamics, consent, setting boundaries, and recognizing warning signs of abuse is essential. Empowering women to assert themselves, prioritize their safety and well-being, and seek support when needed is vital in combating cyber dating abuse. As we progress, society must continue evolving and challenging traditional gender norms and expectations. By promoting equality, fostering a culture of consent and respect, and supporting individuals in developing healthy relationship behaviours, we can create a safer and more empowering environment for women in online dating. Understanding the influence of personality traits and societal dynamics is crucial in addressing cyberdating abuse and promoting healthier and safer experiences for women and individuals in online dating.

REFERENCES

Abbasi, I. S. (2018). Falling Prey to Online Romantic Alternatives: Evaluating Social Media Alternative Partners in Committed Versus Dating Relationships. *Sage, 37*(6), 723–33. doi:10.1177/0894439318793947

Alexopoulos, C., Timmermans, E., & McNallie, J. (2020). Swiping More, Committing Less: Unraveling the Links among Dating App Use, Dating App Success, and Intention to Commit Infidelity. *Computers in Human Behavior, 102*, 172–180. doi:10.1016/j.chb.2019.08.009

Anon. (n.d.-a). *Teen Dating Violence: A Closer Look at Adolescent Romantic Relationships | National Institute of Justice*. National Institute of Justice. (https://nij.ojp.gov/library/publications/teen-dating-violence-closer-look-adolescent-romantic-relationships)

Anon. (n.d.-b). Tinder Revenue and Usage Statistics (2023). *Business of Apps*. https://www.businessofapps.com/data/tinder-statistics/)

Burke, S. C., Wallen, M., Vail-Smith, K., & Knox, D. (2011). Using Technology to Control Intimate Partners: An Exploratory Study of College Undergraduates. *Computers in Human Behavior, 27*(3), 1162–1167. doi:10.1016/j.chb.2010.12.010

Caplan, S. E. (2002). Problematic Internet Use and Psychosocial Well-Being: Development of a Theory-Based Cognitive–Behavioral Measurement Instrument. *Computers in Human Behavior, 18*(5), 553–575. doi:10.1016/S0747-5632(02)00004-3

Castro, Á., & Barrada, J. R. (2020a). Dating Apps and Their Sociodemographic and Psychosocial Correlates: A Systematic Review. *International Journal of Environmental Research and Public Health, 17*(18), 17. doi:10.3390/ijerph17186500 PMID:32906632

Castro, Á., & Barrada, J. R. (2020b). Dating Apps and Their Sociodemographic and Psychosocial Correlates: A Systematic Review. *International Journal of Environmental Research and Public Health, 17*(18), 1–25. doi:10.3390/ijerph17186500 PMID:32906632

Cebollero-Salinas, A., Orejudo, S., Cano-Escoriaza, J., & Íñiguez-Berrozpe, T. (2022). Cybergossip and Problematic Internet Use in Cyberaggression and Cybervictimisation among Adolescents. *Computers in Human Behavior, 131*, 107230. doi:10.1016/j.chb.2022.107230

Choi, E. P. H., Janet, Y. H. W., Herman, H. M. L., Wong, W., Man Chio, J. H., & Daniel, Y. T. F. (2016). The Impacts of Using Smartphone Dating Applications on Sexual Risk Behaviours in College Students in Hong Kong. *PLoS One, 11*(11), e0165394. doi:10.1371/journal.pone.0165394 PMID:27828997

Clayton, H. B., Kilmer, G., DeGue, S., Estefan, L. F., Le, V. D., Suarez, N. A., Lyons, B. H., & Thornton, J. E. (2023). Dating Violence, Sexual Violence, and Bullying Victimization Among High School Students — Youth Risk Behavior Survey, United States, 2021. *MMWR Supplements, 72*(1), 66–74. doi:10.15585/mmwr.su7201a8 PMID:37104527

Gámez-Guadix, M., Orue, I., Smith, P. K., & Calvete, E. (2013). Longitudinal and Reciprocal Relations of Cyberbullying with Depression, Substance Use, and Problematic Internet Use among Adolescents. *The Journal of Adolescent Health, 53*(4), 446–452. doi:10.1016/j.jadohealth.2013.03.030 PMID:23721758

Ilakkuvan, V., Johnson, A., Villanti, A. C., Evans, W. D., & Turner, M. (2019). Patterns of Social Media Use and Their Relationship to Health Risks Among Young Adults. *The Journal of Adolescent Health, 64*(2), 158–164. doi:10.1016/j.jadohealth.2018.06.025 PMID:30269907

Jennings, T. L., Chen, Y.-L., Way, B. M., Borgogna, N. C., & Kraus, S. W. (2023). Associations between Online Dating Platform Use and Mental and Sexual Health among a Mixed Sexuality College Student Sample. *Computers in Human Behavior, 144*, 107727. doi:10.1016/j.chb.2023.107727

Kaakinen, M., Keipi, T., Oksanen, A., & Räsänen, P. (2018). How Does Social Capital Associate With Being a Victim of Online Hate? Survey Evidence From the United States, the United Kingdom, Germany, and Finland. *Policy and Internet, 10*(3), 302–323. doi:10.1002/poi3.173

Kaakinen, M., Koivula, A., Savolainen, I., Sirola, A., Mikkola, M., Zych, I., Paek, H. J., & Oksanen, A. (2021). Online Dating Applications and Risk of Youth Victimization: A Lifestyle Exposure Perspective. *Aggressive Behavior, 47*(5), 530–543. doi:10.1002/ab.21968 PMID:34038595

Lee, C. S., & Kim, J. H. (2020). Latent Groups of Cybersecurity Preparedness in Europe: Sociodemographic Factors and Country-Level Contexts. *Computers & Security, 97*, 101995. doi:10.1016/j.cose.2020.101995

Levesque, D. A., Johnson, J. L., Welch, C. A., Prochaska, J. M., & Paiva, A. L. (2016). Teen Dating Violence Prevention: Cluster-Randomized Trial of Teen Choices, an Online, Stage-Based Program for Healthy, Nonviolent Relationships. *Psychology of Violence, 6*(3), 421–432. doi:10.1037/vio0000049 PMID:27482470

Madigan, S., Ly, A., Rash, C. L., Van Ouytsel, J., & Temple, J. R. (2018). Prevalence of Multiple Forms of Sexting Behavior Among Youth: A Systematic Review and Meta-Analysis. *JAMA Pediatrics, 172*(4), 327–335. doi:10.1001/jamapediatrics.2017.5314 PMID:29482215

Martsolf, D. S., Draucker, C. B., Stephenson, P. L., Cook, C. B., & Heckman, T. A. (2012). Patterns of Dating Violence Across Adolescence. *Sage, 22*(9), 1271–83. doi:10.1177/1049732312449388

Panova, T., & Carbonell, X. (2018). Is Smartphone Addiction Really an Addiction? *Journal ofBehavioral Addictions*, *7*(2), 252–259. doi:10.1556/2006.7.2018.49 PMID:29895183

Sánchez, V., Muñoz-Fernández, N., & Ortega-Ruíz, R. (2015). 'Cyberdating Q_A': An Instrument to Assess the Quality of Adolescent Dating Relationships in Social Networks. *Computers in Human Behavior*, *48*, 78–86. doi:10.1016/j.chb.2015.01.006

Shulman, S., & Connolly, J. (2013). The Challenge of Romantic Relationships in Emerging Adulthood. *Sage, 1*(1), 27–39. doi:10.1177/2167696812467330

Steinberg, L., & Morris, A. S. (2001). Adolescent Development. *Annual Review of Psychology*, *52*(1), 83–110. doi:10.1146/annurev.psych.52.1.83 PMID:11148300

Sumter, S. R., Vandenbosch, L., & Ligtenberg, L. (2017). Love Me Tinder: Untangling Emerging Adults' Motivations for Using the Dating Application Tinder. *Telematics and Informatics*, *34*(1), 67–78. doi:10.1016/j.tele.2016.04.009

Wang, J. L., Hai, Z. W., Gaskin, J., & Hawk, S. (2017). The Mediating Roles of Upward Social Comparison and Self-Esteem and the Moderating Role of Social Comparison Orientation in the Association between Social Networking Site Usage and Subjective Well-Being. *Frontiers in Psychology*, *8*(MAY), 771. doi:10.3389/fpsyg.2017.00771 PMID:28553256

Zweig, J. M., Dank, M., Yahner, J., & Lachman, P. (2013). The Rate of Cyber Dating Abuse Among Teens and How It Relates to Other Forms of Teen Dating Violence. *Journal of Youth and Adolescence*, *42*(7), 1063–1077. doi:10.100710964-013-9922-8 PMID:23412689

Compilation of References

Abad, D., Lucas-Pérez, M. E., Minguez-Vera, A., & Yagüe, J. (2017). Does gender diversity on corporate boards reduce information asymmetry in equity markets? *Business Research Quarterly*, *20*(3), 192–205. doi:10.1016/j.brq.2017.04.001

Abbasi, I. S. (2018). Falling Prey to Online Romantic Alternatives: Evaluating Social Media Alternative Partners in Committed Versus Dating Relationships. *Sage, 37*(6), 723–33. doi:10.1177/0894439318793947

Abidin, C. (2015). Communicative Intimacies: Influencers and Perceived Interconnectedness. *Ada: A Journal of Gender, New Media & Technology, 8*. https://adanewmedia.org/2015/11/issue8-abidin/

Abidin, C. (2016). *Please subscribe!: Influencers, social media, and the commodification of everyday life* [Doctoral dissertation, University of Western Australia].

Adelore, O. (2017). Using WhatApp mobile application as tutorial delivery tool for advanced level learners in adult literacy programmes: Lessons. *AJPSSI*, *20*(1), 131–139.

Adinkrah, M. (2011). Criminalizing rape within marriage; perspectives of Ghanaian University Students. *International Journal of Offender Therapy and Comparative Criminology*, *55*(6), 982–1010. doi:10.1177/0306624X10371800 PMID:20516292

Afful, A. A., & Ricciardelli, R. (2015). Shaping the online fat acceptance movement: Talking about body image and beauty standards. *Journal of Gender Studies*, *24*(4), 453–472. doi:10.1080/09589236.2015.1028523

Agbasiere, C. (2021). Assessing the Role of social media in the Fight Against Sexual Assault. *Path of Science, 7*, 5001–5006.

Agrawal, S. (2020, September 22). Cyber bullying. *ProBono India.* http://probono-india.in/blog-detail.php?id=168

Aiken, L. S., & West, S. G. (1991). Multiple regression: Testing and interpreting interactions. Sage Publications, Inc.

Ajid, L. H., Reni, R., Yunita, D. U., & Dwi, S. (2018). The use of WhatsApp in collaborative learning to improve English teaching and learning process. *International Journal of Research Studies in Educational Technology*, *7*(May), 29–35.

Al-Alosi, H. (2017). Cyber-violence: Digital abuse in the context of domestic violence *Thematic: Cyber-Violence, 40*(4), 1573-1603. https://www.unswlawjournal.unsw.edu.au/wp-content/uploads/2017/11/404_13.pdf

Alberti, R. E., & Emmons, M. L. (1986). Your Perfect Right. A Manual for Assertiveness Trainers. Impact.

Alexopoulos, C., Timmermans, E., & McNallie, J. (2020). Swiping More, Committing Less: Unraveling the Links among Dating App Use, Dating App Success, and Intention to Commit Infidelity. *Computers in Human Behavior*, *102*, 172–180. doi:10.1016/j.chb.2019.08.009

Al-Jenaibi, B. (2016). The Twitter revolution in the Gulf countries. *Journal of Creative Communications*, *11*(1), 61–83. doi:10.1177/0973258616630217

Alkurdi, A., Hussainey, K., Tahat, Y., & Aladwan, M. (2019). The Impact of Corporate Governance on Risk Disclosure: Jordanian Evidence. *Academy of Accounting and Financial Studies Journal, 23*(1).

Allen, K. R. (2022). Feminist theory, method, and praxis: Toward a critical consciousness for family and close relationship scholars. *Journal of Social and Personal Relationships*, *40*(3), 026540752110657. https://doi.org/10.1177/02654075211065779

Alonso, C., & Coe, C. L. (2001). Disruptions of social relationships accentuate the association between emotional distress and menstrual pain in young women. *Health Psychology*, *20*(6), 411–416. doi:10.1037/0278-6133.20.6.411 PMID:11714182

Al-Saggaf, Y., & Simmons, P. (2015). Social media in Saudi Arabia: Exploring its use during two natural disasters. *Technological Forecasting and Social Change*, *95*, 3–15. doi:10.1016/j.techfore.2014.08.013

Al-Shalan, A. (2006). *Cyber-Crime Fear and Victimization: An Analysis of a National Cyber-Crime Fear and Victimization* Mississippi State University. https://scholarsjunction.msstate.edu/td

Al-Shalan, A. (2006). *Cyber-Crime Fear and Victimization: An Analysis of a National Cyber-Crime Fear and Victimization*. Mississippi State University. https://scholarsjunction.msstate.edu/td

Amir, E., Levi, S., & Livne, T. (2018). Do firms underreport information on cyber-attacks? Evidence from capital markets. *Review of Accounting Studies*, *23*(3), 1177–1206. doi:10.100711142-018-9452-4

Amnesty Decoders. (2021). *Troll Patrol India*. Amnesty International. https://decoders.amnesty.org/projects/troll-patrol-india

Amnesty Decoders. (2021). *Troll Patrol*. Amnesty International. https://decoders.amnesty.org/projects/troll-patrol

Amnesty International. (2004). *Turkey: Women confronting family violence*. https://www.amnesty.org/en/documents/eur44/013/2004/en/

Amnesty International. (2018). *Toxic Twitter - A Toxic Place for Women*. Amnesty International. https://www.amnesty.org/en/latest/research/2018/03/online-violence-against-women-chapter-1/

Amnesty International. (2018). *Toxic Twitter - The Psychological Harms of Violence and Abuse Against Women Online*. Amnesty International. https://www.amnesty.org/en/latest/news/2018/03/online-violence-against-women-chapter-6-6/

Amnesty International. (2018). *Toxic Twitter - The Reporting Process*. Amnesty International. https://www.amnesty.org/en/latest/news/2018/03/online-violence-against-women-chapter-4-4/

Amnesty International. (2018). *Toxic Twitter - The Solution - Amnesty International*. (2018). https://www.amnesty.org/en/latest/news/2018/03/online-violence-against-women-chapter-8-8/

Amnesty International. (2018). *Toxic Twitter - Women's Experiences of Violence and Abuse on Twitter*. Amnesty International. https://www.amnesty.org/en/latest/news/2018/03/online-violence-against-women-chapter-3-2/

Anderson, R. C., Reeb, D. M., Upadhyay, A., & Zhao, W. (2011). The economics of director heterogeneity. *Financial Management*, *40*(1), 5–38. doi:10.1111/j.1755-053X.2010.01133.x

Andreassen, S.C., & Pallesen, S. (2014). Social network site addiction-An overview. *Current Pharmaceutical Design, 20*(25), 4053-4061.

Aneja. (2017, May 25). Digital India is no country for women. Here's why. *The Wire*. https://thewire.in/economy/digital-india-women-technology

Anifowose, M., Abdul Rashid, H. M., & Annuar, H. A. (2017). Intellectual capital disclosure and corporate market value: Does board diversity matter? *Journal of Accounting in Emerging Economies*, *7*(3), 369–398. doi:10.1108/JAEE-06-2015-0048

Anon. (n.d.-a). *Teen Dating Violence: A Closer Look at Adolescent Romantic Relationships | National Institute of Justice*. National Institute of Justice. (https://nij.ojp.gov/library/publications/teen-dating-violence-closer-look-adolescent-romantic-relationships)

Anon. (n.d.-b). Tinder Revenue and Usage Statistics (2023). *Business of Apps*. https://www.businessofapps.com/data/tinder-statistics/)

Aranda, M., García-Domingo, M., Montes-Berges, B., & Fuentes, V. (2022). Variables Contributing to the Awareness of Online Gendered Violence: Focus on Observers. SAGE Publications, 8(4).

Armstrong, C. L., & Mahone, J. (2016). *"It's On Us." The Role of Social Media and Rape Culture in Individual Willingness to Mobilize Against Sexual Assault: Mass Communication and Society*. https://www.tandfonline.com/doi/abs/10.1080/15205436.2016.1185127

Arnone, M. P., Small, R. V., Chauncey, S. A., & McKenna, H. P. (2011). Curiosity, interest and engagement in technology-pervasive learning environments: A new research agenda. *Educational Technology Research and Development*, *59*(2), 181–198. doi:10.100711423-011-9190-9

Aryan, A., & Raghavan, P. (n.d.). *Post reports of Co Win leak, IT Min asks CERT 1In to probe*. https://indianexpress.com/article/business /economy/post-reports-of-coin-leak-it min-asks-cert-in-to- probe-7355150/

Aschauer, A. B. (1999). Tinkering with technological skill: An examination of the gendered uses of technologies. *Computers and Composition*, *16*(1), 7–23. doi:10.1016/S8755-4615(99)80003-6

Ash, J., Kitchin, R., & Leszczynski, A. (2016). Digital Turn, Digital Geographies? *Progress in Human Geography*, *42*(1), 25–43. doi:10.1177/0309132516664800

Assunção, C. (2016). "No Girls on the Internet": The Experience of Female Gamers in the Masculine Space of Violent Gaming. *Press Start*. http://press-start.gla.ac.uk

Attanasio, G., Nozza, D., Pastor, E., Hovy, D., & Associates. (2022). Benchmarking post-hoc interpretability approaches for transformer-based misogyny detection. *Proceedings of NLP Power! The First Workshop on Efficient Benchmarking in NLP*. ACL Anthology. 10.18653/v1/2022.nlppower-1.11

Australia News. (2020, April 11). *Cyber abuse up by 50 percent amid COVID-19 restrictions*. https://www.skynews.com.au/australia-news/cyber-abuse-up-by-50-percent-amid-covid19-restrictions/video/0e8534dc15a01707ab2e065cb6a14178

Avery, L. R., Ward, L. M., Moss, L., & Üsküp, D. (2016). Tuning gender. *The Journal of Black Psychology*, *43*(2), 159–191. doi:10.1177/0095798415627917

Aydın, A., Arda, B., Güneş, B., & Erbaş, O. (2021). Psychopathology of Cyberbullying and Internet Trolling. *Journal of Experimental and Basic Medical Sciences*, *2*(3), 380–391.

Baer, H. (2016). Redoing feminism: Digital activism, body politics, and neoliberalism. *Feminist Media Studies*, *16*(1), 17–34. doi:10.1080/14680777.2015.1093070

Bailey, G. (2013). Cyberbullying: Victimization Through Electronic Means. *Current Issues in Middle Level Education*, *18*(1), 1–7.

Bailey, J. (2014). "Sexualized online bullying" through an equality lens: Missed opportunity in AB v. Bragg? *McGill Law Journal. Revue de Droit de McGill, 59*(3), 709–737. doi:10.7202/1025142ar

Bailey, M. (2022). *Misogynoir transformed: Black Women's Digital Resistance*. New York University Press.

Baker & Ryalls. (2016). Technologizing feminist pedagogy: Using blog activism in the gender studies classroom. *Feminist Teacher, 25*(1), 23. doi:10.5406/femteacher.25.1.0023

Baker, C., & Carreño, P. (2016). Understanding the Role of Technology in Adolescent Dating and Dating Violence. *Journal of Child and Family Studies, 25*(1), 308–320. doi:10.100710826-015-0196-5

Baker, N., Gregware, P., & Cassidy, M. (1999). Family killing fields: Honor rationales in the murder of women. *Violence Against Women, 5*(2), 164–184. doi:10.1177/107780129952005

Baker, S. A., & Walsh, M. J. (2018). 'Good Morning Fitfam': Top posts, hashtags and gender display on Instagram. *New Media & Society, 20*(12), 4553–4570. doi:10.1177/1461444818777514

Bali, S. (2023). *Cyber Crime Against Women in India: How can the Law and Technology Help the Victims*. Unleashing the Art of Digital Forensics. Taylor & Francis Publication.

Bamane, A., Bhoyar, P., Dugar, A., & Antony, L. (2023). Enhanced Chat Application. *Global Journals.* https://globaljournals.org/GJCST_Volume12/2-Enhanced-Chat-Application

Banerjee, S., Raja Chakravarthi, B., & McCrae, J. P. (2020). Comparison of Pretrained Embeddings to Identify Hate Speech in Indian Code-Mixed Text. *Proceedings - IEEE 2020 2nd International Conference on Advances in Computing, Communication Control and Networking, ICACCCN 2020*, (pp. 21–25). IEEE. 10.1109/ICACCCN51052.2020.9362731

Banet-Weiser, S. (2018). Empowered: Popular feminism and popular misogyny. In Feminist Media Studies (Vol. 19, Issue 8). Duke University Press. doi:10.1080/14680777.2019.1685190

Banet-Weiser, S., & Miltner, K. M. (2016). # MasculinitySoFragile: Culture, structure, and networked misogyny. *Feminist Media Studies, 16*(1), 171–174. doi:10.1080/14680777.2016.1120490

BargJ. A.DrobetzW.GhoulS. E.GuedhamiO.SchroderH. (2022, March 10). Board ancestral diversity and voluntary greenhouse gas emission disclosure. doi:10.2139/ssrn.3998920

Barker, K., & Jurasz, O. (2019). Online Misogyny: A Challenge for Digital Feminism? *Journal of International Affairs, 72*(2), 95–114. https://www.jstor.org/stable/26760834

Barlett, C., & Coyne, S. M. (2014). A meta-analysis of sex differences in cyber-bullying behavior: The moderating role of age. *Aggressive Behavior, 40*(5), 474–488. doi:10.1002/ab.21555 PMID:25098968

Barlow, C., & Awan, I. (2016). "You need to be sorted out with a knife": The attempted online silencing of women and people of Muslim faith within academia. *Social Media + Society, 2*(4), 2056305116678896. doi:10.1177/2056305116678896

Barthes, R. (1957). *Mythologies.* Paris: Les Lettres nouvelles.

Barton, A., & Storm, H. (2014). *Violence and harassment against women in the news media: A global picture*. International Women's Media Foundation. https://www.iwmf.org/our-research/journalist-safety/violence-and-harassment-against-women-in-the-news-media-a-global-picture/

Basile, V., Bosco, C., Fersini, E., Nozza, D., Patti, V., Pardo, F. M. R., Rosso, P., & Sanguinetti, M. (2019). Semeval-2019 task 5: Multilingual detection of hate speech against immigrants and women in twitter. *Proceedings of the 13th International Workshop on Semantic Evaluation*, (pp. 54–63). ACL Anthology. 10.18653/v1/S19-2007

Basile, K. C. (2002). Prevalence of wife rape and other intimate partner sexual coercion in a nationally representative sample of women. *Violence and Victims*, *17*(5), 511–524. doi:10.1891/vivi.17.5.511.33717 PMID:12477095

Bates, S. (2017). Revenge Porn and Mental Health: A Qualitative Analysis of the Mental Health Effects of Revenge Porn on Female Survivors. *Feminist Criminology*, *12*(1), 22–42.

BBC News. (2018, January 9). India woman kills self "over WhatsApp bullying." *BBC News*. https://www.bbc.com/news/world-asia-india-42617237

Bear, S., Rahman, N., & Post, C. (2010). The impact of board diversity and gender composition on corporate social responsibility and firm reputation. *Journal of Business Ethics*, *97*(2), 207–221. doi:10.100710551-010-0505-2

Beech, M. (2020, March 25). *COVID-19 Pushes Up Internet Use 70% And Streaming More Than 12%, First Figures Reveal*. Forbes. https://www.forbes.com/sites/markbeech/2020/03/25/covid-19-pushes-up-internet-use-70-streaming-more-than-12-first-figures-reveal/#73bc35303104

Ben-Amar, W., Chang, M., & Mcllkenny, P. (2017). Board gender diversity and corporate response to sustainability initiatives: Evidence from the carbon disclosure project. *Journal of Business Ethics*, *142*(2), 369–383. doi:10.100710551-015-2759-1

Bendovschi, A. (2015). Cyber-attacks-trends, patterns and security countermeasures. *Procedia Economics and Finance*, *28*, 24–31. doi:10.1016/S2212-5671(15)01077-1

Bennett, W. L., & Segerberg, A. (2012). The logic of connective action: Digital media and the personalization of contentious politics. *Information Communication and Society*, *15*(5), 739–768. doi:10.1080/1369118X.2012.670661

Berkman, H., Jona, J., Lee, G., & Soderstrom, N. (2018). Cybersecurity awareness and market valuations. *Journal of Accounting and Public Policy*, *37*(6), 508–526. doi:10.1016/j.jaccpubpol.2018.10.003

Betts, L. R. (2016). *Cyberbullying: Approaches, Consequences and Interventions*. Macmillan Publishers Ltd. doi:10.1057/978-1-137-50009-0

Bevans, K., Cerbone, A. B., & Overstreet, S. (2005). Advances and future directions in the study of children's neurobiological responses to trauma and violence exposure. *Journal of Interpersonal Violence*, *20*(4), 418–425. doi:10.1177/0886260504269484 PMID:15722496

Bevir, M. (1999). Foucault, power, and institutions. *Political Studies*, *47*(2), 345–359. doi:10.1111/1467-9248.00204

Bharati, P., Lee, C., & Syed, R. (2018). Trolls and social movement participation: An empirical investigation. *Trolls and Social Movement Participation*, 1-5.

Bharati, P., Lee, C., & Syed, R. (2019, July). Influence of trolling on social media participation: An empirical investigation. In Academy of Management Proceedings (Vol. 2019, No. 1, p. 18645). Academy of Management.

Bhat, C., Suniti, C., Shih-Hua, L., & Jamie, A. (2010). Addressing cyber bullying's media literacy. *New Horizons in Education*, *58*(3), 34–43.

Bhattacharya, S., Singh, S., Kumar, R., Bansal, A., Bhagat, A., Dawer, Y., Lahiri, B., & Kr Ojha, A. (2020). *Developing a Multilingual Annotated Corpus of Misogyny and Aggression*. Kaggle. http://bit.ly/2FhLMVz

Bijker, W. E., & Bijsterveld, K. (2000). Women walking through plans: Technology, democracy, and gender identity. *Technology and Culture*, *41*(3), 485–515. doi:10.1353/tech.2000.0091

Bin Khidmat, W., Ayub Khan, M., & Ullah, H. (2020). The Effect of Board Diversity on Firm Performance: Evidence from Chinese Listed Companies. *Indian Journal of Corporate Governance*, *13*(1), 9–33. doi:10.1177/0974686220923793

Binns, A. (2012). Don't Feed the Trolls! Managing troublemakers in magazines' online communities. *Journalism Practice*, *6*(4), 547–562. doi:10.1080/17512786.2011.648988

Biradar, S., Saumya, S., & chauhan, A. (2022). Fighting hate speech from bilingual hinglish speaker's perspective, a transformer- and translation-based approach. *Social Network Analysis and Mining*, *12*(1), 87. doi:10.100713278-022-00920-w PMID:35911486

Bird, S., Klein, E., & Loper, E. (2009). *Natural language processing with Python: analyzing text with the natural language toolkit*. O'Reilly Media, Inc.

Bishop, C. M., & Nasrabadi, N. M. (2006). Pattern recognition and machine learning (Vol. 4, Issue 4). Springer.

Bishop, J. (2012c). Tackling internet abuse in Great Britain: Towards a framework for classifying severities of 'flame trolling'. In *Proceedings of the 11th International Conference on Security and Management*. SAM.

Bishop, J. (2014a). 'U r bias love:' Using 'bleasure' and 'motif' as forensic linguistic means to annotate twitter and news blog comments for the purpose of multimedia forensics. *Proceedings of the 11th International Conference on Web Based Communities and Social Media*.

Bishop, J. (2014b). 'YouTube if you want to, the lady's not for blogging': Using 'bleasures' and 'motifs' to support multimedia forensic analyses of harassment by social media. *Oxford Cyber Harassment Research Symposium*.

Bist, S. (2020). *Cyber Crime Against Women in India-Investigative and Legislative Challenges*. Wordshrew Press.

Biwa, V. (2021). African Feminisms and co-constructing a collaborative future with men: Namibian women in Mining's discourses. *Management Communication Quarterly*, *35*(1), 43–68. doi:10.1177/0893318920973988

Blau, P. M. (1977). *Inequality and Heterogeneity: A Primitive Theory of Social Structure*. Free Press.

Bohra, A., Vijay, D., Singh, V., Akhtar, S. S., & Shrivastava, M. (2018a). *A Dataset of Hindi-English Code-Mixed Social Media Text for Hate Speech Detection*. Github. https://github.com/deepanshu1995/HateSpeech-Hindi-

Bohra, A., Vijay, D., Singh, V., Akhtar, S. S., & Shrivastava, M. (2018b). *A Dataset of Hindi-English Code-Mixed Social Media Text for Hate Speech Detection*. https://github.com/deepanshu1995/HateSpeech-Hindi-

Bolin, G. (2018). Media use and the extended commodification of the lifeworld. *Technologies of labour and the politics of contradiction*, 235-252.

Bolukbasi, T., Chang, K.-W., Zou, J. Y., Saligrama, V., & Kalai, A. T. (2016). Man is to computer programmer as woman is to homemaker? debiasing word embeddings. *Advances in Neural Information Processing Systems*, 29.

Boluk, S., & Lemieu, P. (2017). Breaking the Metagame Feminist Spoilsports and Magic Circle Jerks. In *Metagaming* (pp. 275–290). University of Minnesota Press. doi:10.5749/j.ctt1n2ttjx.9

Bombak, A. E., Meadows, A., & Billette, J. (2019). Fat acceptance 101: Midwestern American women's perspective on cultural body acceptance. *Health Sociology Review*, *28*(2), 194–208. doi:10.1080/14461242.2019.1604150

Bonanno, R. A., & Hymel, S. (2013). Cyber bullying and internalizing difficulties: Above and beyond the impact of traditional forms of bullying. *Journal of Youth and Adolescence*, *42*(5), 685–697. doi:10.100710964-013-9937-1 PMID:23512485

Bonime-Blanc, A., & Tonello, M. (2017, January 12). A Strategic Cyber-Roadmap for the Board. *The Harvard Law School Forum on Corporate Governance*. https://corpgov.law.harvard.edu/2017/01/12/a-strategic-cyber-roadmap-for-the-board/

Borba, R., & Osterman, A. (2007). Do bodies matter? Travestis' embodiment of (trans)gender identity through the manipulation of the Brazilian Portuguese grammatical gender system. *Gender and Language*, *1*(1), 131–147. doi:10.1558/genl.2007.1.1.131

Bosson, J. K., Vandello, J. A., Burnaford, R. M., Weaver, J. R., & Wasti, S. A. (2009). Precarious manhood and displays of physical aggression. *Personality and Social Psychology Bulletin*, *35*(5), 623–634. doi:10.1177/0146167208331161 PMID:19202132

Bowles Eagle, R. (2015). Loitering, lingering, hashtagging: Women reclaiming public space via #Boardthebus, #Stopstreetharassment, and the #Everydaysexism project. *Feminist Media Studies*, *15*(2), 350–353. doi:10.1080/14680777.2015.1008748

Boyacıoğlu, İ. (2016). Violence against women and the past and present of women's studies in Turkey: A call for psychological research. *Turkish Psychological Articles, 19*(Special Issue), 146-149. https://search.trdizin.gov.tr/tr/yayin/detay/236984/dunden-bugune-turkiyede-kadina-yonelik-siddet-ve-ulusal-kadin-calismalari-psikolojik-arastirmalara-davet

Boyd, D. & Ellison, N. (2007). Social network sites: Definition, history and scholarship. *Journal of Computer-Mediated Communication, 13*(1), 210–230.

Boyd, D. (2008). Why youth (heart) social network sites: The role of networked publics in teenage social life. In D. Buckingham (ed.), *Youth, Identity, and Digital Media* (pp. 119–142). Cambridge, MA: MIT Press.

Boyd, D. (2014). *It's Complicated: The Social Lives of Networked Teens*. New Haven; London: Yale University Press.

Boyer, K. (2021). Sexual Harassment and the Right to everyday life. *Progress in Human Geography*, *46*(2), 398–415. doi:10.1177/03091325211024340

Braidotti, R. (1994). *Nomadic Subjects: Embodiment and Sexual Difference in Contemporary Feminist Theory*. Columbia University Press.

Brathwaite, K. N., & DeAndrea, D. C. (2022). BoPopriation: How self-promotion and corporate commodification can undermine the body positivity (BoPo) movement on Instagram. *Communication Monographs*, *89*(1), 25–46. doi:10.1080/03637751.2021.1925939

Bravo, F. (2018). Does board diversity matter in the disclosure process? An analysis of the association between diversity and the disclosure of information on risks. *International Journal of Disclosure and Governance*, *15*(2), 104–114. doi:10.105741310-018-0040-4

Broadband Commission for Sustainable Development. (n.d.). http://www.broadbandcommission.org/resources/Pages/default.aspx

Brown, S. E. V., & Battle, J. S. (2019). Ostracizing targets of workplace sexual harassment before and after the #MeToo movement. *Equality, Diversity and Inclusion*, *39*(1), 53–67. doi:10.1108/EDI-09-2018-0162

Buchanan, N., & Mahoney, A. (2022). Development of a scale measuring online sexual harassment: Examining gender differences and the emotional impact of sexual harassment victimization online. *Legal and Criminological Psychology*, *27*(1), 63–81. doi:10.1111/lcrp.12197

Buckingham, D. (Ed.). (2008). *Youth, Identity, and Digital Media*. MIT Press.

Bullock, C. F. (2007). Framing domestic violence fatalities: Coverage by Utah newspapers. *Women's Studies in Communication*, *30*(1), 34–63. doi:10.1080/07491409.2007.10162504

Bullock, C. F., & Cubert, J. (2002). Coverage of domestic violence fatalities by newspapers in Washington State. *Journal of Interpersonal Violence*, *17*(5), 475–499. doi:10.1177/0886260502017005001

Burgess, A. W., & Holmstrom, L. L. (1974). Rape Trauma Syndrome. *The American Journal of Psychiatry*, *131*(9), 981–986. doi:10.1176/ajp.131.9.981 PMID:4415470

Burke, S. C., Wallen, M., Vail-Smith, K., & Knox, D. (2011). Using Technology to Control Intimate Partners: An Exploratory Study of College Undergraduates. *Computers in Human Behavior*, *27*(3), 1162–1167. doi:10.1016/j.chb.2010.12.010

Bustos-Ortega, M., Carretero-Dios, H., & Romero-Sánchez, M. (2023). Sexist Attitudes in Online Video Gaming: Development and Validation of the Sexism Against Women Gamers Scale in Spanish and English. *Psychology of Women Quarterly*, *47*(3), 320–342. Advance online publication. doi:10.1177/03616843231162837

Butler, J. (1990). *Gender Trouble*. Routledge.

Butler, J. (1990). *Gender Trouble: Feminism and the Subversion of Identity*. Routledge.

Butler, J. (1993). *Bodies That Matter: On the Discursive Limits of "Sex*. Routledge.

Butler, J. (2005). *Giving an Account of Oneself*. Fordham.University Press. doi:10.5422/fso/9780823225033.001.0001

Cabedo, J. D., & Tirado, J. M. (2004). The disclosure of risk in financial statements. *Accounting Forum*, *28*(2), 181–200. doi:10.1016/j.accfor.2003.10.002

Cambria, E., Chandra, P., Sharma, A., & Hussain, A. (2010). *Do not feel the trolls*. ISWC.

Camélia, R., & Nadia, S. (2022). Board gender diversity and corporate response to cyber risk: Evidence from cybersecurity related disclosure. *Journal of Business Ethics*, *177*(2), 351–374. doi:10.100710551-020-04717-9

Cammaerts, B. (2015). Social Media and Activism. In The International Encyclopedia of Digital Communication and Society. doi:10.1002/9781118767771.wbiedcs083

Campbell, J. L., Chen, H., Dhaliwal, D. S., Lu, H. M., & Steele, L. B. (2014). The information content of mandatory risk factor disclosures in corporate filings. *Review of Accounting Studies*, *19*(1), 394–455. doi:10.100711142-013-9258-3

Campbell, M., Spears, B., Slee, P., Butler, D., & Kift, S. (2012). Victims' perceptions of traditional and cyberbullying, and the psychosocial correlates of their victimization. *Emotional & Behavioural Difficulties*, *17*(3-4), 389–401. doi:10.1080/13632752.2012.704316

Caplan, S. E. (2002). Problematic Internet Use and Psychosocial Well-Being: Development of a Theory-Based Cognitive–Behavioral Measurement Instrument. *Computers in Human Behavior*, *18*(5), 553–575. doi:10.1016/S0747-5632(02)00004-3

Carlyle, K. E., Slater, M. D., & Chakroff, J. L. (2008). Newspaper coverage of intimate partner violence: Skewing representations of risk. *Journal of Communication*, *58*(1), 168–186. doi:10.1111/j.1460-2466.2007.00379.x PMID:21297889

Carrington, K. (2014). *Feminism and Global Justice*. Routledge., doi:10.4324/9781315748368

Carter, D. A., D'Souza, F., Simkins, B. J., & Simpson, W. G. (2010). The gender and ethnic diversity of US boards and board committees and firm financial performance. *Corporate Governance*, *18*(5), 396–414. doi:10.1111/j.1467-8683.2010.00809.x

Case, C. J., & King, D. L. (2017). Internet Trolling in Social Networking Sites: A Preliminary Investigation of Undergraduate Student Victimization. *ASBBS Proceedings, 24*(1), 143.

Castro, Á., & Barrada, J. R. (2020a). Dating Apps and Their Sociodemographic and Psychosocial Correlates: A Systematic Review. *International Journal of Environmental Research and Public Health*, *17*(18), 17. doi:10.3390/ijerph17186500 PMID:32906632

Catherine, A. (2018). They Go for Gender First. *Journalism Practice*, *12*(7), 850–869.

Cebollero-Salinas, A., Orejudo, S., Cano-Escoriaza, J., & Íñiguez-Berrozpe, T. (2022). Cybergossip and Problematic Internet Use in Cyberaggression and Cybervictimisation among Adolescents. *Computers in Human Behavior*, *131*, 107230. doi:10.1016/j.chb.2022.107230

Ceylan-Batur, S., Sakallı, N., & Gunaratne, S. (2021). Predictors of tolerating violence against women: Honor concerns and fundamentalist religious orientation. *Current Psychology (New Brunswick, N.J.)*, *42*(12), 9720–9733. doi:10.100712144-021-02276-4

Chan, S. (2016). Right-Wing Extremist Convicted of Murdering Jo Cox, a U.K. Lawmaker. *The New York Times*. https://www.nytimes.com/2016/11/23/world/europe/thomas-mair-convicted-murder-jo-cox.html

Chandler, D. (2017). *Semiotics: The Basis* (3rd ed.). Routledge.

Chang, J. (2011). Cyberspace and Reconstruction of Women's Identity. *Trans-Humanities Journal*, *4*(2), 125–149. doi:10.1353/trh.2011.0018

Chen, G. M., Pain, P., & Barner, B. (2018). "Hashtag Feminism": Activism or Slacktivism? In D. Harp, J. Loke, & I. Bachman (Eds.), *Feminist Approaches to Media Theory and Research* (pp. 197–218). Palgrave Macmillan. doi:10.1007/978-3-319-90838-0_14

Cheng, J., Bernstein, M., Danescu-Niculescu-mizil, C., & Leskovec, J. (2017). Anyone can become a troll: Causes of trolling behavior in online discussions. *Proceedings of the ACM Conference on Computer Supported Cooperative Work, CSCW*, (pp. 1217–1230). ACM. 10.1145/2998181.2998213

Cheng, J., Danescu-Niculescu-Mizil, C., Leskovec, J., & Bernstein, M. (2017). Anyone can become a troll. *American Scientist*, *105*(3), 152. doi:10.1511/2017.126.152 PMID:29399664

Chesney, M. A., Neilands, T. B., Chambers, D. B., Taylor, J. M., & Folkman, S. (2006). A validity and reliability study of the coping self-efficacy scale. *British Journal of Health Psychology*, *11*(3), 421–437. doi:10.1348/135910705X53155 PMID:16870053

Chin, K. (2023, March 2). *Top cybersecurity regulations in India [Updated 2023]*. Retrieved from UpGuard: https://www.upguard.com/blog/cybersecurity-regulations-india

Cho, C. H., & Patten, D. M. (2007). The role of environmental disclosures as tools of legitimacy: A research note. *Accounting, Organizations and Society*, *32*(7/8), 639–647. doi:10.1016/j.aos.2006.09.009

Choi, E. P. H., Janet, Y. H. W., Herman, H. M. L., Wong, W., Man Chio, J. H., & Daniel, Y. T. F. (2016). The Impacts of Using Smartphone Dating Applications on Sexual Risk Behaviours in College Students in Hong Kong. *PLoS One*, *11*(11), e0165394. doi:10.1371/journal.pone.0165394 PMID:27828997

Chouliaraki, L. (2017). Symbolic bordering: The self-representation of migrants and refugees in digital news. *Popular Communication*, *15*(2), 78–94. doi:10.1080/15405702.2017.1281415

Chouliaraki, L., & Fairclough, N. (1999). *Discourse in Late Modernity: Rethinking Critical Analysis*. Edinburgh University Press.

Chrisler, J. C., & Johnston-Robledo, I. (2018). Woman's embodied self: An introduction. In J. C. Chrisler & I. Johnston-Robledo (Eds.), Woman's embodied self: Feminist perspectives on identity and image (pp. 3–14). American Psychological Association. https://doi.org/10.1037/0000047-001.

Citron, D. K. (2014). *Hate Crimes in Cyberspace*. Harvard University Press. doi:10.4159/harvard.9780674735613

Clark, R. (2016). "Hope in a hashtag": The discursive activism of #WhyIStayed. *Feminist Media Studies*, *16*(5), 788–804. doi:10.1080/14680777.2016.1138235

Clayton, H. B., Kilmer, G., DeGue, S., Estefan, L. F., Le, V. D., Suarez, N. A., Lyons, B. H., & Thornton, J. E. (2023). Dating Violence, Sexual Violence, and Bullying Victimization Among High School Students — Youth Risk Behavior Survey, United States, 2021. *MMWR Supplements*, *72*(1), 66–74. doi:10.15585/mmwr.su7201a8 PMID:37104527

Clifford, P. (2016). *Content Marketing*. John Wiley & Sons, Inc.

Code, L. (2006). Women Knowing/Knowing Women: Crititical-Creative Interventions in the Politics of Knowledge. In K. Davis, M. Evans, & J. Lorber (Eds.), Handbook of gender and women's studies (pp. 146–166). Sage.

Cohen, R., Irwin, L., Newton-John, T., & Slater, A. (2019). #bodypositivity: A content analysis of body positive accounts on Instagram. *Body Image*, *29*, 47–57. doi:10.1016/j.bodyim.2019.02.007 PMID:30831334

Coles, B. A., & West, M. (2016b). Weaving the internet together: Imagined communities in newspaper comment threads. *Computers in Human Behavior*, *60*, 44–53. doi:10.1016/j.chb.2016.02.049

Cooley, C. H. (1918). *Social process*. Scribner's.

Cooper, C. (2008). *What's Fat Activism?* https://www.ul.ie/sociology/docstore/workingpapers/wp2008-02.pdf

Cooper, C. (2011). Fat Lib: How Fat Activism Expands the Obesity Debate. In Debating Obesity (Vol. 1, pp. 164–191). Palgrave Macmillan.

Cooper, S., Estes, R. J., Giardino, A., Kellogg, N., & Vieth, V. (2005). *Medical, legal & social science aspects of child sexual exploitation: A comprehensive review of pornography, prostitution, and Internet crimes*. GW Medical.

Cornell, D., & Limber, S. P. (2015). Law and policy on the concept of bullying at school. *The American Psychologist*, *70*(4), 333–343. doi:10.1037/a0038558 PMID:25961314

Corsini, E. M., Luc, J. G., & Antonoff, M. B. (2021). Women in thoracic surgery: Social media and the value of mentorship. *Journal of Thoracic Disease*, *13*(1), 464–472. doi:10.21037/jtd.2020.04.11

Cott, N. F. (1986). *What is Feminism?* Pantheon Books.

Council of Europe. (2023). *Activities to address gender and gender-based violence with young people*. Available in https://www.coe.int/en/web/gender-matters/activities

Countries with most Twitter users 2022 . (2022). Statista. https://www.statista.com/statistics/242606/number-of-active-twitter-users-in-selected-countries/

Cover, R. (2012a). Performing and undoing identity online: Social networking, identity theories and the incompatibility of online profiles and friendship regimes. *Convergence (London)*, *18*(2), 177–193. doi:10.1177/1354856511433684

Coward, R. (1980). "This Novel Changes Lives": Are Women's Novels Feminist Novels? A Response to Rebecca O'Rourke's Article 'Summer Reading.'. *Feminist Review*, *5*(1), 53–64. doi:10.1057/fr.1980.12

Cowie, H., & Colliety, P. (2010). Cyberbullying: Sanctions or sensitivity? *Pastoral Care in Education*, *28*(4), 261–268. doi:10.1080/02643944.2010.528017

Cox, T. J. Jr. (1991). The multicultural organization. *The Academy of Management Perspectives*, *5*(2), 34–47. doi:10.5465/ame.1991.4274675

Craker, N., & March, E. (2016). The dark side of Facebook®: The Dark Tetrad, negative social potency, and trolling behaviours. *Personality and Individual Differences*, *102*, 79–84. doi:10.1016/j.paid.2016.06.043

Crenshaw, K. W. (1989). Demarginalizing the Intersection of Race and Sex: A Black Feminist Critique of Antidiscrimination Doctrine, Feminist Theory and Antiracist Politics. *University of Chicago Legal Forum*, 149.

Creswell, J. W. (2007). *Qualitative Inquiry & Research Design*. In Sage Publications, Inc. doi:10.1111/1467-9299.00177

Cross-cultural Perspectives. (1996). John Benjamins Publishing Company.

Cross, D., Li, Q., Smith, P. K., & Monks, H. (2012). Understanding and preventing cyberbullying: Where have we been and where should we be going? In Q. Li, D. Cross, & P. K. Smith (Eds.), *Cyberbullying in the global playground: Research from international perspectives* (pp. 287–305). Wiley Blackwell. doi:10.1002/9781119954484.ch14

Cruz, A. G. B., Seo, Y., & Rex, M. (2018). Trolling in online communities: A practice-based theoretical perspective. *The Information Society*, *34*(1), 15–26. doi:10.1080/01972243.2017.1391909

Cunningham, C. M., & Crandall, H. M. (2014). Social Media for Social Justice: Cyberfeminism in the Digital Village. In *Feminist Community Engagement* (pp. 75–91). doi:10.1057/9781137441102_5

Cyber Violence against Women and Girls: A World-Wide Wake-Up Call. (n.d.). https://en.unesco.org/sites/default/files/genderreport2015final.pdf

Cybercrime-Descriptive Portrayal of Crimes against Women in India. (n.d.). https://www.legalserviceindia.com/legal/article-5858-cybercrime-descriptive-portrayal-of-crimes-against women-in-india.html

Cybersafe. (2021), *Cyber Violence against Women & Girls – Report on Cyber VAWG and CYBERSAFE Framework*. Final report on WP2 UL FDV. Funded by the European Union's REC Programme (2014–2020).

Cybersmile. (2022). Young Woman Killed Herself After Being Made To Feel Insecure By Facebook Trolls. *CyberSmile*. https://www.cybersmile.org/news/young-woman-killed-herself-after-being-made-to-feel-insecure-by-facebook-trolls

Daniels, J. (2009, Spring - Summer). Rethinking Cyberfeminism(s): Race, Gender, and Embodiment. *Women's Studies Quarterly*, *37*(1-2), 101–124.

DataReportal. (2022). *Global Digital Insights*. https://datareportal.com/

Davis, A. A., & Patel, V. G. (2019). The role of PD-L1 expression as a predictive biomarker: An analysis of all US Food and Drug Administration (FDA) approvals of immune checkpoint inhibitors. *Journal for Immunotherapy of Cancer*, *7*(1), 1–8. doi:10.118640425-019-0768-9 PMID:31655605

De Bellis, M. D., Keshavan, M. S., Shifflett, H., Iyengar, S., Beers, S. R., Hall, J., & Moritz, G. (2002). Brain structures in pediatric maltreatment-related posttraumatic stress disorder: A sociodemographically matched study. *Biological Psychiatry*, *52*(11), 1066–1078. doi:10.1016/S0006-3223(02)01459-2 PMID:12460690

de GibertO.PerezN.García-PablosA.CuadrosM. (2018). *Hate Speech Dataset from a White Supremacy Forum*. https://arxiv.org/abs/1809.04444 doi:10.18653/v1/W18-5102

de Meco, L., & MacKay, A. (2022, January 19). *Social media, violence and gender norms: The need for a new digital social contract*. https://www.alignplatform.org/resources/blog/social-media-violence-and-gender-norms-need-new-digital-social-contract de Smedt, T., Jaki, S., Kotzé, E., Saoud, L., Gwóźdź, M., de Pauw, G., & Daelemans, W. (2018). *Multilingual Cross-domain Perspectives on Online Hate Speech*. OHCHR. https://www.ohchr.org/EN/ProfessionalInterest/Pages/CCPR.aspx

Dean, J. (2010). Feminism in the Papers. *Feminist Media Studies*, *10*(4), 391–407. doi:10.1080/14680777.2010.514112

Debarati, H., & Jaishankar, K. (2016). *Cyber Crime Against Women in India*. Sage Publications.

Dehue, F., Bolman, C., & Völlink, T. (2008). Cyberbullying: Youngsters' experiences and parental perception. *Cyberpsychology & Behavior*, *11*(2), 217–223. doi:10.1089/cpb.2007.0008

Dennis, P., Connole, H., & Kraut, M. (2015). *The efficacy of voluntary disclosure: A study of water disclosures by mining companies using the global reporting initiative framework*. Academic Press.

Desai, M., & Jaishankar, K. (2007). *Cyber Stalking-Victimization of Girl Student: An Empirical Study*. Academic Press.

DevlinJ.ChangM.-W.LeeK.ToutanovaK. (2018). *BERT: Pre-training of Deep Bidirectional Transformers for Language Understanding*. https://arxiv.org/abs/1810.04805

Dey, A. (2020). Sites of exception: Gender violence, digital activism, and Nirbhaya's zone of anomie in India. *Violence Against Women*, *26*(11), 1423–1444. doi:10.1177/1077801219862633 PMID:31379258

Dhrodia, A. (2017, November 20). Unsocial Media: The Real Toll of Online Abuse against Women. *Medium*. https://medium.com/amnesty-insights/unsocial-media-the-real-toll-of-online-abuse-against-women-37134ddab3f4

Dietz, T. L. (1998). An examination of violence and gender role portrayals in video games: Implications for gender socialization and aggressive behaviour. *Sex Roles*, *38*(5–6), 425–442. doi:10.1023/A:1018709905920

Directorate of Communications, Council of Europe. (2022). *The digital dimension of violence against women as addressed by the seven mechanisms of the EDVAW platform*. https://www.ohchr.org/sites/default/files/documents/hrbodies/cedaw/statements/2022-12-02/EDVAW-Platform-thematic-paper-on-the-digital-dimension-of-VAW_English.pdf

Diseth, T. H. (2005). Dissociation in children and adolescents as reaction to trauma–an overview of conceptual issues and neurobiological factors. *Nordic Journal of Psychiatry*, *59*(2), 79–91. doi:10.1080/08039480510022963 PMID:16195104

Ditch The Label 2016 . (2016). Brandwatch. https://www.brandwatch.com/reports/cyberbullying-2016/

Djuric, N., Zhou, J., Morris, R., Grbovic, M., Radosavljevic, V., & Bhamidipati, N. (2015). Hate speech detection with comment embeddings. *WWW 2015 Companion - Proceedings of the 24th International Conference on World Wide Web*, 29–30. 10.1145/2740908.2742760

Donath, J. S. (2002). Identity and deception in the virtual community. In *Communities in cyberspace* (pp. 37–68). Routledge.

Douglas, H., Harris, B. A., & Dragiewicz, M. (2019). Technology-facilitated Domestic and Family Violence: Women's Experiences. *British Journal of Criminology*, *59*(3), 551–570. https://doi.org/10.1093/bjc/azy068

Downs, E. & Smith, S.L. (2010). Keeping abreast of hypersexuality: A video game character content analysis. *Sex Roles, 62*(11–12), 721–733.

Drüeke, R., & Zobl, E. (2016). Online feminist protest against sexism: The German-language hashtag #aufschrei. *Feminist Media Studies*, *16*(1), 35–54. doi:10.1080/14680777.2015.1093071

Duff, A. S. (2012). *A Normative Theory of the Information Society*. Routledge. doi:10.4324/9780203137758

Dunn, S. (2020). *Technology-Facilitated Gender-Based Violence: An Overview*. https://www.cigionline.org/static/documents/documents/SaferInternet_Paper%20no%201_0.pdf

Durkheim, E. (2016). The rules of the sociological method. In *Social Theory Re-Wired* (pp. 10–15). Routledge.

Dutta, E., Sharma, P., Shah, N., Bharati, A., Sonavane, S., & Desousa, A. (2018). Attitude toward selfie taking and its relation to body image and narcissism in medical students. *Indian Journal of Psychological Medicine*, *40*(1), 17–21. doi:10.4103/IJPSYM.IJPSYM_169_17

Dwivedi, A. (2022, December 18). Crime against women through social media. *The Times of India*. https://timesofindia.indiatimes.com/readersblog/aashank-dwivedi/crime-against-women-through-social-media-48132/

Dwivedi, Y. K., Ismagilova, E., Hughes, D. L., Carlson, J., Filieri, R., Jacobson, J., Jain, V., Karjaluoto, H., Kefi, H., Krishen, A. S., Kumar, V., Rahman, M. M., Raman, R., Rauschnabel, P. A., Rowley, J., Salo, J., Tran, G. A., & Wang, Y. (2021). Setting the Future of Digital and Social Media Marketing research: Perspectives and Research Propositions. *International Journal of Information Management*, *59*(1), 1–37.

Easteal, P., Holland, K., & Judd, K. (2015). Enduring themes and silences in media portrayals of violence against women. *Women's Studies International Forum*, *48*, 103–113. doi:10.1016/j.wsif.2014.10.015

Eco, U. (1976). *A theory of semiotics*. Indiana University Press. doi:10.1007/978-1-349-15849-2

Efe, S. Y., & Ayaz, S. (2010). Domestic violence against women and women's opinions related to domestic violence. *Anatolian Journal of Psychiatry, 11*(1), 23–29. https://www.proquest.com/openview/9adf1e5f0804b9acd8cb7bef255723d5/1?cbl=136214&pq-origsite=gscholar&parentSessionId=hhyqfcP%2FxaqGYN3TR9w4USQToGyvMvOjiDq1ir32N%2FQ%3D

EIGE. (2017). *Cyber violence against women and girls*. https://eige.europa.eu/publications/cyber-violence-against-women-and-girls

EIGE. (2022). *Combating Cyber Violence against Women and Girls*. European Institute for Gender Equality. https://eige.europa.eu/publications/cyber-violence-against-women-and-girls-key-terms-and-concepts

Eijlelenboom, E. V., & Nieuwesteeg, B. F. (2021). An analysis of cybersecurity in Dutch annual reports of listed companies. *Computer Law & Security Report*, *40*, 105513. Advance online publication. doi:10.1016/j.clsr.2020.105513

Eikren, E., & Ingram-Waters, M. (2016). Dismantling "you get what you deserve": Toward a feminist sociology of revenge porn. *Ada: A Journal of Gender, New Media, and Technology*, *10*. https://adanewmedia.org/2016/10/issue10-eikren-ingramwaters/

Elberry, N., & Hussainey, K. (2020). Does corporate investment efficiency affect corporate disclosure practices? *Journal of Applied Accounting Research*, *21*(2), 309–327. doi:10.1108/JAAR-03-2019-0045

Eler, A. (2017). *The selfie generation: How our self-images are changingchange our notions of privacy, Sex, consent, and culture*. Simon and Schuster.

Elfeky, M. I. (2017). The extent of voluntary disclosure and its determinants in emerging markets: Evidence from Egypt. *The Journal of Finance and Data Science*, *3*(1), 45–59. doi:10.1016/j.jfds.2017.09.005

Elisabeth, A., & Utami, W. (2021, May 6). The Effect of Good Corporate Governance, Leverage and Company Profile on Risk Disclosure. *Proceedings of the 1st MICOSS Mercu Buana International Conference on Social Sciences, MICOSS 2020*. https://eudl.eu/doi/10.4108/eai.28-9-2020.2307512

Elleuch, F. L. (2022). Corporate board diversity and carbon disclosure: Evidence from France. *Accounting Research Journal*, *35*(6), 721–736. doi:10.1108/ARJ-12-2021-0350

Elsadda, H. (2010). Arab Women Bloggers: The Emergence of Literary Counterpublics. *Middle East Journal of Culture and Communication, 3*(3), 312–332. doi:10.1163/187398610X538678

Ending Violence is Our Business: Workplace Responses to Intimate Partner Violence in Asia and the Pacific . (2019). UN Women – Asia-Pacific. https://asiapacific.unwomen.org/en/digital-library/publications/2019/10/workplace-responses-to-intimate-partner-violence

Enzer, M. (2023). *Glossary of Internet Terms*. https://www.matisse.net/files/glossary.html

Escosteguy, A. C. (2019). Mídia e questões de gênero no Brasil: pesquisa, categorias e feminismos. *XXVIII Encontro Anual Da Compós*. www.compos.org.brwww.compos.org.br/anais_encontros.php

Essien-Eyo, A., & Ottoh, B. (2011). Semiotics of cartoon in two Nigerian newspapers: the guardian and the punch. *LWATI: Journal of Contemporary Research, 8*(3), 79-90.

Ettredge, M., Guo, F., & Li, Y. (2018). Trade secrets and cyber security breaches. *Journal of Accounting and Public Policy, 37*(6), 564–585. doi:10.1016/j.jaccpubpol.2018.10.006

Ettredge, M., Johnstone, K., Stone, M., & Wang, Q. (2011). The effects of firm size, corporate governance quality, and bad news on disclosure compliance. *Review of Accounting Studies, 16*(4), 866–889. doi:10.100711142-011-9153-8

European Institute for Gender Equality. (2022). *Combating Cyber Violence against Women and Girls*. https://eige.europa.eu/sites/default/files/documents/combating_cyber_violence_against_women_and_girls.pdf

European Parliamentary Research Service (EPRS). (2021). *Combating gender-based violence: Cyber violence European added value assessment*. https://www.europarl.europa.eu/RegData/etudes/STUD/2021/662621/EPRS_STU(2021)662621_EN.pdf

European Union. (2018). *Cyber violence and hate speech online against women*. https://www.europarl.europa.eu/RegData/etudes/STUD/2018/604979/IPOL_STU(2018)604979_EN.pdf

Europol. (2020, April 3). *Catching the virus cybercrime, disinformation and the COVID-19 pandemic*. https://www.europol.europa.eu/publications-events/publications/catching-virus-cybercrime-disinformation-and-covid-19-pandemic

Ezeh, N. C., Chukwuma, N. A., & Okanume, O. B. (2017). Internet and women selfempowerment: Opportunities, strategies, and challenges. *International Journal of Social Sciences and Humanities Review, 17*(1), 203–212.

Fairbairn, J. (2015). Rape threats and revenge porn: Defining sexual violence in the digital age. In J. Bailey & V. Steeves (Eds.), *eGirls, eCitizens: Putting Technology, Theory and Policy into Dialogue with Girls' and Young Women's Voices* (pp. 229–252). University of Ottawa Press. https://www.jstor.org/stable/j.ctt15nmj7f.13

Fairbairn, J., & Dawson, M. (2013). Canadian news coverage of intimate partner homicide: Analyzing changes over time. *Feminist Criminology, 8*(3), 147–176. doi:10.1177/1557085113480824

Fairclough, N. (1999). Linguistic and Intertextual Analysis within Discourse Analysis. In The Discourse Reader (pp. 183-211). Academic Press.

Fairclough, N. (1989). *Language and Power*. Longman.

Fairclough, N. (1992). *Discourse and Social Change*. Polity Press.

Fairclough, N. (1995). *Media Discourse*. Edward Arnold.

Fairclough, N. (2000). *New Labor, New Language*. Routledge.

Fama, E. F., & Jensen, M. C. (1983). Separation of Ownership and Control. *The Journal of Law & Economics, 26*(2), 301–325. doi:10.1086/467037

Fenton, N. (2008). Mediating solidarity. *Global Media and Communication, 4*(1), 37-57.

Ferro, C., Cermele, J., & Saltzman, A. (2008). Current perceptions of marital rape: Some good and not-so-good news. *Journal of Interpersonal Violence, 23*(6), 764–779. doi:10.1177/0886260507313947 PMID:18272725

Fersini, E., Nozza, D., & Rosso, P. (2018). *Overview of the Evalita 2018 Task on Automatic Misogyny Identification (AMI)*. Future Eight. https://figure-eight.com/

Fersini, E., Nozza, D., & Rosso, P. (2020). *AMI @ EVALITA2020: Automatic Misogyny Identification.*

Fersini, E., Rosso, P., & Anzovino, M. (2018). *Overview of the Task on Automatic Misogyny Identification at IberEval 2018*. Figure Eight. https://figure-eight.com/

Fichman, P., & Sanfilippo, M. R. (2016). *Online trolling and its perpetrators: Under the cyberbridge*. Rowman & Littlefield.

Fileborn, B., & Loney-Howes, R. (2019). Introduction: Mapping the Emergence of #MeToo. In #MeToo and the Politics of Social Change (pp. 1–18). Springer International Publishing. doi:10.1007/978-3-030-15213-0_1

Finkelhor, D., Mitchell, K. J., & Wolak, J. (2005). Online victimization: What youth tell us. *Medical, legal, and social science aspects of child sexual exploitation: A comprehensive review of pornography, prostitution, and Internet crimes, 1*, 437-467.

Flood, M., & Pease, B. (2009). Factors influencing attitudes to violence against women. *Trauma, Violence & Abuse, 10*(2), 125–142. doi:10.1177/1524838009334131 PMID:19383630

Fogel, S. (2018, July 11). ESPN, Disney, ABC Airing Overwatch League. *VARIETY*. https://variety.com/2018/gaming/news/espn-disney-abc-overwatch-league-1202870413/

Foleon.com. (2019). *Measuring Digital Development - Gender gap*. https://itu.foleon.com/itu/measuring-digital-development/gender-gap/

Forum, W. E. (2019, October 1). *Cyberattacks and fiscal crises top list of business risks in 2019*. Retrieved from World Economic Forum: https://www.weforum.org/press/2019/10/cyberattacks-and-fiscal-crises-top-list-of-business-risks-in-2019/

Foster, M. D., Tassone, A., & Matheson, K. (2021). Tweeting about sexism motivates further activism: A social identity perspective. *British Journal of Social Psychology, 60*(3), 741–764. doi:10.1111/bjso.12431

Fox & Tang. (2014). *Sexism in Online Video Games: The Role of Conformity to Masculine Norms and Social Dominance Orientation.* doi:10.1016/j.chb.2013.07.014

Fox, J., & Vendemia, M. A. (2016). Selective self-presentation and social comparison through photographs on social networking sites. *Cyberpsychology, behaviorbehaviour, and social networking, 19*(10), 593-600.

Fox, J., Cruz, C., & Lee, J. Y. (2015). Perpetuating online sexism offline: Anonymity, interactivity, and the effects of sexist hashtags on social media. *Computers in Human Behavior, 52*, 436–442. doi:10.1016/j.chb.2015.06.024

Fox, J., & Rooney, M. C. (2015). The Dark Triad and trait self-objectification as predictors of men'smen's use and self-presentation behaviorsbehaviours on social networking sites. *Personality and Individual Differences, 76*, 161–165. doi:10.1016/j.paid.2014.12.017

Franiuk, R., Seefelt, J. L., Cepress, S. L., & Vandello, J. A. (2008a). Prevalence and effects of rape myths in print journalism: The Kobe Bryant case. *Violence Against Women*, *14*(3), 287–309. doi:10.1177/1077801207313971 PMID:18292371

Franiuk, R., Seefelt, J. L., & Vandello, J. A. (2008b). Prevalence of rape myths in headlines and their effects on attitudes toward rape. *Sex Roles*, *58*(11-12), 790–801. doi:10.100711199-007-9372-4

Franklin, C. A. (2016). Sorority affiliation and sexual assault victimization: Assessing vulnerability using path analysis. *Violence Against Women*, *22*(8), 895–922. doi:10.1177/1077801215614971 PMID:26597086

Freeman, R. E. (1984). *Strategic Management: A Stakeholder Approach*. Cambridge University Press.

Frenda, S. (2018). *The role of sarcasm in hate speech. A multilingual perspective*. QCRI. https://alt.qcri.org/semeval2019/index

Frosh, P. (2015). The Gestural Image: The Selfie, Photography Theory, and Kinesthetic Sociability. *International Journal of Communication*, *9*(Feature), 1607–1628. https://doi.org/ doi:1932–8036/2015FEA0002

Gajjala, R. (2018). When an Indian whisper network went digital. *Communication, Culture & Critique*, *11*(3), 1–5. doi:10.1093/ccc/tcy025

Galbraith, P. W. (2017). Adult Computer Games and the Ethics of Imaginary Violence: Responding to Gamergate from Japan. *University of Hawai'i Press on Behalf of International Institute of Gender and Media*, *52*(1), 67–88. doi:10.1353/jwj.2017.0012

Gamble, S. (Ed.). (2004). *The Routledge Companion to Feminism and Post-feminism*. Routledge. doi:10.4324/9780203011010

Gamerschlag, R., Möller, K., & Verbeeten, F. (2011). Determinants of voluntary CSR disclosure: Empirical evidence from Germany. *Review of Managerial Science*, *5*(2), 233–262. doi:10.100711846-010-0052-3

Gámez-Guadix, M., Orue, I., Smith, P. K., & Calvete, E. (2013). Longitudinal and Reciprocal Relations of Cyberbullying with Depression, Substance Use, and Problematic Internet Use among Adolescents. *The Journal of Adolescent Health*, *53*(4), 446–452. doi:10.1016/j.jadohealth.2013.03.030 PMID:23721758

Gandolfia, E., & Sciannamblob, M. (2019). Unfolding female quiet in wargames: Gender bias in Metal Gear Solid V: The Phantom Pain from representation to gameplay. *Feminist Media Studies*, *19*(3), 331–347. Advance online publication. doi:10.1080/14680777.2018.1467476

Garg, A. (2022, January 29). Don't blindly follow West in criminalising marital rape: Govt. *The Times of India*. https://timesofindia.indiatimes.com/india/dont-blindly-follow-west-in-criminalising-marital-rape-govt/articleshow/89188920.cms

Garner, B. A. (2004). *Black's Law Dictionary*. West Group.

Gelles, R. J., & Straus, M. A. (1988). *Intimate Violence*. Simon & Schuster.

General Assembly, United Nations. (2022). *Advancement of women Intensification of efforts to eliminate all forms of violence against women and girls | Report of the Secretary-General*. https://www.unwomen.org/sites/default/files/2022-10/A-77-302-SG-report-EVAWG-en.pdf

Gianniri, L. (2021), "Here too": Some media representations of the intersectoral #Metoo in Greece, in ENA Institute for Alternative Policies (2021). The Greek #Metoo and Public Discourse.

Giddens, A. (2000). *Mundo em Descontmle*. Academic Press.

Gill, R. (2005). Review: Techno feminism! *Science as Culture*, *14*(1), 97–101. doi:10.1080/09505430500042130

Ging, D. (2017). Alphas, Betas, and Incels: Theorizing the masculinities of the Manosphere. *Men and Masculinities*, *22*(4), 638–657. doi:10.1177/1097184X17706401

Ging, D., & Siapera, E. (2018). Special issue on online misogyny. *Feminist Media Studies*, *18*(4), 515–524. doi:10.1080/14680777.2018.1447345

Girl Kills self over Facebook Harassment. (2014). https://timesofindia.indiatimes.com/city/kolkata/girl-kills-self-over-facebook-harassment/articleshow/37211521.cms

Glaser, A., Kesslen, B., & Solon, O. (2020, March 26). *In video chats, familiar forms of online harassment make a comeback*. NBC News. https://www.nbcnews.com/tech/security/video-chats-familiar-forms-online-harassment-make-comeback-n1168806

Glick, P., Sakallı-Uğurlu, N., Akbaş, G., & Metin Orta, İ. (2016). Why do women endorse honor beliefs? Ambivalent sexism and religiosity as predictors. *Sex Roles*, *75*(11), 543–554. doi:10.100711199-015-0550-5

Goel, A. (2006). *Violence and Protective Measures for Women Development and Empowerment*. Deep & Deep Publications.

Goffman, E. (1979). *Gender advertisements*.

Goffman, E. (1969). *The Presentation of Self in Everyday Life*. Allen Lane.

Goffman, E. (1979). *Gender Advertisements*. Harper & Row.

Goffman, E. (2021). *The presentation of self in everyday life*. Anchor.

Golf-Papez, M., & Veer, E. (2017). Don't feed the trolling: Rethinking how online trolling is being defined and combated. *Journal of Marketing Management*, *33*(15-16), 1336–1354. doi:10.1080/0267257X.2017.1383298

Goodfellow, I., Bengio, Y., & Courville, A. (2016). *Deep learning*. MIT press.

Google. (2016, May 27). *Google Photos: One year, 200 million users, and a whole lot of selfies*. Google. https://blog.google/products/photos/google-photos-one-year-200-million/

Gordon, W. J., Fairhall, A., & Landman, A. (2017). Threats to information security—Public health implications. *The New England Journal of Medicine*, *377*(8), 707–709. doi:10.1056/NEJMp1707212 PMID:28700269

Gottman, J., & Mettetal, G. (1986). Speculations about social and affective development: Friendship and acquaintanceship through adolescence. In J. M. Gottman & J. G. Parker (Eds.), *Conversations with friends: Speculations on affective development* (pp. 192–237). Cambridge University Press.

Gqola, P. D. (2001). Ufanele Uqavile: Black women, Feminisms and Postcoloniality in Africa. *Agenda (Durban, South Africa)*, *16*(50), 11–22. doi:10.1080/10130950.2001.9675990

Gradinger, P., Strohmeier, D., & Spiel, C. (2009). Traditional bullying and cyberbullying: Identification of risk groups for adjustment problems. *Zeitschrift für Psychologie. Zeitschrift für Psychologie mit Zeitschrift für Angewandte Psychologie*, *217*(4), 205–213. doi:10.1027/0044-3409.217.4.205

Graewe, D. (2021). *Advisory Boards in Medium-Sized Companies: An International Comparison*. Walter de Gruyter GmbH & Co KG. doi:10.1515/9783110666182

Grasseni, C., Barendregt, B. A., de Maaker, E., Musso, D. F., Littlejohn, A., Maeckelbergh, M., Postma, M., & Westmoreland, M. R. (2022). *Audiovisual and Digital Ethnography: A Practical and Theoretical Guide*. Routledge.

Gray, T., Norton, C., Breault-Hood, J., Christie, B., & Taylor, N. (2018). Curating a public self: Exploring social media images of women in the outdoors. *Journal of Outdoor Recreation, Education, and Leadership, 10*(2), 153–170. doi:10.18666/JOREL-2018-V10-I2-8191

Gruber, M. J., Gelman, B. D., & Ranganath, C. (2014). States of curiosity modulate hippocam- pus-dependent learning via the dopaminergic circuit. *Neuron, 84*(2), 486–496. doi:10.1016/j.neuron.2014.08.060 PMID:25284006

Guest, E., Vidgen, B., Sastry, N., Tyson, G., & Margetts, H. (2021). *An Expert Annotated Dataset for the Detection of Online Misogyny*. Github. https://github.com/ellamguest/

Gul, F. A., & Leung, S. (2004). Board leadership, outside directors' expertise and voluntary corporate disclosures. *Journal of Accounting and Public Policy, 23*(5), 351–379. doi:10.1016/j.jaccpubpol.2004.07.001

Gunning, D., Stefik, M., Choi, J., Miller, T., Stumpf, S., & Yang, G. Z. (2019). XAI-Explainable artificial intelligence. *Science Robotics, 4*(37), eaay7120. doi:10.1126cirobotics.aay7120 PMID:33137719

Gupta, A., Tyagi, M., & Sharma, D. (2013). Use of Social Media Marketing in Healthcare. *Journal of Health Management, 15*(2), 293–302. doi:10.1177/0972063413489058

Gurrieri, L. (2013). Stocky bodies: Fat visual activism. *Fat Studies, 2*(2), 197–209. doi:10.1080/21604851.2013.779554

Gurumurthy, A., & Menon, N. (2009). Violence against Women via Cyberspace. *Economic and Political Weekly, 44*(40), 19-21.

Gurunathan, S. (2022). Cyberfeminism in Online Video Games. *International Journal of Interdisciplinary Research in Arts and Humanities, 7*(2), 4–8. https://www.researchgate.net/publication/361983718

Guthrie, J., Petty, R., Yongvanich, K., & Ricceri, F. (2004). Using content analysis as a research method to inquire into intellectual capital reporting. *Journal of Intellectual Capital, 5*(2), 282–293. doi:10.1108/14691930410533704

Hacettepe Üniversitesi Nüfus Etütleri Enstitüsü. (2015). *Türkiye'de kadına yönelik aile içi şiddet araştırması.* Elma Teknik Basım Matbaacılık.

Hair, J. F., Risher, J. J., Sarstedt, M., & Ringle, C. M. (2019). When to use and how to report the results of PLS-SEM. *European Business Review, 31*(1), 2–24. doi:10.1108/EBR-11-2018-0203

Halbert, D. (2004). Shulamith Firestone: Radical feminism and visions of the information society. *Information Communication and Society, 7*(1), 115–135. doi:10.1080/1369118042000208933

Halder, D., & Jaishankar, K. (2015). *Harassment via WHATsAPP in Urban & Rural India. A Baseline Survey Report (2015).* https://www.cybervictims.org/CCVCresearchreport2015.pdf

Haliday, M. (1978). *Language as Social Semiotic: The Social Interpretation of Language and Meaning*. Edward Arnold.

Halliday, M., & Hasan, R. (1989). *Language Context and Text: Aspects of Language in a Social-Semiotic Perspective* (2nd ed.). Oxford University Press.

Hamad, M. M. (2017). Using WhatsApp to enhance students' learning of English language "Experience to Share.". *Higher Education Studies, 7*(4), 74. doi:10.5539/hes.v7n4p74

Hammond, W. R., Whitaker, D. J., Lutzker, J. R., Mercy, J., & Chin, P. M. (2006). Setting a violence prevention agenda at the Centers for Disease Control and Prevention. *Aggression and Violent Behavior, 11*(2), 112–119. doi:10.1016/j.avb.2005.07.003

Han, S. (2013). Ethnographies of the Videogame: Gender, Narrative and Praxis byHelen Thornham. *American Sociological Association*, *42*(1), 112–114.

Hanton, P. B. (2015). *The lack of women in technology: The role culture and sexism play.*

Haraway, D. (1997). *Modest_Witness@Second_Millennium. FemaleMan©_Meets_OncoMouse™: Feminism and Technoscience*. Routledge.

Haraway, D. J. (1990). *Simians, Cyborgs and Women: The Reinvention of Nature*. Routledge.

Hardaker, C. (2013). "Uh.... not to be nitpicky, but… the past tense of drag is dragged, not drug": An overview of trolling strategies. *Journal of Language Aggression and Conflict, 1*(1), 58-86.

Hardaker, C. (2010). Trolling in asynchronous computer-mediated communication: From user discussions to academic definitions. *Journal of Politeness Research*, *6*(2), 215–242. doi:10.1515/jplr.2010.011

Hardaker, C. (2015). 'I refuse to respond to this obvious troll': An overview of responses to (perceived) trolling. *Corpora*, *10*(2), 201–229. doi:10.3366/cor.2015.0074

Hardaker, C., & McGlashan, M. (2016). "Real men don't hate women": Twitter rape threats and group identity. *Journal of Pragmatics*, *91*, 80–93. doi:10.1016/j.pragma.2015.11.005

Harvey & Fisher. (2015). *"Everyone Can Make Games!": The post-feminist context of women in digital game production.* doi:10.1080/14680777.2014.958867

Hate Crime - Law Commission. (2021). Lawcom. https://www.lawcom.gov.uk/project/hate-crime/

Hatebase. (2023). *Home.* Hatebase. https://hatebase.org/

Hawthorne, S., & Klein, R. (1999). *Cyberfeminism: Connectivity, Critique and Creativity*. Spinifex Press.

Heirman, W., & Walrave, M. (2008). Assessing concerns and issues about the mediation of technology in cyberbullying. *Cyberpsychology (Brno)*, *2*(2), 1.

Henriyan, D., Subiyanti, D., Fauzian, R., Anggraini, D., & Aziz, M. (2016). *Design and implementation of web based real time chat interfacing server*. IEEE. https://ieeexplore.ieee.org/document/7849628

Henry, N., Flynn, A., & Powell, A. (2020). Technology-Facilitated Domestic and Sexual Violence: A Review. *Violence Against Women*, *26*(15-16), 1828–1854. doi:10.1177/1077801219875821 PMID:32998673

Henry, N., & Powell, A. (2015). Embodied harms. *Violence Against Women*, *21*(6), 758–779. doi:10.1177/1077801215576581 PMID:25827609

Hepler, J. B. (Ed.). (2007). *Women in Game Development Breaking the Glass Level-Cap*. CRC Press.

Héroux, S., & Fortin, A. (2022). Board of directors' attributes and aspects of cybersecurity disclosure. *The Journal of Management and Governance*. Advance online publication. doi:10.100710997-022-09660-7

HiggsJ. L.PinskerR. E.SmithT. J.YoungG. (2016). The Relationship between Board-Level Technology Committees and Reported Security Breaches. doi:10.2308/isys-51402

Hill, C. W., & Jones, T. M. (1992). Stakeholder-agency theory. *Journal of Management Studies*, *29*(2), 131–154. doi:10.1111/j.1467-6486.1992.tb00657.x

Hillman, A. J., & Dalziel, T. (2003). Boards of Directors and Firm Performance: Integrating Agency and Resource Dependence Perspectives. *Academy of Management Review*, *28*(3), 383–396. doi:10.5465/amr.2003.10196729

Hinduja, S., & Patchin, J. W. (2014). *Cyberbullying Identification, Prevention, and Response.* Cyberbullying Research Center. www.cyberbullying.us

Hinduja, S., & Patchin, J. W. (2008). Cyberbullying: An exploratory analysis of factors related to offending and victimization. *Deviant Behavior, 29*(2), 129–156. doi:10.1080/01639620701457816

Hingorani, S. (2020, March 26). *Commentary: Isolated with your abuser? Why family violence seems to be on the rise during COVID-19 outbreak.* CNA. https://www.channelnewsasia.com/commentary/coronavirus-covid-19-family-violence-abuse-women-self-isolation-1324466

HjelpdahlA. B. (2020). *Online Gaming: A Successful Life? The Influence of Gaming on Development.* University of South-Eastern Norway Faculty of Health and Social Sciences. doi:10.13140/RG.2.2.34362.41922

Hochreiter, S., & Schmidhuber, J. (1997). Long short-term memory. *Neural Computation, 9*(8), 1735–1780. doi:10.1162/neco.1997.9.8.1735 PMID:9377276

Ho, J., Pang, C., & Choy, C. (2020). Content marketing capability building: A conceptual framework. *Journal of Research in Interactive Marketing, 14*(1), 133–151. doi:10.1108/JRIM-06-2018-0082

Holladay, J. (2011). Cyberbullying. *Education Digest, 76*(5), 4–9.

Holliman, G., & Rowley, J. (2014). Business to business digital content marketing: Marketers' perceptions of best practice. *Journal of Research in Interactive Marketing, 8*(4), 269–293. doi:10.1108/JRIM-02-2014-0013

hooks, b. (2015). *Talking Back: Thinking feminist, thinking black.* Routledge, Taylor & Francis Group.

Humphrey, N., & Symes, W. (2010). A Review of the Literature spectrum disorders (ASDs) in mainstream schools: A qualitative study. *Journal of Research in Special Educational Needs, 10*(2), 82. doi:10.1111/j.1471-3802.2010.01146.x

Hynnä, K., & Kyrölä, K. (2019). "Feel in Your Body": Fat Activist Affects in Blogs. *Social Media + Society, 5*(4). Advance online publication. doi:10.1177/2056305119879983

Ibrahim, A. H., & Hanefah, M. M. (2016). Board diversity and corporate social responsibility in Jordan. *Journal of Financial Reporting and Accounting, 14*(2), 279–298. doi:10.1108/JFRA-06-2015-0065

Ilakkuvan, V., Johnson, A., Villanti, A. C., Evans, W. D., & Turner, M. (2019). Patterns of Social Media Use and Their Relationship to Health Risks Among Young Adults. *The Journal of Adolescent Health, 64*(2), 158–164. doi:10.1016/j.jadohealth.2018.06.025 PMID:30269907

İnam, Ö., & Şahin, N. (2020). Kadına yönelik şiddetin Türk medyasindaki temsil şekli: Sistematik derleme araştirmasi. *Marmara Üniversitesi Kadın ve Toplumsal Cinsiyet Araştırmaları Dergisi, 4*(1), 1–15. doi:10.35333/mukatcad.2020.212

Indian Printer & Publisher. (n.d.). Retrieved June 3, 2023, from https://indianprinterpublisher.com/

International Center for Research on Women (ICRW) & Quilt.AI. (2021). *COVID-19 and Online Violence in India: Digital Intelligence Report.* https://www.icrw.org/wp-content/uploads/2021/10/Online-Violence_Full-Report-Quilt.AI-and-ICRW.pdf

Internet Society. (2017). *Issue Paper: Asia-Pacific Bureau Gender.* Internet Society. https://www.internetsociety.org/wp-content/uploads/2017/08/APAC-Issue-Papers-Gender_0.pdf

Isaac, E. (2023). IAMAI Report: Digital gender divide lingers in India. *Feminism in India.* https://feminisminindia.com/2023/03/08/digital-gender-divide-lingers-in-india-as-per-new-report/

Islam, M. (2020). Investigating the relationship between integrated reporting and firm performance in a voluntary disclosure regime: Insights from Bangladesh. *Asian Journal of Accounting Research*, *6*(2), 228–245. doi:10.1108/AJAR-06-2020-0039

Issa, A., Zaid, M. A., Hanaysha, J. R., & Gull, A. A. (2021). An examination of board diversity and corporate social responsibility disclosure: Evidence from banking sector in the Arabian Gulf countries. *International Journal of Accounting and Information Management*, *30*(1), 22–46. doi:10.1108/IJAIM-07-2021-0137

Ivashkovskaya, I., & Adamu, M. U. (2021). Corporate governance and risk disclosure in emerging countries. *Journal of Corporate Finance Research*, *15*(4), 5–16.

Jackson, C. (2011). Your students love social media ... and so can you. *Teaching Tolerance*, *39*, 38–41.

Jackson, S. (2018). Young Feminists, Feminism and Digital Media. *Feminism & Psychology*, *28*(1), 32–49. doi:10.1177/0959353517716952

Jain, M., & Jamali, D. (2016). Looking inside the black box: The effect of corporate governance on corporate social responsibility. *Corporate Governance*, *24*(3), 253–273. doi:10.1111/corg.12154

Jaji, R. (2021). Youth Masculinities in Zimbabwe's Congested Gerontocratic political space. *Africa Development. Afrique et Developpement*, *45*(3), 77–96. doi:10.57054/ad.v45i3.635

Jane, E. (2017). Misogyny Online: A Short (and Brutish) History. *Sage (Atlanta, Ga.)*. Advance online publication. doi:10.4135/9781473916029

Jankowicz, N. (2022). *How to be a woman online: Surviving Abuse and Harassment and How to Fight Back*. Bloomsbury Publishing.

Jankowicz, N. (2022). *How to Be a Woman Online: Surviving Abuse and Harassment, and How to Fight Back*. Bloomsbury Academic. doi:10.5040/9781350267602

Jeet, S. (2012). Cyber-crimes against women in India: Information Technology Act, 2000. *Elixir Criminal Law*, *47*, 8891–8895.

Jenefa, S. (2017). Social Media as a Tool of Violence against Women. *World Journal of Science and Research*, *2*(2), 77–82.

Jennings, T. L., Chen, Y.-L., Way, B. M., Borgogna, N. C., & Kraus, S. W. (2023). Associations between Online Dating Platform Use and Mental and Sexual Health among a Mixed Sexuality College Student Sample. *Computers in Human Behavior*, *144*, 107727. doi:10.1016/j.chb.2023.107727

Jenny, S. E., Manning, R. D., Keiper, M. C., & Olrich, T. W. (2017). Athletes: Where eSports Fit Within the Definition of "Sport." *Quest*, *69*(1), 1–18. Advance online publication. doi:10.1080/00336297.2016.1144517

Jensen, M. C. (1988). Takeovers: Their causes and consequences. *The Journal of Economic Perspectives*, *2*(1), 21–48. doi:10.1257/jep.2.1.21

Jewkes, Y. (2015). *Media & Crime*. Sage.

Jiao, Y. (2011). Corporate Disclosure, Market Valuation, and Firm Performance. *Financial Management*, *40*(3), 647–676. doi:10.1111/j.1755-053X.2011.01156.x

Jin, X., Wei, Z., Du, J., Xue, X., & Ren, X. (2019). Towards hierarchical importance attribution: Explaining compositional semantics for neural sequence models. *ArXiv Preprint ArXiv:1911.06194*.

Johnson, M. (2015). Digital Literacy and Digital Citizenship: Approaches to Girls' Online Experiences. In *EGirls, eCitizens*. University of Ottawa Press. https://www.jstor.org/stable/j.ctt15nmj7f.17

Jones, S. E., Manstead, A. S. R., & Livingstone, A. G. (2011). Ganging up or sticking together? Group processes and children's responses to text-message bullying. *British Journal of Psychology, 102*(1), 71–96. doi:10.1348/000712610X502826

Jussinoja, T. (2018). Life-cycle of Internet trolls [Unpublished doctoral work]. University of Jyväskylä.

Kaakinen, M., Keipi, T., Oksanen, A., & Räsänen, P. (2018). How Does Social Capital Associate With Being a Victim of Online Hate? Survey Evidence From the United States, the United Kingdom, Germany, and Finland. *Policy and Internet, 10*(3), 302–323. doi:10.1002/poi3.173

Kaakinen, M., Koivula, A., Savolainen, I., Sirola, A., Mikkola, M., Zych, I., Paek, H. J., & Oksanen, A. (2021). Online Dating Applications and Risk of Youth Victimization: A Lifestyle Exposure Perspective. *Aggressive Behavior, 47*(5), 530–543. doi:10.1002/ab.21968 PMID:34038595

Kaloeti, D. V. S., Manalu, R., Kristiana, I. F., & Bidzan, M. (2021). The role of social media use in peer bullying victimization and onset of anxiety among Indonesian elementary school children. *Frontiers in Psychology, 12*, 635725. doi:10.3389/fpsyg.2021.635725 PMID:33995192

Kamath, B. (2008). Intellectual capital disclosure in India: Content analysis of "TecK" firms. *Journal of Human Resource Costing & Accounting, 12*(3), 213–224. doi:10.1108/14013380810919859

KambleS.JoshiA. (2018). *Hate Speech Detection from Code-mixed Hindi-English Tweets Using Deep Learning Models*. https://arxiv.org/abs/1811.05145

Kangere, M., Kemitare, J., & Michau, L. (2017). Hashtag activism: Popularizing feminist analysis of violence against women in the Horn, East and Southern Africa. *Feminist Media Studies, 17*(5), 899–902. doi:10.1080/14680777.2017.1350526

Kang, H., Cheng, M., & Gray, S. J. (2007). Corporate governance and board composition: Diversity and independence of Australian boards. *Corporate Governance, 15*(2), 194–207. doi:10.1111/j.1467-8683.2007.00554.x

Karim, Md. R., Dey, S. K., Islam, T., Sarker, S., Menon, M. H., Hossain, K., Chakravarthi, B. R., Hossain, Md. A., & Decker, S. (2020). *DeepHateExplainer: Explainable Hate Speech Detection in Under-resourced Bengali Language*. https://arxiv.org/abs/2012.14353

Karim, K., Pinsker, R., & Robin, A. (2013). Firm size and the voluntary disclosure of nonfinancial information by private versus public firm managers. *Managerial Auditing Journal, 28*. Advance online publication. doi:10.1108/MAJ-01-2013-0800

Karwowski, M., & Brzeski, A. (2017). Selfies and the (creative) self: A diary study. *Frontiers in Psychology, 8*, 172. doi:10.3389/fpsyg.2017.00172

Katmon, N., Mohamad, Z. Z., Norwani, N. M., & Faroogue, A. (2019). Comprehensive board diversity and quality of corporate social responsibility disclosure: Evidence from an emerging market. *Journal of Business Ethics, 157*(2), 447–481. doi:10.100710551-017-3672-6

Kaufman, M. R., Dey, D., Crainiceanu, C., & Dredze, M. (2021). #MeToo and Google Inquiries Into Sexual Violence: A Hashtag Campaign Can Sustain Information Seeking. *Journal of Interpersonal Violence, 36*(19–20), 9857–9867. doi:10.1177/0886260519868197 PMID:31441695

Kaur, M., & Saini, M. (2022). Indian government initiatives on cyberbullying: A case study on cyberbullying in Indian higher education institutions. *Education and Information Technologies*, *28*(1), 581–615. doi:10.100710639-022-11168-4 PMID:35814802

Keller, J. (2017). Making activism accessible: Exploring girls' blogs as sites of contemporary feminist activism. In Girlhood and the Politics of Place (pp. 261–278). doi:10.2307/j.ctt14jxn16.20

Keller, J. (2012). Virtual feminisms: Girls' blogging communities, feminist activism, and participatory politics. *Information Communication and Society*, *15*(3), 429–447. doi:10.1080/1369118X.2011.642890

Kelly, L. (1988). *Surviving Sexual Violence*. University of Minnesota Press.

Kemp, S. (2018). *Digital in 2018: World's Internet Users Pass the 4 Billion Mark*. https://wearesocial.com/blog/2018/01/global-digital-report-2018

Kemp, S. (2018). *Digital in 2018: World's Internet Users Pass the 4 Billion Mark*. We Are Social. https://wearesocial.com/blog/2018/01/ global-digital-report-2018

Kendall, L. (1998). Meaning and identity in 'Cyberspace': The Performance of Gender, Class and Race Online. *Symbolic Interaction*, *21*(2), 129–153. doi:10.1525i.1998.21.2.129

Khanna, M. (2021, February 24). Female Call Of Duty Player Murdered By Fellow Gamer In Brazil. *The Time of India*. https://www.indiatimes.com/technology/news/female-call-of-duty-player-murdered-by-fellow-gamer-in-brazil-535018.html

Khlifi, F., & Bouri, A. (2010). Corporate disclosure and firm characteristics: A puzzling relationship. *Journal of Accounting. Business & Management*, *17*, 62–89.

Khurana, P., & Knight, T. (2021). Content Analysis of Athletic Brand Posts on Instagram. *Proceedings of the New York State Communication Association*.

Kiani, M., Tavakoli, R., & Mura, P. (2023). Iranian Women Traveling in vTime—A Cyberfeminist Approach. *Journal of Travel Research*. doi:10.1177/00472875221149202

Kılıç, M., & Kuzey, C. (2019). The effect of corporate governance on carbon emission disclosures: Evidence from Turkey. *International Journal of Climate Change Strategies and Management*, *11*(1), 35–53. doi:10.1108/IJCCSM-07-2017-0144

Kilpatrick, D. G., Best, C. L., Saunders, B. E., & Veronen, L. J. (1988). Rape in marriage and in dating relationships: How bad is it for mental health? *Annals of the New York Academy of Sciences*, *528*(1 Human Sexual), 335–344. doi:10.1111/j.1749-6632.1988.tb50875.x PMID:3421605

Kim, H., Lee, M., & Kim, M. (2014). Effects of mobile instant messaging on collaborative learning processes and outcomes: The case of South Korea. *Journal of Educational Technology & Society*, *17*(2), 31–42.

Kim, J., Walsh, E., Pike, K., & Thompson, E. A. (2020). Cyberbullying and victimization and youth suicide risk: The buffering effects of school connectedness. *The Journal of School Nursing: the Official Publication of the National Association of School Nurses*, *36*(4), 251–257. doi:10.1177/1059840518824395 PMID:30665324

Koiso-Kanttila, N. (2004). Digital Content Marketing: A Literature Synthesis. *Journal of Marketing Management*, *20*(1–2), 45–65. doi:10.1362/026725704773041122

Kolsi, M. (2017). The Determinants of Corporate Voluntary Disclosure Policy: Evidence from Abu Dhabi Securities Exchange (ADX). *Journal of Accounting in Emerging Economies*, *7*(2), 249–265. Advance online publication. doi:10.1108/JAEE-12-2015-0089

Konrad, A., Kramer, V., & Erkut, S. (2008). Critical Mass: The Impact of Three or More Women on Corporate Boards. *Organizational Dynamics*, *37*(2), 145–164. doi:10.1016/j.orgdyn.2008.02.005

Koo, J. (2019). South Korean cyberfeminism and trolling: The limitation of online feminist community Womad as counterpublic. *Feminist Media Studies*, *20*(6), 1–16. https://doi.org/10.1080/14680777.2019.1622585

Koss, M. P., Abbey, A., Campbell, R., Cook, S., Norris, J., Testa, M., Ullman, S., West, C., & White, J. (2007). Revising the SES: A collaboration process to improve assessment of sexual aggression and victimization. *Psychology of Women Quarterly*, *31*(4), 357–370. doi:10.1111/j.1471-6402.2007.00385.x

Koss, M. P., & Gidycz, C. A. (1985). Sexual experiences survey: Reliability and validity. *Journal of Consulting and Clinical Psychology*, *53*(3), 422–423. doi:10.1037/0022-006X.53.3.422 PMID:3874219

Koss, M. P., & Oros, C. J. (1982). Sexual experiences survey: A research instrument investigating sexual aggression and victimization. *Journal of Consulting and Clinical Psychology*, *50*(3), 455–457. doi:10.1037/0022-006X.50.3.455 PMID:7096751

Kowalski, R. M. (2008). *Cyber Bullying: Bullying in the Digital Age*. Blackwell Publishing. doi:10.1002/9780470694176

Kowalski, R. M., Limber, S. P., & Agatston, P. W. (2012). *Cyberbullying: Bullying in the Digital Age*. Blackwell Publishing Ltd.

Kravet, T., & Muslu, V. (2013). Textual risk disclosures and investors' risk perceptions. *Review of Accounting Studies*, *18*(4), 1088–1122. doi:10.100711142-013-9228-9

Kress, G., & van Leeuwen, T. (1996). *Reading Images: The Grammar of Visual Design*. Routledge.

Kristeva, J. (1994). *On Yury Lotman* (Vol. 109). Publications of the Modern Language Association.

Kroker, Arthur, & Marilousie. (1993). *The Last Sex: Feminism and Outlaw Bodies*. New World Perspectives Culture Texts Series.

Krook, M. (2022). Semiotic Violence against Women: Theorizing Harms against Female Politicians. *Signs (Chicago, Ill.)*, *47*(2), 371–397. doi:10.1086/716642

Krook, M. L. (2017). Violence against women in politics. *Journal of Democracy*, *28*(1), 74–88. doi:10.1353/jod.2017.0007

Kross, E. (2021). *Talking to Yourself*. Character Lab Tips. doi:10.53776/tips-talking-to-yourself

Kruschek, G. (2019). Stigma in the Comments Section: Feminist and Anti-Feminist Discussions Online. *Computers and Composition*, *54*, 102515. doi:10.1016/j.compcom.2019.102515

Kshetri, N. (2010). Diffusion and effects of cyber-crime in developing economies. *Third World Quarterly*, *31*(7), 1057–1079. doi:10.1080/01436597.2010.518752

Kumar, R., Ojha, A. K., Malmasi, S., & Zampieri, M. (2018). *Benchmarking Aggression Identification in Social Media*. CodaLab. https://competitions.codalab.org/

Kumar, R., Ojha, A. K., Malmasi, S., & Zampieri, M. (2020). *Evaluating Aggression Identification in Social Media*. CodaLab. https://competitions.codalab.org/

Kumari, M. (2020). Social media and women empowerment. *Int. J. Sci. Technol. Res*, *9*(3), 626–629.

Kwon, J., Ulmer, J. R., & Wang, T. (2013). The Association between Top Management Involvement and Compensation and Information Security Breaches. *Journal of Information Systems*, *27*(1), 219–236. doi:10.2308/isys-50339

Lajili, K. (2009). Corporate Risk Disclosure and Corporate Governance. *Journal of Risk and Financial Management, 2*(1), 1. Advance online publication. doi:10.3390/jrfm2010094

Lal, Y. K., Kumar, V., Dhar, M., Shrivastava, M., & Koehn, P. (2019). De-mixing sentiment from code-mixed text. *Proceedings of the 57th Annual Meeting of the Association for Computational Linguistics: Student Research Workshop*, (pp. 371–377). ACL. 10.18653/v1/P19-2052

Lassoued, N., & Khanchel, I. (2023). Voluntary CSR disclosure and CEO narcissism: The moderating role of CEO duality and board gender diversity. *Review of Managerial Science, 17*(3), 1075–1123. doi:10.100711846-022-00555-3

Lee, C. S., & Kim, J. H. (2020). Latent Groups of Cybersecurity Preparedness in Europe: Sociodemographic Factors and Country-Level Contexts. *Computers & Security, 97*, 101995. doi:10.1016/j.cose.2020.101995

Lee, C., & Wong, J. S. (2020). 99 reasons and he ain't one: A content analysis of domestic homicide news coverage. *Violence Against Women, 26*(2), 213–232. doi:10.1177/1077801219832325 PMID:30835161

Lee, F. L. F., Chen, H.-T., & Chan, M. (2017). Social media use and university students' participation in a large-scale protest campaign: The case of Hong Kong's Umbrella Movement. *Telematics and Informatics, 34*(2), 457–469. doi:10.1016/j.tele.2016.08.005

Le, H., Janssen, J., & Wubbels, T. (2018). Collaborative learning practices: Teacher and student perceived obstacles to effective student collaboration. *Cambridge Journal of Education, 48*(1), 103–122. doi:10.1080/0305764X.2016.1259389

Lemanski, C. (2004). A new Apartheid? The Spatial Implications of Fear of Crime in Cape Town, South Africa. *Environment and Urbanization, 16*(2), 101–111. doi:10.1177/095624780401600201

Lenhart, A., Madden, M., Smith, A., Purcell, K., Zickuhr, K., & Rainie, L. (2011). *Teens, kindness and cruelty on social network sites.* Retrieved on 17 March 2015 from https://www.pewinternet.org/2011/11/09/teens-kindness-and-cruelty-on-social-network-sites/

Lenhart, A., Ybarra, M. L., Zickuhr, K., & Price-Feeney, M. (2016). *Online harassment, digital abuse, and cyberstalking in America.* Data & Society Research Institute.

Lestari, N., Fadilah, A. N., & Wuryanta, E. W. (2020). Empowered Women & Social Media: Analyzing #YourBeautyRules in Cyberfeminism Perspective. *Jurnal ASPIKOM, 5*(2), 280–293. doi:10.24329/aspikom.v5i2.664

Leung, A. K. Y., & Cohen, D. (2011). Within-and between-culture variation: Individual differences and the cultural logics of honor, face, and dignity cultures. *Journal of Personality and Social Psychology, 100*(3), 507–526. doi:10.1037/a0022151 PMID:21244179

Levesque, D. A., Johnson, J. L., Welch, C. A., Prochaska, J. M., & Paiva, A. L. (2016). Teen Dating Violence Prevention: Cluster-Randomized Trial of Teen Choices, an Online, Stage-Based Program for Healthy, Nonviolent Relationships. *Psychology of Violence, 6*(3), 421–432. doi:10.1037/vio0000049 PMID:27482470

Li, J., Niu, J., Qian, X., & Liu, Y. (2023). Real-Time Ransomware Detection Method Based on TextGCN. In *2023 6th International Conference on Artificial Intelligence and Big Data (ICAIBD)* (pp. 535-541). IEEE. 10.1109/ICAIBD57115.2023.10206378

Liao, L., Luo, L., & Tang, Q. (2015). Gender diversity, board independence, environmental committee and greenhouse gas disclosure. *The British Accounting Review, 47*(4), 409–424. doi:10.1016/j.bar.2014.01.002

Linabary, J. R., Corple, D. J., & Cooky, C. (2019). Feminist activism in Digital Space: Postfeminist contradictions in #WhyIStayed. *New Media & Society, 22*(10), 1827–1848. doi:10.1177/1461444819884635

Linsley, P. M., & Shrives, P. J. (2006). Risk reporting: A study of risk disclosures in the annual reports of UK companies. *The British Accounting Review, 38*(4), 387–404. doi:10.1016/j.bar.2006.05.002

Lin, X., & Wang, X. (2020). Examining gender differences in people's information-sharing decisions on social networking sites. *International Journal of Information Management, 50*, 45–56. doi:10.1016/j.ijinfomgt.2019.05.004

Lipton, M. (2017, February 15). Risk Management and the board of directors. *The Harvard Law School Forum on Corporate Governance*. https://corpgov.law.harvard.edu/2017/02/15/risk-management-and-the-board-of-directors-4/

Litosseliti, L. (2006). *Gender and Language: Theory and Practice*. Hodder Arnold.

Liu, A. L. (2022). The autoregressive distributed lag model. In Econometric Modelling and Forecasting of Tourism Demand. Routledge.

Liu, H. (2007). Social network profiles as "taste performances.". *Journal of Computer-Mediated Communication, 13*(1), 252–275. doi:10.1111/j.1083-6101.2007.00395.x

Lobinger, K., & Brantner, C. (2015). In the eye of the beholder: Subjective views on the authenticity of selfies. *International Journal of Communication, 9*, 1848-1860.

Look, J. J. (1999). The Virtual Wild, Wild West (www): Intellectual Property Issues in Cyberspace—Trademarks, Service Marks, Copyrights, and Domain Names. *U. Ark. Little Rock. Rev., 22*(49).

Loots, L., Dartnall, E., & Kelly, J. (2020, April 16). Online safety in a changing world – COVID-19 and cyber violence. *Sexual Violence Research Initiative (SVRI)*. http://www.svri.org/blog/online-safety-changing-world-%E2%80%93-covid-19-and-cyber-violence

Lopes, P. T., & Rodrigues, L. L. (2007). Accounting for financial instruments: An analysis of the determinants of disclosure in the Portuguese stock exchange. *The International Journal of Accounting, 42*(1), 25–56. doi:10.1016/j.intacc.2006.12.002

Lopez, K. J., Muldoon, M. L., & McKeown, J. K. L. (2019). One Day of #Feminism: Twitter as a Complex Digital Arena for Wielding, Shielding, and Trolling talk on Feminism. *Leisure Sciences, 41*(3), 203–220. doi:10.1080/01490400.2018.1448022

Lotman, Y. (1990). *Universe of the Mind*. Indiana University Press.

Lövheim, M. (2013). Negotiating Empathic Communication. *Feminist Media Studies, 13*(4), 613–628. doi:10.1080/14680777.2012.659672

Luckman, S. (1999). (En)gendering the Digital Body: Feminism and the Internet. *Hecate, 25*(2), 36–48.

Lundberg, S. M., & Lee, S.-I. (2017). A unified approach to interpreting model predictions. *Advances in Neural Information Processing Systems*, 30.

Luppicini, R. (Ed.). (2012). *Handbook of Research on Technoself: Identity in a Technological Society: Identity in a Technological Society*. IGI Global.

Madigan, S., Ly, A., Rash, C. L., Van Ouytsel, J., & Temple, J. R. (2018). Prevalence of Multiple Forms of Sexting Behavior Among Youth: A Systematic Review and Meta-Analysis. *JAMA Pediatrics, 172*(4), 327–335. doi:10.1001/jamapediatrics.2017.5314 PMID:29482215

MagalhaesI. (2005). Critical Discourse Analysis and the Semiotic Construction on Gender Identities. *DELTA: Documentação de Estudos em Lingüística Teórica e Aplicada*, 179-205. https://doi.org/ doi:10.1590/S0102-44502005000300011

Mahagan, C. A. (2016). Cyberbullying: Feminine Vulnerability in Anonymous Spaces. *Dissenting Voices, 5*, 25–40.

Mahoney, P., & Williams, L. M. (1998). Sexual assault in marriage: Prevalence, consequences, and treatment of wife rape. Academic Press.

Maltby, J., Day, L., Hatcher, R. M., Tazzyman, S., Flowe, H. D., Palmer, E. J., Frosch, C. A., O'Reilly, M., Jones, C., Buckley, C., Knieps, M., & Cutts, K. (2016). Implicit theories of online trolling: Evidence that attention-seeking conceptions are associated with increased psychological resilience. *British Journal of Psychology*, *107*(3), 448–466. doi:10.1111/bjop.12154 PMID:26403842

Maltby, W. (2017). *The reign of Charles V*. Bloomsbury Publishing.

Mandl, T., Modha, S., Shahi, G. K., Kumar Jaiswal, A., Nandini, D., Patel, D., & Schäfer, J. (2020). *Overview of the HASOC track at FIRE 2020: Hate Speech and Offensive Content Identification in Indo-European Languages under Creative Commons License Attribution 4.0 International (CC BY 4.0)*. CEUR. http://ceur-ws.org

Mandl, T., Modha, S., Shahi, G. K., Madhu, H., Satapara, S., Schäfer, J., Ranasinghe, T., Zampieri, M., Nandini, D., Kumar Jaiswal, A., & Zampieri, M. (2021). *Overview of the HASOC Subtrack at FIRE 2021: Hate Speech and Offensive Content Identification in English and Indo-Aryan Languages under Creative Commons License Attribution 4.0 International (CC BY 4.0)*. CEUR. http://ceur-ws.org

Mandl, T., Modha, S., Majumder, P., Patel, D., Dave, M., Mandlia, C., & Patel, A. (2019). Overview of the hasoc track at fire 2019: Hate speech and offensive content identification in indo-european languages. *Proceedings of the 11th Forum for Information Retrieval Evaluation*, (pp. 14–17). IEEE. 10.1145/3368567.3368584

Mantilla, K. (2013). Gendertrolling: Misogyny adapts to new media. *Feminist Studies*, *39*(2), 563–570. doi:10.1353/fem.2013.0039

March, E., & Marrington, J. (2019). A qualitative analysis of internet trolling. *Cyberpsychology, Behavior, and Social Networking*, *22*(3), 192–197. doi:10.1089/cyber.2018.0210 PMID:30720370

March, E., & Steele, G. (2020). High esteem and hurting others online: Trait sadism moderates the relationship between self-esteem and internet trolling. *Cyberpsychology, Behavior, and Social Networking*, *23*(7), 441–446. doi:10.1089/cyber.2019.0652 PMID:32364769

Marcuse, H. (2013). *One-dimensional man: Studies in the ideology of advanced industrial society*. Routledge. doi:10.4324/9780203995211

Markham, A. (2016). The dramaturgy of digital experience. In *The Drama of Social Life* (pp. 297–312). Routledge.

Marret, M. J., & Choo, W. Y. (2017). Factors associated with online victimisation among Malaysian adolescents who use social networking sites: A cross-sectional study. *BMJ Open*, *7*(6), e014959. doi:10.1136/bmjopen-2016-014959 PMID:28667209

Martin, M., Jarvis, H., & Fry, A. (2011, June 9). *"Slutwalk" Goes Global To Protest Sexual Assault*. National Public Radio. NPR.

Martin, E. K., Taft, C. T., & Resick, P. A. (2007). A review of marital rape. *Aggression and Violent Behavior*, *12*(3), 329–347. doi:10.1016/j.avb.2006.10.003

Martínez-Ferrer, B., Moreno, D., & Musitu, G. (2018). Are adolescents engaged in the problematic use of social networking sites more involved in peer aggression and victimization? *Frontiers in Psychology*, *9*, 801. doi:10.3389/fpsyg.2018.00801 PMID:29896139

Martinez-Pecino, R., & Durán, M. (2019). I Love You but I Cyberbully You: The Role of Hostile Sexism. *Journal of Interpersonal Violence*, *34*(4), 812–825. doi:10.1177/0886260516645817 PMID:27118344

Martin, N., & Rice, J. (2012). Children's cyber-safety and protection in Australia: An analysis of community stakeholder views. *Crime Prevention and Community Safety*, *14*(3), 165–181. doi:10.1057/cpcs.2012.4

Martin, P., & Barnard, A. (2013). The experience of women in male-dominated occupations: A constructivist grounded theory inquiry. *SA Journal of Industrial Psychology*, *39*(2). Advance online publication. doi:10.4102ajip.v39i2.1099

Martsolf, D. S., Draucker, C. B., Stephenson, P. L., Cook, C. B., & Heckman, T. A. (2012). Patterns of Dating Violence Across Adolescence. *Sage, 22*(9), 1271–83. doi:10.1177/1049732312449388

Marturana, F., Tacconi, S., & Italiano, G. F. (2013). Cybercrime and Cloud Forensics: Applications for Investigation Processes. Academic Press.

Marwick, A. (2013). *Status Update: Celebrity, Publicity, and Branding in the Social Media Age*. Yale University Press.

Maryana, M., & Carolina, Y. (2021). The Impact of Firm Size, Leverage, Firm Age, Media Visibility and Profitability on Sustainability Report Disclosure. *Jurnal Keuangan Dan Perbankan*, *25*(1). Advance online publication. doi:10.26905/jkdp.v25i1.4941

MathewB.SahaP.YimamS. M.BiemannC.GoyalP.MukherjeeA. (2020). *HateXplain: A Benchmark Dataset for Explainable Hate Speech Detection*. https://arxiv.org/abs/2012.10289

Mathur, P., Ratn Shah, R., Sawhney, R., & Mahata, D. (2018). *Detecting Offensive Tweets in Hindi-English Code-Switched Language*. Github. www.github.com/pmathur5k10/

Matich, M., Ashman, R., & Parsons, E. (2019). #freethenipple–digital activism and embodiment in the contemporary feminist movement. *Consumption Markets & Culture*, *22*(4), 337–362. doi:10.1080/10253866.2018.1512240

Matos, C. (2017). New Brazilian feminisms and online networks: Cyberfeminism, protest and the female 'Arab Spring.'. *International Sociology*, *32*(3), 417–434. doi:10.1177/0268580917694971

Matsuda, M. J., III. C. R., Delgado, R., & Crenshaw, K. W. (1993). Words That Wound: Critical Race Theory, Assaultive Speech, and the First Amendment. Westview.

Mazumder, M. M. M., & Hossain, D. M. (2022). Voluntary cybersecurity disclosure in the banking industry of Bangladesh: Does board composition matter? *Journal of Accounting in Emerging Economies*, *13*(2), 217–239. doi:10.1108/JAEE-07-2021-0237

McArthur, S. A., & Muhammad, G. E. (2020). Pens Down, Don't Shoot An Analysis of How Black Young Women Use Language to fight back. *Urban Education*, *57*(5), 751–778. doi:10.1177/0042085919893734

McBean, J. (2022). *Bryter's Female Gamer Survey* [Infographic]. Bryter Research. https://www.womeningames.org/wp-content/uploads/2021/03/Bryter-Female-Gamers-Survey-2020-12.11.20-SHORT-no-quotes.pdf

McDuffie, K., & Ames, M. (2021). Archiving affect and activism: Hashtag feminism and structures of feeling in Women's March tweets. *First Monday*. Advance online publication. doi:10.5210/fm.v26i2.10317

McGorry, P., Bates, T., & Birchwood, M. (2013). Designing youth mental health services for the 21st century: Examples from Australia, Ireland and the UK. *The British Journal of Psychiatry*, *202*(54), 30–35. doi:10.1192/bjp.bp.112.119214 PMID:23288499

Mckinlay, T., & Lavis, T. (2020). Why did she send it in the first place? Victim blame in the context of 'revenge porn'. *Psychiatry, Psychology and Law*, *27*(3), 386–396. doi:10.1080/13218719.2020.1734977 PMID:33071547

McKinnon-Crowley, S. (2020). Fighting Gendered Battles: On Being a Woman in a Contemporary Gaming Community. *Journal of Contemporary Ethnography*, *49*(1), 118–142. doi:10.1177/0891241619864405

McMillan Cottom, T. (2016). Black CyberFeminism: Ways Forward for Intersectionality and Digital Sociology. In J. Daniels, K. Gregory, & T. McMillan Cottom (Eds.), Digital Sociologies (pp. 211–232). Policy Press.

Media Education Foundation. (1999). *Tough Guise: Violence, Media & the Crisis in Masculinity*. Retrieved from https://www.toughguise2.org/

Mendes, K., Ringrose, J., & Keller, J. (2019). *Digital feminist activism: Girls and women fight back against rape culture*. OUP USA. https://digitalfeministcollective.net/

Menesini, E., & Nocentini, A. (2009). Cyberbullying Definition and Measurement. *Zeitschrift für Psychologie mit Zeitschrift für Angewandte Psychologie*, *217*(4), 230–232. doi:10.1027/0044-3409.217.4.230

Menesini, E., Nocentini, A., Palladino, B. E., Frisén, A., Berne, S., Ortega-Ruiz, R., Calmaestra, J., Scheithauer, H., Schultze-Krumbholz, A., Luik, P., Naruskov, K., Blaya, C., Berthaud, J., & Smith, P. K. (2012). Cyberbullying definition among adolescents: A comparison across six European countries. *Cyberpsychology, Behavior, and Social Networking*, *15*(9), 455–463. doi:10.1089/cyber.2012.0040

Mesch, G. S. (2009). Parental mediation, online activities and cyberbullying. *Cyberpsychology & Behavior*, *12*(4), 387–393. doi:10.1089/cpb.2009.0068 PMID:19630583

Meshi, D., Tamir, D. I., & Heekeren, H. R. (2015). The emerging neuroscience of social media. *Trends in Cognitive Sciences*, *19*(12), 771–782. doi:10.1016/j.tics.2015.09.004 PMID:26578288

Mettler, K. (2023). *Let Her Play, A report on gender-based violence in video games*. Stanford University.

Meyers, M. (1994). News of battering. *Journal of Communication*, *44*(2), 47–63. doi:10.1111/j.1460-2466.1994.tb00676.x

Mey, J. (1985). *Whose Language: A Study in Linguistic Pragmatics*. John Benjamin Publishing Company. doi:10.1075/pbcs.3

Milford, T. S. (2015). Chapter. In J. Bailey & V. Steeves (Eds.), Revisiting Cyberfeminism: Theory as a Tool for Understanding Young Women's Experiences, eGirls, eCitizens (pp. 55–81). University of Ottawa Press.

Miller, J. D., & Hufstedler, S. M. (2009). *Cyberbullying knows no borders*. Australian Teacher Education Association, Paper presented at the Annual Conference of the Australian Teacher Education Association (ATEA) (Albury, Jun 28-Jul 1, 2009). (ED524610).

Miller, O. (2022). *Technology Facilitated Intimate Partner Violence Surged during Covid-19 Pandemic*. University of Kent, News Centre.

Mills, S. (1995). *Feminist Stylistics*. Routledge.

Mills, S. (2005). *Discourse*. Routledge.

Mishna, F., Saini, M., & Solomon, S. (2009). Ongoing and online: Children and youth's perceptions of cyber bullying. *Children and Youth Services Review*, *31*(12), 43. doi:10.1016/j.childyouth.2009.05.004

Mishra, S. (2020). From # MeToo to # MeTooIndia : News Domestication in Indian English Language Newspaper. *Journalism Studies*, *21*(5), 1–19. doi:10.1080/1461670X.2019.1709882

Mitchell, K. J., Ybarra, M., & Finkelhor, D. (2007). The relative importance of online victimization in understanding depression, delinquency, and substance use. *Child Maltreatment*, *12*(4), 314–324. doi:10.1177/1077559507305996 PMID:17954938

Moestue & Muggah. (2014). *Digitally enhanced child protection: How new technology can prevent violence against children in the Global South.* Igarape Institute. https://www.jstor.org/stable/resrep20658

Mogashoa, T. (2014). Understanding critical discourse analysis in qualitative research. *International Journal of Humanities Social Sciences and Education, 1*(7), 104–113. doi:10.5901/mjss.2014.v5n9p452

Mohanty, J. R., & Samantaray, S. (2017). Cyber Feminism: Unleashing Women Power through Technology. *Rupkatha Journal on Interdisciplinary Studies in Humanities, 9*(2), 328–336. doi:10.21659/rupkatha.v9n2.33

Mohurle, S., & Patil, M. (2017). A brief study of wannacry threat: Ransomware attack 2017. *International Journal of Advanced Research in Computer Science, 8*(5), 1938-1940.

Molenda, Z. A., Marchlewska, M., Rogoza, M., Michalski, P., Górska, P., Szczepańska, D., & Cislak, A. (2022). What makes an Internet troll? On the relationships between temperament (BIS/BAS), Dark Triad, and Internet trolling. *Cyberpsychology (Brno), 16*(5). Advance online publication. doi:10.5817/CP2022-5-11

Molla, R. (2020, March 12). *How coronavirus took over social media.* https://www.vox.com/recode/2020/3/12/21175570/coronavirus-covid-19-social-media-twitter-facebook-google

Molluzzo, J. C., Lawler, J., & Manneh, J. (2013). A Comprehensive Survey on Cyberbullying Perceptions at a Major Metropolitan University – Faculty Perspectives. *Information Systems Education Journal, 11*(3), 15-34. https://files.eric.ed.gov/fulltext/EJ1145042.pdf

Mooneeapen, O., Abhayawansa, S., Ramdhony, D., & Atchia, Z. (2022). New insights into the nexus between board characteristics and intellectual capital disclosure: The case of the emerging economy of Mauritius. *Journal of Accounting in Emerging Economies, 12*(1), 29–51. doi:10.1108/JAEE-12-2020-0322

Moor, L., & Anderson, J. R. (2019). A systematic literature review of the relationship between dark personality traits and antisocial online behaviours. *Personality and Individual Differences, 144*, 40–55. doi:10.1016/j.paid.2019.02.027

Moreau, E. (2017, June 2). *10 Popular Social Media Posting Trends.* Retrieved from Life wire: https://www.lifewire.com/popular-social-media-posting-trends-3486028

Moreno, M. A., Gower, A. D., Brittain, H., & Vaillancourt, T. (2019). Applying Natural Language Processing to Evaluate News Media Coverage of Bullying and Cyberbullying. *Prevention Science, 20*(8), 1274–1283. doi:10.100711121-019-01029-x PMID:31414277

Morgan, D. (2006). The Crisis in Masculinity. In K. Davis, M. Evans, & J. Lorber (Eds.), Handbook of gender and women's studies (pp. 109–123). Sage. doi:10.4135/9781848608023.n7

Morgan, J., & Politoff, V. (2012). *Victorian print media coverage of violence against women: A longitudinal study.* VicHealth.

Morris, E. W., & Ratajczak, K. (2019). Critical masculinity studies and research on Violence Against Women: An Assessment of past scholarship and Future Directions. *Violence Against Women, 25*(16), 1980–2006. doi:10.1177/1077801219875827 PMID:31718529

Morrow, J., & Nolen-Hoeksema, S. (1990). Effects of responses to depression on the remediation of depressive affect. *Journal of Personality and Social Psychology, 58*(3), 519–527. doi:10.1037/0022-3514.58.3.519 PMID:2324941

Morse, E. A., Raval, V., & Wingender, J. R. (2018). SEC cybersecurity guidelines: Insight into the utility of risk factor disclosures for investors. *Business Lawyer, 73*, 1–34.

Moya, P. (2014). Habit and embodiment in Merleau-Ponty. *Frontiers in Human Neuroscience*, *8*, 542. https://doi.org/10.3389/fnhum.2014.00542

Mudgway, C., & Jones, K. (2020, April 8). *As use of digital platforms surges, we'll need stronger global efforts to protect human rights online*. The Conversation. https://theconversation.com/as-use-of-digital-platforms-surges-well-need-stronger-global-efforts-to-protect-human-rights-online-135678

Muljadji, Y., Sekarningrum, B., & Muhammad, R. (2017). The Commodification of Religious Clothes Through The Social Media: The Identity Crisis on Youth Muslim Female in Urban Indonesia. *Romanian Journal of Journalism & Communication/Revista Romana De Jurnalism Si Comunicare-RRJC, 12*.

Munster, A. (1999). Is There Postlife After Postfeminism? Tropes of Technics and Life in Cyberfeminism. *Australian Feminist Studies*, *14*(29), 119–131. doi:10.1080/08164649993371

Mutsvairo, B. (2020). *Disenchanting or Demoralizing: Zimbabwean Women Share their Social Media Experience*. Women Empowerment for Leadership (WE4L). https://hivos.org/resource/disenchanting-or-demoralizing-zimbabwean-women-share-their-social-media-experience/

Muttakin, M. B., Khan, A., & Subramaniam, N. (2015). Firm characteristics, board diversity and corporate social responsibility: Evidence from Bangladesh. *Pacific Accounting Review*, *27*(3), 353–372. doi:10.1108/PAR-01-2013-0007

Muttreja & Wojnar. (2023, March 5). India needs to double down on bridging its digital gender gap. *Mint*. https://www.livemint.com/opinion/columns/india-needs-to-double-down-on-bridging-its-digital-gender-gap-11678040421197.html

Myers, C. A., & Cowie, H. (2017). Bullying at university: The social and legal contexts of cyberbullying among university students. *Journal of Cross-Cultural Psychology*, *48*(8), 1172–1182. doi:10.1177/0022022116684208

Myles, D. (2019). Anne goes rogue for abortion rights!: Hashtag feminism and the polyphonic nature of activist discourse. *New Media & Society*, *21*(2), 507–527. doi:10.1177/1461444818800242

Myung, J. W., & Hong, S. (2019). ICS malware Triton attack and countermeasures. *Int. J. Emerg. Multidiscip. Res*, *3*, 13–17.

Nair, S. (2012). *Shame: 2 girls arrested for harmless online comment*. https://timesofindia.indiatimes.com/city/mumbai/shame-2-girls-arrested-for-harmless-online-comment/articleshow/17286105.cms

National Portal of India. (n.d.). *The Group of Twenty (G20)*. Retrieved June 5, 2023, from https://www.india.gov.in/spotlight/group-twenty-g20

Navarro, R., Larranaga, E., & Yubero, S. (2011). S. Bullying-victimization problems and aggressive tendencies in Spanish secondary school students: The role of gender stereotypical traits. *Social Psychology of Education*, *14*(4), 457–473. doi:10.100711218-011-9163-1

NCRB. (n.d.). *Crimes in India 2020: Statistics Volume I*. National Crime Records Bureau (Ministry of Home Affairs). https://ncrb.gov.in/sites/default/files/CII%202020%20Volume%201.pdf

Neifar, S., & Jarboui, A. (2018). Corporate governance and operational risk voluntary disclosure: Evidence from Islamic banks. *Research in International Business and Finance*, *46*, 43–54. doi:10.1016/j.ribaf.2017.09.006

Nielsen. (2022, June 27). *Nielsen's Bharat 2.0 Study reveals a 45% growth in Active Internet Users in rural India since 2019*. Nielsen. https://www.nielsen.com/news-center/2022/nielsens-bharat-2-0-study-reveals-a-45-growth-in-active-internet-users-in-rural-india-since-2019/

Nisbett, R. E., & Cohen, D. (1996). *Culture of honor: The psychology of violence in the South*. Westview Press.

Nixon, C. (2016). Current perspectives: The impact of cyberbullying on adolescent health. *Adolescent Health, Medicine and Therapeutics*, *5*(5), 143–158. https://doi.org/10.2147/ahmt.s36456

Nockleyby, J. (2000). *'Hate speech in Encyclopedia of the American Constitution*. Electron. J. Acad. Spec. Libr.

Nortajuddin, A. (2020, March 30). Virus Lockdown Causing Rise In Domestic Abuse. *The ASEAN Post*. https://theaseanpost.com/article/virus-lockdown-causing-rise-domestic-abuse

Nozza, D., Volpetti, C., & Fersini, E. (2019). Unintended bias in misogyny detection. *Proceedings - 2019 IEEE/WIC/ACM International Conference on Web Intelligence, WI 2019*, 149–155. 10.1145/3350546.3352512

O'Dea, S. (2022). *Global internet user growth 2018-2023*. https://www.statista.com/statistics/1190263/internet-users-worldwide/

O'Kearney, R. (1996). Attachment disruption in anorexia nervosa and bulimia nervosa: A review of theory and empirical research. *International Journal of Eating Disorders*, *20*(2), 115–127. doi:10.1002/(SICI)1098-108X(199609)20:2<115::AID-EAT1>3.0.CO;2-J PMID:8863063

Odia, O. U. (2016). *A Study of University Students' Perceptions and Usage Behaviour of Mobile Media Technologies in Nigeria*. University of Leicester.

OECD. (2018). *Bridging the digital gender divide*. https://www.oecd.org/internet/bridging-the-digital-gender-divide.pdf

Ofcom. (2017). *Rise of the Social Seniors revealed*. Ofcom. Available at: *https://www.ofcom.org.uk/about-ofcom/latest/media/media-releases/2017/rise-social-seniors*

OHCHR. (2011). *Guiding Principles on Business and Human rights Implementing the United Nations "Protect, Respect and Remedy" Framework*. OHCHR. https://www.ohchr.org/Documents/Publications/GuidingPrinciplesBusinessHR_EN.pdf

Oliveira, J., Lima Rodrigues, L., & Craig, R. (2011). Risk-related disclosures by non-finance companies: Portuguese practices and disclosure characteristics. *Managerial Auditing Journal*, *26*(9), 817–839. doi:10.1108/02686901111171466

Ortiz, S. M. (2020). Trolling as a collective form of harassment: An inductive study of how online users understand trolling. *Social Media + Society*, *6*(2). doi:10.1177/2056305120928512

Outlook India Magazine Online- Read News India, Latest News Analysis, World, Sports, Entertainment | Best Online Magazine India. (n.d.). Https://Www.Outlookindia.Com/. Retrieved June 3, 2023, from https://www.outlookindia.com

Outlook India: Best Online Magazine India, Latest News, Story. (2023, May 23). Https://Www.Outlookindia.Com/. https://www.outlookindia.com

Outlook Web Desk. (2022, September 30). *SC's Observations "Welcome" But Marital Rape Still Not Illegal In India, Here Are Countries Where It Is*. Https://Www.Outlookindia.Com/. https://www.outlookindia.com/national/sc-observations-welcome-but-omarital-rape-still-not-illegal-in-india-here-are-countries-where-it-is-news-226913

Oyosoro, F. I., Okafor, C. I., & Aigbe, R. (2022). The #EndSARS protest and Black cyberfeminism: A study of the Feminist Coalition and the rise of cyber-feminist ideologies in Nigeria. *Gender, Technology and Development*, *26*(3), 485–502. Advance online publication. doi:10.1080/09718524.2022.2144099

Paasonen, S. (2011). *Revisiting cyberfeminism. 36*(3), 335–352. doi:10.1515/comm.2011.017

Padte, R. K. (2015, February 19). *Sexist remarks, stalking and rape threats: how women are punished for speaking online*. Scroll.in. https://scroll.in/article/707639/sexist-remarks-stalking-and-rape-threats-how-women-are-punished-for-speaking-online

Panova, T., & Carbonell, X. (2018). Is Smartphone Addiction Really an Addiction? *Journal of Behavioral Addictions*, *7*(2), 252–259. doi:10.1556/2006.7.2018.49 PMID:29895183

Pan, Z., & Kosicki, G. M. (1993). Framing analysis: An approach to news discourse. *Political Communication*, *10*(1), 55–75. doi:10.1080/10584609.1993.9962963

Papapicco, C., & Quatera, I. (2019). "Do not Make to eat to Troll!": The Dark Side of Web. *Online Journal of Communication and Media Technologies*, *9*(2), e201910. doi:10.29333/ojcmt/5764

Park, J. (2012). Cyber Crime: Concepts, Methodologies, Tools, and Applications. Academic Press.

Pasricha, J. (2016). *Violence Online in India: Cybercrimes Against Women and Minorities on Social Media*. https://www.comminit.com/content/violence-online-india-cybercrimes-against-women-and-minorities-social-media

Pasricha, J. (2021). *"Violence" Online in India: Cybercrimes against women and minorities on social media*. https://feminisminindia.com/wp-content/uploads/2021/08/Cyberviolence-Against-Women-in-India_Research-Report_FII.pdf

Pasricha, J. (2021, August). *"Violence" Online in India: Cybercrimes Against Women and Minorities on Social Media*. Retrieved January 25, 2023, from Feminism India: https://feminisminindia.com/wp-content/uploads/2021/08/Cyberviolence-Against-Women-in-India_Research-Report_FII.pdf

Patton, E., & Appelbaum, S. H. (2003). The case for case studies in management research. *Management Research News*, *26*(5), 60–71. doi:10.1108/01409170310783484

Paulhus, D. L. (2014). Toward a taxonomy of dark personalities. *Current Directions in Psychological Science*, *23*(6), 421–426. doi:10.1177/0963721414547737

Pavlopoulos, J., Sorensen, J., Laugier, L., & Androutsopoulos, I. (2021). SemEval-2021 Task 5: Toxic Spans Detection. *Proceedings of the 15th International Workshop on Semantic Evaluation (SemEval-2021)*, (pp. 59–69). ACL. 10.18653/v1/2021.semeval-1.6

Pearson, J. (2016). *Scientists invented a tool to expose 4chan's racist trolling campaigns*. Motherboard. Available at: https://motherboard.vice.com/en_us/article/block-4chan-to-stopthe-alt-right-from-spreading-racist-memes-scientists-say

Peristiany, J. G. (1965). *Honor and shame: The values of Mediterranean society*. Weidenfeld and Nicolson.

Perspective API. (2021). *Home*. Perspective API. https://perspectiveapi.com/

PettyJohn, M. E., Muzzey, F. K., Maas, M. K., & McCauley, H. L. (2018). #HowIWillChange: Engaging Men and Boys in the #MeToo Movement. *Psychology of Men & Masculinity*, (October). Advance online publication. doi:10.1037/men0000186

Pew Research Centre. (2021). *The State of Online Harassment*. Author.

Pew Research Centre. (2021). *The State of Online Harassment*. Pew Research Center.

Pfeffer, J., & Salancik, G. R. (2003). *The External Control of Organizations: A Resource Dependence Perspective*. Stanford University Press.

Pham, M. H. T. (2015). "I click and post and breathe, waiting for others to see what I see": On# FeministSelfies, outfit photos, and networked vanity. *Fashion Theory*, *19*(2), 221–241. doi:10.2752/175174115X14168357992436

Philips, F., & Morrissey, G. (2004). Cyberstalking and cyberpredators: A threat to safe sexuality on the internet. *Convergence (London)*, *10*(1), 66–79. doi:10.1177/135485650401000105

Phillips, W. (2011). Meet the trolls. *Index on Censorship*, *40*(2), 68–76. doi:10.1177/0306422011409641

Phillips, W. (2013). The house that fox built: Anonymous, spectacle, and cycles of amplification. *Television & New Media, 14*(6), 494–509. doi:10.1177/1527476412452799

Phillips, W. (2015). *This is why we can't have nice things: Mapping the relationship between online trolling and mainstream culture.* MIT Press. doi:10.7551/mitpress/10288.001.0001

Pierce, C. S. (1994). Peirce on Signs: Writings on Semiotic. In J. Hoopes (Ed.). University of North Carolina Press.

Pierce, J., & Russell, L. (2022). *Cyberfeminism Index.* Inventory Press.

Pitt-Rivers, J. A. (1977). *The fate of shechem: Or, the politics of sex: Essays in the anthropology of the Mediterranean.* Cambridge University Press.

Plant, S. (1997, January 27). Babes in the Net. *New Statesman & Society*, p. 28.

Plant, S. (2020). On the Matrix: Cyberfeminist simulations. In T. Thomas & U. Wischermann (Eds.), Feminist Theory and Critical Analysis of Media Culture (pp. 337–346). Transcript Verlag. https://doi.org/10.14361/9783839440841-030.

Plant, S. (1995). The Future Looms: Weaving Women and Cybernetics. *Body & Society, 1*(3–4), 45–64. doi:10.1177/1357034X95001003003

Pokin, S. (2007, Nov. 13). Megan Meier story. *St. Charles Journal.*

Polce-Lynch, M., Myers, B. J., Kliewer, W., & Kilmartin, C. (2001). Adolescent self-esteem and gender: Exploring relations to sexual harassment, body image, media influence, and emotional expression. *Journal of Youth and Adolescence, 30*(2), 225–244. doi:10.1023/A:1010397809136

Police suspect cyber bullying behind MBBS student's death TNN. (2017). https://timesofindia.indiatimes.com/city/kozhikode/police-suspect-cyber-bullying-behind-mbbs-students-death/articleshow/61684722.cms

Polivy, J., & Herman, C. P. (2002). Causes of eating disorders. *Annual Review of Psychology, 53*(1), 187–213. doi:10.1146/annurev.psych.53.100901.135103 PMID:11752484

Prime, H., Wade, M., & Browne, D. T. (2020). Risk and resilience in family well-being during the COVID-19 pandemic. *The American Psychologist, 75*(5), 631–643. doi:10.1037/amp0000660 PMID:32437181

Puhakka, A. (2021). Sofie's World: Resistance toward the Thin Ideal in Sofie Hagen's Fat Activist Online Content. In Appearance as Capital: The Normative Regulation of Aesthetic Capital Accumulation and Conversion (pp. 135–148). Emerald Group Publishing Ltd. doi:10.1108/978-1-80043-708-120210009

Punekar. (2021, August 14). Mumbai: Woman Claims Marital Rape Led To Her Paralysis, Court Says "It Is Not Illegal To Have Relationship With Wife Without Her Consent." *Punekar News.* https://www.punekarnews.in/mumbai-woman-claims-marital-rape-led-to-her-paralysis-court-says-it-is-not-illegal-to-have-relationship-with-wife-without-her-consent/

Purba, K. R., Asirvatham, D., & Murugesan, R. K. (2021). Instagram post popularity trend analysis and prediction using hashtag, image assessment, and user history features. *The International Arab Journal of Information Technology, 18*(1), 85–94. doi:10.34028/iajit/18/1/10

Rajagopal, K. (2021, August 14). Courts continue to differ in views on marital rape. *The Hindu.* https://www.thehindu.com/news/national/courts-continue-to-differ-in-views-on-marital-rape/article61430217.ece

Rakow, L. F. (1986). *Feminist Approaches to Technology: Implications for Communications Scholarship.*

Ramakrishnan, N. (2017). Use of Whatsapp for English language proficiency. *International Journal of Research, 5*, 1–6.

Randall, M., & Haskell, L. (1995). Sexual violence in women's lives: Findings from the Women's Safety Project, a community-based survey. *Violence Against Women*, *1*(1), 6–31. doi:10.1177/1077801295001001002 PMID:12346573

Rao, K., & Tilt, C. (2016). Board diversity and CSR reporting: An Australian study. *Meditari Accountancy Research*, *24*(2), 182–210. doi:10.1108/MEDAR-08-2015-0052

Rasul, T., Hoque, M. R., & Arefin, M. S. (2020). Social media for web-communities of female entrepreneurs: A PRISMA-compliant exploration. *International Journal of Web Based Communities*, *16*(4), 396–409. doi:10.1504/IJWBC.2020.111379

Ratele, K. (2016). *Liberating masculinities*. HSRC Press.

Rathi, S., & Chaudhary, V. (2023). Effect of Eye Yoga and Mindful Relaxation Practices on Management of Digital Eye Strain in a Tertiary Care Hospital: A Comparative Interventional Study. *Journal for ReAttach Therapy and Developmental Diversities*, *6*(8s), 40–44.

Ravindra, M. J. P. & S. (n.d.). *Management Principles and Applications (For Sem.- 3rd, Utkal University, Odisha)*. Vikas Publishing House.

Ravishankar, V., Boni, B. V., & Karananou, A. (n.d.). *Engaging on cyber security: Results of the PRI collaborative engagement 2017-2019*. PRI. Retrieved 25 May 2023, from https://www.unpri.org/cyber-security/engaging-on-cyber-security-results-of-the-pri-collaborative-engagement-2017-2019/5680.article

Recognizing and Combating Technology-Facilitated Abuse. (2016, October 13). NNEDV. https://nnedv.org/latest_update/combating-technology-facilitated-abuse/

Reid, S. (2023). *Dealing with Revenge Porn and "Sextortion"*. helpGuide.org

Rentschler, C. (2014). Rape Culture and the Feminist Politics of Social Media. *Girlhood Studies, 7*.

Retallack, H., Ringrose, J., & Lawrence, E. (2016). "Fuck Your Body Image": Teen girls' Twitter and Instagram feminism in and around school. *Learning Bodies - Perspectives on Children and Young People, 2*, 85–103. doi:10.2307/j.ctv62hhgr

Reuters. (2020, January 23). *India Today*. Retrieved February 1, 2023, from https://www.indiatoday.in/india/story/women-politicians-abused-social-media-amnesty-study-1639432-2020-01-23

Ribeiro, M. T., Singh, S., & Guestrin, C. (2016). "Why should i trust you?" Explaining the predictions of any classifier. *Proceedings of the 22nd ACM SIGKDD International Conference on Knowledge Discovery and Data Mining*, (pp. 1135–1144). ACM. 10.1145/2939672.2939778

Richard, G. T. (2017). *Video Games, Gender, Diversity, and Learning as Cultural Practice: Implications for Equitable Learning and Computing Participation Through Games.* Educational Technology Publications. *Inc.*

Richard, G. T., & Gray, K. L. (2018). Gendered Play, Racialized Reality: Black Cyberfeminism, Inclusive Communities of Practice, and the Intersections of Learning, Socialization, and Resilience in Online Gaming. *Frontiers*, *39*(1), 112–148. doi:10.1353/fro.2018.a690812

Rietveld, R., van Dolen, W., Mazloom, M., & Worring, M. (2020). What You Feel, Is What You Like Influence of Message Appeals on Customer Engagement on Instagram. *Journal of Interactive Marketing*, *49*(1), 20–53. doi:10.1016/j.intmar.2019.06.003

Rivers, N. (2017a). Celebrity Feminists: Selling Feminism or Feminism Selling Out? In Postfeminism(s) and the Arrival of the Fourth Wave: Turning Tides (pp. 1–162). doi:10.1007/978-3-319-59812-3

Roberto, K. A., McCann, B. R., & Brossoie, N. (2013). Intimate partner violence in late life: An analysis of national news reports. *Journal of Elder Abuse & Neglect*, *25*(3), 230–241. doi:10.1080/08946566.2012.751825 PMID:23627429

Rodgers, R. F., Paxton, S. J., & Wertheim, E. H. (2021). Take idealized bodies out of the picture: A scoping review of social media content aiming to protect and promote positive body image. In *Body Image* (Vol. 38, pp. 10–36). Elsevier Ltd. doi:10.1016/j.bodyim.2021.03.009

Rodino-colocino, M. (2014). #YesAllWomen: Intersectional Mobilization Against Sexual Assault is Radical (Again). *Feminist Media Studies, 14*(6), 1113–1115. doi:10.1080/14680777.2014.975475

Rodriguez Mosquera, P. M., Fischer, A. H., Manstead, A. S. R., & Zaalberg, R. (2008). Attack, disapproval, or withdrawal? The role of honour in anger and shame responses to being insulted. *Cognition and Emotion, 22*(8), 1471–1498. doi:10.1080/02699930701822272

Rodriguez Mosquera, P. M., Manstead, A. S. R., & Fischer, A. H. (2002a). Honor in the Mediterranean and Northern Europe. *Journal of Cross-Cultural Psychology, 33*(1), 16–36. doi:10.1177/0022022102033001002

Rodriguez Mosquera, P. M., Manstead, A. S. R., & Fischer, A. H. (2002b). The role of honor concerns in emotional reactions to offenses. *Cognition and Emotion, 16*(1), 143–163. doi:10.1080/02699930143000167

Rollero, C., & De Piccoli, N. (2017). Self-objectification and personal values. An exploratory study. *Frontiers in Psychology, 8*, 1055. doi:10.3389/fpsyg.2017.01055

Rose, A. J. (2002). Co-rumination in the friendships of girls and boys. *Child Development, 73*(6), 1830–1843. doi:10.1111/1467-8624.00509 PMID:12487497

RossB.RistM.CarbonellG.CabreraB.KurowskyN.WojatzkiM. (2017). *Measuring the Reliability of Hate Speech Annotations: The Case of the European Refugee Crisis.* doi:10.17185/duepublico/42132

Rosser, S. V. (2004). *The science glass ceiling: Academic women scientists and the struggle to succeed.* Psychology Press.

Rothrock, R. A., Kaplan, J., & van Oord, F. (2018). The board's role in managing cybersecurity risks. *MIT Sloan Management Review, 59*, 12–15.

Rumelhart, D. E., Hinton, G. E., & Williams, R. J. (1985). *Learning internal representations by error propagation.*

Russell, L. (2020). *Glitch Feminism: A Manifesto.* Verso Books.

Saggar, R., Arora, N., & Singh, B. (2022). Gender diversity in corporate boardrooms and risk disclosure: Indian evidence. *Gender in Management, 37*(2), 182–201. doi:10.1108/GM-06-2020-0174

Saggar, R., & Singh, B. (2017). Corporate governance and risk reporting: Indian evidence. *Managerial Auditing Journal, 32*(4/5), 378–405. doi:10.1108/MAJ-03-2016-1341

Sakallı Uğurlu, N., & Akbaş, G. (2013). "Honor" and "honor violence" against women in honor cultures: Social psychological explanations. *Turkish Psychological Articles, 16*(32), 76–91. https://www.psikolog.org.tr/tr/yayinlar/dergiler/1031828/tpy1301996120130000m000089.pdf

Sakallı, N. (2001). Beliefs about wife beating among Turkish college students: The effects of patriarchy, sexism and sex difference. *Sex Roles, 44*(9/10), 599–611. doi:10.1023/A:1012295109711

Salazar, E. (2017). Hashtags 2.0 - An annotated history of the hashtag and a window to its future. *Revista ICONO14 Revista Científica de Comunicación y Tecnologías Emergentes, 15*(2), 16. doi:10.7195/ri14.v15i2.1091

Sameeran, P. (2016). *Arrow Perfect Grammar Class 2.* Arrow Publications Private Limited.

Samundeeswari, S., & Vijaya, K. (2022). Cyberbullying: Harmful impact of technology. *International Journal of Creative Research Thoughts, 10*(2), 850–855. https://ijcrt.org/papers/IJCRT2202339.pdf

Sánchez, V., Muñoz-Fernández, N., & Ortega-Ruíz, R. (2015). 'Cyberdating Q_A': An Instrument to Assess the Quality of Adolescent Dating Relationships in Social Networks. *Computers in Human Behavior*, *48*, 78–86. doi:10.1016/j.chb.2015.01.006

Sandelowski, M. (2011). "Casing" the research case study. *Research in Nursing & Health*, *34*(2), 153–159. doi:10.1002/nur.20421 PMID:21381044

Sanfilippo, M. R., Fichman, P., & Yang, S. (2018). Multidimensionality of online trolling behaviors. *The Information Society*, *34*(1), 27–39. doi:10.1080/01972243.2017.1391911

Sanfilippo, M. R., Yang, S., & Fichman, P. (2017a). Trolling here, there, and everywhere: Perceptions of trolling behaviors in context. *Journal of the Association for Information Science and Technology*, *68*(10), 2313–2337. doi:10.1002/asi.23902

Sanfilippo, M., Yang, S., & Fichman, P. (2017). Managing online trolling: From deviant to social and political trolls. *Proceedings of the 50th Hawaii International Conference on System Sciences*. 10.24251/HICSS.2017.219

Sanjeev, P. (2019). Cyber Crime Against Women: Right to Privacy and Other Issues. *Journal of Legal Studies and Research, 5*(5).

Sargent, K. S., Krauss, A., Jouriles, E. N., & McDonald, R. (2016). Cyber victimization, psychological intimate partner violence, and problematic mental health outcomes among first-year college students. *Cyberpsychology, Behavior, and Social Networking*, *19*(9), 545–550. doi:10.1089/cyber.2016.0115 PMID:27548623

Sarkhel, S., Singh, O. P., & Arora, M. (2020). Clinical practice guidelines for psychoeducation in psychiatric disorders general principles of psychoeducation. *Indian Journal of Psychiatry*, *62*(8, Suppl 2), S319. doi:10.4103/psychiatry.IndianJPsychiatry_780_19 PMID:32055073

Sattar, G., Safeer, A. K., Pasha, M. I., Furqan, K. M. Y., & Riaz, N. (2021). Stereotypical ideologies towards women: Feminist poststructuralist discourse analysis of Malala Yousafzai's political speeches. *Humanities & Social Sciences Reviews*, *9*(3), 1245–1257. doi:10.18510/hssr.2021.93123

Saussure, F. (1959). *Course in General Linguistics*. Columbia University Press.

Schelfhout, Bowers, & Hao. (2021). *Balancing Gender Identity and Gamer Identity: Gender Issues Faced by Wang 'BaiZe' Xinyu at the 2017 Hearthstone Summer Championship.* Sage Publications, Ltd. doi:10.1177/1555412019866348

Schell, B. H., & Melnychuk, J. (2011). Corporate Hacking and Technology-Driven Crime: Social Dynamics and Implications. Academic Press.

Schlesselman-Tarango, G. (2014). Cyborgs in the Academic Library: A Cyberfeminist Approach to Information Literacy Instruction. *Behavioral & Social Sciences Librarian*, *33*(1), 29–46. https://doi.org/10.1080/01639269.2014.872529

Schmidt, A., & Wiegand, M. (2017). *A Survey on Hate Speech Detection using Natural Language Processing*. Wikipedia. https://en.wikipedia.org/wiki/List_

Schubert, R. (2006). Analyzing and managing risks – on the importance of gender differences in risk attitudes. *Managerial Finance*, *32*(9), 706–715. doi:10.1108/03074350610681925

Schuster, J. (2013). Invisible feminists? Social media and young women's political participation. *Political Science (Wellington, N.Z.)*, *65*(1), 8–24. doi:10.1177/0032318713486474

Schwarz, M., Scherrer, A., Hohmann, C., Heiberg, J., Brugger, A., & Nuñez-Jimenez, A. (2020). COVID-19 and the academy: It is time for going digital. *Energy Research & Social Science*, *68*, 101684. doi:10.1016/j.erss.2020.101684 PMID:32839703

Scott, P. (2019). *Introduction to Management Accounting*. Oxford University Press.

SEC cybersecurity disclosure: A how-to guide. (2018, July 9). IFLR. https://www.iflr.com/article/2a63bsmabqyzreejoirk0/sec-cybersecurity-disclosure-a-how-to-guide

SEC. (2018). *Commission statement and guidance on public company cybersecurity disclosures.* Security Exchange Commission. Retrieved from https://www.sec.gov/rules/interp/2018/33-10459.pdf

SEC. (2021a, August 30). *SEC Announces Three Actions Charging Deficient Cybersecurity Procedures.* Retrieved from US Securities and Exchange Commission: https://www.sec.gov/news/press-release/2021-169

SEC. (2021b, June 15). *SEC Charges Issuer With Cybersecurity Disclosure Controls Failures.* Retrieved from US Securities and Exchange Commission: https://www.sec.gov/news/press-release/2021-102

Seets, C., & Niemann, P. (2022, October 2). How cyber governance and disclosures are closing the gaps in 2022. *The Harvard Law School Forum on Corporate Governance.* https://corpgov.law.harvard.edu/2022/10/02/how-cyber-governance-and-disclosures-are-closing-the-gaps-in-2022/

Seets, C., Brorsen, L., & Klemash, S. (2018, October 21). Cybersecurity Disclosure Benchmarking. *The Harvard Law School Forum on Corporate Governance.* https://corpgov.law.harvard.edu/2018/10/21/cybersecurity-disclosure-benchmarking/

Seigfried-Spellar, K. C., & Chowdhury, S. S. (2017). Death and Lulz: Understanding the personality characteristics of RIP trolls. *First Monday.* Advance online publication. doi:10.5210/fm.v22i11.7861

Senft, T. M. (2008). *Camgirls: Celebrity and Community in the Age of Social Networks.* Peter Lang.

Serdar Tekeli, E. (2016). Kadın cinayetlerinin haberleştirilmesi bağlamında medya etiğini yeniden tartışmak: Habertürk gazetesi örneği. *Abant Kültürel Araştırmalar Dergisi, 1*(1), 129-142. https://dergipark.org.tr/en/pub/akader/issue/28202/299477

Sest, N., & March, E. (2017). Constructing the cyber-troll: Psychopathy, sadism, and empathy. *Personality and Individual Differences, 119*, 69–72. doi:10.1016/j.paid.2017.06.038

Seth, K. (2018). *Cyber Crime Against Women.* Published in New Delhi.

Sev'er, A., & Yurdakul, G. (2001). Culture of honor, culture of change: A feminist analysis of honor killings in Turkey. *Violence Against Women, 7*(9), 964–998. doi:10.1177/10778010122182866

Shachaf, P., & Hara, N. (2010). Beyond vandalism: Wikipedia trolls. *Journal of Information Science, 36*(3), 357–370. doi:10.1177/0165551510365390

Shah, B. (2018, June 27). *India snags the first rank—It's the world's most dangerous country for women.* YourStory.Com. https://yourstory.com/2018/06/india-snags-first-rank-list-worlds-worst-places-live-women

Shah, N. (2015). The selfie and the slut: Bodies, technology and public shame. *Economic and Political Weekly*, 86–93.

Shah, R., & Tewari, R. (2016). Demystifying 'selfie': A rampant social media activity. *Behaviour & Information Technology, 35*(10), 864–871. doi:10.1080/0144929X.2016.1201693

Sharma, Nardi, Norton, & Tsaasan. (2019, Sep). Towards safe spaces online: A study of Indian matrimonial websites. *17th IFIP Conference on Human-Computer Interaction (INTERACT),* 43-66. . hal-0255387910.1007/978-3-030-29387-1_4

Shata, A., & Seelig, M. I. (2021). The Dragonfly Effect: Analysis of the Social Media Women's Empowerment Campaign. *Journal of Creative Communications, 16*(3), 331–346. doi:10.1177/09732586211036551

Shaw, A., & Friesem, E. (2016). Where Is the Queerness in Games? Types of Lesbian, Gay, Bisexual, Transgender, and Queer Content in Digital Games. *International Journal of Communication*. https://www.semanticscholar.org/paper/Where-is-the-Queerness-in-Games%3A-Types-of-Lesbian%2C-Shaw-Friesem/9c68711e2af254ffc625f0616f94007b139aad3c

Shimizu, A. (2013). Recent developments: domestic violence in the digital age: Towards the creation of a comprehensive cyberstalking statute. *Berkeley Journal of Gender, Law & Justice*, 116–117.

Shulman, S., & Connolly, J. (2013). The Challenge of Romantic Relationships in Emerging Adulthood. *Sage, 1*(1), 27–39. doi:10.1177/2167696812467330

Silverstein, S. (2019). Women's March Colloquy - On Sirens and Lamp Posts: Sound, Space, and Affective Politics. *Music and Politics, 13*(1). Advance online publication. doi:10.3998/mp.9460447.0013.103

Simon, D., Sweeney, J., Rosenfeld, R., & Mohan, V. (2021, July 25). SEC Increasingly Turns Focus Toward Strength of Cyber Risk Disclosures. *The Harvard Law School Forum on Corporate Governance*. https://corpgov.law.harvard.edu/2021/07/25/sec-increasingly-turns-focus-toward-strength-of-cyber-risk-disclosures/

Singh, R., Choudhary, N., & Shrivastava, M. (2018). Automatic normalization of word variations in code-mixed social media text. *ArXiv Preprint ArXiv:1804.00804*.

Singh, K. A., & Choudhary, J. (2012). *Violence against Women and Children-Issues and Concerns*. Serials Publications.

Slovic, P., Malmfors, T., Mertz, C. K., Neil, N., & Purchase, I. F. (1997). Evaluating chemical risks: Results of a survey of the British Toxicology Society. *Human and Experimental Toxicology, 16*(6), 289–304. doi:10.1177/096032719701600601 PMID:9219024

Smith, P. K., del Barrio, C., & Tokunaga, R. S. (2013). Definitions of bullying and cyberbullying: how useful are the terms? In S. Bauman, D. Cross, & J. Walker (Eds.), *Principles of Cyberbullying Research: Definitions, Measures, and Methodology* (pp. 26–40). Routledge/Taylor & Francis Group.

Snow, D. A., & Anderson, L. (1987). Identity work among the homeless: The verbal construction and avowal of personal identities. *American Journal of Sociology, 92*(6), 1336–1371. doi:10.1086/228668

Sobande, F. (2021). Spectacularized and Branded Digital (Re)presentations of Black people and Blackness. *Television & New Media, 22*(2), 131–146. doi:10.1177/1527476420983745

Song, H., Witt, S. F., & Jensen, T. C. (2003). Tourism forecasting: Accuracy of alternative econometric models. *International Journal of Forecasting, 19*(1), 123–141. doi:10.1016/S0169-2070(01)00134-0

Sontag, S. (2001). *On photography* (Vol. 48). Macmillan.

Sosyalistfeministkolektif.org. (2012). *Şefika Etik davası: Kadın bedeninden ölüme gerekçe yaratmak.* Retrieved from http://www.sosyalistfeministkolektif.org/kampanyalar/istanbul-feminist-kolektif/kadn-cinayetlerine-isyandayz/efika-etik-davas-kadn-bedeninden-oelueme-gerekce-yaratmak/

Spender, D. (1995). *Nattering on the Net: Women, Power and Cyberspace*. Spinifex Press.

Sreelakshmi, K., Premjith, B., & Soman, K. P. (2020). Detection of Hate Speech Text in Hindi-English Code-mixed Data. *Procedia Computer Science, 171*, 737–744. doi:10.1016/j.procs.2020.04.080

Srinidhi, B., Gul, F. A., & Tsui, J. (2011). Female Directors and Earnings Quality*. *Contemporary Accounting Research, 28*(5), 1610–1644. doi:10.1111/j.1911-3846.2011.01071.x

Srmtech. (2022, March 24). *2021 Kerala HC remarks on marital rape that set a precedent*. The Federal. https://thefederal.com/analysis/2021-kerala-hc-remarks-on-marital-rape-that-set-a-precedent/

Staff, F. P. (2020, May 6). Delhi Police arrests Instagram group admin in bois locker room case; 27 other members identified. *Firstpost*. https://www.firstpost.com/india/delhi-police-arrests-instagram-group-admin-in-bois-locker-room-case-27-other-members-identified-8337451.html

Stake, R. E. (1978). The Case Study Method in Social Inquiry. *Educational Researcher*, *7*(2), 5–8. doi:10.3102/0013189X007002005

Stanley, A. (1995). *Mothers and Daughters of Invention: Notes for a Revised History of Technology*. Rutgers University Press.

Starcevic, V., & Aboujaoude, E. (2015). Cyberchondria, cyberbullying, cybersuicide, cybersex: "new" psychopathologies for the 21st century? *World Psychiatry; Official Journal of the World Psychiatric Association (WPA)*, *14*(1), 97–100. doi:10.1002/wps.20195 PMID:25655165

Starmer, K. (2013). *Guidelines on prosecuting cases involving communications sent via social media*. Crown Prosecution Service.

Starr, M. (2016). Beyond Machine Dreams: Zen, Cyber-, and Transnational Feminisms in Ruth Ozeki's *A Tale for the Time Being*. *Meridians (Middletown, Conn.)*, *13*(2), 99–122. doi:10.2979/meridians.13.2.06

Statista. (2022, January 18). *Instagram users worldwide 2022*. Statista.

Steele, C. K. (2021). *Digital Black Feminism*. New York University Press. doi:10.18574/nyu/9781479808373.001.0001

Steeves, V., & Bailey, J. (2015). *EGirls, ECitizens: Putting Technology, Theory and Policy Into Dialogue with Girls' and Young Women's Voices*. University of Ottawa Press.

Steinberg, L., & Morris, A. S. (2001). Adolescent Development. *Annual Review of Psychology*, *52*(1), 83–110. doi:10.1146/annurev.psych.52.1.83 PMID:11148300

Steiner, L. (2014). Feminist Media Theory. In M. Fackler & R. S. Fortner (Eds.), The Handbook of Media and Mass Communication theory (pp. 359–379). John Wiley & Sons, Inc. doi:10.1002/9781118591178.ch20

Stemler, S. (2001). An overview of content analysis. *Practical Assessment, Research & Evaluation*, *7*(17), 1–6. doi:10.7275/z6fm-2e34

Stevens, G. (2007). Tactical Reversal or Re-Centring Whiteness? A Response to Green, Sonn, and Matsebula. *South African Journal of Psychology. Suid-Afrikaanse Tydskrif vir Sielkunde*, *37*(3), 425–430. doi:10.1177/008124630703700303

Stokes, A. M. (2022). Disruption of Library Services Due to Hospital Cyberattack: A Case Study. *Medical Reference Services Quarterly*, *41*(2), 204–212. doi:10.1080/02763869.2022.2054198 PMID:35511424

Stubbs-Richardson, M., Rader, N. E., & Cosby, A. G. (2018). Tweeting rape culture: Examining portrayals of victim blaming in discussions of sexual assault cases on Twitter. *Feminism & Psychology*, *28*(1), 90–108. doi:10.1177/0959353517715874

Sullivan, C. (2011). Digital identity — protection. *Digital Identity: An Emergent Legal Concept*, 107–136. https://www.jstor.org/stable/10.20851/j.ctt1sq5wqb.12

Sumter, S. R., Vandenbosch, L., & Ligtenberg, L. (2017). Love Me Tinder: Untangling Emerging Adults' Motivations for Using the Dating Application Tinder. *Telematics and Informatics*, *34*(1), 67–78. doi:10.1016/j.tele.2016.04.009

Sun, H., & Fichman, P. (2018). Chinese collective trolling. *Proceedings of the Association for Information Science and Technology*, *55*(1), 478–485. doi:10.1002/pra2.2018.14505501052

Susanna, P. (2011). Revisiting cyberfeminism. *Communications*, *36*, 335–352.

Sutikno, T., Handayani, L., Stiawan, D., Riyadi, M. A., & Subroto, I. M. I. (2016). WhatsApp, Viber and Telegram: Which is the best for instant messaging? *Iranian Journal of Electrical and Computer Engineering*, *6*(3), 909–914.

Swinson, K. C. (2013). *The Sexual Assault Severity Scale: A Comprehensive Measure of Assault Severity*. Dissertations. 199.

Synnott, J., Coulias, A., & Ioannou, M. (2017). Online trolling: The case of Madeleine McCann. *Computers in Human Behavior*, *71*, 70–78. doi:10.1016/j.chb.2017.01.053

Ta'amneh, A. (2017). The Effect of Using "Whats App Messenger" in learning English language among university students. *International Journal of Humanities and Applied Social Science*, *2*(2), 15–22.

Talbot, M. (1998). *Language and Gender*. Polity Press.

Tamale, S. (2022). *Decolonization and Afro-Feminism*. Daraja Press.

Tang, S. (2023). Gender Perspectives on Cyberbullying in Different Countries for Comparison. *Journal of Education, Humanities and Social Sciences*, *7*. https://www.researchgate.net/publication/367536292_Gender_Perspectives_on_Cyberbullying_in_Different_Countries_for_Comparison

Taylor, J., Johnston, J., & Whitehead, K. (2016). A Corporation in feminist clothing? Young women discuss the Dove real beaut campaign. *Critical Sociology*, *42*(1), 123–144. doi:10.1177/0896920513501355

Taylor, R. (2009). Slain and slandered: A content analysis of the portrayal of femicide in crime news. *Homicide Studies*, *13*(1), 21–49. doi:10.1177/1088767908326679

Tazi, M., & Oumlil, K. (2020). The Rise of Fourth-Wave Feminism in the Arab region? Cyberfeminism and Women's Activism at the Crossroads of the Arab Spring. *CyberOrient, 14*(1), 44–71. doi:10.1002/j.cyo2.20201401.0002

Terman, L. M., & Miles, C. C. (1936). *Sex and Personality*. McGraw-Hill.

The Dart Center. (2018, May 16). You Can Help! Online Harassment Survey. *Dart Blog*. https://dartcenter.org/blog/2018/05/you-can-help-online-harassment-survey

The New York Times Editorial Staff. (2019). Cyberbullying: A Deadly Trend. New York: The Rosen Publishing Group, Inc.

Thompson, J. (1998). *A Midia e a Modernidade: Uma Teoria Social da Midia*. Academic Press.

Thompson, L. (2018). "I can be your tinder nightmare": Harassment and misogyny in the online sexual marketplace. *Feminism & Psychology*, *28*(1), 69–89. doi:10.1177/0959353517720226

Thrift, N. (2006). Donna Haraway's Dreams. *Theory, Culture & Society*, *23*(7–8), 189–195. doi:10.1177/0263276406069231

Thrift, S. C. (2014). #YesAllWomen as feminist meme event. *Feminist Media Studies*, *14*(6), 1090–1092. doi:10.1080/14680777.2014.975421

Tifferet, S. (2020). Gender differences in social support on social network sites: A meta-analysis. *Cyberpsychology, Behavior, and Social Networking*, *23*(4), 199–209. doi:10.1089/cyber.2019.0516 PMID:32096662

Tifferet, S., & Vilnai-Yavetz, I. (2014). Gender differences in Facebook self-presentation: An international randomized study. *Computers in Human Behavior*, *35*, 388–399. doi:10.1016/j.chb.2014.03.016

Tifferet, S., & Vilnai-Yavetz, I. (2018). Self-presentation in LinkedIn portraits: Common features, gender, and occupational differences. *Computers in Human Behavior*, *80*, 33–48. doi:10.1016/j.chb.2017.10.013

Tiidenberg, K. (2017). "Nude selfies til I die"–making of 'sexy'in selfies. In *Sex in the Digital Age* (pp. 78–88). Routledge. doi:10.4324/9781315446240-8

Tingbani, I., Chithambo, L., Tauringana, V., & Papanikolaou, N. (2020). Board gender diversity, environmental committee and greenhouse gas voluntary disclosures. *Business Strategy and the Environment*, *29*(6), 2194–2210. doi:10.1002/bse.2495

Tiwari, G. (2014). *Understanding Laws Cyber Laws & Cyber Crimes*. Lexis Nexis Publication.

TNN. (2014, June 25). Girl kills self over Facebook harassment. *The Times of India*. https://timesofindia.indiatimes.com/city/kolkata/girl-kills-self-over-facebook%20harassment/articleshow/37211521.cms?utm_source=contentofinterest&utm_medium=text&utm_campaign=cppst

Today, I. (2017). *Gurmehar Kaur's mother to India Today*. https://www.indiatoday.in/india/story/gurmehar-kaur-mother-rajvinder-kaur-ramjas-college-delhi-university-963358-2017-03-01

Tokunaga, R. S. (2010). Following you home from school: A critical review and synthesis on research on cyber bullying victimization. *Computers in Human Behavior*, *26*(3), 277–287. doi:10.1016/j.chb.2009.11.014

Torchia, M., Calabrò, A., & Huse, M. (2011). Women Directors on Corporate Boards: From Tokenism to Critical Mass. *Journal of Business Ethics*, *102*(2), 299–317. doi:10.100710551-011-0815-z

Toto, G. A., & Scarinci, A. (2022). Cyberfeminism: A Relationship between Cyberspace, Technology, and the Internet. *Elementa. Intersections Between Philosophy, Epistemology and Empirical Perspectives*, *1*(1-2), 135–151. doi:10.7358/elem-2021-0102-tosc

Toto, G. A., & Scarinci, A. (2021). Cyberfeminism: A relationship between cyberspace, technology, and the Internet. Elementa. *Intersections Between Philosophy, Epistemology and Empirical Perspectives*, *1*(1-2), 135–151.

Towns, A. R. (2016). Geographies of Pain: #SayHerName and the fear of black women's mobility. *Women's Studies in Communication*, *39*(2), 122–126. doi:10.1080/07491409.2016.1176807

Toyana, M. (2020). Essay Series: African Journalism And Media In The Time Of Covid-19. Hashtags and Spectacles: Zimbabwe's Feminist Activists Find Online Avenues to Tackle Government's COVID-19 Clampdown, 1–13.

Travers, A. (2003). Parallel subaltern feminist counter publics in cyberspace. *Sociological Perspectives*, *46*(2), 223-237.

Tripathi, V. (2014). Cyber Laws India. *Cyber Laws India*. http://www.cyberlawsindia.net/

Trusolino, M. (2022). 'I wanna kill my rapist': Margaret Cho's #12daysofrage campaign as Promotional Digital Activism. *Communication and the Public*, *7*(3), 130–145. doi:10.1177/20570473221111200

Tuna, T., Akbas, E., Aksoy, A., Canbaz, M. A., Karabiyik, U., Gonen, B., & Aygun, R. (2016). User characterization for online social networks. *Social Network Analysis and Mining*, *6*(1), 1–28. doi:10.100713278-016-0412-3

Turay, P., Jr. (2016). *Are messaging apps considered social media?* LinkedIn. https://www.linkedin.com/pulse/messaging-apps- considered-social-media-peter-tur ay-jrc.

Turkle, S. (1999, November). Cyberspace and identity. *Contemporary Sociology*, *28*(6), 643–648. doi:10.2307/2655534

Turley, M. R., & Obrzut, J. E. (2012). Neuropsychological effects of posttraumatic stress disorder in children and adolescents. *Canadian Journal of School Psychology*, *27*(2), 166–182. doi:10.1177/0829573512440420

Twitter's policy on hateful conduct. (2023). Twitter. https://help.twitter.com/en/rules-and-policies/hateful-conduct-policy

Ullman, S. E., & Siegel, J. M. (1993). Victim-offender relationship and sexual assault. *Violence and Victims*, *8*(2), 121–134. doi:10.1891/0886-6708.8.2.121 PMID:8193054

UN Women – Asia-Pacific. (2020). *Social Media Monitoring on COVID-19 and Misogyny in Asia and the Pacific*. UN. https://asiapacific.unwomen.org/en/digital-library/publications/2020/10/ap-social-media-monitoring-on-covid-19-and-misogyny-in-asia-and-the-pacific

UN Women – Asia-Pacific. (2020). *The First 100 Days of the COVID-19 Outbreak in Asia and the Pacific*. UN. https://asiapacific.unwomen.org/en/digital-library/publications/2020/04/the-first-100-days-of-the-covid-19-outbreak-in-asia-and-the-pacific

UN Women. (2019). *Listen, believe, support: the power of mental health care for survivors of violence*. Available in: https://www.unwomen.org/en/news/stories/2019/3/feature-story-mental-health-care

Underberg, N. M., & Zorn, E. (2014). *Digital Ethnography: Anthropology, Narrative, and New Media*. University of Texas Press.

Underwood, M. K., & Ehrenreich, S. E. (2017). The power and the pain of adolescents' digital communication: Cyber victimization and the perils of lurking. *The American Psychologist*, *72*(2), 144–158. doi:10.1037/a0040429 PMID:28221066

United Nations. (1993). *Declaration on the Elimination of Violence against Women*. https://www.un.org/documents/ga/res/48/a48r104.htm

United Nations. (2020). *UN Secretary-General's policy brief: The impact of COVID-19 on women*. https://www.unwomen.org/-/media/headquarters/attachments/sections/library/publications/2020/policy-brief-the-impact-of-covid-19-on-women-en.pdf?la=en&vs=1406

United Nations. (2022). Uncertain times, unsettled lives: Shaping our future in a transforming world. *Human Development Report 2021-22*. https://hdr.undp.org/system/files/documents/global-report-document/hdr2021-22pdf_1.pdf

UNODC. (2020). *UNODC Cybercrime and Anti-Money Laundering Section*. https://www.unodc.org/documents/Advocacy-Section/ES_-_Ciberdelito_y_COVID-19_spanish.pdf

Urban, G. (1981). *Language as Social Semiotic: The Social Interpretation of Language and Meaning*.

Valentini, C., Romenti, S., Murtarelli, G., & Pizzetti, M. (2018). Digital visual engagement: Influencing purchase intentions on Instagram. *Journal of Communication Management (London)*, *22*(4), 362–381. doi:10.1108/JCOM-01-2018-0005

Vandello, J. A., & Cohen, D. (2003). Male honor and female fidelity: Implicit cultural scripts that perpetuate domestic violence. *Journal of Personality and Social Psychology*, *84*(5), 997–1010. doi:10.1037/0022-3514.84.5.997 PMID:12757144

Vandello, J. A., & Cohen, D. (2008). Culture, gender, and men's intimate partner violence. *Social and Personality Psychology Compass*, *2*(2), 652–667. doi:10.1111/j.1751-9004.2008.00080.x

Vandello, J. A., Cohen, D., Grandon, R., & Franiuk, R. (2009). Stand by your man: Indirect prescriptions for honorable violence and feminine loyalty in Canada, Chile, and the United States. *Journal of Cross-Cultural Psychology*, *40*(1), 81–104. doi:10.1177/0022022108326194

Varela, N. (2019). *Feminismo 4.0. La cuarta ola*. Ediciones B.

Veenstra, R., & Laninga-Wijnen, L. (2022). Peer network studies and interventions in adolescence. *Current Opinion in Psychology*, *44*, 157–163. doi:10.1016/j.copsyc.2021.09.015 PMID:34662775

Venditto, B., Set, B., & Amaambo, R. N. (2022). Sexualization and Dehumanization of Women By Social Media Users in Namibia. *Sexes*, *3*(3), 445–462. doi:10.3390exes3030033

Verheijen, A. J. P., & Spooren, W. P. M. S. (2017). *The impact of WhatsApp on Dutch youths' school writing*.

Verma, A. (2021, January 10). Gender, power, and resistance: the diversity in feminism. *IPleaders*. https://blog.ipleaders.in/gender-power-resistance-diversity-feminism/#:~:text=Gender%20resistant%20feminisms%20focus%20on

Verma, M., Haq, F., & Rai, G. (2018). Social media a tool of cyber feminism activism. *International Journal of Research Culture Society*, *2*(2), 488–497. https://ijrcs.org/wp-content/uploads/201802093.pdf

Vernadsky, V. (1926). Biosfera. Leningrad.

Viana, G. de C. S. (2019). *Ciberfeminismo e a (in) visibilidade da mulher negra youtuber*. Universidade Federal do Rio Grande do Norte.

VijayaraghavanP.LarochelleH.RoyD. (2021). *Interpretable Multi-Modal Hate Speech Detection*. https://arxiv.org/abs/2103.01616

Vineyard, J. (2014, October 16). You Don't Need to Care About Video Games to Care About Gamergate. *Vulture*. https://www.vulture.com/2014/10/why-you-should-care-about-gamergate.html

Vitolla, F., Raimo, N., Marrone, A., & Rubino, M. (2020). The role of board of directors in intellectual capital disclosure after the advent of integrated reporting. *Corporate Social Responsibility and Environmental Management*, *27*(5), 2188–2200. doi:10.1002/csr.1957

Wajcman, J. (2006). Review: Wajcman Confronts Cyberfeminism. *Social Studies of Science*, *36*(2), 321–327. doi:10.1177/0306312706058828

Wall, & David S. (2005). The Internet as a Conduit for Criminal Activity. In April Pattavina (Ed.), *Information Technology and the Criminal Justice System* (pp. 77–98). Sage Publications.

Wall, & David S. (2005). The Internet as a Conduit for Criminal Activity. In *Information Technology and the Criminal Justice System* (pp. 77–98). Sage Publications.

Walrave, M., & Heirman, W. (2011). Cyberbullying: Predicting victimisation and perpetration. *Children & Society*, *25*(1), 59–72. doi:10.1111/j.1099-0860.2009.00260.x

Walsh, M. J., & Baker, S. A. (2017). The selfie and the transformation of the public-private distinction. *Information Communication and Society*, *20*(8), 1185–1203. doi:10.1080/1369118X.2016.1220969

Wang, B., & Driscoll, C. (2019). Chinese feminists on social media: Articulating different voices, building strategic alliances. *Continuum (Perth)*, *33*(1), 1–15. doi:10.1080/10304312.2018.1532492

Wang, J. L., Hai, Z. W., Gaskin, J., & Hawk, S. (2017). The Mediating Roles of Upward Social Comparison and Self-Esteem and the Moderating Role of Social Comparison Orientation in the Association between Social Networking Site Usage and Subjective Well-Being. *Frontiers in Psychology*, *8*(MAY), 771. doi:10.3389/fpsyg.2017.00771 PMID:28553256

Warfield, K. (2016). Making the cut: An agential realist examination of selfies and touch. *Social Media + Society*, *2*(2), 2056305116641706. doi:10.1177/2056305116641706

Wargo, J. M. (2017). "Every selfie tells a story…": LGBTQ youth lifestreams and new media narratives as connective identity texts. *New Media & Society*, *19*(4), 560–578. doi:10.1177/1461444815612447

Warner, W., & Hirschberg, J. (2012). *Detecting Hate Speech on the World Wide Web*. Yahoo. http://info.yahoo.com/legal/us/yahoo/utos/utos-173.html

Waseem, Z. (2016). *Are You a Racist or Am I Seeing Things? Annotator Influence on Hate Speech Detection on Twitter*. Spacy. www.spacy.io

Waseem, Z., & Hovy, D. (2016). *Hateful Symbols or Hateful People? Predictive Features for Hate Speech Detection on Twitter*. Github. https://github.com/zeerakw/hatespeech

Watanabe, H., Bouazizi, M., & Ohtsuki, T. (2018). Hate Speech on Twitter: A Pragmatic Approach to Collect Hateful and Offensive Expressions and Perform Hate Speech Detection. *IEEE Access : Practical Innovations, Open Solutions*, *6*, 13825–13835. doi:10.1109/ACCESS.2018.2806394

Webb. (2019, December 18). More than 100 million people watched the "League of Legends" World Championship, cementing its place as the most popular esport. *Business Insider*. https://www.businessinsider.in/tech/news/more-than-100-million-people-watched-the-league-of-legends-world-championship-cementing-its-place-as-the-most-popular-esport/articleshow/72875445.cms

Westlake, E. J. (2008). Friend me if you Facebook: Generation Y and performative surveillance. *The Drama Review*, *52*(4), 21–40. doi:10.1162/dram.2008.52.4.21

Weststar, J., & Marie-Josée, L. (2018). Women's Experiences on the Path to a Career in Game Development. In *Feminism in Play* (pp. 105–123). ResearchGate. doi:10.1007/978-3-319-90539-6_7

What we do: Ending violence against women . (2023). UN Women – Headquarters. https://www.unwomen.org/en/what-we-do/ending-violence-against-women

Whiting, J. B., Davies, B. N., Eisert, B. C., Witting, A. B., & Anderson, S. R. (2022). Online Conversations About Abuse: Responses to IPV Survivors from Support Communities. *Journal of Family Violence*, 1–11.

Wiegand, M., Siegel, M., & Ruppenhofer, J. (2018). *Overview of the GermEval 2018 Shared Task on the Identification of Offensive Language*. Kaggle. https://www.kaggle.com/c/

Wilding, F. (1998). *Where is the Feminism in Cyberfeminism?* Paradoxa, 2.

Wilding, F., & Ensemble, C. A. (1998, Summer). Notes on the Political Condition of Cyberfeminism. *Art Journal*, *57*(2), 46–59. doi:10.1080/00043249.1998.10791878

Wilkinson, S., & Kitzinger, C. (2013). Representing Our Own Experience. *Psychology of Women Quarterly*, *37*(2), 251–255. doi:10.1177/0361684313483111

Willard, N. (2006). *Cyber bullying and cyberthreats: Responding to the challenge of online social cruelty, threats, and distress*. Center for Safe and Responsible Internet Use.

Williams, S. (2015). Digital defense: Black feminists resist violence with hashtag activism. *Feminist Media Studies*, *15*(2), 341–344. doi:10.1080/14680777.2015.1008744

Wilson, K. R., Hansen, D. J., & Li, M. (2011). The traumatic stress response in child maltreatment and resultant neuro-psychological effects. *Aggression and Violent Behavior*, *16*(2), 87–97. doi:10.1016/j.avb.2010.12.007

Winderman, E. (2019). Anger's volumes: Rhetorics of amplification and aggregation in #MeToo. *Women's Studies in Communication*, *42*(3), 327–346. doi:10.1080/07491409.2019.1632234

Women targets in 30% Maharashtra cybercrime cases: NCRB by Narayan Namboodiri. (2022). https://timesofindia.indiatimes.com/city/mumbai/women-targets-in-30-maharashtra-cybercrime-cases-ncrb/articleshow/94124534.cms

Women, U. N. (2020). *Online and ICT-facilitated violence against women and girls during COVID-19*. https://www.unwomen.org/sites/default/files/Headquarters/Attachments/Sections/Library/Publications/2020/Brief-Online-and-ICT-facilitated-violence-against-women-and-girls-during-COVID-19-en.pdf

Women, U. N. (2022). *Frequently asked questions: Tech-facilitated gender-based violence*. https://www.unwomen.org/en/what-we-do/ending-violence-against-women/faqs/tech-facilitated-gender-based-violence#:~:text=TF%20GBV%20can%20also%20exacerbate

Women, U. N. (2023). *Global Database on Violence Against Women*. https://evaw-global-database.unwomen.org/en

Women's Aid. (2022). *Online and digital abuse*. Women's Aid. https://www.womensaid.org.uk/information-support/what-is-domestic-abuse/online-safety/

Women's Media Center (WMC). (n.d.). *Online Abuse 101*. Retrieved May 29, 2023, from https://womensmediacenter.com/speech-project/online-abuse-101/

World Economic Forum. (2022). *Global Gender Gap Report 2022*. https://reports.weforum.org/globalgender-gap-report-2022

World Health Organization. (2018). *Violence against women prevalence estimates*. https://www.who.int/publications/i/item/WHO-SRH-21.9

World Wide Web Foundation. (2020, November 25). *The impact of online gender-based violence on women in public life*. https://webfoundation.org/2020/11/the-impact-of-online-gender-based-violence-on-women-in-public-life/

Wright, M. F., & Wachs, S. (2020). Adolescents' cyber victimization: The influence of technologies, gender, and gender stereotype traits. *International Journal of Environmental Research and Public Health*, *17*(4), 1293. doi:10.3390/ijerph17041293 PMID:32079366

Xavier, S. (2022). Impact of Trolling and Its Effects on the Popularity of social media. *International Journal of Scientific Development and Research*, 760-768.

Xess, G. (n.d.). *Cyber-bullying, cyber-stalking and sexism: A case study of women students of Delhi University*. https://www.jmc.ac.in/uploads/staticfiles/societies/Final%20WSC%20Project%20Report%20(Cyber%20Stalking%20Cyber%20Bullying%20&%20Sexism%20-%20Case%20Study%20of%20Women%20Students%20of%20DU).pdf

Yagnik, B., Kaushal, D., Ballabh, M., Gupta, R., Gayal, S., & Sengupta, V. (2022). *Our take - Navigating the cyber-pass*. Pricewaterhouse Coopers Private Limited.

Yamasaki, N., & Tschanz, B. T. (2005). Rape perception differences between Japanese and American college students: On the mediating influence of gender role traditionality. *Sex Roles*, *52*(5/6), 379–392. Advance online publication. doi:10.100711199-005-2680-7

Yavuz, F. (2016). Do smartphones spur or deter learning: A Whatsapp case study. *International Journal of Educational Sciences*, *15*(3), 408–415. doi:10.1080/09751122.2016.11890551

Yeboah, J., & Ewur, G. D. (2014). The impact of Whatsapp messenger usage on students' performance in tertiary institutions in Ghana. *Journal of Education and Practice*, *5*(6), 157–164.

Yin, S., & Sun, Y. (2021). Intersectional digital feminism: Assessing the participation politics and impact of the MeToo movement in China. *Feminist Media Studies*, *21*(7), 1176–1192. doi:10.1080/14680777.2020.1837908

Yirmibeşoğlu, V. (2007). *Toprağa düşen sevdalar*. Hürriyet Yayınları.

Yousaf, A., Amin, I., Jaziri, D., & Mishra, A. (2021). Effect of message orientation/vividness on consumer engagement for travel brands on social networking sites. *Journal of Product and Brand Management*, *30*(1), 44–57. doi:10.1108/JPBM-08-2019-2546

Yousif, N. (2022, October 15). *Amanda Todd: Dutchman sentenced for fatal cyber-stalking - BBC News*. BBC News, Toronto. https://www.bbc.com/news/world-us-canada-63218797

YouTube users by country 2022. (2022). Statista. https://www.statista.com/statistics/280685/number-of-monthly-unique-youtube-users/

Yuliana, Y. (2022). The importance of cyber-security awareness for children. *Lampung Journal of International Law*, *4*(1), 41–48. doi:10.25041/lajil.v3i2.2526

Zaleski, K. L., Gundersen, K. K., Baes, J., Estupinian, E., & Vergara, A. (2016). Exploring rape culture in social media forums. *Computers in Human Behavior*, *63*, 922–927. doi:10.1016/j.chb.2016.06.036

Zampieri, M., Malmasi, S., Nakov, P., Rosenthal, S., Farra, N., & Kumar, R. (2019a). *Predicting the Type and Target of Offensive Posts in Social Media*. Association for Computational Linguistics. http://bit.ly/2FhLMVz

Zampieri, M., Malmasi, S., Nakov, P., Rosenthal, S., Farra, N., & Kumar, R. (2019b). *SemEval-2019 Task 6: Identifying and Categorizing Offensive Language in Social Media (OffensEval)*. https://competitions.codalab.org/

Zarei, R., Darani, L. H., & Golestan, A. A. (2017). Effect of Telegram application on Iranian advanced EFL learners' vocabulary knowledge and attitude. *International Journal of Foreign Language Teaching and Research*, *5*(20), 9.

Zezulka, L. A., & Seigfried-Spellar, K. (2016). Differentiating cyberbullies and internet trolls by personality characteristics and self-esteem. *Journal of Digital Forensics, Security and Law*, *11*(3), 7–26.

Zhao, R., & Yao, X. (2022). The relationship between bullying victimization and suicidal ideation among Chinese adolescents: The role of depressive symptoms and gender differences. *Journal of School Violence*, *21*(1), 60–80. doi:10.1080/15388220.2021.1985327

Zhao, S., & Zappavigna, M. (2018). Beyond the self: Intersubjectivity and the social semiotic interpretation of the self. *New Media & Society*, *20*(5), 1735–1754. doi:10.1177/1461444817706074

Zhou, Z., Tang, H., Tian, Y., Wei, H., Zhang, F., & Morrison, C. M. (2013). Cyberbullying and its risk factors among Chinese high school students. *School Psychology International*, *34*(6), 630–647. doi:10.1177/0143034313479692

Zonta. (n.d.). *Zonta Says No.* Available in: https://zontasaysno.com/zontasvision/campaign/

Żurawicka, M. (2015, July). *Research World*. Retrieved December 2022, from https://archive.researchworld.com/semiotics-of-brand-gender-what-gender-is-your-brand/

Zweig, J. M., Dank, M., Yahner, J., & Lachman, P. (2013). The Rate of Cyber Dating Abuse Among Teens and How It Relates to Other Forms of Teen Dating Violence. *Journal of Youth and Adolescence*, *42*(7), 1063–1077. doi:10.100710964-013-9922-8 PMID:23412689

About the Contributors

Geeta Ajit is a Researcher, International examiner and an English Language trainer, who has conducted over 25 workshops and training sessions in management and soft skills for professionals, teachers, non-teaching staff and students, including a weeklong FDP in English Language with eminent speakers from seven countries during the pandemic. She has over two decades of teaching experience and is presently teaching at an Engineering college in Mumbai. She is also appointed as an Aviation English Language Expert by the Director General of Civil Aviation, as trainer and examiner, for the Airports Authority of India. Apart from this, she has been invited as a Resource person and Guest speaker at numerous national and international institutions, Faculty Development Programs and Conferences. She has also published numerous research papers in both National and International journals.

Gülçin Akbaş is an Assistant Professor of Psychology at Atılım University, specializing in social psychology. With a background in psychology, she holds a Ph.D. degree in the field. Her research interests encompass a wide array of topics, all of which reflect her unwavering dedication to social justice and addressing critical societal issues including sexism, gender inequality, violence against women, and intergroup relations, particularly examining prejudice and discrimination. Her work explores the role of culture and social influence in shaping human behavior, offering insights into how societal norms and values impact individuals' actions and attitudes. Through rigorous inquiry and empirical analysis, she seeks to shed light on the underlying mechanisms that perpetuate these complex challenges.

Balunkeswari B. is a research scholar pursuing Ph.D., from School of Humanities, KIIT University.

Belem Barbosa received her PhD in Business and Management Studies – Specialisation in Marketing and Strategy from the University of Porto, Portugal. She is Assistant Professor at the School of Economics and Management of the University of Porto. She is full researcher at GOVCOPP, the Research Unit of Governance, Competitiveness, and Public Policies, and Invited Researcher at cef.up Center for Economics and Finance at the University of Porto. Her research interests lie primarily in the areas of digital marketing and consumer behavior.

Cassia Liandra Carvalho earned a Master's in Marketing from the University of Aveiro. She has published several journal articles and book chapters on topics related with feminist hashtags.

Suzan Ceylan-Batur currently holds the position of Assistant Professor at TOBB University of Economics and Technology in Turkey. She is a social psychologist with an interest in investigating how cultural practices influence human behavior, emotions, and cognition. Her research adopts a multifaceted approach, integrating experimental, survey, and qualitative methodologies to gain deeper insights into the impact of socio-cultural factors on critical issues such as violence against women, retaliation, and forgiveness. One of her primary research focuses involves exploring the interplay between social influences and individual differences in shaping attitudes towards these pressing societal concerns. In another research domain, she endeavors to uncover the fundamental mechanisms that underlie these attitudes.

Sanju Choudhary is an Assistant Professor at Department of English, University of Rajasthan, Jaipur. She has more than two decades of teaching experience. She has done her research on the topic Beyond Binaries: Nature, Culture and Language in the Poetic Imagination of Margaret Atwood. Her areas of expertise include Canadian Studies, Indian Writing in English and Diaspora Studies. She has more than 25 publications in reputed journals to her credit. She has presented many papers in national and international seminars and conferences. She has organized many workshops in the university on Communication Skills and Personality Development.

Vishva Chaudhary is presently working as an Assistant Professor in the Department of Psychology, University of Rajasthan located at Jaipur. In the field of teaching from last 12 Years. She has published 15 research articles in various national repute journals. She has presented her research work at many National and International Conferences. Her specialization is in Clinical Psychology. Her interest areas for research majorly focusses on Health psychology, Positive Psychology and Clinical Psychology.

Muhammet Demirbilek is an Professor of Educational Technology in the Faculty of Education at Suleyman Demirel University in Isparta /Turkey. He earned his doctoral and master's degree in Educational Technology from the University of Florida. He also holds B.S. and M.S. degrees in electronics engineering from Istanbul University. He worked as a graduate faculty and visiting Assistant Professor in Digital Worlds Institute at University of Florida (2013-2014) and Post-Doctoral Researcher at Games, Learning, and Society (GLS) at the University of Wisconsin-Madison (2008-2009). His research interests include the impact of digital media and computer games and simulations on teaching and learning. How new media (e.g web 2.0, online social networks, mobile media) . His recent research interests are the effects of online bullying, learning analytic, big data analysis, using mobile games to improve social skills of kids with autism. How augmented reality games on handheld computers designed and used for formal and informal education. How social media, online social networks, and mobile media restructure thinking, values, actions, education, community, and culture.

Soumya Sankar Ghosh holds a doctorate in Linguistics from Jadavpur University's School of Languages and Linguistics, Kolkata, India. He earned a Master's degree in Linguistics from the University of Calcutta in Kolkata and his second Master's degree in English from the IGNOU, New Delhi. In 2021, he completed an Advanced Diploma in TEFL and TESOL from the Asian College of Teachers. He worked as a Pre-Doctoral Fellow at the University of Potsdam in Germany (2018-2019). He has ten years of UG-PG teaching, research, and industrial experience. He is currently employed as an Assistant Professor at VIT Bhopal University, Bhopal. He has over 15 publications in indexed international journals and proceedings such as Scopus, WOS, ACL, and UGC-CARE. Language and Education, Formal Semantics and Pragmatics, Computational Linguistics, Natural Language Processing, and ELT are some of his research interests. He was selected as an Academic Advisor for the West Bengal Government Language Division in 2022. He is a lifetime member of India's Linguistic Society (LSI).

Sandhya Gupta works as Associate Professor in the Department of Psychology, Banasthali Vidyapith, Tonk, Rajasthan, India. She is Doctorate in Psychology and has experience of more than twelve years in teaching and research (excluding Doctoral Research Experience). In these years, she supervised several doctoral thesis, dissertations and research projects; published papers in International and National journals and conference presentations. Dr Sandhya specializes in Educational Psychology and Cognitive Psychology. But her research interest is varied encompassing fields like, Clinical Psychology, Neuropsychology, Health Psychology, Positive Psychology. Moreover, she has organized and conducted several workshops on various topics of Psychology. Her work is extended to administrative responsibilities, of varying nature, as well. Currently she is working on a book on Rehabilitation Psychology.

Anushka Lydia Issac brings a unique perspective. Holding prestigious credentials such as an FHEA and a Lead IQA Certificate, she possesses the skills and knowledge to design, deliver, and assess high-quality learning experiences in higher education. She passion for understanding people and their personalities has propelled her to excel in communications and public speaking at an international level. As an Associate Faculty and Program Leader at Westford University College, she actively contributes to the development of students. Her Ph.D. research from the University of Plymouth, UK focuses on flexible work arrangements.

Kalaivani K. has 14 years of teaching and research experience in the field Computer Science and Engineering. She served as an Assistant Professor in PSNA Colleges of Engineering & Technology, Dindigul, Tamilnadu and in Sree Vidyanikethan Engineering College, Tirupati, Andhra Pradesh. Currently she is serving as Associate Professor in Vignana Bharathi Institute of Technology, Hyderabad. She completed ME., Computer Science & Engineering in Anna University, Chennai, Tamilnadu, India with 8.55 cgpa First Class with Distinction (Anna University Rank Holder) in the year 2013. He was awarded Ph.D. degree in "A Certain Investigations on Heart Disease Prediction System using Soft Computing Techniques." by Anna University, Chennai, Tamilnadu in 2021.

Vijendra Singh Meel is currently working as Deputy Manager (Information Security) at Samsung India Electronics, New Delhi. He has also worked with Bureau of Indian Standards as a Cyber Security expert. His expertise lies in securing Web Applications, Web Servers and Networks and vulnerability assessment. He has also worked with LEA's and delivered training to police officers and officers in various government departments including Air force, Paramilitary forces and many investigating agencies for cybercrime investigations.

Deepanjali Mishra earned her PhD in English from Utkal University, Bhubaneswar. Motivating and Talented English Professor driven to inspire students to pursue academic and personal excellence. Consistently driven towards extensive research and exceptional track record towards contribution to various publication work. Energetic, highly career oriented and focused for attainment of goal. Her Area of interest includes Feminism and Gender Studies, Sociology, Linguistics, Management. She has over 15 years of teaching and research experience. "Published a book titled I am A Woman". Organised a National Workshop and International Conference in Dec 2017. Have published a book titled' I am a

Woman' with Bahri Publishers New Delhi. She is the guest editor of Research Chronicler, Literaria and Indian Journal of Communication. She has published over 26 research papers in reputed International journals and has presented her papers in various International conferences in India and abroad like IIT, IIM, South Korea, China and Nepal.

Pragyan Mohanty is a PhD in Gender Studies and is currently working as an associate professor and dean in Kalinga Institute of social sciences, KISS DU. she has published five books internationally and many articles on social issues in general and gender issues in particular. Her interests include reading, traveling and creative writing.

Kutlwano Mokgwathi is a graduate of Ohio University with a Doctoral degree in Mass Communication. She is a research affiliate at the University of the Western Cape in the Women's and Gender Studies department. Her research focuses on cyberfeminism, masculinity studies, and media technology influences on conceptualizations of gender. She is currently a Media Studies lecturer at the University of Botswana.

Rajni Nair has over 20 years of experience in teaching with Language, Literature and Gender Studies being her core areas of interest and research.

Subhajit Panda is currently pursuing his PhD at Punjabi University, Patiala and also working as an Assistant Librarian in the Central Library, Chandigarh University. Among publications, he has 1 Book, 7 Book Chapters, 28 Journal Articles, and 4 Conference Proceedings. He is a life member of the Indian Library Association (ILA), Madras Library Association (MALA) and Bengal Library Association (BLA). He served as an associate editor for The International Journal of Information Studies & Libraries (IJISL). His areas of interest are e-Learning, Change Management, Cloud Computing, Open Access, Web Accessibility, Virtual & Augmented Reality and Metrics Studies.

Piyush Pandey is currently an Assistant Professor at Arya Mahila PG College, Banaras Hindu University, Varanasi, India. He obtained his PhD degree in Marketing from Faculty of Commerce, Banaras Hindu University, Varanasi, India. He received his master's degree in commerce from Faculty of Commerce, Banaras Hindu University in 2015 and received his bachelor's degree in commerce from Faculty of Commerce, Banaras Hindu University in 2013. He has published research papers in Web of Science and UGC-CARE listed journals and has authors book chapters in national and international publications like Edward-Elgar and Bloomsbury. He also qualified National Eligibility Test from University Grants Commission in the year 2019. His research interests include business management and marketing, specifically customer relationship management. He can be contacted at piyushpandey2592@gmail.com.

Ritu Pareek, Assistant Professor in English at Birla Institute of Technology- Mesra- Jaipur campus has been working in the field of academics for the last fifteen years. Dr. Pareek completed her PhD on the topic "Questioning of Patriarchal Narration and of Female Subjugation in Angela Carter's Short Stories" from Malaviya National Institute of Technology, Jaipur, in 2014. She has published articles on Contemporary British Fiction and on English Language Teaching in reputed journals, and has presented research papers at many international conferences including the University of London, UK, and many national conferences at universities in India. Dr Pareek has also translated various NPTEL Courses and is also associated with Svitlo School, a charitable trust which works for the Ukrainian children.

Pratham Parekh has completed PhD from the Centre for Studies in Society and Development, School of Social Sciences, Central University of Gujarat. He has to his credit 14 research papers published in various international and national journals & 7 book chapters from well-known publishers. He has authored 2 scholarly acclaimed books titled "Epistemes of Death" and "Infrastructure Growth & Human Development in Gujarat". He has presented papers in 43 international, national and state level conferences. His breadth of experience includes working with various private, non-government and government organizations. He has 7 years of experience working at the policy & governance level as a consultant with the Government of Gujarat. He has prepared and contributed to 16 policy intervention documents. He is appraised by the State Government for his contribution in developing Outcome Budget, Gender Budget, Development Program, SDG monitoring system, and CM Dashboard. His interdisciplinary research interests range across sociological aspects related to public policy, governance, information technology, Data Analytics & visualization, Human Resources Management, Labor Laws, Social Policy, Gender & Women Studies, Mythology, Medical & Health Sociology and Development Studies.

Sugyanta Priyadarshini is Assistant Professor in the Department of Humanities, Kalinga Institute of Industrial Technology (KIIT), Deemed to be University, Bhubaneswar, Odisha, India. Dr. Sugyanta has obtained her doctoral (PH.D.) in 2021 and was a University Topper and Gold medalist in masters Examination in 2016. She has successfully published approximately 20 research articles and book chapters in journals and books of high repute. She has participated in more than 30 international/national conferences and has remained a moderator in several workshops and seminars. Presently, she is guiding two doctoral candidates. Her research areas are Gender Economics, Artificial Intelligence in Social issues and behavioral economics. Recently, she has revealed her interest in spiritual interventions by participating in national conference on "spiritualism: a potential key for stress management". She is a potent Reviewer in Journals naming Human Rights Review (Springer Publication House), Lancet Regional Health Southeast Asia (Lancet Journals Group), Technology, Knowledge and Learning (Springer Publication House), Asian Journal of Women's Studies (Taylor and Francis Group) and, International Journal of Qualitative Methods (Sage Publication House). Additionally, she has remained the awardee of Best Paper in 22ND Pattaya International Conference on Economics, Education and Humanities and Social Sciences (PEEHSS-19), Best Paper in International Conference on Education 4.0 (IMHRC 2020) and Best Paper Award in M.S. Gore Centenary Conference 2021 by TISS, Mumbai 2021. She is currently acting as an active member of Odisha Economic Association (OEA).

Anil Kumar Saraswat, IIM Ahmedabad alumni, having more than 22 years of experience in Cyber Security and is currently working as General Manager (Information Security) at Samsung India Electronics, New Delhi. He has also worked with Various MNCs like IBM & SIEMENS as Cyber Security Expert. His domain expertise include Cloud Security, Data Security, and Data Privacy, Network, Web, Servers, and Identity and access management. He also contributed for cyber security incidents handling as well as architecting cyber security solutions for large enterprises. He has also worked with global teams across multiple geo-locations. He is an active security speaker and participated in various global cyber security panel discussions.

Surbhi Sharma is a Senior Lecturer, Orthodontist, author, and an outspoken Pro-feminist.

Manjula Shukla is currently an Assistant Professor at SSSVS Government PG College, Chunar, Mirzapur. She obtained her PhD degree in Finance from Faculty of Commerce, Banaras Hindu University, Varanasi, India. She received her master's degree in commerce from Faculty of Commerce, Banaras Hindu University in 2015 and received her bachelor's degree in commerce from Faculty of Commerce, Banaras Hindu University in 2013. She has published several research papers in Scopus, Web of Science and UGC-CARE listed journals and has authors book chapters in national and international publications. She also received Junior Research Fellowship from University Grants Commission in the year 2014. Her research interests include business management, corporate governance, and marketing.

Rasmita Tripathy, with a Ph.D. degree from Visva-Bharati University, Santiniketan, currently serves as an Associate Professor of Odia Language and Literature and holds the position of Dean at the School of Comparative Tribal Languages and Literatures at KISS Deemed to be University in Bhubaneswar. Over the course of her distinguished 16-year career, she has passionately taught subjects such as Modern Drama and Folklore in PG and Ph.D Programmes. Dr. Tripathy possesses an impressive portfolio of more than 40 research publications, primarily focusing on Modern Drama, Folklore and Tribal Language and Literature. Her academic influence extends beyond publications, having successfully supervised six Ph.D. scholars and four M.Phil. scholars, contributing significantly to the field.

Sargam Yadav is a PhD researcher in Natural Language Processing. Yadav's thesis deals with misogynistic hate speech in code-mixed languages.

Index

D

E

F

G

H

I

J

M

N

O

P

R

S

T

U

V

W

X

Y

www.ingramcontent.com/pod-product-compliance
Lightning Source LLC
LaVergne TN
LVHW060356300926
849162LV00006B/1277